COVENANT, JUSTIFICATION, AND PASTORAL MINISTRY

COVENANT, JUSTIFICATION, AND PASTORAL MINISTRY

Essays by the Faculty of Westminster Seminary California

EDITED BY

R. SCOTT CLARK

P.O. BOX 817 • PHILLIPSBURG • NEW JERSEY 08865-0817

Unless otherwise indicated, Scripture translations are by the authors.

Page design and typesetting by Lakeside Design Plus

Printed in the United States of America

Library of Congress Control Number: 2006934630

Contents

Acknowledgments

The volume is the result of the collaboration of an entire institution. Beginning with the early planning for the conference (April 30–May 1, 2003), the administration, staff, and faculty have shown remarkable discipline and singleness of purpose in this project. Every contributor has done what was necessary to bring this work to completion. As editor, I am grateful for all the labors of all of God's people in this work.

During the time this book was begun and completed we lost one colleague and gained another. Iain Duguid was called to Grove City College in 2005. Joel Kim joined us as assistant professor of New Testament in 2006, too late to contribute to this collection.

Thanks go to Allan Fisher, who encouraged the project from the very beginning. Without his patience and foresight, this project would not have been possible. Thanks also are due to Marvin Padgett, Barb Lerch, and Thom Notaro for their work on this book in various stages of preparation. Special acknowledgment should be given to Bob and Nellie den Dulk for their ceaseless labors for Westminster Seminary California and for Christ, his gospel, and his church.

Contributors

All contributors hold faculty positions in
Westminster Seminary California.

S. M. Baugh (PhD, University of California, Irvine) is professor of New Testament.

R. Scott Clark (DPhil, University of Oxford) is associate professor of historical and systematic theology.

Iain M. Duguid (PhD, University of Cambridge) is visiting professor of Old Testament.

Bryan Estelle (PhD, Catholic University of America) is associate professor of Old Testament.

W. Robert Godfrey (PhD, Stanford University) is president and professor of church history.

Michael S. Horton (PhD, University of Coventry and Wycliffe Hall, Oxford) is J. Gresham Machen Professor of Systematic Theology and Apologetics.

Dennis E. Johnson (PhD, Fuller Theological Seminary) is professor of practical theology and academic dean.

Hywel R. Jones (PhD, University of Wales) is professor of practical theology.

Julius J. Kim (PhD, Trinity Evangelical Divinity School) is associate professor of practical theology and dean of students.

David VanDrunen (JD, Northwestern University; PhD, Loyola University Chicago) is professor of systematic theology and Christian ethics and holds the Robert B. Strimple chair in systematic theology.

Abbreviations

ANF	*Ante-Nicene Fathers*
AV	Authorized (King James) Version
BDAG	Walter Bauer, Frederick W. Danker, William F. Arndt, and F. Wilbur Gingrich, *A Greek-English Lexicon of the New Testament and Other Early Christian Literature* (3rd ed.; Chicago: University of Chicago Press, 2000)
ESV	English Standard Version
HC	Heidelberg Catechism (1563)
Institutes	John Calvin, *Institutes of the Christian Religion* (ed. John T. McNeill; trans. Ford Lewis Battles; 2 vols.; Library of Christian Classics 20–21; Philadelphia: Westminster, 1960)
MT	Masoretic Text
NASB	New American Standard Bible
NIV	New International Version
NPNF[1]	*Nicene and Post-Nicene Fathers*, series 1
NPNF[2]	*Nicene and Post-Nicene Fathers*, series 2
NRSV	New Revised Standard Version
Schaff	Philip Schaff, ed., *The Creeds of Christendom* (1931; 6th ed.; 3 vols.; repr. Rapids: Baker, 1983)
Turretin, *Institutes*	Francis Turretin, *Institutes of Elenctic Theology* (trans. George M. Giger; ed. James T. Dennison Jr.; 3 vols.; Phillipsburg, NJ: P&R, 1992–97)
WCF	Westminster Confession of Faith (1647)
WLC	Westminster Larger Catechism (1647)

PART 1

Orientation

1

How We Got Here

The Roots of the Current Controversy over Justification

R. Scott Clark

Introduction

Presently there is open disagreement within Reformed and Presbyterian churches over the most basic elements of the doctrine of justification. Some are arguing (implicitly and explicitly) that the doctrine of justification contained in the Reformed confessions and catechisms (i.e., symbols) is either inadequate or incorrect.

Some of these revisionists draw upon the work of E. P. Sanders, James Dunn, and N. T. Wright on Second Temple Judaism and Paul's view of the law. Others synthesize threads in covenant theology developed in the Netherlands by Klaas Schilder (1890–1952) and S. G. DeGraaf (1889–1955) and in North America by John Murray (1898–1975) and Norman Shepherd.[1]

1. For an introduction to Schilder's life and work, see J. Geertsma, ed., *Always Obedient: Essays on the Teachings of Dr. Klaas Schilder* (Phillipsburg, NJ: P&R, 1995). For Shepherd's cov-

The Reformed Confessions: A Line of Demarcation

As "Our Testimony on Justification" shows (see the appendix), the teaching of the Reformed symbols is unambiguous on the doctrine of justification. No matter which view of confessional subscription one holds (e.g., system, strict, or good faith), one must agree that the doctrine of justification taught in the Reformed confessions is of the essence of the symbols such that rejection of justification *sola gratia, sola fide* (historically understood) constitutes a deviation from Reformed dogma. As a matter of integrity, then, all who subscribe the Westminster Standards or the *Three Forms of Unity* (as faculty members, we subscribe both) are obligated to uphold and defend the doctrine they contain. The doctrine of justification was, after all, the material principle of the Reformation, and the Reformed symbols were written, published, and adopted as public, ecclesiastically sanctioned summaries of those Reformation doctrines.[2]

To be sure, one may hold one view or another of Second Temple Judaism. Such questions are academic, important background studies for the understanding of Scripture, but without necessary effect upon the doctrine of justification. The same is not necessarily true, however, for every claim concerning covenant nomism and related contentions about the relations of faith to obedience in the act of justification. To conclude that in justification faith justifies *because* it obeys or that Christ did not perform vicarious active obedience or that Paul's doctrine of justification was not primarily about right standing before God has the most serious implications for the historic (and confessional) doctrine of justification. In this case, the question is no longer merely academic, but necessarily ecclesiastical as well.

---

enant theology and doctrine of justification, see Norman Shepherd, *The Call of Grace: How the Covenant Illumines Salvation and Evangelism* (Phillipsburg, NJ: P&R, 2000); idem, "Justification by Faith Alone," *Reformation and Revival* 11 (2002): 75–90; idem, "Justification by Faith in Pauline Theology" and "Justification by Works in Reformed Theology," in *Backbone of the Bible: Covenant in Contemporary Perspective* (ed. P. Andrew Sandlin; Nacogdoches, TX: Covenant Media, 2004), 85–120. For Murray's covenant theology, see John Murray, *The Covenant of Grace: A Biblico-Theological Study* (London: Tyndale, 1953); idem, *Collected Writings of John Murray* (Edinburgh: Banner of Truth, 1976–82), 4.216–40.

2. W. Robert Godfrey, "Westminster, Justification, and the Reformed Confessions," in *The Pattern of Sound Words: Systematic Theology at the Westminster Seminaries: Essays in Honor of Robert B. Strimple* (ed. David VanDrunen; Phillipsburg, NJ: P&R, 2004), 140–43, makes a helpful distinction between the Reformed symbols as ecclesiastical documents and systematic theology.

A Faculty's Role

It is not the function of a seminary faculty to do the work of church courts and assemblies. Ministers who serve in academia have, however, a moral obligation to apply their studies to the life of and for the benefit of the churches. This volume, therefore, seeks to help remedy the confusion by addressing the doctrine of justification from every department of theology: exegetical, historical, systematic, and pastoral. One book will not likely settle all questions, but we hope that it will advance the discussion toward a happy resolution.

Defining "Reformed"

There is, at present, confusion about what constitutes the Reformed doctrine of justification. This is because two sides use the same adjective, "Reformed," to describe incompatible views. One side tends to argue that genuinely Reformed doctrine teaches one covenant before and after the fall, the imputation of Jesus's passive obedience only, and faith that justifies because it obeys.[3] The other side, in contrast, holds that the Reformed doctrine denies those very things. Without equivocating, both sides cannot be correct.

It is the purpose of this book to explain and defend—first from Scripture but also from Reformed history, theology, and practice—the doctrine of justification as expressed in the Reformed confessions. The monocovenantal theology described above, with its denial of the law/gospel distinction and the imputation of Christ's active obedience, cannot be squared with Scripture, the confessions, or Reformed theology. The denial of the law/gospel distinction, the imputation of Christ's active obedience, and the simplicity of faith in justification are not part of Reformed soteriology as defined by the confessions. If this claim is true—that there is within the churches a movement seeking to inculcate in them anticonfessional doctrines of justifica-

3. Godfrey (ibid., 138–39) argues that the rise of a distinctively Reformed approach to biblical theology (e.g., Geerhardus Vos), to pastoral counseling (e.g., Jay Adams), and to apologetics (e.g., Cornelius Van Til) may have given the impression that there should also be a distinctively Reformed doctrine of justification.

tion and covenant theology—it is well to consider how such a state of affairs has come to pass.

Lost: One Grammar and Several Categories

The long conflict between orthodoxy and modernity has left the *corpus reformatum* with some serious wounds. One of those wounds was the reimagination of our identity. Rather than identifying ourselves as Reformed and defining Reformed by the symbols, over time we identified ourselves as conservatives and came to regard our Reformed identity as just a subset of a broader antimodern reaction. Consequently, we have gradually tended to abandon our grammar (ways of speaking) and our categories (ways of thinking) so that now, when they are reintroduced, they appear to some as novelties.

For example, doctrines such as the covenant of works and its relations to the covenant of grace, the *pactum salutis*, and justification suffered the same fate. In this period, respected theologians and their students were able to reject the covenant of works, despite its prominence in the Westminster Confession of Faith, without ecclesiastical consequence.[4] The same sorts of cause-and-effect relations are evident in the current debate over justification. The concerns, vocabulary, convictions, and categories of the Reformed confessions are not dominating the thinking and language of much of the Reformed world. If they were, the state of the question would be different. Instead, a significant number of pastors and theologians are teaching a doctrine of justification obviously at variance with the Reformed confessions. It is not difficult to imagine the uproar if those same people had rejected the confessional doctrine of Scripture, instead of the doctrine of justification.

The Plausibility of Error

These revisions of the doctrine of justification have found a certain degree of plausibility because the context in which we decide what is

4. John Murray took exception to many places in the Westminster Standards, most notably WCF 7.2 and 25.1–3. For a list of his published exceptions, see James E. Urish, "A Peaceable Plea about Subscription: Toward Avoiding Future Divisions," in *The Practice of Confessional Subscription* (ed. David W. Hall; 2nd ed.; Oak Ridge, TN: Covenant Foundation, 2001), 220–21.

credible changed markedly in the twentieth century. The subordination of confessional Reformed and Presbyterian interests in favor of those of broadly conservative Christianity changed what sociologist Peter Berger describes as "plausibility structures," that is, that context in which we decide what is credible.[5]

Part of this shift in plausibility structures occurred when we adopted the categories *liberal* and *conservative* as our primary way of evaluating doctrine and practice. From the point of view of historic Reformed orthodoxy, this turn has not been altogether happy. In business, when a large corporation moves to acquire a useful but smaller company, the latter can remain independent and risk being crushed by the competition, or it can seek the relative safety of merging with a friendlier, but equally large corporation. The danger of such a merger is that the small company may lose its identity. Confessional Reformed Christianity survived the takeover attempt by liberalism, but in order to survive we became a subsidiary of modern American evangelicalism. As J. Gresham Machen and Cornelius Van Til feared, what began as a temporary, strategic alliance became a permanent relation.[6]

It might be objected that Reformed Christians *are* evangelicals and that it is not a matter of *whether* they will be a subset of evangelicalism, but *how*. The response is that it depends on the notoriously difficult definition of *evangelical* as it describes American Protestants since 1720. There are three competing interpretations of the nature of contemporary evangelicalism. The first and dominant view is that American evangelicalism is defined by its relations to the sixteenth-century Protestants and Reformed orthodoxy as it came to expression in old Princeton. Arguing this case in his well-researched and highly influential books, George F. Marsden interprets the rise of early-twentieth-century fundamentalism in relation to old Princeton and the

5. Peter Berger, *A Rumor of Angels: Modern Society and the Rediscovery of the Supernatural* (Garden City, NY: Doubleday, 1969), 42–57. One need not accept Berger's premise that society is a purely human product to recognize the validity of his observations about the situatedness of human knowledge and that human beings form and maintain their views in conversation with others. Michael Polanyi observes the role of authority in learning in *Science, Faith, and Society* (Chicago: University of Chicago Press, 1946).

6. On Machen's ambivalence toward fundamentalism, see D. G. Hart, *Defending the Faith: J. Gresham Machen and the Crisis of Conservative Protestantism in Modern America* (Grand Rapids: Baker, 1994). See Van Til's criticism of evangelicalism in "The New Evangelicalism" (syllabus, Westminster Theological Seminary, Philadelphia, 1960).

rise of neo-evangelicalism (post-1946) relative to old Westminster. Donald Dayton describes this as the "Presbyterian paradigm." For his part, Marsden argues that his interpretation is more complex than Dayton allows and that his view is complementary to Dayton's.[7] This approach is associated with the Institute for the Study of American Evangelicalism and may be seen in the work of Mark Noll and many others.

A second view, advocated by Dayton, is that American evangelicalism is rooted in the sixteenth-century Anabaptist movement and has been more Methodist or Pentecostal than classically Protestant. He argues that American evangelicalism is normed by the revivals of the eighteenth and (especially) the nineteenth centuries. He contends that Marsden's "paradigm" (in the sense that Thomas Kuhn uses the word) unfairly omits the socially radical and theologically deviant (from the Reformed point of view) Wesleyan and Pentecostal (i.e., pietist) mainstream of evangelicalism. In this view, Princeton and Westminster are on the margins of evangelicalism. Dayton calls this a "Pentecostal paradigm" for interpreting American evangelicalism.[8]

The final and perhaps most provocative approach is that of D. G. Hart, who argues that there is no such thing as "evangelicalism." It was a convention, an artificial construct that scholars only recently created and that defies definition.[9] Ironically, the Pentecostal Dayton may

7. See George F. Marsden, *The Evangelical Mind and the New School Presbyterian Experience* (New Haven: Yale University Press, 1970); idem, *Fundamentalism and American Culture: The Shaping of Twentieth-Century Evangelicalism, 1870–1925* (Oxford: Oxford University Press, 1980); idem, ed., *Evangelicalism and Modern America* (Grand Rapids: Eerdmans, 1984); idem, *Reforming Fundamentalism: Fuller Seminary and the New Evangelicalism* (Grand Rapids: Eerdmans, 1987).

8. See Donald W. Dayton, *Discovering an Evangelical Heritage* (New York: Harper & Row, 1976); idem, "The Limits of Evangelicalism: The Pentecostal Tradition" and "Some Doubts about the Usefulness of the Category 'Evangelical,'" in The *Variety of American Evangelicalism* (ed. Donald W. Dayton and Robert K. Johnston; Downers Grove, IL: InterVarsity, 1991). Dayton and Marsden (and others) have engaged in a long-running debate about the roots and nature of modern evangelicalism. See George Marsden, "Demythologizing Evangelicalism: A Review of Donald W. Dayton's *Discovering an Evangelical Heritage*," *Christian Scholar's Review* 7 (1977): 203–11; and the *Christian Scholar's Review* 23 (1993): 12–89, which features essays and responses by Marsden, Dayton, and comments by several evangelical observers.

9. See D. G. Hart, *Deconstructing Evangelicalism: Conservative Protestantism in the Age of Billy Graham* (Grand Rapids: Baker, 2004); idem, *The Lost Soul of American Protestantism* (Lanham: Rowman & Littlefield, 2002); idem, *That Old-Time Religion in Modern America: Evangelical Protestantism in the Twentieth Century* (Chicago: Dee, 2002).

agree with the Presbyterian iconoclast Hart, for Dayton also signaled his dissatisfaction with the term *evangelical* as an adjective in 1991.

To have real meaning, evangelicalism as a universal must have particulars, but it is exceeding difficult to find those particulars, and even when some are nominated, there are multiple filters for determining which are included. If one uses recognized institutions as a barometer (e.g., Evangelical Theological Society, *Christianity Today*, Fuller Seminary) and measures contemporary evangelical theology by something like Reformed orthodoxy, then one will likely agree with the criticisms of evangelicalism (as being in a sort of Babylonian captivity) made by David Wells.[10] Given that the original evangelicals were certainly the sixteenth- and seventeenth-century Protestants, who routinely described themselves as evangelicals, Wells has a point.

When Reformed folk call themselves evangelicals they are thinking of the sixteenth and seventeenth centuries, but almost no one today who might be included under the adjective *evangelical* defines the word according to sixteenth- and seventeenth-century usage. The "Protestant paradigm" is not holding. According to the Institute for the Study of American Evangelicalism there are about 100,000,000 American evangelicals.[11] By contrast, there are no more than 700,000 confessional Reformed Christians in the United States. If, for the sake of discussion, we include this group under rubric of evangelicalism and if more than 99% of American evangelicals do not define themselves by the Reformed Confessions or the convictions of sixteenth- and seventeenth-century Protestantism, then perhaps "evangelical" is no longer a useful adjective to describe those who are confessionally Reformed.

Reformed Christianity defines itself by doctrine and practice. Obviously, given the variety of evangelical theological and ecclesiastical possibilities, neither doctrine nor practice defines evangelicalism. Rather, religious experience defines evangelicalism. What unites evangelicals across ecclesiastical and theological boundaries is their common quest for the immediate (literally "without instruments") experience or

10. See David F. Wells, *No Place for Truth* (Grand Rapids: Eerdmans, 1993); and idem, *God in the Wasteland* (Grand Rapids: Eerdmans, 1994).

11. "Defining Evangelicalism," http://www.wheaton.edu/isae/defining_evangelicalism.html#How%20Many.

knowledge of God. By contrast, what animates Reformed Christianity is not the *immediate* experience of God, but his glory, which he achieves through the means of grace (HC 65 [Schaff 3.328]). Reformed Christianity is organized around mediation: the mediation of revelation in God's covenants and chiefly through the mediator of the covenant of grace—Jesus Christ the Word. Reformed Christianity is nothing if not doctrinal and churchly. To the degree we are defined by our theology and practice, we are not evangelicals, as defined above.[12]

As a member of the conservative evangelical corporation, the Reformed functioned as defenders of Christian theism and the reliability of Scripture, but conservative evangelicalism did not care for our doctrinal peculiarities, namely our Creator/creature distinction (and our definition of theology that followed), our doctrines of God, man, Christ, salvation, and eschatology. This antipathy was especially strong for our doctrines of the church and sacraments.[13] Consequently, over the course of the war with modernity, the Reformed came to identify themselves not by their confessional doctrine and practice, but by those conservative virtues valued by our evangelical patrons.

Tertullian asked famously in the third century, "What has Athens to do with Jerusalem?" We might also ask: What have Reformed and Presbyterian Christians to do with a movement encompassing proponents of plenary inerrancy and limited inerrancy, classical and open theism, divine omniscience and middle knowledge, creedal and social Trinitarianism, Protestants, Roman Catholics, and Eastern Orthodox, those who use the sacraments and those who reject their use?

Therefore, Reformed and Presbyterian folk do better to distinguish between those who are confessional and those who are nonconfes-

12. At root, part of this debate is the question of who "owns" evangelicalism, that is, who belongs to it properly and who does not. This is a question of politics, not theology. With this problem in view, Michael Horton proposes that evangelicalism be regarded as a sort of village green or commons where Christians from a variety of traditions may meet for conversation, owned by no one in particular. In his response to Horton, Roger Olson rejects the "commons" metaphor in favor of the "big tent." The reaction of Olson and others to the proposal to dissolve the evangelical corporation suggests that, at some level, they realize their suzerainty and are reluctant to release Reformed confessionalists from their vassalage. See the Horton-Olson dialogue in "Reflection: Is Evangelicalism Reformed or Wesleyan? Reopening the Marsden-Dayton Debate," *Christian Scholar's Review* 31 (2001): 131–68.

13. According to Marsden's *Reforming Fundamentalism*, Fuller Seminary was founded as a West Coast version of Westminster Seminary, without the ecclesiastical connections to the separating Presbyterians and the Reformed view of the sacraments.

sional.[14] By the former, I mean those who are defined by Scripture as understood by the historic Protestant confessions and catechisms.[15] According to this category, there are Lutheran confessionalists, Reformed confessionalists, and perhaps others. In the nonconfessional category, one finds liberals, that is, those who identify with modern autonomy, and conservatives, who are more traditional. What unifies liberals and conservatives is their relative autonomy to historic symbols of the Reformed and Lutheran churches. Confessionalists, on the other hand, define themselves, their theology, their piety, and their practice according to public, ecclesiastically sanctioned symbolic documents.

Because the Reformed and Presbyterians have used the wrong categories to identify themselves, errors in the doctrine of justification have become more plausible than they might otherwise be. If we examined doctrinal issues through confessional lenses, then, revisions to central doctrines would be less plausible. When, however, we filter doctrine through the categories *conservative* or *liberal*, the definition changes. In the modern period, rather than standing for a full-bodied theology, piety, and practice, the word *Reformed* has come to mean *predestinarian*. With such minimalist doctrinal boundaries, we were ill prepared to anticipate and refute errors that were not obviously liberal or that presented themselves as being consistent with a minimalist boundary marker such as divine sovereignty.

A Preliminary Proposal

Great changes frequently go unnoticed when they happen. The true nature of such changes becomes evident only after the fact. For example, by rights, had the papacy been as powerful in the sixteenth century as it was in the thirteenth century, it seems incredible that Luther would have survived to challenge the existing order in the way

14. See Hart, *Lost Soul of American Protestantism*.

15. The Roman communion does not appear to be a strictly confessional body inasmuch as, since Vatican II at least, she is quite latitudinarian on doctrine and practice. It is not necessary to adhere strictly to the magisterial doctrine as embodied in the conciliar pronouncements or the *Catechism of the Catholic Church* to be regarded as a faithful Roman Catholic. What is essential is to remain in submission to the Roman see. In a similar way, though Anglicans confess the Thirty-Nine Articles, it is not essential to hold them to be regarded as a faithful Anglican or Episcopalian.

he did. In fact, few were conscious of the weakness of the papacy in the sixteenth century, but it was weak and the Reformation survived. More recently, the true weakness of Soviet-bloc communism was made manifest only by the refusal of certain nations and peoples to submit to Moscow. In a similar way, modernity has been mortally wounded, and the need for the broad evangelical coalition has passed. It is time for Reformed Christianity to move out of the evangelical "big tent" and back into our own churches and to take up our own confessions again and recover our own grammar, theology, and piety.

I propose that instead of reading Scripture through the eyes of various contemporary reconstructions of the Reformed faith—for example, the federal vision or covenant nomism—Reformed and Presbyterian Christians do better to read the Scriptures with the visible institutional church as expressed, publicly and authoritatively, in the Reformed and Presbyterian standards.

Protestant Controversies over Justification

Another part of the explanation for the existence of the current crisis over justification is that it is part of a recurring pattern. Almost from the moment Luther first proclaimed the doctrine of justification on the basis of the finished work of Christ for sinners, imputed to sinners and received through faith alone, it came under attack. The first critics were defending of the prevailing medieval doctrine of justification on the joint basis of gracious acceptance of our best efforts (*meritum de congruo*) and Spirit-wrought sanctity (*meritum de condigno*) through *gratia infusa*, with which, of course, the sinner must cooperate for final justification. Luther's doctrine of justification, complained Trent (session 6, chapter 7), is nothing more than a legal fiction. According to the Roman critics of the Reformation, God can declare us "righteous" only if we are actually, intrinsically righteous.[16]

Rome was not the only critic of the Protestant doctrine of justification. Andreas Osiander (1498–1552) argued that the forensic doctrine of justification could not be correct. God could not declare sinners

16. H. Denzinger, *Enchiridion symbolorum* (30th ed.; Barcelona: Herder, 1955), §§799–800.

to be just. They must be intrinsically just; that is, it must be that God actually transforms them by the infusion of the divine nature, with Christ himself, and on that basis declares them to be just.[17] Calvin wrote at great length against this argument (*Institutes* 3.11).

A controversy developed in 1535 over the role of good works in salvation. In a revision of his *Commonplaces* Melanchthon proposed that good works are "necessary" for salvation.[18] He reasoned that if good works necessarily follow salvation, they must be necessary to it. Melanchthon denied that sinners merit justification by good works, but he seems to have made them an efficient cause of justification, at least for a time. Luther reacted by affirming the first part of the proposition but rejecting Melanchthon's conclusion as a non sequitur.

The controversy simmered until the Leipzig Interim (1548), when the qualifier *sola* was omitted from the article on justification.[19] Concerned about antinomianism, Georg Major (1502–74) defended the article in 1551 by arguing that one cannot be saved without good works.[20] In 1553 he modified his formula by saying that good works are necessary *ad retinendam salutem* (to retain salvation). Melanchthon sided with Major in that year, saying that "new obedience is necessary for salvation."[21] Major argued that he was addressing salvation as a broader concept, not the narrower concept of justification, but his critics saw him confusing justification and sanctification.[22] The controversy continued through 1550s and quieted only on Major's death.[23]

It is against the backdrop of this long-running crisis that the doctrine of justification in the Belgic Confession (1561) and the Heidelberg

17. R. Seeberg, *Textbook of the History of Doctrines* (trans. Charles E. Hay; Philadelphia: Lutheran Publication Society, 1904), 2.369–74.

18. F. Bente, *Historical Introductions to the Symbolical Books of the Evangelical Lutheran Church* (St. Louis: Concordia, 1922), 112–24; C. G. Bretschneider, ed., *Corpus reformatorum* (Berlin: Schwetschke, 1834–1941), 21.421, 775.

19. The text of the article is in Robert Kolb and James A. Nestingen, eds., *Sources and Contexts of the Book of Concord* (Minneapolis: Fortress, 2001), 184–89.

20. Seeberg, *History of Doctrines*, 2.364. See also Robert Kolb, "Georg Major as Controversialist: Polemics in the Late Reformation," *Church History* 45 (1976): 455–68; idem, *Nikolaus von Amsdorf (1483–1565): Popular Polemics in the Preservation of Luther's Legacy* (Nieuwkoop: DeGraaf, 1978), 123–71.

21. Seeberg, *History of Doctrines*, 2.366–67.

22. Kolb, "Georg Major," 460–61; idem, *Nikolaus von Amsdorf*, 133. Von Amsdorf equated salvation and justification and did not recognize Major's distinction.

23. Major repudiated these formulations in 1570.

Catechism (1563) must be interpreted.[24] They sided unequivocally with Luther, against Major and Osiander. The only basis for our justification is Christ's obedience to the law imputed to us and received through faith alone. Belgic Confession 24 even went so far as to remind the Reformed that, though it is impossible that a Christian should not produce the fruits of sanctity, nevertheless, that sanctity is "of no account" toward justification. Indeed, we are justified "even before we do good works" (Schaff 3.411). The Heidelberg Catechism explicitly excluded sanctity as any part of the ground or instrument of justification, teaching instead, that sanctification is the only and always the result of justification (see 21, 56, 60).[25]

The first great threat to the doctrine of justification in the early seventeenth century came from Jacobus Arminius (ca. 1560–1609). Though it is often considered that the Synod of Dort was solely concerned with protecting the doctrine of predestination, in the minds of the orthodox the doctrine of justification was just as much in jeopardy.[26] It seemed to the orthodox that Arminius redefined justifying faith so that it changed both the ground and instrument of justification (see chapter 8 below).

Against the Socinian and Arminian revisions of the doctrine of justification, the Westminster Divines reasserted the classical Protestant doctrine of justification. The Westminster Standards categorically repudiated any notion that one is justified on any other basis than the imputation of the "perfect obedience and sacrifice" (WCF 8.5) or the "obedience and satisfaction of Christ" (11.1). Faith justifies not

24. Zacharias Ursinus, the primary author of the Heidelberg Catechism, was Melanchthon's student for seven years and was a witness to this controversy.

25. In reading the Heidelberg Catechism, it is crucial to remember that its doctrine of justification is in the *second* part of the catechism, not the third, where the doctrine of the Christian life is contained. It is wrong to appeal to HC 87, "Can they, then, be saved who do not turn to God from their unthankful, impenitent life?" as proof that the catechism teaches justification by or through sanctity. This question is addressing the *logical* necessity of sanctity as a result of justification and distinguishing between salvation (including justification and sanctification) and the narrower concept of justification. For the catechism to make our dying to self and living to Christ the instrument of justification would contradict flatly the teaching of HC 21 and HC 60. This was Ursinus's interpretation of HC 86–87; see Zacharias Ursinus, *The Commentary of Dr. Zacharias Ursinus on the Heidelberg Catechism* (trans. G. W. Williard; 1852; repr. Phillipsburg, NJ: Presbyterian & Reformed, 1985), 464–67.

26. See W. R. Godfrey, "Tensions within International Calvinism: The Debate on the Atonement at the Synod of Dort, 1618–1619" (PhD diss., Stanford University, 1974), 40–43.

because it is obeying, but because it is "receiving and resting on Christ and his righteousness" (11.2).

Richard Baxter (1615–91) sponsored the second crisis in the doctrine of justification.[27] His 1649 *Aphorisms* on justification taught quite clearly that faith justifies because it obeys.[28] The orthodox (e.g., WLC 70–73) had been explicit that only Christ's obedience is the ground and that in the act of justification faith's only virtue is that it trusts Christ's finished work. Baxter's revision of the doctrine of justification prompted sharp responses from John Owen (1616–83), whose 1677 treatise *On the Doctrine of Justification by Faith* was, in effect, an extended repudiation of Baxter.[29]

The issues fueling the neonomian controversy of the seventeenth century reemerged in the first quarter of the eighteenth century when the Scottish church was convulsed by a complicated debate between two groups, one tending toward neonomianism and the other, who identified with the 1645 *Marrow of Modern Divinity*, known as the "Marrow men." James Buchanan argues that the doctrine of justifi-

27. For a more positive assessment of Baxter's doctrine of justification, see J. I. Packer, *The Redemption and Restoration of Man in the Thought of Richard Baxter: A Study in Puritan Theology* (Studies in Evangelical History and Thought; Carlisle, UK: Paternoster, 2003), 237–65; and Hans Boersma, *A Hot Peppercorn: Richard Baxter's Doctrine of Justification in Its Seventeenth-Century Context of Controversy* (Zoettermeer: Uitgeverij Boekcentrum, 1993). C. F. Allison, *The Rise of Moralism: The Proclamation of the Gospel from Hooker to Baxter* (London: SPCK, 1966), offers a critical assessment. Boersma agrees largely with Packer and seeks to refute Allison's view that Baxter's doctrine of justification is virtually identical to that of the Council of Trent. Packer (261) says that Baxter adapted Hugo Grotius's legal views to argue a "political" view of the law. In this scheme, the demands of the law change under Christ. This view of the law has a long medieval pedigree and was categorically rejected by the Reformation (see chapter 12 below). Carl Trueman notes the need for interpreters of Baxter's theology to account for its medieval roots; see "A Small Step toward Rationalism: The Impact of the Metaphysics of Tommaso Campanella on the Theology of Richard Baxter," in *Protestant Scholasticism: Essays in Reassessment* (ed. Carl R. Trueman and R. S. Clark; Carlisle, UK: Paternoster, 1999), 185n13; idem, *The Claims of Truth: John Owen's Trinitarian Theology* (Carlisle, UK: Paternoster, 1998), 200–205. Boersma concedes (167) that Baxter made evangelical obedience "a secondary part of the condition of the continuation of justification." He also says that Baxter's denial that faith receives Christ's righteousness directly made room for human fulfillment of the conditions of the covenant by the "peppercorn" of evangelical obedience for justification (255). We are declared righteous partly because we are intrinsically righteous (281). Our works are "a condition of continued and consummate justification" (301). Even according to Boersma's sympathetic analysis of Baxter, there is enough evidence to sustain Allison's judgment.

28. Richard Baxter, *Aphorismes of Justification, with Their Explication Annexed* (London, 1649), thesis 74.

29. John Owen, *The Works of John Owen* (ed. W. H. Goold; repr. Edinburgh: Banner of Truth, 1967), vol. 5.

cation was not directly involved in the controversy, since both sides formally affirmed Westminster Confession of Faith 11, but certainly questions touching the nature of justification were not far removed from the debate.[30] Chief among the Marrow men was Thomas Boston (1677–1732), who defended the *Marrow* doctrine of justification by grace alone, through faith alone, and from it a strong doctrine of assurance of faith resting in the promises of the gospel.[31] The Marrow men were opposed by a majority in the Scottish Kirk, who attacked the *Marrow* and its supporters as antinomian and even Amyraldian.

The Oxford Movement (1833–45), led by John Henry Newman (1801–90), challenged the Protestant doctrine of justification in the Church of England. In his 1838 lectures on justification, Newman caricatured Luther and ignored the places where Hooker agreed with confessional Protestants in order to make his case for a distinctively Anglican doctrine of justification.[32] Newman's position, however, was an untenable halfway house to Rome, which even he found unsatisfactory.

In the twentieth century, the foundation of the confessional doctrine of justification, that is, the Protestant distinction between law and gospel, was eroded severely by Karl Barth's "inversion" of law and gospel into grace and law (see chapter 12 below). The effects of this revision reverberated throughout mainline and evangelical Christianity in Europe and in North America.

Thus, one might say that the current controversy arrived more or less on schedule in 1974. There is no need to rehearse the history here, as O. Palmer Robertson and W. Robert Godfrey (both participants) have recently recounted it.[33] What matters here is that in 1981 the board of

30. James Buchanan, *The Doctrine of Justification* (1867; repr. Edinburgh: Banner of Truth, 1997), 184.

31. See, e.g., Thomas Boston, *Human Nature in Its Fourfold State* (1720; repr. Edinburgh: Banner of Truth, 1964), 284–92; *The Marrow of Modern Divinity . . . with Notes by Thomas Boston* (1726; repr. Seoul: Westminster Publishing House, [1991]). See also David C. Lachman, *The Marrow Controversy, 1718–1723: An Historical and Theological Analysis* (Edinburgh: Rutherford, 1988); and Philip Graham Ryken, *Thomas Boston as Preacher of the Fourfold State* (Rutherford Studies in Historical Theology; Edinburgh: Rutherford, 1999), 42–56.

32. Alister McGrath, "The Emergence of the Anglican Tradition on Justification, 1600–1700," *Churchman* 98 (1984): 28–43. See also Allison, *Rise of Moralism*.

33. O. Palmer Robertson, *The Current Justification Controversy* (Unicoi, TN: Trinity Foundation, 2003); Godfrey, "Westminster, Justification," 136–40.

Westminster Theological Seminary found that one of their systematic theologians, Norman Shepherd, was unable to "communicate with unmistakable clarity the doctrine of justification by sovereign grace alone through faith alone on the grounds of Christ's righteousness alone."[34] They also found that "Mr. Shepherd has not been able to satisfy the Board and considerable portions of the Seminary constituency that the structure of his views and his distinctive formulations clearly present the affirmations by which our Standards guard the relation and place of faith and works with respect to salvation."[35]

The board had ample reason for making this judgment. According to board documents, in his 1974 class syllabus Shepherd taught that "justification presupposes faith; faith is not the ground of justification; faith is the instrument of justification. justification presupposes good works; good works are not the ground of justification; good works are the instrument of justification."[36] In a 1975 informal faculty meeting, he "questioned making justification by faith alone a touchstone of orthodoxy, since, as he argued, what can be said of faith can also be said of good works; neither can be the ground of justification, both can be instrument."[37]

In his defense, Shepherd argued in 1976 that "faith coupled with obedience to Christ is what is called for in order to salvation and therefore in order to justification." "Thus, faith and new obedience are in order to justification and salvation."[38] Shepherd continued to defend his views and sustained serious criticism. In 1980 the faculty and board approved a statement on justification for which Shepherd voted and with which he said he agreed. The board was troubled, nonetheless by his 1981 Sandy Cove lectures and concluded that

> by rejecting the distinction between the covenant of works and the covenant of grace as defined in the Westminster Standards, and by failing to take account in the structure of the "covenantal dynamic" of Christ's fulfillment of the covenant by his active obedience as well

34. "Reason and Specifications Supporting the Action of the Board of Trustees in Removing Professor Shepherd" (Westminster Theological Seminary, February 26, 1982), 2.
35. Ibid., 3.
36. Ibid.
37. Ibid.
38. Ibid., 15.

> as by his satisfaction of its curse, Mr. Shepherd develops a uniform concept of covenantal faithfulness for Adam, for Israel, and for the New Covenant people. The danger is that both the distinctiveness of the covenant of grace and of the new covenant fullness of the covenant of grace will be lost from view and that obedience as the way of salvation will swallow up the distinct and primary function of faith. Obedience is nurtured by faith in Christ and flourishes precisely as we trust wholly in him.[39]

Shepherd's critics continue to find in his more recent writings the very same ambiguities, problems, and errors that led to his dismissal.[40]

In the history of theology, there is a short list of those who have concluded, with Shepherd, in favor of a "a uniform concept of covenantal faithfulness for Adam, for Israel, and for the New Covenant people." The traditional adjective for such a view is *Pelagianism*.[41] The board reached the same conclusions about Shepherd's soteriology that Wilhelmus à Brakel reached concerning the Arminians, who denied the covenant of works:

> Whoever errs here or denies the existence of the covenant of works will not understand the covenant of grace, and will readily err concerning the mediatorship of the Lord Jesus. Such a person will very readily deny that Christ by His active obedience has merited a right to eternal life for the elect. This is to be observed with several parties who, because they err concerning the covenant of grace, also deny the covenant of works. Conversely, whoever denies the covenant of works, must rightly be suspected to be in error concerning the covenant of grace as well.[42]

What à Brakel understood—and what we must relearn—is that what is at stake in these distinctions is not some idiosyncratic cov-

39. Ibid. In my judgment, the board suffered a failure of nerve that should not be repeated today, after Shepherd has clearly repudiated the imputation of Christ's active obedience and renewed his siege on the gospel of justification *sola fide, sola gratia, solo Christo*.

40. See David VanDrunen, "Justification by Faith in the Theology of Norman Shepherd," *Katekomen* 14.1 (2002): 23–26.

41. By this I am not suggesting that Shepherd intended to teach Pelagianism, nor am I saying that Shepherd's theology is thoroughly Pelagian.

42. Wilhelmus à Brakel, *The Christian's Reasonable Service* (1700; trans. Bartel Elshout; repr. Ligioner, PA: Soli Deo Gloria, 1992), 1.355.

enant theology, but the doctrine of justification contained in the Westminster Confession of Faith's explicit distinction (and arguably the implicit distinction, in the *Three Forms of Unity*) between the covenant of works as law and the covenant of grace as gospel. Because covenant theology is, as B. B. Warfield says, "architectonic,"[43] it is impossible to make a substantial revision to Reformed covenant theology (such as conflating the covenants of grace and works) without necessarily making wholesale changes to Reformed soteriology.

The Work of This Book

The work of this book is to take up the challenge posed by the various forms of covenant nomism. The introductory essay by David VanDrunen is a comprehensive survey of the various movements seeking to revise the doctrine of justification. He summarizes the arguments raised by the critics of orthodoxy and considers some of the common threads linking these lines of criticism. His essay does not refute the various positions surveyed, but alerts the reader to the issues and authors involved in the current controversy and sets the stage for the rest of the volume.

The Exegetical Argument

One of the most persuasive arguments propounded by covenant nomism is its claim to be more biblical than the traditional doctrines of justification, wherein, for example, Luther is said to have read his own experience back into Paul. In the exegetical section, Iain Duguid tests the soundness of the covenant-nomism hypothesis—that justification is a matter of obtaining and retaining status as God's covenant people—as a description of the Old Testament relations between God and his people and analyzes the crisis that faced God's people during and after the exile. Can covenantal nomism account for the persistence of God's relationship with his people after the exile?

43. Benjamin B. Warfield, *The Westminster Assembly and Its Work* (New York: Oxford University Press, 1931), 56.

Until the modern period, nearly all the Reformed expositors of Scripture found in Scripture a doctrine of the covenant of works (sometimes called covenant of nature, covenant of life, or covenant of law). This doctrine was never received by the Remonstrants or the early critics of Reformed orthodoxy. In the modern period, however, the covenant of works has come under sustained criticism not only from critics but also from many within the Reformed church on the grounds that it is foreign to the theology of Moses and Paul. Bryan Estelle addresses the exegetical and theological questions of its existence and function in the Pentateuch and elsewhere in Scripture. He offers a reassessment of the doctrine based on his exegesis of Genesis 2–3 in the light of recent studies in linguistics and the ancient Near East.

It is a given for many mainline and evangelical New Testament scholars today that Second Temple Judaism has been radically misunderstood until recently and that these misunderstandings have given rise to confusion about the nature of Paul's covenant theology and doctrine of justification. Steven Baugh challenges the methods and claims of the so-called new perspective(s) by examining and criticizing some of the methods common to proponents of covenant nomism and by testing them and their conclusions against a reading of Romans 5.

The Theological Argument

The doctrine of the *pactum salutis* was taught widely in Reformed theology until recently. Since the 1950s, it has come under criticism as speculative, rationalist, unbiblical, and even antitrinitarian. David VanDrunen and Scott Clark restate the doctrine, defend it from its contemporary critics, and show its importance to Reformed covenant theology by interacting with its modern critics. They argue the case for the traditional Reformed doctrine of the *pactum salutis* on exegetical grounds as the best understanding of several biblical passages and on theological grounds as the motive for Christ's active obedience and a necessary constituent to Reformed covenant theology and a covenantal approach to justification.

Contrary to the frequent assertions of older surveys of the history of theology, Reformed federal or covenant theology did not appear *de novo* in the seventeenth century. Rather, it began to appear before the ink of the earliest Protestant theologies was dry. They gathered up threads from across the history of the catholic church and employed them in the service of the Protestant doctrine of justification. Patristic, medieval, and Reformed covenant theologies all take distinct approaches. Michael Horton surveys some of the contemporary competitors to the classic Reformed covenant theology and argues that several of the diverse challenges to the Reformation are properly described as "covenantal nomism" and that they are not very different in substance from what the Reformation repudiated.

Rejected by Rome and rationalist alike, and unlike some other aspects of traditional Reformed theology, the doctrine of the imputation of Christ's active obedience has enjoyed a privileged status among conservative Reformed and Presbyterian churches. Since the mid-1970s, however, this doctrine has been criticized from within the Reformed movement as part of the proposed revision of the doctrine of justification. The questions raised are not new (e.g., what of Jesus's obedience is imputed to believers?) but the mixed response is. Chapter 8 explores the question of Jesus's obedience to the law in the light of the biblical, confessional, and historic doctrine.

The pre-Reformation church taught that only a "formed" faith (*fides formata caritate*) justifies. In response, Luther asserted *sola fide* and argued that faith functions as the instrument of justification because it is "formed," that is, made efficacious by its object, Christ's obedience for sinners. Robert Godfrey places *sola fide* in its historical context and addresses how faith functions in the act of justification and how active is our faith in our standing before God. He also responds to those critics who assert that *sola fide* is not a Reformed doctrine and defends it against some caricatures and misapprehensions.

Before the Reformation, we were said to be justified to the extent that we were sanctified. In the Reformation that pattern was reversed: sanctification was made the result of justification. Today there is considerable confusion as to why and how the Christian should strive to be sanctified. Hywel Jones explains from Paul and James how Scripture relates justification and sanctification. Contrary to those who suspect that the traditional Protestant doctrine of justification leads to immorality, he argues that the doctrine of the Christian life is a vital necessity to sanctity.

The Pastoral Argument

It is one thing to confess the Reformation doctrine of justification, but how should it be practiced? Turning to the life of the church lived institutionally—where theology turns to practice and doxology—Hywel Jones explains the hermeneutical and homiletical implications of *sola fide* and provides concrete help for pastors seeking to preach the gospel more clearly and winsomely.

Is the law/gospel hermeneutic just one among many, and how does it affect the proclamation of the word? How do many modern practices stand up to the homiletical and liturgical implications of the Reformed law/gospel hermeneutic? Scott Clark argues for the unique structural and hermeneutical function of the confessional law/gospel distinction in preaching.

When Luther inveighed against the "theology of glory," he was speaking about the twin dangers of rationalism and moralism. Julius Kim illustrates how segments of well-intentioned seventeenth-century English Protestantism succumbed to the theology of glory. He illustrates how it is possible to jettison the Reformation (and Pauline) message of *sola gratia, sola fide,* precisely because it seems "foolish" and ill suited to motivate Christians to pious living.

The proclamation of the gospel is central to the minister's calling, but there is more to ministry than preaching. Dennis Johnson explores the implications of the distinction for pastoral ministry beyond the pulpit. In particular, he focuses on the relations between the doctrine of justification and the practice of pastoral counseling and the related questions of assurance and sanctification.

Omissions and Audiences

This volume cannot address all issues entailed by the conservative Reformed appropriation of covenant nomism. There are two sorts of books, the perfect and the finished. This collection of essays is not perfect, but it is finished. Astute readers will notice, for example, that no essay touches directly the question of the relation between covenant and election.[44] Other equally important issues might have been but were not addressed. The concern of this collection of essays is perhaps the central matter of the Christian faith: the righteousness of sinners before a just and holy God.

These essays are not intended to be popular. The faculty held a conference in 2003 in which we presented some of this material in a way that is accessible to Christian laity. Those lectures are available from the Westminster Seminary California. Some of the essays in this collection do arise from that conference, but they have been significantly revised to speak to a more academic audience.

Since the submission of this volume to the publisher early in 2005, several titles have appeared that merit discussion. Unavoidable delays in the publication of this volume, however, prevent us from doing more than acknowledging these titles and alerting the reader to them.[45]

With these essays we are attempting to join the conversation that began with the work of Krister Stendahl in 1963 and that has received significant impetus from the pens of E. P. Sanders and James Dunn. In turn, their work has been made more accessibly by evangelical Anglican scholar N. T. Wright. Parallel to that trajectory has been a movement within confessional Reformed circles, beginning in 1974. This discussion flared up for about seven years, went dormant for twenty years, but has been renewed in the public teaching of Norman Shepherd since 1995. His views have been synthesized by evangelical and Reformed students of the new perspective(s) on Paul and certain threads present in confessional Dutch Reformed theology since before World War II.

44. See R. Scott Clark, "Baptism and the Benefits of Christ: The Double Mode of Communion in the Covenant of Grace," *Confessional Presbyterian* 2 (2006): 3–19.

45. Guy Prentiss Waters, *The Federal Vision and Covenant Theology* (Phillipsburg, NJ: P&R, 2006); Cornel Venema, *Getting the Gospel Right* (Edinburgh: Banner of Truth, 2006); D. A. Carson, Peter T. O'Brien, and Mark A. Seifrid, eds., *Justification and Variegated Nomism*, vol. 2: *The Paradoxes of Paul* (Grand Rapids: Baker, 2004); Jeong Koo Jeon, *Covenant Theology and Justification by Faith: The Shepherd Controversy and Its Impacts* (Eugene, OR: Wipf & Stock, 2006); Wayne C. Stumme, ed., *The Gospel of Justification in Christ: Where Does the Church Stand Today?* (Grand Rapids: Eerdmans, 2006); Samuel E. Waldron, *Faith, Obedience, and Justification: Current Evangelical Departures from Sola Fide* (Reformed Baptist Dissertation Series 1; Palmdale, CA: Reformed Baptist Academic Press, 2006); and Richard Gaffin, *By Faith, Not by Sight: Paul and the Order of Salvation* (Oakhill School of Theology Series; Carlisle, UK: Paternoster, 2006).

Many years ago, as a university student I heard a lecture on Calvin and Calvinism during which my professor of European history spoke entirely in the past tense, as if Calvinism had died in the St. Bartholomew's Day massacre in 1572. He seemed genuinely surprised to find that, though we were dead, we yet live. So, we offer these essays with the thought that some readers might find also that that Calvinism is not dead, but offers a vital and persuasive alternative to some of the views offered at present.

2
Where We Are

Justification under Fire in the Contemporary Scene

David VanDrunen

Introduction

Is the doctrine of justification under fire in the contemporary church and academy? If it is, such an attack might seem worthy of no special notice, since the Reformation's doctrine of justification by faith alone, grounded in the imputed righteousness of Christ alone, has been under fire from the Roman Catholic Church ever since Martin Luther, John Calvin, and their theological allies proclaimed this doctrine with such force and eloquence. However, allegations of a contemporary attack on justification point to a different dynamic in recent events. While many Roman Catholics—even many conservative ones—have adopted a remarkably conciliatory tone on justification toward the heirs of the Reformation in recent ecumenical discussions, the alleged attack on justification has come from typically more cordial corners. The field of biblical studies, and particularly Pauline studies, customarily the haven of Protestants in defense of justification by faith alone against Roman Catholic appeals to ecclesiastical tradition, has risen to challenge the Reformation's hegemony over the interpretation of Paul on salvation. Even more noteworthy, perhaps, many self-styled Reformed church leaders have probed various aspects of the traditional Reformation doctrine of justification and found them wanting, proposing various revisions for the sake of greater fidelity to Scripture and their own understanding of Reformed Christianity.

Justification is indeed under fire in the contemporary church and academy, and three distinct lines of attack demonstrate it: recent ecumenical discussions, the new perspective on Paul popular among many biblical scholars, and the proposals of those I call "Reformed revisionists." This essay is not a critique per se of the views expressed in these lines of attack, but rather an attempt to describe these views accurately and fairly, to contrast them with the traditional position of Reformed Christianity, and to identify similarities among these lines of attack in the midst of their differences. In the context of the present book, this essay serves in large part to explain the need for such a book to be written and to set the stage for later essays to defend the Reformed doctrine of justification and to critique its detractors.

Justification in Recent Ecumenical Discussions

Many Roman Catholics have taken a conciliatory tone toward various Protestant groups in recent ecumenical discussions of the doctrine of justification. This does not, however, indicate that Rome has in fact conceded this doctrine to the Reformation. Instead, under the purported goal of moving beyond the old disputes and the condemnations of the sixteenth-century Council of Trent, Roman Catholic ecumenists have offered presentations of the doctrine of justification that are vague and ambiguous enough to win endorsement from many Protestants while not denying key aspects of the traditional Roman doctrine or adopting key Reformational distinctives. In other words, recent ecumenical discussions describe a doctrine of justification that is general enough to please many Catholics and Protestants yet nonspecific enough to avoid offending either side. The result is an optimistic, yet misleading, picture of the amount of agreement on justification that now exists between Roman Catholics and Protestants—at least those Protestants truly committed to confessional, Reformation doctrine.[1] Four matters call for examination: two noteworthy recent ecumenical statements addressing justification (*Joint Declaration on the Doctrine of Justification* and *The Gift of Salvation*), Thomas Oden's ecumenically inspired attempt to identify a consensus on justification through the history of the church, and ecumenical discussions between Lutherans and Eastern Orthodox.

Joint Declaration on the Doctrine of Justification

Signed on Reformation Day 1999 in Augsburg, Germany, by representatives of the Roman Catholic Church and the Lutheran World Federation (an organization consisting of many, though not all, Lutheran denominations worldwide), the *Joint Declaration on the Doctrine of Justification* deserves scrutiny. The *Joint Declaration* and the ecumenical discussions from which it emerged are presented as a culmination of many past discussions and statements produced by Lutherans and

1. One important issue for understanding current ecumenical discussions, though it cannot be considered at length here, is the sensitivity to and interest in the cultural and linguistic contexts in which doctrines are propounded. George A. Lindbeck, for example, a prominent Lutheran ecumenist, argues for a "cultural-linguistic" approach to religion that views doctrines neither as propositional truths nor as expressions of subjective experience, but rather as rules and regulations that define faithful adherence to a community. Given that the communities and their cultural-linguistic contexts have changed since the Reformation era, the mutual Protestant–Roman Catholic condemnations of that era cannot be simply applied today. See Lindbeck's extended argument in *The Nature of Doctrine: Religion and Theology in a Postliberal Age* (Philadelphia: Westminster, 1984). Prominent Roman Catholic ecumenist Avery Dulles, now a cardinal in New York, seems to reflect such an approach in his reflections on the *Joint Declaration on the Doctrine of Justification*: "According to an older theological model, ecumenism would aspire to take the statements of the Lutheran Book of Concord and those of the Catholic councils one by one, and examine them atomistically and fit them into a single internally coherent system. What seems to be surfacing is a willingness to acknowledge that we have here two systems that have to be taken holistically. Both take their departure from Scripture, the creeds, and early tradition. But they filter the data through different thought-forms, or languages. . . . In the dialogues of the past fifty years, Catholics and Lutherans have come to respect one another as Christian believers. We find that in spite of our different thought-forms, our different languages, we can say many things—the most important things—in common. . . . For all these reasons it now seems appropriate to measure the Lutheran theses against some standard other than the decrees of Trent." See "Two Languages of Salvation: The Lutheran-Catholic Joint Declaration," *First Things* 98 (Dec. 1999): 29.

Roman Catholics.[2] To my knowledge, the *Joint Declaration* has attained no official standing in either the Roman Catholic Church or particular Lutheran denominations, yet its bold claims about unity among the participants on justification make it something of an ecumenical landmark.

The stated purpose of the *Joint Declaration* is to summarize the results of these Lutheran–Roman Catholic discussions. Very importantly, it also sets out to show that Lutheran and Roman Catholic churches are able to articulate a common understanding of justification and that whatever differences remain are no longer occasions for doctrinal condemnation.[3] As the *Joint Declaration* itself summarizes, there is "a consensus in the basic truths; the differing explications in particular statements are compatible with it."[4] The *Joint Declaration* does not summarily dismiss the condemnations leveled by both sides in the days since the Reformation—such as the unmentioned, but undoubtedly presupposed, anathematizing of adherents to the doctrine of justification by faith alone by the Council of Trent[5]—but points readers to developments and new insights that require present reexamination of divisive questions.[6] At one point the *Joint Declaration* confesses that the "seriousness" of past condemnations cannot be taken away and somewhat humorously remarks that "some were not simply pointless."[7] In light of such a statement, the thoughtful reader is left wondering whether many of Trent's condemnations—which, in effect, damned Protestants to hell—actually *were* pointless and whether these too should be taken "seriously." Left unclear is whether Reformation-era condemnations hit real targets or were instances, on a grand scale, of parties speak-

2. *Joint Declaration on the Doctrine of Justification* (Grand Rapids: Eerdmans, 2000), §§3, 6.

3. Ibid., §§3–4, 13, 41.

4. Ibid., §14; see also §40.

5. See the canons concerning justification from the sixth session of the Council of Trent, in *Canons and Decrees of the Council of Trent* (ed. H. J. Schroeder; St. Louis: Herder, 1960), 42–46; or *The Sources of Catholic Dogma* (ed. Henry Denzinger; trans. Roy J. Defarrari; St. Louis: Herder, 1957), 258–61.

6. *Joint Declaration on the Doctrine of Justification*, §7.

7. Ibid., §42.

ing past each other.[8] For Roman Catholics who take their church councils seriously and Protestants who take their church confessions seriously, such lack of clarity would seem to be no minor matter, whatever "developments" and "new insights" may have occurred.

What is the doctrine of justification according to the *Joint Declaration*? At several points along the way the *Joint Declaration* makes statements that, from a Reformation perspective, are orthodox on their own terms and seemingly in perfect accord with Reformation doctrine. For example, justification means that "Christ himself is our righteousness," and we are saved by grace alone, "in faith in Christ's saving work and not because of any merit on our part."[9] Furthermore, "Whatever in the justified precedes or follows the free gift of faith is neither the basis of justification nor merits it."[10] Along the same lines, "We confess together that good works . . . follow justification and are its fruits."[11] The idea that Roman Catholics can say these things together with Lutherans may give reason for great encouragement.

Yet at many other points its claims are either in themselves problematic or noticeably missing key aspects of the doctrine of justification. In what seems to be a general definition of justification, the *Joint Declaration* says that "justification is the forgiveness of sins . . . , liberation from the dominating power of sin and death . . . and from the curse of the law. . . . It is acceptance into communion with God."[12] Any mention of the imputed righteousness of Christ is absent here. Included, however, is liberation from the power of sin, which sounds very much like the usual language for sanctification, yet is incorporated here into justification itself. The relationship between justification and sanctification gets no clearer later on. One section reads that Lutherans and Roman Catholics together confess that God both forgives sins and frees from sin's enslaving power, imparts new life, and effects an active love.[13] In the language of the Reformation, this is the claim

8. For an example of the effect of the cultural-linguistic approach to this question, see Karl Lehmann and Wolfhart Pannenberg, *The Condemnations of the Reformation Era: Do They Still Divide?* (Minneapolis: Fortress, 1990).

9. *Joint Declaration on the Doctrine of Justification*, §15.

10. Ibid., §25.

11. Ibid., §37.

12. Ibid., §11.

13. Ibid., §22.

that God both justifies and sanctifies, yet the *Joint Declaration* does not make clear at this point whether both of these actions of God are to be taken as part of justification or as distinct acts—or whether this question is left open as a disagreement that no longer divides. A later section initially offers hope of clarification, yet ultimately does not. In justification, the *Joint Declaration* says, "a distinction but not a separation is made between justification itself and the renewal of one's way of life that necessarily follows from justification. . . . Thereby the basis is indicated from which the renewal of life proceeds, for it comes forth from the love of God imparted to the person in justification. Justification and renewal are joined in Christ, who is present in faith."[14] That God imparts love to a person in justification is decidedly contrary to Protestant doctrine, yet this point is repeated in the following section, which states that justification gives love, faith, and hope.[15] According to the Reformation, faith is the instrument *by which* justification is given, and love is a fruit *flowing out of* justification. In the *Joint Declaration*, justification is that *which gives* faith and love. These are among the more notable examples of how the Reformation's teaching on justification is denied both by omission (no mention of Christ's imputed righteousness) and by confusion of distinct things (justification and sanctification, faith and love). Despite assurances to the contrary, it is difficult to conclude that the Lutheran signatories remained true to their Reformation heritage.

The Gift of Salvation

Another important ecumenical statement of recent years, and one that may hit closer to home for many readers, is *The Gift of Salvation*.[16] This document was released in late 1997 by a group of Roman Catholics and evangelicals, many of whom had previously collaborated on the much-discussed 1994 document *Evangelicals and Catholics Together: The Christian Mission in the Third Millennium*.[17] In this earlier statement, the participants hailed the common cause between Roman

14. Ibid., §26.
15. Ibid., §27.
16. See *First Things* 79 (Jan. 1998): 20–23.
17. See *First Things* 43 (May 1994): 15–22.

Catholics and evangelicals in the cultural battles of the day, acknowledged one another as brothers in Christ, and agreed to cooperate in evangelistic efforts, though they confessed that they had important remaining differences. In *Gift of Salvation*, the participants took up one point of historic disagreement between their two camps: salvation generally and justification in particular. They claim ability "to express a common faith in Christ and so to acknowledge one another as brothers and sisters in Christ" and "together bear witness to the gift of salvation" despite "some persistent and serious differences."

In a way similar to the *Joint Declaration*, *Gift of Salvation* makes many statements that, taken by themselves, seem quite favorable to the Reformation's expression of the doctrine of justification. Many of these statements, however, are left ambiguous enough to be potentially consistent with either traditional Protestant or Roman Catholic understandings. A few examples illustrate. *Gift of Salvation* claims that "justification is not earned by any good works or merits of our own; it is entirely God's gift." As Protestant as this sounds, it is not clear whether this statement rules out the Roman Catholic idea of merit that is attained *after* one's initial justification (and before one's final justification).[18] Shortly thereafter, the document reads: "In justification, God, on the basis of Christ's righteousness alone, declares us to be no longer his rebellious enemies but his forgiven friends, and by virtue of his declaration it is so." Though justification on the basis of Christ's righteousness alone seems to be Protestant language, however, the context never specifies that this means the imputed obedience of Christ as the sole ground of justification. This lack of specification is significant because the Roman Catholic tradition can also speak of Christ's work as the basis for justification—but in the sense of being its meritorious cause—and of Christ's righteousness—but as infused rather than imputed righteousness given to us.[19]

Following on the heels of this statement is a paragraph in which the signatories describe faith, and they claim that "what we here affirm is in agreement with what the Reformation traditions have meant by

18. For Roman Catholic teaching on this point, see, for example, *Catechism of the Catholic Church* (2nd ed.; Rome: Libreria Editrice Vaticana, 1997), §2010.

19. See Council of Trent, session 6, chapter 7, in *Canons and Decrees*, 33–34; and *Sources of Catholic Dogma*, 251–52.

justification by faith alone (*sola fide*)." One might notice that this is not quite the same as saying that what they affirm *is* the Reformation doctrine of *sola fide*. And this is probably not due to careless language, for their description of faith indeed cannot be identified with the Reformation's understanding of faith. Absent from the functions they ascribe to faith is one that most distinguished the Reformation's understanding from Rome's: its extraspective character by which it looks completely outside itself and rests upon the completed work of Christ. Finally, *Gift of Salvation* affirms that sanctification "is not fully accomplished at the beginning of our life in Christ, but is progressively furthered as we struggle, with God's grace and help, against adversity and temptation." Again, taken by themselves, these words might be read as an accurate description of Reformation doctrine. Never specified, however, is whether this progressive sanctification is to be absolutely distinguished from justification itself. Nothing in these words contradicts traditional Roman doctrine, for Rome has taught a progressive sanctification—but one that is in fact an aspect of justification. That idea is not foreclosed by the words of *Gift of Salvation*.

The conclusion to be drawn from *Gift of Salvation*, therefore, is similar to that drawn above about the *Joint Declaration*. Isolated statements sound quite consonant with Reformation teaching about justification, but many of these statements are also consonant with traditional Roman Catholic teaching when ambiguous words and expressions are understood in a slightly different way. Perhaps even more important than what is said is what is not said: there is no fully adequate definition of justifying faith and no description at all of the imputed righteousness of Christ. *Gift of Salvation* itself seems to admit the truth of this last sentence, for the end of the document describes remaining differences among the participants and includes issues of "imputed and transformative righteousness" and "the assertion that while justification is by faith alone, the faith that receives salvation is never alone." From the standpoint of the Reformation's understanding of justification, these are not peripheral issues but the heart of the matter. Despite its claims of expressing basic Roman Catholic–evangelical agreement on the nature of the gospel, *Gift of*

Salvation is misleading insofar as many truly crucial disagreements remain unresolved.

The Oden Proposal

Thomas C. Oden, one of the evangelical signatories of *Gift of Salvation,* presents an intriguing and compelling argument relevant to the present discussion. In his *Justification Reader,* he claims that there is "a textually defined consensual classic Christian teaching on salvation by grace through faith," and hence he sets out to show "how the classic Christian exegetes, mostly of the first five centuries, dealt with Paul's justification doctrine."[20] Oden laments that contemporary evangelical perceptions of the patristic literature dismiss the church fathers as deniers of the imputation of the righteousness of Christ or even as ignorant of the doctrine of justification.[21] Though Oden does not deny that there were ambiguities in the patristic teaching, he argues that a consensus on justification existed among patristic writers that, although distorted in medieval Scholasticism, was recovered in nearly identical form by the Protestant Reformers.[22] The Reformation teaching on justification, says Oden, "was not a rescue from all pre-Protestant interpreters, but rather a rescue from only ancillary distortions of patristic thought that developed in the late middle ages."[23] Oden then mentions contemporary ecumenical statements such as the *Joint Declaration* and claims that "these recent statements are substantially consistent with the consensus established in the patristic period."[24] In summary then, Oden makes the remarkable claim that the patristic, Reformation, and contemporary ecumenical understandings of justification are substantially the same.

Though confident in his claims, Oden is also humble. He asks "Protestant colleagues to admonish me fairly and precisely about what is substantively missing in these patristic justification passages that would be required to pass muster by rigorous classic Protestant teaching stan-

20. Thomas C. Oden, *The Justification Reader* (Grand Rapids: Eerdmans, 2002), 16.
21. Ibid., 19.
22. Ibid., 24.
23. Ibid., 29.
24. Ibid., 30.

dards."[25] The present writer is ill equipped to critique Oden's scholarly expertise in gathering ancient sources, and I am, in fact, very appreciative of Oden's efforts, which I find of great value. Nevertheless, I believe that the evidence he presents of the patristic consensus on justification, while perhaps being substantively similar to documents such as the *Joint Declaration*, demonstrates only continuity, not substantial identity, with the Reformers' teaching. Significantly, Oden clearly includes in the patristic consensus the idea of Christ's imputed righteousness as the ground of justification,[26] but where is the textual evidence? My own reading of his extensive patristic references uncovers only one statement that seems clearly to teach either the active obedience of Christ or the imputation of it to believers, and Oden presents this statement, by Clement of Alexandria, only by way of summary, not quotation.[27] Even if Clement did indeed teach the imputed righteousness of Christ, one example surely does not establish a consensus over five centuries. Other readers can judge for themselves whether I have missed other pieces of evidence in Oden's texts, but at present I must judge that Oden has not proven his case on this point. This means that though the patristic authors said many good and helpful things on justification that were subsequently distorted in medieval theology—and on this narrower claim Oden makes a strong case—they ought to be viewed as forerunners of the more fully developed Reformation position, not as expositors of the full Reformation position itself.[28] From the perspective of Reformation Christianity, this is a very valuable claim to be able to make: the Reformers were not inventing the gospel anew, but picking up the patristic doctrine and strengthening it. If the Reformation's strengthening of the doctrine was biblically accurate, however, present ecumenical reversion to the less developed patristic consensus is hardly more acceptable than would be a present reversion to pre-Nicene expressions of the doctrine of the Trinity at the expense of the more developed Nicene expressions.

25. Ibid., 25.

26. Ibid., 37.

27. Ibid., 92. Oden's two references to Clement on this point, parenthetically in the text and in the footnote (the latter to *ANF*), do not correspond. Having looked at both cited sections of Clement's writings, I am unable to determine the basis for Oden's appeal to them.

28. Oden seems to suggest such a conclusion as a possible alternative should his stronger thesis fail; see ibid., 49–50.

The Finnish School on Luther

In the 1970s, ecumenical discussions between Finnish Lutheran and Russian Orthodox theologians sparked a major theological project at the University of Helsinki, led by Tuomo Mannermaa.[29] Mannermaa and his associates, reading Luther alongside Orthodox literature, claim to have discovered a long-neglected aspect of Luther's theology, namely, his belief in believers' union with Christ such that Christ is really present in salvation and the believer has real participation in him. The Finns contrast this reading of Luther with the idea of justification as purely forensic or legal and assert that the true Luther has more in common with the Eastern Orthodox idea of *theōsis* (deification) than with the soteriology of post-Luther Lutheranism, such as that represented in the Formula of Concord. At one point Mannermaa describes his position:

> Luther does not distinguish between the person and the work of Christ. Christ Himself, both his person and his work, is the righteousness of man before God. Christ is both *favor* (forgiveness of sins, atonement, abolition of wrath) and gift (*donum*), Christ himself present. Faith means justification precisely on the basis of Christ's person being present in it as favor and gift. *In ipsa fide Christus adest*: in faith itself Christ is present, and so the whole of salvation.[30]

Mannermaa explains that this position contrasts with later Lutheranism, which understood justification as a "totally forensic matter" in that Luther "does not separate the person of Christ from his work. Rather, Christ himself, both his person and his work, is the ground of Christian righteousness."[31]

29. See Carl E. Braaten and Robert W. Jenson, "Preface," in *Union with Christ: The New Finnish Interpretation of Luther* (ed. Carl E. Braaten and Robert W. Jenson; Grand Rapids: Eerdmans, 1998), 1.

30. Tuomo Mannermaa, "Why Is Luther so Fascinating? Modern Finnish Luther Research," in *Union with Christ: The New Finnish Interpretation of Luther* (ed. Carl E. Braaten and Robert W. Jenson; Grand Rapids: Eerdmans, 1998), 14–15.

31. Tuomo Mannermaa, "Justification and *Theosis* in Lutheran-Orthodox Perspective," in *Union with Christ: The New Finnish Interpretation of Luther* (ed. Carl E. Braaten and Robert W. Jenson; Grand Rapids: Eerdmans, 1998), 28. Similar understandings of Christ's work and justification are currently being promoted by some in evangelical circles. For a recent example, see Michael F. Bird, "Incorporated Righteousness: A Response to Recent Evangelical Discussion

As a description of the Finnish school on Luther, the above treatment is obviously incomplete. Nevertheless, it exposes another challenge to the Reformation's doctrine of justification in the world of ecumenical dialogue. Though the main conclusions of the Finnish school do not themselves constitute a constructive biblical claim that the idea of forensic justification is incorrect, the claim that Luther himself did not hold the allegedly Reformation view of justification is inevitably troubling for orthodox Protestants. A doctrine of justification that corrupts the great Reformer's thought would seem rather suspicious. Thus, whereas documents such as *Joint Declaration* and *Gift of Salvation* water down and render incomplete the Reformation doctrine of justification, the Finnish school questions whether the received Reformation doctrine is really the Reformation doctrine at all.[32]

Justification and the New Perspective on Paul

A second major front on which battles over justification are being fought in the present day is the field of biblical studies—particularly Pauline studies. The so-called new perspective on Paul is a school of thought whose origins can be traced roughly to the publication of E. P. Sanders's *Paul and Palestinian Judaism* in 1977, a work that has indelibly shaped subsequent New Testament scholarship.[33] Sanders's basic thesis argues that New Testament scholars have incorrectly assumed that the Judaism that Paul confronted was a religion of works-righteousness in which individuals sought to merit their salvation. Picking

concerning the Imputation of Christ's Righteousness in Justification," *Journal of the Evangelical Theological Society* 47 (June 2004): 253–75.

32. Though this is not the place for critique, readers may note that competent scholars have critically evaluated the Finnish proposals. Writing from a Reformed stance, yet focusing particularly on the shortcomings of the Finnish historiography, is Carl R. Trueman, "Is the Finnish Line a New Beginning? A Critical Assessment of the Reading of Luther Offered by the Helsinki Circle," *Westminster Theological Journal* 65 (2003): 231–44. If nothing else, the Finnish ecumenical agenda makes their objective historical study suspect. Mannermaa and several of his associates actually hold positions as professors of *ecumenics* at the University of Helsinki. See Braaten and Jenson, *Union with Christ*, 21, 25, 42n1, for revealing comments on how their ecumenical agenda drives their research. Trueman also picks up on this point in his critique.

33. E. P. Sanders, *Paul and Palestinian Judaism: A Comparison of Patterns of Religion* (Philadelphia: Fortress, 1977).

up this thesis as a virtual starting point for their own work, subsequent writers claim that Paul, in epistles such as Romans and Galatians, neither condemned his Jewish opponents for teaching salvation by meritorious works nor offered justification by faith alone as the alternative to this. Instead, advocates of the new perspective on Paul, in various ways, identify controversies over Jewish exclusiveness and the place of Gentiles in the covenant community as the chief matters of concern to Paul.[34]

Krister Stendahl

Sanders's work was undoubtedly decisive in birthing this movement in New Testament scholarship. His study had precedents, however. One noteworthy work that clearly anticipates Sanders and later advocates of the new perspective on Paul is a 1963 article by Krister Stendahl.[35] According to Stendahl, the introspective conscience has characterized Western religious culture for a very long time. It can be traced back to Augustine's self-reflections and the development of the medieval penitential system, yet perhaps found its most poignant exemplar in Martin Luther. Luther, after long wrestling with how he could be right with God, found his answer in the doctrine of justification by faith alone. Along with so many subsequent interpreters, Luther read back into Paul the same sort of spiritual agony and liberation that he himself experienced. Stendahl argues that such a reading of Paul does not do him justice. He claims instead that Paul experienced no existential angst as a Pharisee, nor was he part of a Jewish religious culture obsessed about individual salvation through obeying the law.

34. In addition to the most important works promoting the new perspective on Paul discussed below, recent significant books offer critical analysis of the new perspective on Paul from different theological perspectives: Stephen Westerholm, *Perspectives Old and New on Paul: The "Lutheran" Paul and His Critics* (Grand Rapids: Eerdmans, 2004); Seyoon Kim, *Paul and the New Perspective: Second Thoughts on the Origin of Paul's Gospel* (Grand Rapids: Eerdmans, 2002); Peter Stuhlmacher, *Revisiting Paul's Doctrine of Justification: A Challenge to the New Perspective; with an Essay by Donald A. Hagner* (Downers Grove, IL: InterVarsity, 2001); D. A. Carson, Peter T. O'Brien, and Mark A. Seifrid, eds., *Justification and Variegated Nomism* (2 vols.; Grand Rapids: Baker, 2001–4); and Mark A. Seifrid, *Christ Our Righteousness: Paul's Theology of Justification* (Downers Grove, IL: InterVarsity, 2000).

35. Krister Stendahl, "The Apostle Paul and the Introspective Conscience of the West," *Harvard Theological Review* 56 (1963): 199–215.

Furthermore, Stendahl argues that Paul's epistles focused much more upon the historical plan of redemption than upon individual experience of redemption, pointing to the importance of Jew-Gentile relations in the plan of God and the significance of the coming of the Messiah. At the end of his article, Stendahl makes clear that he does not view an introspective conscience as necessarily a bad thing, but he calls for readers of the New Testament to do more justice to Paul himself and to leave room in Christianity for other sorts of religious experiences.

E. P. Sanders

E. P. Sanders followed Stendahl's basic trajectory in producing his voluminous comparison of Paul and Palestinian Judaism more than ten years later. Sanders's analysis of Judaism has been more influential than his interpretation of Paul per se, yet his proposal as a whole deserves description. At the beginning of *Paul and Palestinian Judaism,* Sanders announces the several goals of his work. The first goal is to consider, as a general methodological matter, how to compare different but related religions. Sanders then purposes to destroy the view of Palestinian rabbinic Judaism prevalent in the New Testament scholarship of his day and to establish a different interpretation of it. Sanders's last goals are to propose an understanding of Paul's work and to compare Paul to Palestinian Judaism.[36] Important background for Sanders's project was the common assumption in New Testament scholarship that Paul and Judaism were antithetical.[37] Sanders argues that comparing Paul and Judaism in new and different ways will help to overcome this misperception. Instead of comparing what are determined to be the "essences" or special motifs of different religions, Sanders suggests that one religion should be compared to another, each taken as a whole.[38] This may be accomplished, he says, by comparing "patterns of religion":

> A pattern of religion, defined positively, is the description of how a religion is perceived by its adherents to *function*. "Perceived to

36. Sanders, *Paul and Palestinian Judaism,* xii.
37. Ibid., 3.
38. Ibid., 12.

> function" has the sense not of what an adherent does on a day-to-day basis, but of *how getting in and staying in are understood*: the way in which a religion is understood to admit and retain members is considered to be the way it "functions." . . . A pattern of religion thus has largely to do with the items which a systematic theology classifies under "soteriology."[39]

Hence, Sanders intends to describe the relationship between Paul's pattern of religion and that of the Palestinian Judaism contemporary to Paul.[40]

Sanders's analysis of Palestinian Judaism, the longest part of his book and clearly the most important for subsequent scholarship, concludes that its pattern of religion can be described as "covenantal nomism." With one exception, he claims that "in all the literature surveyed, *obedience maintains one's position in the covenant, but it does not earn God's grace as such*. It simply keeps an individual in the group which is the recipient of God's grace."[41] This leads to his summary of the pattern of religion that he calls covenantal nomism:

> (1) God has chosen Israel and (2) given the law. The law implies both (3) God's promise to maintain the election and (4) the requirement to obey. (5) God rewards obedience and punishes transgression. (6) The law provides for means of atonement, and atonement results in (7) maintenance or re-establishment of the covenantal relationship. (8) All those who are maintained in the covenant by obedience, atonement and God's mercy belong to the group which will be saved.

"An important interpretation of the first and last points is that election and ultimately salvation are considered to be by God's mercy rather than human achievement."[42] For Sanders, then, Palestinian Judaism was not about meriting salvation by good works, but about getting into the covenant by God's grace and staying in the covenant by obedience to the law.

39. Ibid., 17.
40. Ibid., 19.
41. Ibid., 420 (emphasis original).
42. Ibid., 422.

Given the common Reformation assumption that combating Judaism's works-righteousness scheme was a chief concern of Paul, Sanders's interpretation of Palestinian Judaism raises significant questions about Paul's epistles. Sanders concludes that Paul technically was not a covenantal nomist and hence that his type of religiousness was different from that of Palestinian Judaism. Sanders claims, however, that on the important issue of grace and works Paul and Palestinian Judaism were actually in agreement. For both parties, "there are two aspects of the relationship between grace and works: *salvation is by grace but judgment is according to works; works are the condition of remaining 'in,' but they do not earn salvation.*"[43] Sanders describes Paul's pattern of religion as "participationist eschatology." This means that God sent Christ to be the Savior of Jew and Gentile alike and that a person comes to participate in salvation by becoming one with Christ in his death and resurrection. Though this union with Christ becomes complete only upon his second coming, one who lives now in Christ is freed from power and defilement of sin and is called to behave accordingly.[44] The charge that Palestinian Judaism was a religion of works-righteousness "is not the heart of Paul's critique." Instead, Paul's polemics against the law were fueled by his "exclusivist soteriology." For Paul, there was nothing wrong with the law itself—such as emphasizing petty things or tabulating merit—but the law was simply worthless in comparison to union with Christ.[45] Likewise, Paul found nothing wrong with Judaism except that it was not Christianity.[46]

Sanders's interpretation of Palestinian Judaism, if not his interpretation of Paul, has become virtually normative for advocates of the new perspective on Paul. Accepting the idea that first-century Judaism was not about keeping the law in order to earn salvation, proponents of the new perspective on Paul conclude that Paul must not have been arguing against such ideas, even in his discussions of justification in Romans and Galatians, as readers of the New Testament have long believed. Therefore, they go about the task of reinterpreting Paul's

43. Ibid., 543 (emphasis original).
44. Ibid., 549.
45. Ibid., 550.
46. Ibid., 552.

thought, including what he meant by justification. Hence, a *new* perspective on Paul.

James D. G. Dunn

James Dunn is perhaps the most accomplished New Testament scholar of the new perspective on Paul circle. In his recent comprehensive study of Pauline theology, he dedicates a large section to justification.[47] Early in this section, Dunn pays his respects to Sanders and notes that readers of the New Testament have long been guilty of reading Luther—his struggles, his theology, and the Reformation debates he spawned—into Paul. Sanders broke important ground in understanding Judaism, but a better understanding of Paul in light of his Jewish context is still necessary.[48]

Dunn views interpretation of Paul's phrase *the righteousness of God* as the obvious place to begin his analysis of justification. He contrasts the understanding of righteousness in the "Greek worldview" as an ideal for measuring action with its meaning in "Jewish thought" as a relational concept. Though the former represents the usual approach to interpreting Paul's use of the term, according to Dunn, Paul in fact understood righteousness in its Hebrew sense.[49] Specifically, Dunn claims that Paul's "righteousness of God" denotes God's faithfulness to his people, his fulfilling the obligations he made in creating the world, calling Abraham, and choosing Israel to be his people.[50] Dunn states, in fact, that Paul could take it for granted that both Jewish and Gentile readers of his epistles would understand his language along these lines.[51] From this point, Dunn launches his initial salvo on justification itself, concluding that this perspective renders much of the Reformation-era disputes on the doctrine "pointless." The concern is not whether God makes people righteous (as in Roman Catholicism) or reckons them righteous (as in Protestantism); instead, the concern is his faithfulness: "The covenant God counts the covenant

47. James D. G. Dunn, *The Theology of Paul the Apostle* (Grand Rapids: Eerdmans, 1998).

48. Ibid., 336–39.

49. Ibid., 340–41.

50. Ibid., 342.

51. Ibid., 343–44.

partner as still in partnership, despite the latter's continued failure. But the covenant partner could hardly fail to be transformed by a living relationship with the life-giving God."[52] Furthermore, Paul's teaching on the initiative of grace in justification was not a polemic against Pharisees or Judaizers, but "was simply a restatement of the first principles of his own ancestral faith."[53]

If Paul was not making arguments about how one is made right with God, but commending the essential teaching of his Jewish heritage on this point, what exactly was he striving against and what fault did he see in those seeking to be justified by "the works of the law"? Dunn points to the importance of understanding the nature of Paul's conversion and asserts that Paul was converted "from measuring righteousness primarily in terms of covenant distinctiveness, and from a competitive practice within Judaism which sought to outdo other Jews in the degree and quality of its Torah-keeping."[54] In other words, Paul reacted against Jewish attempts to use the law to exclude Gentiles and exalt their own status as God's people. When Paul's criticism of the law is understood in terms of its "boundary-defining role, that is, as separating Jew from Gentile," it becomes apparent that his doctrine of justification served "as Paul's attempt to explain why and how Gentiles are accepted by God and consequently should be accepted also by their Jewish fellow believers."[55] Paul's sharp attacks on the works of the law, then, were not attacks on good works done to attain righteousness before God, as Protestant exegesis traditionally contends. Contemporary Jewish theology did not teach this anyway, as Sanders had shown. The phrase *the works of the law* came to have a negative sense in Paul as that by which Israel protected its "privileged status and restricted prerogative."[56] Particularly important among these works of the law were things such as circumcision, Sabbath keeping, and clean/unclean distinctions, which most clearly distinguished Jews from Gentiles.[57] Hence, the works against which

52. Ibid., 344.
53. Ibid., 345; see also 367 in regard to Rom 4:4–5.
54. Ibid., 350.
55. Ibid., 353–54.
56. Ibid., 355.
57. Ibid., 356.

Paul warns were Israel's misunderstanding of its law: using the law to distinguish Jew from Gentile, forcing Gentile Christians to adopt Jewish distinctives, and failing to appreciate God's promise to bless the nations.[58]

Toward the end of his section on justification in Paul, Dunn brings his various lines of analysis together and presents his conclusions on the subject. Some of the things he says are, taken by themselves, consistent with the Reformation's understanding of justification. But, as Dunn himself has already made clear, he thinks that Paul had something else in mind, and his conclusions are certainly different in important respects from the Reformation's. Perhaps Dunn's most thorough summary of Paul's doctrine of justification by faith is this:

> It was a profound conception of the relation between God and humankind—a relation of utter dependence, of unconditional trust. Human dependence on divine grace had to be unqualified or else it was not Abraham's faith, the faith through which God could work his own work. That was why Paul was so fiercely hostile to the qualification which he saw confronting him all the time in any attempt to insist on works of the law as a necessary accompaniment of or addition to faith. God would not justify, could not sustain in relationship with him, those who did not rely wholly on him. Justification was by faith, by faith alone.[59]

The emphasis on the importance of unconditional trust and utter dependence on grace in Paul's view of justification is of course familiar to those accustomed to Reformation teaching. Yet Dunn's divergence from the Reformation is evident here not only in his speaking of justification as the *sustaining* of a relationship with God, but also—and even more striking—in his complete removal of the work of Christ, in his active or passive obedience, from this description of justification. This is perhaps what one would expect from a writer who claims that Paul's conception of individual salvation was a restatement of his pre-Christian, Jewish religion, yet the absence of

58. Ibid., 366.
59. Ibid., 379.

Christ and his atoning work as the object of faith and the source of grace is remarkable.

Further on, Dunn speaks of justification in Paul as "acceptance by God." Though ambiguous, such a notion is not necessarily at odds with Reformation teaching. Dunn, however, again separates himself from traditional Protestant doctrine by recalling his previous claims about the righteousness of God. He derides the "Greek" (read Reformation) understanding of God's righteousness as a law-court metaphor implying "abuse of legal process or a legal fiction." Acceptance by God in justification is not God judicially treating the ungodly as if they were innocent, for in the courtroom there is no place for forgiveness. Instead, along "Hebrew" lines, God graciously decides to continue the relationship that the other covenant partner has breached. In other words, God simply forgives, without the need for justice to be satisfied.[60] To summarize Dunn's conclusions, then, justification in Paul is not a once-for-all completed act, is not ultimately a judicial/forensic concept, and is not based upon the imputation of Christ's obedience.

N. T. Wright

N. T. Wright must be credited with presenting the new perspective on Paul to a wider, popular audience. He has gained a great deal of credibility among evangelicals, much of which can certainly be attributed to his winsome defense of things such as the historical character of Christ's resurrection.[61] In addition, though Wright agrees with much of Dunn's case described above, he attempts to state his view of Paul on justification in a way that appears mostly consistent with, if more developed than, the Reformation's view. In fact, he claims that his view offers all the advantages and basic tenets of the Reformation's doctrine of justification with the added benefit of understanding Paul's own words much more accurately.[62] If true, Wright's version of the new perspective on Paul is understandably attractive to his evangeli-

60. Ibid., 385–86.

61. N. T. Wright, *The Resurrection of the Son of God* (Minneapolis: Fortress, 2003).

62. N. T. Wright, *What Saint Paul Really Said: Was Paul of Tarsus the Real Founder of Christianity?* (Grand Rapids: Eerdmans, 1996), 113.

cal admirers; unfortunately, his differences with the Reformation are considerably more substantive than he sometimes suggests.

Like Dunn, Wright wishes to move beyond Sanders and modify his claims, but he states that he regards Sanders's "basic point as established."[63] The Judaism of Paul's day was not about salvation by works-righteousness, and Saul the Pharisee was no proto-Pelagian worried about getting into heaven by his own efforts. Saul "was not interested in a timeless system of salvation" but above all "wanted God to redeem Israel."[64] Wright claims that Saul the Pharisee, like many other contemporary Jews, believed that Israel was still in a state of exile and that a great day was coming in which God would bring Israel's story to a conclusion by defeating evil and vindicating Israel as the people of God.[65] This hope included the expectation that God would save the entire world—that was his covenant promise. In this context, Wright explains, justification "describes the coming great act of redemption and salvation, *seen from the point of view* of the covenant on the one hand (Israel is God's people) and the law court on the other (God's final judgment will be like a great law-court scene, with Israel winning the case)."[66]

This background illumines Wright's view of Saul's conversion. Saul, of course, was not converted to a different way of attaining personal salvation. Instead, when he saw the resurrected Christ on the road to Damascus, he concluded that God had already done for Jesus what he had thought God was going to do for Israel at the end of history. He had vindicated Jesus after his sufferings rather than Israel after its suffering. This meant that resurrection had occurred and that the age to come had arrived, and thus the converted Paul recognized that the time of the Gentile harvest was now.[67] The Gentile mission upon which Paul then embarked is a very important context for understanding his doctrine of justification. As Wright explains, however, justification was not the focus of the evangelistic message

63. Ibid., 20; see also 114.

64. Ibid., 32.

65. Ibid., 30–31. On this point, see also the exposition in N. T. Wright, *The Climax of the Covenant: Christ and the Law in Pauline Theology* (Minneapolis: Fortress, 1992), chap. 7.

66. Wright, *What Saint Paul Really Said*, 33 (emphasis original).

67. Ibid., 36–37, 82.

that Paul would have announced in the streets of pagan cities. Rather, justification "was the thing *his converts* most needed to know in order to be assured that they really were part of God's people."[68]

What sort of concept was justification, then, if it was not the gospel message that Paul proclaimed to pagans?[69] Wright makes clear that Paul did not mean by justification the imputation of righteousness, as taught by the Reformation. He emphasizes, with Dunn, that the phrase *the righteousness of God* had an obvious meaning: "God's own faithfulness to his promises, to the covenant."[70] In the language of the courtroom, righteousness means different things for the judge and for the defendant, and it is not an object that can be transferred in any way to the defendant from the judge. Though the justified, in Paul's mind, attain the status of righteous, their righteousness is not God the judge's own righteousness. This, Wright sniffs, is "a category mistake" and "makes no sense at all."[71] Hence, the righteousness of God is God's own righteousness, by which he declares the believer to be righteous.[72] Wright concludes: "If we leave the notion of 'righteousness' as a law-court metaphor only, as so many have done in the past, this gives the impression of a legal transaction, a cold piece of business, almost a trick of thought performed by a God who is logical and correct but hardly one we would want to worship."[73]

After taking this shot at his characterization of the Reformation view of justification, Wright reassures his Reformation-sympathizing reader almost immediately thereafter by a cleverly worded piece of reasoning. He says that the popular, common account of justification, which is rooted in the disputes between Augustine and Pelagius and between Luther and Erasmus, is "not entirely misleading." Yet he warns that beginning with the common view will cause one to lose sight of the real Pauline gospel; beginning with his own rediscovery of Paul's gospel, however, allows one to have both the cake and its eating: "If you start with the Pauline gospel itself you will get justification in

68. Ibid., 94 (emphasis added).
69. Ibid., 40–46.
70. Ibid., 96.
71. Ibid., 97–99.
72. Ibid., 107.
73. Ibid., 110.

all its glory thrown in as well."[74] Justification has been used since Augustine as an antidote against Pelagian works-righteousness, yet reading Romans as if it answers the question of how people become Christians has perverted that epistle for hundreds of years.[75] In a very important description of Paul's true doctrine of justification, Wright redefines it as an ecclesiological category:

> "Justification" in the first century was not about how someone might establish a relationship with God. It was about God's eschatological definition, both future and present, of who was, in fact, a member of his people. In Sanders' terms, it was not so much about "getting in," or indeed about "staying in," as about "how you could tell who was in." In standard Christian theological language, it wasn't so much about soteriology as about ecclesiology; not so much about salvation as about the church.[76]

After discussing several Pauline texts relevant to this discussion, Wright offers a helpful summary of his position, specifically in regard to Romans 3:

> Within this context, "justification," as seen in 3:24–26, means that those who believe in Jesus Christ are declared to be members of the true covenant family; which of course means that their sins are forgiven, since that was the purpose of the covenant. They are given the status of being "righteous" in the metaphorical law court. When this is cashed out in terms of the underlying covenantal theme, it means that they are declared, in the present, to be what they will be seen to be in the future, namely the true people of God. Present justification declares, on the basis of faith, what future justification will affirm publicly . . . on the basis of the entire life. And in making this declaration . . . , God himself is in the right, in that he has been faithful to the covenant; he has dealt with sin, and upheld the helpless; and in the crucified Christ he has done so impartially. The gospel—not "justification by faith," but the message

74. Ibid., 113.
75. Ibid., 116–17. See also Wright, *Climax of the Covenant*, 243.
76. Wright, *What Saint Paul Really Said*, 119.

> about Jesus—thus reveals the righteousness, that is, the covenant faithfulness, of God.[77]

For Wright, then, justification involves the forgiveness of sins; that is an "of course." But justification is based upon "the entire life." It does not concern how one becomes right with God, nor is it grounded in the imputed obedience of Jesus Christ or in anything that can rightly be called a theology of the atonement. Whatever kind things Wright occasionally says about the Reformation understanding of justification, his own view of Paul's view is something quite different.

Justification among Reformed Revisionists

Perhaps the most curious aspect of the contemporary attack upon the doctrine of justification is that part of the assault has come from people associated with confessional Reformed Christianity. That those outside the Reformed fold would critique the Reformation doctrine of justification is not stunning, even when their provenance is the relatively friendly field of biblical studies. But that Reformed churchmen and theologians would both implicitly and explicitly attack the Reformation doctrine of justification—sometimes even in the name of Reformed theology itself—is remarkable. Even more remarkable is that many in confessional Reformed circles have expressed support for their positions.

Norman Shepherd

Controversies have surrounded Norman Shepherd's teaching on salvation for more than thirty years. While teaching systematic theology at Westminster Theological Seminary (Philadelphia), Shepherd proposed in a 1974 paper to the faculty that justification was by faith and works. Though he modified his language somewhat in response to criticism, this touched off a long controversy centering around the Westminster board and faculty that finally culminated in 1981 with

77. Ibid., 129.

Shepherd's dismissal from his post.[78] Questions about Shepherd's doctrine of justification lay smoldering for many years, but seem to have been reignited by the 2000 publication of his *Call of Grace* as well as other writing and lecturing that he has done since his retirement from pastoral ministry.[79] Though Shepherd, in his book and elsewhere, sets out on the laudable task of combating the twin evils of legalism and antinomianism, his solution involves both ambiguous teaching on justification and outright conflict with the biblical doctrine as understood by the Reformation.[80]

First, Shepherd's teaching denies, or at least redefines, the idea that justification is *by faith alone*. In his book, Shepherd repeatedly stresses that justifying faith is an active, living, obedient faith. Given the context of debates over justification, such language is inherently ambiguous. By obedient faith does he mean a faith that always produces obedience as its fruit, as Reformation theology teaches? Several lines of evidence, some implicit and others more explicit, attest that Shepherd has something else in mind, a sort of faith/obedience cocktail that differs substantially from Reformed teaching on justifying faith and the obedience that flows from it. In short, whereas Reformed theology teaches that faith alone, defined as an extraspective trust in Christ and his atoning work, justifies and that obedience, which is never to be confused with faith itself, inevitably flows from justifying faith, Shepherd intentionally blurs the distinction between faith and works and hence makes it impossible to speak of faith as the only instrument of justification in any traditional sense.

78. For an account of the Shepherd affair, see O. Palmer Robertson, *The Current Justification Controversy* (Unicoi, TN: Trinity Foundation, 2003). See 74–82 for discussion of the document drawn up by the Westminster Board explaining its dismissal of Shepherd: "Reasons and Specifications Supporting the Action of the Board of Trustees in Removing Professor Shepherd Approved by the Executive Committee of the Board."

79. Norman Shepherd, *The Call of Grace: How the Covenant Illuminates Salvation and Evangelism* (Phillipsburg, NJ: P&R, 2000); idem, "Justification by Faith Alone," *Reformation and Revival* 11 (2002): 75–90. An earlier expression of his views on the subject can be found in "The Grace of Justification" (unpublished paper, 1979).

80. I made several of the following points in David VanDrunen, "Justification by Faith in the Theology of Norman Shepherd," *Katekomen* 14.1 (2002): 23–26. Other reviews of Shepherd's work also make similar points; see especially the thorough review by Cornelis P. Venema in *Mid-America Journal of Theology* 13 (2002): 232–48.

Some statements in Shepherd's earlier writings seem amenable to no other interpretation. He writes, for example, that faith "yields obedience to the commands of Christ" and "forsakes sin and ungodliness" and that the forsaking of sin and rebellion is "an act of faith."[81] Faith is not distinguished from obedience here, but identified with it. Furthermore, "a living and active faith is the fruit of the regenerating and sanctifying work of the Holy Spirit."[82] Whereas the Reformation doctrine has always taught that sanctification is a fruit of justifying faith, here Shepherd says just the opposite—that faith is the fruit of sanctification.

In a recent article Shepherd quite explicitly claims the Westminster Standards for his cause, making much of their never using the exact phrase *justification by faith alone*. He draws a highly questionable divide between Lutherans and Reformed in that the former see all good works as the fruit of faith and the latter do not. He seems to rely here upon the fallacious reasoning that because faith never stands alone, unaccompanied by good works (as the Reformed tradition has taught), therefore good works cannot be (simply) the fruit of faith.[83] Part of Shepherd's agenda in making this claim becomes evident later: justifying faith is not the fount from which all sanctifying blessings flow. For example, Shepherd reasons that because regeneration is the beginning of sanctification, hence saving faith (which is subsequent to regeneration) is produced by sanctification and, therefore, sanctification begins prior to justification.[84] For present purposes, Shepherd's attempt to dismantle the idea of justification by faith alone (and to reinterpret the Westminster Standards) results not only in a denial that good works are to be seen entirely as the fruits of justifying faith but also in the clear affirmation that sanctification actually *precedes* justification in the application of salvation to the Christian.

81. Shepherd, "Grace of Justification," 16, 17, 20.

82. Ibid., 15.

83. Shepherd, "Justification by Faith Alone," 79–81. I call his reasoning fallacious because the mere fact that faith never exists *temporally* apart from good works does not mean that faith is not the fount of good works *causally*.

84. Ibid., 82–83. Along similar lines is Shepherd's claim shortly thereafter that in the Westminster Standards repentance is not simply the fruit and evidence of pardon, but necessary for it, and hence that repentance is "absolutely necessary for" and preached "with a view to" justification (84–85).

Shepherd denies not only the Reformed teaching on the instrument of justification but also its view of the ground of justification, the obedience of Christ imputed to believers. In recent lectures Shepherd becomes more explicit about his rejection of the doctrine of the imputation of Christ's active obedience,[85] but the source of such belief can certainly be traced back to his writings. Shepherd's disagreement with this crucial aspect of Reformed teaching on justification seems to stem at least in large part from his attempt to rid Reformed theology completely of the idea of merit. He recognizes that the Reformation rejected the prevalent Roman Catholic view of merit, involving as it did the Christian's efforts to earn his own justification, but Shepherd claims that the Reformation did not go far enough. He sees lingering ideas of merit in the Reformed doctrine of the covenant of works, in which Adam would have gained eschatological life on the basis of his obedience. Rejecting this idea, Shepherd claims that "God never required his image bearers to earn eternal life by the merit of their good works."[86]

It is not difficult to see how such a view, if taken seriously, makes belief in Christ's active, imputed obedience impossible. If image bearers do not merit anything before God, then the true image bearer, Christ, did not merit anything before God, and his perfect obedience can hardly be reckoned ours as the basis for our justification. What is the point of Christ's obedience then, if it is not to merit the eternal life that we sinners are unable to merit for ourselves? Shepherd turns, at least in part, to the notion of Christ as our great example: "All of this is made possible through the covenantal righteousness of Jesus Christ. His was a living, active, and obedient faith that took him all

85. For example, in his 2003 lectures for the Southern California Center for Christian Studies, Shepherd argues that early Reformed theology, exemplified in the Heidelberg Catechism, for instance, equated justification solely with forgiveness and, therefore, saw justification grounded only in Christ's passive obedience (sacrificial death) and not on his active obedience (law keeping). Shepherd makes clear that he believes this is the biblical position. These lectures were subsequently published as "Justification by Faith in Pauline Theology" and "Justification by Works in Reformed Theology," in *Backbone of the Bible: Covenant in Contemporary Perspective* (ed. P. Andrew Sandlin; Nacogdoches, TX: Covenant Media, 2004), 85–120. This work came into my hands too late to allow more specific interaction with the content of these essays.

86. Shepherd, "Justification by Faith Alone," 88; see also idem, *Call of Grace*, 25–41, in which Shepherd mercilessly misrepresents and caricatures much traditional Reformed teaching on the subject of works in the Mosaic covenant.

the way to the cross. This faith was credited to him as righteousness. . . . But just as Jesus was faithful in order to *guarantee* the blessing, so his followers must be faithful in order to *inherit* the blessing."[87] As Christ was covenantally faithful unto his justification, so we are called to be covenantally faithful unto our justification. But his obedience is not credited to us as the ground of justification.

The Federal Vision

The self-styled federal vision is a movement of sorts that presents another challenge to the Reformed doctrine of justification from the inside. Also referred to as the "Auburn Avenue" theology, after the Auburn Avenue Presbyterian Church in Monroe, Louisiana, that has hosted annual conferences promoting this line of thought, the federal vision is loosely associated with many people whose views are not entirely compatible. Nevertheless, the theology of federal-vision advocates seems to congeal around certain common ideas. Principally, the federal vision emphasizes a revamped covenant theology stressing the objectivity of the promises given to the church, especially in its sacraments. Much attention revolves around understanding election, regeneration, and other salvific blessings through membership in the church as visible covenant community.[88] Though justification per se is not its chief concern, the federal vision does reconfigure the traditional Reformed teaching on this doctrine. Little in the federal vision's handling of justification has not already been seen in other figures surveyed in this essay, particularly in regard to the new perspective on Paul and Shepherd, but a brief account of its justification theology is in order.

First, proponents of the federal vision generally follow the trajectory of the new perspective on Paul, especially in the form presented by Wright, though their debt to him is not always acknowledged. Steve Schlissel, for example, follows the new perspective on Paul extensively,

87. Shepherd, *Call of Grace*, 19 (emphasis original).

88. For a summary of the convictions of the federal vision by one of its most vocal advocates, see Douglas Wilson, "Union with Christ: An Overview of the Federal Vision," in *The Auburn Avenue Theology, Pros and Cons: Debating the Federal Vision* (ed. E. Calvin Beisner; Fort Lauderdale, FL: Knox Theological Seminary, 2004), 1–8.

but fails to make a single reference acknowledging it. He states that the doctrine of justification by faith was already present in Genesis and was presupposed by Paul, but was not what Paul had in mind in Galatians or Romans. Instead, he was concerned that Gentiles as well as Jews were being saved.[89] Schlissel goes on to claim that Paul presented no new *ordo salutis*—in fact, he claims that the *ordo salutis* itself is a more recent, manufactured problem that has helped to make us racists—and that the inclusion of the Gentiles is the major issue of the New Testament.[90] He explains: "Legal justification, far from being 'the heart of the gospel,' let alone identical with it, is hardly ever in view when Paul speaks of justification."[91] Rich Lusk cites and defends many of the sentiments of the new perspective on Paul. He speaks of Luther's misreading of Paul's critique of the law, powered by his "infamous" law-grace antithesis, which was carried on in Reformed Scholasticism.[92] In affirming the new perspective on Paul's views on the law, the problem with the Judaizers, and other issues, Lusk adopts Wright's claim, analyzed above, that the new perspective on Paul does not really deny the Reformation's teaching on justification, but gives a more exegetically nuanced description of Paul's thought.[93]

As was the case with Wright above, however, claims of basic harmony with Reformation concerns sit uneasily with explicit denials and even ridicule of such chief aspects of Reformation doctrine as the imputed righteousness of Christ. Lusk, speaking as a representative of the federal vision, joins his mentors in the new perspective on Paul in harsh critique of this idea.[94] Lusk's difficulties with imputed

89. Steve M. Schlissel, "A New Way of Seeing?" in *The Auburn Avenue Theology, Pros and Cons: Debating the Federal Vision* (ed. E. Calvin Beisner; Fort Lauderdale, FL: Knox Theological Seminary, 2004), 22, 25.

90. Ibid., 32–36.

91. Ibid., 33. Similar claims are also made in Steve Schlissel, "Justification and the Gentiles," in *The Federal Vision* (ed. Steve Wilkins and Duane Garner; Monroe, LA: Athanasius, 2004), 237–61.

92. Rich Lusk, "A Response to 'Covenant and Salvation,'" in *The Auburn Avenue Theology, Pros and Cons: Debating the Federal Vision* (ed. E. Calvin Beisner; Fort Lauderdale, FL: Knox Theological Seminary, 2004), 130.

93. Ibid., 130–36.

94. The doctrines of active obedience and imputed righteousness also come under attack by federal-vision advocate James B. Jordan in "Merit versus Maturity: What Did Jesus Do for Us?" in *The Federal Vision* (ed. Steve Wilkins and Duane Garner; Monroe, LA: Athanasius, 2004), 151–200, esp. 192–95.

righteousness seem to originate in a similar locale as Shepherd's. Like Shepherd, Lusk pummels the idea of merit and the doctrine of the covenant of works.[95] This in turn leads him, naturally, to reject the notion that Christ came to fulfill the broken covenant of works for our sake.[96] Lusk deems "the so-called 'active obedience' of Christ"[97] worthy not only of rejection, but also of outright mockery:

> It ends up looking something like this: In Genesis 1–2, God constructed Pelagian machinery for man to earn his way to blessing. Adam rendered himself incapable of operating that machinery when he sinned. But now God sends his Son into the world as One who can work the machinery flawlessly. In other words, Jesus is the successful Pelagian, the One Guy in the history of the world who succeeded in pulling off the works righteousness plan.[98]

Was Jesus's perfect obedience at all important, then? Lusk affirms that it was, but only in the sense that Jesus's perfection allowed him to be a spotless sacrifice for sin—in other words, simply to make his passive obedience possible.[99] Though advocates of the federal vision at times present their views as a recapturing of genuine Reformed thought,[100] such teaching on justification can hardly be received as anything but direct assault on traditional Reformation doctrine.[101]

95. Lusk, "Response to 'Covenant and Salvation,'" 118–26.

96. Ibid., 137.

97. Ibid., 139–40.

98. Ibid., 137.

99. Ibid., 140.

100. For example, on Lutherans versus the Reformed see Schlissel, "New Way of Seeing?" 23–24; and on Calvin see Lusk, "Response to 'Covenant and Salvation,'" 131, 143–44.

101. Another recent treatment of justification by a federal-vision proponent is Peter J. Leithart, "'Judge Me, O God': Biblical Perspectives on Justification," in *The Federal Vision* (ed. Steve Wilkins and Duane Garner; Monroe, LA: Athanasius, 2004), 203–35. Leithart says that "as far as it goes, the Protestant doctrine is correct." However, he also believes that "the Reformation doctrine of justification has illegitimately narrowed and to some extent distorted the biblical doctrine" (209). He bases this claim on the idea that the Reformation doctrine relies solely on the forensic metaphor used to describe justification in Scripture and not also on other biblical metaphors pertaining to justification. While Leithart is certainly not wrong to recognize the importance of metaphor for human thought and speech, it may well be wondered whether Scripture intends its forensic language about justification to be understood metaphorically. Biblical descriptions of God as judge or of justification as legal verdict are certainly *analogical*, but they are not therefore necessarily *metaphorical*.

Conclusion

Evidence from many different sources shows that the Reformed doctrine of justification is under attack in the present day. Some similarities among these different sources, of varying background, purpose, and sophistication, have already been noted. To help the reader synthesize this material, however, listing the ways in which most or all these various movements and authors agree in their approach to justification identifies common elements in the contemporary attack on the doctrine.

First, and perhaps most importantly, is a point emphasized above: none of the people and movements investigated includes the imputation of Christ's active obedience in the doctrine of justification. Sometimes it is passed over in silence, as in the *Joint Declaration* and the *Gift of Salvation*; other times it is quite openly denied, as in the new perspective on Paul and the Reformed revisionists. Either way, all sides eliminate this crucial aspect of the Reformation's doctrine.

A second element of commonality, not highlighted above but closely related to the first element, is the general sentiment among the various parties that emphasis upon the gracious character of salvation is enough to preserve orthodoxy. Perceiving this point requires a bit of reading between the lines. Nevertheless, all the parties surveyed here—the ecumenical statements, the new perspective on Paul, and the Reformed revisionists—emphasize the gracious character of salvation even while relativizing the importance of defining the instrument or ground of justification carefully. Though most of these parties wish to portray themselves as in harmony with Reformation teaching in one way or another, emphasis upon grace, while obviously important, is not sufficient to capture the heart of the Reformation's concerns.

A third common element among these parties is a strong strain of historical revisionism. Among several examples, the ecumenical statements downplay the traditional significance of the Reformation-era condemnations of Protestants by Roman Catholics; the Finnish school reinterprets Luther; the new perspective on Paul emphasizes a new understanding of first-century Palestinian Judaism; and the Reformed revisionists pit the Reformed against Lutherans on justification.

A fourth element, common at least to advocates of the new perspective on Paul and Reformed revisionists, which is perhaps another example of historical revisionism, is the frequent contrast of "Greek" and "Hebrew" thinking.[102] This appears especially in regard to the concept of righteousness and is portrayed as a key to unlocking past misperceptions of Paul on justification.

A fifth common element, again evident at least in the new perspective on Paul and the Reformed revisionists, is a tendency to express allegiance to the Bible alone in a way that involves antipathy to confessional and systematic theology. Advocates of the new perspective on Paul, as the name of their movement suggests, emphasize their ability to read the Bible anew and rework hundreds of years of Pauline interpretation, much of it embedded in Protestant confessional statements. Perhaps even more explicitly, proponents of the federal vision repeatedly castigate systematic/dogmatic/Scholastic theology and defend their views by claiming that they simply repeat the language of the Bible.[103] Ironically, neither Shepherd nor those associated with the federal vision have produced much detailed exegesis of biblical passages on justification but rely mostly on piling up proof-texts.

A sixth link between the disparate parties investigated here is the ecumenical interest that seems to drive much of the revision of the doctrine of justification. This obviously goes without saying in regard to the ecumenical discussions described above, but it is also evident among several others considered in this essay. Advocates of the new perspective on Paul attempt to transcend Reformation-era debates by their new readings of Paul and even to mend Jewish-Christian

102. For example, Dunn, *Theology of Paul the Apostle*, 341; Wright, *What Saint Paul Really Said*, 95–99; Schlissel, "New Way of Seeing?" 20, 23–26; and Lusk, "Response to 'Covenant and Salvation,'" 130, 147. For critique of such oversimplistic appeals, see James Barr, *The Semantics of Biblical Language* (Oxford: Oxford University Press, 1961), 8–20. More recently, see Mark A. Seifrid, "Righteousness Language in the Hebrew Scriptures and Early Judaism," in *Justification and Variegated Nomism* (ed. D. A. Carson, Peter T. O'Brien, and Mark A. Seifrid; Grand Rapids: Baker, 2001), 1.415–42.

103. For example, Wright, *What Saint Paul Really Said*, 153; Wilson, "Union with Christ," 4–6; Schlissel, "New Way of Seeing?" 20–22, 25; and Lusk, "Response to 'Covenant and Salvation,'" 138, 145. As noted above, of course, Shepherd and federal-vision proponents do at times defend their conformity to the Reformed confessions.

relations.[104] Shepherd himself suggests that his proposed covenantal reading of salvation offers the possibility of transcending the differences between Rome and the Reformation.[105]

The seventh point of commonality is not far removed from this ecumenical interest: concern about social and cultural issues in relation to justification. *Gift of Salvation* emerged out of earlier claims in *Evangelicals and Catholics Together* that alliance in the culture wars unites evangelicals and Roman Catholics in important ways. In general, the new perspective on Paul reconfigures justification around a social issue, Jew-Gentile relations, and Wright specifically makes justification an ecclesiological issue, a definition of who is a member of the covenant community. Schlissel, on behalf of the federal vision, strongly suggests that the culture wars and the perceived collapse of civilization is a much more important issue than—and one that might be overlooked because of—the kind of squabbles about justification described above.[106]

In conclusion, justification is indeed under attack. Whatever the persuasiveness of the views examined in this essay, an issue of such importance deserves careful attention and critical examination. And, if the traditional Reformed view of justification is sound, justification is worthy of a sturdy contemporary defense. Such is what the present book aims to provide.

104. In addition to material already cited, see also Dunn, *Theology of Paul the Apostle*, 336–38.

105. Shepherd, *Call of Grace*, 59.

106. Schlissel, "New Way of Seeing?" 19–21, 35–36.

PART 2

Exegetical and Biblical Theology

3
Covenant Nomism and the Exile

IAIN M. DUGUID

Introduction

According to E. P. Sanders, the core theology of intertestamental Judaism follows a pattern that he calls "covenantal nomism," a view that he explains as follows: "'Covenant' stands for God's grace in election ('getting in'); 'nomism' for the requirement of obedience to the law (*nomos* in Greek: 'staying in')."[1] In other words, according to Sanders, God graciously chose Israel to be his partner in a covenant relationship at the beginning, without any merit on their part, but once that relationship was initiated then Israel's obedience to the law became a necessary condition for continuing the relationship. To quote Sanders again: "Salvation is not earned by obedience, although it may be forfeited by disobedience."[2] To be sure, grace continues to

1. E. P. Sanders, *Judaism: Practice and Belief, 63 BCE–66 CE* (London: SCM, 1992), 262.

2. E. P. Sanders, *Paul and Palestinian Judaism: A Comparison of Patterns of Religion* (London: SCM, 1977), 371.

be a factor in that obedience. The Lord graciously provides forgiveness through the sacrificial system for those who inevitably fell short of perfection, and his mercy would temper his justice, yet without faithfulness on Israel's part the covenant relationship between her and the Lord could not be maintained.[3]

It is not my purpose to assess the correctness of Sanders's version of covenantal nomism as a description of intertestamental Jewish theology.[4] It may be that some, or even many, Jews accepted covenantal nomism during this period. Of more concern is the rise of similar formulations within the modern church. So, for example, Rich Lusk writes (with reference to the reclothing of the high priest Joshua in Zech 3): "The initial clothing in white is received by faith alone. This is the beginning of Joshua's justification. But if Joshua is to remain justified—that is, if the garments he has received are not to become re-soiled with his iniquity—he must be faithful. Thus, initial justification is by faith alone; subsequent justifications include obedience."[5]

My discussion will focus on the accuracy of covenantal nomism as a description of the Old Testament relations between God and his people and in particular on the pastoral crisis that faced God's people during and after the exile. How does the experience of exile and return alter the idea that God's Old Testament people "got in" the covenant by grace and "stayed in" that relationship by their faithful obedience to the law? Can covenantal nomism account for the persistence of God's relationship with his people after the exile?[6] After Israel's unfaithfulness had led to the ultimate sanction of exile, did the prophets promise covenant blessing dependent on human faithfulness, or did they look for something new in which God himself would fulfill the covenant conditions?

3. Sanders, *Judaism: Practice and Belief*, 275–78.

4. For a detailed interaction, see D. A. Carson, Peter T. O'Brien, and Mark A. Seifrid, eds., *Justification and Variegated Nomism* (2 vols.; Grand Rapids: Baker, 2001–4).

5. Rich Lusk, "Future Justification to the Doers of the Law," http://www.hornes.org/theologia/content/rich_lusk/future_justification_to_the_doers_of_the_law.htm. See also the similar stress on the centrality of our faithfulness in Steve M. Schlissel, "A Response to Covenant and Salvation," in *The Auburn Avenue Theology, Pros and Cons: Debating the Federal Vision* (ed. E. Calvin Beisner; Fort Lauderdale, FL: Knox Theological Seminary, 2004), 89–92.

6. As we shall see, there is a distinction between the relationship itself and the blessings associated with that relationship, such as occupation of the land.

Maintenance of Marriage

At first sight, covenantal nomism may seem to be strongly supported by the analogy of a marriage relationship that the Old Testament uses to describe the relationship between the Lord and Israel.[7] In marriage, a husband is not obligated to choose a particular woman as his wife: his choice of her is a matter of unmerited favor, especially if he is of higher social status than she is. Yet once he has chosen this wife, he is bound to her by the covenant relationship, as long as she is faithful. A good husband recognizes that his wife is not perfect and makes allowance for her failings. Minor imperfections do not nullify the marriage covenant. Yet if she is persistently unfaithful, then the covenant relationship is broken; the husband is not bound by his earlier commitment, and the relationship may legitimately be dissolved through divorce. It could well be argued therefore that the wife's faithfulness is necessarily a key element in maintaining the marital relationship and, by analogy, that our faithfulness is a key element in maintaining our relationship with God,[8] even though the initiation of that relationship is entirely of his grace.[9]

7. This marriage covenant finds its full expression at Sinai in the formula "I will be your God and you will be my people" (Exod 6:7; Lev 26:12). This formula is parallel to the ancient Near Eastern marriage contract: "I will be to you a husband and you will be to me a wife"; see Moshe Weinfeld, "*B^{e}rith*—Covenant vs. Obligation," *Biblica* 56 (1975): 125.

8. Thus, Don Garlington asserts: "The very existence of the marriage-covenant is contingent on the righteous/faithful behavior of its partners"; see his review of D. A. Carson, Peter T. O'Brien, and Mark A. Seifrid, eds., *Justification and Variegated Nomism*, vol. 1: *The Complexities of Second Temple Judaism* (Grand Rapids: Baker, 2001) at http://www.thepaulpage.com/Variegated_Nomism.pdf.

9. It is a matter of ongoing debate whether the word *grace* should be used in line with conventional English usage, as many theologians do, to describe God's unmerited favor. Thus, Louis Berkhof defines grace as follows: "The fundamental idea is, that the *blessings* graciously bestowed are *freely given*, and *not in consideration of any claim or merit*. . . . In most of the passages, however, in which the word *charis* is used in the New Testament, it signified the *unmerited operation of God* in the heart of man, effected through the agency of the Holy Spirit"; see *Systematic Theology* (4th ed.; Grand Rapids: Eerdmans, 1949), 427 (emphasis added). Similarly the *New Geneva Study Bible* note on Gal 1:3 states, "'Grace' translates the Greek *charis*, which means 'an undeserved act of kindness.'" Other Reformed theologians insist that the word *grace* should be reserved to describe "demerited favor," God's mercy shown to sinners. See, e.g., Meredith G. Kline, "Covenant Theology under Attack," http://www.upper-register.com/ct_gospel/ct_under_attack.html. Equally insistently, though from a different perspective, is Jerry Bridges, "What Is Grace," *RTS Quarterly* http://www.rts.edu/quarterly/fall98/grace.html. There are certainly advantages in clarity if the word is kept for this more restricted sense, since the broader sense has sometimes been misused in modern theological discussions to blur important distinctions

Ezekiel 16

How, though, is this analogy worked out in Scripture? The description of the Lord's relationship with Jerusalem in Ezekiel 16 explains the analogy of marriage to a faithless partner.[10] The undeserved nature of the relationship is strongly stressed at the outset. Jerusalem was born from pagan Canaanite roots (16:3) and when the Lord found her, she was an abandoned infant, left exposed in the field to die (16:5).[11] She had no inherent beauty or attractiveness and no automatic claim on God's compassion. Left to herself, she would inevitably have died. Yet the Lord did not leave her to her natural fate. Instead, he showed

---

between the biblical covenants. It should also be recognized, however, that the broader sense is a traditional and legitimate rendering of the biblical word חֵן, which has a broad semantic domain. Most commonly חֵן describes favor shown from a superior to an inferior, without the necessary connotation of demerit; see Gen 39:4 AV: "grace," where Potiphar's favor to Joseph actually reflects his diligent service and success; and Prov 3:34 NIV and ESV margin: "grace," where it describes an attitude that God shows to the humble but not to the mocker. Modern translations have followed a dynamic-equivalent approach to translating this word, rendering it by a series of English equivalents such as "favor" or "charm," yet they have generally retained the adjective "gracious" to express the derivative חַנּוּן: this attribute of God likewise describes favor shown to those without claim upon it, rather than favor shown to those who have forfeited God's favor (e.g., Exod 22:27 [MT 22:26]). On this and related words, see T. E. Fretheim, "חנן," in *New International Dictionary of Old Testament Theology and Exegesis* (ed. W. A. VanGemeren; Grand Rapids: Zondervan, 1997), 2.203–6. This varied biblical usage suggests that, at a minimum, we should endeavor to be clear which use of the term we are adopting and recognize that others may use the word in a different sense, without necessarily compromising important doctrines. For the sake of simplicity, I use the word in its conventional sense in this essay, in line with the usage of Sanders and others, rather than in the more technical sense advocated by Kline and Bridges.

10. Jerusalem here stands for the southern kingdom, just as Samaria stands for the northern kingdom in Ezek 16:46; see Moshe Greenberg, *Ezekiel 1–20* (Anchor Bible 22; Garden City, NY: Doubleday, 1983), 274. To be sure, some aspects of the description are particularly fitting for the city of Jerusalem, whose roots in Canaanite culture predate her capture by David, yet there is no ultimate dichotomy in Ezekiel's thinking between the city and the southern kingdom. Together with her northern neighbor, the sisters have a history of rebellion against God that stretches all the way back to Egypt (Ezek 23:27).

11. This is not as apparent to our modern Western sensibilities as it would have been to the original audience. For us it would be unthinkable to find an abandoned infant and leave it to its fate beside the road. In the ancient world, however, the abandonment of girl babies was a common, if unpleasant, fact of life, and most people had no choice but to leave them to their doom. An analogy in our modern world are the many orphaned street children around the world who are malnourished and uncared for. Christian believers and ministries adopt and care for some of these children, yet the scale of the problem far exceeds people's ability to relieve it. As a result, Christians in those locations may be faced regularly with the sight of desperate children whose needs they simply cannot meet, even though they know that without help they are likely to die. Our comfortable location may shield us from these realities, which Old Testament Israel would have recognized as familiar.

her undeserved favor, adopting her just as she was, covered in blood (16:6). He cared for all of her needs and married her when she came of age (16:7–8). Everything she could have wished for was given to her by the Lord: fine food, jewels, and costly garments. She contributed nothing of her own to the relationship. This covenant (16:8) was certainly one that Israel entered by grace.

Having entered by grace, Jerusalem's subsequent behavior became an issue in the relationship. Far from showing faithfulness to her covenant husband, she was the epitome of unfaithfulness. She took the very gifts that the Lord had given her and spent them on her adulterous affairs. She used her clothing to make pagan places of worship and her jewelry to fashion idols (16:16–17). Jerusalem offered the food the Lord had given her to feed the idols she had made and her embroidered garments to dress them (16:18–19). Even the children she had borne the Lord were offered up to the idols (16:20–21). Instead of behaving like a faithful wife, she acted worse than a prostitute: at least prostitutes have a financial motive for their sin, but Jerusalem herself paid her lovers to participate in her abominations (16:32–34). Through her persistent pagan idolatry and covenant-breaking relationships with the nations (Ezek 17), the unfaithfulness of God's people knew no bounds.

If the perspective of covenantal nomism is correct and if staying in the covenant is dependent upon obedience, such behavior as Israel had exhibited throughout her history must necessarily bring the covenant to an end. Indeed, the consequences of her disobedience are severe: Jerusalem will be handed over to her lovers, who will strip her and stone her and hack her in pieces (16:37–40). The Lord's wrath and jealous anger will be poured out upon her, and he will recompense her for her deeds (16:38–43). Yet this is not the end of Israel's relationship with her God. Israel's breaking of the terms of the covenant (16:59) cannot in the end destroy the covenant![12] The Israelites will experience the curses that the covenant threatened, but the covenant relationship itself will not be annulled by their unfaithfulness.

12. On this phrase, see Moshe Weinfeld, "בְּרִית," in *Theological Dictionary of the Old Testament* (ed. G. J. Botterweck and H. Ringgren; trans. J. T. Willis; Grand Rapids: Eerdmans, 1975), 2.261–62.

The reason for this surprising turn of events is that the Lord is not like Israel.[13] Even though Israel has not remembered the days of her youth (16:22, 43), the Lord will remember the covenant he made with her in those days.[14] The conditionality of the Sinai covenant applies only to the experience of the blessings of the covenant, not to the underlying relationship itself. Far from washing his hands of Israel because of her unfaithfulness, the Lord will establish an everlasting covenant with her (16:60, 62). Although Israel has been unfaithful and has provided plentiful grounds for divorce, the Lord will not divorce her, because he is faithful.[15] Israel entered the covenant by grace, and she will remain in it by the Lord's faithfulness—not by her own.

Hosea 2, Isaiah 50, Jeremiah 3

Essentially the same reading of the relationship between Israel and the Lord is evident in other texts. In the book of Hosea, the prophet is instructed to marry an adulterous wife in order to provide a prophetic sign act for the people (1:2). The basis of Hosea's choice of wife was certainly not in any merit that she brought to the relationship but in an act of grace. She was not transformed into a model housewife by his self-sacrificial love, either. On the contrary, she continued to act shamefully with her lovers (2:5). She ascribed the good gifts she had received from the Lord to her idols (2:8). Because of that sin, she faced punishment for her sins in the present, and their husband-wife relationship was temporarily suspended (2:2). Yet divorce could not

13. In view of the contrast in what follows, it is possible that Ezek 16:59 ought to be translated as a question: "Will I deal with you as you have dealt [with me]?"—the implied answer being no, as is evident in what follows; see Leslie C. Allen, *Ezekiel 1–19* (Word Biblical Commentary 28; Dallas: Word, 1994), 232.

14. "The covenant I made with you in the days of your youth" (Ezek 16:60) is a reference to the Sinai covenant, as the parallel passage in Jer 31:31–34 makes clear; see Daniel I. Block, *Ezekiel 1–24* (New International Commentary on the Old Testament; Grand Rapids: Eerdmans, 1997), 517. To the evidence adduced by Block, we may add that Israel's "youth" elsewhere in Ezekiel describes her time in Egypt (compare 23:3, 8, 19, 21).

15. This thought is the fulcrum of hope for the writer of Lamentations. Faced with evidence of God's judgment curse all around him, he clings to this thought: "Because of the steadfast love [חֶסֶד] of the LORD, we are not cut off; his mercies never come to an end; they are new every morning; great is your faithfulness" (Lam 3:22–23). Compare the equally surprising formula in 2 Tim 2:12–13: "If we deny him, he also will deny us; if we are faithless, he remains faithful—for he cannot deny himself."

be the end of the story. Ultimately the Lord would restore her to himself and betroth her to himself forever (2:16–20). That renewed relationship is described as a covenant (2:18) in which the blessings of the relationship promised at Sinai would be experienced in fullness (contrast Hos 2:22 with Deut 28:51). Israel entered the relationship with the Lord by grace, but the relationship will stand only because of the Lord's faithfulness—not her own.

In the book of Isaiah, the Lord asks the people: "Where is your mother's certificate of divorce, with which I sent her away? Or which of my creditors is it to whom I have sold you? Behold, for your iniquities you were sold, and for your transgressions your mother was sent away" (50:1). The implied answer to the prophet's question is clear: it was not the Lord who brought about the present breach in the relationship but Israel, through her transgressions. Nonetheless, even her iniquities and transgressions cannot ultimately destroy the marriage. The Lord has remained faithful to his bride, and as a result the prophet can speak comforting words to Zion regarding her future (51:3–4). The Lord will raise up a servant, who through his faithfulness will bring deliverance to his unfaithful bride (50:2–9).

Even in the book of Jeremiah, where the breach between the Lord and his people is stated in the strongest possible terms, the relationship cannot ultimately be severed by their unfaithfulness. Israel and Judah have been relentless in their adultery (3:1–3, 6–10), to the point where the Lord actually gave the northern kingdom her certificate of divorce (3:8). Judah too deserves the same treatment, for she has behaved even worse than her unfaithful sister (3:11). Yet even this is not the end for the Lord and his people: the Lord remains their husband (3:14), and so he commits himself to bring about a great reversal, not just for Judah but for Israel as well (3:18)! Even though in a human marriage such a thing could not be contemplated—a divorced and unfaithful wife returning to her long-suffering husband (3:1)—such is the Lord's indissoluble unity with his people that this turn of events not only may happen in this case, but inevitably must. The marriage relationship between God and his people cannot ultimately be destroyed by the unfaithfulness of the bride.

Renovation of the Covenant

Nonetheless, the future prospect after the exile is not merely a return to the status ante quo. It would be no comfort to tell a generation who had experienced the full weight of the covenant curses for their disobedience and that of their forefathers that future blessing depended on their future faithfulness. Rather, the prophets repeatedly pointed their hearers to a new intervention of God that would radically alter the constitution of the people.

Jeremiah 31

Thus, the prophet Jeremiah spoke of an act of God so profound that it can be termed a "new covenant" (31:31–34). This new covenant is, in some ways, radically *not* like the covenant made at Sinai. It will not be a covenant whose terms can be broken through the unfaithfulness of God's people (31:32), thereby bringing curse on themselves. It will be a covenant that involves an internal transformation of the people, such that the law is placed in their minds and written on their hearts (31:33), not simply on tablets of stone. It will be a covenant in which the knowledge of God will be universal among his people from least to greatest (31:34), not mediated through Moses and the prophets. In establishing this covenant, the Lord will forgive his people's sin and remember their iniquity no more (31:34).

Yet at the same time the new covenant is, in other ways, simply the fulfillment of the Sinai covenant, especially its central promise: "I will be their God and they shall be my people" (Jer 31:33; cf. Exod 6:7; Lev 26:12).[16] The result of this new covenant will be the fulfillment of all of the blessings of the Sinai covenant and a lifting of all of its curses. The people's yoke will be broken off (Jer 30:8; cf. Lev 26:13); they will have peace and security, with no one to make them afraid (Jer 30:10; cf. Lev 26:6); they will experience healing (Jer 30:17; cf. Exod 15:26) and harvest the grain, new wine and oil, and the young of the flock (Jer 31:12; cf. Deut 28:51). In other words, the new cov-

16. This is a distinctly Sinaitic covenant formula, not found prior to that time in Scripture, although it builds on and develops the promise to Abraham: "I will be your God and the God of your descendants after you" (Gen 17:7).

enant anticipates a time when the blessings of the (conditional) Mosaic covenant will be received unconditionally, through a sovereign act of God's mercy and grace.[17]

The same is true with respect to the Davidic covenant. The prophet had earlier announced the complete rejection of the Davidic king in the person of Jehoiachin (Jer 22:24–27). Hope was to be found in neither Jehoiachin nor his successor, Zedekiah (24:1–10). Yet even though the persistent unfaithfulness of David's heirs had now led to comprehensive judgment, so that they themselves would die in captivity, the prophet promised a renewal of the Davidic covenant in the days to come. A righteous branch would sprout from David's line and bring about the restoration of Jerusalem (33:15–16).[18] Neither God's covenant with David nor his covenant with the descendants of Jacob could ultimately be broken, in spite of all of the unfaithfulness of the human parties, for these covenants were as unbreakable as God's covenant with night and day (33:19–26).

Ezekiel 34

Exactly identical themes emerge in the book of Ezekiel. The prophet speaks of a covenant of peace (בְּרִית שָׁלוֹם) that would bring about a new future for Israel (34:25–31). In line with Jeremiah, Ezekiel foresaw a future of Mosaic covenant blessing for the people, promised precisely to those whom he has been at considerable pains to reveal to be breakers of the Mosaic covenant. No longer would they undergo the curses of the Sinai covenant that they had experienced while they have been under the judgment of God: wild animals, drought,

17. William J. Dumbrell, "The Prospect of Unconditionality in the Sinaitic Covenant," in *Israel's Apostasy and Restoration: Essays in Honor of Roland K. Harrison* (ed. Avraham Gileadi; Grand Rapids: Baker, 1988), 142. Meredith Kline similarly speaks of there being "grace along with the law" in the Deuteronomic covenant; see *By Oath Consigned* (Grand Rapids: Eerdmans, 1968), 19.

18. The import of Isa 11:1 is similar. "There shall come forth a shoot from the stump of Jesse, and a branch from his roots shall bear fruit." We so often focus on the positive side of that promise that we miss the certainty of judgment it conveys. The future of the line of David ends up in a stump, with the tree cut down. Only after the tree's future has been ended, humanly speaking, will there be a divine renewal of the promise. By calling the source of this branch the "stump of Jesse" rather than the "stump of David" the discontinuity in the renewal of the promise is emphasized as well as the continuity; see John Calvin, *Isaiah 1–32* (1843; trans. W. Pringle; repr. Grand Rapids: Baker, 2003), 372.

famine, and the sword (Lev 26:14–35). Now they will experience the blessings of that covenant: safety, rain in its season, fruitfulness, and peace (Ezek 34:25–30; cf. Lev 26:4–13).[19] This state of experiencing the blessings that flow from a harmonious relationship with God makes this distinctively a "covenant of peace." It is a *new* covenant in the sense that they will in future experience the blessings promised in the original (Mosaic) covenant rather than the curses merited by their breaches in the covenant.

What is more, the blessings to be experienced are not limited to the Mosaic covenant. The blessings of the Davidic covenant will also finally be established. In place of the monarchy divided by sin, they will be united under one shepherd. In place of an undistinguished procession of monarchs, they will be given a ruler after God's own heart, a new David. In place of famine, plague, drought, and sword, they will see a new level of peace and prosperity so that they will no longer bear the reproach of the nations (Ezek 34:29).[20] Then they will know that the Lord their God is with them—for blessing and not for curse—and that they are his people. They will be his sheep and he will be their God, the harmonious relationship celebrated in Psalm 100:3. In fact, Ezekiel 34:31 concludes: "You will be 'Adam' and I will be your God," which may suggest that the scope of the prophet's vision reaches even further back to affirm the ultimate restoration of the blessings intended in the original covenant of creation.[21] Adam's

19. For a full table of parallels between Ezek 34:25–30 and Lev 26:4–13, see Daniel I. Block, *Ezekiel 25–48* (New International Commentary on the Old Testament; Grand Rapids: Eerdmans, 1998), 304.

20. The absence of the blessing of victory in war may be due to the new community being now directly under divine protection, as becomes clear in Ezek 38–39; see Moshe Greenberg, *Ezekiel 21–37* (Anchor Bible 22A; New York: Doubleday, 1997), 707.

21. To date, I have yet to see any alternative adequate explanation of the Masoretic Text. אָדָם is absent from the Septuagint, and so it is often read as a clumsy secondary gloss. As such, it would simply identify the Lord's flock as being human, connecting this passage with Ezek 36:38; see W. Zimmerli, *Ezekiel 25–48* (trans. James D. Martin; Hermeneia; Philadelphia: Fortress, 1983), 221. Alternatively, it is argued that the word calls attention to the depth and greatness of the divine condescension in meeting with man who is taken from the earth and returns to it again; see E. W. Hengstenberg, *The Prophecies of Ezekiel Elucidated* (trans. A. C. Murphy and J. G. Murphy; Edinburgh: Clark, 1874), 305. Yet in a context that has just mentioned the fulfillment of the covenant with David and the covenant made at Sinai, it seems that a reference to אָדָם may well be more than simply a random insertion. In fact, the connection with 36:38 may strengthen the Adamic overtones in both passages, since 36:35 promises that the future land will become like the garden of Eden.

original act of unfaithfulness will be undone through a divine act of salvation on the Lord's part.

The central point being made by the prophet is clear: the blessings promised in all of God's covenants—conditional and unconditional—will ultimately be experienced by God's people. This will take place not through their faithfulness but through a sovereign act of God's grace in providing for them a new and faithful shepherd.

Ezekiel 36

This idea is developed further in Ezekiel 36:16–38. The motivation for God's wrath in the past was the unfaithfulness of the people (36:17). They had defiled the land by means of bloodshed and idolatry, making it a place unfit for divine habitation by the living God (36:18). God therefore had no choice but to bring upon them the curses of the covenant they had broken, the Mosaic covenant, in wrath scattering them among the nations and the lands, just as he had threatened (Deut 29:22–28 [MT 29:21–27]).

This action, however, created a new problem for God. He had promised to bring this people, who were called by his name, into the land of Canaan to possess it. He had established a relationship between himself, his people, and the land (Ezek 36:28). Yet now the nations could see that the Lord's people were absent from his land (36:21). The special relationship promised in the Mosaic covenant and symbolized by the tabernacle, the visible dwelling of God in their midst, had been broken. The conclusion that would be drawn by the surrounding nations was natural: the Lord's power was insufficient to bring about that which he promised. Thus, as long as Israel was scattered among the nations, she continually profaned the divine name (36:20). This was now not because of anything particular they did. Rather, she profaned God's name simply by being there in exile, instead of in the land of promise!

This brings Ezekiel to the reasons for God's future mercy. If there had been no other reasoning involved for God than the necessity of dealing with Israel's sin, permanent wrath would have sufficed. Israel could simply and deservedly have been blotted out from the pages of history for her unfaithfulness as an example of the power of God's holiness and his anger against sin. The Israelites of Ezekiel's day, however, were not completely destroyed. Why not? Even though he has no compassion (חָמַל) on Israel, the Lord will nonetheless have concern (חָמַל) for his name, which he had inextricably linked to Israel by entering covenant with them. Because of that sovereign, irrevocable act at Sinai, mercy not only may but must be shown to Israel. The honor of God's name must be vindicated by a show of power among the nations when he brings Israel back to her land (36:21–23). The Lord will act, not for Israel's sake, but for the sake of his own name.

This act through which God's power is demonstrated involves not merely bringing Israel back physically to the land but also a total change in her nature. His people must be redeemed not merely outwardly but inwardly, effectively. First, Israel will indeed be gathered and returned from the nations to her own land (36:24). Then she will be sprinkled with clean water, symbolizing her cleansing from all her past impurities and idolatries, the things that had made the land unclean (Ezek 36:25; cf. Lev 15).

This outward act of initiation is then to be followed by a deeper, internal change, whereby Israel's heart and spirit will be made new. Unresponsive, unyielding stone will be replaced by warm, living, responsive flesh (Ezek 36:26). That which has been defiled will be made clean. The Spirit of God, who brings life and power, will indwell them and create in her both the will and the ability to follow God's decrees and laws (36:27). Then, finally, she will be fit to live in God's land and be his people, and he in turn will not be ashamed to be called her God (36:28). Then Israel will experience the blessings of the Mosaic covenant, the fruitfulness of the land, rather than experiencing the covenant curse of famine that had made them a reproach among the nations (36:30). Such a salvation will not bring about pride in the renewed nation but rather a profound sense of shame, for she will realize that her salvation is not something she has merited or deserved through her faithfulness. Rather, it is a free gift of sovereign grace. Nothing short of such radical divine intervention could have saved such a people.

The Lord's favor toward his people does not flow from this inner transformation but is the cause of it. This change in her status is explicitly not for Israel's sake or based on her deeds, but quite the contrary (36:31–32). Her ways continue to be evil and wicked, yet because of the Lord's concern for the glory of his name, he will sprinkle his defiled people with clean water, making them clean and able to stand in his sight (36:25)—"justified," to use the language of systematic theology. The subsequent inner transformation, "sanctification," flows out of that prior act of God as its fruit. Having cleansed them from their sins in a single day (36:33), the Lord then causes his Spirit to indwell his people and transform them from the inside out (36:26–27).

In addition to the act of self-glorification that results in the restored people being returned to the land, God will also restore the land to a "better-than-original" state, thus fulfilling his purpose in creation. It will become "like the garden of Eden," the ultimate symbol of fertility and fruitfulness (Ezek 36:35; cf. Isa 51:3; Joel 2:3), but the garden land will be filled with restored cities: the places that once were torn down and desolate will be inhabited and fortified (Ezek 36:35). In place of the one original אָדָם and his wife, the new garden land will be filled with "flocks of אָדָם," numerous people who will fill the cities to overflowing (36:38). The fertility and fruitfulness will thus encompass the people as well as the land itself, to the point where it will be as crowded as Jerusalem used to be on the great annual festival occasions, when her streets were crammed with a mass of people and animals (36:38). The end is thus more than a return to the beginning. God's original plan for humanity will find a fulfillment in a way that incorporates and gathers up all of the Lord's mighty acts in redemptive history.

Transformation of the People

Ezekiel 36 pictures the transformation of the people to make them fit for the land God is giving them. This transformation is not, however, something that will take place automatically as a result of the experience of exile and return, but will require a distinct act of God's sovereign power so that both his righteousness and his mercy are satisfied.

Making the Dead Live: Ezekiel 37

The experience of judgment in the exile, when recognized as the consequence of the people's sins, opened up the very real risk of despair. Thus, the people of Ezekiel's day were saying, "Our bones are dried up, and our hope is lost; we are clean cut off" (37:11). They felt themselves to be alienated from God, dead in their transgressions and sins.[22] The prophet's answer was neither to question their assessment of their own state—the bones are indeed very dry and very scattered—nor to exhort them to try harder, but rather to look for a great work of the Lord whereby he would take these dry bones and bring them to life, setting his Spirit within them and commissioning them for his service (37:1–10). The experience that the people need is one that the prophet has already personally experienced: when he was confronted by the majesty of God he was twice prostrated by it, and each time the Spirit entered him and raised him to his feet, just as happens to the bones (1:28; 2:2; 3:23–24). He is himself a kind of firstfruits of this cosmic change.[23] This change is self-evidently from God: dry bones can contribute nothing to their resuscitation, but just as God's life-giving breath first brought Adam to life, so his Spirit can bring about new creation from the dead.

Making the Defiled Clean: Haggai 2

The exiles not only needed resurrection from the dead, they also needed a foundational change in their status before God. They were defiled people who had first to be made clean before any of their works could be accepted. The order of these two acts of God is irreversible: first the people must be made clean and acceptable in God's sight; only after that could the process of being transformed into a new obedience be begun.[24]

22. Perhaps, to paraphrase the title of Krister Stendahl's famous essay, we should speak of "the apostle Ezekiel and the introspective conscience of the exiles." This might help to correct the notion that the concept of people feeling the weight of the law's condemnation and asking how they may be made right with a holy God is somehow a relatively modern Western notion.

23. See Iain M. Duguid, *Ezekiel* (NIV Application Commentary; Grand Rapids: Zondervan, 1999), 427–30.

24. Purification is likewise a key issue in Ezek 40–48. See ibid., 470–86.

This is apparent in Haggai 2, where the prophet is instructed to ask the priests for a "torah" (legal decision). The question he posed is as follows: if someone carries some consecrated meat in the fold of his garment (perhaps the leftovers of a fellowship meal) and there it touches some nonconsecrated items, do they become consecrated? The answer is no: sanctity cannot be so easily transferred (2:12). If, however, these same things come in contact with something defiled, they do become defiled. Defilement is easily contracted, while holiness cannot be conveyed so easily (2:13).

The point of this apparently arcane theological discussion emerges in the following verses. The people of Haggai's day are themselves defiled, which results in whatever they offer the Lord itself becoming automatically defiled (2:14). Because the people themselves were unclean, their offerings became defiled by contact with them and were therefore unacceptable in God's sight. The people must themselves have their status in God's sight changed before their offerings could be accepted by God. That change in status had already begun with the refounding of the temple on that very day.[25] From then on, now that God had once again established his dwelling in their midst, they would experience blessing in place of the former curse.

Making the Defiled Clean: Zechariah 3

The same idea of a cleansing act of God that would change the status of the exiles is developed further in Zechariah 3. There the high priest Joshua was depicted as standing before the Lord in a defiled state. His clothing is not merely filthy, as most English translations render it. It is literally "excrement soiled" (צוֹאִים), which means that it is intrinsically defiling (3:3). This presents a problem not just for Joshua as an individual but for the whole people: if he is unfit to stand before God as their mediator and intercessor on the Day of Atonement, then the whole sacrificial system will be compromised.

25. The twenty-fourth day of the ninth month of the second year of Darius, the date of the oracle in Hag 2, was apparently the day when the temple was formally refounded; see C. L. Meyers and E. M. Meyers, *Haggai, Zechariah 1–8* (Anchor Bible 25B; Garden City, NY: Doubleday, 1987), 63. For the significance of God's sanctuary as a sign of the new order, see Ezek 37:26.

Meanwhile the scene itself is a courtroom setting, with the Angel of the Lord as judge and the Accuser (הַשָּׂטָן) as prosecuting attorney (3:1). It seems that this open-and-shut case against Joshua must lead to his exclusion from the presence of a holy God, yet the Accuser never gets to present his arguments. Instead, the presiding authority, the Angel of the Lord, rules *any and all* charges out of order, because Jerusalem is the Lord's elect (3:2). God's choice of Jerusalem, evidenced by his bringing Joshua out of the fire of the exile safely, means that no further charges can be entertained against him.

Having judicially declared Joshua immune from prosecution, the Lord acts to remove Joshua's iniquity. His excrement-soiled clothes are stripped off, and he is clothed in festival garments (3:4). In order to stand before the judge what is needed is not a neutral nakedness, but pure clothing. Since his filthy garments represent iniquity (עָוֹן) (3:4), his festival garments can represent only a new righteousness, given to him at the orders of the judge as a gift.[26] The act of reclothing is completed by adding a clean turban (צָנִיף) (3:5), which is not distinctively priestly clothing; rather, it has overtones of glory and even royalty (Isa 3:23; 62:3). This is literally the crowning moment of the whole ceremony: Joshua is reclothed in ceremonially pure, festival garments in the presence of the Angel of the Lord as a sign of God's acceptance of him—and in him of the people he represented.

Joshua's reclothing is not an end in itself: he is now fitted to serve, and so he is charged with a task: "If you walk in my ways and if you keep my charge, and if you also judge my house and guard my courts,[27]

26. This clearly disproves Wright's statement that "if we use the language of the law court, it makes no sense whatever to say that the judge imputes, imparts, bequeaths, conveys or otherwise transfers his righteousness to either the plaintiff or the defendant. Righteousness is not an object, a substance or a gas that can be passed across the courtroom"; see N. T. Wright, *What Saint Paul Really Said: Was Paul of Tarsus the Real Founder of Christianity?* (Grand Rapids: Eerdmans, 1996), 98. Here in Zechariah, precisely in a courtroom setting, we have the defendant's defilement removed at the order of the judge and replaced by an alien righteousness. If that is not forensic imputation, then I do not know what would qualify as such.

27. In Hebrew conditional clauses, it is not always clear where the protasis ends and the apodosis begins. Does the "then" clause begin after "if you keep my charge" (with most English translations) or after "if you guard my courts" (with many commentators)? I chose the latter translation since וְגַם does not normally begin the apodosis of a conditional clause; see David L. Petersen, *Haggai, Zechariah 1–8* (Old Testament Library; Philadelphia: Westminster, 1984), 203; and Wolter H. Rose, *Zemah and Zerubbabel: Messianic Expectations in the Early Postexilic Period* (Sheffield: Sheffield Academic Press, 2000), 69.

then I will grant to you access [or men who go][28] among these who stand [before me]" (3:7). The first two requirements are very general ways of describing faithful behavior within a covenant context, while the second pair identifies what that behavior requires of a faithful priest.[29] Joshua is to judge God's house and guard his courts, that is, to ensure that the worship in the temple is pure and undefiled by idolatry (cf. Ezek 44:23–24). If he does these things, then he will be granted privileged access to the Lord. The exact meaning of the word *access* is uncertain: it may be that the access is mediated by angelic messengers, but however the word is translated, Joshua is promised unusually direct communication with the divine council. The important point is that what is dependent upon his faithfulness is not his standing in the covenant community but the experience of extraordinary blessing.[30]

Even such extraordinary blessing on Joshua is merely a shadow of things to come, for the very existence of Joshua and his fellow priests after the exile was a sign of God's blessing (Zech 3:8), a blessing that had far more to give than the people had yet experienced. Specifically, the future blessing involved the coming of a figure named "my servant, the Branch" (3:8), and the complete and instantaneous removal of the iniquity of this land (3:9). When that happened, the complete blessing of the restored (Sinai) covenant relationship would be experienced: each man will invite his neighbor under his vine and under his fig tree. The fertility and peace of the land will be fully restored to levels unknown since the height of the Solomonic empire (1 Kgs 4:25 [MT 5:1]; see also Mic 4:4).

28. Translation of מַהְלְכִים is uncertain since it is a unique form. In the singular, it means "journey" or "walkway" but neither of those fit here. Rose suggests that instead of rendering it as a noun meaning "access," it should be identified as a piel participle with unusual vocalization, meaning "men who go" (*Zemah and Zerubbabel*, 74–79). This is how the ancient versions translated it. The end result of this translation would still be that Joshua had unusual access to the presence of God, albeit in a more mediated form.

29. See Moshe Weinfeld, "The Covenant of Grant in the Old Testament and in the Ancient Near East," *Journal of the American Oriental Society* 90 (1970): 186.

30. Contra, e.g., Lusk, "Future Justification to the Doers of the Law": "This gift is not given apart from the requirement of obedience. Joshua can only continue to stand in the Lord's presence if he obeys the Lord (3:6)." "Standing in the Lord's presence" in Zech 3:7 has more in common with the privilege of the prophets than of a normal Israelite and is thus clearly a blessing beyond mere salvation.

The Lord's actions would not only ensure the blessings of the Sinai covenant for the people but would also renew the blessings of the Davidic covenant. The name of this coming future figure, the Branch, is almost certainly a reference to Jeremiah 23:5, which itself promises a reversal of the rejection of Jehoiachin by the Lord in 22:30. Through the prophet Jeremiah, the Lord had declared that none of Jehoiachin's seed will sit on his throne. Nonetheless, God would yet raise up a righteous descendant for David who will reign with justice and will establish salvation for his people (23:7–8). This promise is reiterated by Zechariah and linked to the sign of the existence of Joshua and his fellow priests.

Finally, Joshua's attention is directed to an engraved stone (Zech 3:9). This stone is most probably part of the high priest's clothing, a gemstone with seven facets (or "eyes") associated with the turban and inscribed with an inscription.[31] Aaron's turban had just such an ornament, engraved with the words *Holy to the LORD*, which enabled him to bear the iniquity of the people before the Lord (Exod 28:36–38).[32] This stone has been prepared by God and engraved by him, for he is the one who will act to remove the iniquity of the land definitively.

Rewards for Faithfulness

Since the Lord is going to bring about this definitive work, does this mean that there is nothing for his human servants to do? Not at all. The theme of faithfulness is very important to the exilic and postexilic literature, not as the means of staying within the covenant relationship but as the source of receiving reward. We have already seen this in Zechariah 3, with the promise of special access to God for Joshua the

31. There may be a play on words here. The seven eyes recall the seven eyes of the Lord that roam throughout the earth in Zech 4:10. It is not only Joshua's attention that is directed toward the stone but the Lord's attention also.

32. Meyers and Meyers, *Haggai, Zechariah 1–8*, 205. It is also possible that this stone is not part of Joshua's clothing but is the same stone found in Zech 4:7, where it is an essential part of the temple. Since priest and temple function together in the removal of sin and since both point us forward to the work of Christ, there is not a great deal of difference in the exposition of the passage, whichever alternative is chosen.

high priest as a reward for faithful service, but it is equally prominent elsewhere in the literature.

Haggai 2

Because of his faithfulness in obeying the Lord during the day of small things (Zech 4:10), the civil governor, Zerubbabel, is promised special status on the day of cosmic shaking (Hag 2:6–7). On that day, Zerubbabel need not fear. The Lord would take him and make him like a signet ring (חוֹתָם), for he had chosen him (Hag 2:23). The language used reinforces the point that Zerubbabel, as a descendant of the Davidic line (1 Chr 3:19), represents the renewal of that ancient commitment on God's part. Though the Lord had cast away Jehoiachin like a signet ring (Jer 22:24), now that rejection would be reversed. The language of "taking" and "choosing" is the language of election, especially the initial election of David (Ps 78:70). The Lord is declaring in this oracle that the presence of Zerubbabel is evidence that the stump is not dead; he is, as it were, a green shoot emerging from the stump of the old line (an image that will be developed further by Zechariah).

What has Zerubbabel done to deserve this mark of approval? He has simply done what the kings of Judah ought to have done, but often failed to do, namely listen to God's word through the prophet and obey it. The role that Zerubbabel has played in the refounding of the temple has earned him the title *my servant*, a title that was used particularly of David and of the expectation of an ideal successor in his line (2 Sam 3:18; Ps 78:70).[33] He has not built his own house but has labored to rebuild God's house, precisely the calling he received in Haggai 1. His reward was to hear God say to him, in effect: "Well done, good and faithful servant! You have been faithful over a little; I will set you over much. Enter into the joy of your master" (Matt 25:21). Even though there was no earthly reward for his faithfulness, his obedience was not useless or unobserved. It may not yet have been the day for shaking the world, but his present faithfulness would in due time receive a heavenly reward.

33. Ibid., 68.

Ezekiel 40–48

The principle of reward for faithful service is a key element behind the construction of the book of Ezekiel, in which the plan for the future in Ezekiel 40–48 reflects the critique of Ezekiel 1–39.[34] Those who are privileged with closest access to the center of the temple are those who have been most faithful in the past. This is especially true of the Zadokite priests, who have been faithful and are rewarded with the central role in the new temple (44:15–16). To be sure, their faithfulness is not perfect (22:26), and therefore they have no access to the most holy place.[35] Nonetheless, they have been the most faithful of the Lord's people and so may expect a reward in the heavenly realm.

The Levites, on the other hand, had been unfaithful, serving the people in their spiritual adultery (44:6–8). Yet far from being excluded from the visionary Promised Land for their unfaithfulness, they are restored to their honorable, God-given place as ministers of the sanctuary (44:9–13).[36] The covenant between the Lord and the tribe of Levi cannot be broken through their faithlessness (Jer 33:21). The prince (נָשִׂיא) also has an honored, although limited, place in the new society, in spite of the covenant breaking of his forerunners. Meanwhile, the laity, whose leaders are charged with the prime responsibility for the abominations that led up to the exile, are pushed to the margins of the new society. In contrast to their former rights of access, they are now limited to a mere procession through the outer court of the temple, separated from the inner court by a high wall with strong gates (46:8–10). Yet even they are not excluded from this new world order: through God's grace and mercy, all twelve of the tribes find a place in the renewed land. All of God's chosen people enter and

34. I argue this point at length in *Ezekiel and the Leaders of Israel* (Leiden: Brill, 1994).

35. There is no sacrificial ritual carried out within the most holy place of Ezekiel's temple, unlike the Mosaic tabernacle and the Davidic temple. In fact, no one—not even the prophet himself—has access to that holy space. This is one aspect of the design that marks it out as "theology as architecture," rather than a blueprint for an actual building. On the theological ideas being expressed, see Duguid, *Ezekiel*, 464–551.

36. On the restoration of the Levites, see Duguid, *Ezekiel and the Leaders of Israel*, 133–39. On Ezekiel's purpose in this section, see idem, "Putting Priests in Their Place: Ezekiel's Contribution to the History of the Old Testament Priesthood," in *Ezekiel's Hierarchical World: Wrestling with a Tiered Reality* (ed. Stephen L. Cook and Corinne L. Patton; SBL Symposium Series 31; Atlanta: Society of Biblical Literature, 2004), 41–57.

remain in the covenant relationship through the Lord's faithfulness, yet there are greater rewards for those who have been more faithful in that service. Faithfulness in the Lord's service finds its reward in enhanced access to the presence of the Lord.

Theological Reflections

All of the Old Testament covenants, both conditional and unconditional, would have ended in failure if left to the faithfulness of sinful human beings. The covenant with Abraham was endangered on several occasions by Abraham himself before Isaac was even born (Gen 12:10–16; 16:1–15; 20:1–2) and then by Isaac and Jacob (Gen 27). The people of Israel's unfaithfulness led God to threaten their total annihilation on several occasions before they even reached the Promised Land (Exod 32:9–10; Num 14:11–12; 16:21, 45 [MT 17:10]).[37] At the end of Deuteronomy, the Lord renewed the Sinai covenant with the people, rehearsing the alternatives: blessing or curse (Deut 28). Yet it was already evident which of these prospects faced the people. In spite of Moses's impassioned appeal to "choose life!" (30:19), the people had already demonstrated many times over their inability to keep the terms of the covenant. If their unfaithfulness could have negated the relationship, then it would have done so already. The same is true of the Davidic covenant: it is no coincidence that David's sin with Bathsheba is recounted (2 Sam 11–12) immediately after the account of the Davidic covenant (2 Sam 7). The narrator is showing us that human unfaithfulness cannot annul God's covenant commitment.[38]

37. Had God really intended to destroy the people he could have done so immediately, without further discussion. His threats provide the cue for Moses to intercede on behalf of the people, so that they may receive his mercy and grace instead of the judgment their unfaithfulness deserved; see Jacob Milgrom, *Numbers* (Jewish Publication Society Torah Commentary; Philadelphia: Jewish Publication Society, 1990), 109.

38. In a similar fashion, the author of Genesis follows the Noahic covenant with the story of Noah's drunkenness; see Bruce K. Waltke, "The Phenomenon of Conditionality within Unconditional Covenants," in *Israel's Apostasy and Restoration: Essays in Honor of Roland K. Harrison* (ed. Avraham Gileadi; Grand Rapids: Baker, 1988), 131. One could also add Israel's apostasy with the golden calf immediately after the giving of the covenant documents on Mount Sinai. It is as if in every covenant the human parties are immediately put to the test and demonstrated to be lacking in faithfulness, yet the covenant relationship persists.

Jesus Christ, the Fulfiller of the Covenants

If Israel is a nation of promise breakers, though, how then will these covenants be fulfilled and bring about the blessing that God has irrevocably committed himself to give his people? To use N. T. Wright's apt phrase, "What happens when promise and Torah meet?"[39] How could a conditional covenant, whose blessings could be enjoyed only by the faithful, be good news for a deeply flawed people?[40] The answer of the Old Testament is twofold: there must be a substitute who suffers in place of his people and a covenant keeper who takes Israel's place (and, even more profoundly, Adam's place) in fulfilling the righteousness that God demands as the condition of blessing. The answer of the New Testament is that that suffering substitute and obedient servant is Jesus Christ, the fulfiller of all of God's covenants.

In the first place, there must be a suffering substitute. This is depicted visually in the various sacrifices given as part of the Sinai covenant. Sin must be atoned for by the shedding of blood, as these sacrifices vividly and regularly made clear (Lev 17:11). Covenantal nomists regularly refer to these sacrifices as part of the obligation of man's faithfulness, one of the aspects of the covenantal relationship that made imperfect obedience to its terms acceptable to God.[41] Yet this seems to place too much weight on the efficacy of these old covenant sacrifices, which as Hebrews 10:11 reminds us "can never take away sins." The value of these sacrifices and their efficacy, such as it was, lay in their ability to point old covenant believers forward by faith to the single efficacious sacrifice that Christ would offer in the

39. N. T. Wright, *The Climax of the Covenant: Christ and the Law in Pauline Theology* (Minneapolis: Fortress, 1992), 138.

40. Wright may be correct in saying that this problem "is more than the plight of the sinner convicted by a holy law" (ibid., 142), but at the same time it is not *less* than the plight of the sinner convicted by a holy law. Even though the question has a context in redemptive history, it is still essentially the same question that faces every person who stands in the presence of a God whose standard is absolute perfection. There is in fact no conflict between the individual and the corporate (or covenantal) perspective. The exiles needed to know that God had not rejected his people as a whole, but they also needed to know that they themselves as individuals were welcome to return. On the balance between corporate and individual categories, see Duguid, *Ezekiel*, 239–41.

41. See Rich Lusk, "Response to Morton Smith," in *The Auburn Avenue Theology, Pros and Cons: Debating the Federal Vision* (ed. E. Calvin Beisner; Fort Lauderdale, FL: Knox Theological Seminary, 2004), 128. Similarly, Sanders, *Paul and Palestinian Judaism*, 422.

fullness of time (10:10). In fact, the old covenant sacrifices themselves could not atone for the sins that the people were committing, which is why the people ended up in exile.

This is precisely what Deuteronomy 30 anticipated would be the result of the renewed Sinai covenant. Because of their rebellion and apostasy, the people would end up in exile (29:16–28 [MT 29:15–27]), from where the Lord would have to restore them by a sovereign act of his grace (30:1–6). Their history of apostasy would inevitably climax in covenant judgment and renewal in the form of exile and restoration.[42] And so indeed the history of Israel unfolded. Yet the historical exile to Babylon effected no such change in the people. They were the same Israel after the exile as they had been before, still experiencing the effects of the curse because of their sin (Hag 1:10). This should have made the lesson abundantly evident to all from their historical experience, that there was no way to blessing through their faithfulness to works of Torah. What Deuteronomy warned, history had validated: those who rely on their own efforts to keep the Sinai covenant as the means of blessing would find there nothing other than curse (Gal 3:10).

In order for there to be such a profound change in the people, God himself, in the person of Israel's Messiah, had to take upon himself the curse of the Torah and endure exile on their behalf. As Messiah, Jesus represented Israel and so was able to take upon himself Israel's curse and exhaust it.[43] That is why his death took the form of the covenantally cursed death on a tree (Deut 21:23). Through his death, in which his alienation from God on the cross was the profoundest experience of exile ever, Jesus paid for Israel's sins and removed their curse.

Yet, it is not enough to remove the curse and return God's people to, as it were, neutral ground. The goal of the covenant is not simply removing the threat of God's wrath from his people; it is bringing about the full blessing that all of the covenants promised to covenant keepers. From where does the righteousness required to earn these blessings come? The answer is that Messiah Jesus not only bore the

42. Wright, *Climax of the Covenant*, 140.
43. Ibid., 151.

curse of the law against covenant breakers, but he himself was the covenant keeper. That is why he could not simply be beamed down to the cross or crucified in infancy, but needed to be born of a woman, under the law, to redeem those under the law (Gal 4:4–5).[44] Just as in his death and resurrection Jesus is Israel, undergoing exile and restoration, so also in his earlier life, Jesus is Israel, perfectly fulfilling all of the demands of Torah.

This depiction is particularly prominent in Matthew's gospel, where the genealogy's three foci (Abraham, David, and exile) serve as structuring devices for the whole gospel. The first part (Matt 1:18–4:16) shows us Jesus the son of Abraham, going down to Egypt (2:14–15), passing through the waters (3:13–17), and enduring the wilderness just as Israel did (4:1–11), yet without sin. In the next section (4:17–16:20), after the Sermon on the Mount in which Jesus recapitulates the law-giving role of Moses, the attention increasingly focuses on the question, "Could this be the son of David?" (12:23). Meanwhile, the third section (16:21–28:20) shows us Jesus the son of exile as he turns his face to the cross. In his faithful life, Jesus thus reenacts the entire course of Israel's history, remaining faithful where they failed.[45]

This is exactly what we should have expected from passages like Zechariah 3. It is not enough for the high priest's filthy garments to be removed and for him to be left naked. He must also be reclothed in pure festival garments if he is to serve before a holy God. In the light of the New Testament, we may go further and observe that every privilege assigned to Joshua is matched by a move in the opposite direction by Christ. Joshua was clothed in festival garments, his shame removed; Jesus had the clothing stripped from his back and divided among his crucifiers, exposing him to their mockery. Joshua received a clean turban on his head; Jesus was crowned with thorns, pressed down into his forehead until the blood ran down his face. Joshua was judged and declared clean on the basis of God's choice of him for salvation, found not guilty of defilement that was really his;

44. S. M. Baugh, "Galatians 3:20 and the Covenant of Redemption," *Westminster Theological Journal* 66 (2004): 68.

45. As is observed correctly by Craig L. Blomberg, *Matthew* (New American Commentary; Nashville: Broadman, 1992), 67.

Jesus was judged by sinners, found guilty on trumped up charges, and handed over to be scourged and despised—because of God's choice of him to be the sin bearer (Acts 4:28). Joshua's sin was taken away: he was declared innocent, able to stand before God as high priest for his people, bearing their name before God; Jesus, our true and holy high priest, was made sin by God (2 Cor 5:21) and separated from God the Father so that he cried out in agony, "My God, my God, why have you forsaken me?" At the cross, Joshua's filth was removed and imputed to Jesus, and Jesus's perfect Torah keeping was imputed to Joshua. In Christ, the sign of Joshua found its fulfillment, as the Lord "removed the sin of this land in a single day" (Zech 3:9).

The Place of Human Faithfulness

The treatment of reward in the exilic and postexilic materials has a reflex in the New Testament that helps us to understand where our faithfulness belongs. Our faithfulness is not the condition by which we remain in the covenant; nonetheless, there is covenantal reward for those who are faithful, a reward that is related in some manner to our faithfulness. This gradation of reward should be neither overstressed nor understressed: there is real differentiation on the basis of our faithfulness, yet at the same time all the renewed people of God receive the fundamental blessing of being in God's presence eternally.[46]

Both of these aspects are present in the New Testament. In the vision of the New Jerusalem in Revelation 21, it is the equal reward of all the saints that is prominent. All believers are made perfect and granted equal entrance into the very presence of God himself, in the heavenly most holy place itself, which is the entire city. Likewise, in the parable of the workers in the vineyard, the same reward is given to those who are hired at the eleventh hour as to those who have worked hardest and longest (Matt 20:1–16). This fundamental

46. When we speak of *our* faithfulness, we should remember that all of our good works flow not from ourselves but from the work of the Spirit of Christ within us (WCF 16.3) and are always a long way short of perfect obedience. Nonetheless, as WCF 16.6 points out, because believers are accepted in Christ, God is pleased to reward their sincere works, although they are accompanied with many weaknesses and imperfections. See also HC 63, which teaches a doctrine of rewards but adds that these rewards "come not of merit, but of grace."

equality of reward flows from our being united to Christ, and it is his righteousness that is the basis for our full inheritance.

Yet on the other hand, some texts also affirm gradation in reward. Paul draws a contrast between two builders, each of whom is building up God's church on the only possible foundation, Jesus Christ (1 Cor 3:11). One of the builders builds with gold and precious stones, while the other builds with wood and straw (3:12). The works of each will be exposed on the day of judgment, their quality tested with fire (3:13). If what he has built survives, he will receive his reward. If it is burned up, he will suffer loss (3:14). Both are equally saved (3:15), but they receive different rewards.[47]

Suggestively, the two versions of the parable of the talents in the Gospels present complementary pictures. In Matthew, the focus is on the faithful stewards receiving exactly the same reward: the man who has been faithful with two talents, hears his master say exactly the same words as the one who was faithful with five: "Well done, good and faithful servant! You have been faithful with a few things; I will put you in charge of many things. Come and share your master's happiness!" (25:21). Their common faithfulness over differing amounts receives a common reward. Yet in Luke's account, the one whose faithful stewardship of the money resulted in a tenfold increase is rewarded with charge of ten cities, while the servant whose stewardship resulted in a fivefold increase is awarded charge over five cities (Luke 19:17, 19). Their differing fruitfulness with the same initial amount receives a graded reward.

As with so many other biblical metaphors, these images present complementary truths that together express a richer picture than any single image could.[48] Either image on its own is open to misunderstanding, while taken together they give a fuller picture. The function of the scriptural teaching of rewards is similarly twofold: the equality of inheritance stresses that all who enter heaven have a glorious reward, while the principle of gradation of reward stresses the accountability

47. Anthony A. Hoekema, *The Bible and the Future* (Grand Rapids: Eerdmans, 1979), 263.

48. Another example of this phenomenon is the slain lamb who is paradoxically also the Lion of Judah (Rev 5:5–6). Together, the images present a richer picture than either image taken on its own.

of the saints to God and the certainty of their future vindication by him.[49] On the one hand, God expects fruitfulness from his servants and will hold everyone accountable for their use of the resources and opportunities that he has entrusted to their care, while on the other hand no one who has trusted Christ will be disappointed by the inheritance he receives. There is only one way to enter this reward of eternal life in the close presence of God: through faith in Christ that looks to his righteousness imputed to us and depends on his faithfulness—not our own—to bring to completion our salvation.

49. Darrell L. Bock, *Luke* (NIV Application Commentary; Grand Rapids: Zondervan, 1996), 488.

4

The Covenant of Works in Moses and Paul

BRYAN D. ESTELLE

Power as such is a relational concept and requires relation.
—*Hans Jonas*

A writer who neglects the work of his predecessors and contemporaries is wasting his time and the time of his readers.
—*E. H. Sturtevant*

Introduction

Novelist Frederick Buechner,[1] hardly known for his strident orthodoxy, expressed the tremendous significance of the Eden narrative:

Most references to the secondary literature on Genesis, Romans, and Galatians are representative, since the literature is vast. Sometimes I cite both German and English versions of commentaries; however, the reader is reassured that the latest English versions are always cited since most will be referring to those works. Hebrew Bible text is quoted from *Biblia Hebraica Stuttgartensia*. Hebrew quotations from the Hebrew Bible and Mishnah are pointed; Qumran Hebrew quotations are unpointed.

1. See Maire-Hélène Davies, *Laughter in a Genevan Gown: The Works of Frederick Buechner, 1970–1980* (Grand Rapids: Eerdmans, 1983). Buechner was influenced by Barth, Tillich, and others.

> The old covenant of law grows out of God's telling Adam and Eve that all Eden is theirs if only they will not eat of that one fatal tree; and the whole tragic history of Israel, not to mention of the rest of us, stems from their eating it anyway; and out of those garments of skins as emblematic of the love that will not let them go grows the new covenant of grace where nothing is asked of them except that they allow themselves to be clothed. As Saint Paul understood it, in the face of Adam, who went wrong, are already faintly visible the features of Jesus, who went right, was right, lived and died to make all things finally right and whole.[2]

Those words allude indirectly to a doctrine that has often received an esteemed pride of place in Reformed theology but is increasingly coming under criticism: the doctrine of the covenant of works.

So we begin by asking: Was there a prelapsarian covenant of works? Could Adam have merited something from God and been placed in a state of permanent confirmed righteousness? Was this covenant arrangement a matter of grace or justice?[3] Was the covenant legal or relational?[4] Are there differences and distinctions that must be

2. Frederick Buechner, "The Bible as Literature," in *A Complete Literary Guide to the Bible* (ed. Leland Ryken and Tremper Longman III; Grand Rapids: Zondervan, 1993), 42.

3. See, e.g., Rich Lusk, "A Response to 'the Biblical Plan of Salvation,'" in *The Auburn Avenue Theology, Pros and Cons: Debating the Federal Vision* (ed. E. Calvin Beisner; Fort Lauderdale, FL: Knox Theological Seminary, 2004), 118–48. Lusk comments in response to those who argue in favor of a meritorious covenant claim: "As Aquinas pointed out, strict justice can only exist between equals. The creature is indebted to the Creator for his very existence; the creature can never indebt the Creator, no matter how much he serves or obeys. Unless we are going to exalt man to the same level as God, we must maintain a basic asymmetry" (121–22). I agree with Lusk's statement that "we must maintain a basic asymmetry"; nevertheless, it is clear that Lusk is unfamiliar with Aquinas and should have noted, so as not to prejudice the issue, that this is not all that Aquinas says about justice and merit. For example, in *Summa theologiae* I-II Q.114 Aquinas also states: "And so man can only merit before God on the presupposition of a divine ordination, of such a kind that by his work and action man is to obtain from God as a sort of reward that for which God has allotted him a power of action. . . . Since our actions have a meritorious character only on the presupposition of a divine ordination, it does not follow that God becomes simply obliged by debt to us but to himself, in the sense that an obligation of debt holds that his ordination should be fulfilled"; see Thomas Aquinas, *Summa theologiae* (ed. Thomas Gilby; New York/London: Blackfriars, 1972), 30.203. This statement would comfortably fit within a conception of merit from a covenantal perspective.

4. For example, see C. G. Berkouwer, *Sin* (Grand Rapids, Eerdmans, 1971), 208: "If we drive a wedge between these concepts of *works* and *grace* [in the Edenic narrative] we interpose the notion of an impersonal legalism within the original relation of God and man" (emphasis original).

maintained between the prefall covenant and the postfall covenant? What is the relationship between these covenants?

The classic Reformed view of the covenant of works is not a weak doctrine needing to be revised; rather, its classical expression as found in the Westminster Confession of Faith and elsewhere is the teaching of Scripture, and this position is only strengthened when carefully examined in light of modern biblical studies and linguistics. Indeed, good descriptions of the covenant of works may be found elsewhere.[5] Oswald T. Allis gives a brief and simple description of the covenant of works: "God Commanded; Adam and Eve disobeyed; the penalty of sanction attached to the command was invoked; and the guilty pair, under sentence of death, were driven from the presence of God."[6]

My presentation, however, is unique in some respects: it incorporates modern research in biblical studies in order to supplement the traditional presentation of the doctrine; it is concerned with the exegesis of some of the ideal biblical passages (*sedes materiae*); it describes the doctrine with current objections and objectors in view; it includes exegetical theology, biblical theology, and systematic theology

5. See, e.g., J. Gresham Machen, *The Christian View of Man* (London: Banner of Truth, 1965), 149–60; Geerhardus Vos, *Biblical Theology* (Grand Rapids: Eerdmans, 1948), 27–44; Oswald T. Allis, "The Covenant of Works," in *Basic Christian Doctrines* (ed. Carl F. H. Henry; New York: Holt, Rinehart & Winston, 1962), 96–102; E. J. Young, *In the Beginning: Genesis Chapters 1 to 3 and the Authority of Scripture* (Edinburgh: Banner of Truth, 1976), 111–17; Meredith G. Kline, *Kingdom Prologue: Genesis Foundations for a Covenantal Worldview* (Overland Park, KS: Two Age Press, 2000), 91–117; O. Palmer Robertson, *The Christ of the Covenants* (Phillipsburg, NJ: Presbyterian & Reformed, 1980), 55–57, 67–87 (although Robertson has exceptions to the nomenclature *works* because of his view of the role of grace in both the covenant of works and grace); Louis Berkhof, *Systematic Theology* (Grand Rapids: Eerdmans, 1984), 211–18; Charles Hodge, *Systematic Theology* (1873; repr. Grand Rapids: Eerdmans, 1982), 2.117–22; A. A. Hodge, *The Confession of Faith: A Handbook of Christian Doctrine Expounding the Westminster Confession of Faith* (Edinburgh: Banner of Truth, 1983), 120–24; Robert L. Dabney, *Lectures in Systematic Theology* (Grand Rapids: Zondervan, 1972), 302–5; William G. T. Shedd, *Dogmatic Theology* (Grand Rapids: Zondervan, 1950), 2.152–67; Turretin, *Institutes* 1.574–89 §8.3–7. Very instructive as well is *Institutes* 2.189–92 §12.4, where Turretin discusses the distinctions between the covenant of works and grace. In response to the adherents of the federal vision, see Morton H. Smith, "The Biblical Plan of Salvation, with Reference to the Covenant of Works, Imputation, and Justification by Faith," in *The Auburn Avenue Theology, Pros and Cons: Debating the Federal Vision* (ed. E. Calvin Beisner; Fort Lauderdale, FL: Knox Theological Seminary, 2004), 96–117.

6. Allis, "Covenant of Works," 97.

in its methodology; and it supplements the traditional disciplines of biblical interpretation with modern linguistics.

Various theologians, some Reformed, have criticized the covenant of works in the past.[7] In the present day, it is asserted that the doctrine is both a novelty and an abstraction in the history of the Reformed church that "deviated considerably from Calvin's more pastoral, organic approach to biblical theology."[8] I will not take up the historical question,[9] nor will I comment in any significant way upon the Mosaic covenant.[10] I am concerned with criticisms that

7. Herman Hoeksema, *Reformed Dogmatics* (Grand Rapids: Reformed Free Publishing Association, 1966), 214–26; Berkouwer, *Sin*, 207–8; John Murray, *Collected Writings of John Murray* (Edinburgh: Banner of Truth, 1976–82), 2.49; Klaas Schilder's and S. G. DeGraaf's views are easily accessible in Clarence Stam, *The Covenant of Love: Exploring Our Relationship with God* (Winnipeg: Premier, 1999), 40–54. On Schilder's views, see also S. A. Strauss, "Schilder on the Covenant," in *Always Obedient: Essays on the Teachings of Dr. Klaas Schilder* (ed. J. Geertsema; Phillipsburg, NJ: Presbyterian & Reformed, 1995), 19–34, esp. 23–25; and C. Van Der Waal, *The Covenantal Gospel* (Neerlandia, AB: Inheritance Publications, 1990), 47–64. In consideration of whether the "inborn law of nature [was] repeated at Sinai," Van Der Waal writes: "The doctrine of a covenant of works, despite the fact that it has been adhered to for ages, must yield to the glad tidings. The idea of contrasting covenant of works and covenant of grace, law and gospel, Old and New Testament, is to be rejected. There is but *one* history of grace, and *one* covenant" (59, emphasis original). See also Daniel P. Fuller, *The Unity of the Bible: Unfolding God's Plan for Humanity* (Grand Rapids: Zondervan, 1992), 179–84; Anthony A. Hoekema, *Created in God's Image* (Grand Rapids: Eerdmans, 1986), 119–21; W. J. Dumbrell, *Covenant and Creation: An Old Testament Covenantal Theology* (Carlisle, UK: Paternoster, 1984), 43–46; and Gerard Van Groningen, *From Creation to Consummation* (Sioux Center, IA: Dordt College Press, 1996), 65–71. Van Groningen, who denies that the covenant with Adam was one of works and probation and who denies the possibility of eschatological reward, says: "They [Adam and Eve] had nothing to merit. No reward was given" (68; see also 98).

8. Lusk, "Response to 'the Biblical Plan of Salvation,'" 119. Lusk reaches the pinnacle of his vitriolic criticism of the covenant of works when he says: "In short, the doctrine of a meritorious covenant of works has a dangerous Gnosticizing tendency on theology as a whole" (148).

9. This criticism suffers from many weaknesses that are beyond the scope of this essay. Suffice it to say, however, that Geerhardus Vos attributes an ancient pedigree to the doctrine at least in its seminal form; see "Doctrine of the Covenant in Reformed Theology," in *Redemptive History and Biblical Interpretation: The Shorter Writings of Geerhardus Vos* (ed. Richard B. Gaffin Jr.; Phillipsburg, NJ: Presbyterian & Reformed, 1980), 234–67. Vos does not fail to upbraid those who would assert that the doctrine is merely a relatively recent doctrine: "Whoever has the historical sense to be able to separate the mature development of a thought from its original sprouting and does not insist that a doctrine be mature at birth, will have no difficulty in recognizing the covenant of works as an old Reformed doctrine" (237).

10. Indeed, a responsible serious and sustained study of the Mosaic covenant with respect to the possibility of the principle of republication of the covenant of works in some manner, apparent in many Reformed luminaries in the past, is *still* a desideratum for both exegetical and historical theology. As is well known, Murray rejects such a notion: "The first or old covenant is the Sinaitic. And not only must this confusion in denotation be avoided,

touch most closely on the covenant of works in the Scriptures and in Westminster Confession of Faith 19.1 and 7.2–3, which are described by some as unclear or "at best confusing and at worse misleading."[11] Such statements are themselves open to criticism.

What is wanted from all sides in the current debates is a serious investigation of the *very words of the text* themselves, in their cultural and canonical context.[12] This leads me to another concern: an understanding of speech utterances and narrative in the Bible that attempts to minimize legal description in favor of familial and relational categories.

---

but also any attempt to interpret the Mosaic covenant in terms of the Adamic institution. The latter could apply only to the state of innocence, and to Adam alone as representative head. The view that in the Mosaic covenant there was a repetition of the so-called covenant of works, current among covenant theologians, is a grave misconception and involves an erroneous construction of the Mosaic covenant, as well as fails to assess the uniqueness of the Adamic administration" (*Collected Writings*, 2.50). Nevertheless, the significant parallel between the Eden narrative and the potential gift of rest in Eden in connection with obedience to God's commands and the land of Canaan in connection with the Israelites' obedience later in the Pentateuch has not gone unnoticed by modern scholars in addition to many Reformed luminaries in the past. Cf. Eckart Otto, "Die Paradieserzählung Genesis 2–3: Eine nachpriesterschriftliche Lehrerzählung in ihrem religionshistorischen Kontext," in *"Jedes Ding hat seine Zeit . . .": Studien zur israelitischen und altorientalischen Weisheit: Diethelm Miche zum 65. Geburtstag* (Beihefte zur Zeitschrift für die alttestamentliche Wissenschaft 241; Berlin: de Gruyter, 1996), 167–92, esp. 182. Whether the principle of works was merely hypothetical or actually operative in some manner during the Mosaic economy is the main question I have in mind, and the answer to that issue has systemic ramifications for covenant theology as a whole.

11. James Jordan, "Merit versus Maturity: What Did Jesus Do for Us?" in *The Federal Vision* (ed. Steve Wilkins and Duane Garner; Monroe, LA: Athanasius, 2004), 154. Jordan sees himself as taking up Murray's call for continued reformation of covenant theology: "The purpose of this paper is to take up Murray's challenge, and provide a better systematic construction of the nature of the Adamic Covenant and of how Jesus fulfilled it for us" (155). Jordan seems to have ignored Gerhard von Rad's comments, *Genesis: A Commentary* (trans. J. H. Marks; rev. ed.; Old Testament Library; Philadelphia: Westminster, 1972), 81: "Nothing [in Gen 2:15] is said to indicate that God combined pedagogical intentions with this prohibition (in the sense of a 'moral' development of man). On the contrary, one destroys the essential part of the story with such rationalistic explanations. Man in his original state was completely *subject* to God's command, and the question, 'Who will say to him, What doest thou?' (Job 9:12; Dan 4:35b) was equally out of place in Paradise" (emphasis original).

12. See, e.g., Steve Schlissel's appeal for systematicians to return to the text of Scripture in its original context in "Justification and the Gentiles," in *The Federal Vision* (ed. Steve Wilkins and Duane Garner; Monroe, LA: Athanasius, 2004), 237–61. The fact of the matter is, as Moisés Silva says, that "all interpreters recognize the crucial importance of context for exegesis. The meaning of every utterance depends, to a greater or lesser degree, on the setting of which it is a part"; see *Interpreting Galatians: Explorations in Exegetical Method* (2nd ed.; Grand Rapids: Baker, 2001), 103.

I will challenge the widely received notion that financial, legal, or forensic metaphors often used in descriptions of the covenant of works and justification must now be transcended and replaced in theological, philosophical, and pastoral discourse. Indeed, in the current ecclesiastical and academic climate, one gains the impression that legal language has little explanatory power for such crucial topics as the doctrine of God, atonement, forgiveness, or justification any longer "after the philosophical 'turn to relationality.'"[13] I contend, however, that we must be rigorously fair with the full panoply of linguistic categories presented in Scripture. Otherwise, our potentially *thick* descriptions of the biblical content will be reduced to *thin* descriptions.[14]

Related to these methodological questions, but not exactly tantamount to them, is the antipathy for abstract theological frameworks and systematic theology in both the new perspective on Paul and the so-called federal-vision adherents and others.[15] The contention often

13. Quoting F. LeRon Shults in Shults and Steven J. Sandage, *The Faces of Forgiveness: Searching for Wholeness and Salvation* (Grand Rapids: Baker, 2003), 105. One can appreciate Shults and Sandage's sophistication in and appreciation for understanding the fascinating play of individuals in the systemic dynamics of relational intersubjectivity. It seems, nevertheless, that their opinion that legal and financial metaphors are insufficient for describing the Christian doctrine of salvation in the practice of forgiveness is overworked as a theme in their book (cf. 12, 72, 123, 125, 133, 136, 139, 147, 148, 158, 172). For another example in systematic theology from a German theologian at Ruhr-Universität Bochum, see Christian Link, "Providence: An Unsolved Problem of the Doctrine of Creation," in *Creation in Jewish and Christian Tradition* (ed. Henning Graf Reventlow and Yair Hoffman; Journal for the Study of the Old Testament Supplement 319; Sheffield: Sheffield Academic Press, 2002), 266–76. Link proposes adopting a model of God as king along relational lines as developed in process theology *rather than* the model of an almighty God with its similes and metaphors of absolute king or victorious general or "perhaps even that of good shepherd." For Link, this shift provides the solution for overcoming the problems of causality associated with our traditional categories of providence. Kevin J. Vanhoozer, *First Theology: God, Scriptures, and Hermeneutics* (Downers Grove, IL: InterVarsity, 2002), questions the viability of the more "populist" metaphor, that is, "God is not over his people but among them" (although here he is polemicizing against Farley, Kelsey, and Barr). Vanhoozer states: "This personal-relational model of conceiving God's presence and activity is not, however, without its problems" (149).

14. See Kevin Vanhoozer, *Is There a Meaning in This Text?* (Grand Rapids: Zondervan, 1998), 328–31.

15. See, e.g., N. T. Wright, *What Saint Paul Really Said: Was Paul of Tarsus the Real Founder of Christianity?* (Grand Rapids: Eerdmans, 1996), 79–80. Cf. Steve M. Schlissel, "A New Way of Seeing?" in *The Auburn Avenue Theology, Pros and Cons: Debating the Federal Vision* (ed. E. Calvin Beisner; Fort Lauderdale, FL: Knox Theological Seminary, 2004), 18–39. Schlissel sets up a false dichotomy between "story" and the doctrine of justification by faith (see esp. 22, 25, 27, 33). Also see Peter Leithart, "Trinitarian Anthropology: Toward a Trinitarian Re-Casting of Reformed Theology," in *The Auburn Avenue Theology, Pros and Cons: Debating the Federal*

made in the current discussions is that the methods and practice of biblical theology entail demurring from the findings of systematic theology. I reassert, however, in the most emphatic terms that the proper use and application of the science of biblical theology, rather than supplanting systematic theology, will actually support and serve its purposes. In short, a wise use of biblical theology will usually not lead a scholar to the implication that the church has, all this time, "been chasing her own shadow."[16]

This essay is divided into two unequal parts. More discussion is devoted to an exposition of the doctrine of the covenant of works from the Hebrew Bible[17] (with primary reference to Gen 2–3) than to its

---

Vision (ed. E. Calvin Beisner; Fort Lauderdale, FL: Knox Theological Seminary, 2004), 58–71, at 65: "All this has one main implication for the current debate: Insofar as the Auburn Avenue conferences have proposed refinements of Reformed theology, we have done so in order to purge Reformed theology of pagan impersonalism and to replace it with more thoroughly Trinitarian and more thoroughly Calvinistic formulations. Abstraction, especially Enlightenment abstraction, is the great bogeyman of the Auburn Avenue speakers. The claim that Reformed theology has compromised with the Enlightenment is controversial (I believe it is true in many respects), but if it is true, then I trust all Christians will agree it is imperative to continue the process of purgation." See also Steve Schlissel, "Justification and the Gentiles," in *The Federal Vision* (ed. Steve Wilkins and Duane Garner; Monroe, LA: Athanasius, 2004), 237–61, esp. 239–44. For an example of polemicizing against "bare law" abstraction and the law/gospel contrast, see Joseph P. Braswell, "Covenant Salvation: Covenant Religion vs. Legalism," *Journal of Christian Reconstruction* 16 (1994): 204.

16. Geerhardus Vos, "The Idea of Biblical Theology as a Science and as a Theological Discipline," in *Redemptive History and Biblical Interpretation: The Shorter Writings of Geerhardus Vos* (ed. Richard B. Gaffin Jr.; Phillipsburg, NJ: Presbyterian & Reformed, 1980), 3–24, esp. 23. An insightful article and comments on "bottom-up relationships" and "top-down relationships" by Al Wolters is germane: "Confessional Criticism and the Night Visions of Zechariah," in *Renewing Biblical Interpretation: Scripture and Hermeneutics Series* (ed. Craig Bartholomew, Colin Green, and Karl Möller; Grand Rapids: Zondervan, 2000), 1.90–117. For a simple and clear description of the necessity of relating systematic theology to exegesis and the problems entailed in the process, see Silva, *Interpreting Galatians*, 204–10.

17. The Old Testament has always been open to significant criticism throughout the history of the church. At times, there have even been attempts at wholesale rejection. Beginning with Marcion, who renounced so much of the Old Testament, and continuing to famous German scholar Adolf von Harnack, who challenged Christians to admit the irrelevance of the Old Testament, the function of the Old Testament for Christian theology has been challenged. See, e.g., Bernhard W. Anderson's introduction to *The Old Testament and Christian Faith: Essays by Rudolph Bultmann and Others* (ed. Bernhard W. Anderson; London: SCM, 1964). To understand the significance of the Old Testament for a proper understanding of the New is not simply one theological problem among many; it may be argued that it is *the* problem of Christian theology. Anderson, for example, says with respect to the relationship between the Old Testament and the New that it is no exaggeration to say that "on this question hangs the meaning of the Christian faith." See also A. H. J. Gunneweg,

exposition from the Greek Bible. In the New Testament, I give primary attention to Paul's letters to the Romans (especially Rom 5) and Galatians (especially 3:10). I take great pains to describe the setting of the Eden narrative before discussing one of the crucial texts (Gen 2:15–17) for the covenant of works. My premise is that if one understands the Edenic scenario and Adam's role in it for what it is, then the gravity of that first sin and its entailments for the human race and Christ's mission on earth become more vividly clear and dramatically weighty.

Covenant of Works in Moses

Terminology

We begin with the definition of "covenant." Surveying the recent definitions of several scholars will help clarify the issues before us. The venerable John Murray (1898–1975) saw a need to revise traditional Reformed ideas about the covenants, especially with respect to the covenant of works.[18] He protested against the nomenclature *covenant of works* because it "is not designated a covenant in Scripture."[19] For Murray, therefore, a covenant was "a sovereign administration of promise and grace."[20] Murray saw God's interactions expressed within

Understanding the Old Testament (trans. John Bowden; Old Testament Library; Philadelphia: Westminster, 1978), 2.

18. Cf. John Murray, "The Theology of the Westminster Confession of Faith," in *Scripture and Confession: A Book about Confessions Old and New* (ed. J. H. Skilton; Nutley, NJ: Presbyterian & Reformed, 1973), 146: "The term 'covenant of works' to designate the Adamaic administration [WCF 7.2] is not an accurate designation. If the term 'covenant' is used, the designation in the Shorter Catechism 'covenant of life' is preferable"; idem, "Covenant Theology," in *The Encyclopedia of Christianity* (Marshalton: National Foundation for Christian Education, 1972), 199–216; idem, "The Adamic Administration," in *Collected Works*, 2.47–59; idem, "Covenant Theology," in *Collected Works*, 4.216–40; and especially idem, *The Covenant of Grace: A Biblio-Theological Study* (1953; repr. Phillipsburg, NJ: Presbyterian & Reformed, 1988), 5: "However architectonic may be the systematic constructions of any one generation or group of generations, there always remains the need for correction and reconstruction so that the structure may be brought into closer approximation to the Scripture and the reproduction be a more faithful transcript or reflection of the heavenly exemplar. It appears to me that covenant theology, notwithstanding the finesse of analysis with which it has been worked out and the grandeur of its articulated systematization, needs recasting."

19. Murray, "Adamic Administration," 2.49.

20. See Murray, *Covenant of Grace*, 29. Murray comments earlier in this work: "As we study the biblical evidence bearing upon the nature of divine covenant we shall discover that

biblical covenants as always redemptive in design.[21] The first part of Murray's definition is satisfactory but the latter part is wanting since it is too restrictive. Murray's definition, simply stated, does not fit all the administrations of covenant in the Bible.

O. Palmer Robertson defines covenant as a "bond-in-blood sovereignly administered."[22] For Robertson, the relational bond is the crucial factor, but this definition does not adequately cover all covenants described in the Bible either. For example, in Genesis 9, the Noahic covenant is described as a common-grace covenant. It is made with believers and unbelievers alike and with all of creation for that matter (cf. 9:9–10).[23] This common-grace covenant does not fit well with Robertson's definition. Moreover, biblical covenants were bonds in the sense of being obligatory rather than merely religious community bonds.

A final definition of covenant, a very simple and yet comprehensive one, is a "commitment with divine sanctions."[24] This definition has the advantage of being general enough to incorporate various biblical covenants. Its strength also lies in emphasizing the sanction, that is, the oath, that gives the covenant its binding force. The "swearing of an oath" is the sine qua non of covenants, in which the "relational"

the emphasis in these theologians upon God's *grace* and *promise* is one thoroughly in accord with the relevant biblical data" (8, emphasis original).

21. Murray, "Adamic Administration," 2.49: "Scripture always uses the term covenant, when applied to God's administration to men, in reference to a provision that is redemptive or closely related to redemptive design. Covenant in Scripture denotes the oath-bound confirmation of promise and involves a security that the Adamic economy did not bestow."

22. O. Palmer Robertson, *The Christ of the Covenants* (Phillipsburg, NJ: Presbyterian & Reformed, 1980), 15. A cursory search of Palmer's most recent release, *The Christ of the Prophets* (Phillipsburg, NJ: Presbyterian & Reformed, 2004), does not give any indication that he has significantly altered his definition.

23. See Claus Westermann, *Genesis 1–11: A Commentary* (trans. John J. Scullion; Minneapolis: Augsburg, 1984), 471: "The assurance is extended expressly and in detail to all species of animals which are once more bracketed with humans in the concluding words: 'all that have come out of the ark.' . . . It is this very verse, which extends the 'covenant' to all species of animals." Cf. the striking comment of Hermann Gunkel, *Genesis* (trans. Mark E. Biddle; Macon, GA: Mercer University Press, 1997), 150: "God gives this promise to all those who were impacted by the Flood, that is, humans and animals. This idea that God's covenant also applies to animals sounds amazingly profane for P, who otherwise thinks of a 'history of salvation' in relation to covenants." An appreciation for common grace would have rescued Gunkel from his bewilderment. Finally, Umberto Cassuto's philological comments in *A Commentary on the Book of Genesis*, vol. 2: *From Noah to Abraham* (trans. Israel Abrahams; Jerusalem: Magnes, 1964), 131–32, drive the point home further.

24. Kline, *Kingdom Prologue*, 1–7.

aspect is already assumed, or, more precisely, a covenant provides the context, or arrangement, in which a relationship may proceed.

True, the lexical term for covenant (בְּרִית) does not occur in the biblical text until Genesis 6:18.[25] When doing biblical studies, however, one needs to discriminate between a term and the idea behind a term. If there is no explicit term, a historical covenant may still be assumed even without explicit lexical references (i.e., בְּרִית) to that covenant.[26] This touches on an axiom (i.e., a principle that does not need to be proven) of both theology and linguistics: a term or word does not necessarily have to be present in order for the substance of a concept to be present.[27] This is crucial to our discussion and the current debate.[28]

25. This can sometimes be an obstacle to those wrestling with the constructions of Reformed theology. For example, before he became Reformed, Bruce Waltke concluded in "An Evangelical Christian View of the Hebrew Scriptures," in *Evangelicals and Jews in an Age of Pluralism* (ed. Marc H. Tanenbaum, Marvin R. Wilson, and A. James Rudin; Grand Rapids: Baker, 1984), 105–39 at 131 that "we should reckon only with the historic covenants of the Old Testament and not construct abstract, theological covenants such as the covenant of grace or redemption and confound them with the historic covenants (Noahic, Abrahamic, Mosaic, Davidic, New)." A similar principle (although applied to a discussion about the covenant of redemption and not the covenant of works) can be observed operating in Murray's writing as well: "It is not strictly proper to use a biblical term to designate something to which it is not applied in Scripture itself" (*Collected Writings*, 2.130). See also John H. Stek, "'Covenant' Overload in Reformed Theology," *Calvin Theological Journal* 29 (1994): 12–41. Stek suggests that Reformed theology needs a radical reassessment of its emphasis on covenant as an organizing principle in Scripture. For a rejoinder (which starts down the right track but doesn't go far enough) to Stek's challenge to the covenant tradition in Reformed theology, see Craig G. Bartholomew, "Covenant and Creation: Covenant Overload or Covenantal Deconstruction," *Calvin Theological Journal* 30 (1995): 11–33.

26. See, e.g., Berkhof, *Systematic Theology*, 213: "It must be admitted that the term 'covenant' is not found in the first three chapters of Genesis, but this is not tantamount to saying that they do not contain the necessary data for the construction of a doctrine of the covenant. . . . All the elements of a covenant are indicated in Scripture, and if the elements are present, we are not only warranted but, in a systematic study of the doctrine, also in duty bound to relate them to one another, and to give the doctrine so construed an appropriate name."

27. See Bartholomew, "Covenant and Creation," 28, who correctly says: "The absence of the word *covenant* does not necessarily indicate its absence."

28. It is not an illegitimate endeavor to talk in the realm of concepts; one needs to be careful, however, not to do injustice to the linguistic facts in such a process. Cf. James Barr, *Biblical Words for Time* (2nd ed.; Studies in Biblical Theology 33; Edinburgh: SCM, 1969), 54. For an accessible treatment of possible errors stemming from the confusion over the relationship of words and concepts and an introduction to the foundation-shaking work of Barr's linguistics in biblical studies, see Peter Cotterell and Max Turner, *Linguistics and Biblical Interpretation* (Downers Grove, IL: InterVarsity, 1989), 109–28. See also Moisés Silva's review of Cotterell

Genesis 2–3

The Edenic scenario is the proper place to begin.[29] Both the setting of Eden and the role of the humans placed in that garden have been discussed at length. Describing accurately the scene itself is all important to our exegesis. We could turn to Genesis 1 itself to prove our upcoming point;[30] first, however, we will take up the setting of the garden of Eden and discuss it at length, since proper understanding of the context illumines the key texts, before proceeding to man's role in that garden.

---

and Turner's book in *Westminster Theological Journal* 51 (1989): 389–90, who considers it "a great success."

29. Vos, *Biblical Theology*, 16, in his discussion of the method of biblical theology, recognizes the benefits of a proper starting place: "The main problem will be how to do justice to the individual peculiarities of the agents in revelation. These individual traits subserve the historical plan. Some propose that we discuss each book separately. But this leads to unnecessary repetition, because there is so much that all have in common. A better plan is to apply the collective treatment in the earlier stages of revelation, where the truth is not as yet much differentiated, and then to individualize in the later periods where greater diversity is reached."

30. See, e.g., Jon Levenson, *Sinai and Zion: An Entry into the Jewish Bible* (San Francisco: Harper & Row, 1985), 142–43 (a section entitled "Sacred Space and Sacred Time"): "If the Temple is a form of the world, then the construction of the Temple, and of its predecessor, the Tabernacle, should mirror the creation of the world. In fact, exactly such a parallelism can be seen from a comparison of the language describing the two building programs." Levenson's comparison of biblical passages is illustrative:

A1. The heaven and the Earth were finished, and all their array. On the seventh day God finished the work that he had been doing, and he rested on the seventh day from all the work he had done. (Gen 2:1–2)	A2. All the work of the Tabernacle, the Tent of Encounter, was finished. The Israelites had done everything exactly as YHWH had commanded Moses: Thus had they done it. (Exod 39:32)
B1. And God saw all that he had made and found it very good. And there was evening and there was morning, a sixth day. (Gen 1:31)	B2. And Moses saw all the work and found that they had made it as YHWH had commanded: Thus had they made it. And Moses blessed them. (Exod 39:43)
C1. And God blessed the seventh day and made it sacred, for on it God had ceased from all the work of creation that he had done. (Gen 2:3)	C2. Same as B2.
D1. Same as C1.	D2. You shall take the anointing oil and anoint the Tabernacle and all that is in it, and you shall make it sacred, along with all its furnishings. It shall be sacred. (Exod 40:9)

Sanctuary Symbolism

The garden was first and foremost a place of *fellowship* with God.[31] Moreover, the garden of Eden is to be viewed as a prototypical sanctuary.[32] Significant data supports this contention. First are various verbal hints that suggest sanctuary imagery.[33] For example, the verb מִתְהַלֵּךְ in Genesis 3:8 (traditionally translated "walking") is used in similar forms in other sanctuary contexts as well (Lev 26:12; Deut 23:14 [MT 23:15]; 2 Sam 7:6–7)[34] and is often used in connection with righteousness (e.g., with Enoch, Noah, and Abraham).[35]

Second, references to cherubim (כְּרֻבִים) are significant since these creatures are the guardians of the divine sanctuary.[36] The "cheru-

31. Vos, *Biblical Theology*, 27–28, writes: "The garden is 'the garden of God,' not in the first instance an abode for man as such, but specifically a place of reception of man into fellowship with God in God's own dwelling place. The God-centred character of religion finds its first, but already fundamental, expression in this arrangement."

32. Gordon J. Wenham, "Sanctuary Symbolism in the Garden of Eden Story," in *I Studied Inscriptions from before the Flood* (ed. Richard S. Hess and David Toshio Tsummra; Winona Lake, IN: Eisenbrauns, 1994), 399–404. Wenham actually uses the word *archetypal*, but because in theological discourse this term often means "known only to God," I avoid it to prevent confusion. See also Gary A. Anderson, "The Cosmic Mountain: Eden and Its Early Interpreters in Syriac Christianity," in *Genesis 1–3 in the History of Exegesis: Intrigue in the Garden* (ed. Gregory Allen Robbins; Lewiston: Mellen, 1988), 187–224 at 199: "Eden, as a luxuriant cosmic mountain becomes an archetype or symbol for the earthly temple."

33. Wenham, "Sanctuary Symbolism," 400–401.

34. The allusion to 2 Sam 7:6–7 is evident enough; the references to the other two passages may, however, need further explanation. Lev 26:12 is clearly in the context of sanctuary, as indicated in Carl F. Keil, *The Pentateuch* (trans. James Martin; repr. Grand Rapids: Eerdmans, 1991), 2.471, commenting on 26:11: "'I will make My dwelling among you, and My soul will not despise you.' מִשְׁכָּן [is] applied to the dwelling of God among His people in the sanctuary." Likewise, a superficial reading Deut 23:14 may not immediately seem as though it is in the context of sanctuary or the presence of the ark; when, however, Deuteronomy says that Yahweh is walking in the "midst of your camp," the connotation is that God is present sometimes explicitly through the presence of the ark. The exact expression is found only here, Num 14:44, and Deut 2:14–16. See William L. Moran, "The End of the Unholy War and the Anti-Exodus," in *A Song of Power and the Power of the Song: Essays on the Book of Deuteronomy* (ed. Duane Christensen; Winona Lake, IN: Eisenbrauns, 1993), 149.

35. Ithamar Gruenwald, "The Creation of the World and the Shaping of Ethos and Religion in Ancient Israel," in *Creation in Jewish and Christian Tradition* (ed. Henning Graf Reventlow and Yair Hoffman; Journal for the Study of the Old Testament Supplement 319; Sheffield: Sheffield Academic Press, 2002), 179–218 at 217: "The verb הִתְהַלֵּךְ really deserves a full-scale semantic study."

36. Umberto Cassuto, *A Commentary on the Book of Genesis* (trans. Israel Abrahams; Jerusalem: Magnes, 1961), 1.174, notes that the garden was entered from the east and that is why the guardian cherubs were stationed on that side. Also see Wenham, "Sanctuary Symbolism," 401, who notes that "the tabernacle and Jerusalem temple were also entered from the east. That the entrance of the garden was guarded by *kĕrûbîm* is another indication that it is viewed

bim denote God's physical presence throughout the Hebrew Bible. Wherever one finds a cherub (whether as a decorative feature or a mythical creature), one finds divine presence."[37] Ronald Hendel draws attention to the flame of the whirling sword, which, although less recognized, is also significant based on comparative data from the ancient Near East.[38]

Additionally, the compound name יְהוָה אֱלֹהִים, which is predominately used in a *cultic* context, occurs frequently in Genesis 2.[39] The tree of life and the tree of the knowledge of good and evil also indicate that the garden is to be viewed as a prototypical sanctuary. Adam's function in the garden, however, is of the greatest significance.

The correct understanding of the phrase לְעָבְדָהּ וּלְשָׁמְרָהּ in Genesis 2:15 is of paramount importance. The passage intends to say that God took the man and placed him in the garden "to tend it and guard it." This meaning (especially "guard it") is lost in most English translations. It is important, however, that the only places in the Pentateuch where these two verbs occur together are in contexts where the Levites' duties include guarding and protecting the sanctuary.[40]

as a sanctuary, for *kěrûbîm*, Akkadian *kuribu*, were the traditional guardians of holy places in the ancient Near East." Cf. 1 Kgs 6:23–38; Exod 25:18–22; 26:31.

37. Benjamin D. Sommer, "Conflicting Constructions of Divine Presence in the Priestly Tabernacle," *Biblical Interpretation* 9.1 (2001): 41–63, esp. 49. Cf. the discussion by T. Stordalen, *Echoes of Eden: Genesis 2–3 and Symbolism of the Eden Garden in Biblical Hebrew Literature* (Contributions to Biblical Exegesis and Theology 25; Louvain: Peeters, 2000), 458–59, who cites many other passages where "cherubs are almost exclusively connected to cultic entities."

38. Ronald Hendel, "'The Flame of the Whirling Sword': A Note on Genesis 3:24," *Journal of Biblical Literature* 104 (1985): 671–74. I am unsure, however, that his argument that the flame of the whirling sword is an independent fiery being in the service of Yahweh is successful.

39. Stordalen, *Echoes of Eden*, 287 (see footnotes for numerous biblical justifications) and 458–59, where he demonstrates that in the history of Chronicles the compound name is almost exclusively associated with cultic situations.

40. Wenham, "Sanctuary Symbolism," 401, draws attention to Num 3:7–8; 8:26; 18:5–6 and concludes: "If Eden is seen then as an ideal sanctuary, then perhaps Adam should be described as an archetypal Levite." Noteworthy on this point is the book of Jubilees, one of the oldest and most important Jewish texts in the Pseudepigrapha (a group of writings from approximately 250 BC to AD 200 that help students understand early Judaism). James VanderKam dates Jubilees between 170 and 140 BC. Although the text was probably originally written in Hebrew and translated into Greek and possibly Syriac, the only entire extant version is the Ethiopic rendition. The text is heavy with sacerdotalism. Although this might be because the author himself was a priest, significantly, Jubilees has Adam and Eve observing certain levitical laws in the garden (cf. 3.8–14) "because it is the holiest [sanctuary] in the entire earth, and every tree which is planted in it is holy." See James C. Vanderkam, ed., *The Book of Jubilees: A Critical Text* (Corpus scriptorum christianorum orientalium 510–11; Scriptores aethiopici 87–88; Louvain:

Thus, the cherubim are stationed east of the garden (following the fall of mankind) "to guard" (לִשְׁמֹר) the way to the tree of life (Gen 3:24).

Other evidence demonstrates that the garden was a holy sanctuary, one to be guarded by the priest placed in the garden, namely Adam. Gordon Wenham, for example, brings attention to the tunics in Genesis 3:21 and the ordination clothing of priests (Exod 28:41; 29:8; 40:14; Lev 8:13). Additionally, the geography of the garden, especially with its description of rivers (Gen 2:10–14) and its precious jewels (2:12), demonstrates that the garden was conceived after a sanctuary design.[41] Not only was the garden a sanctuary and Adam primarily a priest who had the duty to maintain the purity of the garden, but Adam was also a king who fulfilled a royal function.[42]

Royal Ideology

The garden scene is imbued with themes of royal ideology. The idea of God as sovereign ruler and king over all his kingdom of creation is, unarguably, "totally unreasonable to the modern consciousness."[43] Moreover, whether the text emphasizes that mankind is the possessor of kingship or whether Yahweh himself is king is the topic of debate. The answer to this apparent dilemma lies not in putting the two options on the horns of a false dilemma; rather, the key is the middle way. Throughout the Old and New Testaments, God is portrayed as the

Peeters, 1989), 17–18. Cf. also Stephen N. Lambdin, "From Fig Leaves to Fingernails: Some Notes on the Garments of Adam and Eve in the Hebrew Bible and Select Early Postbiblical Jewish Writings," in *A Walk in the Garden: Biblical, Iconographical, and Literary Images of Eden* (Journal for the Study of the Old Testament Supplement 136; Sheffield: JSOT Press, 1992), 74–90. Lambdin catalogues the numerous postbiblical Jewish writings, targumim, Samaritan, and rabbinic literatures that develop Adam's exalted primordial priesthood and the significance of his garments and the coverings provided by God following the fall.

41. Wenham, "Sanctuary Symbolism," 401–3. On Eden and the cosmography of Gen 2:10–14, see Stordalen, *Echoes of Eden*, 270–86. By the term *cosmography* Stordalen means a mixture of topography and cosmology that was common in the way the ancient Near Eastern cultures conceived of their geography and the way they perceived space, which was different from the modern interpreter's view of topographic apprehension.

42. Which takes precedence—the priestly or the kingly—will have tremendous ramifications for one's overall system of theology and one's view of the relationship of cult to culture; but this is not an issue immediately in view in this essay.

43. Link, "Providence," 272.

king of creation and history.[44] Although dominion belongs ultimately and solely to God, the concept of kingship belongs also to mankind, to whom God commands and delegates responsibility.[45]

Even if the accent is on man's kingship in the early chapters of Genesis (which it probably is given the portrayal of Ezekiel discussed below), the text clearly takes pains to demonstrate that Yahweh owns the garden.[46] Additionally, this becomes even more conspicuous when Psalm 8, which is clearly commenting on Genesis, is brought into the discussion. As Randall Garr states in his recent tour de force on Genesis 1:26: "Created 'in our image' and 'in the image of God' represents both levels of divine authority that governs the cosmos. Humankind represents God's community of co-rulers, responsible for performing the justice and enacting the sovereign will of God."[47] These themes are familiar to those who are familiar with Reformed theology and modern scholarship, since they are discussed in numerous places in the secondary literature.[48]

Much has been written about the prominent idea in Mesopotamian cosmogonies that human beings were created to do the work of the gods.[49] This is probably a distinct difference between the Hebrew

44. See, e.g., Charles H. H. Scobie, *The Ways of Our God: An Approach to Biblical Theology* (Grand Rapids: Eerdmans, 2003), 106–8.

45. Ibid., 156–59.

46. As demonstrated by Alan Jon Hauser, "Genesis 2–3: The Theme of Intimacy and Alienation," in *I Studied Inscriptions from before the Flood* (ed. Richard S. Hess and David Toshio Tsummra; Winona Lake, IN: Eisenbrauns, 1994), 383–98. Significantly, Hauser demonstrates that numerous stylistic devices are used by the author to convey the theme of intimacy in Gen 2. This seems to contradict the facile interpretation of the early chapters of Genesis that sets the relational against the forensic.

47. W. Randall Garr, *In His Own Image and Likeness: Humanity, Divinity, and Monotheism* (Culture and History of Ancient Near East 15; Leiden: Brill, 2003), 219. Garr adds: "Like Gen 1, this psalm ascribes 'image' to human beings. God ensures that they dominate terrestrial, aviary, and marine life (vv. 8–9; see Gen 1:26b.28b). They collaterally hold the power to place everything under their control (v. 7b; see Gen 1:26babβ.28aβb). God even assigns royal status and royal rule comparable to his own (e.g., v. 6b)" (220–21).

48. For further bibliography in Reformed scholarship, see Hoekema, *Created in God's Image*, 78–80. For bibliography on royal ideology from modern scholarship, see David P. Wright, "Holiness, Sex, and Death in the Garden of Eden," *Biblica* 77 (1996): 305–29, esp. 310.

49. The Atrahasis Epic (and not *Enuma Elish*, as usually imagined) contains the standard account of man's creation from the Babylonian sources. See W. G. Lambert, "A New Look at the Babylonian Background of Genesis," in *I Studied Inscriptions from before the Flood* (ed. Richard S. Hess and David Toshio Tsummra; Winona Lake, IN: Eisenbrauns, 1994), 107. See also W. G. Lambert and A. R. Millard, *Atra-Ḫasīs: The Babylonian Story of the Flood* (repr. Winona Lake, IN: Eisenbrauns, 1999).

conception and the surrounding cultures.[50] The Genesis account, very frankly, stands in glaring contrast to the Sumerian and Babylonian counterparts with respect to whether God needed any assistance in his sovereign fiat creation.[51] This emphasis on man as surrogate worker for the gods is said to be absent from the Egyptian conception.[52] In contrast to these nearest creation accounts, in the biblical narrative God portrays man as the priestly, guardian, vassal-king who watches over the sanctuary of Eden entrusted to him. In fact, as Walter Brueggemann argues, "creation of man is in fact enthronement of man."[53]

Eden: The Cosmic Mountain of God in Ezekiel's Vision

As emphasized above, Eden was a sacred place because God revealed himself there: Eden was holy space. God's presence sanctified Eden. This external reign of God over Eden constituted the garden as a theocracy.[54] Eden, however, according to later biblical passages was also understood as a cosmic mountain. Although it may not be immediately evident from a superficial reading of Genesis, it is clear that it was understood in this manner, especially in Ezekiel 28:11–19. The literary typological similarities between Ezekiel 28 and Genesis 2 are striking indeed. Not only is there the overlap of the precious stones and cherubim but the allusion to Eden,[55] with its attendant rivers, is

50. The notion of a distinct difference is challenged, however, by Edward L. Greenstein, "God's Golem: The Creation of the Human in Genesis 2," in *Creation in Jewish and Christian Tradition* (ed. Henning Graf Reventlow and Yair Hoffman; Journal for the Study of the Old Testament Supplement 319; Sheffield: Sheffield Academic Press, 2002), 219–39. I do not think that Greenstein's argument is successful, although it is very illuminating with regards to the history of understanding Gen 2.

51. See, e.g., G. Castellino, "The Origins of Civilization according to Biblical and Cuneiform Texts," in *I Studied Inscriptions from before the Flood* (ed. Richard S. Hess and David Toshio Tsummra; Winona Lake, IN: Eisenbrauns, 1994), 75–95 at 91: "The spiritual and monotheistic conception of God (the anthropomorphism should not deceive us) could not permit the notion that God had need of material help from humanity."

52. John D. Currid, *Ancient Egypt and the Old Testament* (Grand Rapids: Baker, 1997), 72. See also Hans-Peter Hasenfratz, "Patterns of Creation in Ancient Egypt," in *Creation in Jewish and Christian Tradition* (ed. Henning Graf Reventlow and Yair Hoffman; Journal for the Study of the Old Testament Supplement 319; Sheffield: Sheffield Academic Press, 2002), 174–78.

53. Walter Brueggeman, "From Dust to Kingship," *Zeitschrift für die alttestamentliche Wissenschaft* 84 (1972): 1–18, esp. 12.

54. Kline, *Kingdom Prologue*, 49.

55. Both the Septuagint and the Ezekiel Targum (containing in all probability tannaitic traditions) saw the jewels as referring to a jeweled garment worn by the Edenic figure. See Lambdin, "From Fig Leaves to Fingernails," 79.

highly significant as well.[56] Although this passage's immediate point of reference is a dirge for the king of Tyre, whose pretensions have led to him setting himself up "as the first (and therefore foremost) of all men, an *Urmensch* become *Übermensch* (original man become superman)";[57] nevertheless, Ezekiel's allusion views Eden as the central (indeed, cosmic) mountain of God, the place where his name—and hence his presence—dwells upon the throne, exalted and lifted up.[58] Furthermore, the early church was sensitive to these themes and developed them extensively.[59]

The Trees

Two trees in the garden warrant special comment: the tree of the knowledge of good and bad and the tree of life. Although they contain great mystery, in their quintessential double signification are the seminal teachings of law and gospel (Turretin, *Institutes* 1.582 §8.5.6).[60] What is the tree of the knowledge of good and evil, and why did God insist that mankind not eat from it? Essentially, the tree

56. See Levenson, *Sinai and Zion*, 111–35, esp. 129–31.

57. Iain Duguid, *Ezekiel* (NIV Application Commentary; Grand Rapids: Zondervan, 1999), 346.

58. For a full review of the scholarly treatment on this passage, see Stordalen, *Echoes of Eden*, 332–63.

59. See, e.g., Anderson, "Cosmic Mountain," 202–3, who demonstrates this based on "Hymns on Paradise" and "Cave of Treasures" (mistakenly attributed to Ephraim the Syrian but in fact anonymous): "The holiness of Eden becomes a very important factor in the interpretation of the Bible. Eden, as cosmic mountain, becomes a hermeneutical tool . . . on the largest possible scale, that of the entire Bible, Eden is both the image of the ideal first time, and the eschatological goal of the end-time. . . . The identification of the temple in Jerusalem with Eden is as old as the Bible itself. The important new development for these writers is the equation of Eden with the church." A question that has exercised scholars recently is whether Gen 2 (esp. 2:4b–14) fits the cosmic mountain model found in Ezek 28 and in the Ugaritic literature (i.e., Northwest Semitic). Some scholars argue that Northwest Semitic material should not be considered because of the likelihood of Mesopotamian influence in this section of Genesis; see Richard J. Clifford, *The Cosmic Mountain in Canaan and the Old Testament* (Cambridge: Harvard University Press, 1972), 98–103. Clifford's conclusion is that "the joining of the theme of the Garden of Eden and of the holy mountain in Ezekiel 28 appears to be late and peculiar to the Ezekielian passage" (103). See, however, Jon D. Levenson, *Theology of the Program of Restoration of Ezekiel 40–48* (Harvard Semitic Monograph 10; Atlanta: Scholars Press, 1976), 25–36, who demolishes Clifford's arguments.

60. Bolton reminds us with great felicity that, in the postlapsarian period, with the advent of the covenant of grace, the function of law and gospel shifts so that "the law sends us to the gospel for our justification; the gospel sends us to the law to frame our way of life"; cf. S. Bolton, *The True Bounds of Christian Freedom* (London: Banner of Truth, 1964), 11.

of the knowledge of good and evil shows that God takes a tree out of the plant kingdom where he had designated those things for our good (Gen 1:29–30) and then assigns a particular meaning to that that tree in order to sharpen the test.[61]

The tree of the knowledge of good and evil would become the quintessential testing tree wherein mankind would be faced with the absolute lordship of his God. Good and evil would become the opposites between which a choice must be made and a right judgment would become evident (cf. 1 Kgs 3:9, 28; Mic 3:1–2).[62] Would Adam, the federal (representative) head of the human race, listen to the apocryphal word (mediated through his soul mate!) of the unholy intruder, that is, the snake, thus betraying his allegiance to another, or would he maintain fealty to his Lord and king and yield his will, his love, and his veneration to only his Creator?[63]

The Qumran writings, some of the clearest examples of how the biblical text was studied and interpreted in the ancient world, provide early corroboration for this interpretation.[64] Only certain significant

61. Dabney, *Lectures in Systematic Theology*, 154, states: "The tree thus became 'the tree of the knowledge of good and evil,' not because it was a particular species of tree, but because it had been selected as the tree whereby to test the implicit obedience of Adam." See Herbert Chanan Brichto, *The Names of God: Poetic Readings in Biblical Beginnings* (Oxford: Oxford University Press, 1998). If erudite modern Jewish exegetes are able to answer the question "why did God make this tree available in the first place?"—without equivocation—namely, "as a test of man; clearly as of his obedience" (74), then perhaps the Westminster Divines and their frequently maligned heirs of classic covenant theology were not so ignorant after all.

62. Significant to our discussion, especially the relationship between 1 Kgs 3:9 and Gen 2, is the point made by Meir Malul, *Knowledge, Control, and Sex: Studies in Biblical Thought, Culture, and Worldview* (Tel Aviv/Jaffa: Archaeological Center Publication, 2002), 196, that Solomon's prayer in 1 Kings is clearly in a "forensic context." Ranier Albertz draws attention to the expression לִשְׁמֹעַ הַטּוֹב וְהָרָע (to discern between good and evil) in 2 Sam 14:17, where the wise discerning choice contemplated by the king is likened in 14:20 and 19:27 (MT 19:28) to the angel of God (כְּמַלְאַךְ הָאֱלֹהִים); see "'Ihr werdet sein wie Gott . . .': Gen 3,1–7 auf dem Hintergrund des alttestamentlichen und des sumerisch-babylonischen Menschenbildes," *Welt des Orients* 24 (1993): 95. Not without significance, additionally, is the learned S. R. Driver comparing 2 Sam 14:17 with the phrase for a discerning heart (לֵב שֹׁמֵעַ) in 1 Kgs 3:9! Cf. *Notes on the Hebrew Text and the Topography of the Books of Samuel* (2nd ed. Oxford: Oxford University Press, 1913), 309.

63. Murray, *Collected Writings*, 2.49, states: "We know that Adam acted in a public capacity. Not only his destiny but that of the whole human race was bound up with his conduct for good or for evil (Rom 5:12–19; 1 Cor 15:22, 45, 46)."

64. See, e.g., John J. Collins, *The Apocalyptic Imagination: An Introduction to Jewish Apocalyptic Literature* (Grand Rapids: Eerdmans, 1998), 39: "Our clearest illustrations of the use of scripture in this period are found in the Qumran writings, which reflect the constant study of the sacred

biblical themes stemming from the biblical creation account are evident at Qumran: "insight of good and evil" is related to Genesis 2:17 and at Qumran, the notion being that "the ability given to man to distinguish between good and evil made man himself responsible for choosing the path of good rather than evil."[65]

The other tree, the tree of life, stood in the midst of the garden. There, in the garden of Eden, was God's presence, and consequently

---

writings that was practiced by the members of the community." See Bilha Nitzan, "The Idea of Creation and Its Implications in Qumran Literature," in *Creation in Jewish and Christian Tradition* (ed. Henning Graf Reventlow and Yair Hoffman; Journal for the Study of the Old Testament Supplement 319; Sheffield: Sheffield Academic Press, 2002), 240–64, esp. 241. A wisdom text, "Meditation on Creation" (4Q303), is instructive for Gen 2:15–17. The editio princeps was published by Timothy Lim, "4Q Meditation on Creation A," in *Qumran Cave 4.XV: Sapiential Tests, Part 1* (ed. T. Elgvin et al.; Discoveries in the Judaean Desert 20; Oxford: Clarendon, 1997), 151–53. See also H. Jacobson, "Notes on 4Q303," *Dead Sea Discoveries* 6.1 (1999): 78–80. The following translation from Nitzan integrates readings suggested by Jacobson:

]מבינים שמעו ו◦[	(1)	] those of understanding pay heed and [
]מים וישביתו מעל נ[	(2)	] . . . and cause them to cease treachery . . . [
]א{ס◦ר◦◦} נפלאות אל אש[ר	(3)	] I {will tell} the wonderful acts of God whi[ch
]לאור עולם ושמי טוה[ר	(4)	] for eternal light and cle[ar] heaven [
או]ר במקום תהווב[הו	(5)	ligh]t in place of emptiness and vo[id
]כולמעשיהם עד ק◦[	(6)	] all their deeds until . . . [
]ר בם מלך לכולם[	(7)	] among them, a king for all of them [
]ר ושכל טוב ורע ל[	(8)	] . . . and insight of good and evil, to [

65. Nitzan, "Idea of Creation," 254. Also interesting in this respect is the meaning given to the notion of choosing the path of good rather than evil by *2 Enoch*, a pseudepigraphal apocalypse whose only extant version is attested in Slavonic; see Christopher Rowland, *The Open Heaven: A Study of Apocalyptic in Judaism and Early Christianity* (New York: Crossroad, 1982). Albeit extrabiblical, *2 Enoch* suggests the answers to many issues that early Christians were interested in discussing and debating (e.g., the creation of angels, Adam's role in paradise and the fall). Rowland says that according to Slavonic Enoch "Adam from the very start has the ability to distinguish between good and evil (Slav. Enoch 30:15, cf. Gen 2:16f.) The reason for God giving man the ability to distinguish between good and evil is itself explained. God did not create man simply as a being who would do only that which was acceptable to him. The reason for this is that God wished to ascertain whether the man whom he had created did in fact have love and obedience toward himself. Thus the responsibility for the human plight is placed fairly and squarely on man, and God is in no way held responsible. The opportunity for obedience and disobedience was given to man by God, and there was no reason why man should not choose to follow the ways of God of his own volition" (*Open Heaven*, 150). In other words, he was up to the task to obey. This suggests that early readers of the Genesis account interpreted the testing dimension of the tree of knowledge of good and evil as not demonstrating a new acquisition of knowledge; rather, it was a matter of putting into practice what Adam knew. Although it could prove profitable, we are not venturing into a detailed discussion here of the issue of Adam's potential maturation with respect to attaining knowledge of good and evil. For a discussion on that subject, which is very different from Jordan's discussion on maturation, see Vos, *Biblical Theology*, 31–33.

fellowship, or *relationship*, with God existed—both actual fellowship and potential fellowship. It was potential because "man was created in a state of *relative* perfection, a state of righteousness and holiness."[66] The tree of life pointed beyond the immediate life that Adam and Eve presently had to a consummated period: eternal life. What did it signify? It signified life consummated through eschatological blessing.[67] It did not merely signify endless existence, for that could be a curse as well as blessing.[68] Indeed, had man passed the probation, he would have received the approbation of God and no longer been

66. Berkhof, *Systematic Theology*, 209 (emphasis added). Relative perfection, Berkhof explains, "does not mean that he had already reached the highest state of excellence of which he was susceptible. It is generally assumed that he was destined to reach a higher degree of perfection in the way of obedience. He was, something like a child, perfect in parts, but not yet in degree. His condition was a preliminary and temporary one, which would either lead on to greater perfection and glory or terminate in a fall." H. Witsius, *The Economy of the Covenants between God and Man* (trans. William Crookshank; 1803; repr. Phillipsburg, NJ: P&R, 1990), 75 §1.4.7 states: "Now Adam enjoyed in paradise all imaginable, natural, and animal happiness, as it is called. A greater, therefore, and a more exalted felicity still awaited him." Eschatology, therefore, clearly is present from the beginning and consequently precedes soteriology. Thus, Vos writes: "In so far as the covenant of works posited for mankind an absolute goal and unchangeable future, the eschatological may be even said to have preceded the soteric religion"; *The Pauline Eschatology* (Phillipsburg, NJ: Presbyterian & Reformed, 1979), 325n1. See also idem, *Biblical Theology*, 22: "Man had been created perfectly good in a moral sense. And yet there was a sense in which he could be raised to a still higher level of perfection."

67. This is implied in the prohibition as well as in the signification of the tree. Berkhof, *Systematic Theology*, 213, states: "Some deny that there is any Scripture evidence for such a promise. Now it is perfectly true that no such promise is explicitly recorded, but it is clearly implied in the alternative of death as a result of disobedience." Cf. Machen, *Christian View of Man*, 154: "But although the covenant [Gen 2:16–17] is directly put only in a negative form, the positive implications are perfectly clear. When God established death as the penalty of disobedience, that plainly meant that if man did not disobey he would have life. Underlying the establishment of the penalty there is clearly a promise." Turretin says with respect to the promise: "The covenant of works promises life only to the man perfectly just and deserving; but the covenant of grace promises not only life, but also salvation to the man altogether undeserving and unworthy (namely to the sinner)" (*Institutes* 1.585 §8.6.13). Dabney states that the "promise of life was clearly implied . . . for the soul not to live, is to die; not to die, is to live" (*Lectures in Systematic Theology*, 303). After marshalling numerous arguments concerning the implied promise, Witsius, *Economy of the Covenants*, 75 §1.4.7 states: "I therefore conclude, that to Adam, in the covenant of works, was promised the same eternal life, to be obtained by the righteousness which is of the law, of which believers are made partakers through Christ."

68. Turretin says: "Far better [than those who maintain it had in itself some kind of vivifying power] therefore is the opinion of others that the tree obtained this name [i.e., the tree of life] principally by reason of signification. It was a sacrament and symbol of the immortality which would have been bestowed upon Adam if he had persevered in his first state. . . . Therefore the life which this tree signified and sealed was not properly either the longevity or the immortality of the body alone; rather it was the eternal happiness to be obtained at length in heaven" (*Institutes* 1.581 §8.5.3–4).

under the probation of God. Mankind would have been established in righteousness and holiness. Faith and works function quite differently *before* the fall than *after* it.[69]

Interestingly, the tree of life in John's Apocalypse functionally serves an illuminating role for the interpretation of the tree in the primeval garden: only the eschatological community may partake.[70] This, together with other evidence, seems to support the notion that Adam and Eve had not eaten of the tree of life prior to the fall.[71] With this setting and Adam's role in it clearly described, we are now prepared to talk about the crucial text.

Genesis 2:15–17: A Seminal Text

Careful examination of Genesis 2:15–17 demonstrates that a superior (the Lord God) gave a specific prohibition to an inferior addressee (Adam), with an implied promise. Understanding the nature of the communication in the garden enables the reader to evaluate the claims

69. Turretin felicitously comments: "Nor can it be objected here that faith was required also in the first covenant and works are not excluded in the second. . . . They stand in a far different relation. For in the first covenant [i.e., the covenant of works], faith was required as a work and a part of the inherent righteousness to which life was promised. But in the second [i.e., the covenant of grace], it is demanded—not as a work on account of which life is given, but as a mere instrument apprehending the righteousness of Christ (on account of which alone salvation is granted to us). In the one, faith was a theological virtue from the strength of nature, terminating on God, the Creator; in the other, faith is an evangelical condition after the manner of supernatural grace, terminating on God, the Redeemer. *As to works*, they were required in the first as an antecedent condition by way of a cause for acquiring life; but in the second, they are only the subsequent condition as the fruit and effect of the life already acquired. *In the first, they ought to precede the act of justification; in the second, they follow it*" (*Institutes* 2.190–91 §12.4.7, emphasis added).

70. Elke Toenges, "'See, I Am Making All Things New': New Creation in the Book of Revelation," in *Creation in Jewish and Christian Tradition* (ed. Henning Graf Reventlow and Yair Hoffman; Journal for the Study of the Old Testament Supplement 319; Sheffield: Sheffield Academic Press, 2002), 138–52.

71. Vos, *Biblical Theology*, 28; W. H. Propp, "Eden Sketches," in *The Hebrew Bible and Its Interpreters* (ed. W. H. Propp, B. Halpern, and D. N. Freedman; Winona Lake, IN: Eisenbrauns, 1990), 189–203, esp. 192. Also see the classic work by Paul Humbert, *Études sur le récit du paradis et de la chute dans la genèse* (Mémoires de l'université de Neuchâtel 14; Neuchâtel: Secrétariat de l'Université, 1940), 131. After studying all 131 cases of פֶּן in the Hebrew Bible, he concludes that it never means implementing a measure to prevent the continuation of an action, contra, for example, Augustine, who saw nourishment supplied from the tree of life for Adam. Dabney, *Lectures in Systematic Theology*, 303, sees Adam in his rectitude enjoying the use of the tree of life, as does Stewart E. Lauer, "Was the Tree of Life Always Off-Limits? A Critique of Vos's Answer," *Kerux* 16 (2001): 42–50.

of those who support the traditional Reformed exposition of the covenant of works with respect to those who are challenging the traditional understanding of the doctrine.[72]

The first significant point in this text is the question of the nature of the command in 2:16–17,[73] for it is more than a "preemptive warning":[74]

וַיְצַו יְהוָה אֱלֹהִים עַל־הָאָדָם לֵאמֹר מִכֹּל עֵץ־הַגָּן אָכֹל תֹּאכֵל וּמֵעֵץ הַדַּעַת טוֹב וָרָע לֹא תֹאכַל מִמֶּנּוּ כִּי בְּיוֹם אֲכָלְךָ מִמֶּנּוּ מוֹת תָּמוּת	And the LORD God commanded the man, saying, "You may eat freely[75] from every tree of the garden; but as for the tree of knowledge of good and evil, you shall not eat from it; for on the day of your eating, you will deserve to die."[76]

The command, in terms of speech-act theory, is an exercitive, a wide class of speech acts made use of especially by judges.[77] Genesis

72. Jordan, "Merit versus Maturity," 158: "I believe that part of the failure of traditional Reformed theology lies right at this point [i.e., Gen 2–3]."

73. Discerning how speech is being *used* in any given utterance is essential to interpretation. J. L. Austin, whose influence on the philosophy of language has been enormous, states: "It makes a great difference whether we were advising, or merely suggesting, or actually ordering, whether we were strictly promising or only announcing a vague intention, and so forth"; "How to Do Things with Words," in *Pragmatics: Critical Concepts* (ed. Asa Kasher; London: Routledge, 1998), 2.7–28 at 10.

74. Kenneth A. Mathews, *Genesis 1–11:26* (New American Commentary 1A; Nashville: Broadman & Holman, 2001), 211. Also, D. R. G. Beattie, "*Peshat* and *derash* in the Garden of Eden," *Irish Biblical Studies* (1985): 62–75, esp. 71, following Westermann.

75. The use of the infinitive absolute in this text contributes force and emphasis to the liberty of action expressed in the modal imperfect: "you *may* eat freely"; see Paul Joüon, *A Grammar of Biblical Hebrew* (trans. and rev. Takamitsu Muraoka; Subsidia biblica 14; Rome: Pontifical Biblical Institute Press, 1991), 370 §113l and 423 §123h.

76. Following Albert Soggin, "Philological-Linguistic Notes on the Second Chapter of Genesis," in *Old Testament and Oriental Studies* (Biblica et orientalia 29; Rome: Pontifical Biblical Institute Press, 1980), 169–78, esp. 175.

77. J. L. Austin, *How to Do Things with Words* (ed. J. O. Urmson and Marina Sbisà; Cambridge: Harvard University Press, 1962), 155–56. See Vanhoozer, *First Theology*, 159–203, for a discussion that factors theology, specifically the covenant, into the equation of speech-act philosophy and theories, including in a limited manner relevance theory, the influential new paradigm of Sperber and Wilson that addresses the obvious deficiencies of the widely held "message model" of linguistic communication. For a good brief introduction to relevance theory, see Dan Sperber and Deidre Wilson, "Précis of Relevance: Communication and Cognition," *Behavioral and Brain Sciences* 10 (1987): 697–754; Deirdre Wilson and Dan Sperber, "An Outline of Relevance Theory," *Notes on Linguistics* 39 (1987): 5–24; Ernst-August Gutt, *Translation and Relevance: Cognition and Context* (Cambridge, MA: Blackwell, 1991). For more on the importance of relevance theory, see the discussion below on Galatians. For an excellent introductory treat-

2:16 is a command, but it is not the technical expression for the issuing of a law. That would have been expressed by a different arrangement: צִוָּה אֶת.[78] Nevertheless, the expression used here, צִוָּה עַל, typically denotes "a provisional instruction from a ruler (or father) concerning subordinates."[79]

Stating it this way does not remove the obligatory and legal character of the discourse.[80] Indeed, the attached motive clause is a common characteristic of later Israelite law.[81] Additionally, מוֹת תָּמוּת in 2:17 is not a motivation separated from the legal death sanction proclaimed;[82] it is "in clear relation to the divine command."[83] What is more, the constellation of terms used here in the Eden narrative reflects a command (צִוָּה) that often occurs with the collocation שָׁמַע בְּקוֹל mean-

---

ment of the message model and its limitations together with a fine introduction to pragmatics and speech-act theories, see Adrian Akmajian et al., *Lingusitics: An Introduction to Language and Communication* (Cambridge: MIT Press, 1995), 346–93. For a global review of recent work in biblical interpretation and theology using speech-act theory, see Richard S. Briggs, "The Uses of Speech-Act Theory in Biblical Interpretation," *Currents in Research: Biblical Studies* 9 (2001): 229–76. Along similar lines to Vanhoozer, see Michael S. Horton, *Covenant and Eschatology: The Divine Drama* (Louisville: Westminster John Knox, 2002).

78. Stordalen, *Echoes of Eden*, 226, states that צִוָּה אֶת would be used as the "technical term for YHWH's issuing laws . . . used with Moses some 85 times, see for instance Exod 35:1; 38:22; 39:1; 40:21." See Ludwig Koehler, Walter Baumgartner, Johann Jakob Stamm, et al., *The Hebrew and Aramaic Lexicon of the Old Testament* (trans. M. E. J. Richardson et al.; Leiden: Brill, 1996), 3.1010–11, for various collocations used when an order or command is addressed to humans.

79. Stordalen, *Echoes of Eden*, 226. Cf. Gen 12:20; 44:1; 2 Sam 14:8; 1 Kgs 2:43; Jer 39:11; Esth 2:10, 20. See also F. Zorell, *Lexicon hebraicum et aramaicum veteris testamenti* (Rome: Pontifical Biblical Institute Press, 1963), 685–86, who lists biblical references under צִוָּה עַל, with particular nuances.

80. Stordalen, *Echoes of Eden*, 226, states interestingly (and most likely correctly, at least in some instances) that "in the book of Esther, צִוָּה is used as a test of being faithful while not perceiving (fully) the reason behind an instruction." Cf. Vanhoozer, *First Theology*, 181, on the covenantal responsibility entailed for communicants in any given speech act, whether the participant be the addressee (i.e., the recipient) or the one issuing the utterance.

81. So B. Gemser, "The Importance of the Motive Clause in Old Testament Law," in *Congress Volume: Copenhagen 1953* (Vetus Testamentum Supplement 1; Leiden: Brill, 1953), 50–66. Gemser demonstrates that not all motive clauses are the same; however, the most frequent kind do begin with כִּי (because), as in the passage under consideration. Gemser is followed by Gordon J. Wenham, *Genesis 1–15* (Word Biblical Commentary 1; Waco: Word, 1987), 67.

82. Otto, "Die Paradieserzählung Genesis 2–3," 181.

83. Cf. Soggin, "Philological-Linguistic Notes," 174, who writes, after his exhaustive search of Mandelkern's concordance, that "in the majority of cases, there is a context of strong juridical tenor, while the crime tends to have certain typical theologico-religious configurations. . . . Here [Gen 2:17] the expression clearly establishes the sanction to which the culprit is liable."

ing "obey, be in subjection to, or comply with."[84] When the reason is stated for the banishment from the garden (3:17), therefore, we hear divine judgment: "Because you listened to the voice [לְקוֹל שָׁמַעְתָּ][85] of your wife, and you ate from the tree I had commanded you [צִוִּיתִיךָ]." In short, the underlying *social-legal* significance of the verb שָׁמַע in Biblical Hebrew is conspicuous here as it is elsewhere in the Hebrew Bible.[86]

Consequently, what we have in these verses, stated succinctly, is צִוָּה עַל introducing "a provisional instruction, headed with a positive allowance which is followed by one specific prohibition."[87] This explanation comports well with a traditional reading of the covenant of works. If Adam, as the federal head of the human race, had passed his temporary probation, he would have justly merited God's approval and moved on to a higher state, contrary to Daniel Fuller, who wants to redefine merit.[88] In other words, something potentially greater—

84. Luis Alonso Schökel et al., *Diccionario bíblico hebreo-español* (Madrid: Trotta, 1994), 776. The syntagmatic options for שָׁמַע קוֹל include use with or without a particle, meaning "hear, listen, obey" (775). The use of this phrase with בְּ (i.e., שָׁמַע בְּקוֹל) clearly means "obey," and some form of צִוָּה also occurs in the same context; see Gen 27:8; Deut 30:2; Josh 22:2; Jer 35:8. I am indebted to Otto, "Die Paradieserzählung Genesis 2–3," for this particular insight.

85. The use of שָׁמַע לְקוֹל instead of שָׁמַע בְּקוֹל in Gen 3:17 is no problem since the use of לְ instead of בְּ can mean "obey" as well; see Exod 3:18; Judg 2:20; Ps 81:11 (MT 81:12); Koehler et al., *Hebrew and Aramaic Lexicon of the Old Testament*, 4.1572.

86. See Malul, *Knowledge, Control, and Sex*, 194–97. One of the clearest contexts among many listed by Malul is Deut 21:18–21, where the rebellious son does not "hear the voice of" (שָׁמַע בְּקוֹל) his parents, and therefore, Malul says, the phrase has the "meaning of to obey and abide by the rules of law or of custom. . . . The son who does not 'hear the voice of his parents' is an unruly son who challenges their accepted authority, and in a way strikes at the foundations of society" (194). Clear uses of שָׁמַע (with or without קוֹל) in a legal-technical sense occur in Exod 15:26; Deut 4:1; 5:1; 1 Kgs 22:19; Isa 30:9. Malul also draws attention to Isa 48:8, where not hearing means to rebel.

87. Stordalen, *Echoes of Eden*, 226. This conclusion drawn from the philological evidence supports the important theological claim that the probation had to have temporal limits. Testing, by very definition, had to be temporally defined and limited. Furthermore, the principles of federal representation (i.e., that mankind, represented by Adam, underwent probation) kept the probation short. Dabney, *Lectures in Systematic Theology*, 305, says: "Such a covenant, with an indefinite probation, would have been no covenant at all." The reductio ad absurdum arguments he applies to the notion of an indefinite probation are forceful.

88. In his critique of classical covenant theology and dispensationalism, Daniel Fuller, *Law and Gospel: Contrast or Continuum? The Hermeneutics of Dispensationalism and Covenant Theology* (Grand Rapids: Eerdmans, 1980), 113, states: "Legalism, then, is no longer defined, as it has been in these two systems [dispensationalism and covenant theology], as doing things 'in order to . . .' gain a blessing from God." Fuller asserts that God never uses a works principle

namely, the state of permanent, confirmed righteousness—was waiting for him if he passed this probation.[89]

Even so, in light of the current debates, in which there has often been more fuzziness than clarity, something still further needs to be said in the light of the above exegesis. Whenever an utterance is analyzed, the question of social status is significant.[90] Sociolinguistics can be a helpful supplement to traditional exegesis in this regard.[91] Most people understand "status" as an element of power having something to do with "roles" and "role-sets."[92] Applicable to the analysis of our crucial text (Gen 2:15–17), E. J. Revell defines status as "the combination of factors which determine the treatment of one individual as the superior or subordinate of another, or as neither, and so as equal."[93] This definition is inclusive of power but not limited to that important indicator.[94] What is the significance of these insights

---

in Scripture; however, as will be shown below, God does use a works principle (cf. Rom 5:18), and it matters greatly that there was something meritorious about the Last Adam's work.

89. Berkhof, *Systematic Theology*, 209, and many others along similar lines.

90. See, e.g., Ahouva Shulman, "The Particle נָא in Biblical Hebrew Prose," *Hebrew Studies* 40 (1999): 57–82 at 59: "The relative status of speaker and addressee is a major consideration in the analyses of utterances, since the intention of the speaker and the understanding of the utterance by the addressee involve their recognition of the role relationship that exists between them, and of the rights and obligations that they have toward each other at any particular time." See further the influential article by Roger Brown and Albert Gilman, "The Pronouns of Power and Solidarity," in *Style in Language* (ed. Thomas A. Sebeok; Cambridge: MIT Press, 1960), 253–76.

91. See, e.g., Roger Fowler, "Power and Language," in *International Encyclopedia of Linguistics* (ed. William Bright; Oxford: Oxford University Press, 1992), 3.257–59. For a helpful survey of contributions that sociolinguistics and related disciplines can make to biblical exegesis, see M. O'Connor, "Discourse Linguistics and the Study of Biblical Hebrew," in *Congress Volume: Basel 2001* (Vetus Testamentum Supplement 92; Leiden: Brill, 2002), 17–42. For a linguistic analysis of deference, see Penelope Brown and Stephen C. Levinson, *Politeness: Some Universals in Language Use* (Studies in Interactional Sociolinguistics 4; Cambridge: Cambridge University Press, 1987). The most important studies for Hebrew Bible are E. J. Revell, *The Designation of the Individual: Expressive Usage in Biblical Narrative* (Contributions to Biblical Exegesis and Theology 14; Kampen: Kok Pharos, 1996); Cynthia L. Miller, *The Representation of Speech in Biblical Hebrew Narrative: A Linguistic Analysis* (Harvard Semitic Monograph 55; Atlanta: Scholars Press, 1998). Noteworthy is Vanhoozer's recognition of the social dimension of his view of covenantal discourse; see *First Theology*, 182.

92. See Brown and Levinson, *Politeness*, 74–84 at 78–79.

93. Revell, *Designation of the Individual*, 43.

94. Peter Mülhläusler and Rom Harré, *Pronouns and People: The Linguistic Construction of Social and Personal Identity* (Cambridge, MA: Blackwell, 1990), 19, recognize the profound implications of Roger Brown and Albert Gilman's famous 1964 paper; nevertheless, they propose an even more nuanced way of approaching the issues: "The idea of a *system* or rights, duties and obligations can be taken further [than Brown and Gilman take it]. It is usual to call such a system a 'moral order.' A convenient way of expressing the details of a moral

from sociolinguistic analysis for our interpretation of 2:15–17 and the covenant of works?

Recognizing the status of participants in this speech utterance enables a reader to understand the significance of social interactions encoded in a piece of language.[95] In 2:15–17, God is portrayed as the owner and king of the garden who delivers a provisional command to his vassal-king, that is, Adam. Because God spoke as the king, there were consequences to violating his spoken word. The language is command, legal, and judicial: the language is simultaneously relational because the king, that is, the Lord, delivers it.[96]

In short, the two—the language and the Lord who pronounces it—cannot be severed without destroying the story. The Lord God is superior, and it is entirely fitting that he should speak in commands. Adam, the inferior in relation, is not in a position to tell the superior what to do. God, the royal superior, is entitled and expected to give commands in such a situation.[97] Such a construal of the status structures with appropriate recognition of expected speech utterances in the given situation does not undermine the relational character of the passage; it actually establishes and upholds the communication intent

---

order is to assign people to roles. A role is a coherent set of conventions of speech and action by reference to which a person can be seen as behaving in an orderly fashion, in particular with respect to the activities of another. One needs to express the role idea in the cautious fashion to *avoid facile assumptions about the kind of causality that explains role performances*" (29, emphasis added).

95. With O'Connor, I am not saying that social structures can always be read off the page of the biblical text, but I am saying that "social structure is reflected there"; cf. O'Connor, "Discourse Linguistics," 24.

96. These particular exegetical conclusions, arrived at independently of Vanhoozer's work assuming that language itself is a covenantal affair, nevertheless correlate with his notion of the "presumption of covenantal relation"; cf. Vanhoozer, *First Theology*, 200–203. Germane to our present discussion and the alleged dichotomy between "relational" vis-à-vis "abstract/forensic" categorization are Vanhoozer's comments: "This goes beyond the presumption of relevance. The latter states that implied in every speech act is the claim that it is relevant. The covenantal presumption states that implied in every speech act is a certain covenantal relation—a tacit plea, or demand, to understand. Language itself cannot make this demand on us. Language, considered in the abstract, holds no rights. No, the presumption of covenantal relation stems from the fact that we are obliged to do justice to the words of a communicative agent in order to do that *person* justice" (201, emphasis original).

97. Therefore, it is not just a grasp of "bare" language or culture that is necessary for a keen understanding of a discourse, but whether a speech utterance occurs in the realm of the king (e.g., in a king's court). See, e.g., the conclusions of University of Munich Assyriologist Walther Sallaberger, *"Wenn Du mein Bruder bist . . . ": Interaktion and Textgestaltung in altababylonischen Alltagsbriefen* (Cuneiform Monographs 16; Groningen: Styx, 1999), esp. 210–11.

of the passage. Understanding these discourse-pragmatic functions of the language,[98] therefore, may help readers and writers avoid fruitless discussions regarding the relational and legal aspects of the language used here in Genesis.[99]

Theophany, Death, and the Protevangelium

It should now be clear how great the heights were from which Adam, our federal head, fell. This first sin, indeed, was "willful and wanton in a high degree."[100] Violation of, breach of, and disregard for the covenant brought theophany, particularly in the form of a storm,[101] judgment, common curse, and expulsion from God's Eden sanctuary, but mercy and grace—in a word, redemption—were the corollary of the curse.

Since the terrible fall of mankind, the mission of Christ became necessary (WCF 6.2). The gospel, therefore, was given in the protevangelium, in Genesis 3:14–20. Calvin himself clearly recognized it as such.[102] In fact, when Adam declares in 3:20 that Eve (חַוָּה) is "mother of all that lives" (אֵם כָּל־חָי), this means much more than mere life or sexual fecundity.[103] It was indeed, Adam's "confessional

98. This is not to exaggerate the help of linguistics for traditional biblical exegesis; it is merely to understand such a perspective from the field of language study as a helpful supplement. Cf. Silva's comments in *Interpreting Galatians*, 110–11.

99. See, e.g., John Barach, "Covenant and Election," in *The Federal Vision* (ed. Steve Wilkins and Duane Garner; Monroe, LA: Athanasius, 2004), 15–46 at 36: "Covenant membership is not just a bare legal relationship." Noteworthy also is Richard B. Gaffin, "Paul the Theologian," *Westminster Theological Journal* 62 (2000): 121–41, who helpfully describes and catalogues how some of the scholars in the new perspective eschew the use of judicial metaphors (esp. 137).

100. See Shedd, *Dogmatic Theology*, 2.154–58.

101. See, e.g., Jeffrey Niehaus, "In the Wind of the Storm: Another Look at Genesis 3.8," *Vetus Testamentum* 44 (1994): 263–67. Also note Christopher Grundke, "A Tempest in a Teapot: Genesis 3.8 Again," *Vetus Testamentum* 51 (2001): 548–51, who offers counterarguments to Niehaus's article based on text-critical, semantic, and literary grounds, but his rebuttal does not succeed. Strengthening the awareness of storm theophanies in the Bible through meteorological analysis is the important work by Aloysius Fitzgerald, *The Lord of the East Wind* (Catholic Biblical Quarterly Monograph 34; Washington, DC: Catholic Biblical Association of America, 2002). Also instructive is M. G. Kline, *Images of the Spirit* (Grand Rapids: Baker, 1980), 97–131.

102. Calvin states: "The Lord held to this orderly plan in administering the covenant of his mercy: as the day of full revelation approached with the passing of time, the more he increased each day the brightness of its manifestation. Accordingly, at the beginning when the first promise of salvation was given to Adam [Gen 3:15] it glowed like a feeble spark. Then, as it was added to, the light grew in fullness, breaking forth increasingly and shedding its radiance more widely. At last—when all the clouds were dispersed—Christ, the Sun of Righteousness, fully illumined the whole earth [cf. Mal., ch. 4]" (*Institutes* 2.10.20).

103. Wright, "Holiness, Sex, and Death," 316.

'Amen' to the Genesis 3:15 promise of restoration from death to life through the woman's seed."[104] That seed is Christ, as is demonstrated when we turn to Paul's letter to the Romans.

Covenant of Works in Paul

The Adam-Christ Typology and the Law's Continuing Requirement for Perfect Obedience

The apostle Paul makes only selective use of Genesis 1–3: he "does not cite extensively passages of the biblical story of the creation of the world in Genesis 1–3. . . . He only gives single aspects and central points."[105] Even so, Paul's use of creation themes in Romans 1–8 provides an important frame that integrates various creation themes highlighting a great reversal of the consequences brought about by Adam's autonomy and rebellion.[106] In the important connection between 5:1–11 and 5:12–21 Christ reverses the damage and death wrought by Adam and changes our legal status before God, thereby reintroducing us into fellowship and communion with God.[107]

104. Kline, *Kingdom Prologue*, 150.

105. Gottfried Nebe, "Creation in Paul's Theology," in *Creation in Jewish and Christian Tradition* (ed. Henning Graf Reventlow and Yair Hoffman; Journal for the Study of the Old Testament Supplement 319; Sheffield: Sheffield Academic Press, 2002), 115.

106. Steve Kraftchick, "Paul's Use of Creation Themes: A Test of Romans 1–8," *Ex auditu* 3 (1987): 72–87 at 84–85: "This frame, created by chaps. 1 and 8, involves the relationship between the creation and the Creator as it is manifested in the human response to its created status. It is especially the case that the idea of rebellion can be seen in chap. 1. As a result of the human refusal to recognize the creation as God's, and itself as part of the created order, the human removes itself from proper relationship to God and the created order. It is in this state of rebellion where the Christ encounters us (chap. 5), and it is from this state of rebellion from which we will ultimately be redeemed (chap. 8). . . . The argument of Rom 1–8 suggests that for Paul the history and state of the creation and the human are intertwined in such a way that redemption necessarily includes both. . . . Of the above mentioned themes the *controlling theme is that of reversal* . . . the verdict against the humanity is reversed, for it will gain the glory to come, and the state of creation is reversed, for it will regain freedom, a freedom which is the product of the coming glory" (emphasis added).

107. See Neil B. MacDonald, "The Philosophy of Language and the Renewal of Biblical Hermeneutics," in *Renewing Biblical Interpretation: Scripture and Hermeneutics Series* (ed. Craig Bartholomew, Colin Green, and Karl Möller; Grand Rapids: Zondervan, 2000), 123–40. Although typological interpretation fell on hard times after the Enlightenment, typology as a method of biblical interpretation has a time-honored pedigree practiced by many churchmen and scholars in the past. MacDonald demonstrates how recent studies in the philosophy of language have confirmed its validity as a method for understanding bibli-

Romans 5:12–21 and Its Context

Paul is the undisputed author of the letter to the Romans, and although he himself had not visited Rome yet, he is particularly well suited to explain its theme of grace (Rom 1:1, 16–17; 15:25–29).[108] Although little exegesis hinges on the date and place of origin, most authorities agree that it was written toward the end of the apostle's third missionary journey in or around Corinth around 57.[109]

Perhaps no passage in the Bible is clearer in its reference and understanding of Adam's function in the Edenic situation as is Romans 5:12–21.[110] Even so, before discussing the Adam-Christ typology described in this passage, we must situate it in the context of Paul's argument. The text of 5:1–11 is perhaps one of the most pristine statements on justification.[111] Therefore, we begin here.

A preliminary survey of 5:1–11 shows that 5:1–2 is the conclusion and natural consequence to what the apostle had just summed up, signaled by the postpositive inferential conjunction οὖν. This connects the text back to the conclusion reached in 4:23–25. The apostle is gathering up his thoughts with respect to justification, but not to the

---

cal literature. He uses the Adam-Christ typology as an example of how recent philosophy language—"in conjunction with the right kinds of ontological Christian truth-claims—may well provide one particular rational means of affirming one particular example of typological interpretation" (137).

108. First, Paul knew as well as anyone Roman's theme after his Damascus road encounter. When Paul is wrestling with these doctrines, therefore, we need to remember that he is engaged personally in its expression. Second, Paul was a well-educated, Greek-speaking Jew, a yeshiva boy and a gymnasium boy, so to speak. He was therefore notably qualified to write to a church consisting of both Jews and Gentiles (cf. Rom 2:17–29 and 11:13).

109. With respect to the purpose of the letter, James Dunn warns against overemphasizing one purpose to the neglect of one or more others. He points out three purposes that hang together: missional (15:18–24, 28); apologetic, since Paul seems concerned to set out for the believers a specific statement of the gospel (1:16–17); and pastoral, assuming that the names mentioned in Rom 16 are indeed a part of the original letter. Cf. James D. G. Dunn, *Romans 1–8* (Word Biblical Commentary 38A; Dallas: Word, 1988), lv–lviii.

110. See John Murray, *The Imputation of Adam's Sin* (Phillipsburg, NJ: Presbyterian & Reformed, 1959).

111. The text of Rom 5:1–11 has for some time been respected as the consummate, climactic conclusion to the discussion of doctrine that has preceded this section in 3:21–4:25. Although this rich passage does in fact give a summary statement on justification by faith, it also addresses at length or in part such themes as peace, hope, suffering, death, and reconciliation. This passage is related not only to Paul's discussion in the previous sections but also to and moreover pointing toward the arguments that follow in Romans.

neglect of passing over the vital expression about resurrection.[112] In 5:1, the apostle asserts that we are justified.[113] We have peace with God, the theme of the immediate context.[114] Of course, "peace" derives its evocation from the rich Old Testament background.[115]

Ralph Martin notes that the preposition πρός emphasizes the relational nature of the gift of grace and is reiterated in the noun

112. Vos, *Pauline Eschatology*, 151: "Resurrection thus comes out of justification, and justification comes, after a manner most carefully to be defined, out of the resurrection; not, be it noted out of the spiritual resurrection of the believer himself, but out of the resurrection of Christ. On the basis of merit this is so. Christ's resurrection was the *de facto* declaration of God in regard to his being just. His quickening bears in itself the testimony of his justification. God, through suspending the forces of death operating on Him, declared that the ultimate, the supreme consequence of sin had reached its termination." See also Richard B. Gaffin Jr., *Resurrection and Redemption: A Study in Paul's Soteriology* (2nd ed.; Phillipsburg, NJ: Presbyterian & Reformed, 1987), 122–24. Cf. B. McNeil, "Raised for Our Justification," *Irish Theological Quarterly* 42 (1975): 97–105. The cross and the resurrection are intimately connected, so much so that McNeil writes: "We may indeed say that the death of Jesus means life" (105).

113. It is not insignificant that the apostle uses the aorist passive participle because it states facticity.

114. Although the external evidence on this much debated verse is stronger for the subjunctive—and therefore hortatory—ἔχωμεν at this juncture, most opt for the indicative ἔχομεν on the grounds of internal evidence, namely, that Paul is describing and not exhorting at this point. Such a move is not necessary, however. One may follow the indicative since reasonable explanations can be made on other grounds. See Kurt Aland and Barbara Aland, *The Text of the New Testament* (trans. E. F. Rhodes; Grand Rapids: Eerdmans, 1987), 281: "With regard to ἔχομεν and ἔχωμεν the evidence of the Greek manuscripts (and therefore also of the versions based on them) remain ambiguous: ω can stand for ο, as well as ο for ω." There is significant internal evidence for the indicative in Rom 5:1, since Paul significantly uses the perfect two times in 5:2, ἐσχήκαμεν and ἑστήκαμεν, emphasizing that the access won in the past is still valid.

115. H. Beck and C. Brown, "Peace," in *The New International Dictionary of New Testament Theology* (ed. Colin Brown; Grand Rapids: Zondervan, 1976), 2.778–79. The peace of God in this context is not the subjective state of peaceful feelings but rather the resultant state of no longer being enemies of God, now having been justified. In the rabbinic literature, peace becomes the very essence of salvation. Moreover, the Jews were to pursue it with others. See, e.g., Hillel's statement in Mishnah, tractate *Avot* 1.12: "Be of the disciples of Aaron, loving peace and pursuing peace, loving human beings, and bringing them near to Torah" (trans. Estelle). For a general introduction to this important tractate, see Jacob Neusner, *Introduction to Rabbinic Literature* (New York: Doubleday, 1994), 572: "The document serves as the Mishnah's first and most important documentary apologetic, stating in abstract and general terms the ideals for the virtuous life that are set forth by the Mishnah's sages and animate its laws." Throughout this essay, *Avot* (Fathers) is cited from the most reliable manuscript: manuscript Kaufmann. See Moshe Bar-Asher, "The Study of Mishnaic Hebrew Grammar Based on Written Sources: Achievements, Problems, and Tasks," in *Studies in Mishnaic Hebrew* (Scripta Hierosolymitana 37; Jerusalem: Magnes, 1998), 9–42 at 30: "Research into Mishnaic Hebrew that is based on excellent manuscripts differs from that based on printed editions."

προσαγωγήν, which essentially means "access" or a privileged introduction to a VIP.[116] Paul now makes his first positive use of καυχώμεθα in Romans: "we boast/exult." In what are we to exult? In the "hope of the glory of God." Here is the first major introduction of the eschatological theme in this section of Paul's letter.

The eschatological theme of hope has provided a bridge to the causal chain in 5:2b–5. Having emphasized this glorious future, Paul the realist now affirms that the Christians are to rejoice in their tribulations. Paul proceeds through this "chain syllogism" and then comes back full circle to hope, which does not disappoint.[117] The next clause is introduced by ὅτι, which is causal in this case: "Because [ὅτι] the love of God has been poured out into our hearts."[118]

The basic structure of 5:6–8 is that 5:6 begins with a statement regarding Jesus's sacrificial death on the cross; 5:8 is Paul's interpretation of that death; and 5:7 is a strange and difficult statement sandwiched in between.[119] Paul begins his thesis with a qualifying statement: "While we were weak."[120] Then comes the punch line: "Christ died for the ungodly."[121] This is a repetition of the main themes

116. Ralph P. Martin, *Reconciliation: A Study in Paul's Theology* (Atlanta: John Knox, 1981), 140. This relational aspect of the gift of peace is significant and will be discussed further below. Two other passages are significant for this expression of "access": 1 Pet 3:18, where the purpose of Christ's death is said to bring us "access" (ποσαγάγῃ) to God; and Eph 2:18.

117. Joseph A. Fitzmyer, *Romans* (Anchor Bible 33; New York: Doubleday, 1993), 397, sees allusions to Ps 22:5 (MT 22:6) and 25:20.

118. This is clearly a subjective genitive, not an objective genitive. In other words, it is God's love to us (contra Augustine and many following), not ours to God, which is being discussed here. Rom 5:8 makes this clear as well.

119. The main purpose of Rom 5:7 is to illustrate the superlative nature of Christ's sacrificial death. On the hand, it is stated that someone might die for a righteous (δικαίου) man although this is hardly necessary. On the other hand, some admirable person might gather the courage to die on behalf of a good man (or possibly good cause, since ἀγαθοῦ may be neuter). Even so, the really astonishing thing is that no one would dare to die for a helpless man, let alone their enemy!

120. The genitive absolute clause ὄντων ἡμῶν ἀσθενῶν reiterates what Paul has been emphasizing throughout the book—that mankind is helpless when left to himself to effect any remedy for sin.

121. The term ἀσεβῶν (lit. without reverence) is to be linked with ἐχθροί (enemies) in 5:10, as C. E. B. Cranfield, *The Epistle to the Romans* (International Critical Commentary; Edinburgh: Clark, 1975), 1.264 notes: "In dying for us, Christ died for those who were helpless, ungodly, sinners, enemies. What Paul is here concerned to bring out is the fact that the divine love is love for the undeserving, love that is not the result of any worth in its objects but is self-caused and in its freedom itself confers worth upon them." The phrase ἀποθανεῖν ὑπέρ was

in the epistle so far.[122] Then, after marshalling one point after another, the apostle drives home his main point in 5:8:[123] "Christ died for us" (Χριστὸς ὑπὲρ ἡμῶν ἀπέθανεν).

Even so, 5:8 begins with the present tense verb συνίστησιν: but God *demonstrates* his love, which seems to be Paul's way of emphasizing the continuing emphasis of the past event of the cross. Then, another genitive absolute clause, "while we were sinners" (ἁμαρτλῶν ὄντων ἡμῶν), which echoes the previous genitive absolute in 5:6 ("while we were weak").

The next three verses form a confluence of much of what has gone before in our passage. Immediately, in 5:9, we are introduced to the verb δικαιωθέντες (having been justified) with the phrase ἐν τῷ αἵματι (by his blood). This hearkens back both to 5:1, where the same verb introduced this section, and also to 3:25, where reference was also made to the same essential components of the atonement.[124]

Romans 5:9 and 5:10 are obviously parallel. Both use a form of a minori ad maius argument or a fortiori argument.[125] Both verses establish their argument with an aorist passive participle and are connected to the next verb, σωθησόμεθα, with the phrase πολλῷ μᾶλλον (how much more), which expresses the confident assertion: "Having been reconciled we will be saved in his life."

---

already well established as martyr terminology and would have had a very moving affect upon the listeners; see Dunn, *Romans 1–8*, 255.

122. The concept was introduced previously in Rom 3:25 and 4:25.

123. Ernst Käsemann, *Commentary on Romans* (trans. and ed. Geoffrey W. Bromiley; Grand Rapids: Eerdmans, 1980), 137.

124. Analysis of chiastic arrangement is an often overworked method in biblical studies. Nevertheless, prominent motifs of Rom 5:1–2 are "taken up again chiastically in the final verse [5:11]," as recognized by Käsemann, *Romans*, 132. Charles Davison Myers, "The Place of Romans 5:1–11 with the Argument of the Epistle" (PhD diss., Princeton Theological Seminary, 1985), 183, sketches the chiastic relationship between 5:1–2 and 5:11.

125. The phrase קַל וָחוֹמֶר (lit. light and heavy) was common in rabbinic literature as a rule for interpretation of Scripture. For example, it is the first of Hillel's rules for the interpretation of Scripture. It sets up a parallelism, or actually an antiparallelism, between things being compared. See Miguel Pérez Fernández, *An Introductory Grammar of Rabbinic Hebrew* (trans. John Elwolde; Leiden: Brill, 1999), 201, 30. Although the argument here in Paul's transition may proceed from the major to the minor—in contrast to proceeding from the minor to the major—both directions of argument are subsumed in the rabbinic קַל וָחוֹמֶר. See Douglas Moo, *Romans 1–8* (Wycliffe Exegetical Commentary; Chicago: Moody, 1991), 317–18.

In 5:10–11, therefore, we are introduced to the new theme of reconciliation, and several points are brought together again. The noun καταλλαγήν (reconciliation) brings the reader back to εἰρήνην (peace) in 5:1.[126] The English word *reconciliation*, however, may obscure the truths of the Greek: that reconciliation is objective in character and God initiates it.[127] It is difficult for English to render the one-sidedness of the Greek terms here since, to our minds, reconciliation connotes a mutual resolution of terms on the part of both parties involved. Nevertheless, Paul says that while we were enemies, we have received (ἐλάβομεν) the reconciliation.

The description of our status prior to being justified and reconciled in 5:10 as ἐχθροί (enemies) amplifies and echoes humanity's plight while being at enmity with God and under his wrath. Reconciliation, therefore, here means to be restored to the favor of God with whom we were formerly in a state of enmity, by means of "the removal of objective legal obstacles."[128]

The apostle now begins his section in 5:12 with διὰ τοῦτο (therefore). What is the apostle doing at this point? Is it a transition to a new

126. See Cranfield, *Romans*, 1.256–57: "The reconciliation Paul is speaking of is not to be understood as simply identical with justification . . . nor yet as a consequence of justification, a result following afterwards. The thought is rather that—in the case of the divine justification of sinners—justification necessarily involves reconciliation. Whereas between a human judge and an accused person there may be no really deep personal relationship at all, the relation between God and the sinner is altogether personal, both because God is the God He is and also because it is against God Himself that the sinner has sinned. So God's justification of sinners of necessity involves their reconciliation, the removal of enmity, the establishment of peace." Cf. the role of peace and reconciliation in Eph 2:15–22 and Col 1:19–22.

127. See Leon Morris, *The Apostolic Preaching of the Cross* (Grand Rapids: Eerdmans, 1956), 186–223 at 198: "There is an aspect of reconciliation which is outside of man, an objective element; for we are said to have received the reconciliation, which therefore is in some sense independent of us. . . . There is a sense in which a reconciliation can be said to be proffered to us."

128. See Geerhardus Vos, "The Pauline Conception of Reconciliation," in *Redemptive History and Biblical Interpretation: The Shorter Writings of Geerhardus Vos* (ed. Richard B. Gaffin Jr.; Phillipsburg, NJ: Presbyterian & Reformed, 1980), 361–66 at 364: "The two passages discussed [2 Cor 5 5:18–19 and Rom 5:9–11] not merely prove the objective character of the reconciliation, they also determine *its essence*. It consisted in the removal of objective legal obstacles, which not withstanding God's love for sinners yet compelled Him to treat them on the basis of enmity" (emphasis added). Interestingly, Calvin comments on reconciliation in the following manner: "Now let us examine how true that statement is which is spoken in the definition, that the righteousness of faith is reconciliation with God, which consists solely in the forgiveness of sins" (*Institutes* 3.11.21).

thought[129] or concluding a previous argument such as 5:11, 5:1–11, 1:16–5:11, or something else? Here, διὰ τοῦτο is not a transitional particle, but rather introducing the new reasoning as the conclusion to what had gone before.[130]

In 5:1–11, the instrumentality of Christ had been emphasized time and time again (5:1, 2, 6, 8, 9, 10 [twice], 11 [twice]). Specifically, therefore, what the apostle is doing in 5:12–21 is explaining the instrumentality of Christ's work, which is stressing the righteousness of Christ "over against the instrumentality of Adam with respect to sin and death."[131]

Having the exegesis of 5:1–11 present before our minds, now the theme of the great reversal emerges. In short, mankind's alienated state before God, brought about by the high-handed sin of the First Adam is reversed by means of the righteous work of the Last Adam.[132]

Murray argues that 5:12–19 must be treated as a complete unit. In other words, when the apostle says in 5:12 that "death came to all men because all sinned," is *this sin* to be understood as referring to the *same sin* that Paul alludes to later in 5:15: "By the sin of the one the many died" (εἰ γὰρ τῷ τοῦ ἑνὸς παραπτώματι οἱ πολλοὶ ἀπέθανον), and similarly also in 5:16–18? The answer is yes.[133]

Paul leaves his unfinished comparison in 5:12 and then returns to it later in the same section. Reformed exegetes have rightly inter-

129. Cf. Myers, "Place of Romans 5:1–11," who by dint of his chiastic analysis sees 5:12 not as logically consecutive to 5:1–11; rather, he sees 5:12 as beginning a new phase in the apostle's argument and picking up his earlier arguments in 3:9b–20, whereas 5:1–11 restates important ideas in 3:21–28. I am not sure that Myer's arguments are successful. Cranfield and others seem to be on point.

130. See Ulrich Wilckens, *Der Brief an die Römer* (Evangelisch-Katholischer Kommentar 6; Einsiedeln: Benziger/Neukirchen-Vluyn: Neukirchener Verlag, 1978–82), 1.314. Dunn, *Romans 1–8*, 272, understands the function of διὰ τοῦτο "to indicate that vv. 12–21 serve as a conclusion to the compete argument from 1:18–5:11." Moo, *Romans 1–8*, 328, says: "Most commentators agree, then, that the phrase functions to introduce 5:12–21 as a conclusion or inference drawn from something in the preceding context." See also Cranfield, *Romans*, 1.271, followed by Fitzmyer, *Romans*, 411.

131. Brendan Byrne, *Romans* (Sacra Pagina 6; Collegeville, MN: Liturgical Press, 1996), 173.

132. Moo, *Romans 1–8*, 327, states that 5:12–21 shows why those who have been justified and reconciled can be so certain that they will be saved from wrath and share in "the glory of God": it is because Christ's act of obedience ensures eternal life for all those who are "in Christ."

133. Murray, *Imputation of Adam's Sin*, 19–21.

preted 5:12 as representing the federal headship of Adam.[134] Romans 5:13–14 has been understood as a parenthesis, at the end of which Adam is identified as a type of the coming Christ (lit. who is a type of the one coming). In 5:15–21, this typological relationship between Adam and Christ is explained further. The acts of Adam and Christ are "considered to have determinative significance for those who belong to each."[135]

The description of the work of Christ is put into striking grammatical parallelism with the destructive act of Adam. There is parallelism, but there is contrast. These contrasts may be summed up in two basic ways: *degree* and *consequence,* with each one introduced by οὐχ ὡς (not as).[136] Paul's first contrast, one of degree, is set forth in 5:15a: "not as the trespass, so also is the free gift," which he then explains in the subsequent verses, with the climax coming in 5:19. In other words, "the work of Christ, being a manifestation of grace, is far more powerful than that of Adam."[137]

The second contrast is one of consequence. Although death reigned by dint of the transgression of one, that is, Adam (ὁ θάνατος ἐβασίλευσεν διὰ τοῦ ἑνός) (5:17a), Paul uses another a minori ad maius argument to drive home his point of the great reversal in 5:17b: "Much more" will those who receive the abundance of grace and the gift of righteousness (τῆς δωρεᾶς τῆς δικαιοσύνης λαμβάνοντες). In other words, this contrast is one of consequence: it is a gift of righteousness, a free gift, being received or bestowed.

134. But see Joseph A. Fitzmyer, "The Consecutive Meaning of ἐφ' ᾧ in Romans 5:12," in *To Advance the Gospel: New Testament Studies* (Grand Rapids: Eerdmans, 1988), 349–68. Based on an exhaustive study of the phrase in contemporary Greek, Fitzmyer's study may have advanced our understanding of the phrase: it is to be taken in a consecutive sense, introducing a result clause: "Therefore, just as sin entered the world through one man, and through sin death, and so death spread to all human beings, with the result that all have sinned." Even if this interpretation is correct, it does not vitiate the point that Reformed interpreters drove home, as Fitzmyer himself makes clear: "Thus Paul in v. 12 would be ascribing death and human sinfulness to two causes, not unrelated: to Adam and to the conduct of all human beings. The fate of sinful humanity ultimately rests on what its head, Adam, has done to it, the primary causality for its sinful and mortal condition is ascribed to him, but a secondary resultant causality is attributed to the sinful conduct of all human beings. . . . Yet no matter how one understands 5:12d, the universal causality of Adam's sin is presupposed in 5:15a, 16a, 17a, 18a, and 19a" (362).

135. Moo, *Romans 1–8*, 347.

136. For details, see ibid.

137. Ibid.

Although Adam existed in a state of demerit and death reigned through the one and the result was condemnation to all persons, the necessary work for restored communion with God was achieved by another Adam—Christ himself. Through the Last Adam, there results justification to those whom he represents: "Now, therefore [so then], just as through the trespass of the one man, condemnation came to all mankind, so also through the righteous deed of the one man did justification and life come to all mankind." It is here at 5:18, with some foreshadowing in 5:17, that "the full, balanced statement of the comparison [between the figures of Adam and Christ] emerge[s]."[138]

In 5:18, the apostle affirms that the one man Jesus Christ has secured, through his obedience, the promises of God talked about in 5:1–11. In 5:19, the apostle elaborates further. After describing Adam's transgression as "disobedience" (παρακοή) resulting in "many made sinners," the apostle characterizes Christ's act as "obedience" (ὑπακοή) resulting in "many made righteous." In another epistle, the apostle makes it clear that we become righteous by virtue of our union with Christ (2 Cor 5:21).[139]

In the final two verses of Romans 5, the apostle deals with a clarification about the role of the law of Moses (5:20) and then concludes with a summary about the comparison between Adam and Christ (5:21). Christ, by reversing the consequences brought about by Adam's disobedience, has triumphed over sin by his obedience. We are justified and have "peace with God through our Lord Jesus Christ" (5:1).

The Riddle of Galatians 3:10 Revisited Again

A final question remains in our discussion of the covenant of works: Did the apostle Paul understand the law as requiring perfect obedience? Traditional readings of Galatians 3:10 understood it to teach man's inability to keep the law:[140]

138. Byrne, *Romans*, 174.

139. See Murray, *Collected Writings*, 2.212–15.

140. Other New Testament passages teaching the necessity of perfect obedience could have been examined as well. For a recent treatment of issues of special introduction (i.e., history, date, relationship to the book of Acts), see Silva, *Interpreting Galatians*, 101–39. Silva's more recent work, "Faith versus Works of Law in Galatians," in *Justification and Variegated Nomism* (ed. D. A. Carson, Peter T. O'Brien, and Mark A. Seifrid; Grand Rapids: Baker, 2001–4), 2.217–48,

Ὅσοι γὰρ ἐξ ἔργων νόμου εἰσίν, ὑπὸ κατάραν εἰσίν· γέγραπται γὰρ ὅτι ἐπικατάρατος πᾶς ὃς οὐκ ἐμμένει πᾶσιν τοῖς γεγραμμένοις ἐν τῷ βιβλίῳ τοῦ νόμου τοῦ ποιῆσαι αὐτά.	For as many as are of the works of the law, they are under a curse; for it stands written, "Cursed is everyone that does not abide by all the things written in the book of the law by doing them."

My interest at this point is only the narrow question of the demand for legal perfection.[141] Generally it is agreed that Paul never comes closer elsewhere to expressing the law's requirement for perfect obedience than he does in Galatians 3:10.[142] My thesis is that this verse teaches the necessity of perfect obedience to the law, *albeit only hypothetical,* since all mankind descending from Adam by ordinary generation is under its curse and unable to keep the law.[143]

---

appeared too late for consideration in this essay. For bibliographies of older commentators and recent scholarship taking this position and recent responses to it, see the footnotes in Thomas R. Schreiner, "Is Perfect Obedience to the Law Possible? A Re-examination of Galatians 3:10," *Journal of the Evangelical Theological Society* 27 (1984): 151–60; and Michael Cranford, "The Possibility of Perfect Obedience: Paul and an Implied Premise in Galatians 3:10 and 5:3," *Novum Testamentum* 36 (1994): 242–58.

141. For a clear introduction to the larger issues at stake in this passage and its context, see Silva, *Interpreting Galatians*, 217–35; or J. Gresham Machen, *Machen's Notes on Galatians, and Other Aids to the Interpretation of the Epistle to the Galatians from the Writings of J. Gresham Machen* (ed. John H. Skilton; Philadelphia: Presbyterian & Reformed, 1972), 176–81. A more satisfactory exegesis of this section, especially as it relates to the works principle contrasted with the promise-grace-faith principle in the Mosaic economy in particular, would require a much more complete treatment than is possible here (see note 10 above).

142. Cranford, "Possibility of Perfect Obedience," 244. Other New Testament passages could have been examined as well, however, my focus in this essay will be on Gal 3:10 alone and not even the following verses. Gal 3:10 may be treated as a single argument (as will become clear below), with 3:11–14 presenting a separate but related argument.

143. This assumes that certain aspects of the covenant of works are still in force, that man always owes God perfect obedience, in spite of no person, save Christ, being able keep the law perfectly. That it is only hypothetical in the postlapsarian period (with respect to being impossible for persons to keep the law perfectly, although not touching on the issue of the law's function in the Mosaic economy) does not indict the system. Vos says: "These [i.e., several Pauline passages that demonstrate the ineffectiveness of the law method of justification] are commonplaces of the Pauline theology. But it is plain that judgments of this class imply nothing derogatory to the law method of securing eternal life in the abstract. The disability under which the legal system labors is not inherent in the system itself, but arises wholly *from the fact that men attempt to put it in operation in a state of sin*"; see Geerhardus Vos, "'Legalism' in Paul's Doctrine of Justification," in *Redemptive History and Biblical Interpretation: The Shorter Writings of Geerhardus Vos* (ed. Richard B. Gaffin Jr.; Phillipsburg, NJ: Presbyterian & Reformed, 1980), 383–99 at 388 (emphasis added). See also Stephen Westerholm, in *Perspectives Old and New on Paul: The "Lutheran" Paul and His Critics* (Grand Rapids: Eerdmans, 2004), 380–81: "Judaism in Galatians is life lived under the Sinaitic law. As a present manifestation of that life, it is in error, Paul implies, in fostering the belief that people can

This is Paul's "anthropological pessimism" stated most baldly.[144] And according to Stephen Westerholm, at least one antecedent of this is Genesis 3.[145]

Even so, different opinions with respect to Paul's attitude toward the law began with E. P. Sanders's paradigm-breaking book.[146] Andrew Wakefield writes: "It is evident that Sanders has changed the landscape of Pauline scholarship."[147] And N. T. Wright speaks of "the Sanders revolution."[148] Sanders writes that the rabbis taught that human perfection was not achievable and that there was no hint of Paul's view of human inability with respect to fulfilling the law's requirements as expressed in Galatians 3:10 in rabbinic literature.[149] Indeed, since 1977 scholars have begun to reinterpret this verse—which has been the subject of much attention[150]—and other passages along nontraditional lines.[151]

---

be declared righteous on the basis of their faithfulness to the Sinaitic law; moreover, though Paul voices no criticism of *Jews* on this score, one may wonder what point he would see in continuing to observe the distinctively Jewish practices prescribed by the Sinaitic law now that its mission has been accomplished, its validity ended. But he does not fault the Sinaitic law per se. Its operative principle—that life is theirs who do what it commands—is found articulated in Scripture itself. And though that principle is different from that of faith, it is not *wrong* for that reason (or any other). After all, *that* God places demands for righteous behavior on his moral creatures is presupposed in everything Paul writes; the law, in spelling them out, performs a divine function" (emphasis original).

144. Therefore, the Westminster Shorter Catechism 19 says: "*All mankind* by their fall lost communion with God, are under his wrath and curse" (emphasis added).

145. Westerholm, *Perspectives Old and New on Paul*, 420.

146. E. P. Sanders, *Paul and Palestinian Judaism* (Philadelphia: Fortress, 1977). It goes without saying that Sanders's book is an impressive engagement of primary and secondary sources of Judaism. Through his serious and sustained engagement of the sources, Sanders raises a whole host of issues with which New Testament scholars and scholars in related fields must now grapple and perhaps even nuance or adjust previously held opinions.

147. Andrew Wakefield, *Where to Live: The Hermeneutical Significance of Paul's Citations from Scripture in Galatians 3:1–14* (Academia biblica 14; Atlanta: Society of Biblical Literature, 2003), 39. Wakefield is referring to the seismic changes that have come in the wake of Sanders's *Paul and Palestinian Judaism*.

148. Wright, *What Saint Paul Really Said*, 114.

149. Sanders, *Paul and Palestinian Judaism*, 137. E. P. Sanders, *Paul, the Law, and the Jewish People* (Minneapolis: Fortress, 1993), 17–29, has demurred from his earlier position (that the law cannot be fulfilled), treating Gal 3:10–13 as subordinate to 3:8 in the totality of the apostle's argument.

150. Silva, *Interpreting Galatians*, 217: "Few passages in the Pauline literature have received as much attention as Gal 3:10–14."

151. For a quick global survey of how Wright, Dunn, Fuller, and others understand Gal 3:10 as not teaching the necessity of perfect obedience, see A. Andrew Das, *Paul, the Law, and the Covenant* (Peabody, MA: Hendrickson, 2001), 145–70.

Several issues need to be addressed in examining the exegesis of Galatians 3:10: whether there is an (intentionally) omitted premise link in the argument of the apostle; whether the meaning of the quotation from Deuteronomy implies that the potential curse in Galatians 3:10 applies to corporate or individual obligation; and whether Sanders's thesis about rabbinic Judaism and the traditional interpretation of Galatians 3:10 is correct.

First, is a premise omitted from Paul's argument? In other words, is Paul's argument here an abbreviated syllogism? Or, more precisely, is Paul's argument in Galatians 3:10 an example of what is called a rhetorical enthymeme as opposed to a strict logical syllogism?[152] It was common practice in the ancient world to supply only one premise in an enthymeme, leaving out a minor premise. Paul's argument looks like this:[153] "Premise: Cursed is everyone who does not observe and obey all the things written in the book of the law. Conclusion: All who rely on the works of the law are under a curse."

According to Andrew Das, the implied reconstructed minor premise would possibly look like this: "All who rely on the works of the law do not observe and obey all the things written in the book of the law."[154] Calvin puts it succinctly: "Either Paul reasons badly or it is impossible for men to fulfil the law."[155] In other words, Paul is

152. This Aristotelian distinction between logical and rhetorical enthymemes is discussed at length by Kjell Arne Morland, *The Rhetoric of Curse in Galatians* (Emory Studies in Early Christianity 5; Atlanta: Scholars Press, 1995), 117–19, 201–12. Also see Das, *Paul*, 145–48.

153. The following reconstruction of Paul's argument is adopted from Das, *Paul*, 146.

154. Although Morland, *Rhetoric of Curse*, 203–4, says that it is difficult to identify exactly the omitted premise (and gives a nice summary of the way recent scholars have construed the missing premise), his reconstruction is very similar to Das's reconstruction of the missing specific premise at this point: "All who rely on the works of the law do not abide by all things written in the book of the law and do them." The argument has been made by many scholars, not least among them Machen, *Notes on Galatians*, 177–78: "It is evident that one link is here omitted from the argument . . . the argument depends, of course, altogether upon the assumption that no one has obeyed the law. If anyone had obeyed the law, then the curse which the law pronounces upon disobedience would not apply to him . . . the argument in verse 10 is complete in itself and that that argument depends on the expressed but obviously valid assumption that no one has really kept the law. The law pronounces a curse upon disobedience; no one has really obeyed; therefore all are under the curse."

155. John Calvin, *The Epistles of Paul the Apostle to the Galatians, Ephesians, Philippians and Colossians* (trans. T. H. L. Parker; Grand Rapids: Eerdmans, 1965), 53. Calvin fills in the

expressing himself in a common rhetorical practice of the day. It was not uncommon for Paul to use this technique in other places, even in the immediate context.[156] In short, all, according to Paul, are under a curse because they have not kept the law.[157] This verse, along with many others in Paul, teaches the necessity of perfect obedience, albeit hypothetical this side of the fall.[158]

Perhaps one might ask why the apostle would express it this way. Das may indeed be on the right path when he states that Paul "leaves it to the Galatians to figure out for themselves . . . all who rely on the works of the law (Israel and anyone else who would try) fail (and failed) to observe and obey all that is written in the book of the law."[159] Paul is not trying to obfuscate here.[160] He knew what he is doing, and he is actually being quite clear, though not as *easy as*

syllogism in the following manner: Whoever has come short in any part of the law is cursed. All are held chargeable of this guilt. Therefore all are cursed.

156. See Morland, *Rhetoric of Curse*, 198–201.

157. Contra Fuller, *Law and Gospel*, 99, who indicts Calvin for "inserting a proposition into the middle of verse 10 which does not render this passage 'most clear.'" This misses the point of the communication intention of the Galatians' passage.

158. Even though this obedience is hypothetical, it is not without significance, as will be discussed below. Hodge, *Systematic Theology*, 2.375, states felicitously: "It is as true now as in the days of Adam, it always has been and always must be true, that rational creatures who perfectly obey the law of God are blessed in the enjoyment of his favour; and that those who sin are subject to his wrath and curse. Our Lord assured the young man who came to Him for instruction that if he kept the commandments he should live. And Paul says (Rom. ii.6) that God will render to every man according to his deeds; tribulation and anguish upon every soul of man that doeth evil; but glory, honour, and peace to every man who worketh good. This arises from the relation of intelligent creatures to God. It is in fact nothing but a declaration of the eternal and immutable principles of justice. If a man rejects or neglects the gospel, these are the principles, as Paul teaches in the opening chapters of his Epistle to the Romans, according to which he will be judged. If he will not be under grace, if he will not accede to the method of salvation by grace, he is of necessity under the law." See also Machen, *Notes on Galatians*, 178: "So when the Scripture says that a man is justified by faith, that involves saying that he is *not* justified by anything that he does. There are two conceivable ways of salvation. One way is to keep the law perfectly, to *do* the things which the law requires. No mere man since the fall has accomplished that. The other way is to *receive* something, to receive something that is freely given by God's grace. That way is followed when a man has faith. But you cannot possibly mingle the two. You might conceivably be saved by works or you might be saved by faith; but you cannot be saved by both. It is 'either or' here not 'both and.' But which shall it be, works or faith? The Scripture gives the answer. The Scripture says it is faith. Therefore, it is *not* works" (emphasis original).

159. Das, *Paul*, 54–55.

160. Cf. Daniel P. Fuller, "Paul and 'the Works of the Law,'" *Westminster Theological Journal* 38 (1975–76): 28–42, esp. 32, who says that Paul could have stated more clearly what he

possible.[161] Paul is engaging his readers in a mental exercise that has their best interest at heart. Whatever difficulties are left in Paul's writing in Galatians 3:10 actually enhances the communication since the reader would have to consider what Paul is actually saying, a *mental and psychological process.*[162]

This position may now be supported from modern linguistic theories of communication. And this modern communication theory, *relevance theory*, and what it teaches us about communicative intentions, is very helpful at this point in Scripture.[163] Dan Sperber and Deidre Wilson distinguish between two types of implicatures, which in linguistic terms may be defined generally as "inductive inferences which the hearer draws."[164] For Sperber and Wilson, there is a distinction between implicated premises and implicated conclusions. The present example from Galatians 3:10 fits clearly under the former category.[165]

---

intended. This misses the point, however: what would the potential response of the Galatians be? Cf. Das, *Paul*, 155.

161. Much of the argumentation back and forth between scholars on this verse, especially considering the likelihood of an omitted premise, misses the whole point of Paul's argument because they are searching for the allegedly easiest reading.

162. See, e.g., Sperber and Wilson, "Précis of Relevance," 701: "Often in human interaction weak communication is found sufficient or even preferable to the stronger forms."

163. Relevance theory is rooted in Gricean pragmatics; however, it also addresses certain deficiencies in Grice's theories. Paul Grice (1913–90), a British-American linguistic philosopher who taught at Oxford, Harvard, Berkeley, and elsewhere, was extremely influential in his teaching and lectures, especially in America. Over against the simplistic "message model" of communication, Grice emphasized the inferential nature of communication. Sperber and Wilson and others focussed on the psychological processing side of communication and therefore addressed certain weaknesses in the "message model" as well. In other words, their theory is based on human cognition. Building on the work of pragmatics, psycholinguistics, and the philosophy of language, they explain the importance of understanding the *inferential process*, which includes ostension and inference. Basically, they contend that the more complex a speech utterance is, then the more necessary and complex the psychological processing (through inference) in order to understand the intentions of the speaker. In other words, a complex statement with fewer contextual implications renders a statement *less relevant* and therefore more mental energy is needed to process the communication. In Gal 3:10, the audience must expend mental energy to consider what the extra-communication implications are (i.e., the omitted minor premise). My argument is that this was intentional on Paul's part in *this* communication context.

164. Peter Gundry, *Doing Pragmatics* (London: Arnold, 1995), 44.

165. Sperber and Wilson, "Précis of Relevance," 705: "Implicated conclusions are deduced from the explicit content of an utterance and its context. What makes it possible to identify such conclusions as implicatures is that the speaker must have expected the hearer to derive them, or some of them, given that she intended her utterance to be manifestly relevant to the

The reader, a sinner, whether an individual or group, must understand and contemplate Paul's saying in both its explicitness and its implicitness. In short, their inability to keep the law is what is at stake. Far from making the "whole question of perfect obedience irrelevant,"[166] this fact contributes significantly to Paul's argument about the necessity of faith.

Second, with regard to whether the curse cited from Deuteronomy applies to the individual or corporate Israel, the issue is whether Israel as a whole has kept the law or whether the expectation of Galatians 3:10 is about individual obedience. Paul's quotation is not verbatim but reflects the broader context of Deuteronomy 27–30.[167] Paul's wording may have been for the purposes of improving the rhetorical parallelism in Galatians 3:10–13.[168]

Wright and others argue that Galatians 3:10 is not about individual obedience but rather Israel as a whole. When the context of the quotation from Deuteronomy is considered closely, however, recent scholarship shows that the sins and retribution for those sins listed in Deuteronomy are actually mixed between corporate and individual. Deuteronomy 27:26, for example, occurs in a series of sins and retributive curses, some of which are related to sins that are clearly individual, not corporate.[169] Moreover, Joel Kaminsky demonstrates that the common tendency of scholarship to view indi-

---

hearer. *Implicated premises* are added to the context by the hearer, who either retrieves them from memory or constructs them ad hoc. What makes it possible to identify such premises as implicatures is that the speaker must have expected the hearer to supply them, or some of them, in order to be able to deduce the implicated conclusions and thereby arrive at an interpretation consistent with the principle of relevance" (emphasis added). See also Dan Sperber and Deirdre Wilson, *Relevance: Communication and Cognition* (2nd ed.; Oxford: Blackwell, 1995), 172–202, for a discussion with many examples and full argumentation.

166. Cranford, "Possibility of Perfect Obedience," 252.

167. Morland, *Rhetoric of Curse*, 208.

168. Christopher Stanley, *Paul and the Language of Scripture: Citation Technique in the Pauline Epistles and Contemporary Literature* (Society for New Testament Studies Monograph 69; Cambridge: Cambridge University Press, 1992), 239. In addition to Stanley's thorough treatment of Gal 3:10, see Morland, *Rhetoric of Curse*, 206–10, for a description and analysis of Paul's quotation from Deuteronomy.

169. See Elizabeth Bellefontaine, "The Curses of Deuteronomy 27: Their Relationship to the Prohibitives," in *A Song of Power and the Power of Song: Essays on the Book of Deuteronomy* (ed. Duane L. Christensen; Sources for Biblical and Theological Study 3; Winona Lake, IN: Eisenbrauns, 1993), 256–68, who demonstrates that many of the sins listed in the context of Deuteronomy were committed secretly and therefore must have been individual.

vidualizing retribution as more superior and late in the history of Israel is probably not an accurate reflection of Deuteronomy and the Deuteronomistic history.[170] Therefore, interpreting Galatians 3:10 as concerned only with corporate Israel over against the individual is an oversimplification.

The third issue is Sanders's assessment of rabbinic Judaism with respect to expressions of the divine standard of justice and the possibility of rabbinic Judaism's views mirrored in Galatians 3:10 along the lines of the traditional interpretation. Sanders says, for example, "Human perfection was not considered realistically achievable by the rabbis, nor was it required."[171]

Sanders's views, however, have not gone unchallenged. One of the focal points of discussion is Mishnah tractate *Avot*, cited earlier. Arguing that Sanders cannot be so dismissive of Akiba's words, Charles Quarles demonstrates that the statement in question in *Avot* "is probably the most systematic soteriological explanation in the Mishnah."[172] Moreover, Quarles concludes that "older rabbis such as Gamaliel II clearly held the views of the divine standard of justice expressed by Paul in Gal 3.10."[173] At stake in this disagreement is the correct interpretation of *Avot* 3.15–16:[174]

170. Joel S. Kaminsky, *Corporate Responsibility in the Hebrew Bible* (Journal for the Study of the Old Testament Supplement 196; Sheffield: Sheffield Academic Press, 1995), 116–38. That there may have been a growing movement toward a more individualistic model of retribution in the history of Israel and especially in the prophets does not negate, according to Kaminsky, that some concepts of divine retribution against individuals were very ancient. The problem, as Kaminsky demonstrates, is more complicated than the standard communal view portrayed in much modern scholarship. According to Kaminsky, we see evidence in Deuteronomy of divine retribution individualized and the principle of corporate responsibility side by side, even at an early date in Israel's history.

171. Sanders, *Paul and Palestinian Judaism*, 136–47.

172. Charles L. Quarles, "The Soteriology of R. Akiba and E. P. Sanders's *Paul and Palestinian Judaism*," *New Testament Studies* 42 (1996): 185–95.

173. Ibid., 195.

174. There are many slight differences in manuscript Kaufmann and later critical editions of *Avot* 3.15–16. The most interesting one is Kaufmann's לִסְעוֹדָה as the final word in these two verses. Could this be translated "visitation," under either Aramaic (סעורא) or Modern Hebrew (סְעוֹרָא) influence? If so, the final phrase may not be talking about the eschatological banquet: "Everything is set for the final accounting visitation."

הַכֹּל צָפוּי וְהָרְשׁוּת נְתוּנָה וּבְטוֹב הָעוֹלָם נִדּוֹן וְהַכֹּל לְפִי רֹב הַמַּעֲשֶׂה הוּא הָיָה אוֹמֵר הַכֹּל נָתוּן בָּעֵרָבוֹן וּמְצוּדָה פְּרוּסָה עַל כָּל הַחַיִּים הֶחָנוּת פְּתוּחָה וְהַחֶנְוָנִי מַקִּיף וְהַפִּנְקָס פָּתוּחַ וְהַיָּד כּוֹתֶבֶת וְכָל הָרוֹצֶה לִלְווֹת יָבֹא וְיִלְוֶה וְהַגַּבָּאִים מַחֲזִירִים תָּדִיר בְּכָל יוֹם וְנִפְרָעִין מִן הָאָדָם מִדַּעְתּוֹ וְשֶׁלֹּא מִדַּעְתּוֹ וְיֵשׁ לָהֶם עַל מַה שֶּׁיִּסְמֹכוּ וְהַדִּין דִּין אֱמֶת וְהַכֹּל מְתֻקָּן לַסְּעוּדָה	Everything is foreseen, but freedom of choice is granted and the world is judged in righteousness.[175] Yet all is in accord with the abundance of deed[s]. He used to say, everything is given as a pledge and a net is spread over all the living.[176] The tradesman's shop is open and the shop-keeper gives credit; the ledger is open and the hand is writing. Whoever wants to borrow may come and borrow. And the collectors make their daily rounds and exact payment whether one knows it or not and they have support for what they do and the judgment is a judgment of truth. And everything is ready for the final banquet.[177]

Quarles argues that careful exegesis of *Avot* 3.15 in its immediate context (especially 3.16) and the wider context of this tractate and rabbinic Judaism demonstrate that Sanders "went too far in his assertion that no one in the early Rabbinical context held to the view of Paul."[178] Still others approaching the question from a more global appraisal of the evidence in rabbinic Judaism have also questioned Sanders's conclusions.[179]

In summary, Galatians 3:10 has been interpreted by Calvin and a whole entourage of Reformed luminaries as stating that the law of God

175. I translate טוֹב "righteousness," following Quarles's argumentation that "grace" or something similar is unsupported when read in the context of the entire *Avot* tractate.

176. Meaning that none can escape judgment.

177. Quarles, "Soteriology of R. Akiba," 191, states: "The illustration [of this verse following the previous one] offered an analogy by which one may understand judgment according to the majority of works. Like a shopkeeper, God maintains a careful record of a person's moral debits and credits. Sins, for which there are no corresponding good works, create a debit on a person's eternal count. Payment will be exacted in the day of judgment."

178. Quarles, "Soteriology of R. Akiba," 195. Quarles expresses his bewilderment: "It is puzzling that Sanders completely ignored Akiba's own explanation of this theological maxim in *m. Aboth* [3.16]" (191). Those demanding a more accurate portrayal of the complexities of rabbinic Judaism are lining up behind Quarles as well. For the possibility of optional systems of soteriology (election/membership vis-à-vis reward/retribution) in rabbinic Judaism, see Friedrich Avemarie, "Erwählung und Wergeltung: Zur Optionalen Struktur rabbinischer Soteriologie," *New Testament Studies* 45 (1999): 108–26.

179. Guy Prentiss Waters, *Justification and the New Perspective on Paul: A Review and Response* (Phillipsburg, NJ: P&R, 2004), 43–46, 152.

is a curse only to its transgressors since all human beings are subject to its curse and unable to perform its requirement. The solution to this plight,[180] as stated in Galatians and elsewhere by the apostle, is faith in Jesus Christ, who has "ransomed us from the curse of the law by becoming a curse for us" (Gal 3:13).[181]

Conclusion

By way of synthesis, I ask what the preceding treatment can do for us with regard to the question asked at the beginning of this essay: Was there a prelapsarian covenant of works?[182] As a reply to that question, the evidence offered above suggests an unequivocal yes.[183]

The choice of the word *works* by the Westminster Divines and the older classical Reformed theologians is indeed felicitous for at least two reasons. First, by designating the prelapsarian covenant as one of "works," the divines helped to highlight that which is particularly important in the covenant: namely, that certain probationary conditions were placed upon Adam if he was to remain in good favor and covenantal communion with his Lord.

Second, such language helps maintain the vital distinctions and the necessary differences between the prefall covenant and the subsequent postfall covenant of grace. Many recent writers make it their custom

180. Based upon the evidence presented by Quarles, it seems to be more than an anachronistically designed etiology to explain the relevance of the Christ event in the apostle's life.

181. Even though "us" in this passage probably refers to the Jewish Christians, this does not mitigate this text's application to Jews and Gentiles alike; cf. Machen, *Notes on Galatians*, 179. This is true even if Paul had the Judaizers primarily in mind regarding the reference ὅσοι ἐξ ἔργων νόμου, as Silva argues in *Interpreting Galatians*, 232; nevertheless, this does not do away with its wider application. Westerholm, *Perspectives Old and New on Paul*, 442–43, summarizes Paul's view succinctly: "It was, however, when his Galatian converts were told to get circumcised and submit to the Mosaic law that Paul first clarified the relationship between Israel's law and the church's faith. All human beings, Paul insisted, are the subjects of sin (Gal 3:22). The law God gave to Israel, though offering life to its doers (3:12), can only curse its transgressors (3:10) and consign sinners to their doom (3:21–23). But Christ bore the curse of the law (3:13). Now God will declare righteous those who put their faith in him (2:16; 3:24)."

182. Some of the statements in this section of the essay occurred previously in *Evangelium* 3.1 (Jan./Feb. 2005), a bimonthly publication of Westminster Seminary California.

183. WCF 7.2: "The first covenant made with man was a covenant of works, wherein life was promised to Adam, and in him to his posterity, upon condition of perfect and personal obedience."

to flatten out the necessary distinctions between the prelapsarian and postlapsarian covenants. Such leveling tendencies make opaque the biblical portrayal of original mankind created in upright sinless integrity, now alienated from God by means of his own fall into sin and disobedience and, consequently, left in a condition of desperate and helpless need for reintroduction into communion with God.

If Adam as the federal representative head of the human race had passed his temporary probationary testing, he would then have justly merited God's approbation and moved on to Sabbath consummation and a new state: had he fulfilled his probation with obedience, Adam would have been confirmed in righteousness. As it was, he failed the test. Since God's claim for obedience on his creatures has not ceased since the fall and since man's inability to now keep the law is universally evident (as exegesis of Gal 3:10 makes clear), the curse of the law rests on mankind.

Consequently, now existing in a state of demerit and deserving of God's just wrath, Adam's sin and failure (imputed to all his posterity) rendered the promises of God inaccessible except for the provision of the meritorious achievement of another Adam—Christ himself, the Last Adam. Paul clearly states in Romans 5:15–21 that the work of the Last Adam (i.e., Christ) undoes the damage, death, and destruction wrought by the First Adam. The cornucopia of justification for those in Christ, described in 5:1–11, is brought about by the instrumentality of Christ's work.

Christ is the federal head of the covenant of grace just as Adam was the federal head of the covenant of works. Christ has rendered a passive and active obedience that is full of perfect merit. The sins of the people of God have been imputed to their redeemer. The satisfaction of Christ meets the demands of justice. Christ has paid the penalty for the sins of the people. Moreover, he has earned the reward. God has graciously supplied the mediator. All demands and obligations have been met and fulfilled completely in the Savior, and now the righteousness of Christ is imputed to his people. Those who are in Christ have been brought into fellowship and communion with God.

The righteous obedience of Christ alone, the substitutionary atonement of Christ alone, is the ground of our justification and our kingdom inheritance. Such alien righteousness (i.e., belonging to another), moreover, necessitates and maintains the extraspective (looking outward) character of biblical faith, "the alone instrument of justification" (WCF 11.2).

The history of redemption is "an astonishing drama indeed."[184] Valiant for truth, it is crucial to the advance of theology that innovations should be suggested (with due propriety) where previous conclusions about doctrine need recasting. This essay demonstrates, however, that the innovators and innovations suggesting revision to the covenant of works have been weighed in the scales of classic Reformed orthodoxy, modern biblical scholarship, and modern linguistics and have been found wanting.

In conclusion, the biblical evidence supports the covenant of works. Consequently, the covenant of works, as described by the Westminster Divines, will not fall on its own sword in order to die an honorable death as some critics and distinguished professors have proposed and as their epigones would also currently wish. From its ancient inception and down to the present day, the covenant of works has displayed the penalty-paying substitution and probation keeping of the Last Adam in the wake of the failures of the First Adam. With the queen of essayists we say, "Let us, in Heaven's name, drag out the Divine Drama from under the dreadful accumulation of slipshod thinking and trashy sentiment heaped upon it, and set it on an open stage to startle the world into some sort of vigorous reaction."[185]

184. Dorothy L. Sayers, *Creed or Chaos?* (New York: Harcourt, Brace, 1949), 7.
185. Ibid., 24.

5

The New Perspective, Mediation, and Justification

S. M. Baugh

Introduction

After all these centuries the Reformation's doctrine of justification is still disputed in some circles, particularly among a relatively small but vocal group associated with the so-called new perspective on Paul.[1] The various positions of this group have been subject to considerable critique and rebuttal in scholarly literature, for its underlying analysis of both ancient Judaism and Paul's theology.[2]

1. Normally traced to Krister Stendahl, "The Apostle Paul and the Introspective Conscious of the West," *Harvard Theological Review* 56 (1963): 199–215; reprinted in idem, *Paul among Jews and Gentiles and Other Essays* (Philadelphia: Fortress, 1976); and E. P. Sanders, *Paul and Palestinian Judaism: A Comparison of Patterns of Religion* (Philadelphia: Fortress, 1977). The label was coined in 1983 by James D. G. Dunn; see his "The New Perspective on Paul," in *Jesus, Paul, and the Law: Studies in Mark and Galatians* (Louisville: Westminster/John Knox, 1990), 183–214. A view over thirty years old is hardly "new" anymore. Cf. the overview by Michael B. Thompson, *The New Perspective on Paul* (Cambridge: Grove, 2002).

2. General critiques include Peter Stuhlmacher, *Revisiting Paul's Doctrine of Justification: A Challenge to the New Perspective; with an Essay by Donald A. Hagner* (Downers Grove,

Because of the wide availability of thorough reviews and critiques of the new perspective, I will not rehearse it in detail here.[3] I will briefly describe the new perspective's core ideas and methods, comment on a few of these, and then spend the bulk of my time on an exposition of key notions in Paul recognized in the Reformed view on justification, which often get overlooked in the debate today. It is my opinion that confessional Reformed and Lutherans are fundamentally agreed on the essence of justification as consisting of the forgiveness of sins and the imputation of Christ's righteousness as a gift by grace through faith alone, but that the Reformed wing of Protestantism has from very early on expressed this in distinctive ways through biblical notions of the covenant mediation of Christ.[4] I will illustrate this viewpoint with a survey exegesis of Romans 5.

IL: InterVarsity, 2001); Seyoon Kim, *Paul and the New Perspective: Second Thoughts on the Origin of Paul's Gospel* (Grand Rapids: Eerdmans, 2002); Stephen Westerholm, *Israel's Law and the Church's Faith: Paul and His Recent Interpreters* (Grand Rapids: Eerdmans, 1988); idem, *Perspectives Old and New on Paul: The "Lutheran" Paul and His Critics* (Grand Rapids: Eerdmans, 2004); D. A. Carson, Peter T. O'Brien, and Mark A. Seifrid, eds., *Justification and Variegated Nomism* (2 vols.; Grand Rapids: Baker, 2001–4); A. Andrew Das, *Paul, the Law, and the Covenant* (Peabody, MA: Hendrickson, 2001); Mark Seifrid, *Justification by Faith: The Origin and Development of a Central Pauline Theme* (Novum Testamentum Supplement 68; Leiden: Brill, 1992); and Richard Gaffin, "Paul the Theologian," *Westminster Theological Journal* 62 (2000). 121–41. Francis Watson's recent work, "Not the New Perspective" (paper presented at the British New Testament Conference, Sept. 2001), is particularly interesting since he had previously defended a new perspective position in his *Paul, Judaism, and the Gentiles: A Sociological Approach* (Cambridge: Cambridge University Press, 1986). For critique of Sanders's analysis of ancient Judaism, see, e.g., Mark A. Elliott's massive work: *The Survivors of Israel: A Reconsideration of the Theology of Pre-Christian Judaism* (Grand Rapids: Eerdmans, 2000). A review of this book by a scholar of ancient Judaism, Johannes Tromp, expresses doubt that E. P. Sanders's views are all that influential except possibly among New Testament scholars, but "I have never noticed much of it among students of Judaism"; see *Journal of Theological Studies* 52 (2001): 772. Cf. the rather strident review of Sanders by another expert in ancient Judaism, Jacob Neusner in *History of Religions* 18 (1978): 177–91.

3. Many shorter critiques by other notable scholars are handily available through a web page devoted to discussion of the issues both pro and con: "The Paul Page," http://www.thepaulpage.com (accessed Sept. 2004).

4. Significant work on this has been done in the past by the Reformed (e.g., Cocceius, Witsius, Owen), but it is, alas, lost from view in modern debates. Cf. covenant mediation expressed as "surety" in WLC 71: "How is justification an act of God's free grace? Although Christ, by his obedience and death, did make a proper, real, and full satisfaction to God's justice in the behalf of them that are justified; yet inasmuch as God accepts the satisfaction from a *surety*, which he might have demanded of them, and did provide this *surety*, his own only Son, imputing his righteousness to them, and requiring nothing of them for their justification but faith, which also is his gift, their justification is to them of free grace" (emphasis added).

The Fundamentals of the New Perspective

While new perspective scholars differ in many particulars, at least three points derived from E. P. Sanders form nonnegotiable ideas for their position.[5] First, Protestant analysis of Paul's Jewish-Christian opponents (or even of Judaism itself) consistently presents them as what could be called "rank" legalists. That is, one's acceptance by God into eternal life is based solely on one's own meritorious obedience to the law: *solis operibus*. Sanders writes: "The frequent Christian charge against Judaism, it must be recalled, is not that some individual Jews misunderstood, misapplied and abused their religion, but that *Judaism necessarily tends* toward petty legalism, self-serving and self-deceiving casuistry, and a mixture of arrogance and lack of confidence in God."[6] Instead, Sanders identifies ancient Judaism, including Paul's Jewish-Christian opponents, as holding to what he describes as a nonlegalistic "covenant nomism," identified by the language of "getting in" by grace but "staying in" by works of obedience to God's law.[7] N. T. Wright summarizes: "Judaism, he [Sanders] insisted, was and is a perfectly valid and proper form of religion. Paul's only real critique of Judaism, according to Sanders, was that it was 'not Christianity.'"[8]

Second, what began as a new perspective on Second Temple Judaism against a supposed Protestant misinterpretation turns without further ado into a complete recasting of Paul's theology.[9] Notably,

5. See N. T. Wright's remarks on Sanders's importance in *What Saint Paul Really Said: Was Paul of Tarsus the Real Founder of Christianity?* (Grand Rapids: Eerdmans, 1996), 20: "He [Sanders] nevertheless dominates the landscape, and, until a major refutation of his central thesis is produced, honesty compels one to do business with him. I do not myself believe such a refutation can or will be offered; serious modifications are required, but I regard his basic point as established."

6. Sanders, *Paul and Palestinian Judaism*, 427 (emphasis original).

7. Sanders writes: "The pattern is this: God has chosen Israel and Israel has accepted the election. In his role as King, God gave Israel commandments which they are to obey as best they can. Obedience is rewarded and disobedience punished. In case of failure to obey, however, man has recourse to divinely ordained means of atonement, in all of which repentance is required. As long as he maintains his desire to stay in the covenant, he has a share in God's covenantal promises, including life in the world to come. The intention and effort to be obedient constitute the *condition for remaining in the covenant*, but they do not *earn* it" (ibid., 180, emphasis original).

8. Wright, *What Saint Paul Really Said*, 19.

9. Sanders and others give very little attention to classic Protestant authors when rejecting Protestantism's views on ancient Judaism. For example, Martin Luther is cited only once in

Sanders himself did little exegesis of Paul, and his own sketch of Paul's theology has gained few followers. Nevertheless, we are confidently told that Sanders's conclusions on ancient Judaism lead necessarily to a complete reworking of Paul and—relevant for our purposes here—a reworking of Paul's doctrine of justification in all of its essential elements. Wright, for example, indicts the church—principally because it has misunderstood ancient Judaism and has "ransacked" Paul for mere proof-texts; therefore the Christian church has misunderstood Paul on justification "for nearly two thousand years" and "has systematically done violence to that text [Romans] for hundreds of years."[10]

Third, in consequence of the other two points, any reading of Paul that looks suspiciously like the Protestant view is ipso facto mistaken and excluded from consideration in the new perspective.[11] Correlative with this point is the curious fact that the new perspective Paul looks remarkably like his "covenant nomist" opponents described in Sanders's portrait of ancient Judaism. If the Judaism of Sanders teaches that one "gets into" covenant fellowship and salvation through a gracious, corporate divine election, one retains title to these blessings only through a sort of nonmeritorious obedience through works of law keeping.

Paul and Palestinian Judaism (492n57), when Sanders argues that Paul does not have a forensic view of imputed righteousness as found in Luther's commentary on Galatians.

10. Wright, *What Saint Paul Really Said*, 115–17. Wright cites no sources as examples of the offenders he has in mind.

11. This is not my opinion alone, but is illustrated very pointedly by Watson: "In interpreting the relevant Pauline texts, the new perspective repeatedly performs a characteristic exegetical manoeuvre in three steps. Here's how it works. *Step one*: we observe that a Pauline text appears to be contrasting the logic of the gospel with the logic of a Jewish or Jewish Christian understanding of the law. Paul speaks of grace over against law, faith over against works; he seems to set believing the gospel of divine saving action over against practising the law. *Step two*: we know, however, that the point of these Pauline antitheses *cannot* be to contrast the gospel's emphasis on divine agency with a Jewish emphasis on human agency. If we think we see this antithesis between divine and human agency in Paul, we're still held captive by the ideology of the Reformation, resulting as it must do in a hostile caricature of Judaism. But how do we know that an antithesis between divine and human agency *cannot* be present in Paul's texts? Because Sanders has taught us that Judaism was and is a religion of grace; and, on this matter, Sanders speaks not only the truth but also the whole truth and nothing but the truth. *Step three*: we must therefore read the Pauline antithesis differently, as an 'ecclesiological' statement about the nature of the people of God. For Paul, 'faith' represents an *inclusive* understanding of the people of God as including non-law-observant Gentiles; 'works' represents an *exclusive* understanding of the people of God according to which full conversion to the practice of Judaism is a necessary precondition of salvation. What Paul is propounding is, in effect, an inclusive, universal, liberal form of Jewish covenant theology"; "Not the New Perspective," 14 (emphasis original).

"In Paul, as in Jewish literature," Sanders writes, "good deeds are the *condition* of remaining 'in,' but they do not *earn* salvation."[12]

Methodological Difficulties in the New Perspective

Four consistent methodological problems in the new perspective literature should at least give one pause when accepting their conclusions. Many people regard exegesis as a neutral or even a scientific procedure that, if done correctly, will yield consistently true results, but exegesis is performed by human beings who begin with their own prejudices, areas of expertise as well as of ignorance, and prior theological commitments that inevitably shape their exegetical conclusions.[13] One can always learn something valuable from careful exegesis no matter how much the interpreter's viewpoint and conclusions diverge from one's own, but it is far less satisfying and instructive to read exegetes who time and again evidence errors of exegetical method and dismiss carefully researched positions out of hand. It leads to the suspicion that the conclusions are not as self-evident and well established as claimed.

The first methodological problem is a pervasive tendency in new perspective scholars to use a word, word group, or a phrase in Paul as levers to shift our understanding of Paul's doctrines from what has been painstakingly established to their own eccentric interpretations. The exact way this is done may vary, but the leverage takes place in significant ways nevertheless. Here are some examples.

Occurring several places in Paul (e.g., Rom 3:22; Gal 2:16; 3:22; Phil 3:9), the phrase πίστις Χριστοῦ is the subject of ongoing dispute and is variously interpreted: (1) the believer's trust in Christ (brought out by rendering "faith *in* Christ" as found in most English versions); (2) Christ's own fidelity or faithfulness to God; (3) Christ's own faith in God; and (4) faith that has a more generic relation to Christ,

12. Sanders, *Paul and Palestinian Judaism*, 517.

13. This conclusion is supported by Wright in a most candid statement: "Many New Testament scholars use detailed exegesis as a way of escaping from heavy-handed and stultifying conservatism; any attempt to reconstruct the sort of system from which they themselves are glad to be free" (*What Saint Paul Really Said*, 21). Exegesis in this light is not the neutral *Wissenschaft* as often imagined.

communicated by "Christic faith."[14] I am not interested in entering this debate here, but merely showing how this phrase is used to pry too large a load.[15] For example, Douglas Campbell, after discussing πίστις in Romans 1:17 ("from faith to faith") and in Paul's citation of Habakkuk 2:4 ("the righteous one will live from faith"), claims that this use of πίστις settles not only the πίστις Χριστοῦ debate in favor of meaning 2, but actually leads to an inevitable reworking of everything we thought Paul has said.[16] Here is Campbell's own breathtaking conclusion:

> With the establishment of this equation between ἐκ πίστεως, Hab 2:4, and the faithfulness of the Messiah in [Rom] 1:17, much in the rest of Paul's argument within Romans is both resolved and clarified. . . . Probably all that can be claimed at this point is that the burden of proof now rests firmly on those who would read many of these genitives and arguments in a way that does *not* link πίστις with Χριστός in a subjective fashion, that is, as an elliptical reference, mediated by the terminology of Hab 2:4, to his death on the cross. Yet even this minimal concession opens up the possibility of a *major reevaluation of Paul's argument in Romans* (especially chaps. 1–4), *and of his theology as a whole*.[17]

Time does not allow us to illustrate this methodological problem more fully. Yet one will find the phrase δικαιοσύνη θεοῦ (righteousness of God), the whole δικαιο- word group (righteous, righteousness, justify), and ἔργα νόμου (works of law) receiving particular attention in new perspective literature as words and phrases that warrant the recasting of Paul's whole theology and especially his

14. For a survey of the options, see Richard B. Hays and Luke Timothy Johnson, *The Faith of Jesus Christ: The Narrative Substructure of Galatians 3:1–4:11* (Grand Rapids: Eerdmans, 2001).

15. Is it improper to recall Virgil's *mens agitat molem* here (*Aeneid* 6.727)?

16. Douglas A. Campbell, "Romans 1:17: A *Crux Interpretum* for the Πίστις Χριστοῦ Debate," *Journal of Biblical Literature* 113 (1994): 265–85. By the way, meaning 2 for πίστις Χριστοῦ would communicate what the Reformed called "the active obedience of Christ" (discussed in chapter 8 below) and is therefore not a revolutionary concept for us, though I still prefer meaning 1 for other linguistic and exegetical reasons.

17. Ibid., 284–85 (emphasis added). For follow-up critique, see Brian Dodd, "Romans 1:17: A *Crux Interpretum* for the Πίστις Χριστοῦ Debate?" *Journal of Biblical Literature* 114 (1995): 470–73.

doctrine of justification in the way in which new perspective adherents desire.[18]

In all this flurry of claims about a few pivotal words and phrases, however, an exegete must firmly grasp and act upon this fundamental truth: a complex conception like justification in the teaching of Paul cannot be constructed in whole or even in large part by simple analysis of a few words or phrases.[19] Word and phrase studies certainly have their place in the process, but a complex conception must be established by *statements* and larger units of discourse. As just one simple example of this, even a surface reading of Romans 4:5–8 shows that Paul views justification to be a multifaceted concept that involves "the one who does not labor" but instead "trusts in the one who justifies the ungodly" and receives a "reckoning of righteousness" that can, as its flip side, be described as "not reckoning sins" because "blessed are those whose sins are forgiven" (quoting Ps 32). Works, faith, ungodliness (*simul iustus et peccator*), reckoning righteous, the forgiveness of sins, and more must all factor into our grasp of Paul's conception of justification. These issues are not established by simple analysis of words alone, but by reading contexts and evaluating larger units of discourse.[20]

18. Cf. Sanders, *Paul and Palestinian Judaism*, 544: "The debate about righteousness by faith or by works of law thus turns out to result from the different usage of the 'righteous' word-group." For Dunn and others the supposed Hebrew meaning of Paul's phrase δικαιοσὺνη θεοῦ becomes "a key to his exposition in Romans"; James D. G. Dunn, *Romans 1–8* (Word Biblical Commentary 38A; Dallas: Word, 1988), 41. One extreme example of a similar methodological problem is Wright's attempt to fix the content of Paul's gospel (εὐαγγέλιον) by locating "the Jewish usage of the relevant root" in two verses in Isaiah. In consequence, he believes that the referent of Paul's gospel is the announcement that Gentiles join Israel in return from (Babylonian?) exile; see *What Saint Paul Really Said*, 43. If this procedure were valid we could just as likely trace Paul's gospel to Jer 20:15, where the prophet curses the man who brought the "gospel" of his birth to his father; hence, the gospel would be viewed as a curse.

19. We are not talking here about concrete objects in the world but complex theological conceptions. In other realms of life, one would need to perform similar global analysis to grasp ideas such as democracy, freedom, common law, and the like.

20. N. T. Wright warns that Rom 4 is not "a mere proof from scripture of the abstract doctrine of justification by faith"; *The Climax of the Covenant: Christ and the Law in Pauline Theology* (Minneapolis: Fortress, 1992), 36, though we are not told why this doctrine must be "abstract" here. See also his conflation (e.g., *What Saint Paul Really Said*, 160) of the conceptions of "faith" and "faithfulness" simply because the term πίστις in Greek can have either (discrete) meaning—as clear an example of Barr's "illegitimate totality transfer" as any, though Wright provides several others in his writings.

A second common methodological problem in new perspective interpreters involves something more subtle and entails many interrelated issues. Put simply, justification for them is not a definitive declaration by God that the sinner is accounted righteous in Christ by faith alone, but—and here the new perspective interpreters will vary in the details—it is some sort of ongoing relationship in covenant involving both God's obligation to save his covenant people and the individual's own obedience to maintain covenant with God. One of the linchpins of this argument is that the Jewish conception of justify, righteousness, and so on (all in the δικαιο- word group in Greek) differs from "the typical Greek worldview" as follows: "For whereas in Greek thought 'righteousness' or 'justice' was an ideal norm by which particular claims or duties could be measured, in Hebrew thought 'righteousness' was more a concept of relation."[21] Specifically, these conceptions for the Jew worked within "a relationship of mutual obligation" so that for us it means "to be acquitted, recognized as righteous, . . . to be counted as one of God's own people *who had proved faithful* to the covenant."[22] Hence, Paul turns out to be a "covenant nomist" like his opponents.

While Dunn quotes many secondary sources to justify this claim of the opposition of Jewish and Greek thought on the issues of justice and justification, one will be hard pressed to find a "typical Greek" who held to an abstract notion of justice or a typical Jew—including Paul himself—who did not conceive of the law of Moses as a norm by which sin was accounted as transgression.[23] This latter view is clearly taught in Romans 5:13–14. The Greeks, however, had a longstanding debate over whether societal norms were rooted merely in νόμος (custom) (i.e., arbitrary human inventions and changing societal norms) or φύσις (nature) (i.e., the unchanging nature of reality and fundamental existence), and their popular conception of certain transgressions as personal affronts to certain gods (e.g., violation of the strict demands of hospitality overseen by Zeus Xenios) is ignored

21. James D. G. Dunn, *The Epistle to the Galatians* (Black's New Testament Commentaries; London: Black, 1993), 134; cf. idem, *The Theology of Paul the Apostle* (Grand Rapids: Eerdmans, 1998), 341–42.

22. Dunn, *Theology of Paul*, 342; and idem, *Galatians*, 134–35 (emphasis added).

23. For Dunn's sources, see *Theology of Paul*, 341–42n27.

by new perspective advocates. Even the most idealized conception of law by the Greeks (e.g., Plato's *Laws*) recognized that each *polis* had its own distinct ancestral laws (similar to Rome's *mos maiorum*) that were not abstract but operated within the whole Mediterranean notion of *eusebeia* or *pietas* toward parents and superiors in complex interrelations of patronage or formal friendship. One could easily assert that the Greek (and Roman) notion of justice was relational and not abstract if given to oversimplification,[24] but a more accurate evaluation of Paul's historical backdrop would be inconvenient for the rhetorical appeal of the new perspective.

The third methodological problem haunting new perspective exegesis is the consistent tendency to limit the meaning of Paul's own teaching to what his supposed Jewish contemporaries either taught or what they would have understood. We are told that this is reading Paul historically in light of his contemporaries rather than through the improper lenses of the Reformation or of contemporary Western theological interests foreign to the ancient Jewish world. The last thing I want to do is commend reading the New Testament in a historical vacuum,[25] but there are obvious limits here when the Paul of the new perspective becomes indistinguishable from his opponents.[26] Let me illustrate with one notable example.

In Galatians 5:3, Paul reasserts his most dire warning to the Galatians by testifying that to accept the way of law keeping for justification embodied in taking on circumcision (cf. Acts 15:1, 5) means that they would then be personally under obligation "to perform the whole law," for they will have been cut off from Christ (the covenant mediator) and have fallen from grace (Gal 5:2, 4). This text, in association with Galatians 3:10, has been taken to indicate that Paul interpreted the

24. This is not to say that there was no differences of thought between Paul and, say, contemporary Greeks like Epictetus or Plutarch or Romans like Seneca or Pliny the Younger. One will also need to take into account the heavy influence of pagan philosophy on Jewish authors such as Philo (Platonism) or the author of 4 Maccabees (Stoicism). All of this, however, is another essay. See "Nomos," in *Der Neue Pauly: Enzyklopädie der Antike* (ed. Hubert Cancik and Helmuth Schneider; Stuttgart/Weimar: Metzler, 2000), 8.982–85, esp. 984.

25. See Steven Michael Baugh, "Paul and Ephesus: The Apostle among His Contemporaries" (PhD diss., University of California, Irvine, 1990).

26. See Watson's telling statement quoted above that the theology of the new perspective Paul "is, in effect, an inclusive, universal, liberal form of Jewish covenant theology"; "Not the New Perspective," 14.

law to require perfect and entire obedience "that neither our fathers nor we have been able to bear" (Acts 15:10). Yet, this interpretation does not fit Sanders's view that both Paul and contemporary Judaism taught a more relaxed view of the law in the form of covenant nomism. In other words, Paul cannot be interpreted to view the law as imposing an exacting and exhaustive requirement for personal obedience for Sanders or his whole analysis of Paul's opponents would end in failure.[27]

Initially in *Paul and Palestinian Judaism*, Sanders saw Paul in Galatians 3:10 holding "that one must achieve legal perfection." In contrast, "The Amoraic literature always emphasizes that one should confirm the law, not keep it without error. . . . Human perfection was not considered realistically achievable by the Rabbis, nor was it required."[28] Later on, however, Sanders changed his view to assert that Paul too did not believe that the law required perfection.[29]

This seems to run against the obvious import of Galatians 3:10 and even more clearly 5:3, where Paul says that the Galatian who "attempts to be justified by the law" (5:4) is severed from Christ and from divine grace and would be under personal obligation to fulfill the whole law (ὀφειλέτης ἐστὶν ὅλον τὸν νόμον ποιῆσαι). The question has its own importance for reading Paul, but what is under review here is merely how Sanders deals with this verse and its context. He does give 5:3 a few pages of treatment in his later book, *Paul, the Law, and the Jewish People*.[30] Sanders's conclusion is that Paul is merely "reminding his converts that, if they accept circumcision, the consequence would be that they would have to begin living their lives according to

27. For citation of literature and discussion of this issue, see my "Galatians 5:1–6 and Personal Obligation: Reflections on Paul and the Law," paper read at the 2004 national meeting of the Evangelical Theological Society in San Antonio, Texas.

28. Sanders, *Paul and Palestinian Judaism*, 137. As an aside, Sanders's treatment here of the Hebrew verb יָקִים (confirm) in Deut 27:26 cited by Paul in Gal 3:10 can be challenged. קוּם in the Hifil is found in very interesting connections with oath and covenant stipulations in the Old Testament to show that the law imposed a rigid obligation for personal performance of its commandments (e.g., 1 Sam 15:11; 2 Kgs 23:3), which is transgression of the covenant by not "keeping" (הֵקִים) its terms (Jer 34:18).

29. Sanders notes that he changed his view in *Paul, the Law, and the Jewish People* (Philadelphia: Fortress, 1983), 23.

30. Ibid., 27–29.

a new set of rules for daily living."[31] Paul's anguished, dire, and blunt warning of 5:1–6 (i.e., ἴδε ἐγὼ Παῦλος λέγω ὑμῖν ὅτι in 5:2) becomes for Sanders a mild bit of advice about a change of ethics of very little consequence. What is important to us here, however, is how Sanders arrives at this unsatisfying interpretation. Here is the sum of his argument in his own words:

> It would, in short, be extraordinarily un-Pharisaic and even un-Jewish of Paul to insist that obedience of the law, once undertaken, must be perfect. Such a position would directly imply that the means of atonement specified in Scripture itself were of no avail. Appeal to Paul's pre-Christian views lends no support to the position that the weight of Paul's argument in Galatians 3 rests on the word "all" in 3:10, or to the position that Paul came to his negative stance on righteousness by the law because it cannot be adequately fulfilled. Paul's Pharisaic past counts heavily against both positions.[32]

In other words, the new perspective Paul can never break out of the box of his supposed pre-Christian convictions about the nature of the law and its righteousness. Paraphrased, the reconstructed ancient Judaism of the new perspective acts as a filter through which Paul must pass. Anything he says that does not conform to the views of this censorship board must be scrubbed of all offending material. In the end, it seems obvious to conclude that if Sanders and his followers were right we would be left with the urgent question of why this Paul, doomed to his Pharisaic prison, has not faded into the same obscurity and anonymity as his nameless opponents at Galatia rather than being a continuing major contributor to the most robust and exciting theology on the planet two millennia later.

A fourth methodological problem is the rather abrupt way we are told that justification is not a definitive, judicial act of God but a process connected with continuance in the covenant relationship. Though the exact nuance will vary from one new perspective propo-

31. Ibid., 29.

32. Ibid., 28. This stratagem is used often by new perspective interpreters, for instance: "When Paul speaks of justification he is operating within the whole world of thought of second-temple Judaism" (Wright, *What Saint Paul Really Said*, 117). Rather Paul is operating in the thought world of Christianity (cf. 1 Cor 2:8–13 or 2 Cor 3:14–18).

nent to another, continuance in the relationship is made to depend on some form of the believer's obedience and works.[33] In Sanders's terminology one may "get in" by grace, but one "stays in" by works of obedience.[34]

The viewpoint of justification as a process is substantiated by the previously discussed issue of "justify" and related Greek words as distinctively relational terms for Paul. Support for justification as a process is said to come from the verb tenses Paul uses when expressing δικαιόω (justify) in various contexts in his epistles. This point comes up particularly in Dunn's treatment of the aorist participle δικαιωθέντες in Romans 5:1, so I will use this as the occasion to begin our survey of Romans 5.

Covenant Mediation in Romans

We open Romans 5 conscious of entering Paul's epistle in progress, with some key notions already carefully laid down by the apostle. All the world, both Jew and Greek, is under indictment to God's law, condemnation, and wrath (3:9, 19–20), so that only through the one mediator between God and man (1 Tim 2:5) through whose propitiatory death (Rom 3:25) and fulfilling of the law's demands can God's forgiveness and justification extend as a free gift to the profane and ungodly who put their trust in the Savior (3:26; 4:5–12; cf. 2 Cor 5:21; Eph 2:8–9; Titus 2:14).[35]

33. Here Paul's often misunderstood "obedience of faith" (Rom 1:5; 16:26) is sometimes invoked as "one of Paul's key phrases" (Wright, *What Saint Paul Really Said*, 160) to show that "faith" is really tantamount to "faithfulness" or works of obedience; cf. Dunn (*Theology of Paul*, 360–61 [esp. n107] and 635), who via the etymology of the word ὑπακοή (obedience) derived from ὑπό (under) and ἀκοή (hearing) connects the phrase *obedience of faith* with the Hebrew word שָׁמַע and Paul's phrase *hearing of faith* (Gal 3:2, 5). This is an extreme example of the well-known etymological fallacy; cf. D. A. Carson, *Exegetical Fallacies* (2nd ed.; Grand Rapids: Baker, 1996), 28–33.

34. Never mind that this is precisely what Protestants have labeled "legalism" rather than the scarecrow easily knocked over by champions of the new perspective.

35. One will note that I accept the Pastoral epistles and other so-called deuteropauline books as Pauline in origin. Dunn defends his rejection of these books in a brief footnote, *Theology of Paul*, 13n39, which necessarily skews the results of his so-called Pauline theology. In my mind, significant works such as E. Randolph Richards's *Secretary in the Letters of Paul* (Wissenschaftliche Untersuchungen zum Neuen Testament 2.42; Tübingen: Mohr, 1991) or Anthony

Having Been Justified

Romans 5 then opens with the stunning words: "Therefore, since we have been justified by faith, we have peace with God through our Lord Jesus Christ. Through him we have also obtained access by faith into this grace in which we stand, and we rejoice in hope of the glory of God" (5:1–2 ESV). Paul says that we have *now* been justified and in consequence have peace, access, and standing in God's grace, which gives us sure hope for the future. This means that God has already rendered his verdict of the last day in our favor through Jesus Christ. Justification is accomplished. To all appearances, this seems to be communicated rather neatly by the lead aorist adverbial (or circumstantial) participle in 5:1: δικαιωθέντες, rendered "since we have been justified."[36]

Two issues need to be briefly addressed before going further: the meaning of the word δικαιόω and the significance of the aorist tense form of the participle δικαιωθέντες. While I have already stated that our grasp of Paul's complex conception of justification by faith alone cannot rest on such questions alone, it is still necessary to treat them.

The verb δικαιόω has four identifiably distinct meanings in the Greek New Testament:[37]

1. To judicially pronounce acquittal from charges of wrongdoing and, consequently, to declare someone's just status according to a legal or moral standard. In most New Testament contexts, the final judgment is the setting, and the legal

Kenny's *Stylometric Study of the New Testament* (Oxford: Oxford University Press, 1986) must be answered by those who reject Pauline authorship of these New Testament books.

36. All major English versions render the participle δικαιωθέντες causally: "*Since* we have been justified." NRSV infelicitously renders the aorist participle as "since we *are* justified by faith" (emphasis added), which would be appropriate if the participle had been expressed in its perfect tense form.

37. Cf. BDAG 249: (1) to take up a legal cause, *show justice, do justice, take up a cause* (no New Testament examples); (2) to render a favorable verdict, *vindicate*; (3) to cause someone to be released from personal or institutional claims that are no longer to be considered pertinent or valid, *make free/pure*; (4) to demonstrate to be morally right, *prove to be right*. Henry George Liddell, Robert Scott, and H. Stuart Jones, *A Greek-English Lexicon* (9th ed.; Oxford: Clarendon, 1996), in both the main text (429) and the supplement (42), point to other meanings: "demand as a right," "consent," "punish," "brought to justice," in addition to the Septuagint and New Testament meanings (e.g., "pass sentence; pronounce and treat as righteous").

standard is the divinely issued law (from general or special revelation) (Matt 12:36–37; Luke 18:14; Rom 8:33–34). The antonym is "condemn" (Rom 8:33–34).[38]

2. To set someone free from some offense or guilt; to purify from sin, rendered "to clear" or "to purify from" (Acts 13:38–39; Rom 6:7).
3. To demonstrate that one is right in word or deed. The setting may be a formal public setting (courtroom). The idea carries with it the proving of one's veracity or rightness. "Vindicate" is the closest English rendering (Matt 11:19; Luke 10:29; Rom 3:4 [quoting Ps 51]; 1 Tim 3:16; Jas 2:21, 24).
4. To publicly acknowledge the rightness of someone (Luke 7:29).[39]

In Romans 5:1 (and 5:9), meaning 1 is clearly intended by δικαιωθέντες. When we look at what Paul says through this verb with this meaning, we find that the rendering of this positive verdict about believers is before God (versus man as Luke 16:15) (Rom 2:23; 3:20; Gal 3:11) as a gift (Rom 3:24) to those deserving condemnation (4:5; 5:6–10) by faith alone in Christ (3:26, 28, 30; 4:2; 1 Cor 6:11; Gal 2:16–17; 3:8, 24; 5:4; Titus 3:7) and is tantamount to "credit righteousness to someone" or "account someone as righteous" (λογίζεσθαι τινί [εἰς] δικαιοσύνην; e.g., Rom 4:3, 6) and involves the forgiveness of sins (4:6–8). This surely informs how we must read δικαιωθέντες in 5:1 and 5:9.

The issue of the aorist tense form of δικαιωθέντες in 5:1 arises because of Dunn's warning:

> Somewhat surprisingly, this is the first time Paul uses δικαιόω in the aorist in Romans—apart from 3:4 (God) and 4:2 (Abraham). In more general references and references to fellow believers the present indicative (3:24, 26, 28; 4:5) and future (2:13; 3:20, 30)

38. See esp. Prov 17:15: מַצְדִּיק רָשָׁע וּמַרְשִׁיעַ צַדִּיק תּוֹעֲבַת יְהוָה גַּם־שְׁנֵיהֶם (he who justifies the wicked and he who condemns the righteous / are both alike an abomination to the Lord) (ESV), which is rendered rather freely in the Septuagint as ὃς δίκαιον κρίνει τὸν ἄδικον, ἄδικον δὲ τὸν δίκαιον, ἀκάθαρτος καὶ βδελυκτὸς παρὰ θεῷ.

39. BDAG 249 §2a renders "tax-collectors affirmed God's uprightness." This meaning is possibly subsumed under #3 above.

> have predominated. The tense here certainly indicates an act of God in the past, but that should not be allowed to dominate the doctrine of justification drawn from Paul to the extent that it has, or to overwhelm the force of the other tenses.[40]

It is not easy to see what it is that concerns Dunn here about how the aorist in 5:1 has "dominate[d] the doctrine of justification" or "overwhelm[ed] the force of the other tenses," but he feels strongly enough about the issue to repeat his warning in his book on Paul's theology:

> Too much weight should not be put on the aorist tense at the beginning of 5.1—"having been justified from faith. . . ." For that simply emphasizes the *beginning* of the salvation process. As the whole conception of God's righteousness has indicated, *justification is not a once-for-all act of God*. It is rather the initial acceptance by God into restored relationship.[41]

In the end, it seems that Dunn wants to color his doctrine of justification with relational hues, and in this last quotation one can see how he uses his relational understanding of "the righteousness of God" (1:17) to lever the whole concept of justification. What is particularly lacking here is the imputation of Christ's righteousness to the sinner as the sine qua non of Paul's view of justification in favor of more generic relational ideas.[42]

To get back to δικαιωθέντες, the question of Greek verb tense forms and the present and future collocations of δικαιόω elsewhere in Romans that Dunn mentions is a complex one that requires more discussion than can be spared here. Suffice it to say that specialists on the Greek verb system would admonish us against making precipitate conclusions on the mere occurrence of a verb in different tense forms.[43]

40. Dunn, *Romans 1–8*, 246.

41. Dunn, *Theology of Paul*, 386 (and n212) (emphasis added). It should be noted that many of the things in Dunn's book are perfectly sound.

42. For example, note the apposition in this statement: "God would not justify, could not sustain in relationship with him, those who did not rely wholly on him" (*Theology of Paul*, 379). Are "justify" and "sustain in relationship" truly synonymous ideas for Paul?

43. Cf. Buist M. Fanning, *Verbal Aspect in New Testament Greek* (Oxford: Clarendon, 1990); Stanley Porter, *Verbal Aspect in the Greek of the New Testament* (Studies in Biblical Greek

In my own view, one must be particularly careful comparing verb tense forms from one mood to another, since factors often guide the use of a "default" or "unmarked" form in particular situations. This is true even within the same mood depending on the construction.

Careful examination shows that what Dunn identifies as "the present indicative (3:24, 26, 28; 4:5)" of δικαιόω in Romans turns out, in fact, to be three participles and one infinitive with no use of the present indicative for δικαιόω in Romans at all.[44] The present tense form of the attributive and substantive participles of δικαιόω in Romans (3:26; 4:5; and 8:33) can all be accounted for as characteristics of God: he is the justifier. This is not because justification is a present process, but because in Greek the present participle in this use signifies a characteristic action or feature of someone: one who judges (2:1, 3), one who labors for wages (4:4), one who wills or runs (9:16), one who believes (10:11), one who teaches (12:7), one who exhorts (12:8), one who loves (13:8), and so on. This is why some common participles became nouns or acted as labels for individuals.[45]

The causal participle δικαιωθέντες in 5:1 and 5:9 is adverbial, however, and the aorist form has a straightforward sense: the event to which it refers is antecedent to the main verb's statement: "We have [ἔχομεν] peace with God." In other words, the justifying verdict referenced by the participle must be viewed as completed in order to lead to the consequence of peace with God and the other benefits of access and standing in grace leading to confident boasting even

1; New York/Bern: Peter Lang, 1989); idem, *Idioms of the Greek New Testament* (Sheffield: Sheffield Academic Press, 1992); K. L. McKay, *A New Syntax of the Verb in New Testament Greek: An Aspectual Approach* (Studies in Biblical Greek 5; New York/Bern: Peter Lang, 1994); idem, "Time and Aspect in New Testament Greek," *Novum Testamentum* 34 (1992): 209–28; Stanley E. Porter and D. A. Carson, eds., *Biblical Greek Language and Linguistics: Open Questions in Current Research* (Journal for the Study of the New Testament Supplement 80; Sheffield: Sheffield Academic Press, 1993); and Albert Rijksbaron, *The Syntax and Semantics of the Verb in Classical Greek: An Introduction* (2nd ed.; Amsterdam: Gieben, 1994).

44. The forms are δικαιούμενοι (Rom 3:24), δικαιοῦντα (3:26), δικαιοῦσθαι (3:28), and δικαιοῦντα (4:5). It is worth adding that δικαιόω appears several times in Galatians as present indicative forms expressing a "gnomic" or "omnitemporal" truth (2:16; 3:8, 11) or a connative nuance (5:4); cf. Porter, *Idioms of the Greek New Testament*, 32–33.

45. That is, the noun ὁ ἄρχων (the ruler) began life as a participle; and ὁ βαπτίζων (the Baptist) became a title for John even after he died, showing that this was not some sort of ongoing process; cf. Judas who was labeled ὁ παραδιδούς (the betrayer) in the Gospels (e.g., Matt 26:25).

in tribulation as Paul's discussion moves ahead in 5:2–5. While this one participle does not conclusively settle the whole issue of when believers are justified, it must not be preemptively muzzled of its contribution to the doctrine.[46]

What is most interesting about δικαιωθέντες in 5:1 is that Paul repeats it in a fascinating and unequivocal statement in 5:9. In fact, the whole of this section (5:1–11) is building to a unified climax from the foundation of what proceeds, because we are justified by faith. Let us look at this development in 5:1–11, then return to δικαιωθέντες in 5:9.

Paul claims that in consequence of being justified by faith, we have peace with God through Christ (5:1). This peace is the consummate benefit of covenant blessing won for us by Christ's death (5:10a) and life (5:10b). Peace, access to God, and permanent standing in his grace as a sure possession (5:1–2) are the great benefits conveyed in the covenant of grace,[47] which are expressed in its great "covenant formula," God is our God and we become his prized possession.[48] As a result, we "boast in hope of the glory of God" (5:2). Our versions want to avoid the negative implications of the English word *boast* for καυχάομαι in 5:2–3 by rendering the word as "rejoice" (AV [5:2], NIV, ESV), "exult" (NASB), or "glory" (AV [5:3]) and so are trying to capture the exultant, joyful confidence that flows from the sure foundation of being justified and standing in grace.[49] This confidence is so powerful and unshakable that even tribulations are turned from

46. For a parallel example of a causal participle with a present tense main verb within Romans itself see 6:9: "Since Christ was raised from the dead, he cannot die again" (NIV) for Χριστὸς ἐγερθεὶς ἐκ νεκρῶν οὐκέτι ἀποθνῄσκει. Clearly, "being raised" must be a prior event to "not dying again."

47. The continuing state or condition of "standing" in grace is implied in the perfect tense form of ἑστήκαμεν (in which *we stand* or exist) (cf. BDAG 483 §5) and confirmed by the "confident boasting" that follows in 5:2b–5.

48. See esp. Ezek 37:24–28 for these themes clearly expressed of the new covenant. Old Testament scholars today recognize the covenant formula (*Bundesformel*) as "the chief thread through the labyrinth of the Bible"; see Otto Kaiser, "The Law as Center of the Hebrew Bible," in *"Sha'arei Talmon": Studies in the Bible, Qumran, and the Ancient Near East Presented to Shemaryahu Talmon* (ed. M. Fishbane and E. Tov; Winona Lake, IN: Eisenbrauns, 1992), 96 (and 93–103 for the broader argument). This is not a new observation; see, e.g., the discussion of the *formula foederis* by Turretin, *Institutes* 2.179–80 §12.2.17; 2.232 §12.8.3.

49. See the brief but helpful note in Douglas Moo, *The Epistle to the Romans* (New International Commentary on the New Testament; Grand Rapids: Eerdmans, 1996), 301–2.

their expected course as threats to our hope to become instruments of endurance, proven character, and further *hope* (5:3–4). The links of this chain of confident hope to an even more sure hope are tempered by tribulation's fires through the Holy Spirit poured out upon us (5:5).

Justification and Mediation

In Romans 5:6–11, Paul grounds these glorious blessings of 5:1–5 in the mediation of Christ.[50] In this section, Christ's mediation is not the shocking thing; the objects of his mediation are. Contrast here the psalmist's righteous indignation: "Do I not hate those who hate you, O LORD? / And do I not loathe those who rise up against you? / I hate them with complete hatred; / I count them my enemies" (Ps 139:21–22 ESV). Yet it is precisely the morally incapacitated (Rom 5:6a), the ungodly (5:6b) who are not only not righteous but not even good (5:7), the sinners (5:8) who are God's enemies (5:10) and therefore prime objects for the psalmist's loathing for whom Christ died to deliver from God's well-deserved wrath (5:9).[51]

This stunning section, 5:6–11, performs two vital functions for Paul's argument on justification. First, it shows how God can be just and the justifier of the wantonly corrupt (5:6; cf. τὸν ἀσεβῆ in 4:5) who nevertheless turns in trust to Christ (cf. 3:25–26). How can this be, since to justify the guilty is declared to be abominable to God (Prov 17:15)? The answer Paul supplies in Romans 5:6–11 is the effective intervention of Christ as our substitutionary mediator (cf. 1 John 1:9; 2:1–2). The stress here shows Paul's vital second point: it was *while* we were in this forlorn state that Christ intervened. One may die for a worthwhile (ἀγαθός) individual (Rom 5:7), but Paul's relentless argument is that we cannot even make that claim as the

50. Rom 5:6 begins with γάρ (for), signaling that what follows are the underlying truths of the previous assertions. The variation ἔτι γάρ in the beginning of 5:6 is caused by the repetition of ἔτι later in the verse, not because γάρ was in doubt.

51. The adjective ἀσθενής is normally rendered "weak," but the idea here is our incapacity and helplessness to redeem ourselves (cf. BDAG 142–43 §2), while ἀσεβής (ungodly) has negative connotations of someone who is wantonly evil and corrupt (so Rom 1:18–32, issuing from ἀσέβεια). Paul contrasts starkly with Greek moral philosophy, where a "good man" (καλοκἀγαθός) was a very obtainable ideal. For God's mercy toward his enemies, see esp. Christ's teaching in Matt 5:43–45 and Luke 6:27–36.

reason for Christ pitying us. This shows beyond any doubt or confusion that Paul thoroughly repudiates any kind of synergism in his soteriology, including what Sanders labels "covenant nomism." We can have no claim on God derived from anything in ourselves as worthy of redemption. In contrast, Christ's mediation is so thoroughly effective that Paul moves us to conclude that not only are we *now* justified and reconciled through Christ, but the ultimate outcome is a guaranteed salvation from divine wrath in the future (5:9–11).

The temporal dynamic in what was just said should not be minimized. If our being justified is presented as the grounds for current blessings in 5:1, this is underlined unambiguously in 5:9 when he says that we are *now* justified (δικαιωθέντες νῦν), leading to future deliverance ("salvation") from divine wrath.

If we were unsure of the completed character of justification (δικαιωθέντες) in 5:1 (due to Dunn's warning to the contrary), we cannot be so now. The blood of Jesus is the ground of this justification that we possess *now*—in this era. For us the last-day verdict has already been rendered at the resurrection of Jesus "for our justification" (4:25), so that we possess it now in anticipation of that future day of God's righteous judgment when his wrath is unleashed upon the unjustified, according to Paul's gospel (2:16; cf. 2:4–5 and 1:18). We possess it *now*, because the blood of our mediator has *now*, in this age, been spilt as the propitiation of wrath (cf. 3:25).

Paul hammers this present justification home with an unequivocal parallel in 5:10–11: "For if while we were enemies *we were reconciled* [κατηλλάγημεν] to God by the death of his Son, much more, *now that we are reconciled* [καταλλαγέντες], shall we be saved by his life. More than that, we also rejoice in God through our Lord Jesus Christ, through whom *we have now received reconciliation* [νῦν τὴν καταλλαγὴν ἐλάβομεν] (ESV, emphasis added). The force of the aorist participle καταλλαγέντες in 5:10 is a current reality shaping the future (σωθησόμεθα, we will be saved); reconciliation is clearly *now* (νῦν in 5:11) our possession as a gift flowing from Christ's mediation analogous with justification in 5:1 and 5:9.[52]

52. Another parallel later in Romans has virtually the same aorist participle and particle construction: "And, having been set free [ἐλευθερωθέντες] from sin, [you] have become slaves of righteousness. . . . But now that you have been set free [νυνὶ δὲ ἐλευθερωθέντες] from sin

While we have not discussed the full *doctrine* of justification by way of δικαιωθέντες in 5:1 and 5:9, we have looked carefully at this evidence, which must form a significant part of the foundation for the doctrine. The completed character of this referent is all the more evident both because of the linguistic evidence we have reviewed and because of Paul's *statements* connected to this concept linking justification *now* with the finished, effective mediation of Christ in this age guaranteeing the future blessings for his people.

The Development of Paul's Thought

Nothing is more important for the successful interpretation of Paul's epistles than the ability to explain the development of his thought. This comes to play in Romans 5 in relating 5:12–21 with what he has said before. In 5:12, the marker of this development is the phrase διὰ τοῦτο, which is usually not difficult to understand—but it is here: "More than that, we also rejoice in God through our Lord Jesus Christ, through whom we have now received reconciliation. *Therefore*, just as sin came into the world through one man . . ." (5:11–12 ESV, emphasis added). Wright notes: "Perhaps the most important point about the whole section is the significance of διὰ τοῦτο at the start of 5.12."[53]

Normally, διὰ τοῦτο draws out a conclusion from the foregoing and is rendered "therefore" (e.g., Matt 6:25; 12:27; Luke 14:20; cf. BDAG 225 §B2b), even if the reason for the conclusion follows the clause marked by διὰ τοῦτο.[54] But as the commentators note, διὰ τοῦτο seems "peculiar" in Romans 5:12, since, as Douglas Moo says, 5:12–21 "makes better sense when viewed as the *basis* for what has just been said" in 5:1–11 rather than vice versa.[55] Normally, one marks the basis or rationale for what has just been said with γάρ (for) or equivalent expressions, but not διὰ τοῦτο.

---

and have become slaves of God, the fruit you get leads to sanctification and its end, eternal life" (6:18, 22 ESV).

53. Wright, *Climax of the Covenant*, 35.

54. E.g., John 5:16: "And this was why [διὰ τοῦτο] the Jews were persecuting Jesus, because [ὅτι] he was doing these things on the Sabbath."

55. Moo, *Romans*, 317, with detailed discussion of διὰ τοῦτο on 316–18, esp. n17. The phrase is "peculiar" according to Otto Michel, *Der Brief an die Römer* (14th ed.; Kritisch-exegetischer Kommentar über das Neue Testament 14; Göttingen: Vandenhoeck & Ruprecht, 1978), 186.

The problem, however, with seeing 5:12–21 as a conclusion arises because of the difficulty of seeing what exactly it connects to in the foregoing discussion of Romans to that point. Various proposals include that Paul is making only a general summary conclusion of all of 1:17–5:11, or that he is concluding 5:1–11 in a general way, or that he is more specifically picking up something from 5:11 alone.[56]

Because we are more acclimatized to the gospel than they would have been in Paul's day, perhaps we have lost the sense of just how radical Paul's statements about Christ's substitutionary mediation are in 5:6–11. While Jesus and the prophets did announce his redemptive death (e.g., Mark 10:45; Isa 53:10–11), nevertheless, it ran counter to other Scripture principles:

> Son of man, when a land sins against me by acting faithlessly, and I stretch out my hand against it and break its supply of bread and send famine upon it, and cut off from it man and beast, even if these three men, Noah, Daniel, and Job, were in it, they would deliver but their own lives by their righteousness, declares the Lord GOD. . . .
>
> Or if I send a pestilence into that land and pour out my wrath upon it with blood, to cut off from it man and beast, even if Noah, Daniel, and Job were in it, as I live, declares the Lord GOD, they would deliver neither son nor daughter. They would deliver but their own lives by their righteousness. (Ezek 14:13–14, 19–20 ESV)

> Truly no man can ransom another,
>   or give to God the price of his life,
> for the ransom of their life is costly
>   and can never suffice,
> that he should live on forever
>   and never see the pit. (Ps 49:7–9 ESV [MT 49:8–10])

The question now stands out a little more urgently from what Paul has just said in Romans 5:6–11: How can it be then that Jesus Christ the Righteous One (1 John 2:2) could give himself for us? Notice the repeated emphasis in Romans 5:6–11:

56. See Moo, *Romans*, 316–17, for survey of different opinions. The view I advance here is similar to Moo's and Michel's, but I express it a little differently.

> *Christ died for the ungodly*. For one will scarcely die *for a righteous person*—though *perhaps for a good person* one would dare even to die. . . . *Christ died for us*. . . . Shall we be saved *by him* from the wrath of God. . . . We were reconciled to God *by the death of his Son*, much more, now that we are reconciled, shall we be saved *by his life*. More than that, we also rejoice in God *through our Lord Jesus Christ, through whom* we have now received reconciliation. (ESV, emphasis added)

The same emphasis on mediation of both condemnation and justification is found in 5:12–21:

> Therefore . . . through one man . . . through one man's trespass . . . by the grace of that one man Jesus Christ. . . . one man's sin . . . one trespass . . . because of one man's trespass . . . through that one man . . . through the one man Jesus Christ . . . one trespass . . . one act of righteousness . . . by the one man's disobedience . . . by the one man's obedience. (ESV)

The point of 5:12–21 is to explain how it is that Christ *could* die on our behalf (ὑπὲρ ἡμῶν).[57] More pointedly, how could his mediation be effective for those who have *no active involvement* at the time when the intervention is accomplished, yet the intervention forms the *sufficient ground* of the tremendous results obtained? Paul has strongly asserted the principle of substitutionary mediation in 5:1–11, and in 5:12–21 he is indeed making a conclusion, but the conclusion is not what one might have thought. The conclusion Paul is eliciting from 5:1–11 is not the comparison between Adam and Christ given in the second half of the chapter. Instead, Paul is concluding that Christ's obedience and mediation bring *saving results* that can be explained only on analogy with Adam. In other words, much of Paul's statements in 5:12–21 are a restatement of the effective mediation of Christ already taught in 5:1–11. Where he wants to take us in concluding his earlier thought is to the infallible outcome of this free, gracious substitutionary mediation.

57. This phrase from Rom 5:8 occurs elsewhere in key places: Rom 8:31–34; 2 Cor 5:21; Gal 3:13; Eph 5:2; 1 Thess 5:10; and Titus 2:14.

Here are the results in isolation from the argumentation of the passage:

> The free gift . . . the grace of God and the free gift by the grace of that one man Jesus Christ abounded for many. And the free gift . . . the free gift . . . much more will those who receive the abundance of grace and the free gift of righteousness reign in life through the one man Jesus Christ . . . justification and life for all men . . . the many will be made righteous . . . grace abounded all the more . . . grace also might reign through righteousness leading to eternal life through Jesus Christ our Lord. (Rom 5:15–21 ESV)

Paul is saying that if Christ died for us when we were utterly incapacitated to contribute to the saving outcomes we enjoy (justification, reconciliation, salvation from wrath), then we must conclude that—just as in Adam all die—in Christ we enjoy a wholly free and gracious justification based upon his comprehensively effective mediation. The conclusion from *this* conclusion must await a few chapters of explanatory material (Rom 6–7), but Paul says it very succinctly: "There is therefore now no condemnation for those who are in Christ Jesus" (8:1 ESV).

Part of what makes this understanding of 5:12–21 work is a particular analysis of its internal structure and its subsequent main point. As I have already stated, the main point of 5:12–21 is not exactly the comparison of Christ to Adam. The comparison serves to underline Paul's real point that Christ's mediation on our behalf—while we were yet God's enemies—was categorically effective wholly apart from our personal involvement through our works in obedience to the law.

Almost all interpreters today see that 5:12 introduces a comparison that is broken off in order for Paul to explain important material (5:12b–14) and to qualify how Adam and Christ are *not* comparable (5:15–17), before resuming the comparison in 5:18–21.[58] Paul signals that he is resuming his point introduced in 5:12 in two ways. First, he repeats the introductory phrase of 5:12 (ὥσπερ δι' ἑνὸς ἀνθρώπου

58. So commentaries by Dunn, Wright, and Moo; cf. Cranfield, Michel, Murray, and F. Blass, Albert Debrunner, and Robert W. Funk, *A Greek Grammar of the New Testament and Other Early Christian Literature* (Chicago: University of Chicago Press, 1961), §451.1.

. . . εἰς πάντας ἀνθρώπους) with only slight variation in 5:18 (ὡς δι' ἑνὸς παραπτώματος εἰς πάντας ἀνθρώπους). Repeating the substance of an earlier statement is one way an author signals a return to a suspended point.[59] Second, Paul introduces 5:18 with the conjunctive combination ἄρα οὖν (so then [NASB]). Versions that render ἄρα οὖν as "therefore" (AV, ESV, NRSV) or "consequently" (NIV) do not express the nuance well, since this makes 5:18 seem like a conclusion from the foregoing rather than Paul bringing us back after a digression: "Now then! [back to the point]."[60] Paul uses ἄρα οὖν together with the same function, for example, in 7:25 (resuming the discussion in 7:15–18) and 8:12 (resuming the point of 8:4–5).

It is important to understand ἄρα οὖν correctly in 5:18, because it shows that the main point of 5:12–21 is expressed in 5:18–21. We often focus on the earlier section, particularly on the densely packed 5:12, at the expense of fuller examination of 5:18–21, which is the heart of the issue and a particularly clear expression of Christ's substitutionary mediation in both its positive and negative aspects—what is termed in Reformed theology as the active and passive obedience of Christ elaborated elsewhere in this volume. It is also here that Paul's view of justification is further elaborated.

Justification cannot rely in any way upon personal obedience to God's law. Interpreters sometimes point to Paul's expression *the obedience of faith* in 1:5 as communicating that *our* obedience expressed as covenant fidelity is the operative means for our justification.[61] They may further point to πίστις (faith) also communicating "faithfulness" and try to blend the two meanings together,[62] but in our Romans text Paul clearly attributes our "justification of life"—which is contrasted with "condemnation" in Adam—to the obedient performance of righteousness (δικαίωμα) through the one man, Jesus Christ (5:18). In all

59. One of the clearest and most interesting examples of this is Eph 2:1, which introduces an idea with καὶ ὑμᾶς ὄντας νεκροὺς τοῖς παραπτώμασιν καὶ ταῖς ἁμαρτίαις ὑμῶν and does not give its main verb until 2:5 after repetition of the same words with slight variation: καὶ ὄντας ἡμᾶς νεκροὺς τοῖς παραπτώμασιν συνεζωοποίησεν [= main verb governing accusative participle phrase in 2:1 and in 2:5] τῷ Χριστῷ.

60. Cf. J. D. Denniston, *The Greek Particles* (2nd ed.; Oxford: Clarendon, 1978), 32–43.

61. For recent discussion, see Moo, *Romans*, 51–53; cf. C. E. B. Cranfield, *The Epistle to the Romans* (International Critical Commentary; Edinburgh: Clark, 1975), 1.66–67. The same phrase occurs in Rom 16:26, but the authenticity of the text is uncertain.

62. E.g., both points are made by Wright, *What Saint Paul Really Said*, 45, 109, 160.

of Romans 5, we have been led inexorably to see that our justification and all of its soteriological concomitants have no dependence upon our personal performance of the law's demands whatsoever, but are wholly dependent on our mediator's effective intervention, which we appropriate by faith alone.

Hence, Paul can unequivocally denominate us as "those who receive the abundance of grace and *the free gift of righteousness* . . . through the one man Jesus Christ" (5:17 ESV, emphasis added). When Paul says that we receive righteousness as a gift, he is expressing what Protestants have all along described as the imputation of Christ's righteousness to sinners *sola gratia, sola fide*. Righteousness is bestowed upon us as a divine gift.[63] To deny this and to attribute even a part of our righteousness to our own obedience to the law's demands is to make Christ's death pointless and to nullify God's grace (Gal 2:21; cf. 3:21; 5:1–6). Christ's substitutionary mediation is nowhere more clearly expressed by Paul than when he says, "I have been crucified with Christ. It is no longer I who live, but Christ who lives in me" (2:20 ESV).

Both Dunn and Wright work very hard to show that the phrase *the righteousness of God* (δικαιοσύνη θεοῦ) in Romans 1:17 and elsewhere (Rom 3:21–22; 10:3; 2 Cor 5:21) refers to God's own fidelity to his covenant promises. It may not be immediately clear why this is so important to them, but it appears that they see this as the Protestant claim of imputed righteousness: that somehow God's own righteousness is imputed to us directly. Wright expresses this most clearly when he discusses righteousness and justification in an imagined Hebrew law court: "To imagine the defendant somehow receiving the judge's righteousness is simply a category mistake. That is not how the language works." God's people will be justified, "*but the righteousness they have will not be God's own righteousness*. That makes no sense at all. God's own righteousness is his covenant faithfulness."[64] This is nice rhetoric, but it misses the point entirely. The Protestant understanding of imputed righteousness is that we receive the gift of *Christ's*

63. Cf. Rom 5:11, where it is said that we also receive reconciliation: τὴν καταλλαγὴν ἐλάβομεν.

64. Wright, *What Saint Paul Really Said*, 98–99 (emphasis original). Cf. Dunn, *Romans 1–8*, 40–42.

righteousness through his obedient life and death as Second Adam in our stead. It is the genuinely *human* righteous obedience to all of God's righteous commands as one born under the law (Gal 4:4) that he performed on our behalf and in our stead and, as Paul explicitly says in Romans 5:17, that we receive as a divinely initiated gracious gift through Jesus Christ.[65] "To be in Christ is to have *his* (and only his) faithfulness as the mark of one's own covenant fidelity."[66]

Conclusion

In fairness, the methodological and exegetical weaknesses found in representatives of the new perspective on Paul would be problematic in members of any school. The defenders of the new perspective, however, are energetic and effective rhetoricians, which covers over their interpretive blemishes with an appealing veneer and results in some popular appeal for their ideas.

Paul's forcefully clear focus on Christ's substitutionary mediation in Romans 5 relates to justification. While there is room for a fuller presentation of Paul's doctrine of justification or a fuller discussion of Romans 5 (e.g., Paul's presentation of the law, imputation, transgression, Adam in 5:13–14), I concentrated here on clear and necessary conclusions from Romans 5: the righteousness resulting in divine approval at the last day comes to us as a free gift of the righteousness of Christ as Second Adam and our mediator. It is his obedience to the covenant stipulations of the law imputed to us that forms the only ground of our justification, an eschatological verdict rendered now in Christ. The soteriology offered by Paul's opponents insofar as it is evidenced in Romans (and Galatians)—whether one sees it as Sanders's "covenant nomism" or as any other kind of synthesis that somehow imports our works of obedience into our justification—is just what Paul's teaching in Romans 5 decisively undercuts. Any syn-

65. Paul expressed the same concept in other places as well, even if by slightly different wording; e.g., Rom 10:6; 1 Cor 1:30; Gal 5:5; Phil 3:9; 2 Tim 4:8; and Titus 3:5–7.

66. Bruce W. Longenecker, "Defining the Faithful Character of the Covenant Community: Galatians 2.15–21 and Beyond," in *Paul and the Mosaic Law: The Third Durham-Tübingen Research Symposium on Earliest Christianity and Judaism* (ed. James D. G. Dunn; Tübingen: Mohr, 1996), 83 (emphasis original).

thesis makes Christ's substitutionary life and death gratuitous and undermines God's grace (Gal 2:21).[67]

Justification is indeed based on a human obedience to the law of God, and that loving obedience was entire and perfect in every respect, but no human after Adam—being helpless, impious enemies of God (cf. Rom 3:9–20) who have defaced the divine image and are therefore devoid of the glory of God (3:23)—did or even could ever fulfill God's holy law for righteousness, except one: the one man, Jesus Christ. That is Paul's incontestable message in Romans 5 and has been a continuing hallmark of Reformed interpretation to this day.

Wright begins one of his books by saying, "Covenant theology is one of the main clues, usually neglected, for understanding Paul."[68] By "covenant theology" he probably means the theology of Second Temple Judaism as described by Sanders rather than the thoroughly biblical covenant theology surveyed in this collection. Nevertheless, Wright and other new perspective proponents have indeed done New Testament scholarship a service by discussing justification as a decidedly covenant issue. This is precisely the insight of confessional Reformed theology, whose insights should no longer be overlooked.[69] This is particularly urgent today because of the isolation of Old Testament and New Testament scholarship from each other, which was not the case when the main lines of Reformed covenant theology were being worked out, with its soteriology centering on the suretyship of our covenant mediator Jesus Christ.[70]

67. See esp. James D. G. Dunn, "Paul's Understanding of the Death of Jesus," in *Reconciliation and Hope: New Testament Essays on Atonement and Eschatology Presented to L. L. Morris on His 60th Birthday* (ed. Robert Banks; Grand Rapids: Eerdmans, 1974), 125–41, esp. 139–41, where he raises objections to the idea of Christ's substitution.

68. Wright, *Climax of the Covenant*, xi.

69. See also the remarks of Kim (*Paul and the New Perspective*, 83) in this regard: "The traditional interpretation may need to be augmented by the consideration of the fundamental covenantal dimension of the doctrine of justification which the New Perspectivists stress. It appears that further work is needed to clarify the relationship between the covenantal and forensic dimensions of justification."

70. For a stimulating introduction to an important covenant theologian and biblical scholar, see Willem J. Van Asselt, *The Federal Theology of Johannes Cocceius (1603–1669)* (trans. Raymond A. Blacketer; Leiden: Brill, 2001).

PART 3

Systematic Theology

6
The Covenant before the Covenants

David VanDrunen and R. Scott Clark

Introduction

Those not well read in sixteenth- and seventeenth-century Reformed theology might be forgiven their ignorance of the covenant of redemption or for concluding that it is an arcane doctrine long abandoned. Judging by its absence from some contemporary systematic theologies and its idiosyncratic treatment or rejection in others, one might not realize that the eternal covenant of redemption (*pactum salutis*), also known as the counsel of peace (the Vulgate translates עֲצַת שָׁלוֹם in Zech 6:13 as *consilium pacis*), among the trinitarian persons was not only one of the most fascinating aspects of the development of Reformed federalism in the sixteenth and seventeenth centuries, but also one of the most important and widely taught aspects of Reformed covenant theology and a cornerstone of its soteriology.[1]

1. Since the late 1960s several monographs on covenant theology have appeared wherein the discussion has centered entirely on the *historia salutis*. Writers from a variety of perspectives

In Reformed theology, the *pactum salutis* has been defined as a pretemporal, intratrinitarian agreement between the Father and Son in which the Father promises to redeem an elect people. In turn, the Son volunteers to earn the salvation of his people by becoming incarnate (the Spirit having prepared a body for him), by acting as the surety (ἔγγους, *sponsor*, *fideiussor*, or *expromissor*) of the covenant of grace for and as mediator of the covenant of grace to the elect. In his active and passive obedience, Christ fulfills the conditions of the *pactum salutis* and fulfills his guarantee (*sponsio*, *vas*, or *fideiussio*), ratifying the Father's promise, because of which the Father rewards the Son's obedience with the salvation of the elect. And because of this, the Holy Spirit applies the Son's work to his people through the means of grace.

For the Son, the *pactum salutis* is a legal/works covenant of obligation, merit, and reward wherein, as Louis Berkhof says, "eternal life could only be obtained by meeting the demands of the law." In this, God the Son incarnate served as our representative, surety, sponsor, and guarantee. With respect (considered prospectively) to sinners,

omit any discussion of the *pactum salutis*; see Jacob Jocz, *The Covenant: A Theology of Human Destiny* (1968; repr. Eugene, OR: Wipf & Stock, 1999); Delbert R. Hillers, *Covenant: The History of a Biblical Idea* (Baltimore: Johns Hopkins University Press, 1969); C. K. Campbell, *God's Covenant* (Phillipsburg, NJ: P&R, 1974), who uses the term *covenant of redemption* strictly to denote the *historia salutis*; John M. Zinkand, *Covenants: God's Claims* (Sioux Center, IA: Dordt College Press, 1984); Thomas Edward McComiskey, *The Covenants of Promise: A Theology of the Old Testament Covenants* (Grand Rapids: Baker, 1985); C. Van Der Waal, *The Covenantal Gospel* (Neerlandia, AB: Inheritance Publications, 1990); Clarence Stam, *The Covenant of Love: Exploring Our Relationship with God* (Winnipeg: Premier, 1999); Rowland S. Ward, *God and Adam: Reformed Theology and the Creation Covenant* (Wantirna, Australia: New Melbourne Press, 2003); Donald G. Bloesch, *God the Almighty: Power, Wisdom, Holiness, and Love* (Downers Grove, IL: InterVarsity, 1995); idem, *Jesus Christ: Savior and Lord* (Downers Grove, IL: InterVarsity, 1997); Gordon J. Spykman, *Reformational Theology: A New Paradigm for Doing Dogmatics* (Grand Rapids: Eerdmans, 1992); Dewey D. Wallace Jr., "Federal Theology," in *The Encyclopedia of the Reformed Faith* (ed. Donald K. McKim; Louisville: WJK, 1992); Peter A. Lilback, "Covenant," in *New Dictionary of Theology* (ed. Sinclair B. Ferguson and David F. Wright; Downers Grove, IL: InterVarsity, 1988), who makes only a passing reference to the *pactum salutis*; Hendrikus Berkof, *Christian Faith: An Introduction to the Study of the Faith* (trans. Sierd Woudstra; Grand Rapids: Eerdmans, 1979), who mentions (and rejects) the covenant of works but ignores the *pactum salutis* completely; Jürgen Moltmann, *Trinity and the Kingdom* (trans. Margaret Kohl; Minneapolis: Fortress, 1993), 83, 111–28, who writes of intratrinitarian relations in Hegelian terms so that history is not so much the outworking of the divine counsel of redemption as it is the self-realization of God and the inclusion of humanity with him; and Otto Weber, *Foundations of Dogmatics* (trans. Darrel L. Guder; 2 vols.; Grand Rapids: Eerdmans, 1981), who is aware of federal theology but does not mention the *pactum salutis*.

however, it is a gracious covenant, the condition of which is extra-spective faith.[2]

The function of the *pactum salutis* in Reformed theology is, first, to synthesize and explain a series of biblical passages that indicate a pretemporal covenant of the sort described above. Second, it accounts for the covenants of works and grace in Scripture being not mere conventions or *nomina*, but rather covenants made in history being grounded in the nature of the intratrinitarian relations. Third, and most important for this volume, the *pactum salutis* provides an essential part of the biblical and theological context for the doctrine of active obedience and hence the doctrine of justification. When Jesus Christ earned the righteousness to be imputed to his people, he was fulfilling not only the historical covenant of works as the Second Adam (Rom 5:12–21; 1 Cor 15:45) but also the covenant he made with his Father.

Jacobus Arminius (1560–1609) is sometimes credited with first using the noun *pactum* to describe this arrangement between the Father and the Son.[3] Arminius, however, was not the first to use the term. Rather, it was Johannes Oecolampadius (1482–1531), who in his 1523–24 lectures on Isaiah first spoke of a *pactum* between the Father and "his Son, our Lord Jesus Christ," describing an eternal, legal, intratrinitarian agreement, and again in the early 1530s in lectures on Hebrews.[4] Given that this language and conception

2. Louis Berkhof, *Systematic Theology* (Grand Rapids: Eerdmans, 1939), 268.

3. B. Loonstra, *Verkiezing-Versoening-Verbond: Beschrijving en beoordeling van de leer van het pactum salutis in de gereformeerde theologie* (The Hague: Boekencentrum, 1990), 21–31. In 1603 Arminius was voicing support for the doctrine, but by 1608 he was at least ambivalent toward it. He argued that Christ's righteousness—rather than Christ's obedience—made it possible for our faith to be imputed to us as righteousness. See Jacobus Arminius, *Opera theologica* (Leiden, 1629), 1.16, 39, 66, 963; idem, *The Works of James Arminius* (trans. James Nichols and William Nichols; Grand Rapids: Baker, 1996), 1.343, 365, 410–31; 2.727.

4. Johannes Oecolampadius, *In iesaiam prophetam hypomnematon* (Basle, 1525), 268b: "Pactum cum filio suo domino nostro Ihesu Christo." Two things about the passage in which this language occurs strike the reader. The first is the casual way Oecolampadius introduces the idea. The tone of the passage suggests that he did not consider the idea controversial or novel. The second is that he appeals to the *pactum* between the Father and the Son in support of his exposition of the covenant of grace. In other words, for Oecolampadius, the nature of the covenant of grace is grounded in the *pactum salutis*; see idem, *In epistolam ad hebraeos* (Strasbourg, 1534), 78. See also A. A. Woolsey, "Unity and Continuity in Covenantal Thought: A Study in the Reformed Tradition to the Westminster Assembly" (PhD thesis; Glasgow University, 1988), 1.262.

occur so early in the development of Protestant (and Reformed) theology, rather than thinking of the *pactum salutis* as a late transplant we should think of the *pactum salutis* as indigenous to Reformed theology.[5]

The *pactum salutis* has appeared in every era of Reformed theology and in every region where Reformed theology flourished, beginning in the early orthodox period in Germany (Caspar Olevianus, Zacharias Ursinus), Switzerland (Amandus Polanus), and the Netherlands (William Ames, Gijsbertus Voetius, Johannes Cocceius, Abraham Heidanus).[6] In the period of high orthodoxy, it was found in Britain (John Owen, Edward Leigh), Geneva (Francis Turretin), Germany and the Netherlands (Peter Van Mastricht, Franz Burman), and Switzerland (J. H. Heidegger). Throughout the seventeenth and eighteenth centuries, the *pactum salutis* found support among a variety of Reformed schools. For example, both the Cocceians and the Voetians taught it, as did Herman Witsius, who sought to mediate between them. In Scotland, the leader of the so-called Marrow men, Thomas Boston, taught the *pactum salutis*, and Jonathan Edwards, the leader of the New Side revival, taught it in New England. In the nineteenth century, the *pactum salutis* was a staple of the old-school theology at Princeton (Charles Hodge, A. A. Hodge, B. B. Warfield) and of the southern Presbyterians (John L. Girardeau, Robert L. Dabney). In the early twentieth century, Dutch neo-Calvinists Abraham Kuyper, Herman Bavinck, Geerhardus Vos, and M. J. Bosma all taught the *pactum salutis*.

The thing not to be missed in this taxonomy is that it covers virtually every school, major subgroup, era, and location in the history of the Reformed theology from the late sixteenth century up to the early twentieth century. Support for the *pactum salutis* in the Reformed tradition has been virtually universal and constant until quite recently.

5. Herman Witsius addressed this question in *De oeconomia foederum dei cum hominibus* (Leeuwarden, 1677), 2.2.16; for English translation see *The Economy of the Covenants between God and Man* (trans. William Crookshank; 1803; repr. Phillipsburg, NJ: P&R, 1990).

6. On Olevianus, see R. Scott Clark, *Caspar Olevian and the Substance of the Covenant: The Double Benefit of Christ* (Rutherford Studies in Historical Theology; Edinburgh: Rutherford House, 2005), 168, 177–80, 209.

Confessional Teaching on the Covenant of Redemption

The earlier Reformed confessions did not present a detailed covenant theology in formal terms, but shared many of the assumptions exploited by the more mature covenant theology, including the basic ideas behind the covenant of works and the *pactum salutis*.

The most explicit covenant theology in the Belgic Confession (1561) concerns the covenant of grace. The term *covenant* occurs in the explanation of the sacraments. Baptism is, according to the Latin text adopted at Dort (1619), a "sign of the covenant" (*signum foederis*) (Schaff 3.427).[7] Bearing in mind the theological context in which the confession was written, we should not miss the import for covenant theology of terms such as *mediator* and *high priest*. When, according to the Belgic Confession, did Jesus become our "high priest forever" and mediator (21)? According to Belgic Confession 26, the Father has "constituted" (*constituit*) the Son as "mediator" between "himself and us" (Schaff 3.413).[8] The confession regards this constituting as eternal, interpersonal, legal, and covenantal.

The formal covenant theology of the Heidelberg Catechism (1563) was also rudimentary. The terms *testament* and *covenant* (*Bund* in the German edition and *foedus* in the Latin) occur only in conjunction with questions concerning the sacraments (HC 68, 77, 79, 82, 84).[9] The Heidelberg Catechism assumed the covenant of works/covenant of grace scheme taught by Ursinus and Olevianus. In this context, then, we should read the catechism's references to Christ as mediator (e.g., HC 15, 18) as implying the *pactum salutis*. This is especially true regarding the catechism's reference to Christ's office as high priest (HC 31), which teaches the foreordination of Christ as the revealer of God's "secret counsel and will . . . concerning our redemption" and our "only high priest."[10] This language reveals the same conceptual

7. The Latin text is found in J. N. Bakhuizen Van Den Brink, ed., *De nederlandsche belijdenisgeschriften* (Amsterdam: Uitgeversmaatschappij Holland, 1945), 129.

8. Ibid., 109.

9. Schaff 3.329–37 (German-English text); H. A. Niemeyer, *Collectio confessionum in ecclesiis reformatis publicatorum* (Leipzig, 1840) (Latin text).

10. Schaff 3.317; Niemeyer, *Collectio confessionum*, 437. If it is objected that the term *pactum salutis* does not occur in the Heidelberg Catechism and thus it is improper to interpret it to teach the *pactum salutis*, we respond by noting that the Heidelberg Catechism also does

framework that supported the *pactum salutis* in orthodox Reformed theology.

The Canons of Dort (1619), however, were more explicit. In 1.7, as part of the definition of election, synod ruled that the Reformed churches believe that God has "elected . . . a certain number of persons . . . to salvation in Christ." Christ is he "whom also, from eternity, God constituted mediator and head of all the elect, and the ground of salvation." This was the very language used by the orthodox to teach the *pactum salutis*: "God has decreed to give [them, the elect] to Christ to be saved by him, and effectually to call and draw them . . . by his Word and Spirit" and to give them the benefits of Christ (Schaff 3.582).[11] Canons of Dort 2.2 removes any ambiguity about the commitment of the canons to the *pactum salutis* when it says that God "from his infinite mercy" gives his "only begotten Son as our surety [*sponsor*]" (Schaff 3.586).[12] No one familiar with the basics of Reformed orthodoxy in this period could miss the force of this language.

The Westminster Divines were even more explicit in their endorsement of the ideas behind the *pactum salutis*. Westminster Confession of Faith 8.1 says that "God, in his eternal purpose, . . . [chose] and ordain[ed]" Christ "to be the Mediator between God and man" to "whom he did, from all eternity, give a people to be his seed, and to be by him in time redeemed, called, justified, sanctified, and glorified" (Schaff 3.619). This is the essence of the *pactum salutis*: that the Father gave a people to the Son upon certain conditions, namely, that the Son should redeem them and that his work should be applied to those elect. Westminster Confession of Faith 8.2 makes it clear that the Son performed those very stipulations as mediator. The confession's conception of the *pactum salutis* is explicitly trinitarian. Christ was not only conceived by the Holy Spirit (WCF 8.2), but he was "thoroughly furnished" by the Holy Spirit "to execute the office of a

---

not use the words *Trinity* or *triune* and yet it would obtuse to refuse to see that doctrine in the catechism.

11. "Ad salutem elegit in Christo, quem etiam ab aeterno Mediatorem et omnium electorum caput, salutisque fundamentum constituit; atque ita eos ipsi salvandos dare, et ad eius communionem per verbum et Spiritum suum efficaciter vocare ac trahere" (Schaff 3.553).

12. "Deus ex immensa misericordia Filium suum unigenitum nobis Sponsorem dedit" (Schaff 3.561).

mediator and surety" (8.3 [Schaff 3.620]).[13] This language reflected the Reformed orthodox doctrine of the *pactum salutis* as expressed in the period.[14]

Modern Literature on the Covenant of Redemption

Geerhardus Vos (1862–1949) taught the *pactum salutis* not only in his 1891 essay but also in the classroom in Grand Rapids, as evidenced by his 1910 *Dogmatiek*.[15] He argued that the work of salvation was covenantal "at its roots" and that the "rest of its unfolding was bound to correspond to it."[16] This had also been the approach of Herman Bavinck.[17]

The theologian of the Netherlands Reformed Congregations, G. H. Kersten (1882–1948), defended the *pactum salutis* as established with Christ as the federal head of the elect.[18] He was highly critical of South

13. The Latin text has *mediatoris vadisque* (mediator and surety). This latter term, *vas, vadis,* is a commercial-legal term denoting a bail or guarantee. It seems to have been relatively rare word in Reformed use, so its appearances here and in Calvin are interesting. See also Johannes Cloppenburg, "Exercitationes super locos communes theologicos," in Cloppenburg's *Theologica opera omnia* (ed. Johannes Marckius; Amsterdam, 1684), 10.2.13, where Christ is described as both *sponsor* and *vas*.

14. A distinction is to be made between Christ's offices as mediator and surety. They are related closely, however, in the Westminster Confession of Faith since in the *pactum salutis* the Son is appointed to be mediator of the covenant of grace. On the relations between these two offices, see John Owen, *The Works of John Owen* (ed. W. H. Goold; Edinburgh: Johnstone & Hunter, 1850–53), 21.495–512. On the Spirit's role in the *pactum salutis* in Reformed theology, see Carl R. Trueman, *The Claims of Truth: John Owen's Trinitarian Theology* (Carlisle: Paternoster, 1998), 96–97, 133–40, 146–50.

15. Geerhardus Vos, *Dogmatiek* (Grand Rapids: N.P., 1910), 2.88–90.

16. Geerhardus Vos, "Doctrine of the Covenant in Reformed Theology," in *Redemptive History and Biblical Interpretation: The Shorter Writings of Geerhardus Vos* (ed. Richard B. Gaffin Jr.; Phillipsburg, NJ: Presbyterian & Reformed, 1980), 252. William Hendriksen (1900–1982) followed this view in *The Covenant of Grace* (Grand Rapids: Eerdmans, 1932).

17. See Herman Bavinck, *Magnalia dei* (Kampen: Kok, 1909), 261; idem, *Our Reasonable Faith* (trans. Henry Zylstra; Grand Rapids: Baker, 1956), 273.

18. G. H. Kersten, *Reformed Dogmatics: A Systematic Treatment of Reformed Doctrine* (1947; repr. Grand Rapids: Netherlands Reformed Book and Publishing Committee, 1980), 1.233–58. He recognized that there were "sound divines" who taught that the covenant of grace is established with the elect (and taught the internal/external distinction) and should be regarded as anti-Arminian and anti-Pelagian (1.237). On the debates in the *Christelijke Gereformeerde Kerken in Nederland* on these issues, see J. Van Genderen, *Covenant and Election* (Neerlandia, AB/Pella, IA: Inheritance Publications, 1995). On the doctrinal distinctives of the liberated, see Jelle Faber, "The Liberation: The Doctrinal Aspect," in *The Liberation: Causes and Consequences: The Struggle in the Reformed Churches in the Netherlands in the 1940s* (ed. Cornelis Van Dam; Winnipeg: Premier, 1995), 1–29.

African theologian J. A. Heyns (1928–94) and Gereformeerde Kerken Nederland (Vrijgemaakt/Liberated) theologian Klaas Schilder (1890–1952) among others for distinguishing between the *pactum salutis* and the covenant of grace[19] and also for failing to distinguish between those who are in the covenant of grace only externally and those who are in the covenant of grace both externally and internally.[20] As a result, in Schilder's view, all baptized persons, elect and nonelect, are in the covenant of grace "head for head" in precisely the same way. One is either baptized and therefore in "the covenant"—or not. It is *alles of niks* (all or nothing), to use Schilder's famous expression. The results of Schilder's view were that the covenant of grace could be "broken" such that Schilder seemed to make remaining in "the covenant" (for Schilder there was only one) a matter of works, and further Schilder had the Son acting as "the Surety of the covenant" for elect and reprobate alike.[21]

Louis Berkhof (1873–1957) affirmed and defended the covenant of redemption, adopting the three-covenant view.[22] He recognized that

19. The approach Kersten takes in not distinguishing the *pactum salutis* from the covenant of grace has a long and honorable pedigree, but it is not our approach, in which the *pactum salutis* and the covenant of grace are distinguished clearly without divorcing them. For example, Caspar Olevianus, Herman Witsius, and Charles Hodge taught the *pactum salutis* within a three-covenant scheme (i.e., *pactum salutis*, covenant of works, covenant of grace), whereas Zacharias Ursinus, the Westminster Larger Catechism, and A. A. Hodge taught the *pactum salutis* within a two-covenant scheme (i.e., covenant of works, covenant of grace). Both approaches have been used by orthodox Reformed theologians, and the thing to emphasize here is that both approaches held and taught the *pactum salutis*. The differences were *pedagogical* not *theological*.

20. Citing Calvin, Gomarus, Voetius, Van Mastrict, and others, Kersten argues for the traditional distinction between those who are in the covenant of grace "internally" and those reprobates and hypocrites who have merely an "external" relation to the covenant of grace. Those whom Scripture describes as having "broken" the covenant (Gen 17:14; Jer 31:32; Hos 6:7; 8:1) are those who have been initiated into the covenant of grace (1 Cor 10:1–5; John 15; 2 Pet 2:1) and who have become responsible persons before God; see *Reformed Dogmatics*, 1.250–55. See also R. Scott Clark, "Baptism and the Benefits of Christ: The Double Mode of Communion in the Covenant of Grace," *Confessional Presbyterian* 2 (2006): 3–19.

21. Ibid., 1.236; see also 235, 252. R. L. Dabney makes this same criticism in *Lectures in Systematic Theology* (Grand Rapids: Zondervan, 1972), 432. If Kersten's analysis is correct, Schilder's approach to covenant theology would seem to have paved the way for the so-called Auburn Avenue or federal-vision theology (see chapter 9 below). On Schilder's covenant theology, see J. Mark Beach, "The Doctrine of the *pactum salutis* in the Covenant Theology of Herman Witsius," *Mid-America Journal of Theology* 13 (2002): 111–13; and S. A. Strauss, "Schilder on the Covenant," in *Always Obedient: Essays on the Teachings of Klaas Schilder* (ed. J. Geertsma; Phillipsburg, NJ: P&R, 1995). For a review of modern *Afscheiding* thought on covenant and baptism, see Jelle Faber, *American Secession Theologians on Covenant and Baptism* (Neerlandia, AB/Pella, IA: Inheritance Publications, 1996).

22. Berkhof, *Systematic Theology*, 266–71.

the term *pactum salutis* was not in Scripture, but he argued that the substance of the doctrine is present (i.e., contracting parties, promises, and conditions). The *pactum salutis* is a sort of archetype for the historical covenants. He argued that the eternal plan was *covenantal* in form on the basis of the promises made to Christ (John 5:30, 43; 6:38–40; 17:4–12), most particularly Luke 22:29.[23] Following Cocceius and others, he noted the verbal connection in Jesus's language between the verb διέθετο (to appoint) and the noun διαθήκη (covenant). He argued in defense of the Voetian view that Christ as *expromissor* (as distinct from *fideiussor*) earned complete forgiveness (ἄφεσις) rather than a mere overlooking (πάρεσις) of the sins of Old Testament believers. For Berkhof, the *pactum salutis* entailed that the Son appeared "in this covenant" as surety, head of his people, and the Last Adam and did "what Adam failed to do by keeping the law and thus securing eternal life" for the elect. This is the ground of the active obedience of Christ in which he entered into natural, penal, and federal relations to the law in order to merit eternal life for his people.[24]

Since the middle of the twentieth century, reception of the *pactum salutis* among Reformed theologians has been mixed, and it has received more than one idiosyncratic reformulation. According to Herman Hoeksema (1886–1965) the *pactum salutis* (he preferred "counsel of peace") is "the eternal decree of God to reveal His own Triune covenant life in the highest possible sense of the word in the establishment of and realization of a covenant outside of Himself with the creature in the way of sin and grace, of death and redemption, to the glory of His holy name."[25] Though retaining the expression *pactum salutis*, he rejected the essence of the traditional doctrine as a legal transaction involving "mutual stipulations, conditions and promises."[26] He distinguished between the "covenant God establishes with Christ as the Servant of the Lord" and "the eternal covenant of the Three Persons of the Holy Trinity." He charged that the traditional

23. Perhaps *prototype* might be a better word here than *archetype* since, in Reformed theology, what is archetypal belongs to God and the *pactum salutis* is revealed and therefore ectypal and belongs to us (Deut 29:29 [MT 29:28]).

24. Berkhof, *Systematic Theology*, 269.

25. Herman Hoeksema, *Reformed Dogmatics* (Grand Rapids: Reformed Free Publishing, 1966), 330.

26. Ibid., 292.

failure to make this distinction has led to the practical denial of "the co-equality of the Son with the Father."[27]

The biblical passages traditionally cited for the *pactum salutis* really apply to the covenant between the Father and the Son, not to the *pactum salutis* as Hoeksema conceived of it. It is clear that Hoeksema taught that there was an eternal arrangement between the Father and the Son, with the Son as the head of the elect for their redemption. He simply wanted to strip that arrangement of the title *pactum salutis* and of any contractual implications. Of course, this criticism flowed from his definition of covenant as "the communion of friendship."[28] According to Hoeksema, implicit in Berkhof's formulation was an unintentional "denial of the Trinity" and subordination of the Son to the Father, making the work of redemption the Father's alone. He advocated a covenant between the triune God and Christ.[29] In his redefinition of the *pactum salutis*, however, it is apparent that he did exactly what Vos rejected, making it nothing other than a "reworking of the doctrine of election."[30]

In his famous excursus on federal theology in the *Church Dogmatics* 4/1, Karl Barth (1886–1968) expressed cautious appreciation for aspects of traditional Reformed federalism, but rejected much of it as unbiblical.[31] He rejected the covenant of redemption and the classic distinction between the covenant of works and the covenant of grace as legalistic. In particular he criticized the *innergöttlichen Pakt*, asking provocatively:

> Can we really think of the first and second persons of the triune Godhead as two divine subjects and therefore as two legal subjects who can have dealings and enter into obligations with one another? This is mythology, for which there is no place in a right understanding of the doctrine of the Trinity as the doctrine of the three modes of

27. Ibid., 319, 297.

28. Ibid., 318, 322.

29. Ibid., 293.

30. Geerhardus Vos, "The Doctrine of the Covenant in Reformed Theology," in *Redemptive History and Biblical Interpretation: The Shorter Writings of Geerhardus Vos* (ed. Richard B. Gaffin Jr.; Phillipsburg, NJ: Presbyterian & Reformed, 1980), 251.

31. Karl Barth, *Church Dogmatics* (trans. G. W. Bromiley; Edinburgh: Clark, 1956), 4/1.54–78.

> being of the one God, which is how it was understood and presented in Reformed orthodoxy itself.[32]

Barth did understand the tension between the traditional covenant theology and his reformulation of it. He did not seem to see the irony of claiming to uphold the Reformed tradition concerning "modes of being" (a groundless assertion) and his rejection of one of the principal expressions of the Reformed doctrine of the Trinity, the *pactum salutis*.

John Murray (1898–1975) also adopted a definition of covenant that precluded the sort of conditional or legal relations entailed in the traditional view. Using the postdiluvian Noahic covenant as his paradigm, he defined covenant as a "sovereign administration of grace and promise."[33] Further, he restricted the term *covenant* to purely "temporal administration," arguing that it is "not strictly proper to use a biblical term to designate something to which it is not applied in the Scripture itself."[34]

In his 1980 covenant theology, O. Palmer Robertson also adopted a definition of covenant ("a bond in blood sovereignly administered") that precluded the *pactum salutis*. He argued that the eternal counsel of God should not be construed as a "pre-creation covenant between Father and Son" because a "sense of artificiality flavors effort to structure in covenant terms the mysteries of God's eternal counsels." To speak of a *pactum salutis* "is to extend the bounds of scriptural evidence beyond propriety."[35]

Bert Loonstra's 1990 monograph explores the *pactum salutis* from historical, biblical, and systematic perspectives.[36] His diachronic survey of the history of the doctrine argues that the *pactum salutis* was developed as a response to Arminian universalism.[37] In the

32. Ibid., 65. The English translation *intertrinitarian* is infelicitous at best; see Karl Barth, *Die kirchliche Dogmatik* (Zürich: Evangelischer Verlag, 1953), 4/1.69.

33. John Murray, *The Covenant of Grace* (London: Tyndale, 1953), 31.

34. John Murray, *Collected Writings of John Murray* (Edinburgh: Banner of Truth, 1976–82), 2.130–31.

35. O. Palmer Robertson, *The Christ of the Covenants* (Phillipsburg, NJ: P&R, 1980), 4, 54.

36. For a critical analysis of Loonstra's *Verkiezing-Versoening-Verbond*, see Hans Boersma's review in *Calvin Theological Journal* 26 (1991): 241–44.

37. Loonstra, *Verkiezing-Versoening-Verbond*, 28–31.

biblical and systematic sections, Loonstra rejects any location of the *pactum salutis* in the being of God and proposes a revision of the traditional *pactum salutis* by removing any notion of contract from covenant theology, excluding Christ's suretyship. According to Loonstra, the traditional construction has the two divine parties equal in the contracting but unequal in the administration of the *pactum salutis*, which tends toward Nestorianism.[38] Loonstra wants to reshape the *pactum salutis* to focus on the history of redemption in Christ and to serve as an account of the Son's voluntary self-humiliation.[39]

In 1993 Robert Letham claimed that Johannes Cocceius invented the *pactum salutis* in 1648 and criticized the doctrine for omitting the Holy Spirit, introducing elements of subordinationism with respect to the Son, and containing tendencies to tritheism.[40] In his 1994 *Systematic Theology*, Wayne Grudem essentially restated the classic view of the *pactum salutis*, but made more explicit than some (e.g., Berkhof) the role of the Spirit in the *pactum salutis*.[41] Bastiaan Wielenga criticized the traditional Reformed doctrine of the *pactum salutis*, arguing instead that, in the Old Testament, the covenant of peace is nothing but the Noahic covenant, which is part of the Abrahamic covenant.[42] Robert Reymond addressed the *pactum salutis* as a way of accounting for the economic subordination of the Son and identified it with the divine plan of salvation.[43] He also used it as a synonym for the "eternal order of the decrees."[44] He did not, however, define the *pactum salutis*, nor did he describe its exact relations to the historical covenants. Meredith Kline taught and defended the *pactum salutis* from an exegetical perspective, as part of his research into the historical administration of the covenants

38. Ibid., 343–45.

39. Ibid., 347–51.

40. Robert W. Letham, *The Work of Christ* (Downers Grove, IL: InterVarsity, 1993), 53, who cites and follows G. C. Berkouwer, *Divine Election* (trans. Hugo Bekker; Grand Rapids: Eerdmans, 1960), 162.

41. Wayne Grudem, *Systematic Theology* (Grand Rapids: Zondervan, 1994), 519.

42. Bastiaan Wielenga, "Over het vredesverbond als noachitisch verbond: *pactum salutis* in Vetere Testamento," *In die Skriflig* 30 (1996): 457–69.

43. Robert L. Reymond, *A New Systematic Theology of the Christian Faith* (Nashville: Nelson, 1998), 227–28, 337–38.

44. Ibid., 502.

of works and grace.[45] J. Mark Beach called attention to the *pactum salutis* in the theology of Herman Witsius.[46] Most recently, S. M. Baugh has published a vigorous exegetical defense of the *pactum salutis* based on his interpretation of Galatians 3:15–20, which shall be considered below, and Michael S. Horton has restated the classic Reformed view.[47]

Criticisms of the pactum salutis

Since the middle of the twentieth century, five major criticisms have been leveled against the covenant of redemption:

- It is speculative, unbiblical, rationalist, and even grotesque.[48]
- It confuses the ontological Trinity with the economic Trinity.
- It tends to tritheism.
- Its biblical proofs refer not to pretemporal, intratrinitarian relations but to redemptive history.
- It ignores the person of the Holy Spirit and construes redemption in binatarian terms.

In response, we argue that the traditional doctrine of the *pactum salutis* is essentially correct and necessary not only to understand Reformed federal theology properly but also to provide the best explanation of a series of biblical passages.

Biblical Teaching on the Covenant of Redemption

The Reformed tradition developed the doctrine of the covenant of redemption under the conviction that it accurately expresses the

45. Meredith G. Kline, *Kingdom Prologue: Genesis Foundations for a Covenantal Worldview* (Overland Park, KS: Two Age Press, 2000), 145; idem, *Glory in Our Midst: A Biblical Theological Reading of Zechariah's Night Visions* (Overland Park, KS: Two Age Press, 2001), 219–40.

46. Beach, "Doctrine of the *pactum salutis*."

47. S. M. Baugh, "Galatians 3:20 and the Covenant of Redemption," *Westminster Theological Journal* 66 (2004): 49–70.; and Michael S. Horton, *God of Promise: Introduction Covenant Theology* (Grand Rapids: Baker, 2006), 78–82, 87.

48. Cornelius Plantinga describes the *pactum salutis* as "grotesque," in "The Threeness/Oneness Problem of the Trinity," *Calvin Theological Journal* 23 (1988): 37–38.

teaching of Scripture, and, as we shall see, this conviction was correct. Taken together, three principal points establish the main contours of the doctrine. First, Scripture describes the relationship between the Father and Son as one conditioned on the obedience of the Son with the promise of a reward upon obedience. Second, this relationship is portrayed in Scripture as covenantal in nature. Finally, this covenant is properly understood in Scripture as established in eternity, even while executed in time.

A Relationship of Obedience and Reward

The catholic doctrine of the Trinity holds that the God who is one is also three distinct persons or subsistences and that these persons exist eternally in perichoretic (i.e., the Son is eternally begotten, the Spirit is eternally proceeding) personal relations with one another. That such relations exist, specifically here between the Father and the Son, seems justified, given the copious material in Scripture, and particularly in the Gospel of John, testifying to the conscious fellowship between them. The crucial and more difficult question is how to describe the nature of this relationship. Scripture describes this relationship as one in which the Father promises a reward to the Son upon his fulfilling the condition of perfect obedience, which condition the Son accepts voluntarily on behalf of his people. More specifically, the Father promises to the Son, by the power of the Holy Spirit, both his own exaltation and the salvation of a people to share in his glory, to be given on the basis of the Son's obedience to the will of his Father.[49]

That the relationship of Father and Son entailed *some* sort of obedience on the part of the Son to his Father's will is clear from many places in Scripture. In John, for example, Christ speaks of the commandment(s) (ἐντολή, ἐντέλλω) given to him by the Father (10:18; 12:49; 14:31; 15:10) and of finishing the work that his Father entrusted to him (17:4). Both Paul and the author of the epistle to the Hebrews speak of the "obedience" that Christ rendered during his earthly sojourn (Phil 2:8; Heb 5:8). Hebrews also adds, in interpreta-

49. See Charles Hodge, *Systematic Theology* (New York: Scribner, Armstrong, 1873), 2.360.

tion of Psalm 40, that Christ came to do the "will" of his Father (Heb 10:5–10). Therefore, that Christ was offering obedience to the will and commandments of his Father seems unobjectionable.

A more challenging question is how to describe the context of that obedience. Why exactly was Christ obeying and what were its consequences? The Reformed doctrine of the covenant of redemption posits that Christ obeyed in order to obtain from his Father a reward: his exaltation and the salvation of a chosen people. Hence, Christ's obedience was the *cause* of the reward bestowed such that his obedience is meritorious in the eyes of his Father. Witsius puts it succinctly yet clearly: "The *obedience* of Christ bears to these *blessings,* not only the relation of *antecedent* to *consequent,* but of *merit* to *reward*; so that his obedience is *the cause,* and *the condition* now fulfilled, by virtue of which he has *a right* to the reward, as several express passages of scripture declare."[50] Two Scripture passages that Witsius mentions in support of this claim, along with a few other texts, are perhaps the most powerful biblical testimonies to the truth of this aspect of the doctrine.

First, the quotation and exposition of Psalm 40:6–8 (MT 40:7–9) in Hebrews 10:5–10 provides initial evidence for the idea that the Son's obedience was the cause of his reward. The context of this passage occurs within a discussion of the perfection of Christ's sacrifice in comparison with the sacrifices of the old covenant. Hebrews 10:1–4 discusses these old covenant sacrifices and concludes that, though they positively served to remind the people of their sin, they could not take sin away, as evidenced by their being offered repeatedly. In 10:5–10, the author contrasts this with Christ's sacrifice, concluding with the claim that Christ's once-for-all sacrifice has provided true sanctification for his people. Important for present purposes, Hebrews grounds this efficacy of Christ's sacrifice in the Son's commitment to accomplish the will of his Father. Hebrews 10:5 identifies Christ as the speaker of Psalm 40, which concludes with the Son's promise: "Behold, *I have come*—it is written about me in the scroll of the book—*to do your will,* O God." Hebrews 10:9, continuing the author's exposition of Psalm

50. Witsius, *Economy of the Covenants,* 1.190 (emphasis original). See also Beach, "Doctrine of the *pactum salutis,*" 129–37.

40, repeats these words without the parenthetical comment: "I have come to do your will." In the conclusion of this pericope, the author brings his reasoning to a head: "By that will we have been sanctified, through the offering of the body of Jesus Christ once-for-all." The author reasons, therefore, that Christ's accomplishment of the will of God, in his atoning sacrifice, is precisely what brought about the Holy Spirit's sanctification of God's people, one aspect of the reward promised to the Son according to the covenant of redemption doctrine. The author's progression of thought here is this: God's will impels Christ's work, Christ's sacrifice fulfills God's will, and the result of Christ's obedient sacrifice is our salvation. The basis of the blessing is Christ's accomplishing his Father's will.

The beautiful conclusion to Isaiah 53 is perhaps even clearer on Christ's obedience to his Father's will as the cause and basis of his reward. In this extended prophecy about the sufferings of the Servant of Yahweh, attention turns in 53:10 to the will of Yahweh, a familiar idea just observed in Hebrews 10. Isaiah 53:10, in fact, speaks of the will of God both as verb and as noun: "Yahweh willed to crush him. . . . The will of Yahweh will flourish in his hand." In these phrases, a similar idea is communicated from different angles. Yahweh wills the suffering of the Servant, and the Servant's actions bring about the accomplishment of Yahweh's will. And Yahweh's will in Isaiah 53:10 is directed at exactly the same thing as it is in Hebrews 10, namely, the offering up of the Messiah for sin. Though even stronger causal language appears in the following verses, already in Isaiah 53:10 the Servant's suffering is described as the basis for subsequent reward: "When [*or* if] his soul makes an offering for sin, / he shall see his offspring; he shall prolong his days; / the will of the Lord shall prosper in his hand" (ESV). Isaiah 53:11 continues the recitation of blessings that will flow out of the Servant's accomplishment of Yahweh's will: not only the seeing of his offspring and the prolongation of his days but also his seeing the light, his satisfaction, and the justification of his people.

Finally, in Isaiah 53:12, the causality becomes explicit: the atoning work of the Servant—identified in 53:10 as Yahweh's will for him—is the cause of the Servant's subsequent victorious exaltation. Isaiah 53:12 begins with a strong causal conclusion: "Therefore [לָכֵן] I will divide him a portion with the many, / and he shall divide the spoil with the strong" (ESV). Isaiah here portrays the Servant as a conquering king, one resembling a warrior who joins the mighty in taking plunder from the vanquished. Why does God appoint the Servant to seize the booty? The use of "therefore" suggests that this appointment is the consequence of what has just been said at the end of 53:11: "He shall bear their iniquities" (ESV). Because the Servant bears his people's sins, God will give him the plunder of the enemy. But the causal language becomes yet more explicit. Immediately following the statement at the beginning of 53:12 concerning the Servant's appointment as the plunder-taking conqueror, Isaiah continues: "Inasmuch as he offered up his soul to death / and was counted with transgressors, / and he bore the sins of many / and makes intercession for transgressors." This phrase begins with a striking expression: Because (תַּחַת אֲשֶׁר)—inasmuch as—the Servant did these things, Yahweh has made him the seizer of spoils. The causal force of this Hebrew phrase is evident in Deuteronomy 28:47–48: "Because [תַּחַת אֲשֶׁר] you did not serve the LORD your God . . . therefore you shall serve your enemies" (ESV). The disobedience was the basis for the curse. Likewise in Isaiah 53:12: the Servant's soul-offering, transgressors-identifying, sin-bearing, intercession-making is the basis for the glorious riches that God will give to him.

A third passage that testifies to the Son's obedience as earning the reward from his Father is Philippians 2:5–11. Many significant doctrinal matters are addressed in this *carmen Christi*, yet perhaps none as significant as the obedience-reward pattern that characterizes the covenant of redemption. The two aspects of the Father-Son relationship under consideration in this section—obedience and reward—dominate this passage. Philippians 2:7–8 speaks explicitly of the Son's obedience: his emptying himself, taking the form of a servant, being found in human appearance, and humbling himself. These verses then conclude with the profound proclamation that he became *obedient* unto death, even the death of the cross. The next verses, however, turn immediately to speak of how God exalted the Son following this obedience, giving him the name above every name so that every knee might bow and tongue confess that Jesus Christ is Lord (2:9–11). Just how does this passage characterize the relationship of the Son's obedience and the Father's exalting him? Curiously, advocates of the federal-vision theology argue that Philippians 2 establishes that the Father exalted the Son as a matter of grace rather than merit or reward, based on the word used for the Father's giving in 2:9, ἐχαρίσατο (bestowed [ESV]), being etymologically related to the common Greek word for "grace" (χάρις).[51] Such an exegetical conclusion rests upon the fallacy that etymological relationship determines the meaning of a word, apart from consideration of the context in which the word appears. In Philippians 2, the context is incompatible with the conclusion that the Father's exaltation of the Son is a gift of grace that excludes the idea of merit. Instead, Paul speaks of the exaltation as the consequence of the obedience and, conversely, the obedience as the cause of the reward. Immediately upon finishing his thoughts on Christ's obedience in 2:8 ("having become obedient unto death, the death of the cross"), Paul uses a strong causal conjunction to make his transition to the exaltation: "And therefore [διό] God exalted him." Why did the Father exalt the Son? Not because he is a gracious God (though he is), but because the Son drank the cup of God's wrath down to the very dregs, because he was obedient even unto the horrific death of the cross.[52] The Son obeyed, and *therefore* his Father exalted him.[53]

51. See Rich Lusk, "A Response to 'the Biblical Plan of Salvation,'" in *The Auburn Avenue Theology, Pros and Cons: Debating the Federal Vision* (ed. E. Calvin Beisner; Fort Lauderdale, FL: Knox Theological Seminary, 2004), 137–38; and James B. Jordan, "Merit versus Maturity: What Did Jesus Do for Us?" in *The Federal Vision* (ed. Steve Wilkins and Duane Garner; Monroe, LA: Athanasius, 2004), 193. Geerhardus Vos, who held a traditional Reformed understanding of the *pactum salutis*, does speak in a way somewhat similar to Lusk and Jordan by noting that ἐχαρίσατο suggests a gracious act on God's part; see *The Pauline Eschatology* (Grand Rapids: Baker, 1979), 275n13. Vos was not, however, throwing out the idea of merit altogether. Immediately before the footnote just cited he writes that "the gracious bestowal of the name above every name upon the Saviour is placed by Paul without the slightest hesitation on the footing of work rendered and value received" (275).

52. N. T. Wright, *The Climax of the Covenant: Christ and the Law in Pauline Theology* (Minneapolis: Fortress, 1992), 86–97, interprets these verses as evidence of Paul's "Adam Christology," wherein Christ is presented as "the obedient man," not only undoing what Adam did (snatching equality with God), but undoing the damage of Adam's snatching but refusing to cling to his divine prerogative. Such a reading is consonant with the argument made here and is quite superior to that offered by Wright's federal-vision followers.

53. Many other passages could be added to the three considered in this section; for example, Heb 2:9; 5:7–10; John 17:4–5; and perhaps Ps 2:7–8. See also Geerhardus Vos, "'Legalism' in Paul's Doctrine of Justification," in *Redemptive History and Biblical Interpretation: The Shorter Writings of Geerhardus Vos* (ed. Richard B. Gaffin Jr.; Phillipsburg, NJ: Presbyterian & Reformed, 1980), 398–99.

A Covenantal Relationship

A second aspect of this intratrinitarian relationship that calls for detailed biblical discussion is its covenantal nature. Even within the Reformed community, where relations between Father and Son, following an obedience-reward pattern, have long been recognized, the propriety of understanding these relations in covenantal terms has been called into question, as noted earlier.[54] Scripture gives multiple lines of warrant for viewing these relations as covenantal: implicit covenantal language, the analogy with God's legal covenant with the First Adam, and explicit covenantal language.

First, Scripture uses implicit covenantal language in describing this relationship. The implicit nature of the language considered in the passages below ought not to be viewed as making this evidence necessarily less persuasive than that from explicit language. Scripture teaches many doctrines without using traditional theological language, but its testimony is nonetheless persuasive. Thus it is in the present case, where some of the most compelling covenantal descriptions of the Father-Son relations speak not of covenant explicitly but of *oath*. Throughout Scripture, covenant and oath bear the closest relations, covenants typically being sealed by oaths and the taking of oaths between parties ordinarily indicating the initiation of covenants.[55] To see the oath-bound character of the relationship between Father and Son is to see its covenantal nature.

Perhaps no better place to begin on this point is Isaiah 45:23, for it connects us directly with the previous section. The closing verses of Philippians 2:5–11 (discussed above to demonstrate the obedience-reward pattern) are a reference to the prophecy of Isaiah 45:23: "For to me every knee will bow, / every tongue will swear." Isaiah presents a promise of what God will do for himself, and Paul

54. Murray, *Collected Writings*, 2.130–31.

55. For literature on the interdependence of covenant and oath, see M. G. Kline, *Treaty of the Great King* (Grand Rapids: Eerdmans, 1963); idem, *The Structure of Biblical Authority* (Grand Rapids: Eerdmans, 1972); idem, *By Oath Consigned* (Grand Rapids: Eerdmans, 1968); G. E. Mendenhall, *Law and Covenant in Israel and the Ancient Near East* (Pittsburgh: Presbyterian Board of Colportage of Western Pennsylvania, 1955); Dennis J. McCarthy, *Treaty and Covenant: A Study in Form in the Ancient Oriental Documents and in the Old Testament* (Analecta biblica 21A; Rome: Pontifical Biblical Institute Press, 1981).

presents this as fulfilled in the reward that God has given to Christ for completing his course of obedience. What Isaiah 45:23 makes clear is that the obedience-reward pattern described in Philippians 2 occurs in oath-bound context: "By myself *I have sworn*; / from my mouth has gone out in righteousness / a word that shall not return: / 'To me every knee shall bow, / *every tongue shall swear* allegiance'" (ESV, emphasis added).

This oath-bound, and hence covenantal, context of the Father-Son relationship is seen also in the rich verses of Psalm 110. In this psalm, the theme of Christ's kingship is pervasive, as well as the themes of conquest and triumph. As king, the promised Messiah is seated at God's right hand (110:1), and his scepter goes forth from Zion as he rules in the midst of his enemies (110:2). As conqueror, he destroys kings and judges the nations (110:5–6). In the mysterious yet awesome closing verse, the Messiah drinks from a brook and lifts up his head—a metaphorical description of one, with no enemies left to defeat, who can refresh himself without fear and stand up in triumph (110:7). All of this hearkens back again to the material in the previous section, where Christ's royal exaltation was part of the reward for his obedience. Further connecting Psalm 110 with the discussion above is its identification of the Messiah not only as a victorious king, but also as a priest (110:4), and therefore as a suffering king. His exaltation cannot be disconnected from his priestly suffering. Therefore, it seems evident that Psalm 110 speaks about the relationship between Father and Son under consideration in this essay, not only by means of prophesying his suffering and exaltation but also by means of the intratrinitarian communication revealed in 110:1 and 110:4. Of special interest, however, is that Psalm 110 speaks of this relationship as oath-bound. As in Isaiah 45:23, the Father seals this relationship with an oath: "The Lord *has sworn* / and will not change his mind, / 'You are a priest forever / after the order of Melchizedek'" (ESV, emphasis added).[56] Thus Psalm 110 also points us to the covenantal nature of this Father-Son relationship. Were the context of Psalm 110

56. Another interesting similarity between Ps 110:4 and Isa 45:23 is God's promise that he will not repent, an idea inherent in an oath but not necessary to say explicitly: "The Lord has sworn / *and will not change his mind*" and "by myself I have sworn . . . / *a word that shall not return*" (ESV, emphasis added).

not enough, Hebrews 7:21–22 explicitly interprets Psalm 110:4 in covenantal terms.[57]

Another piece of evidence for the covenantal nature of the intra-trinitarian relations implicit in the language of Scripture is Christ's frequent practice of calling the Father "my God." Examples of this language can be drawn from both Old Testament prophecy and the New Testament: Psalm 22:1–2 (MT 22:2–3); 40:8 (MT 40:9); 45:7 (MT 45:8); and John 20:17. The high privilege of calling the Almighty "my God" is a covenantal privilege. The great covenant promise echoed throughout Scripture, "I will be your God and you will be my people" (e.g., Jer 31:33; Rev 21:7), captures this point, and the adoption of similar language characterizes various Old Testament covenant renewal ceremonies (e.g., Deut 26:17; Josh 24:18). Also significant here is Hebrews 10:5–10, one of the passages considered above in regard to the obedience-reward pattern, being a quotation and interpretation of one of the passages in which the Son addresses the Father in this covenantal manner (Ps 40:8 [MT 40:9]). The obedience is rendered and the reward is given in the context of covenant.

A third and final example of implicit language in Scripture testifying to the covenantal nature of the Father-Son relationship is the reference to the "counsel of peace" in Zechariah 6:13. Though a popular proof-text for the covenant of redemption in some older Reformed literature, the relevance of this verse is dismissed by many recent Reformed theologians—even by some committed to the doctrine itself.[58] The ESV translates this verse as follows: "It is he [the

57. In Heb 7, the Levitical priests of the weak and useless old covenant (7:11, 18) could not bring consummation precisely because it was never intended that they should (7:19). Jesus introduced a "better hope" (7:19). His priesthood was grounded in the power of his "indestructible life" (7:16) and involved an "oathtaking" (7:20). The writer quotes Ps 110:4, of which he concludes: "This [oath] makes Jesus the *sponsor* of a better covenant" (Heb 7:22). Though the broader context of this passage speaks of the relationship between two administrations of the covenant of grace, the old and new covenants, the discussion in 7:21–22 seems not to be discussing an oath-swearing in history (what incident would be in mind?). Instead, the author suggests a pretemporal oath-swearing that underlies the efficacious character of the new covenant.

58. As examples of those who used this text to support the *pactum salutis*, see Johannes Cocceius, *Summa de foedere*, 5.27 in *Omnia opera* (Amsterdam, 1673), 6.27; Abraham Heidanus, *De origine erroris* (Amsterdam, 1678), 7.2.398; Witsius, *Economy of the Covenants*, 1.167–70; idem, *Exercitationes sacrae in symbolum quod apostolorum dicitur* (Amsterdam, 1697), 14.17.241; Johannes Heidegger, *Corpus theologiae* (Zurich, 1700), 2.12, cited in Heinrich Heppe, *Reformed Dogmatics* (trans. G. T. Thomson; London: Allen & Unwin, 1950), 376; and Johannes Marckius,

Branch—see 6:12] who shall build the temple of the LORD and shall bear royal honor, and shall sit and rule on his throne. And there shall be a priest on his throne, and the counsel of peace [שָׁלוֹם עֲצַת] shall be between them both." The ambiguity in the language is evident even in this English translation: who or what are the "both" between which there is a counsel of peace? Seeing this verse as a reference to the covenant of redemption seems to require that "both" speaks of the messianic Branch and Yahweh—that is, the Son and the Father. Others suggest, however, that "both" refers instead to the kingship and priesthood of Christ the Branch (e.g., Turretin, *Institutes* 2.393 §14.5.6). In other words, the two offices of king and priest, ordinarily separated so that no one person would hold them both, are to be united in the Messiah. While this latter interpretation is happily orthodox, it seems to be a much weaker exegetical option. Two figures are mentioned at the beginning of the verse: the Branch and Yahweh. Explicitly, the Branch will build Yahweh's temple, and thus "his throne" upon which the Branch will sit refers to the throne of Yahweh. Hence, "there shall be a priest on his [Yahweh's] throne." The emphasis of the verse lies upon the work that the Branch does for Yahweh and the honor that Yahweh bestows upon the Branch. The foci of this verse are not abstract notions of king*ship* or priest*hood*, but the concrete persons of Father and Son. The compelling interpretation of the end of 6:13 remains, therefore, that a counsel of peace exists between these two persons—Yahweh and the Branch.

Given that this verse situates us in the context of the Father-Son relationship, the language of "counsel of peace" has subtle, yet strong, covenantal, and legal overtones. Scripture at times associates the taking of counsel with covenant making. Psalm 83:5 (MT 83:6), for example, reads: "For they conspire [נוֹעֲצוּ] with one accord; / against you they make a covenant" (ESV). In addition to this, Scripture also speaks in many places of peace as a defining characteristic or purpose

Compendium theologiae christianae didactico-elencticum (Amsterdam, 1749), 18.18.362. Among those who rejected this text as a support for the *pactum salutis* is Berkhof, *Systematic Theology*, 266. On Cocceius's use of the *pactum salutis*, see Willem J. Van Asselt, *The Federal Theology of Johannes Cocceius (1603–1669)* (Leiden: Brill, 2001), 299–300; and Brian J. Lee, "Biblical Exegesis, Johannes Cocceius, and Federal Thought: Developments in the Interpretation of Hebrews 7:1–10:18" (PhD diss., Calvin Theological Seminary, 2003), 151–53.

of covenantal relationships. In Joshua 9:15 Joshua's making peace with the Gibeonites is bound up in his making a covenant with them. Later, several of the Old Testament prophets use explicit language of a "covenant of peace" to describe God's relationship to his people. Among several other examples (e.g., Ezek 34:25; 37:26; Mal 2:5; and perhaps Zech 9:10–11), Isaiah 54:10 reads: "For the mountains may depart / and the hills be removed, / but my steadfast love shall not depart from you, / and my covenant of peace [בְּרִית שְׁלוֹמִי] shall not be removed, / says the LORD, who has compassion on you" (ESV). Given this Old Testament prophetic background, therefore, the reference in Zechariah 6:13 to a "counsel of peace" strongly suggests a covenant relationship. Beyond the terminology itself, some broader considerations of the teaching of this bolster this conclusion. The description of Christ as both priest and king, in context of Yahweh's relationship to the promised Messiah, evokes recollection of Psalm 110, with its oath formula, considered above.[59] Therefore, Scripture has already indicated that such matters are to be read in covenantal fashion.

A second reason for speaking of the relationship under consideration here as covenantal is the biblical analogy between the First and Second Adams. Paul makes explicit analogy between Adam and Christ in two places: briefly in 1 Corinthians 15:21–22 and more elaborately in Romans 5:12–19. In the latter, Paul shows the similarity between the coming of disobedience and condemnation into the world and the coming of obedience and justification. As the work of one man brought the former, so the work of one man brought the latter. Here we observe the representative, federal principle so important for the doctrine of the covenant of redemption: the Son, on behalf of "the many," obeys his Father so that the many might be righteous. The word *covenant* is not used here or in 1 Corinthians 15, of course. However, that Christ's representative work purposefully resembles that of Adam—or vice versa, as Romans 5:14 suggests—brings us again squarely within the covenantal realm. As explored in another essay in this book, Scripture speaks not only explicitly

59. See M. G. Kline, *Glory in Our Midst: A Biblical-Theological Reading of Zechariah's Night Visions* (Overland Park, KS: Two Age Press, 2001), 219–40.

(Hos 6:7) but also implicitly in many ways of God's dealings with Adam at his creation as a covenant.[60] According to the overwhelming consensus of Reformed theology, Adam's establishment as representative head of the human race, the testing of his obedience, and the promise of eschatological life stands at the heart of this creation covenant. That Christ came as the Second Adam as head of a new humanity, to have his obedience tested and to earn eschatological life, offers strong reason to speak of this in covenantal terms.

A third and final reason for speaking of this relationship of Father and Son as a covenant is grounded in the explicit language of Scripture. Christ himself spoke of his relationship with his Father as covenantal in nature in Luke 22:29 (Turretin, *Institutes* 2.177 §12.2.14). The significance of the language in this verse is likely to be missed if it is read only in English. The profound relationship of the Father and Son is certainly evident even in English renditions: "I assign to you, as my Father assigned to me, a kingdom" (ESV). Luke's use of covenantal language, however, is not easy to communicate in translation. What the ESV translates as "assign" is διατίθεμαι, a verbal form of the New Testament's common word for "covenant," διαθήκη, and indicates activity of covenant conferral (see Acts 3:25; Heb 8:10; 9:16–17; 10:16). In other words, therefore, Christ speaks of his Father conferring a kingdom upon him by way of covenant, and he in turn conferring a kingdom upon his people by way of covenant. The former, of course, is of particular interest here. Both the words of this verse itself and its immediate context suggest its relevance for the very things this essay has been examining. Reading Luke 22:29 along with 22:30 shows that this kingdom that the Father confers upon the Son is an eschatological kingdom that he will enjoy with his people. Thus, here is a similar picture to that seen above concerning the Son's reward: the king in his eternal glory. What is more, 22:28 anticipates 22:29 by speaking of the trials of Christ as the backdrop to this covenantal conferral of an eternal kingdom. Thus, the pattern of suffering obedience followed by an eternal reward is evident in these verses as well, and here the language of covenant is specifically used.

60. On the use of Hos 6:7, see B. B. Warfield, "Hosea VI.7: Adam or Man?" *Bible Student* 8 (1903): 1–10, repr. in *Selected Shorter Writings of Benjamin B. Warfield* (ed. J. E. Meeter; Nutley, NJ: Presbyterian & Reformed, 1970), 2.116–29.

Another example of explicit covenant language used to describe this relationship of Father and Son is Galatians 3:15–22, as S. M. Baugh argues.[61] The words of 3:20, "Now an intermediary implies more than one, but God is one" (ESV), has long baffled interpreters. As Baugh contends, however, Paul's principal point in 3:15–22 is the inability of the Mosaic law to mediate the promise given to Abraham and his seed, whom Paul identifies as Christ. Paul makes his point in two ways. First, in 3:15–18 he draws upon an analogy with human covenants to show that covenants once ratified cannot be annulled or added to. Then, in 3:19–20 he appeals to God's essential unity. Baugh effectively argues how Paul's claim that "a mediator is not of one (party), but God is one," is an argument that the law, with its mediator Moses, is not able to mediate the covenant promise made to Abraham and Christ his seed. The reason is that God the Father, the promisor, and God the Son, the promisee, are one in the divine being. Hence, Paul had in mind the deity of Christ and the intra-trinitarian relations when bringing his argument to a climax in 3:20. Baugh summarizes his exegetical conclusions: "The Father made his promissory oath to the covenant Head in whom all his promises are refracted (2 Cor 1:19–20). And until that One should come into the world, no third party could intervene, because the first two parties to this transaction—the *pactum salutis*—are actually one in inseparable divinity."[62]

In the end, then, the evidence from Scripture points us overwhelmingly to the conclusion that this relationship of Father and Son, characterized by the obedience-reward pattern, ought to be referred to in covenantal terms. As suggested throughout, such covenantal relations among the trinitarian persons entails the *legal* nature of the covenant of redemption. Whether in equilateral (as in the case of Abraham's defense alliance in Gen 14:13) or bilateral covenants (as in the case of the covenant of works with Adam in Gen 2:8–16) conditioned by obedience, there is always a legal aspect to covenantal relations. Thus, in the nature of the case, to speak of "covenantal" relations between trinitarian persons is but another way of saying that

61. S. M. Baugh, "Galatians 3:20 and the Covenant of Redemption," *Westminster Theological Journal* 66 (2004): 49–70.

62. Ibid., 54. Readers are encouraged to read this article for Baugh's full argument.

the Father's promise and the Son's obedience occurred in the context not only of intimate personal fellowship but also legal relations, in the same way that a marriage is simultaneously personal and legal.

An Eternal Covenant

This leaves one final but significant question left to address, albeit more briefly: can we, and in what sense, refer to this covenant of redemption as an *eternal* covenant, as the Reformed tradition has done, and hence distinguish it from the covenant of grace executed by God with his people in time? Some recent Reformed theologians raise objections to the doctrine of the covenant of redemption on this point. They claim that while traditional Reformed teaching has spoken of the *pactum salutis* as an eternal covenant, the typical proof-texts speak instead of the relationship of the Father with the *incarnate* Son and hence as a historical rather than eternal covenant.[63] This objection has some plausibility and deserves a few remarks in response.

No Reformed participants in this discussion would dispute that God has ordained the way of salvation through the work of Christ from all eternity. Ephesians 1:3–14, for example, sets forth redemption in Christ and all its benefits as eternally foreordained. At the very least, this means that the covenantal, obedience-reward patterned relationship examined above was foreordained in the divine council. Ephesians 3:8–12 suggests a similar conclusion. The administration of the mystery (Christ) was kept hidden *from eternity* (3:9), and God has made known his manifold wisdom through the church, in Christ, according to his *eternal* purpose (3:10–11). This eternal mystery/purpose results in time in our enjoying confident access to God by faith (3:12), which is one of the saving benefits won for us by the covenant of redemption. Once again, the things we have considered under the covenant of redemption appear as eternally purposed. Many other passages of Scripture may come to mind about which similar conclusions could be drawn.[64] In addition, Zechariah 6:13 may again be considered. This verse, as seen above, refers to the relationship of

63. E.g., Hoeksema, *Reformed Dogmatics*, 285–336.

64. 2 Thess 2:13; 2 Tim 1:9; and 1 Pet 1:2 are mentioned by Berkhof, *Systematic Theology*, 266.

Father and Son in terms of עֵצָה, a plan or strategy. Whatever execution of their tasks the Father and Son might perform in time, the idea of a plan or strategy indicates that counsel stands behind it.[65] The actions of obedience and reward in time do not exhaust the scope of the covenant of redemption.

The objection has not really been answered yet. Though the covenant of redemption is undoubtedly purposed from eternity, in this it does not differ from the covenant of grace or anything else. The covenant of redemption might be purposed in eternity and yet still be entered into only in time with the incarnate Christ. Several passages of Scripture, however, answer this objection more specifically. The covenant of redemption was not entered into in time with the incarnate Christ, for the *incarnation itself* was a consequence of this covenant, the beginning of Christ's obedience to his Father's will. John 6:38, for example, states that Christ has come down (καταβέβηκα) from heaven *in order to do the will* of the one who sent him. The very obedience observed at the heart of this relationship between Father and Son is set into motion not subsequent to the incarnation, but by it. Such testimony makes it difficult to speak of Christ's coming apart from an already-existing covenantal relationship that he was coming to execute. Hebrews 10:5–7 is similar. Here Christ, adopting the words of the psalmist in Psalm 40, says: "A body you have prepared for me. . . . I have come to do your will, O God." Again, Christ's very act of becoming incarnate by the Holy Spirit cannot be understood except in terms of his covenantal obedience. The Son of God obeyed because that is why he was "sent," as so often described in the Gospels (e.g., Matt 10:40; 15:24; 21:37; Luke 4:18, 43; 10:16; and dozens of times in John).

In addition to these considerations, Hebrews offers reasons for viewing this covenant as eternal. Hebrews 5:5–6 reflects on Psalm 2:7 ("you are my Son, / today I have begotten you" [ESV]) and Psalm 110:4 ("you are a priest forever / after the order of Melchizedek" [ESV]). In Hebrews 7:21 the writer appeals to the intratrinitarian covenant revealed in Psalm 110:4. When, in the conception of Hebrews, did this

65. For other Old Testament examples of this use of עֵצָה, see 2 Sam 15:31; Ps 33:11; Isa 11:2; 19:17; 25:1; 28:29; 40:13; Mic 4:12.

begetting, oath-swearing, and ordination occur? There is no particular event in redemptive history to which these things obviously refer. We are thus driven to understand them as revealed accounts of pretemporal relations that underlie the historical acts of redemption and that Reformed theology has described as the covenant of redemption.

Thus, there is good biblical warrant for speaking of this covenant as an eternal covenant. It was purposed from eternity, and the promise of obedience and reward was established from eternity, so that, in time, the Father might send the Son and the Son might obediently become incarnate and fulfill the work of redemption. The eternal character of this covenant offers one way in which to describe the distinction between the covenant of redemption and the covenant of grace, established in time between God and his people. In considering this, however, the intimate connection between these covenants ought never be lost. As Christ related in Luke 22:29, he has covenanted a kingdom upon his people as his Father has covenanted one upon him. And as passages such as Isaiah 53:10–12 and Hebrews 10:5–10 reveal, the very justification and sanctification of Christ's people (in the covenant of grace) are precisely among the rewards given to Christ upon the completion of his obedience.

Conclusions and Responses to Objections

On the basis of the foregoing historical and exegetical arguments we are prepared to respond briefly to three of the most pressing objections. First, G. C. Berkouwer (1903–96) criticizes the *pactum salutis* as a speculative doctrine.[66] In this case, "speculative" seems to mean something like "not sufficiently grounded in divine revelation." The *pactum salutis* is a deduction resulting from the analysis and synthesis of several biblical passages and strands of revelation. A synthetic doctrine is what Westminster Confession of Faith 1.6 calls a "good and necessary consequence." The alternative would seem to be a sort of Socinian-biblicist approach to theology that neither Berkouwer nor any other significant Reformed theologian has ever followed.

66. G. C. Berkouwer, *Divine Election* (trans. Hugo Bekker; Grand Rapids: Eerdmans, 1960), 162.

Second, and perhaps more substantively, Berkouwer also criticizes the doctrine as tending to tritheism by confusing the economic and ontological distinction.[67] This criticism is ironic because one of the chief theological functions of the covenant of redemption has been to express this very distinction. Indeed, in his essay "The Biblical Doctrine of the Trinity," B. B. Warfield appeals to the *pactum salutis* as a way of explaining "modes of operation" peculiar to the divine persons or subsistences. *Theologoumena* such as the *pactum salutis* are essential to explaining subordinationist passages such as John 14:28: "My Father is greater than I." This language is either economic or ontological. If it is economic, what are the implications? Warfield argues that the subordination evident in John 14 and elsewhere is due more to "a convention, an agreement, between the Persons of the Trinity—a 'Covenant' as it is technically called—by virtue of which a distinct function in the work of redemption is voluntarily assumed by each."[68] Far from confusing a distinction, the *pactum salutis* relies on it. Those who impute ontological subordination of the Son to the Father have lost the distinction. Surely, Berkouwer and Letham would not have us think that the economic distinction has no basis in the divine subsistence.

This question leads to the next issue: whether the *pactum salutis* tends to tritheism. This criticism could have force only in the case that consideration of the distinct work of the trinitarian persons in the history of creation and redemption tends to tritheism, but such is not the case. If consideration of the Spirit's distinct role in creation and redemption meant tritheism, then all study of creation and redemption would have to cease.

By analogy, the covenant of redemption imputes the very same economic relations back into pretemporal existence. The Son's eternal filiation is ontologically necessary but, by contrast, the Son's subordination for our salvation was *voluntary* but not ontologically necessary. The Father can promise and the Son can accept the covenant only if both are "very God of very God," but they can enter into a covenant

67. Ibid., 163. See also Letham, *Work of Christ*, 53.

68. B. B. Warfield, *Biblical Doctrines* (New York: Oxford University Press, 1929), 166.

only if they are distinct persons. This seems more Athanasian than tritheist.

In response to Socinianism and the Remonstrants, theologians such as Owen and Witsius argued that the subordination was not ontological but economic and used the *pactum salutis* to express those economic relations.[69] Therefore, the traditional discussion of the *pactum salutis* quite naturally tends to focus on the Father and the Son. Nevertheless, as Vos argued over a century ago, the *pactum salutis* emerges "from the depths of the divine Being Himself." God the Father issues the "requirement of redemption," God the Son "becomes the guarantor," and to God the Holy Spirit belongs the application of redemption. This is a thoroughly trinitarian scheme that illumines the intrapersonal relations within the Trinity serving as an analogy of the archetypal *perichoresis* or interpenetration of the trinitarian persons.[70]

69. See Trueman, *Claims of Truth*, 133–39, 189–222; Owen, *Works*, 10.163–74; Witsius, *Economy of the Covenants*, 1.180.

70. Vos, "Doctrine of the Covenant," 247.

7

Which Covenant Theology?

MICHAEL S. HORTON

Introduction

Covenant theology seems to be all the rage these days. According to E. P. Sanders, the "pattern of religion" known as Second Temple Judaism can be described as "covenantal nomism."[1] N. T. Wright's *Climax of the Covenant* captures his own summary of the New Testament (especially Paul), and Norman Shepherd and his followers advocate a covenantal approach that stands over against both a medieval theology of merit and a Lutheran doctrine of justification.[2] A small but vocal group in our own circles even calls its position the "federal-vision" theology, despite frequently sweeping denunciations of the classic

1. All references to E. P. Sanders are to his *Paul and Palestinian Judaism* (Minneapolis: Fortress, 1977).

2. See also N. T. Wright, *What Saint Paul Really Said: Was Paul of Tarsus the Real Founder of Christianity?* (Grand Rapids: Eerdmans, 1996), 117: "First, it [justification] is covenant language—not in the sense of that word made famous through some sixteenth- and seventeenth-century discussions, but in the first-century Jewish sense." Typically, Wright dismisses a long-established view with a considerable consensus as something other than "the first-century Jewish [i.e., biblical] sense," without any argumentation. We are to simply accept that he has a direct access to the Bible that apparently our predecessors and we ourselves do not have.

federal theology that dominated Reformed instruction all the way to Louis Berkhof's *Systematic Theology*.

Not only Second Temple Judaism but all of these somewhat diverse challenges to the evangelical doctrine of justification may be accurately described as "covenantal nomism." This pattern of religion is united by three principal theses: (1) our personal obedience is a condition of justification, but that this does not mean that justification is strictly merited; (2) there is no qualitative distinction between law and gospel or a covenant of works and a covenant of grace; and (3) we "get in by grace, but stay in by obedience" (Sanders)—that is, a final justification by works.[3] While we cannot do justice to the various aspects of this argument, it will hopefully become clearer that Paul, the Reformers, and the federal theology that forms the warp and woof of the Reformed system stand on one side, while the revised covenant theologies espoused by the new perspective on Paul, Norman Shepherd, and the federal vision—despite their differences—reflect together something very similar to the covenantal nomism that the Reformation repudiated. If true, this would be important because it would mean that the Reformers were at least close to getting it right when they compared the Galatian heresy to medieval theology and, further, that the only reason that such historical confusion over law and gospel is less objectionable to many today is that a similar confusion is widely accepted within our ranks.

Is Obedience a Condition of Justification?

Sanders argues that the Jews of Paul's day did not believe in merit, strictly speaking, and so were not trying to justify themselves by legalistic works. Yet, his own magisterial study shows just how crucial was the concept of merit. Since, however, for Sanders "merit" can mean

3. There is considerable debate over Sanders's method ("types of religion") and his tendency (especially in Wright's view) to be too interested in soteriology: in other words, he is still asking Protestant questions of Jewish texts. Here I am less interested in taking a stand in this debate, which is beyond my competence, than in using Sanders's typology as a marker for the broad similarities that unite the otherwise different movements described here. For a more extensive discussion of some of these issues, see Michael S. Horton, *Justification and Participation: A Covenant Soteriology* (Louisville: Westminster John Knox, forthcoming).

only *strict* merit (i.e., an exact quid pro quo), he tries (unsuccessfully) to exonerate Second Temple Judaism from that charge. The mere presence of references to God's grace and provisions for forgiveness leads Sanders to conclude that Judaism was far from the medieval theology targeted by the Reformers. However, as we will see, Rome was no less committed to a halfhearted works-righteousness that far fell short of a full-blown Pelagianism.

Thus, part of the difficulty that we encounter in all of the versions of covenantal nomism surveyed here is the remarkably poor scholarship in treating the Reformers and their successors. Despite Sanders and his diverse students having made the Reformation views part of their thesis (viz., the Reformers missed Paul's point), not a single representative of the new perspective on Paul demonstrates any scholarly familiarity with primary or secondary sources in the field.

The presence of forgiveness, divine assistance, grace, and repentance as a means of restoration after sin makes Second Temple Judaism nothing like medieval Rome, we are told. One will find this thesis persuasive, however, only if one misunderstands the latter as a purely Pelagian works-righteousness. Rome, too, affirmed the need for forgiveness and grace, with its own provisions for sin through sacrifices and penance. Furthermore, the Reformers never argued that Paul's opponents had no place for grace, forgiveness, and sacrifice. Rather, they were convinced that, like the medieval church, the Jewish believers in Galatia had confused law and gospel, grace and works, promise and conditionality, Abraham and Sinai.[4]

Both forms of covenantal nomism, ancient and medieval, certainly did hold to the necessity of our own meritorious obedience in some sense as a condition of justification. Even Sanders concedes this much concerning Second Temple Judaism. The difference is one's theological perspective: for Paul and the Reformers, this position—whatever we want to call it—amounted to works-righteousness. Justification is either by works or by grace, but it cannot be by both. A debilitating habit of the representatives considered here, from Sanders to Wright, Shepherd, and the federal vision, is the pretense to be simply

4. See, e.g., the commentaries of Luther (his second commentary) and Calvin on Galatians, although this is part of their running polemic through their writings more generally.

reading the text, while others are "doing theology." Everyone in this debate, however, is working with biases that shape their exegetical labors. Sanders is semi-Pelagian; that comes across quite clearly in his dogmatic pronouncements. If one believes that semi-Pelagianism avoids works-righteousness and is therefore acceptable as a religion of grace, one will hardly challenge as works-righteousness a position that admits some notion of grace. If, on the other hand, one maintains that Scripture prohibits this semi-Pelagianism as a distortion of the gospel, then a religion need not be fully Pelagian in order to qualify as works-righteousness. Though I have no difficulty assigning the label *semi-Pelagian* to Sanders, I am not at all making a sweeping judgment about everyone else I will be considering. Those, however, who depend on Sanders's thesis—even if they are not themselves semi-Pelagian—should recognize the theological assumptions that make that thesis plausible. Sanders's so-called discoveries are hardly new, except to the generations of biblical scholars who have heard distorted versions of Reformation theology only secondhand or thirdhand and assumed a crude view of Judaism as "law without grace," which the Reformers were too well informed to have adopted.[5]

Monocovenantalism (one covenant simultaneously evangelical and legal in its basis) simply collapses the Abrahamic promise and the Sinaitic law. What results is covenantal nomism. Even after—indeed especially after—reading Montefiore's and Sanders's descriptions of Second Temple Judaism, the contrast with Paul's preaching could not be greater. Paul does not believe that Judaism had no place for God's grace or provisions for forgiveness, but he emphatically declares that the earthly Jerusalem is in bondage to works-righteousness just the same and that the law cannot bring about peace with God, even with the assistance of the Spirit, grace, and provisions in case of transgression (Gal 4). If our obedience in any respect is a condition of our justification, we are condemned—since the law does not exonerate hearers but only doers of the law (Rom 2:13; Gal 3:10–11). Monocovenantalism old and new attempts to combine merit and grace, and the result is that both concepts are weakened. The place traditionally

5. Admittedly, this is a sweeping claim, the defense of which is beyond the scope of this essay. It receives some treatment in Horton, *Justification and Participation*.

given in Reformed theology to Christ's full and meritorious obedience as our representative is eclipsed or even denied, while our own obedience (however weak) is seen as a condition of justification. Thus, both the justice of God in upholding his righteous law and his mercy in satisfying its conditions himself are eclipsed—or, better, both his justice and his mercy are relativized by each other instead of being held together simultaneously in their integrity. The end product is a relaxed law and a demanding gospel.

Shepherd and others within our circles share the view of advocates of the new perspective on Paul that merit—a crucial category in Reformation theology (particularly with respect to Christ's)—is an idea we can live without. Not surprisingly, the crucial doctrine of the imputation of Christ's active obedience—indeed, imputation of Christ's righteousness at all—is denied. (Interestingly, even Wright is unwilling to go quite that far: he does not deny imputation; he just does not see it as the point of λογίζομαι in Paul.)[6]

Reformed theology simply failed to eliminate merit from its medieval vocabulary, we are told. Typical of the caricatures, federal-vision advocate Richard Lusk summarizes the classic Reformed position:

> In other words, Jesus is the successful Pelagian, the One Guy in the history of the world who succeeded in pulling off the works righteousness plan. Jesus covered our demerits by dying on the cross and provides all the merits we need by keeping the legal terms of the covenant of works perfectly. Those merits are then imputed to us by faith alone. . . . Such is the view of bi-covenantal federalism.[7]

Aside from Calvin and the Reformed orthodox repeatedly distinguishing between human ability before and after the fall and aside from Pelagianism being the view *that after the fall* we can obey God perfectly apart from grace, Lusk here seems to have trouble accepting the very notion that Christ's representative work included his life of obedience. Lusk affirms Jesus's sinlessness, substitutionary

6. Wright, *What Saint Paul Really Said*, 123.

7. Rich Lusk, "A Response to 'the Biblical Plan of Salvation,'" in *The Auburn Avenue Theology, Pros and Cons: Debating the Federal Vision* (ed. E. Calvin Beisner; Fort Lauderdale, FL: Knox Theological Seminary, 2004), 137.

atonement, and "the infinite value of his obedience," but denies that his own obedience is in any way a meritorious feat that is then imputed to us.[8]

In the bicovenantal system of classic Reformed theology, says Lusk (correctly), "Jesus is regarded as a dutiful servant who has to earn favor."[9] (There *is* a prominent messianic-Servant theme in the Old Testament, is there not?) He appeals to Philippians 2:9, of all texts, to say that "Paul writes the Father *graced* him with such a name as a gift."[10] That passage, however, actually says that "Christ became obedient even to death, even the death of the cross. *Therefore* [on the basis of that obedience] God also has highly exalted him and given him the name above every name."

The covenant of works, Christ's meritorious obedience, and imputation stand or fall together in Reformed theology, Lusk rightly recognizes:

> Those who advocate a meritorious covenant of works put a great deal of weight on the so-called "active obedience" of Christ. I remember hearing sermons in which I was told "Jesus' thirty-three years of law-keeping are your righteousness. They were credited to you! He kept the law, the covenant of works, on your behalf!" . . . But the notion of his thirty-three years of Torah-keeping being imputed to me is problematic. After all, as a Gentile, I was never under Torah and therefore never under obligation to keep many of the commands Jesus performed. . . . God's righteousness is his own righteousness, not something imputed or infused. . . . Paul is *not* identifying the gospel with the doctrine of imputed righteousness.[11]

Yet, again there is a contradiction: "He was raised up *on the basis of* his flawless obedience to the Father," Lusk says.[12] But "on the basis of" means "ground." Lusk does not even refer to this flawless obedience as a *means*, but as the *ground*, yet he has told us that the ground was *grace*. What is the difference between saying that Jesus

8. Ibid., 137–38.
9. Ibid., 137.
10. Ibid.
11. Ibid., 141 (emphasis original).
12. Ibid., 142.

was raised because he had *merited* everlasting life by his obedience and saying that he was raised *on the basis of* his flawless obedience to the Father? If his flawless obedience is the basis, then, it is clearly a matter of deserts. Whatever it means to say that Christ was raised on the basis of his flawless obedience, it surely cannot be grace; "otherwise grace is no longer grace" (Rom 11:6). The inevitable tendency of Lusk's argument is to diminish the uniqueness of Christ's justification by personal, loving, faithful, devoted, filial obedience to his Father and to view Christ simply as the first Christian—one who in some vague sense "deserved" to be rewarded with salvation, but in no sense meriting it. As we will see, this amounts not to the end of the category of merit but a shift from condign (strict) to congruent (graciously accepted) merit.

Lusk himself says, again contradicting his statements above, "Christ 'deserved' to be rewarded after he suffered and died, not because of some abstract justice (or 'merit'), but because the Father had freely promised him such (cf. Isaiah 53:10–11; Philippians 2:9)."[13] Although he puts it in scare quotes, even Lusk concedes some notion of Christ's "deserving" to be rewarded. And who says that it is "because of some abstract justice" as opposed to "the Father's promise"? Certainly not Reformed theology, according to which Jesus, like Adam, was promised the consummation on the condition of his successful completion of the probation.

Such sweeping contrasts between "abstract justice" and relational categories—applied to the character of God, the atonement, justification, and future destinies—have a long but quite unhelpful career in the history of modern theology. Lusk never clarifies what he means by "abstract," so the assumption is simply that it describes the position that Christ actually fulfilled a covenant of works. That there really are abstract theories of atonement and justification out there I do not doubt. I am familiar with popular presentations in which the atonement and justification are treated as impersonal transactions. We do need to reflect more on the covenantal context of these truths. For example, we are repeatedly reminded in the epistles of the words reported first in the Psalter: "I desire obedience and not sacrifice." The

13. Ibid., 147.

imputation of Christ's active obedience is the ground upon which the Father can receive from his human servant (representatively in Jesus Christ) the full love, loyalty, and obedience in which he delights and his law requires, so that he can receive as "sons" those who "in Christ" are as yet in themselves sinful. It is about relationship after all: adoption, filial devotion—and the restoration of sinners to God in such a way that in Christ even their feeble and sin-stained works can be nevertheless acceptable to the Father precisely because they are merely a response to and in no way condition of that acceptance. So much for abstract justice. Further, Lusk's claim that Gentiles were never under Torah is refuted by Paul's argument in Romans 1–3, that "all the world" is swept into Israel, condemned by the law, whether written on the conscience (Gentiles) or on tablets (Jews).

With the covenant of works and the concept of strict merit denied, the imputation of Christ's perfect obedience to God's covenant law is no longer a relevant category. According to Lusk, "This justification requires no transfer or imputation of anything."[14] We also encounter another false choice: either imputation *or* union with Christ.[15] Citing Calvin and Richard Gaffin, Lusk says that believers are righteous by virtue of their union with Christ.[16] Protestantism, however, avoided the false choice between imputation *or* union, making imputed righteousness the legal ground of the union.[17]

At this point Lusk appeals to Shepherd's contrast between a merit principle and a covenantal approach.[18] Yet like the new perspective on Paul, Lusk (and Shepherd) ignores not only that the Reformed held to the principle of merit (Christ's) within a thoroughly covenantal theology, but also fails to recognize that Rome *had* a covenantal paradigm—very much like the covenantal nomism already described.

Identified especially with the school of nominalism, the slogan of this medieval covenant theology was this: "God will not deny his grace to those who do what lies within them."[19] Strictly speaking,

14. Ibid., 142.
15. Ibid., 142–43.
16. Ibid., 143.
17. See Horton, *Justification and Participation*, for an elaboration of this theme.
18. Ibid., 144.
19. See Heiko Oberman, *Forerunners of the Reformation: The Shape of Late Medieval Thought Illustrated by Key Documents* (Philadelphia: Fortress, 1966), 123–74. For a fuller treat-

no one merits salvation (*condign* merit). Rather, God accepts the imperfect obedience of those who belong to the church as if it were satisfactory for final justification (*congruent* merit). Although no one is strictly meritorious of final justification, God has instituted a covenant in which cooperation with infused grace will be accepted in place of perfect fulfillment of the law. Grace was provided through the sacraments, just as it had been through the sacrifices of the old covenant. As faith became formed by love—in other words, as faith became obedience—it became justifying. The "new law," as the New Testament was called, is a kinder, gentler form of conditionality than is the old covenant. Jesus is a new Moses, but a milder one (evidently, the Sermon on the Mount, with its far more demanding interpretation of Torah, was not determinative). Similarly, the Arminians on the Continent and neonomians (such as Richard Baxter) in England sought a rapprochement with Rome on justification by saying that faith—construed as obedience—was the only work substituting for full obedience. The law now relaxed, one could be justified simply by having the beginnings of holiness. It was a "kinder, gentler" justification by works.

While Shepherd and the federal-vision proponents oppose the category of merit in principle, they do insist that faith *and* obedience (or faith *as* obedience) are the instruments of final justification, which amounts to the *congruent* merit advocated by late medieval theology. While our confessions affirm that the faith that justifies is a living, active, and obedient faith, they universally insist that faith is justifying only in its act of resting in Christ's merits. In the words of John Murray, "It is this resting, confiding, entrusting quality of faith that makes it appropriate to and indeed exhibitive of the nature of justification. . . . Faith terminates upon Christ and his righteousness and it makes mention of his righteousness only. . . . This is both the stumbling block and the irresistible appeal of the gospel."[20]

It is impossible to read Sanders's description of Second Temple Judaism and Heiko Oberman's description of late medieval nominal-

---

ment, see idem, *The Harvest of Medieval Theology: Gabriel Biel and Late Medieval Nominalism* (Durham, NC: Labyrinth, 1983), esp. 167–220.

20. John Murray, *Principles of Conduct: Aspects of Biblical Ethics* (1957; repr. Grand Rapids: Eerdmans, 1991), 217.

ism and not recognize striking similarities. This covenantal nomism is the official position of post-Tridentine Rome, as the most recent *Catechism of the Catholic Church* illustrates:

> With regard to God, there is no strict right to any merit on the part of man. Between God and us there is an immeasurable inequality, for we have received everything from him, our Creator. The merit of man before God in the Christian life arises from the fact that God has freely chosen to associate man with the work of his grace. The fatherly action of God is first on his own initiative, and then follows man's free acting through his collaboration, so that the merit of good works is to be attributed in the first place to the grace of God, then to the faithful.[21]

This is not a new position, however; it has been the long-standing Counter-Reformation interpretation: neither fully Pauline nor fully Pelagian.

Lusk confidently declares that Calvin "clearly repudiated the notion that Christ merited God's favor in any strict sense," citing Alister McGrath.[22] Both Lusk and McGrath, however, are wrong. Of course, Calvin did deny that *our* works were meritorious, but Calvin speaks clearly of Christ's meritorious obedience, without which (says the Reformer) there could have been no salvation: "By his obedience, however, Christ truly *acquired and merited* grace for us with the Father. Many passages of Scripture surely and firmly attest this." In fact, he adds: "*I take it to be a commonplace* that if Christ made satisfaction for our sins, if he paid the penalty owed by us, if he appeased God by his obedience . . . then he *acquired* salvation for us by his righ-

21. *Catechism of the Catholic Church* (2nd ed.; Rome: Libreria Editrice Vaticana, 1997), 486 §§2007–8.

22. Lusk, "Response to 'the Biblical Plan of Salvation.'" All of Lusk's confident assertions are not only based on secondary research, but on dated research that does not take into account the massive contradiction of the discontinuity thesis (i.e., the assertion that Calvin and the Calvinists did not see things eye to eye). See especially Richard Muller, *The Unaccommodated Calvin* (Oxford: Oxford University Press, 2000); idem, *After Calvin: Studies in the Development of a Theological Tradition* (Oxford: Oxford University Press, 2003). The work of Lyle Bierma, Carl Trueman, Joel Beeke, and R. Scott Clark represent a significant reevaluation of the unfounded assumptions of discontinuity between Calvin and the Reformed tradition, while a fresh wave of first-rate scholars has emerged within European universities greatly substantiating Muller's "continuity" thesis: namely, Irena Backus, Willem Van Asselt, and Anton Vos, among others.

teousness, which is tantamount to *deserving* it. . . . *Hence it is absurd to set Christ's merit against God's mercy*" (*Institutes* 2.17.3, 1, emphasis added). Christ's meritorious obedience is the basis upon which God can justly show mercy to sinners.

Merit is the category for Christ's saving work that one finds in the Reformed and Presbyterian confessions. Not only is it found in the more fully developed federal theology of the Westminster Divines, it is just as clearly articulated in the Belgic Confession 22–24, which refer repeatedly to Christ's having merited our salvation. And according to Heidelberg Catechism 17, Christ came to "earn for us and restore to us righteousness and life."

The Canons of Dort rejected those "who teach that Christ, by the satisfaction which he gave, did not certainly *merit* for anyone salvation itself and the faith by which this satisfaction of Christ is effectively applied to salvation, but only acquired for the Father the authority or plenary will to relate in a new way with men and to impose such new conditions as he chose. . . . For they have too low an opinion of the death of Christ, do not at all acknowledge the foremost fruit or benefit which it brings forth, and summon back from hell the Pelagian error" (Rejection of Errors 2.3, emphasis added). Ironically, Lusk and his colleagues accuse the Reformation appeal to Christ's meritorious obedience of being "Pelagian," while Dort refers this charge to its denial. Rejection of Errors 2.4 is especially pertinent in its rejection of those

> who teach that what is involved in the new covenant of grace which God the Father made with men through the intervening of Christ's death is not that we are justified before God and saved through faith, insofar as it accepts Christ's merit, but rather that God, having withdrawn his demand for perfect obedience to the law, counts faith itself, and the imperfect obedience of faith, as perfect obedience to the law, and graciously looks upon these as worthy of the reward of eternal life. . . . And along with the ungodly Socinus, they introduce a new and foreign justification of man before God, against the consensus of the whole church.

Christ not only merited our salvation in a congruent sense—that is, in the sense that God graciously *accepted* his work as satisfactory—

but also in the condign sense: he actually *fulfilled* the obedience that God required of us all in Adam.

Lusk claims that the teaching of Christ's active obedience and the covenant of works was never heard of in the church until the federal theologians. As early as the second century, however, Irenaeus distinguishes between a covenant of law and a covenant of promise, identifying the former with the first arrangement with Adam as well as the Sinai covenant, while linking the latter to the protevangelium, Abraham, and the new covenant in Christ.[23] John of Damascus makes a similar statement.[24] And Augustine says: "The first covenant was this, unto Adam: 'Whensoever thou eatest thereof thou shalt die the death,'" which is why all his children "are breakers of God's covenant made with Adam in paradise."[25] In fact, Augustine elaborates this point in considerable detail in these two passages, contrasting the creation covenant with the covenant of grace as we find it in the promise to Abraham. To be sure, federal theology represents a refinement and greater elaboration, but not a new idea. More importantly, these distinctions between promise and law, the Abrahamic and Sinaitic covenants, faith and works, are explicit in the Old and New Testaments.

Finally, says Lusk, the covenant of works and its category of Christ's meritorious obedience leads inevitably to antinomianism—a charge with which Paul was not unacquainted. In a sweeping indictment of the entire Reformed tradition (including the Puritans who framed the Westminster Standards), Lusk writes:

23. Irenaeus, *Against Heresies* 4.25; 5.16.3; 4.13.1; 4.15.1; 4.16.3 (*ANF* 1.24–26, 554); cf. Ligon Duncan, "The Covenant Idea in Irenaeus of Lyons" (paper presented at the North American Patristics Society annual meeting, May 29, 1997); Everett Ferguson, "The Covenant Idea in the Second Century," in *Texts and Testaments: Critical Essays on the Bible and the Early Church Fathers* (ed. W. E. March; San Antonio: Trinity University Press, 1980), 135–62.

24. John of Damascus, *An Exact Exposition of the Orthodox Faith* 2.30 (*NPNF*[2] 9.43).

25. Augustine, *City of God* (trans. Henry Bettenson; ed. David Knowles; New York: Penguin, 1972), 688–89 §16.28; cf. Augustine, *On Christian Doctrine* 3.33 (*NPNF*[1] 2.569). Augustine commends the hermeneutical rules of Tichonius: "The third rule relates to the promises and the law, and may be designated in other terms as relating to the spirit and the letter, which is the name I made use of when writing a book on this subject. It may be also named, of grace and the law. This, however, seems to me to be a great question in itself, rather than a rule to be applied to the solution of other questions. It was the want of clear views on this question that originated, or at least greatly aggravated, the Pelagian heresy. And the efforts of Tichonius to clear up this point were good, but not complete. For, in discussing the question about faith and works, he said that works were given us by God as the reward of faith, but that faith itself was so far our own that it did not come to us from God."

> Talk about obedience is always suspect because it smells of merit. . . . The entire federalist theological construction creates massive dichotomies that make it virtually impossible to tie together faith and works, justification and Christian growth, grace and new obedience, and so on, in any organic, covenantal whole. . . . Sanctification comes to fit only very awkwardly into our theological system and the pressures towards (theoretical, if not practical) antinomianism become greater and greater.[26]

A typical argument used by Paul's opponents (and by the medieval church) was that justification on the basis of an alien righteousness, simply received and not acquired by oneself—even with God's help—would lead inexorably to license. Lusk too assumes that if one accepts the traditional Reformed position one would simply be antinomian. To deduce is one thing, but to actually make the sweeping historical claim that the Westminster Divines (i.e., the Puritans) were afraid to talk about obedience, "Christian growth, grace and new obedience, and so on, in any organic, covenantal whole" goes beyond any criticism leveled even by the tradition's staunchest opponents.[27]

Aside from the obvious historical inaccuracies in such sweeping denunciations of Reformed theology, the most pressing problem with this challenge is that when Christ's fulfillment of meritorious obedience of the covenant of works/law on our behalf is categorically denied, it is not that the *concept* of merit disappears, but only the *term*. "Thus, in Christ, our faith-wrought good works have *value* before God, but not *merit*," Lusk says.[28] Just what is that "value" that is not "merit"? And is that "value" in reference to justification? According to Rome, the category of "final justification" answers that question. Although believers "get in by grace"—even grace *alone*, through a regenerative baptism—they are justified on the last day according to their works. Not only do federal-vision advocates such as Lusk endorse something close to baptismal regeneration (emphasizing that this is by grace alone), we find in these writers comments such as the following from Lusk:

26. Lusk, "Response to 'the Biblical Plan of Salvation,'" 145.
27. Ibid.
28. Ibid., 146.

> Biblically, judgment according to works comes at the end of history, not the beginning. Only after we have had time to mature into fruit bearers does God give a full evaluation of our covenant fidelity. Judgment according to works is eschatological, not protological. But the proponents of the covenant of works put this mature judgment at the beginning! The New Covenant sacramental system reveals this basic progression [toward a judgment according to works at the end]. God, not man, makes the water used in baptism. The one baptized has no works to offer. He is completely passive. But due to the Lord's Supper man must "make" bread and wine out of the raw materials of creation. The elements of the Supper represent human labor and are offered to God as a sacrifice of praise and thanks. Man is active in eating and drinking at the table, and God judges us according to our "works" therein (cf. 1 Corinthians 11:17ff.). So baptism, as the sacrament of initiation, grants initial justification apart from works. But the Supper, as the sacrament of nourishment and maturation, includes an evaluation of our works.[29]

This is a classic statement of the unfortunate consensus at the Council of Trent. And in some important respects, once different sacraments are substituted, it fits Sanders's definition of covenantal nomism in Second Temple Judaism. The notion of two justifications—one by grace, the other by works—distinguishes all these forms of covenant nomism from biblical faith.

Critics of the Reformation doctrine like to quote Paul's reference to "the obedience of faith" (Rom 1:5) as if this were a proof-text for justification by faithfulness.[30] Yet this is not a new insight but an old error. The Canons of Dort condemn the view that "the imperfect obedience of faith" is "a condition of salvation" or "worthy of the reward of eternal life. For by this pernicious error the good pleasure of God and the merit of Christ are robbed of their effectiveness and people are drawn away, by unprofitable inquiries, from the truth of

29. Ibid.

30. Paul is not suggesting that faith justifies because it is obedience, but is simply treating "obedience" at least in reference to faith (and therefore justification) as believing in Christ. If critics are willing to limit their definition of obedience (in reference to justifying faith) as Paul does here, and as Jesus does in John 6:29, we would have no quibble. But, in fact, their "obedience of faith" is actually a "faith of obedience."

undeserved justification and the simplicity of Scripture" (Rejection of Errors 1.3).

Related to the question of merit is the argument that Paul's polemics against works are not as sweeping as the Reformers assumed. Since the Reformers did not have Sanders, Dunn, and Wright at hand, they could not have known that "works of the law" referred to circumcision and dietary laws—that is, ethnic badges, rather than to any and all works. Yet once more, when we read the Reformers, we soon encounter the same debates. For example, Calvin says of Galatians 2:15: "[Others] hold that this [i.e., works of the law] does not refer to moral works. The context, however, shows clearly that the moral law is also comprehended in these words, for almost everything that Paul adds relates to the moral rather than the ceremonial law."[31] The new perspective on Paul unwittingly repeats the medieval arguments as if they were fresh exegetical discoveries, and the federal vision demonstrates no greater familiarity with the sources that they assume to have gotten Paul so badly wrong.

Is There a Qualitative Distinction between Law and Gospel?

Monocovenantalism is a common distinctive of the various forms of covenantal nomism we are describing. Yet, as already noted, biblical scholarship is increasingly aware of the differences between conditional and unconditional covenants in Scripture. Even such a seminal architect of the new perspective on Paul as James Dunn recognizes this: "The more obvious line of reasoning is that Paul was so remembered [as chief heretic of Judaism] because he was in fact the one who brought the tension between law and gospel (already present in Jesus's own ministry—Mark 7:1–23; Matt 15:1–20) to its sharpest and indeed antithetical expression."[32] Dunn acknowledges a law/gospel antithesis in Paul.[33] Similarly, even Wright makes a distinction between

31. John Calvin, *Commentaries on the Epistles to the Galatians and Ephesians* (trans. William Pringle; Grand Rapids: Eerdmans, 1948), 37–39.

32. James D. G. Dunn, *Jesus, Paul, and the Law: Studies in Mark and Galatians* (London: SPCK/Louisville: Westminster, 1990), 93.

33. Ibid., 95.

commands and promises.[34] In fact, although he would not wish to be seen aiding and abetting a confessional dogmatic system, throughout *Climax of the Covenant* Wright repeatedly strengthens the exegetical case for the Mosaic theocracy as a law-covenant distinguished from the Abrahamic promise-covenant.[35] On Romans 7:7–12, Wright states the argument: "The law is not sin, but its arrival, in Sinai as in Eden, was sin's opportunity to kill its recipients."[36] Many of these representatives of the new perspective on Paul are far more careful in their exegesis and often less radical in their repudiation of Reformation theology than those of the federal vision.

Yet on the subject of election in Galatians 3, Wright's view seems to be that Paul modified the single Jewish doctrine of election and covenant.[37] Classic federal theology has generally held that two covenants are in view (as Paul says explicitly): national (Sinai) and individual-global (Abrahamic). This is already an Old Testament concept that Paul simply draws out and expands. They are not just two *successive* covenants, but two covenants that coexist *side by side*. In fact, even Jesuit Old Testament scholar Dennis J. McCarthy complains that the failure to recognize and distinguish unconditional and conditional covenants in the Old Testament leads to enormous exegetical confusion.[38]

The problem with Paul's opponents was precisely that they were monocovenantalists (covenantal nomists, just as Sanders describes the position) and confused the blessings of Abraham with the Mosaic covenant described in Deuteronomy 27–30, failing to realize that in this way they were under only covenant curses rather than blessings. Wright even says that "the temporary status of the Torah has given way to the permanent creation, in Christ, of a worldwide people

34. Wright, *What Saint Paul Really Said*, 23.

35. Paul's point, then, is that Israel as a nation has failed to keep Torah and is thus as a nation under its curse, so that Torah can hardly be the means of returning after exile and retaining membership and becoming a blessing to the world. This can happen (Gal 3:10–14) only when Israel becomes "the means of blessing the world in accordance with the promise to Abraham"; N. T. Wright, *The Climax of the Covenant: Christ and the Law in Pauline Theology* (Minneapolis: Fortress, 1992), 146.

36. Ibid., 197.

37. Ibid., 171.

38. Dennis J. McCarthy, *Old Testament Covenant: A Survey of Current Opinions* (Atlanta: John Knox, 1972), 5.

characterized by faith. This people is the single family promised to Abraham. We may compare Romans 8.3f.: what the law could not do, being weak because of human sinfulness, God has done in Christ and by the Spirit."[39] Then Wright returns to the false dilemma that seems to result from his abiding commitment to Dunn's "membership identity" thesis.[40] This, again, is based on his restrictive view that "the law" has reference to only Israel's Torah—and only the ceremonial aspects at that—which is, as we have seen, an argument that the Reformers also encountered.[41]

The Reformers, however, spoke of νόμος (Torah) in both a wide and a narrow sense: law as a principle of works-righteousness and law as God's specific commandments to Israel. They did not maintain that law and gospel are antithetical *in principle*, whether understood in terms of the old and new covenants or in terms of commands and promises, which are after all present in both covenants. When, however, it comes to the principle by which sinners are to appear before a holy God in his righteous judgment, says Calvin, we must heed the gospel and not the law, "forgetting all law righteousness. . . . If consciences wish to attain any certainty in this matter [of justification], they ought to give no place to the law." The law still guides believers in the way of holiness: "But where consciences are worried how to render God favorable, what they will reply, and with what assurance they will stand should they be called to his judgment, there we are not to reckon what the law requires, but Christ alone, who surpasses all perfection of the law, must be set forth as righteousness" (*Institutes* 3.19.2). Romans 10:5–6 drives this point home, Calvin says: "Do you not see how he [Paul] makes this the distinction between law and gospel . . . ? This is an important passage, and one that can extricate us from many difficulties if we understand that that righteousness which is given us through the gospel has been freed of all conditions of the law. . . . The gospel promises are free and dependent solely upon God's mercy, while the promises of the law depend upon the condition of works" (*Institutes* 3.11.17).

39. Wright, *Climax of the Covenant*, 172.
40. Ibid., 173.
41. Ibid., 182.

Remarkably, given the recurring polemics, Wright goes so far as to conclude: "The Lutheran wants to maintain the sharp antithesis between law and gospel; so does Paul, but within the context of a single plan of God, and with no suggestion that the Torah itself is a bad thing."[42] Further, "the Lutheran view is not without its merit; it simply needs setting in a wider context," namely, seeing the relation as "contained within the sense of climax, of 'goal.' When I reach my goal I stop traveling; not because my journey was a silly idea but because it was a good idea now fully worked out."[43]

This is less radical, of course, than denying the law/gospel distinction altogether, as many even in our circles are now doing. Yet, even this fails to recognize that the Reformers regularly referred to law and gospel in precisely these two ways, which may be fairly described in terms (albeit anachronistically) of the *historia salutis* and the *ordo salutis*. Calvin also speaks of "the law" in both senses: redemptive-historical (old covenant) and as a principle of works.[44] The Reformers assert both with great hermeneutical sophistication and nuance, while covenantal nomism simply collapses the latter into the former. A thorough treatment of Paul's understanding of the law in these broader and narrower senses is provided by Stephen Westerholm, among others.[45]

42. Ibid., 241.

43. Ibid., 244.

44. For more on this, see my "Calvin and the Law-Gospel Hermeneutic," *Pro ecclesia* 6 (1997): 27–42.

45. Stephen Westerholm, *Perspectives Old and New on Paul: The "Lutheran" Paul and His Critics* (Grand Rapids: Eerdmans, 2004), 105–20. For example, regarding the question as to whether "works of the law" is restricted to ethnic distinctives: "That Paul could use 'law' and 'works of law' interchangeably [Rom 3:28] makes it highly unlikely that, with the latter phrase, he has in mind only a few specific statutes or, indeed, a distortion of the law. . . . But the only commandments of the law mentioned by Paul before his reference to 'works of the law' in Rom 3:20 are taken from the Decalogue (2:21–22), and do not refer to Jewish 'identity markers'" (118). "The 'works of the law' which do not justify are the demands of the law that are not met, not those observed for the wrong reasons by Jews. If in Rom 2 the Jews are condemned for not fulfilling the works of the law, that can hardly fit circumcision, dietary laws, etc., which they did in fact keep scrupulously. That Paul supports his rejection of the 'works of the law' in Rom 3:20, 28 by showing that Abraham was justified by faith, not works (4:1–5), is positively fatal to Dunn's proposal, as it was to that of Gaston. For the 'works' by which Abraham could conceivably have been justified, and of which he might have boasted (4:2), were certainly not observances of the peculiarly Jewish parts of the Mosaic code. Paul is here demonstrating that the broad category of 'works' cannot be a factor in salvation in order to exclude the subcategory, 'works of law.' Not particular works which set Jews apart, but works in general—anything 'done'

Neither Paul nor the Reformers thought that the law was itself the problem, contrary to the position of Hans Dieter Betz, Rudolf Bultmann, and others against whom the new perspective on Paul is reacting, as if their negative view of the law as law was that of the Reformers.[46] According to Paul, the law is good, but we are not (Rom 7:12). This is why "law"—*any* imperative—cannot bring life. If any law could have, then Torah surely would have done it (Gal 3:21). Justification and new life depend on a divine indicative, and not just any such indicative, but God's deed in Christ as offered in the covenant of grace. In fact, Paul's own use of the phrase *principle* of law versus *principle* of faith (as in Rom 3:27 and 9:30–32) is not inimical lexically to substituting the term *covenant*, where *principle* (νόμος) is used to refer to a regime, order, or economy. Steve Schlissel, however, simply rejects the validity of such a distinction:

> God has peppered his Word with a lot of "or-elses," so many that no one could miss them. But while the or-elses couldn't be missed, they could be mis-assigned, as if they belonged to the Law and not to the Gospel. This is a false division, of course. It is a division, however, famously *rejected* by Calvinists! . . . Of course Christ has become a new Moses![47]

At this point, the federal-vision writers are simply confused. On one hand, they repeatedly reject Reformed bicovenantalism (works and grace), realizing that it rests on the law/gospel distinction. Yet, by calling it "Lutheran" they think that they can create a new "Reformed" doctrine out of whole cloth. John Frame similarly exaggerates the

---

that might deserve a recompense (μισθός, 4:4) or justify pride (καύχημα, v. 2)—are meant, and that in contrast with the 'faith' of one who 'does not work' but benefits by divine grace without any consideration of personal merit" (119). While Paul's law does not include Jesus's commands but is restricted to the Mosaic law, Luther's "contrast between 'law' and 'gospel,' though never explicit in the epistles, does not distort Paul's point" (122).

46. Hans Dieter Betz, *Galatians* (Hermeneia; Minneapolis: Fortress, 1979), 145–46. For an excellent treatment of Paul's use of the phrase, see C. E. B. Cranfield, "'The Works of the Law' in the Epistle to the Romans," *Journal for the Study of the New Testament* 43 (1991): 325–86; cf. Douglas Moo, "'Law,' 'Works of the Law,' and Legalism in Paul," *Westminster Theological Journal* 45 (1983): 94–97.

47. Steve M. Schlissel, "A New Way of Seeing?" in *The Auburn Avenue Theology, Pros and Cons: Debating the Federal Vision* (ed. E. Calvin Beisner; Fort Lauderdale, FL: Knox Theological Seminary, 2004), 23.

Lutheran view of the law/gospel relation in the name of a Reformed covenantalism. "Reformed" seems to be defined by Frame's own idiosyncratic view rather than by that tradition's typical way of speaking about this issue, since he says: "The view that I oppose, which sharply separates the two messages [of law and gospel], comes mainly out of Lutheran theology, *though similar statements can be found in Calvin and in other Reformed writers*. . . . I believe that we should stand with the Scriptures against this tradition."[48] This, of course, puts Frame at odds with classic Reformed theology, whose covenant of works/covenant of grace scheme is a redemptive-historical elaboration of the law/gospel distinction.[49] This claim, however, places him at odds even with such modern representatives as Murray, who writes concerning the distinction between law and gospel: "In the degree to which error is entertained on this point, in the same degree is our conception of the gospel perverted. . . . What was the question that aroused the apostle to such passionate zeal and holy indignation, indignation that has its kinship with the imprecatory utterances of the Old Testament? In a word it was the relation of law and gospel."[50]

This was also Shepherd's argument in the controversy at Westminster Seminary: we need a distinctly Reformed (covenantal) doctrine of justification, not the so-called Lutheran one found in the Reformed confessions![51] Whatever results from a "non-Lutheran Reformed" doctrine of justification, however, cannot be called Reformed. Schlissel claims that "Paul's point, therefore, was not to prove justification by faith, but rather to prove justification for Gentiles. . . . *Obedience and faith are the same thing, biblically speaking*."[52] Again the federal vision asks us to make a false choice: either a faith *divorced from* obedience or a faith that *is* obedience, the same false choice demanded by the Counter-Reformation and by Paul's antagonists. In Rome's construction, faith itself is mere assent to church teaching. (This, by the way,

48. John Frame, "Law and Gospel," *Chalcedon Report* (Jan. 4, 2002): 1, 7 (emphasis added).

49. See Michael Horton, "Law, Gospel, and Covenant," *Westminster Theological Journal* 64 (2002): 279–88.

50. Murray, *Principles of Conduct*, 181.

51. See, e.g., the more recent argument (or assertion) by Norman Shepherd, "Justification by Faith Alone," *Reformation and Revival* 11 (2002): 81.

52. Schlissel, "A New Way of Seeing?" 26 (emphasis added).

seems virtually indistinguishable from Wright's definition of faith.)[53] Therefore, in order for faith to be "fully formed" it must become a work: *fides formata caritate* (faith formed by love). So too for the federal vision: not only does genuine faith *yield* obedience, but faith justifies a person only insofar as it *is* obedience. This is nothing more than a repristination of the covenantal nomism that Paul, the Reformers, and our confessions condemn.

Further, all of these challenges ignore the careful way in which mainstream Reformed theology has dealt with the obvious conditionality in Scripture, including Paul. This tradition has never said that there are no conditions in the covenant—or even in justification. Rather, it argued that the condition of justification is faith and that the conditions of salvation as a whole process are many: lifelong repentance and faith, sanctification, and glorification. This theology, however, emphasized that these conditions are fulfilled by the gifts that come to us through union with Christ. Thus, God promises to give faith and perseverance, justification and sanctification, throughout the course of our life, all the while distinguishing justification from the process of inner renewal. Furthermore, even the law that accused us now appears to us as a delight. Luther writes: the law "no longer terrifies us with death and hell but has become our kind friend and companion." Christ has turned the prison into a palace. "He did not destroy and abrogate the Law; but He so changed our heart . . . and made the Law so lovely to it that the heart now delights and rejoices in nothing more than the Law. It would not willingly see one tittle of it fall away."[54] Thus, even the law depends on the gospel for its efficacy. The distinction between law and gospel, works and faith, and the covenant of works and covenant of grace does not, at least in Reformed theology, imply an absolute antithesis except at the point of how one is accepted by

53. Furthermore, as Wright sees the matter, faith is defined not as trust in the person and work of Christ, but as assent to Paul's redefinition of Jewish monotheism. Paul is arguing for "justification by *belief*, i.e., covenant membership demarcated by that which is believed." He recognizes that this amounts to "my redefinition of what 'justification' thus actually *means*" (*Climax of the Covenant*, 2–3). How does this not represent the Roman Catholic view of faith as mere *assent* to church teaching?

54. See *Luthers Werke Kritische Gesamtausgabe* (ed. J. K. F. Knaake, G. Kawerau, et al.; Weimar: Böhlau, 1883–), 10^1, 1.459; and Ewald M. Plass, *What Luther Says* (St. Louis: Concordia, 1956), 2.766.

God. To distinguish the respective nature and role of command and promise is not to denigrate, much less repudiate, either.

The new covenant is a covenant of promise or gospel—that is, of what God will do for us—not only the promise to forgive all sins but to give a new heart (Jer 31:30–31). Yet God's gift of new obedience can in no way serve as a second instrument of justification, nor can faith be defined as obedience (faith formed by love) in the act of justifying sinners. Certainly not on every point, but *where justification is concerned*, faith and works are absolutely antithetical (Rom 3:20–28; 4:4–5, 13–17; 10:1–13; 11:6; Gal 2:16–21; 3:2–14, 21–4:31; Eph 2:8–9; 2 Tim 1:9).

Summarizing Wright almost verbatim, Schlissel asserts:

> The lenses through which the Letters of Paul must be read are not those supplied by systematic theology, abstract or otherwise. They must be the lenses provided by the Story, by Scripture itself. "Justification" in Galatians and Romans deals with the status of Gentiles. . . . Legal justification, far from being "the heart of the Gospel," let alone identical with it, is hardly ever in view when Paul speaks of justification. Paul's concern is the status of the Gentiles as Israelites indeed, through faith, not through ritual circumcision or the various identity markers uniquely connected with it.[55]

Commenting on Luke 10:25–37, Schlissel writes: "It is effrontery, an insult, to suggest that Jesus's answer, 'Do this and you will live,' was anything other than plain truth. . . . It was Christ teaching that obedience to the law was something very do-able and that such obedience, which includes repentance and faith, does save."[56] Yet Schlissel so overstates his case that not even Wright would concur. The federal vision is so reactionary in its rejection of the so-called Lutheran paradigm that its own systematic-theological prejudices render responsible exegesis of Jesus as well as of Paul an impossible quest. As for the Reformed confessions, Christopher Hutchinson rightly

55. Schlissel, "A New Way of Seeing?" 33.

56. Cited by Christopher Hutchinson, "A Reply to 'A New Way of Seeing?'" in *The Auburn Avenue Theology, Pros and Cons: Debating the Federal Vision* (ed. E. Calvin Beisner; Fort Lauderdale, FL: Knox Theological Seminary, 2004), 53, quoting Steve Schlissel's comments in *Christian Renewal* (April 28, 2003): 11.

concludes: "The assertion that the law-gospel formula is a 'Lutheran' scheme is discredited just three questions into the 1563 Heidelberg Catechism: 'Q. 3. How do you come to know your misery? A. The law of God tells me.'"[57] Ursinus's own opening arguments in his commentary on the Heidelberg Catechism—"the law and the gospel as the two parts of the Word of God"—serve only to confirm this point.[58]

Lusk seems to be a little more open to exegetical nuance than Schlissel, who sees no significant discontinuity between the old and new covenants. There is some need to distinguish the Mosaic and Abrahamic covenants, says Lusk.[59] Yet "the fundamental requirement of the Mosaic covenant was not any different from the basic requirements of the Abrahamic or Christic covenants: the obedience of faith." Further, "the law did not require perfect obedience," and "the sacrificial system clearly offered a remedy for sin." Thus, "the law was a pre-Christian revelation of the gospel." Lusk then cites passages from Paul and Hebrews, indicating what we have called the redemptive-historical use of law and gospel, but as if this were the only use these apostolic writers made of those categories and as if there were no contrast at all.[60] So the sweep from Moses to Christ is continuum, never contrast.[61]

We are surely better served with the more nuanced claim that Paul employs both a redemptive-historical and a principled (dogmatic) strategy (1) reflecting law and gospel as a continuum of promise/type leading to fulfillment (infancy to adulthood) and (2) reflecting contrasting means of justification. Just as the Reformed view does not pose a false choice between justification and sanctification or between the *historia salutis* and the *ordo salutis*, it offers a far richer and broader way of accounting for the diversity of the biblical material. This diversity should not be exchanged for the reductionism that results from the imposition of any a priori dogmatic scheme. Paul's (or Jeremiah's)

57. Hutchinson, "Reply to 'A New Way of Seeing?'" 57.

58. Zacharias Ursinus, *Commentary on the Heidelberg Catechism* (1852; 2nd ed.; repr. Phillipsburg, NJ: P&R, 1985), 1.

59. Lusk, "Response to 'the Biblical Plan of Salvation,'" 127.

60. Ibid., 128.

61. Ibid., 129.

statements about the *differences* between the Abrahamic covenant of promise and the Mosaic covenant of law is simply lost in the fog of a one-sided emphasis on redemptive-historical progress of a *single* covenant. At the end of the day, Christ is simply a new Moses.

Why then did Paul say in Galatians that the Mosaic covenant could not *annul* the Abrahamic? Why would that question even arise unless there was some contrast and tension? Whatever differences there might be between the Abrahamic and Mosaic covenants, they do not seem to be a matter of principle, says Lusk: "Or to put it another way, the New Covenant is just the Old Covenant in mature, glorified form."[62] Does this characterization, however, come close to the contrasts that are drawn by Paul and the writer to the Hebrews or John 1:17? Actually, "law and gospel actually perform the same (rather than contradictory) functions . . . [and] are simply two phases in the same redemptive program."[63] Once again, this simply does not accord with the facts, with respect to either Luther or Paul. And because this distinction is confused in the new perspective on Paul and federal vision, there is no longer any acknowledgement of even a difference between imperatives and indicatives. The law does not equal condemnation, says Lusk:

> The flip side, though, is that the gospel is not a pure unconditional message of grace and blessing, as the law/gospel dichotomy seems to imply. The gospel can condemn every bit as much as the law. . . . Thus, whether or not a particular piece of God's revelation is comforting ("gospel") or condemning ("law") depends on the state of the person's heart to which it comes.[64]

To be sure, we must recognize that there certainly is an existential aspect: the sinful tendency of human nature to "suppress the truth in unrighteousness" will lead unbelievers to turn even the gospel into law, but should the hermeneutic of unbelief be normative? Ironically, having correctly rejected Bultmann's existentialist hermeneutics, the new perspective on Paul and some of its federal-vision supporters

62. Ibid., 130.
63. Ibid., 131.
64. Ibid., 131–32.

inadvertently return to something like it at just this point. Is there really no such thing as indicative and imperative moods encoded into the text? Does it all depend on reader response? The systematic-theological grid seems to impose itself over even obvious rules of Greek grammar.

Is Final Justification by Works?

Again, this position is identical to the covenant theology of the late middle ages. Unlike the strict justice of the old covenant, the new covenant reflects a relaxation in God's demands. As the new perspective on Paul and federal-vision advocates have told us, God's law is very "do-able" (Schlissel). It is easy: get in by grace, stay in by cooperating with God's grace—doing whatever lies within you. If this is the view of new perspective on Paul and federal vision, then it is the height of arrogance to criticize the medieval church for its version of covenantal nomism. According to the Council of Trent, one "got in" by baptism, which could hardly be regarded as a human work of the infant. This is the "first justification," but one's subsequent status ("second justification") depended on cooperation with infused grace. "Final justification" referred to the last judgment, which involves a divine weighing of good works against transgressions. Ironically, even the term *final justification* is employed by Wright, and a final justification by works is endorsed by the new perspective on Paul, Shepherd, and the federal vision.[65]

With Paul, the Reformers challenged this entire paradigm by insisting that one not only gets in but stays in by grace *alone*. They realized that the law, which we could *not* fulfill, nevertheless *had* to be fulfilled. Clearly, this involves some notion of merit: either Christ's or our own personal obedience. Paul's contrast between "the righteousness that is by the law" and "the righteousness that is by faith" (Rom 10:5–6) is

65. Wright, *What Saint Paul Really Said*, 126: "It is strange, above all, that the first mention of justification in Romans is a mention of justification by works—apparently with Paul's approval (2:13: 'It is not the hearers of the law who will be justified before God, but the doers of the law who will be justified'). The right way to understand this, I believe, is to see that Paul is talking about the final justification." It is interesting to see that Wright does have a place for talking about how one is actually justified before God after all.

also that of the Reformers, as is the apostle's criticism of Judaism as a energetic zeal without the knowledge of God's justifying righteousness in Christ alone (10:2–4). The traditional Protestant interpretation does not deny that Paul has in mind the boundary markers that separate Jews from Gentiles, but it recognizes that he also speaks more broadly of works-righteousness.[66]

Of course, there is a final vindication of God's elect on judgment day, but the point of the doctrine of justification is to say that this eschatological verdict has already been rendered in the present. There are not two verdicts: one dependent on Christ's obedience, the other on ours—getting in by grace, staying in by obedience. Like Paul's critics, the Reformers' opponents, "being ignorant of God's righteousness, and seeking to establish their own righteousness, [have] not submitted to the righteousness of God. For Christ is the end of the law for righteousness to everyone who believes" (10:3–4). "This only I want to learn from you," Paul demands of the Galatians:

> Did you receive the Spirit by the works of the law, or by the hearing of faith? Are you so foolish? Having begun in the Spirit [getting in by grace], are you now being made perfect by the flesh [staying in by obedience]? . . .
>
> For as many as are of the works of the law are under the curse; for it is written, "Cursed is everyone who does not continue in all things which are written in the book of the law, to do them." But that no one is justified by the law in the sight of God is evident, for "the just shall live by faith." Yet the law is not of faith, but "the man who does them shall live by them." Christ has redeemed us from the curse of the law, having become a curse for us. (Gal 3:2–3, 10–12)

Those who seek to be justified by works, even congruently, with the assistance of grace, are not children of Abraham (the father of faith). In fact, they are slaves, not sons, heirs of Hagar the slave rather than

66. That election is of grace, for example, is illustrated in Jacob's being chosen "before the twins were born and had done [anything] either good or bad—in order that God's purpose of election might continue, not because of works but because of his call" (Rom 9:11). Clearly, it is works of any kind that Paul has in mind here, as also in 11:6: "But if it is by grace, it is no longer on the basis of works; otherwise grace would no longer be grace." With reference to election and justification, grace and works are not only distinguished but completely antithetical.

of Sarah the free woman. Or, to change the metaphor, Paul says that the Jerusalem below is in bondage, while the Jerusalem above is free. There are two covenants, says Paul, not one: a covenant of law (Sinai) and a covenant of promise (Abraham and his Seed) (4:21–31).

All of this is consistent with the prophets, especially Jeremiah 31, where God reissues the unilateral promise that the new covenant "will not be like the covenant I made with their fathers" at Sinai, "my covenant that they broke, though I was a husband to them, says the LORD" (31:32). Paul does not invent the gospel; he is simply reminding them that the covenant of promise (Abrahamic) cannot be annulled by the later covenant at Sinai (Gal 3:15–18). Evidently, Paul thought that his opponents had collapsed the Abrahamic covenant of promise, which was unconditional and global, into the covenant at Sinai, which was conditional and limited to the nation. This confusion of law covenants and promissory covenants creates a single covenantal nomism. The new perspective on Paul gets the second half of Paul's polemic: the Abrahamic covenant is global rather than restricted to the nation, but misses the first half upon which the second is predicated, namely, that the Abrahamic covenant is global precisely inasmuch as it is determined by the work of Christ and not by Israel's fidelity to the conditions of national status and possession of the land.

It is important to assert once again that the new perspective on Paul is often to be faulted not in what it affirms, but in what it denies. Covenant theology, whether covenantal nomism or the Reformed variety, is inherently communal.[67] It resists *reduction to* "me and my personal relationship with God"—or to the question, "How can I be saved?" There is no doubt that a one-sided interest in the *ordo salutis* and individual salvation has threatened to eclipse the *historia salutis* and the cosmic horizon. Reformed theology has been urging balance

67. We should note Wright's alteration of Sanders's thesis: "At this point the categories of 'getting in' and 'staying in,' made popular by E. P. Sanders, seem to need more nuances: 'getting *back in*,' for instance, or 'staying in when it looked as though one had been ejected'" (*What Saint Paul Really Said*, 155). There is all this continuity: "But Paul is not simply offering another form of 'covenantal nomism.' The covenant is now the renewed covenant; and the badge of membership is faith" (156). The majority of Israelites, Paul laments, are headed toward the curse of AD 70, but many ("Israel in principle") is entering into the restoration promised in the prophets through Messiah (156n61, in discussing 1 Thess 2). Concerning Sanders's thesis, Wright adds: "I do not myself believe such a refutation can or will be offered; serious modifications are required, but I regard his basic point as established" (20).

in this area long before the appearance of Wright's work. At the same time, *Reformed* covenant theology resists the opposite reduction to the question of covenant membership.[68] The gospel is not "a description of how people get saved," Wright insists, but is rather "*the return of Israel from exile*."[69] Again, we do not doubt that this redemptive-historical (biblical-theological) aspect is crucial, nor has it been lacking in Reformed covenant theology, but does this narrow definition exclude equally important elements in the prophets: forgiveness of sins, reconciliation with God, a new heart, adoption, the resurrection of individual bodies, all of which were both issues of individual salvation *and* the fulfillment of God's promise to restore Israel? Jesus spoke of the publican returning "to his house justified rather than" the Pharisee (Luke 18:14). "What must I do to be saved?" was clearly a question that Jesus and the apostles were asked, and answered, in the New Testament. Since not only Paul but Jesus says, "None of you keeps the law" (John 7:19), this especially becomes a paramount personal crisis. Even if revivalism has sacrificed ecclesiology to the quest for personal salvation, "How can I be saved?" is not the question of Luther's tortured subjectivity, but is asked and answered in the Gospels (Matt 19:25) and Acts (2:40; 16:30). In fact, says Paul, "This is a faithful saying and worthy of all acceptance, that Christ Jesus came into the world to save sinners, of whom I am chief" (1 Tim 1:15).

The Gentile mission would hardly have made sense if the gospel were simply the announcement of Israel's return from exile. And the Jewish mission would not have had any better success with

68. Heikki Räisänen, *Paul and the Law* (2nd ed.; Tübingen: Mohr, 1987), 147. Räisänen points out, however, that this thesis itself is unraveling, especially with the appearance of M. A. Elliott's *The Survivors of Israel: A Reconsideration of Pre-Christian Judaism* (Grand Rapids: Eerdmans, 2000): "This fresh and thorough study of pre-Christian Jewish literature effectively repudiates the notion of 'nationalistic election theology' in Judaism, i.e., 'covenantal nomism' in Sanders' terms, and convincingly demonstrates 'a highly individualistic and conditional view of covenant.' . . . Thus the work deprives the New Perspective School of its basis in Judaism and so makes its proposed revolution in Pauline studies abortive." Whether this overstates Elliott's achievement, my approach is able to give place to the new perspective's emphasis on a national election theology and, with it, a covenantal nomism. It distinguishes, however, between this (Sinaitic covenant) and the earlier (Abrahamic) covenant. This distinction, anchored so explicitly in the text (especially in Gal 3), allows us to account for both strands of exegetical data: a covenant of works and a covenant of grace.

69. Wright, *What Saint Paul Really Said*, 43 (emphasis original).

the "good news" reduced to the imperative to relax the entrance requirements.

So what happens if Paul's polemics against "works of the law" refers only to ethnic markers? Do we not end up with salvation by works, just not these particular works unique to Jewish identity? Schlissel and others actually go further than Wright in refusing any distinction between the principles of command and promise or between old and new covenants. Jesus is a new Moses; all discontinuity is eclipsed, even though the very announcement is that this new covenant "will not be like the covenant I made with [their] fathers" at Sinai. Included in a list of proof-texts for Schlissel's systematic-theological proposition that the gospel is full of conditions is Deuteronomy 28:

> If you fully obey the LORD your God and carefully follow all his commands I give you today, the LORD your God will set you high above all the nations on earth. All these blessings will come upon you and accompany you if you obey the LORD your God. . . .
>
> However, if you do not obey the LORD your God and do not carefully follow all his commands and decrees I am giving you today, all these curses will come upon you and overtake you. (28:12, 15 NIV)

Once more, however, we see that the question is not systematic theology versus the Bible, but careful systematic theology versus careless systematic theology. We have already affirmed conditionality. We do not deny it. There is even obvious conditionality in the new covenant, although conditions function differently: they are means of administering the covenant, not of election or justification, whose only ground is Christ's person and work, the latter received through faith alone. Schlissel thinks that the law expressed in Deuteronomy is easy to fulfill, whereas even Moses realizes its impossibility due to Israel's sin (Deut 7–9). So we appeal to Paul by way of response:

> For as many as are of the works of the law are under the curse; for it is written [in Deut 27:26, just cited by Schlissel as pertaining to believers], "Cursed is everyone who does not continue in all things which are written in the book of the law, to do them." But that no one is justified by the law in the sight of God is evident, for "the just

> shall live by faith." Yet the law is not of faith, but "the man who does them shall live by them." Christ has redeemed us from the curse of the law, having become a curse for us (for it is written, "Cursed is everyone who hangs on a tree"), that the blessing of Abraham might come upon the Gentiles, in Christ Jesus, that we might receive the promise of the Spirit through faith. . . .
>
> Tell me, you who desire to be under the law, do you not hear the law? (Gal 3:10–14; 4:21)

Schlissel believes that the law as well as the gospel makes alive, but Paul maintains, "For if there had been a law given which could have given life, truly righteousness would have been by the law" (Gal 3:21). If the Sinai covenant's conditions are for everlasting rest, as Schlissel suggests, then we are still under its curse. There are not two justifications, one based on Christ's righteousness and another based on our own. A final justification based on our own works, even those works done in faith, would reverse the verdict pronounced in our present justification.

Conclusion

These challenges of covenantal nomism represent both a threat and an opportunity. Seyoon Kim says that the new perspective on Paul is attempting to overturn the entire "Reformation interpretation of Paul's gospel."[70] Yet Kim also points up the important contributions of this debate: "It appears that further work is needed to clarify the relationship between the covenantal and forensic dimensions of justification."[71] This is precisely where the classic Reformed version of covenant theology makes a contribution that has often been overlooked on both sides in these related debates. Union with Christ in the covenant of grace is the context within which justification makes sense and is given both its cosmic-eschatological and individual horizon. In this covenant theology, the *historia salutis* and *ordo salutis* come together, as do justification and sanctification, the church and the individual.

70. Seyoon Kim, *Paul and the New Perspective: Second Thoughts on the Origin of Paul's Gospel* (Grand Rapids: Eerdmans, 2002), xiv.

71. Ibid., 83.

Union with Christ is not an *alternative* to the Reformation doctrine of justification, but its proper horizon.

The new perspective on Paul raises a host of important themes and makes some important contributions to our understanding of Paul and Israel. Furthermore, even the federal-vision circle is right to encourage us to appreciate more fully an objectivity to the covenant and its sacraments that has been severely weakened by revivalism. The cure, however, may be worse than the disease. That we must be always reforming according to God's word is not to be denied, but what we find in our classic Reformed resources is far more reflective of the whole counsel of God than the reactionary tendencies of our day. If we are to recover a genuinely Reformed covenant theology, it will require patient exegesis, not reactionary and dismissive polemics that derive from false dilemmas, reductionism, and caricatures. Clearly, we all have a lot more work to do, but at least we can rejoice in that the most decisive work, namely, the perfect fulfillment of the law, has already been done for us.

8

Do This and Live

Christ's Active Obedience as the Ground of Justification

R. Scott Clark

Introduction

In the controversy between Protestants and Roman Catholics there has been no question whether Jesus obeyed God's law, but only to what effect. Did Jesus obey the law so as to make it possible for us to cooperate with grace toward future justification, or did he obey God's law *for* us (*pro nobis*) to accomplish our justification once for all? The Protestants affirmed the latter and denied the former.

Nevertheless, despite the unity among confessional Protestants on justification, questions have persistently arisen among them concerning the nature, intent, and effect of Jesus's law keeping and its relation to the justification of sinners. What of Jesus's obedience is imputed to believers? Did Jesus obey the law as a qualification for his sacrifice on the cross only or did he accomplish more? Is it proper to distinguish between two or more aspects of his obedience? Are believers only forgiven, or are we also positively righteous before God? Should we say that Jesus has earned our righteousness and a place in heaven for us?

Given their opposition in this discussion, the terms *active* and *passive* might tend to create the impression that the work of Christ is being distinguished chronologically, but this is not the intent at all. These terms might also be misunderstood to denote a distinction between something done by Christ and something done to him.[1] Again, no such distinction is intended. In this context, *active* denotes Christ's intentional and positive fulfillment of God's law for his people at every moment of his life, and *passive* (from the Latin adjective derived from the verb *patior*, to suffer) speaks to the concept that, in the course of his obedience, "all the time he lived on earth, but especially at the end of his life, he bore, in body and soul, the wrath of God against the sin of the whole human race" (HC 37 [Schaff 3.319]). Christ's was, as Jürgen Moltmann says, "no unwilling fortuitous suffering; it is a *passio activa*."[2] Both adjectives are meant to describe, from different aspects, the entirety of Christ's work from the moment of his conception until his resurrection.[3]

History

The essence of the doctrine of the imputation of active obedience is the view that Christ's obedience and our justification have two parts: the remission of sins and the imputation to sinners of Christ's obedience to the law for believers. This is what one finds in the major Reformers.[4] From the moment Luther became a Protestant he taught that Christ's merits, which was nothing more than shorthand for "Christ's

1. Robert Reymond seems to reject the terms *active* and *passive* on the grounds that *passive* refers to something done to Christ; see *A New Systematic Theology of the Christian Faith* (Nashville: Nelson, 1998), 631.

2. Jürgen Moltmann, *Trinity and the Kingdom* (trans. Margaret Kohl; Minneapolis: Fortress, 1993), 75.

3. See Charles Hodge, *Systematic Theology* (New York: Scribner, Armstrong, 1873), 3.143.

4. J. I. Packer argues for an organic development of the doctrine of the imputation of active obedience out of the Protestant doctrine of justification; see "The Doctrine of Justifica-

obedience to the law for me," are imputed to the believer.[5] Calvin was heartily one with Luther on the doctrine of justification and from him inherited the foundation of what came to be articulated as the doctrine of the imputation of active obedience. The mere absence of the later technical terms *obedientia activa et passiva* (which did not come into use until the 1570s) should not deter us from observing the substance of the doctrine in Calvin. It should also be remembered that the Karg controversy did not begin until 1563, just one year before his death and after he had finished the final revisions to the *Institutes of the Christian Religion*.[6]

In fact, Calvin wrote repeatedly of Christ's entire obedience, under which discussion he included Christ's obedient life before his passion and by which he says Christ earned our redemption. This is evident in his 1539 commentary on Romans (at 5:19) and in the 1559 edition of *Institutes of the Christian Religion*, where he argued that it is not sanctity that forms faith (makes it efficacious) but rather Christ's obedience to the law (*Institutes* 3.11.23). God accepts sinners only because the *obedientia Christi* is imputed to us.[7] Against Osiander's doctrine of justification by "essential justice" (the infusion of Christ's person into the Christian), Calvin argued that the righteousness that is "reputed" (*reputari*) is the obedience and sacrificial death of Christ.[8]

Among the early orthodox, the doctrine of the imputation of active obedience is found in Ursinus (e.g., *Summa theologiae* [1561]) and Olevianus (e.g., *De substantia* [1585]).[9] Certainly the substance

---

tion among the Puritans," in *By Schisms Rent Asunder: Papers Read at the Puritan and Reformed Studies Conference, 1969* (London: N.P., 1970), 21.

5. See *Luther's Works* (trans. and ed. J. Pelikan and H. T. Lehmann; Philadelphia: Fortress/ St. Louis: Concordia, 1955–), 44.286–87; 26.122–33. See also *Luthers Werke Kritische Gesamtausgabe* (ed. J. K. F. Knaake, G. Kawerau, et al.; Weimar: Böhlau, 1883–), 391, 82–126.

6. The question "what did Calvin say on active obedience?" is anachronistic. I am not arguing that Calvin taught the later doctrine in all its detail. Rather, I am arguing only that ideas that the orthodox later exploited were present seminally in Calvin.

7. T. H. L. Parker and D. C. Parker, eds., *Ioannis calvini commentarius in epistolam pauli ad romanos* (Opera omnia series 13; Geneva: Droz, 1999), 115.8–14; P. Barth and W. Niesel, eds., *Joannis calvini opera selecta* (Munich: Kaiser, 1926–54), 3.485.38–39, 486.1, 486.4–13, 511.7–8; 4.207.6–9. Francis Turretin appealed to this locus in Calvin for support of his doctrine of the imputation of active obedience (*Institutes* 2.454 §14.13.32).

8. *Institutio* 3.11.5; *OS* 4.186.13–15. See also 3.11.8; *OS* 4.189.16–21.

9. See *Catechismus minor* 42 and *Summa theologiae* 16, 18, 23, 63, 131–39, 211 in K. Sudhoff, *C. Olevianus and Z. Ursinus: Leben und ausgewählte Schriften* (Elberfeld: Friderichs, 1857), 154–55, 160, 171–72, 206. For Olevianus, see Caspar Olevianus, *In epistolam d. pauli apostoli ad*

of the imputation of active obedience is present in the Heidelberg Catechism, when it says that God "grants and imputes to me the perfect satisfaction, righteousness, and holiness of Christ, as if I had never committed nor had any sin, and had myself accomplished all the obedience which Christ has fulfilled for me" (HC 60 [Schaff 3.326–27]).[10] It hard to imagine what other expression the catechism might have used to teach the substance of the imputation of active obedience more clearly. This is certainly how the catechism was understood by Johannes Wollebius (1586–1629) and Amandus Polanus (1561–1610), who also taught the imputation of active obedience.[11] A few, however, within confessional circles (e.g., the Lutheran Karg; and Pareus, Gattaker, and Twisse among the Reformed) denied the imputation of active obedience. Outside confessional circles, there have been more critics, among them Socinians, Arminians, Amyraldians, and neonomians of the seventeenth and eighteenth centuries.

Johannes Piscator (1546–1625), an influential German Reformed theologian of the late sixteenth and early seventeenth century, defined justification as *only* the forgiveness of sins (*remissio peccatorum*).[12] In his *scholia* in Romans 5:19 he argued that Paul was speaking of only justification through Christ's blood, not his law keeping.[13] Christ owed obedience to the law for himself and therefore could not have rendered it purely for the elect.[14] Piscator's reasoning was that it is unjust that God should punish Christ twice for Adam's sin by requiring of him

romanos notae, ex concionibus G. *Oleviani excerptae* (ed. T. Beza; Geneva, 1579), 196, 197, 205, 206, 209, 210; idem, *In epistolam d. pauli apostoli ad galatas notae, ex concionibus* G. *Oleviani excerptae* (ed. T. Beza; Geneva, 1578), 57.

10. David Pareus (1548–1622) said he wanted to reconcile both positions, but on every essential question he sided with Piscator. He adopted Piscator's definition of justification as only the remission of sins and appealed to HC 37 in support of his contention that the catechism teaches the same thing. His explanation of HC 60 ignored the language of the catechism and begged the question. See his letter on active obedience written in 1598 to Count Ludwig of Wittgenstein (a patron of the seminary in Heidelberg) in Zacharias Ursinus, *The Summe of Christian Religion* (trans. H. Parrie; London, 1645), 791–806.

11. Johannes Wollebius, *Compendium christianae theologiae* (ed. E. Bizer; Munich: Moers, 1935), 1.18.8; 1.30.15–18.

12. Johannes Piscator, *Aphorismi doctrinae christianae* (3rd ed.; London, 1595).

13. Johannes Piscator, *Analysis logica epistolae pauli ad romanos* (Herborn, 1595).

14. Johannes Piscator, *Theses theologicae de iustificatione hominis coram deo* (Herborn, 1612).

both active and passive obedience. Further, if Christ fulfilled the law for us, then his death was meaningless.[15] He rejected the conclusion that because sin is *duplex* Christ's obedience must also be *duplex*. He also rejected the argument that because of Christ's virgin birth he owed active obedience for only the elect. Piscator also took issue with the language of Heidelberg Catechism 60, which God imputes Christ's obedience to believers "as though we ourselves had performed it, the consequence will be, that *we are delivered from yielding obedience to the law*, since according to the hypothesis, Christ has performed it for us, or in our stead."[16]

According to W. Robert Godfrey, one of the chief concerns of the orthodox Reformed about Jacobus Arminius (1560–1609) was his doctrine of justification.[17] For example, most of his 1609 *Apology* concerned not predestination, but justification.[18] Whatever he actually believed (the Reformed accused him of redefining faith so that it justifies because of some quality in it or us), it is clear that he understood the issues surrounding the imputation of active obedience.[19]

Though Arminius professed ambivalence about the imputation of active obedience, the trajectory of his soteriology certainly led away from it, and the Remonstrants became active defenders of Piscator. Like Thomas Aquinas (ca. 1224–74), they taught the necessity of *gratia praeveniens et cooperans* but also the resistibility of that grace.[20] In this case, Christ made redemption possible for all who will cooperate,

15. See the editors' note in *The Works of James Arminius* (trans. James Nichols and William Nichols; Grand Rapids: Baker, 1996), 1.696–700.

16. Quoted in ibid., 1.698n (emphasis original).

17. W. R. Godfrey, "Tensions within International Calvinism: The Debate on the Atonement at the Synod of Dort, 1618–1619" (PhD diss., Stanford University, 1974), 40.

18. See Jacobus Arminius, *Opera theologica* (Leiden, 1629), 135–39, 145–46, 151–52, 156–61, 171–78, 180–83; idem, *Works of James Arminius*, 1.738–50, 763–65; 2.6–9, 16–25, 42–63.

19. See Arminius, *Opera theologica*, 127; *Works of James Arminius*, 1.696. The Remonstrants certainly took up that position, and it was rejected flatly by the Synod of Dort (Rejection of Errors 2.4) and the Westminster Divines. WCF 11.1 denies that we are justified "by imputing faith itself, the act of believing, or any other evangelical obedience to them, as their righteousness," and WLC 73 says that it is not as if "the grace of faith, or any act thereof were imputed to him for his justification" (quoted from *Westminster Confession of Faith* [Glasgow: Free Presbyterian Publications, 1994], 57, 167). Unless noted, all references are to this edition.

20. See Arminian Articles 4–5 (Schaff 3.547–48).

but not certain for anyone. From this platform, the rejection of the imputation of active obedience necessarily followed.

In response, the Synod of Dort (1618–19) repudiated the doctrine that God has willed to save those "who would believe and would persevere in faith and in the obedience of faith" (Rejection of Errors 1.1).[21] Rather, they argued, we believe and persevere because we are elect. Believing and persevering do not, however, become grounds or instruments of justification.[22] Dort declared that if the "act of faith" or our "incomplete obedience" is a condition of justification, the "merit of Christ is enervated" (*meritum Christi enervatur*) (1.3 [Schaff 3.557]). They turned again to Christ's "merits" (2.1) and rejected explicitly the idea that Christ merited only the *possibility* of the salvation of the elect (2.3). Rather, they declared, he achieved it for them (Schaff 3.563). The merits of our faith are contrasted with the merits of Christ's obedience (2.4; see also Canons of Dort 5.8).

In the Irish Articles of Religion (1615) Archbishop Ussher spoke for the Reformed mainstream when he wrote that "we are accounted righteous . . . for the merit of our Lord and Saviour Jesus Christ, applied by faith" (34). He defined that merit this way: "Christ is now the righteousness of all them that truly believe in him. He, for them, paid their ransom by his death. He, for them, fulfilled the law in his life" (35 [Schaff 3.532]).

Gijsbertus Voetius (1589–1676) understood Christ's merits as a synonym for Christ's active obedience. "Merit," he argued, "is the work provided, to which a reward or retribution is due proportionate to the work." This is, in effect, a Protestant version of condign merit, that is, the merit that God rewards because it meets the terms of divine

21. Since the proponents of the so-called federal vision seem to affirm both an eternal, unconditional election *and* a historical, conditional election that can be lost without perseverance, it is difficult to see how they escape the strictures of the Synod of Dort on at least half of their position. See John Barach, "Covenant and Election"; Steve Wilkins, "Covenant, Baptism, and Salvation"; and Rich Lusk, "New Life and Apostasy: Hebrews 6:4–8 as Test Case," all in *The Federal Vision* (ed. Steve Wilkins and Duane Garner; Monroe, LA: Athanasius, 2004), 15–44, 47–69, 271–99; Norman Shepherd, *The Call of Grace* (Phillipsburg, NJ: P&R, 2000), 79–91.

22. "Qui docent, 'Voluntatem Dei de servandis credituris, et in fide fideique obedientia perseveraturis, esse totum et integrum electionis ad salutem decretum" (Rejection of Errors 1.1 [Schaff 3.557]; see also 1.5. It is hard to ignore the similarities between the program of the federal vision and the very thing condemned by the Synod of Dort here.

justice.[23] Christ's work, he said, was "voluntary," and he provided "utterly perfect obedience" "in our behalf as sponsor of everything which God's law required of us."[24]

As the position of the Remonstrants, Amyraldians, and Socinians against the imputation of active obedience became fixed, the confessional Reformed response became more explicit in defense of the imputation of active obedience. For example, Johann Heinrich Alsted (1588–1638) taught the imputation of active obedience under the heading *De Christo mediatore* (locus 30).[25] It is significant that the Reformed treated the imputation of active obedience under Christ's priesthood since it called attention to the vicarious nature of Christ's obedience for us. Those who rejected the imputation of active obedience seemed to be shortchanging Christ's work *for* us in favor of his work *in* us. Reformed resolve would be tested by the opponents of the imputation of active obedience, eventually forcing a verbal compromise at the Westminster Assembly, but the center held, and the language of the confession remained sufficiently strong.[26] According to Westminster Confession of Faith 11.1 both Christ's obedience and satisfaction are imputed. Both "by his obedience and death" Christ

> did fully discharge the debt of all those that are thus justified, and did make a proper, real, and full satisfaction to his Father's justice in their behalf. Yet, inasmuch as he was given by the Father for them; and his obedience and satisfaction accepted in their stead, and both freely, not for any thing in them; their justification is only of free

23. Gijsbertus Voetius, *Selectarum disputationum theologicarum* (Utrecht, 1648–69), 2.228.

24. Ibid., 2.229.

25. J. H. Alsted, *Synopsis theologiae* (Hanau, 1627), 75.

26. On the controversy over the imputation of active obedience among the Westminster Divines, Packer, "Doctrine of Justification among the Puritans," 22, says: "Though the phrase 'formal cause,' and the distinction between active and passive obedience, do not appear in the statement on justification in the Westminster Confession, nonetheless this statement is a classic indication of the precision and balance of thought, as well as the polemical thrusts that were learned in these exchanges." I agree and am suggesting here that the Westminster Divines removed the more explicit language (i.e., "the whole obedience of Christ") regarding active obedience to allow the opponents of the imputation of active obedience (Twisse, Vines, and Gattaker) to subscribe the confession while providing language sufficient for the preservation of the doctrine. I am indebted to Tom Wenger and Chad Van Dixhoorn for their help on this issue, though I am not suggesting that they agree with my conclusion.

> grace; that both the exact justice and rich grace of God might be glorified in the justification of sinners. (WCF 11.3)

Westminster Larger Catechism 70 says that there is no ground in us for our justification, but rather the only ground is Christ's "perfect obedience and full satisfaction" that is "imputed" to believers and "received by faith alone." This bipartite logical distinction between obedience and satisfaction is substantially what the orthodox wanted.[27]

After the Westminster Assembly, John Owen defended the imputation of active obedience against Piscator, turning to Christ's active obedience as a source of encouragement and consolation for the Christian.[28] According to Owen, Christ had to provide active obedience because Adam was under the law ("do this and live"). The life promised to him "is not to be obtained unless all be done that the law requires." By analogy, just as our first federal head, Adam, actively disobeyed God, so Christ our surety necessarily provided active obedience in our place. If he provided only remission of sins, then we still owe active obedience ourselves for justification. In other words, for Owen, either Jesus is a compete Savior or he is not.

Piscator had suggested that the imputation of active obedience might lead to less sanctity among believers, but Owen argued that because of Christ's active obedience for us we are right with God, which is the basis for our communion with him and from which flows sanctity and the Christian life. Far from being a hindrance to a vital spiritual life, according to Owen, the imputation of active obedience is the source of it.[29]

27. Pareus recognized that this distinction was the essence of the argument for the imputation of active obedience; in Ursinus, *Summe of Christian Religion*, 793.

28. John Owen, *The Works of John Owen* (ed. W. H. Goold; New York: Carter, 1851–53), 5.254; 1.482. See also his reflection on the spiritual benefits of Christ's obedience in *Works* 2.133–35, 154–57.

29. Ibid., 2.162–63; see also 5.240–75. Owen's approach is in contrast to that proposed by the new perspective on Paul (and the federal vision), who in the words of Peter Stuhlmacher "propagate afresh the old two-part analysis of Pauline soteriology in terms of a juristic stream and a participatory stream, already proposed by William Wrede and above all by Albert Schweitzer." According to Stuhlmacher, "this distinction becomes superfluous as soon as we notice Paul's own clear connection between justification, atonement and reconciliation and furthermore recall that Christ Jesus is for Paul always a corporate, representative figure, even as the Messiah and the Son of Man are"; Peter Stuhlmacher, *Revisiting Paul's Doctrine of*

In the later seventeenth century, the European Reformed theologians continued to advocate the imputation of active obedience. Francis Turretin (1623–87) in his *Institutes of the Elenctic Theology* (1679–85) argued against Piscator and Karg by name (*Institutes* 2.445 §14.13.1). By the last quarter of the century, Turretin could justly claim that the imputation of active obedience was "the common opinion and the one received in our churches" (*sed communis et in Ecclesiis nostris recepta sententia*) (2.445 §14.13.2). He rejected Piscator's argument that the imputation of active obedience has God demanding a double payment. Christ's righteousness is one, though complex. The law binds sinners to obedience and punishment, and thus Christ's obedience liberates us from death and merits our right to life (2.454 §14.13.29).

Modern Discussion

Supporters

Certainly one of the strongest twentieth-century advocates for the imputation of active obedience was J. Gresham Machen (1881–1937). He argues that without the imputation of active obedience, we would be worse off than Adam, but because of the imputation of active obedience, we are better off than Adam before the fall, since now, for Christ's sake, "we are beyond the possibility of becoming unrighteous."[30]

Despite his discomfort with the traditional and confessional doctrine of the covenant of works, John Murray (1898–1975) affirmed the imputation of active obedience repeatedly.[31] He reminded readers that

Justification: A Challenge to the New Perspective; with an Essay by Donald A. Hagner (Downers Grove, IL: InterVarsity, 2001), 57.

30. J. G. Machen, *God Transcendent and Other Sermons* (ed. N. B. Stonehouse; Grand Rapids: Eerdmans, 1949), 172–80.

31. See John Murray, *The Epistle to the Romans* (New International Commentary on the New Testament; Grand Rapids: Eerdmans, 1959–65), 1.204–5; idem, *Redemption Accomplished and Applied* (Grand Rapids: Eerdmans, 1955), 26–29. James B. Jordan, "Merit versus Maturity: What Did Jesus Do for Us?" in *The Federal Vision* (ed. Steve Wilkins and Duane Garner; Monroe, LA: Athanasius, 2004), 152, makes much of Murray and others, such as Herman Hoeksema, S. G. DeGraaf, and C. Van Der Waal, rejecting the covenant of works as unbiblical and says that "a rejection of the idea of a meritorious covenant of works was commonly entertained in Continental Reformed circles." It is true that Murray was uncomfortable with the traditional formulations of covenant theology, but he remained orthodox in his doctrine of justification. See John Murray, *Collected Writings of John Murray* (Edinburgh: Banner of Truth, 1976–82), 2.202–22. Jeong Koo Jeon, *Covenant Theology: John Murray's and Meredith G. Kline's Response*

the terms *active* and *passive* are but aspects of his one obedience.[32] He argued that the imputation of active obedience was not just a biblical teaching, but a category, a way of comprehending all of Christ's work for us: "The Scripture regards the work of Christ as one of obedience and uses this term, or the concept that it designates, with sufficient frequency to warrant the conclusion that obedience is generic [i.e., general] and therefore embracive enough to be viewed as the unifying or integrating principle."[33] Murray used and defended the terms *active and passive obedience* and noted with the tradition that all Christ did was both active and passive, inasmuch as he suffered in all he did and all he did was voluntary and active.[34]

Emil Brunner (1889–1966) described as "intolerably pedantic" and a "complete misunderstanding" the claim that only the passive obedience is imputed to the believer. He rejected the distinction between the active and passive obedience itself as "impossible."[35]

Louis Berkhof (1873–1957) also followed the tradition by placing the imputation of active obedience in the context of the covenant of works and a twofold conception of justification as remission and imputation of Christ's righteousness and in terms of Christ's threefold relation to the law.[36] He stressed a complementary relation between the two aspects of Christ's obedience for us and argued for a "constant interpenetration" of the two.[37]

---

to the Historical Development of Federal Theology in Reformed Thought (Lanham: University Press of America, 1999), shows that Murray used a range of expressions throughout his career. That Hoeksema and the followers of Klaas Schilder rejected the covenant of works is beyond dispute, but Jordan's conclusion does not follow. The Kuyperians continued to hold to the covenant of works, as did others such as Bavinck, Vos, Berkhof, Kersten, and Bosma, all of whom were Dutch. More importantly, the notion that so-called Continental Reformed theology did not hold the covenant of works contradicts mountains of evidence in the primary sources of Reformed theology. Continental Reformed theologians (e.g., Olevianus and Ursinus, who were German and Silesian and therefore Continental) were among its most important developers in the sixteenth century, and it was universally held by Continental Reformed theologians (e.g., Polanus, Wollebius, Voetius, Cocceius, Turretin, Witsius, Rijssen, Heidanus, Heidegger, à Brakel, Van Mastricht, Marckius, and Cloppenburg) in the seventeenth century.

32. Murray, *Redemption Accomplished and Applied*, 27.

33. Ibid., 19.

34. Ibid., 20–23.

35. Emil Brunner, *The Christian Doctrine of Creation and Redemption* (trans. Olive Wyon; Philadelphia: Westminster, 1952), 282–83.

36. Louis Berkhof, *Systematic Theology* (Grand Rapids: Eerdmans, 1939), 214, 379.

37. Ibid., 379–80.

G. C. Berkouwer (1903–96) asked whether the dogmatic distinction between active and passive obedience is "subtle, scholastic, unfounded, and irreverent"? Properly understood, however, he concluded that it is not. He argued for the mystery of Christ's "entire" and "uninterrupted" obedience. Denial of active obedience violates that mystery.[38]

New Testament scholar Richard Longnecker traces the New Testament and patristic uses of the ὑπακοή (obedience) and the adjective ὑπήκοος (obedient) and their cognates.[39] Taken together with the understanding of πίστις as Christ's faithfulness (following A. G. Herbert and T. F. Torrance) in certain passages, they denote Christ's active obedience.[40]

Robert Letham advocates Christ's "vicarious obedience" from, among other grounds, Jesus's claim to sinlessness and his role as Second Adam.[41] Robert L. Reymond affirms strongly the substance of

38. G. C. Berkouwer, *The Work of Christ* (trans. C. Lambregste; Grand Rapids: Eerdmans, 1965), 319–27.

39. Richard N. Longnecker, "The Obedience of Christ in the Theology of the Early Church," in *Reconciliation and Hope: New Testament Essays on Atonement and Eschatology Presented to Leon Morris on His 60th Birthday* (ed. Robert Banks; Grand Rapids: Eerdmans, 1974), 142–52. Stuhlmacher, *Revisiting Paul's Doctrine of Justification*, 64–66, takes the opposite approach to πίστις Ἰησοῦ Χριστοῦ (e.g., Gal 2:16), arguing that it refers not to Jesus's "own faith or faithfulness, but rather our faith in Jesus." While Stuhlmacher's understanding seems to accord better with the sense of the text, in either case the vicarious active obedience of Christ is upheld, either as the faithful one or the obedient one in whom sinners trust. On the contemporary turn to the subjective reading of the genitive, see C. E. B. Cranfield, "On the Πίστις Χριστοῦ Question," in *On Romans and Other New Testament Essays* (Edinburgh: Clark, 1998), who concludes: "The absence of any clear statement that Jesus 'believed,' 'had faith' (πιστεύειν) and of any unambiguous use of πίστις of Christ's own faith, and the fact that there are quite unambiguous references to faith in Christ are surely persuasive arguments against the subjective genitive interpretation and for the objective" (95). Contrast Cranfield's careful judgment with Norman Shepherd, *The Call of Grace* (Phillipsburg, NJ: P&R, 2000), 19, who recklessly assumes the subjective genitive in speaking of Jesus's "living, active, and obedient faith" as if he were more Christian than Christ. The popular penetration of this view and its effects on the doctrine of justification are also evident in John Armstrong, "The Obedience of Faith," in *Trust and Obey: Obedience and the Christian* (ed. Don Kistler; Morgan, PA: Soli Deo Gloria, 1996), 79–117.

40. Longnecker, "Obedience of Christ," 146–47.

41. Robert Letham, *Contours of Christian Theology: The Work of Christ* (Downers Grove, IL: InterVarsity, 1993), 113–21; see also G. H. Kersten, *Reformed Dogmatics: A Systematic Treatment of Reformed Doctrine* (Grand Rapids: Netherlands Reformed Book and Publishing Committee, 1981), 1.262–71.

the doctrine of double imputation.[42] And William Berends defends active obedience by interpreting Philippians 2:5–11 in light of Paul's two-Adam scheme.[43]

The publication of "The Gospel of Jesus Christ: An Evangelical Celebration" in June 1999, with its endorsement of the imputation of Jesus's "flawless obedience" and his righteousness, sparked a controversy that continues to reverberate in the broad evangelical world, with some effect in the confessional Reformed community.[44] Robert H. Gundry responded with a declaration that he would not sign it because of its doctrine of the imputation of Christ's righteousness. Thomas C. Oden responded by defending the doctrine of imputation, sparking a further exchange with Gundry.[45] John Piper entered the fray in 2002 by restating the traditional Reformation doctrine of the imputation of active obedience.[46] This triggered further responses from Gundry and Mark A. Seifrid, among others.

Nicolaas H. Gootjes argues for Christ's active obedience as a biblical and confessional (e.g., Belgic and French Confessions) doctrine and the basis for Christian obedience.[47] In dialogue with the proponents of the so-called federal-vision theology, Morton Smith also defends the imputation of active obedience.[48]

42. Reymond, *New Systematic Theology*, 631.

43. William Berends, "The Obedience of Jesus Christ," *Vox reformata* 66 (2001): 26–51. See also Herman Hoeksema, *Reformed Dogmatics* (Grand Rapids: Reformed Free Publishing Association, 1966), 365. Berends, "Obedience of Christ," 42, says that Hoeksema denied active obedience.

44. *Christianity Today* (June 14, 1999): 51–56.

45. See Robert H. Gundry, "Why I Didn't Endorse 'The Gospel of Jesus Christ: An Evangelical Celebration' . . . Even Though I Wasn't Asked To," *Books and Culture* (Jan./Feb. 2001): 6–9; Thomas C. Oden, "A Calm Answer . . . to a Critique of 'The Gospel of Jesus Christ: An Evangelical Celebration,'" *Books and Culture* (March/April 2001): 12–13, 39; Robert H. Gundry, "On Oden's Answer," *Books and Culture* (March/April 2001): 14–15, 39; Thomas C. Oden, "Answering Critics of 'An Evangelical Celebration,'" *Books and Culture* (May/June 2001): 6–7. See also the debate in the pages of *Pro ecclesia* 9 (Spring 2000): 133–49; and Oden's discussion of active obedience in his *Word of Life: Systematic Theology* (San Francisco: Harper, 1992), 2.358–62.

46. John Piper, *Counted Righteous in Christ: Should We Abandon the Imputation of Christ's Righteousness?* (Wheaton, IL: Crossway, 2002), esp. 121–25.

47. Nicolaas H. Gootjes, "Christ's Obedience and Covenant Obedience," Κοινωνία 19 (2002): 2–22.

48. Morton H. Smith, "The Biblical Plan of Salvation, with Reference to the Covenant of Works, Imputation, and Justification by Faith," in *The Auburn Avenue Theology, Pros and*

Critics

In his analysis of John Owen's doctrine of justification, Amyraldian theologian A. C. Clifford suggests that the doctrine of the imputation of active obedience removes the necessity for the Christian's own obedience.[49] He argues that the orthodox quite misunderstood Calvin, who actually taught that justification is "no less dependent on the believer's obedience than it is on Christ's righteousness."[50] According to Clifford, Piscator and not Theodore Beza (and the Reformed orthodox following him) understood Calvin's doctrine of justification correctly. Clifford links Calvin, Piscator, Arminius, and Wesley in support of his own rejection of the doctrine of double imputation.[51]

Among New Testament scholars, Mark Seifrid, influenced by Clifford's interpretation of Protestant orthodoxy, says that it "added the imputation of Christ's righteousness to the forgiveness of sins." The distinction between active and passive righteousness is "unnecessary and misleading" and arose from a "failure to grasp that Christ's work represents the prolepsis of the final judgment and an entrance of the age to come."[52] N. T. Wright rejects the imputation of active obedience on the ground that it "gives the impression of a legal transaction, a cold piece of business, almost a trick of thought performed by a God who is logical and correct but hardly one we would want to worship."[53]

Some federal-vision proponents also reject the imputation of active obedience.[54] Rich Lusk argues that the imputation of active obedience

---

Cons: Debating the Federal Vision (ed. E. Calvin Beisner; Fort Lauderdale, FL: Knox Theological Seminary, 2004), 109.

49. A. C. Clifford, *Atonement and Justification* (Oxford: Oxford University Press, 1990), 174.

50. Ibid., 175.

51. Ibid., 190–91. From a dispensational perspective, Andrew V. Snider argues that the doctrine of Christ's vicarious obedience is unbiblical and turns the focus away from Christ's penal substitution and death on the cross; "Justification and the Active Obedience of Christ: Toward a Biblical Understanding of Imputed Righteousness" (MA thesis, Master's Seminary, 2002).

52. Mark A. Seifrid, *Christ Our Righteousness: Paul's Theology of Justification* (Leicester: Apollos/Downers Grove, IL: InterVarsity, 2000), 175. Clifford's account of Reformed orthodoxy is substantially discredited by Carl R. Trueman, *The Claims of Truth: John Owen's Trinitarian Theology* (Carlisle, UK: Paternoster, 1998).

53. N. T. Wright, *What Saint Paul Really Said: Was Paul of Tarsus the Real Founder of Christianity?* (Grand Rapids: Eerdmans, 1996), 110. I am grateful to David VanDrunen for directing me to this quotation.

54. For example, Norman Shepherd, a former professor of systematic theology at Westminster Theological Seminary (Philadelphia), gave public speeches in 2003 and 2004 rejecting

is premised on post-Reformation federal theology, which, he suggests, makes it illegitimate.[55] More importantly, he says that "justification requires no transfer or imputation of anything" suggests that the very notion of merit "has some incoherencies."[56] Any notion of "strict merit," he says, runs afoul of many biblical passages and has been rejected by leading Reformed theologians such as Herman Bavinck.[57]

Because creation is inherently gracious, Adam, Lusk argues, could never have merited life with God. Grace is before all. Adam's relation to God was not legal, it was filial—family relations are not legal.[58] His sin was a not a failure to obey, but a failure to trust and obey.[59] The traditional view, he argues, introduced an unbiblical nature/grace dualism.[60] He denies that Jesus performed active obedience for us, since such a notion would rely on unbiblical notions about law and gospel and merit and on a contractual construction of the covenant. According to Lusk, Reformed dogmatics erred rather seriously by placing such freight on the imputation of active obedience, when it should have

---

the doctrine of the imputation of active obedience for the same reasons as Piscator. In his book *The Call of Grace* (Phillipsburg, NJ: P&R, 2000), Christ is not presented as our law keeper, whose obedience is imputed to us, but rather as the first believer whose faithfulness we are to emulate.

55. Rich Lusk, "A Response to 'the Biblical Plan of Salvation,'" in *The Auburn Avenue Theology, Pros and Cons: Debating the Federal Vision* (ed. E. Calvin Beisner; Fort Lauderdale, FL: Knox Theological Seminary, 2004), 120. Lusk relies on the research of those influenced by J. B. Torrance (1924–2004), who saw Reformed federal theology as a corruption of Calvin's theology. Lusk makes many sweeping historical claims, concluding that the historic doctrine of the covenant of works is a "minority report in the Reformed world today." In so doing, he ignores a considerable amount of modern scholarship that corrects the claims made by Torrance and others; see Richard A. Muller, *Christ and the Decree: Christology and Predestination in Reformed Theology from Calvin to Perkins* (Grand Rapids: Baker, 1986); idem, *Post-Reformation Reformed Dogmatics: The Rise and Development of Reformed Orthodoxy, ca. 1520 to ca. 1725* (2nd ed.; 4vols.; Grand Rapids: Baker, 2003); Carl R. Trueman and R. S. Clark, eds., *Protestant Scholasticism: Essays in Reassessment* (Carlisle, UK: Paternoster, 1999); Willem J. Van Asselt and Eef Dekker, eds., *Reformation and Scholasticism: An Ecumenical Enterprise* (Grand Rapids: Baker, 2001); Lyle D. Bierma, *German Calvinism in the Confessional Age* (Grand Rapids: Baker, 1997); and R. Scott Clark, *Caspar Olevian and the Substance of the Covenant: The Double Benefit of Christ* (Rutherford Studies in Historical Theology; Edinburgh: Rutherford House, 2005).

56. Lusk, "Response to 'the Biblical Plan of Salvation,'" 142.

57. Ibid., 120, 125. Lusk supplies no proof for this claim. See Herman Bavinck, *Our Reasonable Faith: A Survey of Christian Doctrine* (trans. H. Zylstra; Grand Rapids: Baker, 1956), 452–68, who argues for the very classical Protestant doctrines Lusk rejects, including the imputation of active obedience and *sola fide*.

58. Lusk, "Response to 'the Biblical Plan of Salvation,'" 122, 124–25, 137.

59. Ibid., 125.

60. Ibid., 126.

been placed on the resurrection. Machen's famous telegram should have read, "So thankful for the resurrection," not "so thankful for the active obedience of Christ."[61] According to Lusk, the great problem with the imputation of active obedience is that it "de-eschatalogizes" the work of Christ: "The new age is not brought by the fulfillment of the old law, it is inaugurated in his resurrection."[62]

The solution, Lusk says, is to turn away from the imputation of active obedience and toward union with Christ: "With regards to justification, this means that my right standing before the Father is grounded in Christ's own right standing before the Father. So long as I abide in Christ, I can no more come under the Father's negative judgment than Jesus himself can!" He continues: "This justification requires no transfer or imputation of anything. It does not force us to reify 'righteousness' into something that can be shuffled around in heavenly accounting books." This approach, he says, does not downplay Christ's active obedience, since without it "his body would still be in the tomb."[63]

In an even more improbable essay, James Jordan rejects the covenant of works as Pelagian.[64] Because he was created immature, Adam's probation was not to obey the law but to *mature*.[65] In this scheme, merit per se is inappropriate and unnecessary, and Jordan concludes that Jesus did not "earn" anything from God's justice. Rather, he says, Jesus "became the first mature man.[66]

Thesis

I contend that, as the voluntary surety entailed by the covenant of redemption between the Father and the Son (*pactum salutis*) and as

61. Ibid., 140–41.

62. Ibid., 141.

63. Ibid., 142.

64. Jordan, "Merit versus Maturity," 152–53. Among the more fanciful elements of his account of prelapsarian existence are Jordan's hypotheses that God promised to Adam and Eve that, upon maturity, they would be allowed to eat from the tree of the knowledge of good and evil and that Adam might have had to die to protect Eve from continued onslaughts from Satan (180–81).

65. Ibid., 158, 178–82.

66. Like Lusk, Jordan too commits the etymological fallacy of deducing the meaning of ἐχαρίσατο in Phil 2:9 from its root rather than its usage and context (ibid., 193).

the Second Adam required by the covenant of works, God the Son became incarnate to fulfill the legal obligations of these covenants. By his active suffering obedience to God's law as expressed in these covenants, he not only propitiated the divine wrath and expiated sin but also merited justification and eternal life for his people.

Biblical Teaching of the Imputation of Active Obedience

According to Romans 1:18–2:16, the divine demand for obedience has existed since before the fall.[67] From creation (1:19) the divine attributes and requirement for justice have been manifest (φανερόν). The phrase ἀπὸ κτίσεως κόσμου (1:20) frames the discussion in terms of Adam and the fall. Even in paradise, the demands were unequivocal and the standard unforgiving: "You may eat from any tree in the garden except from the tree of the knowledge of good and evil. The day you eat of it, you shall surely die" (Gen 2:16–17). The essence of the law (Rom 2:6) is that God shall "give to each man according to his works [κατὰ τὰ ἔργα αὐτοῦ]." In this case, the formal "doing" required by the law was abstinence, but the material obedience was loving God and obeying him completely.

Those who lived under the Mosaic system will be judged accordingly (2:12–13), and those who did not (2:15) shall face judgment on the basis of the "law written on their hearts" (τοῦ νόμου γραπτὸν ἐν ταῖς καρδίας), but they are substantially identical. All humans live under the same law: "do."[68]

67. Paul did not have Barth's opinion of natural law. See Karl Barth, *Nein! Antwort an Emil Brunner* (Munich: Kaiser, 1934); see Brunner's response in *Natural Theology* (London: Bles, 1956).

68. Paul refers to such principles as στοιχεῖα (elemental principles) (Gal 4:3, 9; Col 2:8). The στοιχεῖα are ruthless taskmasters requiring performance. These are difficult verses to be sure, but the best reading of Paul's use of στοιχεῖα is not to infuse it with the classical meaning (i.e., the four natural elements) or a philosophical sense, but rather to understand it as a shorthand reference to the natural-law principle of creation under which all humans who are not in Christ exist. Eduard Schweizer, "Slaves of the Elements and Worshipers of Angels: Gal 4:3, 9 and Col 2:8, 18, 20," *Journal of Biblical Literature* 107 (1988): 455–68, correlates Paul's use of στοιχεῖα to the classical and pagan use. Philipp Veilhauer, "Gesetzesdienst und Stoicheiadienst im Galaterbrief," in *Rechtfertigung: Festschrift für Ernst Käsemann zum 70. Geburtstag* (ed. J. Friedrich, W. Pöhlmann, and P. Stuhlmacher; Tübingen: Mohr/Göttingen: Vandenhoeck & Ruprecht, 1976), 543–55, takes roughly the same view as espoused here.

Because the moral law issues from the divine nature, Jesus was categorical about its demands, its unbending nature, and constitutional function. Not a "yod or dot shall pass from the law until all is accomplished" (Matt 5:18–19). Whoever tries to "loose" (λύσῃ) the law or teaches others that the requirements of the law have been relaxed will be called least in the kingdom of heaven. The law must be "accomplished" and "fulfilled"; it must be "done." What the law requires must be performed. To the self-righteous lawyer, Jesus did not say, "Do your best," but rather, "Do this and live" (Luke 10:25–28).

Paul says that the one "having done" (ποιήσας) righteousness (Rom 10:5) shall live "by the law" (ἐκ [τοῦ] νόμου).[69] This is why it is "not the hearers of the law who are righteous before God, but the *doers* of the law who will be justified" (2:13, emphasis added). This is how Paul interprets Deuteronomy 27:26: "For all who rely on works of the law are under a curse; for it is written, 'Cursed is everyone who does not continue to do [ποιῆσαι] everything that is written in the book of the law'" (Gal 3:10).[70] This "doing" is essential to understanding the perfect performance of his law that God expects of his image bearers. The demand is not only for the absence of sin or even just punishment for sin but also for positive performance of all requirements.

Our Lord summarized his entire earthly *missio* by saying that, as the Son, he was "unable [οὐ δύναται] to do" anything on his own initiative. He does only "what he sees the Father doing" (John 5:19). To John the Baptist he declared that he had come "to fulfill all righteousness" (πρέπον ἐστὶν ἡμῖν πληρῶσαι πᾶσαν δικαιοσύνην) (Matt 3:15). Righteousness was something he had to do. Inaugurating formally his threefold office at his baptism was part of that fulfilling. To hungry disciples he declared, "My food is to do the will of him who sent me and to accomplish his work" (John 4:34). In the key terms in this verse, ἵνα ποιήσω, Jesus did not say he came to "trust" his Father, though he certainly did, but he said he was sent to "do" his Father's will and to "fulfill his work" (τελειώσω αὐτοῦ τό ἔργον).

69. James noted three times that the law requires "doing," not just "hearing" (Jas 1:22–27; 4:11).

70. The examples of the demand for justice come from postlapsarian revelation, but are fairly considered here since the demand published before the fall has never been revoked.

This is also why Jesus did not simply appear in history as an adult and promptly die, nor did he obey the law only as preparation for his passion. Rather, we should say with the Heidelberg Catechism that he suffered "all the time he lived on earth" (HC 37), and in so doing he "accomplished all the obedience" we owed (60). Christ was born "under the law" (Gal 4:4), to redeem those under the στοιχεῖα (4:3), that is, those "under the law." God the Son became incarnate for the purpose of performing the demands of the law (John 6:38–40; 17:3–6; Gal 4:4–5).

This is how we should read Romans 5:12–21. According to Paul, there are two heads of humanity—one disobedient and the other obedient. Sin and death entered the world through Adam, the first head of all humanity (5:12).[71] He broke the law (5:13). His disobedience became the instrument through which death entered the world.

The disobedience of ὁ πρῶτος ἄνθρωπος (the first man) (1 Cor 15:47) creates an expectation concerning remedial obedience to be performed by ὁ ἔσχατος Ἀδάμ (the final Adam) (15:45). Thus, Paul says, "through the obedience of the one" (διὰ τῆς παρακοῆς τοῦ ἑνός) the many, that is, those who are united to Christ through faith alone (Gal 2:16), "shall be constituted righteous" (δίκαιοι κατασταθήσονται)

71. Though most of the Western church has followed some version of Augustine's interpretation (e.g., *City of God* 16.27), the grammar of ἐφ' ᾧ in Rom 5:12 has not historically been decisive for its interpretation. On the history of interpretation, see C. E. B. Cranfield, *Romans* (International Critical Commentary; Edinburgh: Clark, 1975), 1.274–79. The logical connection tends to be interpreted in the light of one's broader reading of Scripture. Calvin took an Augustinian (anti-Pelagian) position, interpreting 5:12 somewhat realistically, but with his conclusion the Reformed agreed that Paul here describes how Adam "in himself vitiated, corrupted, and depraved our nature." For Calvin, there was not a strict parallel between the fall and justification; the fall was partly forensic and partly realistic; John Calvin, *Commentarius in epistolam pauli ad romanos* (Geneva: Droz, 1999), 108.33–34; 1013.30–34. Justification, however, is totally forensic. The ground is Christ's righteousness, not ours. James Dunn rejects the strict Augustinian/realistic view but is vague about the link between Adam and us; *Romans 1–8* (Word Biblical Commentary 38A; Dallas: Word, 1988), 273–74. Murray, *Romans*, 1.184–87, argued that this passage teaches not inherent original sin and inherent righteousness (Augustine's view); rather it teaches that the sin of 5:12 refers to the same event as the "one trespass" of 5:15–19. For Murray, the frame of reference was not realistic but forensic, with realistic effects. Murray eliminated the tension in Calvin's view between the forensic and the realistic in favor of a totally forensic view; see Meredith G. Kline, "Gospel until the Law: Romans 5:13–14 and the Old Covenant," *Journal of the Evangelical Theological Society* (1991): 433–46.

(Rom 5:19).[72] We are declared righteous because Jesus's obedience was that δικαίωμα and met the terms of divine justice.

Paul's grammar, contrasting the calamity that came δι' ἑνὸς παραπτώματος (through the one unrighteous act) or διὰ τῆς παρακοῆς (through the disobedience) and the δικαίωμα (righteous act) of another, is particularly pointed here.[73] The force of this contrast is to establish a forensic frame of reference. The events in view are justification and condemnation (cf. Prov 17:15, which has a similar structure).

There is discernable logical progression in Romans 5 from the general to the particular, from cost/benefit of gift/trespass in 5:15 to obedience/disobedience in 5:19.[74] In 5:15–16 Paul contrasts the παραπτώματα (transgression) and παρακοῆς (disobedience) with the χάρισμα (grace). Adam brought penalties and death, but Jesus brought gifts (δωρεά) and life. The legal and logical basis for the gifts that accrue to believers is Christ's ὑπακοή (obedience).[75]

In 5:16 the nature of the gifts (δώρημα) and graces (χάρισμα) come into focus. The end of the gifts is our δικαίωμα (justification). In 5:17, what Christ earned is described as "the gift of righteousness" (δωρεᾶς τῆς δικαιοσύνης).

In 5:18 Paul is a more precise about how the penalty was incurred and how the benefit was acquired. The penalty was incurred "by

72. Longnecker, "Obedience of Christ," 145, is right to see "obedience" (ὑπακοή) here as referring to Jesus's active obedience, to Christ's "humble submission to the Mosaic law" and his fulfillment "of its obligations." N. T. Wright, *The Climax of the Covenant: Christ and the Law in Pauline Theology* (Minneapolis: Fortress, 1992), 37–39, connects Jesus's obedience with his role as the Second Adam and as the true Israel. This view seems to support the very doctrine he elsewhere rejects.

73. This same logic is evident in Rom 6:23. The "wages" (ὀψώνια) of sin is death. Wages, as Paul said, are not a gift, but earned (4:4). Disobedience is not something that happened to Adam. He was not a recipient of sin but its perpetrator. In 1:32 and 2:26 δικαίωμα refers to legal righteousness. In Rom 4:25 and Eph 2:1 παράπτωμα stands for transgressions of law. B. F. Westcott, *St. Paul and Justification* (London: Macmillan, 1913), 226–28, takes these nouns as neuter. Cranfield takes δικαίωμα as "righteous conduct" in parallel to παράπτωμα (*Romans*, 1.289–90); so too Peter Stuhlmacher, *Paul's Letter to the Roman: A Commentary* (trans. Scott J. Hafemann; Louisville: WJK, 1994), 88. Dunn (*Romans 1–8*, 283) and others take these nouns as a masculine, thus "through one man's trespass." Westcott traces the masculine reading to the influence of the Vulgate: *per unum delictum* (228–29).

74. I am grateful to David VanDrunen for comments that stimulated this reading of these verses.

75. Murray, *Romans*, 1.194–96; Calvin, *Ad romanos*, 113.6–8.

one act of disobedience" (δι' ἑνὸς παραπτώματος). The benefit was accrued "by one act of obedience" (δι' ἑνὸς δικαιώματος). Both phrases express instrumentality. Both use abstract nouns concerning legal unrighteousness and righteousness. Both refer to historical actions by historical persons, not to the divine decree.[76] Adam's "act" was "unto judgment" (εἰς κατάκριμα), but Christ's "act" was "unto righteousness of life" (εἰς δικαίωσιν ζωῆς). In 5:19, Jesus's one act is specified as his ὑπακοή (obedience).[77]

The case for the imputation of active obedience is further strengthened when one considers that Paul does not compartmentalize Jesus's obedience chronologically or logically. He does not describe Christ's obedience as if it began only at Golgotha or on the cross. Obedience characterizes Jesus's entire existence, just as Adam's entire life to that point is characterized by his disobedience.

This same logic also appears in Philippians 2:8.[78] Paul's appeal to redemptive history comes in the service of moral argument. He grounds his parenesis in the gospel of the obedience of Christ. Jesus humbled (ἐταπείνωσεν) himself, and this humiliation began with the incarnation: "having been found in human form" (καὶ σχήματι εὑρεθείς). The Son came to be "obedient" (ὑπήκοος), all the way to the holocaust of the cross. For Paul, Christ's crucifixion was not the totality of his obedience, it was its consummation. This the force of the grammar and meter of the last clause of 2:8: μέχρι θανάτου, θανάτου δὲ σταυροῦ (unto death, even the death of the cross). In the context (2:1–4, 12–17) Paul's exhortation is most compelling if the model to which obedience appealed was vicarious. Just as Jesus poured himself out

76. Barth's reading of δικαίωμα as "righteous decision" is quite implausible, as it moves the sphere of discourse from Christ's saving work in history back to the decree; *Christ and Adam: Man and Humanity in Romans 5* (trans. T. A. Smail; New York: Harper, 1957), 41–42. The focus is not on election here but on obedience to the law.

77. Calvin, *Ad romanos*, 113.38–114.1, says that this verse "signifies the gracious imputation of righteousness." "The righteousness of Christ is regarded in its compact unity in parallelism with the one trespass" (Murray, *Romans*, 1.201).

78. See, e.g., Caspar Olevianus, *Expositio symbolici apostolici* (Frankfurt, 1576), 111; idem, *In epistolas d. pauli apostoli ad philippenses et colossenses* (ed. Theodore Beza; Geneva, 1580), 19–20; William Ames, *The Marrow of Sacred Divinity* (London, 1642), 91–92; Owen, *Works*, 2.156; Leonard Van Rijssen, *Compendium theologiae didactio-elencticae* (Amsterdam, 1695), 149; Johannes Marckius, *Compendium theologiae christianae didactico-elencticum* (Amsterdam, 1749), 397–98.

(ἐκένωσεν) as a drink offering for us (2:7), so Paul is being poured out (σπένδομαι), and so ought we to be (2:17).[79]

Theological Context of the Imputation of Active Obedience

It seems clear that the two sides in this discussion hold different views of divine justice, sin, and the nature of Christ's work.[80] According to the proponents of the imputation of active obedience, divine justice requires both obedience and punishment for sin such that Christ had to provide obedience and suffer the penalty for his elect. Proponents of the imputation of active obedience held to a twofold nature of sin and consequently a twofold remedy: the imputation of active obedience and remission of sins.

Divine Justice and Sin

Is God's justice such that not breaking the law is the same as keeping it? This was the argument of Piscator and Pareus. They argued that either not breaking the law or "punishment is the fulfilling of the law."[81] They argued that it is unjust to require both obedience to the law and punishment. It must be one or the other. This approach, however, fundamentally misconstrues the nature of divine justice as expressed in the law. The command in the garden was a prohibition, but according to Paul, we owed more to God than mere abstinence: "For although they knew God, they did not honor him as God or give thanks to him, but they became futile in their thinking, and their foolish hearts were darkened" (Rom 1:21 ESV).

79. See Robert B. Strimple, "Philippians 2:5–11 in Recent Studies: Some Exegetical Conclusions," *Westminster Theological Journal* 41 (1979): 247–68. Wright, *Climax of the Covenant*, chap. 4, presents a useful survey of interpretations of this passage.

80. Geerhardus Vos notes this same connection; "'Legalism' in Paul's Doctrine of Justification," in *Redemptive History and Biblical Interpretation: The Shorter Writings of Geerhardus Vos* (ed. Richard B. Gaffin Jr.; Phillipsburg, NJ: Presbyterian & Reformed, 1980), 399.

81. Pareus, in Ursinus, *Summe of Christian Religion*, 797–800. Given Pareus's patent concern to eliminate ammunition for Counter-Reformation critics (e.g., Robert Bellarmine, 1542–1621), it is quite surprising that he compared justification to "whitening" a wall, thus inviting unhappy comparisons to our Lord's teaching in Matt 23:27 and strengthening the Roman complaint that the Protestant doctrine of justification really depends on a "legal fiction."

This understanding of divine justice best explains the sanctions promised to disobedience: "Cursed is anyone who does not continue to do [יָקִים] everything written in the book of the law" (Deut 27:26). So Paul says that it is not the hearers, but the *doers* (ποιηταί) of the law who shall be justified (Rom 2:13). In James those who profess faith in Christ (2:14) must "put away [ἀποτίθημι] impurity and the abundance of evil" (1:21–22). The notion of active obedience to the law conditions James's use of "doers."

Adam owed total, active obedience to the law, and the law continues to require nothing less than active and perfect fulfillment. Before the fall, God demanded obedience and threatened death for disobedience. After the fall, God continued to insist on total obedience to his law (Deut 11:1; 13:3 [MT 13:4]).

First John 3:4 says that "sin is lawlessness [ἀνομία]." To be sure, lawlessness is the absence of righteousness, but it is more. It is, as Westminster Larger Catechism 24 has it, "any want of conformity unto, or transgression of" God's law. Sin incurs guilt, that is, moral stain and punishment. The threatened punishment was executed. Adam died and we in him (Rom 5:12; Eph 2:1). As a consequence of our sin, "no good dwells" in us (Rom 7:18), and where we are required to will and do the good, we will and do the opposite (7:20).[82] We are no longer capable of the required performance, thus further exposed to liability (Deut 27:26; 28:58). This is why it is "evident that no one is justified before God by the law" (Gal 3:11).

Christ's Work

Criticisms of the imputation of active obedience raise fundamental questions about the work of Christ. Rome and the Remonstrants argued that Jesus came to make salvation possible for those who do their part by cooperation with divine grace. Such soteriology is a serious challenge to the Reformation doctrine of justification and at

82. The general confession of sin in the Book of Common Prayer (1662) captures the Spirit of Paul's lament: "We have erred, and strayed from thy ways like lost sheep. We have followed too much the devices and desires of our own hearts. We have offended against thy holy laws. We have left undone those things which we ought to have done; And we have done those things which we ought not to have done; And there is no health in us."

variance with the language of Scripture. Our Lord said he came to be the perfectly obedient Son of Man for two purposes: "to seek and to save the lost" (Luke 19:10). The verb *save* (σῶσαι) does not denote *make possible*, but *accomplish* (see Matt 1:21; 8:25; Mark 13:13; John 3:17; 12:47; Acts 2:21, 47; 11:14; 16:31; Rom 5:9–10; 10:9, 13; 1 Tim 1:15). Before he went to the cross, Jesus testified to his Father that he had "completed" (τελειώσας) the work that the Father had given him (John 17:4).

Like Arminian theologian Richard Watson, some critics of the imputation of active obedience call into question Jesus's mediatorial office and work.[83] According to the apostle Paul, however, "there is one mediator [μεσίτης] between God and man, the man Christ Jesus" (1 Tim 2:5). Hebrews 9:15 and 12:24 say that Jesus is the "mediator of a new covenant" (διαθήκης καινῆς μεσίτης). The result of calling Jesus's mediatorial work into question is to subvert the doctrine of Jesus's representative work *for* us and imputed to us.

The intention of the incarnation was Christ's substitution for his people. Paul says that in the "fullness of time, God sent his Son, born of a woman, born under the law" in order to "redeem those under the law" (Gal 4:4–5). Contra Piscator, the implication of 4:5 is not that, by virtue of his humanity, Jesus was under the law for himself, but rather, the implication is that he came as our federal head, our high priest, our mediator, solely to obey the law in our place. To say that he was "under the law" for himself ignores the substitutionary force implied in the combination of "born of a woman" and "under the law" and turns the passage on its head. It makes more sense of Paul's language to interpret it as another example of his doctrine of Christ's substitutionary obedience.

Paul repeatedly describes Jesus's obedience and death as being ὑπὲρ ἡμῶν (for us). Nowhere does he say or imply that Christ obeyed for his own sake. He was "constituted" (ἐποίησεν) sin "for us" (2 Cor 5:21). Christ "gave himself for us" (Titus 2:14) and "died for us" (Eph 5:2; 1 Thess 5:10). He became "a curse for us" (Gal 3:13). This last phrase especially corresponds very closely to Galatians 4:4–5. Both

83. Richard Watson, *Theological Institutes* (New York: Carlton & Lanahan, 1850), 2.216.

passages use the same verb: ἐξαγοράζω (redeem). Christ came "in the fullness of time" not to qualify himself to be a redeemer, but to redeem those under the law.

Objections to the Imputation of Active Obedience

It Makes God Unjust

Since Piscator, critics of the imputation of active obedience have all assumed a priori that God is unjust, but it is an assumption that Scripture will not tolerate. Scripture does not consider that punishment is a substitute for obedience. Rather, punishment is the consequence of disobedience, but obedience is still required. The demand remains: "do." It is not as if one can break a law, suffer the punishment, and then carry on as if the law no longer requires active obedience. After the fall, we were still obligated to perform righteousness either personally or vicariously (Rom 8:3–4; Gal 3:12).

It Leads to Antinomianism

The assumption behind the charge of antinomianism needs close examination. Implied in this objection is the premise that Christians will pursue sanctity only if their justification depends upon it. Therefore, critics conclude, the message that Christ kept the law vicariously for believers can only weaken the Christian's motivation for piety. This question was at the heart of the Protestant Reformation.[84] The material question of the Reformation was whether our sanctity (both Spirit-wrought and the result of our cooperation with grace) is in any way instrumental in or a part of the ground of our justification. Hence the Council of Trent (session 6, canon 24) declared: "If any one says, that the justice received is not preserved and also increased before God through good works; but that the said works *are merely the fruits and signs of justification* obtained, but not a cause of the increase thereof: let him be anathema" (Schaff 2.115, emphasis added).[85] Rome

84. This is implicit in Council of Trent, session 6, canons 11 and 24 (Schaff 2.112–13, 115).

85. H. Denzinger, *Enchiridion symbolorum* (30th ed.; Freiburg: Herder, 1955), §834.

understood the Protestant position: good works are *merely* evidence of sanctity and nothing more.[86] Those who subscribe this criticism of the imputation of active obedience have to choose whether they wish to agree with the Reformation or Trent.

Those who confess the imputation of active obedience should find this criticism encouraging. It is, after all, the same criticism Paul faced (Rom 6:1). Regarding justification, "we are not under law, but under grace" (6:14). We know the terrible and righteous demands of the law. It does not say "try," but "do." Christians confess that Christ has "done" for us.

The law word of Scripture, "do this and live" (Luke 10:28), is neither designed nor has the power to produce sanctity. This much is evident from the structure of Paul's epistles. He typically speaks the imperative (i.e., the law) after and on the basis of the indicative (i.e., the gospel). For example, the first three chapters of Ephesians are essentially gospel proclamation, *sola gratia, sola fide*. It is not until Ephesians 4 that Paul turns to urge (παρακαλέω) believers to sanctity on the basis of what Christ has accomplished for us, following a benediction (see also Rom 12:1; Gal 5:1; 1 Thess 4:1; 2 Thess 2:17). This is because through the gospel word "Christ has done" God the Spirit "works [faith] in our hearts by the preaching of the holy Gospel" (HC 65 [Schaff 3.328]). This scheme may be counterintuitive, but true nonetheless. Paul says, "It pleased God through the folly of what we preach to save those who believe" (1 Cor 1:21). It is foolishness to Greeks and a stumbling block to Jews, but "the power of God and the wisdom of God" (1:24).

It Diminishes the Cross

Piscator, Pareus, and the Arminians alleged that if Christ achieved our righteousness before the cross then his death was superfluous. The charge reveals a basic misunderstanding of Christ's work. The distinction between active and passive obedience is logical, a distinction between aspects of the one, whole, complete obedience—not between chronological phases in his work.

86. See John Calvin, *John Calvin's New Testament Commentaries* (trans. J. W. Fraser et al.; ed. D. W. Torrance and T. F. Torrance; Grand Rapids: Eerdmans, 1960–75), 3.282–88.

In the orthodox scheme, the cross is the highest expression of Christ's righteousness for us. This is just how Paul connects the two. When Paul says that Christ "humbled himself" (ἐταπείνωσεν), "having become obedient" (γενόμενος ὑπήκοος), he does not restrict it to the cross. Rather the logical movement of Philippians 2 is from eternity to incarnation to humiliation, of which the cross is the culmination, not the beginning. In Philippians 2 the cross qualifies Christ's obedience: "until death, even the death of the cross" (μέχρι θανάτου, θανάτου δὲ σταυροῦ).

The same logic is evident in Galatians 3:13, where Paul says that "Christ redeemed us from the curse of the law by becoming a curse for us—for it is written, 'Cursed is everyone who is hanged on a tree'" (ESV). Jesus did not become accursed only on the cross. The cross was the seal of his accursedness that endured for us. Scripture says that Jesus was born under the law and under the curse (Gal 4:4). This is the paradox of the gospel. Only because he is the beloved Son (Matt 3:17) is he eligible to bear the curse for us. Because of the curse he had to flee to Egypt and make his exodus as the obedient Son (2:15), battle Satan in the wilderness (Mark 1:13), and suffer the humiliation of being hunted by the scribes and Pharisees (John 5:18; 7:1). The cross was not the beginning but the consummation of the execution of the sanctions brought by the curse. Because of sin, there is a "record of debt." Paul reckons that Christ canceled that record on the cross because he actively obeyed the law for us (Col 2:14).

It Relies on Roman Categories of Merit

Shepherd and his followers have suggested for thirty years that the category of "merit" is unbiblical and illegitimate.[87] If this complaint

87. About 1974, Norman Shepherd began criticizing the notion that Adam might have merited a reward in the covenant of works. The Board of Trustees of Westminster Seminary (Philadelphia) concluded in their "Reason and Specifications Supporting the Action of the Board of Trustees in Removing Professor Shepherd" (February 26, 1982) that "Mr. Shepherd rejects not only the term 'covenant of works' but the possibility of any merit or reward attaching to the obedience of Adam in the creation covenant. He holds that faithful obedience is the condition of all covenants in contrast to the distinction made in the Westminster Confession." They further concluded that "by rejecting the distinction between the covenant of works and the covenant of grace as defined in the Westminster Standards, and by failing to take account in the structure of the 'covenantal dynamic' of Christ's fulfillment of the covenant by his active

were conceded then we should have to reverse not only the Reformation doctrine of justification, which was premised on the notion of Christ's merits, but we should also have to repudiate most of two millennia of Western theology. In fact, merit is a central theological and hermeneutical category.[88]

Contrary to Jordan's claim that merit is a "hangover of Medieval theology,"[89] the notion of Christ's worthiness is rooted deeply in Scripture. Where Revelation 4:11 proclaims Christ the Lamb to be "worthy" (ἄξιος), the Vulgate translated it with *dignus*.[90] According to the writer to the Hebrews, Jesus was "made a lower than the angels" but because of his suffering (διὰ τὸ πάθημα τοῦ θανάτου) he was "crowned with glory" (2:9) In order for "many sons" to be led to glory, the τὸν ἀρχηγὸν τῆς σωτηρίας had to "be made perfect [τελειῶσαι] through suffering [διὰ παθημάτων]" (2:10). As used in Hebrews τελειόω does not denote deification, but rather completion of an assignment, that is, the semantic field is moral rather than ontological. The expression διὰ τὸ πάθημα establishes the causal link between Jesus's completion of his obedience and the "bringing of many sons to glory."

Jesus was "faithful in all things" (3:2) to his Father who appointed him. Therefore, he is "worthy" (ἠξίωται) of more glory than Moses (3:3). Hebrews does not suggest that the Father *graced* Jesus with a reward, but quite the opposite. The Father recognized Jesus's accomplishment of righteousness, and the reward is commensurate. More than that, his worthiness is the basis of our confidence and boldness before God (3:6).

We find a complementary conceptual framework in the Apocalypse. In 5:4 we read of the crisis of the sealed scroll. No one is "worthy"

---

obedience as well as by his satisfaction of its curse, Mr. Shepherd develops a uniform concept of covenantal faithfulness for Adam, for Israel, and for the New Covenant people. The danger is that both the distinctiveness of the covenant of grace and of the new covenant fullness of the covenant of grace will be lost from view and that obedience as the way of salvation will swallow up the distinct and primary function of faith. Obedience is nurtured by faith in Christ and flourishes precisely as we trust wholly in him" (15).

88. The Reformed confessions appeal to the category of merit repeatedly. See HC 21, 60, 63, 84, 86; Belgic Confession 22–24, 35; Canons of Dort, Rejection of Errors 1.3; 2.1, 3–4, 6–7; 5.8; WCF 16.5; 17.2; WLC 55, 174, 193.

89. Jordan, "Merit versus Maturity," 192.

90. In the Vulgate, Rom 8:18 uses *condignus* for ἄξιος.

(ἄξιος) to open the scroll, that is, no one is qualified to do it.[91] The resolution comes in the next verse, however, when we are told, that "the Lion of the tribe of Judah, the Root of David," is qualified to open the scroll. His qualification is that he has "conquered" (ἐνίκησεν) sin, death, and hell.

Interpreting this vocabulary within a realistic philosophical context, the medieval theologians distinguished between condign merit (*meritum de condigno*), whereby a work was said to have met the standard of divine justice, and congruent merit (*meritum de congruo*), whereby a work does not meet the standard of justice, but justice is graciously imputed to it nonetheless (Thomas Aquinas, *Summa theologiae* I-II Q. 114.6). The Protestants rejected the medieval doctrine of justification through sanctification (or deification), but they did not reject the *category* of merit.[92] They rejected the notion of congruent merit altogether and said that Jesus alone has condign merit that is imputed to us.[93]

91. See G. K. Beale, *The Book of Revelation: A Commentary on the Greek Text* (New International Greek Testament Commentary; Grand Rapids: Eerdmans, 1999), 350, who connects Christ's worthiness to his overcoming of the enemy.

92. "Deus solus deificet" (*Summa theologiae* I-II Q. 112.1). The Reformed churches all confess that we are justified on the basis of Christ's merits imputed to us and reject any notion that sinners can merit anything before God either condignly or congruently.

93. Pace Peter Lillback, *The Binding of God: Calvin's Role in the Development of Covenant Theology* (Texts and Studies in Reformation and Post-Reformation Thought; Grand Rapids: Baker, 2001), 171, who argues that Calvin taught that, under Christ, the law is no longer a harsh taskmaster demanding perfection, but now through faith in the gospel, the Spirit helping us, we can keep the law in a way that God will accept. This suggests that Calvin taught a version of congruent merit. Lillback continues (204) this argument and argues that Calvin appropriated and modified the Franciscan "covenant of acceptance" (*facientibus quod in se est, Deus non denegat gratiam*) so as to teach that God graciously accepts the works of Christians not merely as a response of gratitude, as Protestantism has traditionally taught (e.g., HC 2), but as a part of the way of justification. If this interpretation is true, one can only wonder why Calvin complained so vociferously about the Roman doctrine of the congruity of works as taught in session 6 of the Council of Trent. See C. G. Bretschneider, ed., *Corpus reformatorum* (Berlin: Schwetschke, 1834–1941), 35.429–86; John Calvin, *Selected Works of John Calvin: Tracts and Letters* (trans. H. Beveridge; Grand Rapids: Baker, 1983), 3.116–17. See also Calvin's rejection of congruent merit in his *Articuli a facultate sacrae theologiae parisensi determinati . . . cum antidoto* (*Corpus reformatorum* 35.12–13; the English text is *Articles Agreed upon by the Faculty of Sacred Theology of Paris . . . with the Antidote* [*Selected Works*, 1.80–82]), where he argued that God accepts only those with perfect righteousness and contrasts the system of condign and congruent merit with doctrine of the "Lutherans," who "place the righteousness of faith in the predicament of a relation, saying that we are righteous merely because God accepts us in Christ." See also the Canons of Dort, Rejection of Errors 1.3; 2.4 (Schaff 3.557, 563). According to Herman Witsius (1636–1708), Christ's active obedience merited a reward for himself and

What does Jordan offer in place of Christ's merit imputed to sinners? By reinterpreting Adam's probation in terms of "maturity" and immaturity," he seems to be turning to Plotinus (204–70) and Aquinas (ca. 1224–74). Such a conception makes the human problem ontological (i.e., a lack of divinity) rather than legal. There is evidence for this claim within Jordan's own essay. Following Scotus (ca. 1265–1308), he says that our humanity per se, not the fall, required God the Son to become incarnate.[94] This ontological turn is quite at odds with confessional Reformed theology, which affirms that creation was טוב (good), that Adam was created "in righteousness and true holiness," by nature able to love and obey God (HC 6 [Schaff 3.309]).[95]

---

his elect, by virtue of the covenant of strict justice he made with his Father—Jesus earned his righteousness and ours by works—and by virtue of the condignity, that is, the inherent worth of his obedience; see Herman Witsius, *De oeconomia foederum dei cum hominibus* (Leeuwarden, 1677), 2.3.32–33; idem, *The Economy of the Covenants between God and Man* (trans. William Crookshank; 1803; repr. Phillipsburg, NJ: P&R, 1990), 1.190–92.

94. Jordan, "Merit versus Maturity," 184–86.

95. Historically, the turn to ontology has threatened the Creator/creature distinction since salvation becomes *theōsis* (deification). It was to avoid the problem of *theōsis* and the Thomistic (*Summa theologiae* I Q. 95.1) scheme of prelapsarian *donum super additum* that the Westminster Divines spoke not of a gracious covenant with Adam, but of God's "voluntary condescension" (WCF 7.1) in establishing a legal covenant with Adam (see also 26.3). According to WCF 4.2 we were created with the "power to fulfill" the law in the covenant of works. Richard Muller observes similarities between the Reformed orthodox and Thomas on this point; see *After Calvin: Studies in the Development of a Theological Tradition* (Oxford: Oxford University Press, 2003), 184–85, 256–57n62. For example, Ursinus's argument, in his exposition of HC 7, that God "withdrew" his grace from Adam is similar to Thomas's doctrine of the *donum*; see Zacharias Ursinus, *Opera theologica* (ed. Q. Reuter; Heidelberg, 1612), 1.64–65 §II; and Lyle D. Bierma, "Ursinus' Doctrine of the Natural Covenant," in *Protestant Scholasticism: Essays in Reassessment* (ed. Carl R. Trueman and R. S. Clark; Carlisle, UK: Paternoster, 1999), 96–110. One might add, however, that prelapsarian grace did not function for Ursinus exactly as it did for Thomas. For Ursinus, the primary function of prelapsarian grace was *apologetic*. It did not lead to a conception of salvation as deification, as it did for Thomas. Ursinus used it as part of a theodicy, that God is not morally liable for the fall since grace, being undeserved, was properly withdrawn. This is distinct from Thomas's nature/grace dualism whereby grace suppresses *vires inferiores*, which exist by the fact of creation. For Thomas, Adam fell from grace, but Ursinus did not assume that grace perfects nature. For Ursinus, Adam violated the law (e.g., *Summa theologiae* 23). Ursinus's use of prelapsarian grace occurred in the context of the Protestant law/gospel distinction, which he expressed in terms of the covenant of works as law and the covenant of grace as gospel (*Summa theologiae* 36; *Opera* 1.325). See also R. Scott Clark and Joel Beeke, "Ursinus, Oxford, and the Westminster Divines," in *The Westminster Confession into the 21st Century: Essays in Remembrance of the 350th Anniversary of the Publication of the Westminster Confession of Faith* (ed. Ligon Duncan; Ross-Shire, Scotland: Mentor, 2004), 2.1–32. By contrast, Aquinas thought in terms of old law/new law. After Dort, the Reformed orthodox spoke of God's grace in making the covenant of works, and some (e.g., William Bucanus, John Ball, Anthony Burgess) said grace was necessary for Adam to complete it, but others (e.g., Caspar

According to Reformed theology, our need of a mediator was not ontological, but legal and moral. In Romans 5:12–21, Paul characterizes the human condition in legal categories: death, sin, trespass, and condemnation. Reformed theology is not Hegelian. Adam was not commanded to "become" but to "do."

It Relies on a Legal Fiction

Critics charge that the imputation of active obedience assumes a sort of philosophical realism (i.e., God can say what he does only because things are what they are) that Scripture does not teach, assume, or permit. In this scheme, God's justice must be correlate to an extrinsic, eternal moral standard. This approach has been widely held by realists such as Aquinas, that is, those who would have the human intellective faculty intersect with the divine (*Summa theologiae* I-II Q. 1).[96] The argument runs thus: The world is composed of universals and particulars. We abstract universals from particulars, but Thomas argued that a created intellect, with the help of grace, can see the essence of God. The contact between the human intellect and the divine substance occurs when the intellect apprehends *universalia*, which are expressions of the divine essence.[97]

However tempting such a scheme might be, for it seems to vindicate God's justice, we should resist it because it necessarily subordinates God to some other entity, which contravenes the doctrine of God in Deuteronomy 6:4: "Hear O Israel, Yahweh our God, Yahweh is one." Yahweh is God and there is none like or beside him (32:39), and none other is to be worshiped (Exod 20:3). In Scripture and in confessional Reformed theology, God is not said to be accountable to any moral standard outside himself.

We do not live in a universe where God acts and speaks according to some extrinsic standard, by which both he and we can judge his

---

Olevianus, Robert Rollock, Johannes Wollebius, Amandus Polanus, James Ussher, John Owen, Johannes Cocceius, J. H. Heidegger, H. Witsius, W. à Brakel) said that Adam, by virtue of his creation, had natural ability to meet its terms.

96. See Jeffrey Stout, "Truth, Natural Law, and Ethical Theory," in *Natural Law Theory: Contemporary Essays* (ed. Robert P. George; Oxford: Clarendon/New York: Oxford University Press, 1992), 72; and R. S. Clark, "Calvin on the *lex naturalis*," *Stulos* 6 (1998): 4–8, 13n43.

97. On the *visio dei* see *Summa theologiae* I Q. 12.1, 9, 12–13.

speech-acts. Rather, we live in a world in which God acts and speaks according to his own nature. His speech-acts are creative, constitutive, and nominative. In this universe, the imputation of Christ's righteousness to those who are not intrinsically and fully sanctified is no more a legal fiction than was God's *fiat lux* (Gen 1:3) or naming of the first creation (1:5) or the new creation (2 Cor 5:17). God's powerful word makes things so.[98] Reformed theology has typically taught a sort of consequent realism. Having willed to justify his people on the basis of Christ's righteousness, God grounds his declaration in the highest expression of his will, an actual, earned righteousness whereby justice was, in time and space, satisfied by the obedience and death of Jesus (*Institutes* 3.23.2). It is that actual righteousness that is imputed (Rom 5:12–19) to believers, and on that basis believers gain a right to eternal life. It is a gift to us, but that gift was earned by the obedience of our Savior (4:4–5).[99]

It Makes the Filial Superior to the Legal

German liberalism set Jesus's religion of the love and fatherhood of God against justice and an allegedly "legalistic" doctrine of justification in Paul.[100] As we have seen, however, Jesus made no such dichotomy between the filial and the legal. In one breath he speaks of the mutual interpenetration and intimate fellowship between the Father and the Son, and in the next he speaks of a judicial event. For Jesus, the two are inseparable (John 5:26–27).[101]

Jesus repeatedly described his own mission both in terms of his relation to the Father as Son and in terms of obligation to the performance of righteousness. In the case of a family business, the father may well love his son, and the son his father, but even in a family business,

98. The medieval scheme of *meritum de congruo*, at least within the nominalist context, and *meritum de condigno* really did rely on a legal fiction.

99. Turretin, *Institutio*, 16.3.8., distinguished between "imputed" and "putative" righteousness (*distinguendum est imputatum à putativo seu fictitio*). Such a charge ignores the reality of a judicial action. If God pronounced us *iustos in nobis*, that *would* be a judicial fiction. Christ's *iustitia* is the *solidum fundamentum* for our justification.

100. E.g., Paul Wernle, *Der Christ und die Sünde bei Paulus* (Freiburg/Leipzig: Mohr, 1897). See also Vos, "'Legalism' in Paul's Doctrine of Justification."

101. See also Meredith G. Kline, *Kingdom Prologue: Genesis Foundations for a Covenantal Worldview* (Overland Park, KS: Two Age Press, 2000), 110.

an implicit contract exists between father and son. As much as they love one another, the son's obligation to perform and the father's obligation to justice remains. In this case, for the love of his people the Son has voluntarily taken on certain obligations, which neither his love for his Father nor his Father's love for him precludes. Rather, the Father's love for those whom he elected ἐν Χριστῷ (in Christ) (Eph 1:1–15; Rom 8:39; John 3:16) necessitates the Son's "personal, perfect, and perpetual conformity and obedience" to the law for us (WLC 93).

The juxtaposition of the filial and the legal is nothing new. What is new, however, is the naïve adaptation of this scheme by some in confessional Reformed circles in order to rescue Paul by transforming his doctrine into that of the pietists and liberals. This question arises as part of broader move either to diminish the forensic element of justification in favor of the relational or to replace the forensic with the relational altogether.[102] Luther and Calvin

102. See, e.g., Michael F. Bird, "Incorporated Righteousness: A Response to Recent Evangelical Discussion concerning the Imputation of Christ's Righteousness in Justification," *Journal of the Evangelical Theological Society* 47 (2004): 253–75, who follows Mark Seifrid's argument in *Christ, Our Righteousness* that, as Bird puts it, "there can be no justification of the believer without the simultaneous justification of God." See also Stephen Strehle, "*Imputatio iustitiae*: Its Origin in Melanchthon, Its Opposition in Osiander," *Theologische Zeitschrift* 50 (1994): 201–19, who argues that Osiander was more faithful than Melanchthon to Luther's doctrine of justification. Mark Seifrid, "Paul, Luther, and Justification, in Gal 2:15–21," *Westminster Theological Journal* 65 (2003): 229n45; and idem, "Luther, Melanchthon, and Paul on the Question of Imputation," in *Justification: What's at Stake in the Current Controversies?* (ed. Mark Husbands and Daniel J. Trier; Downers Grove, IL: InterVarsity, 2004), 137–52, argues for a split between Luther and Melanchthon by 1536. Melanchthon is said to have moved to a doctrine of justification by the "imputation of Christ's righteousness" while Luther continued to teach that imputation is a divine declaration that includes our believing and union with Christ. According to Seifrid, Luther's view agrees with Robert H. Gundry's Arminian view in "The Nonimputation of Christ's Righteousness," in *Justification: What's at Stake in the Current Controversies?* (ed. Mark Husbands and Daniel J. Trier; Downers Grove, IL: InterVarsity, 2004), 17–45, and Melanchthon's is said to agree with John Piper's Melanchthonian-Calvinist view in *Counted Righteous in Christ*. Calvin's doctrine of justification is also being radically reconsidered; see Carl Mosser, "The Greatest Possible Blessing: Calvin and Deification," *Scottish Journal of Theology* 55 (2002): 36–57; and Julie Canlis, "Calvin, Osiander, and Participation in God," *International Journal of Systematic Theology* 6 (2004): 169–84, who argue that Calvin's doctrine of union with Christ was more ontic and relational than legal. Craig B. Carpenter, "A Question of Union with Christ: Calvin and Trent on Justification," *Westminster Theological Journal* 64 (2002): 363–86, argues that Calvin's problem with Rome was not so much Rome's doctrine of justification, but its doctrine of union with Christ.

both had a vibrant doctrine of union with Christ, as did Reformed orthodox such as Zanchi, Wollebius, Owen, Turretin, and Witsius, but they never found it necessary to juxtapose the forensic with the filial.[103] We should agree with Geerhardus Vos that a "forensic treatment of man and a loving treatment of man are not to Paul in any sense mutually exclusive in God."[104] Indeed, as Vos observes, in Paul's theology "the transfer of the fulfillment of the law from the sinner to Christ . . . safeguards the interests of the divine righteousness" while protecting the faith from the self-righteousness to which Paul was so opposed. This is why Christ's active obedience is so important—because the "earthly life of Christ offers the only instance of the working of the scheme under normal conditions, outside of the original state of rectitude." In his "perfect obedience," Christ was aware of the eschatological glory that awaited him "as the prize of his obedience." This vision, however it strengthened him, did not corrupt his motives.[105]

In this regard, the language of Hebrews 5:8 is instructive. The writer makes an point to contrast Jesus's sonship (υἱός) with the discipline he suffered *pro nobis*. If critics of the imputation of active obedience are correct, one should not expect this contrast, since, they argue, he was obligated to offer obedience for himself. This verse, however, makes no sense in such a scheme. The point of the argument here is that he was serving as our *representative*. Hence, "Although [καίπερ] he was a son, he learned obedience by the things that he suffered." The concessive particle καίπερ implies a state of things contrary to expectation. Given his status as son and not servant (3:5), one might have expected that Jesus would have received honor rather than discipline, but he was disciplined throughout his life, not for his sake but for ours. This vicarious federal obedience is the essence of the imputation of active obedience.

103. Though it is an important category in Calvin's theology, his discussion of union with Christ as a locus proper is very brief (*Institutes* 3.11.10). This is all the more remarkable given the elaborate constructions given to his doctrine of union with Christ in some recent scholarship.

104. Vos, "'Legalism' in Paul's Doctrine of Justification," 392–93.

105. Ibid., 398.

It Should Be Replaced by Union with Christ

The federal-vision advocates suggest that we are justified so long as we are united to Christ, but we retain that union partly by cooperating with grace. Here is a subtle shifting of the indicative (gospel) "is" ("we *are* united to Christ") into an imperative (law): "We *must* remain united to Christ."[106]

There is no question whether we need both a legal and vital union with Christ, but these must be distinguished. By virtue of legal union with Christ our federal head and substitute, his obedience is credited to believers. This union is distinct (not separate) from that union that increases, of which Heidelberg Catechism 76 speaks when it says that, having been justified, we are now "united more and more to his sacred body by the Holy Ghost" (Schaff 3.332–33; this is also the view of WCF 26.3 and WLC 65–69, 79, 168). Like election, union with Christ is a precondition of regeneration (i.e., renewal from death to life), and regeneration is precondition of faith, since the dead do not believe. A precondition is not, however, identity. Union with Christ is *not* the same thing as faith, and faith is the sole instrument of justification.

Our legal union with Christ is objective (*extra nos*). This is the category at work in Romans 5:8. Christ died *pro nobis* (also 1 Thess 5:10). He became a curse "for us" (Gal 3:13). He gave himself up "for us" (Eph 5:2; Titus 2:14; 1 John 3:16). He opened a living way "for us," into the *sanctum sanctorum* (Heb 10:20). In turn, we are accepted and regarded as righteous *propter Christum*.[107] Vital union speaks of the subjective, progressive realization of Christ's benefits and is premised on the objective accomplishment of redemption by Christ.

It Is Not Confessional

In the late sixteenth and early seventeenth centuries, both Piscator and Pareus argued that the imputation of active obedience is not confessional. In both cases, however, they either ignored or challenged

106. See, e.g., Lusk, "New Life and Apostasy."

107. This expression goes to the essence of Reformed federalism. See, e.g., Ursinus, *Summa theologiae* 31, 36, 141, 225, 232, 255, 284.

Heidelberg Catechism 60 and ignored the theological function of merit in the standards.

This is not only how most Reformed theologians have interpreted the Reformed symbols; it is how some synods have done. We have already seen that the Synod of Dort affirmed Christ's merits as the ground of justification. In 1603 the 17th National Synod of the French Reformed Churches rejected Piscator's view soundly, reaffirmed the imputation of active obedience, and remonstrated with the major Reformed schools to support them in their rejection of Piscator's view.[108] In 1604 Piscator answered the synod's questions and restated his conviction that Scripture teaches that "the perfect obedience which Christ performed to the law is not imputed to us and his righteousness and purity are not given to us for the price of eternal salvation."[109] In 1607 the 18th National Synod rejected Piscator's reply and his division of Christ's work in favor of the statement that "the whole obedience of Christ, both in his life and death, is imputed to us for the full remission of our sins, and acceptance into eternal life: and in short, that this being but one and the self-same obedience, is our entire and perfect justification."[110] In 1612 the synod required ministers and professors to subscribe an authorized interpretation of the 1559 French Confession 18, which bound all ministers to teach that justification is not just the *remissio peccatorum*, but that it also consists in "the imputation of his active righteousness," that Christ obeyed the law vicariously for believers, that his "whole obedience" is imputed to us.[111]

Following Calvin, Olevianus, and Ursinus, the synod interpreted Mark 10:45 (and Phil 2:5–11) to teach that, because he born of a virgin, Christ did not owe active obedience for himself, but rather he lived his entire life as our mediator and representative so that all his obedience is vicarious. They rejected the assumption implicit in Piscator's denial of the imputation of active obedience that Christ

108. John Quick, *Synodicon in gallia; or, The Acts, Decisions, Decrees, and Canons of Those Famous National Councils of the Reformed Churches in France* (London, 1692), 1.227.

109. Quoted in *Works of James Arminius*, 1.697n.

110. Quick, *Synodicon in gallia*, 1.265.

111. Ibid., 1.348.

made salvation possible and the explicit argument that the imputation of active obedience would subvert Christian sanctity.

In 1614 the Synod of Tonneins settled the matter finally by propounding an authoritative explanation of French Confession 18 and of the oath of 1612, affirming that Jesus was "obedient unto his Father from the first moment of his birth, unto the last of his ignominious death upon the Cross, having most perfectly both in his life and death, fulfilled the whole Law given unto men." They understood the "merit of this whole obedience" by which "we have, and shall obtain the forgiveness of all our sins" as an affirmation of the imputation of active obedience.[112] The decrees of these synods make the doctrine of the imputation of active obedience more than just another *theologoumenon*. The imputation of active obedience is ecclesiastical doctrine.

That the Westminster Divines graciously formed the confession to allow a small minority who denied the imputation of active obedience to affirm it should not blind us to the external evidence (from the minutes) that the majority held and understood the Westminster Standards to teach the imputation of active obedience.[113] The internal evidence supports this interpretation. Westminster Confession of Faith 7.2 speaks of Adam's obligation to "perfect and personal obedience."[114] In that context, the force of the distinction between "perfect obedience" and "sacrifice of himself" (8.5), between "obedience" and "sacrifice" (11.1), and between "obedience and death" and "obedience and satisfaction" (11.3) seems clear.[115] In other words, in this reading, "perfect obedience" refers to the active aspect of his obedience and "satisfaction" refers to the passive aspect of Christ's obedience. This is how the majority of the Westminster Divines understood it.[116]

112. Ibid., 1.401.

113. See A. F. Mitchell and J. Struthers, *Minutes of the Sessions of the Westminster Assembly of Divines* (Edinburgh/London: Blackwood, 1874), lxv–lxvii; and A. F. Mitchell, *The Westminster Assembly: Its History and Standards* (Philadelphia: Presbyterian Board of Publication, 1884), 148–57.

114. WLC 20 has "personal, perfect, and perpetual obedience."

115. WLC 38, 39, 70, 71 makes the same distinction. This is the same distinction with virtually the same language used by William Ames, *The Marrow of Theology* (trans. John D. Eusden; Durham, NC: Labyrinth, 1983), 92.

116. Mitchell, *Westminster Assembly*, 155.

Conclusion

This is not just another intramural Reformed scrimmage. In the nineteenth century, James Buchanan (1804–70) reminded his readers that by denying Christ's active obedience as the "believer's title to eternal life" Piscator thus "left a door open for the introduction of his own personal obedience, as the only ground of his future hope, after he had obtained the remission of his past sins."[117] With this temptation in view, it is well to remember that at his death our Lord did not say "I have made justification possible for those who cooperate with grace" when he cried, "It is finished!" (John 19:30). He testified to his performance of the law. The gospel is not just that we are forgiven, but that believers are reckoned as law keepers for the sake of Christ's law keeping credited them (Rom 4:3; 2 Cor 5:19–21; Gal 3:6). Whoever trusts in Jesus and rests in his finished work alone *is* righteous before God. It is as if the Christian has performed all that the law requires.

117. James Buchanan, *The Doctrine of Justification* (repr. Edinburgh: Banner of Truth, 1997), 175. Of course, this was not just a theoretical problem. The Socinian Racovian Catechism (1605) taught this very doctrine; see *The Racovian Catechism* (trans. Thomas Rees; 1818; repr. Lexington: American Theological Library Association, 1962), 21–24, 280, 302–25.

9

Faith Formed by Love or Faith Alone?

The Instrument of Justification

W. Robert Godfrey

Introduction

In 1522 Martin Luther published his German translation of the New Testament. He had been at work on this translation for about a year and would eventually translate the entire Scripture into the German language, providing for German-speaking people the version of the Bible that would have roughly have the same influence, authority, and life as the AV did among English-speaking people. Whereas it took a whole committee of Englishmen to translate the Bible, Martin Luther did it alone. In his translation of Romans 3:28 he rendered the Greek in these words: "So halten wir nun dafür dass der Mensch gerecht werde ohne des Gesetzes Werke, allein durch den Glauben" (therefore we maintained that a man is justified, not by the works of the law, but by faith alone).[1]

1. *Die Bibel oder die Ganze Heilige Schrift des Alten und Neuen Testaments: Nach der Deutschen Übersetzung Martin Luthers* (Stuttgart: Württembergische Bibelanstalt, 1956), my translation.

Luther's influential translation of Romans 3:28 became the subject of a great deal of controversy. Roman Catholic critics responded that the word *alone* (*allein*) was not in the Greek text. They argued that the only place in the Bible where the phrase *faith alone* occurred was in James 2:24, where the apostle James rejected the idea. Luther and many other Protestants answered this criticism. John Calvin in particular responded in a powerful way in his commentary on Romans: "Those, too, who falsely accuse us of asserting that according to Scripture we are justified by faith alone, since the exclusive particle *alone* is nowhere to be found in Scripture, are refuted by this same argument. But if justification does not depend either on the law, or on ourselves, why should it not be ascribed to mercy alone? And if it is of mercy alone, then it is of faith alone."[2] Defending *sola fide*, Calvin put it more simply in his *Institutes of the Christian Religion*: "Does not he who takes everything from works firmly enough ascribe everything to faith alone?" (*Institutes* 3.11.19). In other words, Calvin and Luther said in effect that the use of the word *alone* in the translation is to make clear the force of the Greek, which the medieval commentators and interpreters never understood.

What did the Reformers mean by "faith alone"? In answering that question, we will focus attention on the teaching of Calvin. For this reason, it is important to underscore that the Reformation speaks with one voice on this point. Luther and Reformed theologians are agreed about justification and about faith alone. The contention that the Reformed somehow have a distinctive doctrine of justification is simply false and can be articulated and defended only by those who do not understand either Lutheran or Reformed theologies. Herman Bavinck, one of the great Dutch Reformed scholars and theologians of the late nineteenth and early twentieth centuries, writes in his *Reformed Dogmatics*: "There is no essential difference on the doctrine of justification between the Lutheran and the Reformed theology."[3] Bavinck's is not an idiosyncratic view; rather it is the almost universal

2. John Calvin, *The Epistles of Paul the Apostle to the Romans and to the Thessalonians* (ed. D. W. Torrance and T. F. Torrance; Grand Rapids: Eerdmans, 1973), *ad Rom* 3:21.

3. Herman Bavinck, *Gereformeerde Dogmatiek* (Kampen: Kok, 1911), 4.208: "In de leer der rechtvaardigmaking is er zakelijk tusschen de Luthersche en de Gereformeerde theologie geen verschil."

testimony of Reformed theologians. The Reformed do not have a theology of justification or of faith alone different from that of the Lutherans, but there is a common Reformation theology, a common Reformation doctrine here, that the Lutheran and Reformed uphold together.

In responding to those who are critical of justification by faith alone, the doctrine can be examined in three ways: the medieval definition of faith, what Calvin taught on faith alone, and the apostle Paul's doctrine. It is good to know what Calvin said; it is much more important to know what Paul said. To anticipate our conclusion: we will find that Calvin faithfully summarized what Paul taught.

The Roman Doctrine of *fides formata*

The medieval church consistently taught that faith, in its essence, was simply or implicitly a mental category or habit to which the believer must assent, *fides informis*. Thomas Aquinas writes: "Hence if anyone wishes to reduce these words to the form of a definition, he may say: 'Faith is a habit [*habitus mentis*] of the mind, whereby eternal life is begun in us, and which causes the intellect [*intellectum*] to assent to things not seen'" (*Summa theologiae* II-II Q. 4.1).[4] For medieval theology, faith alone means mental assent to doctrinal truth. Such assent is a necessary beginning to salvation, but by no means saving in itself.

Saving faith must be more than unformed faith. To unformed faith must be added love, which gives form, life, and saving effect to faith. Again Thomas Aquinas: "Charity is not the intrinsic form of faith, but that which brings the act of faith to its form" (*Summa theologiae* II-II Q. 4.4). This doctrine of *fides formata caritate* teaches that as unformed faith perfects the intellect so formed faith perfects the will. A faith that is "formed by love" is that infused into man and makes him capable of producing good works. Thomas summarizes: "Unformed faith is the cause of servile fear. Formed faith is the cause

4. Quoted from *Nature and Grace: Selections from the Summa Theologica of Thomas Aquinas* (trans. A. M. Fairweather; Philadelphia: Westminster, 1956), 265. See also Thomas Aquinas, *Summa theologiae* (New York: Blackfriars, 1972), 31.116–17.

of filial fear, since it is through charity that faith causes man to adhere to God, and to be subject to him" (*Summa theologiae* II-II Q. 7).

The medieval understanding of faith, taught clearly by Thomas, was officially adopted by the Council of Trent: "For faith, unless hope and charity be added thereto, neither unites man perfectly with Christ, nor makes him a living member of his body" (session 6, chapter 7 [Schaff 2.96]). Trent's canons on justification also address this matter:

> If any one saith, that men are justified, either by the sole imputation of the justice of Christ, or by the sole remission of sins, to the exclusion of the grace and *the charity which is poured forth in their hearts by the Holy Ghost,* and is inherent in them; or even that the grace, whereby we are justified, is only the favor of God: let him be anathema.
>
> If any one saith, that justifying faith is nothing else but confidence in divine mercy which remits sins for Christ's sake; or, that this confidence alone is that whereby we are justified: let him be anathema. (session 6, canons 11–12 [Schaff 2.112–13, emphasis original])

When the Reformers wrote of faith alone, they, of course, did not mean that we are justified by doctrinal assent alone. They meant something quite different by faith than what the medieval theologians had meant. Trent understood their doctrine of faith alone and anathematized it clearly in session 6, canon 12.

Calvin's Doctrine of *sola fide*

In his great work *Institutes of the Christian Religion,* Calvin focused the third book formally on the work of the Holy Spirit, but the third book is almost entirely a book on faith. Calvin begins: "The Holy Spirit is the bond by which Christ effectually unites us to himself" (*Institutes* 3.1.1). The Holy Spirit is the Christian's union with Jesus Christ. Some contemporary Reformed theologians make much of union with Christ as a key doctrine.[5] Specifically how did Calvin understand the

5. See, e.g., Craig B. Carpenter, "A Question of Union with Christ? Calvin and Trent on Justification," *Westminster Theological Journal* 64 (2002): 363–86.

union of the believer with Christ by the power of the Holy Spirit? He writes: "All that he [Christ] possesses is nothing to us until we grow into one body with him. It is true that we obtain this by faith" (3.1.1). And: "Faith is the principal work of the Holy Spirit" (3.1.4). The union that the Holy Spirit creates with Christ for us is through the gift of faith.

All the rest of book 3 of the *Institutes of the Christian Religion* is on faith: a definition of faith (*Institutes* 3.2), the effect of faith in sanctification (3.3–10), the effect of faith in justification (3.11–18), freedom as an effect of faith (3.19), prayer as an effect of faith (3.20), the source of faith in divine election (3.21–24), and the outcome of faith in the Christian's resurrection at the last day (3.25).

As Calvin begins his discussion of faith, he indicates the centrality of faith to the saving plan of God:

> First, God lays down for us through the law what we should do; if we then fail in any part of it, that dreadful sentence of eternal death which it pronounces will rest upon us. Secondly, it is not only hard, but above our strength and beyond all our abilities, to fulfill the law to the letter; thus, if we look to ourselves only, and ponder what condition we deserve, no trace of good hope will remain; but cast away by God, we shall lie under eternal death. Thirdly, it has been explained that there is but one means of liberation that can rescue us from such miserable calamity: the appearance of Christ the Redeemer, through whose hand, the Heavenly Father, pitying us out of his infinite goodness and mercy, willed to help us; if, indeed, with firm faith we embrace this mercy and rest in it with steadfast hope. (*Institutes* 3.2.1)

In book 2 of the *Institutes of the Christian Religion,* Calvin writes in great detail about the work of Christ, and in book 3 he examines the character of the faith that unites us to Christ and the benefits of his work under four headings. The first heading is faith and knowledge. Faith is knowledge. This knowledge is not just knowledge of historical facts, rather this knowledge is above all else knowledge of God's attitude toward us in Christ and for Christ's sake: "Faith rests not on ignorance, but on knowledge. And this is, indeed, knowledge not only of God but of the divine will. . . . We know that God is our merciful Father, because of reconciliation effected through Christ" (*Institutes* 3.2.2). Faith knows about Christ and his reconciling work on our behalf. It knows that because of Christ's work the Father is reconciled to us. The Father who loved us and gave Christ for us is now reconciled to us through that work of Christ. We need to know that gospel promise.

Calvin's teaching here opposes the medieval teaching known as "implicit faith." The doctrine of implicit faith taught that Christians did not need to know the teaching of the Scriptures and the church, but needed to believe only that whatever the church teaches is true (cf. *Institutes* 3.2.2–5).[6] By contrast, Calvin and the whole Reformation insist that Christianity was not ignorance or blind obedience to the church. Christianity is knowing what Christ has done for us and how God now sees us in Christ. So in Calvin's basic definition of faith, knowledge is fundamental: "Now we shall possess a right definition of faith if we call it a firm and certain knowledge of God's benevolence toward us, founded upon the truth of the freely given promise in Christ, both revealed to our minds and sealed upon our hearts through the Holy Spirit" (3.2.7).

Calvin's second concern was to teach clearly that faith is trust. It is a trusting and confident knowledge:

> As faith is not content with a doubtful and changeable opinion, so it is not content with an obscure and confused conception; but requires full and fixed certainty, such as men are wont to have from things experienced and proved. For unbelief is so deeply rooted in our hearts, and we are so inclined to it, that not without hard struggle is each one able to persuade himself of what all confess with the mouth: namely, that God is faithful. (*Institutes* 3.2.15)

6. Following the editorial notes in John Calvin, *Opera selecta* (ed. P. Barth and G. Niesel; Munich: Kaiser, 1962), 3.10n1, John T. McNeill in *Institutes* 1.544n8 cites Lombard's *Sentences* 3.25.1–4 and Aquinas's *Summa theologiae* II-II Q. 2.5–8, as examples of those of whom Calvin might have been thinking when he attacked the "Schoolmen" who "ruinously delude poor, miserable folk" with their doctrine of "implicit faith" (*Institutes* 3.2.2). Calvin's relations to medieval Scholasticism were more complicated, however, than these notes suggest. See Richard A. Muller, *The Unaccommodated Calvin* (Oxford Studies in Historical Theology; New York: Oxford University Press, 2000), 46–61.

Especially as a pastor, Calvin understood the trusting character of faith. He knew that in the trials and difficulties of life, it is hard to believe that God is faithful. God sometimes seems as much absent as faithful, as much forgetful as remembering, as much indifferent as caring. So, the essence of faith is that we know and trust that God in Christ is faithful to us and will redeem us.

When Calvin declares that faith is "full and fixed certainty," he does not mean that Christians do not struggle in this life:

> Surely, while we teach that faith ought to be certain and assured, we cannot imagine any certainty that is not tinged with doubt, or any assurance that is not assailed by some anxiety. On the other hand, we say that believers are in perpetual conflict with their own unbelief. Far, indeed, are we from putting their consciences in any peaceful repose, undisturbed by any tumult at all. Yet, once again, we deny that, in whatever way they are afflicted, they fall away and depart from the certain assurance received from God's mercy. (*Institutes* 3.2.17)

Christians do face doubt and anxiety, but faith always triumphs in the end: "The end of the conflict is always this: that faith ultimately triumphs over those difficulties which besiege and seem too imperil it" (*Institutes* 3.2.18). Calvin expands this thought:

> For faith does not certainly promise itself either length of years or honor or riches in this life, since the Lord willed that none of these things be appointed for us. But it is content with this certainty: that, however many things fail us that have to do with the maintenance of this life, God will never fail. Rather, the chief assurance of faith rests in the expectation of the life to come, which has been placed beyond doubt through the Word of God. (*Institutes* 3.2.28)

Faith in all struggles looks to the righteousness of Christ to avoid eternal death and to possess eternal life: "Faith properly begins with the promise, rests in it, and ends in it. For in God faith seeks life: a life that is not found in commandments or declarations of penalties, but in the promise of mercy, and only in a freely given promise" (*Institutes* 3.2.29).

Third, Calvin teaches that faith was the gift of God's grace. The Christian's faith comes from God's plan and from the working of the Holy Spirit: "Therefore, as we cannot come to Christ unless we be drawn by the Spirit of God, so when we are drawn we are lifted up in mind and heart above our understanding" (*Institutes* 3.2.34). Christians know and trust what they could have never known and trusted left to themselves apart from the Spirit of God.

Fourth, Calvin explains the relation of faith and love. As noted above, the medieval doctors suggested that an implicit faith became saving only when formed by love. Calvin sees that this teaching reversed the proper relationship of faith and love: "Also, they pointlessly strive after the foolish subtlety that we are justified by faith alone, which acts through love, so that righteousness depends upon love. Indeed, we confess with Paul that no other faith justifies 'but faith working through love' [Gal 5:6]. But it does not take its power to justify from that working of love. Indeed, it justifies in no other way but in that it leads us into fellowship in the righteousness of Christ" (*Institutes* 3.11.20). Calvin also writes: "The teaching of the Schoolmen, that love is prior to faith and hope, is mere madness; for it is faith alone that first engenders love in us" (3.2.41). Where Rome conflated faith and love, justification and sanctification, Calvin teaches that it is faith alone that *produces* love.

Faith, Calvin argues, looks away from self to rest in Christ for justification. Therefore, even a weak and imperfect faith still connects with Christ and his perfection when it is genuine. (By contrast our love is always weak and imperfect in itself and as a virtue in us cannot stand in God's judgment because of that imperfection.) True faith is also the fountain of sanctification, love, and repentance. Calvin contemplated no kind of Christian life that was not progressing in holiness.

What Calvin taught on faith and love is also what Luther taught. Luther complained that some people were abusing the doctrine of justification by faith alone. Luther was adamant at this point: "To preach as follows (as some have formerly done, and some mad spirits are still doing) would be wrong and intolerable: Although you do not keep the commandments, do not love God and your neighbor, aye, although you are an adulterer, this does not matter; if you believe, you will be saved." Luther utterly rejected such a notion: "No, my good man, this will not do! You will not possess the kingdom of heaven."[7] Luther, like Calvin, taught that the true faith that justifies is a faith that leads also to sanctification. Those who totally lack sanctification can make no claim of having true faith. Calvin and Luther are at one on this point.

After defining faith (*Institutes* 3.2), Calvin develops the sanctifying effect of faith (3.3–10). In this way, he makes clear how important sanctification was in true religion. Then he comes to the subject of justification as the effect of faith:

> Let us sum these up. Christ was given us by God's generosity, to be grasped and possessed by us in faith. By partaking of him, we principally receive a double grace: namely, that being reconciled to God through Christ's blamelessness, we may have in heaven instead of a Judge a gracious Father; and secondly, that sanctified by Christ's spirit we may cultivate blamelessness and purity of life. Of regeneration, indeed, the second of these gifts, I have said what seemed sufficient. The theme of justification was therefore more lightly touched upon because it was more to the point to understand first how little devoid of good works is the faith, through which alone we obtain free righteousness by the mercy of God. . . . Therefore we must now discuss these matters [i.e., justification] thoroughly. And we must so discuss them as to bear in mind that this is the main hinge on which religion turns, so that we devote the greater attention and care to it. For unless you first of all grasp what your relationship to God is, and the nature of his judgment concerning you, you have neither a foundation on which to establish your salvation nor one on which to build piety toward God. (*Institutes* 3.11.1)

The pious life rests on the foundation of its relationship with God. For the Reformation, reconciliation precedes sanctification.

Calvin insists that reconciliation means that the Christian is connected to the perfect righteousness of Christ by that faith that looks away from itself, which is only an instrument of receiving the work of Christ:

7. Martin Luther, *What Luther Says: An Anthology* (ed. Ewald M. Plass; St. Louis: Concordia, 1959), 1.494.

> Faith, even though of itself it is of no worth or price, can justify us by bringing Christ, just as a pot crammed with money makes a man rich. Therefore, I say that faith, which is only the instrument for receiving righteousness, is ignorantly confused with Christ, who is the material cause and at the same time the Author and Minister of this great benefit. Now we have disposed of the problem as to how the term "faith" ought to be understood when justification is under consideration. (*Institutes* 3.11.7)

In an arresting image here, Calvin teaches that as money, not the pot, makes one rich, so Christ's work held by faith reconciles the Christian to God.

Calvin again notes that this faith alone, which looks to Christ alone, has its works, but its works, its fruit, or its outcome are in no way part of justification:

> For, according to them [the Sophists], man is justified by both faith and works provided they are not his own works but the gifts of Christ and the fruit of regeneration. . . . Still they do not observe that in the contrast between the righteousness of the law and of the gospel, which Paul elsewhere introduces, all works are excluded, whatever title may grace them [Gal 3:11–12]. For he teaches that this is the righteousness of the law, that he who has fulfilled what the law commands should obtain salvation; but this is the righteousness of faith, to believe that Christ died and rose again [Rom 10:5, 9]. . . .
>
> From this it follows that not even spiritual works come into account when the power of justifying is ascribed to faith. (*Institutes* 3.11.14)

In his discussion of works, Calvin anticipates the great error of many contemporary critics of the Reformation doctrine. They think that as long as they say that salvation is by grace alone they have said all they need to say theologically, but many medieval theologians said exactly that. They taught that grace alone worked to transform and sanctify the life and that all the works of the Christian are the fruit of grace. Such an improved life, however, is still an imperfect life and cannot stand in the judgment. Calvin summarizes the situation succinctly: "If righteousness is revealed in the gospel, surely no mutilated or half righteousness but a full and perfect righteousness is contained there. The law therefore has no place in it" (*Institutes* 3.11.19). What one needs to stand in the judgment, Calvin declares over and over again, is a perfect righteousness. No matter how much progress one makes in grace during this life, so that one's life becomes holier, holier, and holier, it will never get to the point where it will be able to stand in the judgment.

Calvin's teaching on faith alone is clear. He believed that he was simply teaching what the apostle Paul had taught in his letter to the Romans. Following Calvin and the Reformation, we now turn to Paul's letter to the Romans to examine what the apostle taught about justification.

The Biblical Doctrine of *sola fide*

In the current situation, however, we must pause to ask whether, as the people of God, we can turn to the book of Romans with the expectation of understanding the apostle's basic teaching there. Many voices suggest that we cannot, but that we can understand Paul only if some expert explains him to us. We need to be renewed in the true Protestant conviction that God has spoken clearly in his word. Psalm 119:105 assures us, "Your word is a lamp to my feet / and a light to my path" (ESV). God is successful in revealing himself. Too much of modern theology rests on the idea that somehow God has failed to be clear in his revelation. We must utterly reject that notion.

Still, we must explain why there are so many competing interpretations of the Bible. In Romans 1:18 Paul gave a clear answer: sinners suppress the truth in unrighteousness. Why do people fail to understand the Bible? They have a moral problem as much as an intellectual problem. They suppress the truth. They do not want to see it. There is deep in the hearts of sinners a conviction that they do not want to acknowledge that they are utterly lost in sin and unable to help themselves. They do not want to have to acknowledge that they can do nothing to help themselves. They do not want to acknowledge that Christ alone has done everything for their salvation.

In our day, this moral problem has affected much biblical scholarship and further weakened itself by divorcing itself from the church, the confessions, and the orthodox community of faith. Biblical scholarship too often has become indifferent to theology, indifferent to the responsibility to explain how one section of Scripture relates to other sections of Scripture, and indifferent to the spiritual implications of its work for the life of the church. We must reject a biblical scholarship that asks us to trust experts and abdicate our own responsibility to read and reflect. We have to beware of biblical scholars who are constantly creating a speculative environment and context for understanding the Bible by which they make the Bible say the opposite of what it says.[8]

This has happened in contemporary discussions of whether women can hold the offices of minister and elder in the church. Paul says, "I do not permit a woman to teach" (1 Tim 2:12 ESV), but some scholars create a context for that statement so that Paul is read as saying, "I want women to teach."[9] The same thing has happened with the issue of homosexuality.[10] Scholars create a speculative context in which to interpret Paul's prohibitions against homosexuality, so that they discover that Paul supports committed homosexual relationships. Such scholarship turns the Bible on its head and suppresses the truth in unrighteousness. By contrast, scholars who listen carefully to the Word greatly aid the church in understanding the Bible, but the church is not dependent even on faithful scholars to understand the Bible's basic message of redemption.[11]

That basic message of redemption is clear in Paul's letter to the Romans. He began this letter, as he began several of his letters, by introducing major themes of the letter in a noncontroversial context.

8. In his refutation of the new perspective on Paul, Guy Prentiss Waters exposes this tendency; *Justification and the New Perspective on Paul* (Phillipsburg, NJ: P&R, 2004), 193.

9. Cf. Susan T. Foh's *Women and the Word of God* (Phillipsburg, NJ: Presbyterian & Reformed, 1979) and James B. Hurley's *Man and Woman in Biblical Perspective* (Grand Rapids: Zondervan, 1981), who cite scholars who argue in this way.

10. Cf. Robin Scroggs, *The New Testament and Homosexuality: Contextual Background for Contemporary Debate* (Philadelphia: Fortress, 1983).

11. This is not to say that the church should ignore scholarly reflection on exegetical or theological matters. After all, this volume contains the reflections of scholars trained in their particular academic fields. Scholarly reflection should, however, never be elevated as an authority above Scripture and the church's confessions of faith.

He wrote of the gospel (1:1–2), the Jewish background of the gospel (1:2–3), his particular ministry to the Gentiles (1:5, 13), and the common application of the gospel to Jews and Gentiles (1:14, 16).

Intriguingly, Paul summarized his ministry as calling Gentiles to "the obedience that comes from faith" (1:5 NIV) or, more literally, "the obedience of faith" (ESV). What did Paul mean by this phrase? He might simply have meant, as the NIV translators concluded, that obedience is the fruit of faith. He might also be saying something a little ironic here. To his critics who accused him of antinomianism and stressed the necessity of obedience as foundational to justification, Paul might have wanted to show them what true gospel obedience was. It is as if Paul implicitly asked them: what obedience does God want of you? His answer, summarized in 1:5 and developed in the next chapters of the letter, is that the gospel obedience that God calls for is faith. Paul was not suggesting that believing is the one work God rewards, but rather was ironically teaching that faith looks away from itself and rests in the obedience of another. His gospel is the gospel of Jesus's work (1:2–5).

Paul's expression *the obedience of faith* is parallel to the way in which Jesus taught in John 6. The crowd asked Jesus, "What must we do, to be doing the works of God?" (6:28 ESV). Jesus replied—possibly with an ironic smile—"This is the work of God, that you believe in him whom he has sent" (6:29 ESV). The work of God for Christians is that they believe in Jesus.

Paul's introduction to Romans is particularly appropriate for a letter to a church that was largely Gentile and in which his apostolic ministry and teaching had been much maligned. He wrote in Romans 3:8: "And why not do evil that good may come?—as some people slanderously charge us with saying" (ESV). His critics were claiming that the apostle Paul's message was, "Do evil, that good may result." They maintained that Paul was antinomian and antiholiness and that he preached a gospel of grace so free that he did not care how one lived. Some critics actually said that Paul wanted Christians to do evil, because then they would really understand grace.

Paul was writing to the Romans, at least in part, to set the record straight. He utterly rejected his critics' characterization. Paul not only addressed their slander in Romans 3, but he returned to it in 6:1: "Are we to continue in sin that grace may abound?" (ESV). The intriguing conclusion that we must draw from 3:8 and 6:1 is that people could conceive that Paul was indifferent to holiness. We see that Paul taught a gospel—and a doctrine of justification—so full, complete, free, and glorious in Christ that some people could mishear him as if he were indifferent to holiness.

This misunderstanding of Paul suggests a critical question for some of his interpreters. Would anyone ever read the federal-vision writers or Norman Shepherd or the new perspective on Paul or Thomas Aquinas or the Council of Trent and come with the question to them: Should we sin that grace may abound? That question would never, could never, arise for anyone who has read these teachers. As Martyn Lloyd-Jones and other defenders of the Reformation doctrine of justification say: If no one ever comes to you after you preach the gospel and asks, "So should we sin so that grace may abound?" you have probably never preached the gospel.

The true biblical doctrine of justification by faith has to be formulated with great precision and care to teach both the glorious free justification that we have in Christ and its fruit in holiness. True doctrine is like walking a tight rope. One can fall off the tight rope of justification in two directions: the antinomian direction and the neonomian direction. Both the antinomian and the neonomian miss the biblical doctrine of justification.

As Paul vindicated himself from the charge of antinomianism, so he warned the Roman church against neonomianism. He refuted the teaching of his opponents, which seemed to be saying that Gentiles could be right with God only if they would become Jews and keep the law of Moses. Paul's opponents taught that the gospel was the good news that Gentiles at long last could become Jews and enter into the inheritance of the preferred status of Jews, but Paul insisted that this was not the gospel.

Paul readily acknowledged that Jews enjoyed certain priorities and privileges in redemptive history (Rom 1:16; 3:1–2). He went on to argue, however, that in a fundamental sense Jews and Gentiles were in exactly the same situation before God. Paul stressed that point in part to refute his critics, who were constantly teaching the superiority of Judaism and insisting that Gentiles needed to become Jews.

In contrast, Paul declared that Jews and Gentiles were in the same situation. They both have law and they both were obligated to live by it. Obviously, the Jews had the law in the Torah, but Paul belabored the point in Romans to make clear that Gentiles also know at least something of the holy will of God. The Gentiles know the truth (1:18, 25), they possess knowledge of God (1:19, 28), and they have derived understanding from creation (1:20) or from nature (1:26). Gentiles know the righteous decree of God (1:32), and indeed they have the law written in their hearts (2:14–15).

For our purposes, we do not need a detailed discussion of all the implications of the law to which Paul referred in Romans. His basic point was simply this: the Jews have law, the Gentiles have law, and they are all obligated to live according to the law that they have. He went on to conclude that everyone would be judged according to the law that they had, in terms of how their lives measured up to law.

In his discussion in Romans 2, Paul recognized that those who broke the law would be judged by it and that those who kept the law would be vindicated by it. Some interpreters get so lost in the forest looking for trees that they actually seem to think that Paul was arguing that some people could keep the law and be vindicated by it. Unless Paul lost his mind somewhere between Romans 1 and Romans 3 he could not be saying that. In Romans he repeatedly taught the universality of human sin and destituteness (1:18, 20, 28–29; 2:12). Paul summarized all that he had been teaching in Romans 1–3: "For all have sinned and fall short of the glory of God" (3:23 ESV). Paul did not add a footnote to this statement: "Except those who actually keep the law and therefore are vindicated by it." It is a violation of logic, clear thinking, theology, and exegesis not to allow Paul's conclusion in Romans 3 to determine what he is arguing in Romans 2. In Romans 2, Paul spoke hypothetically about being vindicated by the law. Certainly, anyone who kept the law would be vindicated by it, but could anyone keep the law? The conclusion in Romans 3 was crystal clear—no one could: "None is righteous . . . no one seeks for God . . . no one does good" (3:10–12 ESV). All have sinned and fallen short of the glory of God. Paul concluded: "For by works of the law no human being will be justified in his sight, since through the law comes knowledge of sin" (3:20 ESV).

Is the law good? Of course it is (7:12). By its very goodness, however, the law shows sinners their sin and inability to be righteous. By contrast, the gospel, as Paul taught in Romans 1–3, is this: sinners who do not and cannot have a righteousness of their own can find righteousness in another: "But now the righteousness of God has been manifested apart from the law, although the Law and the Prophets bear witness to it" (3:21 ESV). The good news is that God has provided a righteousness of his own apart from the law and all of its demands.

Is the "righteousness of God" that is "apart from law" really apart from the whole law? Is the "law" (3:21) equivalent to the "works of the law" (3:20, 28)? Many clever interpreters, from the ancient church period until the twentieth century, argue that "law" and "works of the law" here in Paul are just part of the law. These works of the law are the ceremonial requirements of the law, such as circumcision, dietary laws, or special holidays. These interpreters argue that no one can be justified by those ceremonial works of the law, but they say that one can be justified by the moral law. They deny that Paul was talking about the moral law when he rejected works of the law. They ignore in their interpretation the comprehensive character of 3:21 and the contrast Paul repeatedly drew between faith and law (3:27–4:6). For Paul, works of the law and the law are indeed synonymous in Romans 3, but the works of the law are the moral works of the law as well as every other kind. Calvin demonstrates this very effectively in *Institutes* 3.11.20. Jonathan Edwards also argues the case brilliantly and convincingly in his treatise "Justification by Faith Alone."[12] Paul has argued that God will judge our works by the law to determine whether they are good, acceptable, and deserving a reward (4:2). The contrast Paul made in 3:27–31 is between a righteousness that comes by law and a righteousness that comes from Christ and is received by faith alone. Paul really could not be clearer. Paul indeed taught that faith stands alone in receiving justification from the work of Christ (3:24–26). Justification is not received or maintained by any kind of working, any kind of moral improvement, or any kind of sanctifying development.

12. Jonathan Edwards, *The Works of Jonathan Edwards* (Edinburgh: Banner of Truth, 1979), 1.630–35; and idem, *Works* (New Haven: Yale University Press, 2001), 19.167.

Calvin believes that Paul used Abraham as an example to press justification by faith alone. For Paul, Abraham was the father of the faithful. Abraham believed both before he was circumcised and after he was circumcised, so he was the father of the uncircumcised and of the circumcised. He was the father of all Christians, whether Jew and Gentile. Therefore, what is true of Abraham is true of all of Christians. The truth about Abraham is that he had nothing about which to boast. Abraham could not boast because he was justified by faith alone: "Abraham believed God, and it was counted to him as righteousness" (4:3 ESV). Faith was foundational for Abraham.

Paul made clear at the beginning of Romans 4 that the justification of Abraham was the justification of the "ungodly" (4:5 ESV) or "wicked" (NIV). Calvin presses the question: Where do we read in Scripture that Abraham believed that it was reckoned to him as righteousness? Obviously Paul was citing Genesis 15, but, Calvin notes, Abraham had become a follower of God in Genesis 12. Abraham had long been a faithful believer before the statement in Genesis 15: "Even though the life of the patriarch [Abraham] was spiritual and well-nigh angelic, he did not have sufficient merit of works to acquire righteousness before God" (*Institutes* 3.11.14). It was Abraham the faithful, Abraham the obedient, Abraham the godly, whom Paul called wicked. No matter how much progress Abraham made in godliness, he could not stand in the judgment. He needed to be a believer. His righteousness was to be found in the faith that rested in Christ's righteousness. That was Paul's argument.

Paul made this point even more clearly in quoting from Psalm 32. David there referred to God's people as godly (32:6), righteous (32:11), and trusting (32:10). Who are the godly, the righteous, the trusting? They are the ones blessed by having their transgressions forgiven and their sins covered (32:1–2). This David, as God's servant, as the man after God's own heart, and as an Israelite who was called forgiven, godly, righteous, and trusting, still had to plead with God: "Enter not into judgment with your servant, / for no one living is righteous before you" (143:2 ESV). Abraham in the best of his service and David in the best of his service had to plead with God not to judge them for their continuing failure in sin and wickedness, and David and Abraham looked away from themselves to rest in the righteousness that comes from God in Jesus Christ.

Conclusion

Justification is by faith alone. The Reformation got the biblical doctrine of justification exactly right. The new perspective on Paul and the federal vision are not really new, but a reiteration of medieval theological errors. When Thomas Aquinas asked whether God justifies the wicked, he responded that God justifies those who used to be wicked and now have become righteous (Aquinas, *Summa theologiae* I-II Q. 113.1). Such an answer, however, is not faithful to Paul. Paul taught that God justifies wicked people, like godly Abraham and godly David, by faith alone, because only faith receives the imputation of the perfect righteousness of Christ.

Only the doctrine of faith alone can lead someone to say with Paul in Romans 5:1: "Therefore, since we have been justified through faith, we have peace with God through our Lord Jesus Christ" (NIV). The truth of Christ and the perfection of his work is critical in the current debates about faith alone, but the peace of the Christian heart and conscience is also at stake. Paul declared that Christians should enjoy a sense of peace with God through faith in Christ. Any claim to teach or preach the gospel that does not lead to such peace is no gospel at all. So Luther was right in understanding Paul: "A man is justified, not by the works of the law, but by faith alone."

10
Justification by Faith Alone

No Christian Life without It

Hywel R. Jones

Introduction

Whenever the doctrines of justification and sanctification are to be considered, the instinctive reaction of a Protestant ought to be to draw a distinction between them. This is because the great good news of salvation that is about Jesus Christ and what he has done and the terms on which God will receive sinners who approach him lies at the very point where these two doctrines are to be differentiated. There is but one Savior and one way for a sinner to obtain salvation from him. That way is "through faith alone," which means not only "*simply* to thy cross I cling" but also "*nothing* in my hand I bring"—and that applies to every occasion when God's mercy is sought through Jesus Christ.

The distinction between justification and sanctification is therefore absolutely crucial. The Christian needs to be reminded of it every bit as much as the non-Christian needs to know of it. And Satan strives to make the one forget it and to keep the other in ignorance of it! Its truth should therefore be made clear repeatedly in preaching and pastoral work and especially when it is being blurred—as it is at the present time in both pedobaptist and Baptist circles.[1]

The object of this essay, however, is to consider how justification and sanctification are to be connected with each other—and that is important too. The distinction between them touches the vitals of how a person *becomes* a Christian; the connection between them goes to the heart of what is involved in *being* a Christian, which is another name for living the Christian life. These are core matters in Christianity, and they are hand in glove with each other.

Even so, a notion has been current for some time that they are incompatible. It has been expressed in terms of an emphasis on a free and final justification in this life inevitably cutting the nerve of pursuing Christian holiness with a view to the life to come. This goes back at least to the Roman Catholic and Arminian objections to *sola fide* (by faith alone) voiced in the sixteenth and seventeenth centuries.[2] But the idea has a longer pedigree than that. We may hear an echo of it in the words of the apostle Paul: "Shall we continue in sin, that grace may abound?" (Rom 6:1 AV). The idea is therefore almost as old as *sola fide* itself, but that is not something to trumpet proudly, because both Paul and the Reformers rejected it.[3] It is the standard reaction of those who do not understand the truth and power of *sola fide*. But it survives from generation to generation because, as was said in the seventeenth century, "there is an Arminian scheme of salvation in every unrenewed human heart."[4] For professing Christians therefore to be thinking it or voicing it still is an indication of a powerful misunderstanding and even of a potential defection from orthodox belief.

1. See Norman Shepherd, *The Call of Grace* (Phillipsburg, NJ: P&R, 2000); John Armstrong, "The Obedience of Faith," in *Trust and Obey: Obedience and the Christian* (ed. R. C. Sproul and D. Kistler; Morgan, PA: Soli Deo Gloria, 1996), 79–117; and Don B. Garlington, *Faith, Obedience, and Perseverance* (Tübingen: Mohr, 1994), 96.

2. See John Calvin, *A Harmony of the Gospels, vol. 3 and the Epistles of James and Jude* (trans. A. W. Morrison; Grand Rapids: Eerdmans, 1972), 324–26 (on Jude 4). See also Robert Traill, *Justification Vindicated* (repr. Edinburgh: Banner of Truth, 2002), 6.

3. *Sola fide* is explicitly as old as Abraham (Gen 15:6), and an anticipation of it is present in Adam's renaming of Eve (3:20).

4. Traill, *Justification Vindicated*, 60.

As has been hinted, the charge that *sola fide* (rightly understood) is an obstacle to holiness has been denied, and what follows will demonstrate that at least on the conceptual level. As far as its outworking on the personal and practical level is concerned, two things need to be borne in mind. First, everyone had better be cautious when the matter of personal holiness is under consideration because there is no one, irrespective of his views on this matter, who could not have done better. Second, sinning is not traceable in principle to the truth of *sola fide*. As Paul said to Peter in Galatians 2:18, "If I rebuild what I tore down, I prove myself to be a transgressor" (ESV). Sinning is not traceable to any biblical truth but to a misuse or a neglect of it. The fault is always to be laid at one's own door and not God's.

The testimony of the Protestant doctrinal standards of the sixteenth and seventeenth centuries shows an integral connection between justification and sanctification, and they describe it conceptually and experientially. To take just one example, the Westminster Confession of Faith contains the following statement: "Faith, thus receiving and resting on Christ and his righteousness, is the alone instrument of justification; yet is it not alone in the person justified, but is ever accompanied with all other saving graces, and is no dead faith, but worketh by love" (11.2).

This essay will concentrate more on how these truths connect on the personal than on the doctrinal level because of the terms in which the objection to a strong emphasis on *sola fide* is cast. It will seek to show that far from its being the case that an emphasis on *sola fide* is inimical to the pursuit of holiness, the truth is rather the opposite. The truth of *sola fide* plays *no less* significant a role in sanctification than it does in a sinner's acceptance by a holy God. The question to be considered therefore is the following: What role does justification play in sanctification? The answer can be summarized in advance as follows: The realization that one is pardoned and accepted by God on the basis of Christ's righteousness, without any works of one's own, motivates and supports one in doing the will of God—*as nothing else does or can do*.

Two biblical subjects have to be considered in this essay, and care must therefore be taken to ensure that neither is minimized in the interests of the other. That being so, the natural thing to do is to turn for help and guidance to a place in the New Testament where both are dealt with. The epistle to the Romans would of course be suitable, but Paul's epistle to the Galatians will be more helpful because Paul's burden in writing it was to emphasize *sola fide*: "Knowing that a man is not justified by the works of the law but through faith in Christ Jesus, even we have believed in Christ Jesus, that we may be justified by faith and not by the works of the law; since by the works of the law shall no flesh be justified" (2:16).

Given such statements it can therefore be said that if the message of sanctification is going to be shortchanged anywhere in the New Testament because of an emphasis on justification, then Galatians is most likely to be that place. But if, on the other hand, sanctification is also emphasized there—and it is—then the way in which the apostle deals with both justification and sanctification sets a pattern that all who uphold *sola scriptura* should follow—and a benchmark for all their attempts. This essay will therefore look at how Paul deals with justification and sanctification in Galatians, beginning with the distinction between them and moving on to their correlation.

Distinction between Justification and Sanctification

In 1575 Luther's *Sermons on Galatians* appeared in English. In the foreword, the translators gave their readers a useful piece of advice. They urged them to note:

> How and in what sence he [Luther] excludeth good works, and how not; how he neglecteth the law & how he magnifieth the law. For as in the case of justifying before God the free promise of the Gospell admitteth no condition but faith onely in Christ Jesu: so in the case of dutifull obedience, Luther here excludeth no good workes, but rather exhorteth thereunto, and that in many places. Thus times and cases discreetly must be distincted.[5]

5. Martin Luther, *Commentary on Galatians* (trans. Philip S. Watson; repr. London: Clarke, 1961), 11.

This advice about distinguishing between "times and places" is important for understanding not only Luther but also Paul—and therefore for understanding the mind of God, the Holy Spirit, in Scripture. If only this advice had been followed with a humble spirit, much of the confusion that arose in the sixteenth and seventeenth centuries and that has continued until the present time could have been avoided.

Luther himself cannot be completely exonerated on this account, of course, given his typical broadside against the epistle of James, but his dismissive swat at the "right strawy epistle" should not be made so much of, seeing that he presents and commends its teaching so well in his summary of Paul's argument in Romans. What his well-known remark was intended to highlight was the difference between the "chief books" of the New Testament (that included Romans and Galatians) and James, and if we are going to err that is by far the safer side to err on. It maintains the distinction between justification and sanctification with which we began, and doing that is basic to correlating them properly.

Over the years, however, a proper balance between James and Paul has not been maintained, with both a contradiction between them and a conflation of them being posited—and *sola fide* has suffered on both counts. Douglas Moo identifies what is said about the noun *faith* and the verb *justify* as causing "the *appearance* of . . . conflict," with "their arguments [being] advanced against different errors."[6] These terms provide a focus for considering the distinction between justification and sanctification.

The Noun Faith

It is well known that what James says in the second chapter of his letter about faith and its relationship to works has been set in opposition to what Paul affirms in Romans and Galatians. This has been done so loudly and for so long that any one who is not familiar with the New Testament might well be pardoned for thinking that those men never had the opportunity of talking to each other. That of course

6. Douglas J. Moo, *James* (Tyndale New Testament Commentary; Downers Grove, IL: InterVarsity, 1988), 100 (emphasis original).

is not the case. According to the opening chapters of Galatians, they were in each other's company on two occasions before the Council of Jerusalem, although whether James had written his letter before the first of these is a moot point. What is clear is that they did not disagree with each other.

Both meetings took place in Jerusalem. The first was semiprivate, and we do not know what they spoke about. At the second, the leaders of the Jerusalem church were present and the question of faith and works was discussed. Paul had gone there because "false brothers" from Jerusalem had arrived at the church in Syrian Antioch requiring Gentiles who believed in Jesus to be circumcised—that is, to become Jews or else they would not be saved (Acts 15:2, 5). They required them to keep other laws as well, such as those related to "days and months and seasons and years" (Gal 4:10 ESV), and they falsely claimed to have James's authorization (2:9). That was openly repudiated later in the council's letter: "Since we have heard that some persons have gone out from us and troubled you with words, unsettling your minds, although we gave them no instructions" (Acts 15:24 ESV).

Paul acquainted James, Peter, and John with the message that he had been preaching (Gal 2:2), and Barnabas, a former Levite, and Titus, a Gentile, whom he had taken with him provided the evidence of divine attestation of it. Having heard Paul, they "added nothing" to him (2:6 ESV), that is, they did not ask him to supplement his message of faith in Christ with a requirement to submit to the law. In addition, they made their position crystal clear by not requiring Titus to be circumcised (2:3) and by giving Paul "the right hand of fellowship" (2:9 ESV) in the one-gospel ministry. They were all in agreement that acceptance with God was by means of faith alone in Christ alone, and this was confirmed later at the Jerusalem Council (Acts 15). Given this history, the idea that Paul and James were at loggerheads should never have arisen.

The misconstruction referred to was corrected in the sixteenth century by Calvin, who writes in his summary of the argument of James that "what seems in the second chapter to be inconsistent with the doctrine of a free justification we shall easily explain in its place."[7] John Owen and others did the same in the following century, but the fiction rumbled on and was greatly fueled by higher critics in the nineteenth century.[8] It is now claimed that recent New Testament scholarship shows that "properly interpreted, Paul and James are united in their understanding of faith and works and their relationship to justification."[9]

When James speaks about "faith alone" (2:24), he is not thinking of Paul's emphasis at all. What he has in view he identifies as "faith by itself" (2:17 ESV), and he describes it as being akin to the demons' apprehensive knowledge that there is only one God (2:19). Such faith has knowledge and even some assent (or inability to dissent), but it is a faith destitute of trust. It is not true faith. Over against this, he depicts a faith that is genuine, that has works to manifest its reality. James and Paul are addressing different pastoral situations, and that means that each should be allowed to make his point in a way independent of but complementary to the other.

But that is what has not been happening for many a long day. We have already referred to the way in which James was used to contradict Paul and to cancel out his teaching. Although it would be too bold to declare that this view is no longer being held, it is not the pitch that is being made. Instead a quiet conflation is proceeding in which proper weight is not being given to *sola fide* when James 2 is being considered, and then that has a knock-on effect with regard to an understanding of both Romans and Galatians. Two examples of this tendency can be offered.

First, in *The Call of Grace,* Norman Shepherd describes the faith credited to Abraham as "a living and obedient faith."[10] He then uses this definition to explain James 2:21, where Abraham is said to have been "justified by works" in offering Isaac, concluding that justification is by faith plus works. He then carries this over to 2:23 and to the quotation from Genesis 15:6—"Abraham believed God, and it

7. John Calvin, *Commentaries on the Catholic Epistles* (trans. John Owen; Grand Rapids: Eerdmans, 1948), 276.

8. John Owen, *The Works of John Owen* (repr. Edinburgh: Banner of Truth, 1966), 5.384–400.

9. Moo, *James,* 100.

10. Shepherd, *Call of Grace,* 16.

was counted to him as righteousness" (ESV)—but Paul interprets this in Romans 4:1–5 as referring to righteousness being reckoned without works being done! By using "living and obedient faith" (or being faithful) as a working definition of faith, Shepherd prevents any distinction between made between faith and works in relation to justification, and that failure impacts justification adversely. It is a distinction that simply must be made.

Second, John Armstrong provides another example of this tendency in an essay that examines Paul's terse expression *the obedience of faith* (Rom 1:5).[11] He presents but (respectfully) sets aside two interpretations of this succinct (better than "ambiguous") phrase, which he describes as (a) "the obedience which comes from faith" and (b) "the obedience which is directed towards faith or the faith, or which is faith."[12] Each of these is exegetically possible and in addition has the advantage of leaving room for the distinction between *sola fide* and works of faith that Paul subsequently makes in Romans on the basis that the first has the moment of conversion in view whereas the second looks to the postconversion life. Armstrong, however, advocates an interpretation that he describes as "a richer and more contextually accurate understanding of the phrase and its use."[13] Quoting Don Garlington, he says that "the obedience of faith" is "*both* the obedience which *consists* in faith" and "the obedience which is the *product* of faith."[14]

As has been said, Paul includes more in this letter about the gospel than an account of justification. Consequently, his use of the term *faith* in Romans has more scope than how it relates to justification. For example, the terse expression with arguably the same intent—namely,

11. Armstrong, "Obedience of Faith."

12. Armstrong refers to several commentators as advocating one or other of these views: William Hendriksen, *Romans 1–8* (New Testament Commentary; Grand Rapids: Eerdmans, 1980); F. F. Bruce, *The Epistle to the Romans* (Grand Rapids: Eerdmans, 1963); C. E. B. Cranfield, *A Critical and Exegetical Commentary on the Epistle to the Romans* (International Critical Commentary; 2 vols.; Edinburgh: Clark, 1979); idem, *Romans: A Shorter Commentary* (Grand Rapids: Eerdmans, 1985); and John Murray, *The Epistle to the Romans* (New International Commentary on the New Testament; Grand Rapids: Eerdmans, 1968). He also includes references to Charles Hodge and D. M. Lloyd-Jones.

13. Armstrong, "Obedience of Faith," 85–86.

14. Garlington, *Faith, Obedience, and Perseverance*, 96 (emphasis original).

"from faith to faith" (1:17 AV)—also reminds his addressees that they "bec[a]me obedient from the heart . . . to which [they] were committed" (6:17 ESV), that is, "handed over" by God. The whole of the Christian life is indeed one of "trusting and obeying," but that does not mean that the term *faith* means *both whenever* it is used. Each context must be examined because, as every schoolboy knows, Paul sets them in opposition to each other sometimes. For example, he writes: "Now to the one who works, his wages are not counted as a gift but as his due. And to the one who does not work but trusts him who justifies the ungodly, his faith is counted as righteousness" (Rom 4:4–5 ESV). Armstrong's "richer" interpretation therefore contains the built-in potential of destroying justification by faith without works *unless some distinctions are clearly made* in relation to God's justifying declaration.

The Verb Justify

Moving over into the realm of ecclesiastical dogma, mention must be made of the Council of Trent, where the Roman Catholic response to *sola fide* was formulated. Trent spoke of two justifications, namely "initial" and "continuing," which it connected with Paul and James respectively. The first was related to faith as assent and to a contrition that is meritorious, and it consisted in a removal of original corruption and the implanting of a principle of love. The second was connected with works wrought (formed) in love, which establishes a righteousness before God.[15] This twofold justification was something that the Reformers and Puritans rejected, even though Calvin does have a chapter in his *Institutes of the Christian Religion* entitled "The Beginning of Justification and Its Continual Progress" (*Institutes* 3.14). What is in view there is a continuing to believe that one has been justified, and not anything ongoing about the justifying declaration of God or increasing in the state it inaugurates.[16]

Owen responds to this Roman Catholic construction in a most pointed and effective manner: "This distinction was coined unto no

15. This way of thinking is found in *Catechism of the Catholic Church* (2nd ed.; Rome: Libreria Editrice Vaticana, 1997), §2010.

16. We are indebted to W. R. Godfrey for this observation.

other end but to bring in confusion into the whole doctrine of the gospel. Justification, through the free grace of God, by faith in the blood of Christ, is evacuated by it. Sanctification is turned into a justification and corrupted by making the fruits of it meritorious."[17] He then goes on to record that some Protestants "embraced this distinction . . . although not absolutely." He accuses them of "sophistical cavills [word games]," and although he acknowledged that they put justification before good works he notes that they spoke of "a continuation of . . . justification . . . an increase of it as to degrees." He objects strongly whenever and wherever he saw an "inherent righteousness" being regarded as "the cause of or [having] any influence into our justification before God": "And if they may be allowed to turn *sanctification* into *justification,* and to make progress therein, or an increase thereof, either in the root or the fruit, to be a new justification, they may make twenty justifications as well as two for aught I know" (emphasis original). Owen is therefore asserting that there is only one justification. This is an emphasis that needs to be made today because a trend is developing of using the adjectives *initial* and *final* with regard to it. This two-part way of speaking about justification is quite alien to the classic Protestant tradition. On what grounds is this done with regard to James and Paul?

In a guarded way Moo presents a case for "initial-final" justification and refers to John Wesley's doing so.[18] He bases his view on an understanding of the verb *justify* in James 2, which he acknowledges can have one of two senses, both of which are attested in Jewish literature and in the New Testament: the demonstrative sense points to something being validated as just and right, and the declarative sense points to someone being declared by God to be just in his sight. Moo opts for the declarative sense mainly because he regards James as addressing the question "What kind of faith secures righteousness?" and not "How can righteousness be demonstrated?" In answer to his preferred question, works have to be included, but because Moo understands James to be referring to the last judgment and not to a response to the gospel message, any collision with Paul's teaching

17. Owen, *Works*, 5.138 (emphasis original).

18. Moo cites Minutes of 1744 in J. Wesley, *Works* 8.277, as supplying the source of his remark, but the details of his reference are not sufficient to confirm this claim.

in Romans and Galatians on justification in the present is avoided. Whether this exegesis succeeds in keeping safe and clear all that is important is open to question; in our view it is exegetically unnecessary and potentially dangerous. It also diminishes justification as the final verdict announced ahead of time!

We prefer the demonstrative sense for two reasons. First, nowhere in James 2:14–26 is the verb *justify* in the active mood. It therefore never has the noun *God* for a subject; there is nothing here like "God justifies the ungodly" in Romans 4:5, which is plainly declarative. But that of course does not mean that God may not be the unidentified agent of any or all of those passive verbs. Whether he is or is not has to be shown. In our view, in only one place in James 2 must a divine passive be understood and that is in 2:23, where James quotes from Genesis 15:6—the monumental verse that says, "[Abraham] believed the LORD, and he counted it to him as righteousness" (ESV). This establishes a divine imputation of righteousness through believing God's word about a promised seed and not from doing anything that God says.

Second, and as we have already mentioned, the question James is concerned about is "How can faith be demonstrated?" and not "How can righteousness be demonstrated?"—pace Moo. That is what James begins with in 2:14, and he concentrates on it throughout the passage. When he refers to works he does so by way of demonstrating faith's reality, whether in time or at the last day. That seems to be the integrative focus of this section. Works "justify" faith just like "wisdom is justified [by] her children" (Matt 11:19 AV). In the same way, Jesus said, "By your words you will be justified, and by your words you will be condemned" (12:37 ESV).

It is highly significant that our confessional documents do not use the word *justification* concerning the final judgment. Instead, they speak of "perfection" or of "open acknowledgment and acquittal" (WLC 90). This choice of language makes clear that justification—full, free, and final—takes place in the present world. Spiritual realities cannot last much longer than those terms that express and safeguard them. For all the reasons given, any and every attempt to speak of justification in two stages should be given up.

Armstrong goes further in connection with his views on "the obedience of faith" when he acknowledges that his "thought about the biblical language of redemption" has changed.[19] He wants to use the term *vindication* rather than *justification* and to speak of two related "vindications." In addition, he wishes to dispense with the doctrinal category of "merit"—and not merely with it as a term but also with the idea of a covenant that man has broken and that Christ must keep in order for man to be saved. This strikes a blow not only at the necessity of obedience but also at required righteousness as the condition of salvation. It means revising the terms and concepts that have been used throughout the history of the church in order to speak of redemption—and now is not a good time to be doing that. If this new terminology were to be adopted, the result will be the loss of the finality of justification in the here and now, and with it all the glorious blessings of peace of conscience and assurance of salvation, in spite of Armstrong's protestations to maintain them. Justification is as "once for all" as atonement is—and it is the launchpad for sanctification.

Correlation of Justification and Sanctification

Given that the distinction between justification and sanctification is vital for a proper interconnection, how should they be properly associated? The apostle Paul makes the statement that bears most relevantly and decisively on our subject: "For you were called to freedom, brothers. Only do not use your freedom as an opportunity for the flesh, but through love serve one another. For the whole law is fulfilled in one word: 'You shall love your neighbor as yourself'" (Gal 5:13–14 ESV). In these words he declares that the Christian life is a life of freedom from the law and also a life of "fulfillment of the law." There is of course no contradiction between those two statements; they are complementary and provide an example of those fine distinctions that are important to make. Each part of this statement is an essential component of genuine Christian living, set out in proper order. Freedom is clearly prior to fulfillment. Legalism is the consequence

19. John Armstrong, "Weekly Messenger," *Reformation and Revival* (April 5, 2004).

of forgetting the first; Antinomianism follows upon the second—and neither is what the Christian life is about.

Each part must therefore be given its proper place and weight. And what is that? The words of the middle portion of 5:13—"only do not use your freedom as an opportunity for the flesh"—help in that regard. There is no verb in this clause in the original text. One has to be supplied to convey the sense of the whole, and "use" is the word commonly employed. But that apart, what needs to be noted is that this clause indicates what Christians should not do with the freedom that *they have*; the clause that follows indicates what they *should do* with or by means of it. Living the Christian life therefore consists of using gospel liberty appropriately.[20] The basic fact—the glorious fact—is that the Christian has freedom from the law and is able to live a life that seeks to fulfil the law. Freedom connects with justification, fulfillment with sanctification.

Freedom from the Law

Before inquiring into the sense in which Christians are free from the law, attention ought first to be given to the stupendous reality of the fact. Paul does this in the opening words of Galatians 5 by using both the noun *freedom* and the verb *set free*.[21] In addition, he is at such pains to be specific as well as emphatic that he uses the noun *bondage*, which conceivably might have been left unmentioned, seeing that it is the necessary alternative to freedom. What is more, he follows his ringing assertion with "Now I, Paul say" and then "I testify again." Strong stuff!

Freedom from what? It is freedom from the law, and although he does not specify this in the opening of Galatians 5, it is borne out by what he has been saying in the preceding chapter (and by the verses that follow 5:1). Paul's allegory of Abraham's two wives is constructed around freedom and slavery language, and it is addressed specifically

20. By way of parallel, reference could be made to Eph 4:17–32; 5:8, 15–21, where Paul reminds Christians that they are to live wisely because they have been enlightened. Similarly, the apostle Peter writes: "Live as people who are free, not using your freedom as a cover-up for evil, but living as servants of God" (1 Pet 2:16).

21. This is a Hebraism comparable to "dying you will die" (Gen 2:17) and "blessing I will bless" (22:17). It describes fullness as well as certainty.

to those "who desire to be under law" (4:18 and 5:18). In 5:1 (which is generally read as if it were the last verse of Galatians 4 rather than the opening verse of a new chapter), he describes the slavery as being connected with "a yoke," which was a synonym for law to so many Jews. In the Council of Jerusalem, Peter referred to the yoke that neither those present nor their forefathers "have been able to bear"—and described an attempt to impose it on believing Gentiles as "putting God to the test" (Acts 15:10 ESV). That matches and explains Paul's determination in Galatians 2:4 to resist the Judaizers' demands for circumcision as maintenance of a newfound freedom or as a refusal to be enslaved again in 5:1.

Up to the coming of Christ, Jews had been "held captive under the law" (3:23 ESV) or under its disciplinary function (3:24). Something similar was also true of Gentiles because they were "enslaved to the elementary principles of the world" (4:3 ESV) and to "those that were by nature no gods," that is, to idols (4:8). Life before Christ was therefore life "under law" for Gentile as well as Jew. There was a universal obligation to obey however much of God's law that had been made known, by whatever means it had been disclosed, and on pain of awful penalty if it was not fully kept (Rom 1:18–32; 2:14–16; 3:9–20). It was also life without Christ for all who did not believe in the promised deliverer (Gen 3:15). That bondage comprising law, sin, and guilt shapes the freedom that Christ gives all those who believe.

The basis on which this freedom rests, together with believing appreciation of it, is expressed so harmoniously and movingly by Paul: "For through the law I died to the law, so that I might live to God. I have been crucified with Christ. It is no longer I who live, but Christ who lives in me. And the life I now live in the flesh I live by faith in the Son of God, who loved me and gave himself for me" (Gal 2:19–20 ESV). Although he uses the first-person singular, Paul intends all Galatians to echo his words, and especially Peter whom he had opposed on account of his inconsistency and insincerity. Galatians 2:19 implies that it is not possible "to live to the law" *and* "to live to God." "To live to the law" means having the law front and center, and always as the rule and guide for one's life, for one's own obedience as the way to God and blessing. And it is a hard taskmaster (3:24) because it demands total obedience.

One must therefore die to the law before one can live to God, but how can anyone "die to the law"? Paul tells us that it was "through the law" and by being "co-crucified with Christ." It was therefore by law and gospel. The law's shackle was struck off by a believing sight of the one who was thrust through with the Lord's sword (Zech 13:7)—and that pierced Saul's heart too. He became Paul, willingly bound to Jesus Christ, who had kept the law and borne the curse for each one of his people. Rejecting himself as no more than "death warmed up" and entrusting himself to the Christ who died, Paul lives by the power of the resurrected Christ who now lives in him, in his flesh. So he lives for the one who loved him and gave himself for him.

This is what becomes actual and personal by the effectual call of the gospel. That is what Galatians 5:13 says: "You were called to freedom, brothers" (ESV). This does not mean that freedom lies in the future as something that it is yet to be possessed. Rather, the cell door swings open by virtue of the call, and the prisoner steps out—and there is no longer any punishment to be faced. He is a "dead man walking" to freedom not execution.

There are three references to this call in Galatians. The first says that it is a call "into the grace of Christ" (1:6 AV), and the second refers to its actualization in the case of Paul (1:15). It therefore joins to the grace that is in Christ and in him alone. The first step a former condemned sinner takes is therefore a step "into Christ." It is not a step into no-man's-land. The third refers to the one who does the calling and to its power, its persuasive effect (5:8), namely, God himself. This is what has been designated the effectual call—the Spirit of God takes the word of law and gospel and makes it invincible in the conscience, producing a most willing reception of it. He justifies the ungodly, that is, he pardons the guilty, absolves the condemned, and graciously joins them as they are to Christ in all the fullness of his merit and might (Rom 4:5, 17; 1 Cor 1:9, 26–30; 2 Thess 2:13–14).

Now the all-important question is this: What does this freedom mean for the believer as he thinks about living as a Christian, that is, about sanctification? In what sense is a believer in Jesus Christ free from the law? Because Christ has honored it (Isa 42:21), restoring what he did not take away (Ps 69:4 [MT 69:5]), the believer should realize that no obedience is required of him for acceptance with God and that he has no liability to penalty for his disobedience. He is therefore to be free in conscience before God's law, refusing its right to require any obedience of him or threaten him with damnation if he does not comply—and only because the life of Jesus offered up in death to God is his obedience and curse. This should be so well known that the believer "stands fast" on it (Gal 5:1).

Luther puts this so well, clearly and often, as in this memorable example:

> If the law shall presume to creep into thy conscience, see thou play the cunning logician, and make the true division. Give no more to the law than belongeth unto it and say thou: O law, thou wouldest climb up into the kingdom of my conscience, and there reign and reprove it of sin, and wouldest take from me the joy of my heart, which I have by faith in Christ, and drive me to desperation, that I might be without all hope, and utterly perish. This thou dost besides [outside] thine office; keep thyself within thy bounds. . . . I will not suffer thee, so intolerable a tyrant and cruel tormentor to reign in my conscience, for it is the seat and temple of Christ, the Son of God, who is the king of righteousness and peace, and my most sweet saviour and mediator; he shall keep my conscience joyful and quiet in the sound and pure doctrine of the gospel, and in the knowledge of this passive and heavenly righteousness.[22]

Luther then goes on immediately to say: "When I have this righteousness reigning in my heart, I descend from heaven as the rain making fruitful the earth: that is to say, I come forth into another kingdom, and I do good works, how and whensoever occasion is offered." And after listing various stations and professions in life he says: "To conclude: whosoever he be that is assuredly that Christ is his righteousness, doth not only cheerfully and gladly work well in his vocation, but also submitteth himself in love." This means that God's verdict of "not guilty" echoes in the sinner's conscience. Believing in Christ, he hears it and is as good as in heaven as a result of it. A legal fiction? Preposterous!

22. Luther, *Commentary on Galatians*, 28.

Fulfillment of the Law

Proceeding straight to Galatians 5:14, where the fulfillment of the law is referred to, it should be noted that this is summed up by just one word—"love." So far, what has been said about the law and the gospel might make it appear as if the good gospel has got rid of the bad law but, of course, it is not that the law is bad but that people are. In that situation, the only good that it can do for them is to show them how guilty and helpless they are and to point them to Jesus Christ so that they may turn from self and sin (i.e., repentance) and turn to trust in Christ (i.e., faith). In doing so, not only do they die to their attempts to keep the law as a way to God, but they also begin to live to God through Christ's law keeping and curse bearing for them.

Wonder of wonders, the effect of this is that a glad and grateful desire to serve God and neighbor to the glory of our Savior and Lord is generated in the heart. And how can that be done? By love fulfilling the law. Not loving instead of law keeping, but loving to keep the law.

From where does that obedient love that is so essential to sanctification come? It is not native to the unregenerate human heart, because self-love and self-will reign there. The whole life of the sinner is, as Luther says, turned in upon himself. Whatever unbelievers may do is therefore with themselves in view. Even if they try to obey by being religious or moral, it is in order to gain merit and to obligate God. This was the case with Saul of Tarsus, as he himself admitted: "If anyone else thinks he has reason for confidence in the flesh, I have more: circumcised on the eighth day, of the people of Israel, of the tribe of Benjamin, a Hebrew of Hebrews; as to the law, a Pharisee; as to zeal, a persecutor of the church; as to righteousness, under the law blameless. But whatever gain I had, I counted as loss for the sake of Christ" (Phil 3:4–7 ESV).[23]

So where does such love come from? It can come only from the bosom of the God who is love. How is it transplanted in the human heart? It is done by the action of the regenerating Spirit, and it surfaces in the conscience as a sinner places faith in Jesus Christ, the Son of

23. Jesus taught the same in the parable of the Pharisee and the tax collector (Luke 18:9–14).

God "who loved me and gave himself for me" (Gal 2:20 ESV). It is therefore inseparably bound up with being justified, as Paul goes on to confess:

> Indeed, I count everything as loss because of the surpassing worth of knowing Christ Jesus my Lord. For his sake I have suffered the loss of all things and count them as rubbish, in order that I may gain Christ and be found in him, *not having a righteousness of my own that comes from the law, but that which comes through faith in Christ, the righteousness from God that depends on faith*—that I may know him and the power of his resurrection, and may share his sufferings, becoming like him in his death, that by any means possible I may attain the resurrection from the dead. (Phil 3:8–11 ESV, emphasis added)

The only people who can truly love are therefore those who have been justified. In Galatians this is summed up by these words: "For through the Spirit, by faith, we ourselves eagerly wait for the hope of righteousness. For in Christ Jesus neither circumcision nor uncircumcision counts for anything, but only faith working through love" (5:5–6 ESV).[24] Faith is described as waiting and also as working. Again there is no contradiction, because it waits for one thing and works for another. It waits for the righteousness that is perfection and vindication at the last day, whereas it works in loving service every day. The first relates to justification and the second to sanctification. With regard to vindication in heaven, it waits expectantly and *does not work*; with regard to sanctification, it *does not wait* but works energetically on earth.

The position in which the justified believer now finds himself can be depicted in three interrelated terms mentioned in Galatians 5:13–14: the "law" of God as summarized by the second great commandment, the believer's "love," and the believer's "flesh." They relate in the following ways. God's law and the believer's love now go together

24. This is a statement of how faith functions and not how it is formed. This distinction was at the heart of Protestant and Roman Catholic debate in the sixteenth century. An indication of how grievous the slippage has become is that in the recent Lutheran-Roman Catholic dialogue, Luther's Ninety-Five Theses were evoked and effectively rescinded by a statement entitled "Ninety-Five Reasons Why We Ought to Love One Another"!

most happily (Ps 119:97; John 15:10; 1 John 5:3). God's law and the believer's flesh oppose each other most strongly, as is indicated by the way in which "the works of the flesh" are set over against the reign of God and in that there is no law against the fruit of the Spirit, which is "love, joy, peace, patience, kindness, goodness, faithfulness, gentleness, self-control" (Gal 5:23 ESV).

How do the believer's love and his flesh relate? What is flesh? The term has more than a physical connotation in Scripture. It is more than a body. This can be seen from "the works" that are attributed to it—"sexual immorality, impurity, sensuality, idolatry, sorcery, enmity, strife, jealousy, fits of anger, rivalries, dissensions, divisions, envy, drunkenness, orgies" (Gal 5:19–21 ESV). It is therefore associated with deeds and words of the body but also with its "desires," even strong ones (5:16–17, 24). Flesh is therefore the unrenewed nature of the justified believer. Consequently, flesh and love are not wholly separate in the Christian—nor are they easily separable. They tangle with each other most frustratingly and sometimes even shamefully.

This does not mean, however, that the Christian has not been "crucified with Christ" or that he is no longer free, because all "who belong to Christ Jesus have crucified the flesh with its passions and desires" (5:24 ESV). That is something an unbeliever cannot do. It is the conscious, reflex act of having been "crucified with Christ," namely, nailing one's own sinful self to the cross that it might die. That is what it means to repent and believe, to turn from sin and trust in Christ. A Christian is therefore a new person with an old lifestyle that refuses to die merely on his say-so. This spells conflict, even all-out war, in the inner life of the believer and not merely his speech and conduct, between what he now loves and what he formerly lived for. Satan has a hand in it too. The pathway to personal holiness is a fight.

This war is unremitting and lifelong, but its issue is not uncertain and there are victories along the way. This is because those who have been justified have not only been absolved from guilt, but they have been adopted into the family of God and are indwelt by the Holy Spirit. Paul writes:

> But when the fullness of time had come, God sent forth his Son, born of woman, born under the law, to redeem those who were under

> the law, so that we might receive adoption as sons. And because you are sons, God has sent the Spirit of his Son into our hearts, crying, "Abba! Father!" So you are no longer a slave, but a son, and if a son, then an heir through God. (Gal 4:4–7 ESV).

Jesus has died for sin, and a life in the Spirit results for all who have put their trust in him. The life they live "in the flesh" (or the fight they fight) is "by faith in the Son of God" (2:20 ESV). The justified, adopted believer is a conqueror, even though he is sometimes overcome. He stumbles and falls whenever he remembers only *that* he is free and not *why* he was freed and uses his liberty in a way that is contrary to both the gospel and the law. That is what is pointed out in 2:13.

Freedom after slavery is a heady thing. A sinner who knows he is freed from the duty to keep the law and from the fear of death (Heb 2:15) can (as Luther said) seem to be "in heaven" already. To know that there is no condemnation now (Rom 8:1), no separation ever (8:35, 38–39), and no opposition worth speaking about in the interval (8:31, 37)—that takes some holding! It is intoxicating stuff. It is eternal life—heavenly as well as everlasting. But every Christian has an Achilles' heel: his flesh, the sinful nature that still has power but "no dominion" over him (6:14). That is where he must stand guard, for it provides an opportunity that is a vantage point, a position from which an attack may be effectively launched against the Spirit and what he desires to produce in the believer. Walking in the Spirit—that is, doing the law out of gratitude for the gospel—the believer becomes more and more righteous in his character and conduct. The sevenfold fruit of the Spirit will increasingly displace the works of the flesh and will enable the believer to do his last work well, which is to depart this life in confidence in Christ alone through faith alone and to the glory of God alone.

Conclusion

Our aim in preaching and in living is therefore twofold: sanctification must be (a) kept from where it does not belong and (b) given its proper place where it does belong. The apostle Paul brackets them memorably in Romans 8:1–4:

> There is therefore now no condemnation for those who are in Christ Jesus. For the law of the Spirit of life has set you free in Christ Jesus from the law of sin and death. For God has done what the law, weakened by the flesh could not do. By sending his own Son in the likeness of sinful flesh and for sin, he condemned sin in the flesh, in order that the righteous requirement of the law might be fulfilled in us, who walk not according to the flesh but according to the Spirit. (ESV)

With regard to the first aim, a strenuous effort is to be made to exclude any works of any kind from the way in which a guilty sinner is accepted by a holy God, in time and for eternity. Faith is the only instrument by which Christ's spotless righteousness is received, and it is imputed to everyone who trusts him. *Sola fide* therefore safeguards *solo Christo*! The camel's nose of human merit must be kept out of the tent in the interests of maintaining the Savior's voluntary and meritorious obedience in life and death as the only ground of a sinner's acceptance with God.

With regard to the second aim, equally strenuous efforts are to be made to enthrone sanctification as every professing believer's goal in life. The pursuit of holiness and living the Christian life are synonymous. There is no Christian life if there is no obedience to the will of God, and if there are no good works there is no faith. Every professing believer should be as energetic and extensive in his obedience to all the will of God as Jesus was to his Father's will, in accomplishing the salvation of his sinful people.

So just as morality is not to be preached as a way to acceptance with God, so moralism is to be rejected as a way to live the Christian life. "Be good" and "do good" is not a summary of Christianity. "Try harder" is even worse. Faith in Christ is the dynamic for "perfecting holiness in the fear of God" (2 Cor 7:1 AV), and his precepts are the directive for it. We hold to justification in order to make progress in sanctification. Every Christian should be able to say, "Jesus Christ lived and died for my sake, for my lasting good; I live for his sake, according to his precepts and for his eternal glory." That is the soul of Christianity. What could be simpler? What could be stronger? What could be sweeter? Without it, the life that some professing Christians seek to live is hard drudgery, whereas for others it might even be unperceived bondage. In reality, it is a life of glorious liberty.

PART 4

Pastoral Theology

11

Preaching *sola fide* Better

HYWEL R. JONES

The confession of divine justification touches man's moral life at its heart, at the point of its relationship to God. It defines the preaching of the Church, the existence and progress of the life of faith, the root of human security and man's perspective of the future.

—*G. C. Berkouwer*

If there is one thing that the Church needs today it is the republication with faith and passion of the presuppositions of the doctrine of justification, and the reapplication of [it], the article of a standing or falling church.

—*John Murray*

Introduction

The above statements by two respected Reformed theologians of the last century set the stage for our inquiry.[1] The first indicates how *sola*

1. See G. C. Berkouwer, *Faith and Justification* (trans. Lewis B. Smedes; Grand Rapids: Eerdmans, 1954), 17; and John Murray, *Collected Writings of John Murray* (Edinburgh: Banner of Truth, 1976–82), 2.202.

fide is central to almost everything Christian; the second appeals for a clearer proclamation of its truth (for a more comprehensive discussion of *sola fide* as a doctrine see chapter 9 above). This essay is about those matters: the message and its proclamation. They will be dealt with in turn and in the conviction that one must be a *sola fide* preacher in order to be a preacher of the gospel of Christ.

The Need for Preaching **sola fide** *Better*

After a conference address that expounded the doctrine of justification by faith and showed its contemporary importance, the following comments were overheard during a coffee break. Someone said, "What is all the fuss about? The terms *justification*, *righteousness*, *grace*, and *faith* are still being used aren't they? And the terms *active obedience* and *imputation* can't matter that much, surely?" Another replied, "Theologians are always quibbling over terms. So, let them argue about it and not trouble us with the matter or disturb the churches."

To hear such comments at all was a shock to the system, but even more disturbing was the realization that they were being made by folk who would have listened to many sermons in their lifetime and who belonged to the very tradition represented by Berkouwer and Murray. It is not only in Reformed churches, however, that the message of *sola fide* needs to be preached, but also in every strand of the ecclesiastical spectrum, especially the evangelical. Richard Lovelace points this out by way of a breathtaking claim:

> Only a fraction of the present body of professing Christians are solidly appropriating the justifying work of Christ in their lives. Many have so light an apprehension of God's holiness and of the extent and guilt for their sin that consciously they see little need for justification, although below the surface of their lives they are deeply guilt-ridden and insecure. Many others have a theoretical commitment to this doctrine, but in their day to day existence they rely on their sanctification for justification drawing their assurance of acceptance with God from their sincerity, their past experience of conversion, their recent religious performance or the relative infrequency of their conscious, willful disobedience. Few know enough to start each day with a thoroughgoing stand on Luther's platform; you are

> accepted, looking outward in faith and claiming the wholly alien righteousness of Christ as the only ground for acceptance, relaxing in the quality of trust which will produce increasing sanctification as faith is active in love and gratitude.[2]

The message of *sola fide* is therefore vital in the life of the Christian and the church and, by extension, her mission in the world. Much good work has recently been done by way of explaining and maintaining it on both the scholarly and popular levels, but more needs to be done at the level of the local congregation via the regular pulpit ministry. In a word, the message of *sola fide* needs to be preached—and preached better.

The Benefits of Preaching sola fide *Better*

Some benefits have already been alluded to in general terms, but there are three that we want to specify in the hope of generating interest in the subject matter of this essay. First, when ordinary folk possess the message of *sola fide* as *their* gospel—the light of their minds and the life of their souls—they will have a firm assurance of their salvation and make progress in holiness and evangelistic zeal. Second, the church's worship will become more fervent and her orthodoxy will be guarded as office bearers pay particular attention to the preservation of this biblical teaching, even initiating disciplinary procedures against any who present a revision of it. Third, a generation of preachers will be raised up who can declare the message well, promoting vigorous outreach into the world. If, as some argue, there is need for another reformation, then this is where one is greatly needed. Interestingly, it is also where the old one started!

The Method of Preaching sola fide *Better*

In light of our title and what has already been said, it will be no surprise that we are going to consider this subject from the standpoint of the preacher. After all, it is he who has the great privilege and

2. Richard F. Lovelace, *Dynamics of Spiritual Life: An Evangelical Theology of Renewal* (Downers Grove, IL: InterVarsity, 1979), 101.

chief responsibility for ensuring that *sola fide* is the lifeblood of the church. In what follows we will address two questions: What does the preacher need to be believe about this doctrine? How can it be preached more effectively to a congregation?

Doctrinal Distinctions

What Is Justification by Faith All About?

Every gospel preacher must be able to answer the question what justification by faith is all about, because there is no hope of preaching the message any better than it is clearly understood. However, raising this specific question goes against the tide, because the prevailing tendency in today's church wants to deal with justification *only* in its relationship to other doctrinal loci and not by focusing on it particularly. One example of this trend is the second phase of the Anglican and Roman Catholic International Commission, whose assignment was to study this very doctrine.[3] Its report was awaited with keen interest because of the known Protestant-Roman divide on the subject, in spite of the attempted narrowing of the gap following Hans Küng's work and Karl Barth's comment on it.[4] When the report appeared, however, its title did not even include the term *justification*, but bore the title *Salvation and the Church*.[5] Ecclesiology is important, but if the truth of justification and the need for it are never allowed to challenge the visible church, then somehow its message has been neutralized or even lost. Sadly, the biblical theme of covenant has also been used to that unhappy effect by spokesmen from the Episcopalian, Reformed, Presbyterian, and Baptist traditions,

3. The Anglican–Roman Catholic International Commission was a theological study group inaugurated following the visit of Archbishop A. M. Ramsey to Rome in 1966. It received fresh impetus after Archbishop F. D. Coggan's visit to Pope Paul VI and their Common Declaration in 1977. Three areas were identified for attention: Eucharist, ministry, and authority, and all three are available in *The Final Report* (London: Catholic Truth Society/SPCK, 1992).

4. Hans Kung, *Justification: The Doctrine of Karl Barth and a Catholic Reflection; Together with a Letter from Karl Barth* (trans. Thomas Collins, Edmund E. Tolk, and David Granskou; New York: Nelson, 1964), ix–xxvi.

5. *ARCIC II: Salvation and the Church* (London: Church House Publishing/Catholic Truth Society, 1987). See also Hywel R. Jones, *Gospel and Church: An Evangelical Evaluation of Ecumenical Documents on Church Unity* (Bridgend: Evangelical Press of Wales, 1989).

as *sola fide* has become conditioned by the view that there is only one kind of covenant in Scripture.[6]

In our ecumenical and revisionist age, theologizing no longer proceeds in terms of the old, well-founded, and well-tested categories, and to draw lines of differentiation between various religious communions is not welcome at all. (If this trend merges with political correctness, orthodoxy is, to use a colloquial British expression, on a hiding to nothing—in other words, no outcome would be favorable and success would be impossible!) Earlier ages, however, were not so squeamish or cagey about *sola fide*. This was because people recognized that it was specifically mentioned in Scripture by way of both question and answer (Job 9:2; John 6:27–29; Acts 16:29–30), and also because they knew something of its importance and worth in their own souls. They were therefore more protective of the truth than about the survival of their churches as institutions or even about their own lives, for that matter. This is, of course, implicit in the well-known phrase that *sola fide* is "the article of the standing or falling church"[7] and also in Calvin's view of it as the "hinge on which religion turns" (*Institutes* 3.11.1).

J. I. Packer made this same point some twenty years before the second Anglican and Roman Catholic International Commission. Borrowing an analogy from the world of classical mythology, he compared *sola fide* to Atlas bearing "a whole world on his shoulders, the entire evangelical knowledge of saving grace." Setting this in opposition to Roman dogma, which he described as "committed by its official creed to pervert the doctrine of justification, [and so sentencing] itself to a distorted understanding of salvation at every point," he proceeded to warn Protestants that they too would lose "the true knowledge of salvation" if they "let the thought of justification drop out of their minds." Memorably he wrote, "When Atlas falls everything else comes crashing down too."[8]

6. There is no lack of names that could be mentioned, as is evident from other essays in this volume.

7. On the history of this phrase, see Alister E. McGrath, *Iustitia dei: A History of the Christian Doctrine of Justification* (Cambridge: Cambridge University Press, 1991–93), 2.193n3.

8. J. I. Packer, "Foreword" to James Buchanan, *Introduction to the Doctrine of Justification* (Edinburgh: Banner of Truth, 1967), 7.

This concern to focus narrowly on *sola fide* did not, however, result in its links with other doctrines going unidentified or unappreciated. Far from it! Over the last five hundred years, scholars have indicated that many primary Christian truths are inseparably connected with the message of *sola fide*. Robert Traill did so in his 1692 *Vindication of the Protestant Doctrine concerning Justification from the Unjust Charge of Antinomianism*: "All the great fundamentals of Christian truth centre in this of justification."[9] As noted at the head of this essay, Berkouwer said much the same, and so did Packer:

> This theme is theological, declaring a work of amazing grace; anthropological, demonstrating that we cannot save ourselves; Christological, resting on incarnation and atonement; pneumatological, rooted in Spirit-wrought faith-union with Jesus; ecclesiological, determining both the definition and the health of the church; eschatological, proclaiming God's truly final verdict on believers here and now; evangelistic, inviting troubled souls into everlasting peace; pastoral, making our identity as forgiven sinners basic to our fellowship; and liturgical, being decisive for interpreting the sacraments and shaping sacramental services. No other biblical doctrine holds together so much that is precious and enlivening.[10]

What Is Special about Justification by Faith?

Given that there are so many connections between *sola fide* and other doctrines (are any doctrines not connected with it, one may wonder?), in what way can it be distinguished from them all? It does this for us by its very terms—almost. It tells us that justification is "by faith." Could it be put any more clearly? Only by the addition of the word *alone*, which brings out what is implicit in its being said that it is "by faith"—period: "Not of works lest anyone should boast" (Eph 2:9).

Justification is therefore distinguishable from all the other blessings of salvation because while they all have some connection with faith, *only* justification can be said to be by faith *alone*. Some of the others like election and foreordination precede and anticipate faith.

9. Robert Traill, *Justification Vindicated* (repr. Edinburgh: Banner of Truth, 2002), 5.
10. J. I. Packer, *Here We Stand* (London: Hodder & Stoughton, 1986), x–xi.

Regeneration is productive of faith. Sanctification proceeds by faith and works, while glorification consummates both, albeit in different ways. Only justification is "by faith"—alone—and that entails reconciliation and adoption.

Another way of highlighting the uniqueness of justification is to say that while all saving blessings are traceable to the grace of God and not to any merit or accomplishment by human beings, only one of them is received by faith alone, but this blessing conveys a title to all the rest! It installs a sinner in God's favor and gives access to God and joy at the prospect of his glory (Rom 5:1–2).

This is the one distinctive point that is absolutely crucial for a preacher to bear in mind, because it enables him to make a genuine offer of a salvation that is not only free but also full to everyone who hears the word that he preaches. Without an appreciation of this, no preacher will ever preach *sola fide* properly, let alone preach it better.

As is well known, several sixteenth- and seventeenth-century confessions state what justification is in the most succinct and lucid of terms, and their agreement is remarkable, given their differing ecclesiastical provenance (Belgic Confession, Heidelberg Catechism, Westminster Standards, Savoy Declaration, and London Confession). They all affirm that justification is a divine verdict, based on Christ's obedience that is imputed to the guilty sinner by faith. While each of these items needs explaining and applying, they can all be presented and defended as the essential lineaments of the doctrine. They are closely connected, especially in terms of the all-embracing reality of union with Christ, but they are not to be conflated. Indeed, distinctions between them must be maintained:

1. The first element is the verdict of God: it is *altogether divine*. Justification is the declaration of God, the judge of mankind. He declares a sinner to be "not guilty" with reference to the law; he forgives all his sins and installs him in his favor. It is his judicial verdict, announced in heaven.
2. The second element is *divine-human*, namely, the life and death of God's incarnate son, Jesus Christ. Being just, God cannot absolve sinners without upholding the demands of

his law and executing its penalty, or else he himself ceases to be just. So he must find (provide) a substitute who acts for the transgressor with respect to both the demands and liabilities of the law that bear upon him. This righteousness is the ground of atonement and the object of faith.

3. The third element is a *fully human* act—faith, that is, trust. In making this assertion, such faith as the gift of God is not being minimized, let alone denied (Eph 2:8). It is true that no one can believe for himself apart from regeneration and effectual calling, which are divine acts, but the point stressed here is that no one can believe for another; neither God nor Christ does so for the sinner. While one can stand proxy for another in a marriage, no one can stand proxy for another in the matter of union with Christ being actualized. Christ's righteousness is imputed to every sinful individual who, knowing he or she is guilty before God and is hopeless and helpless, believes the gospel message.

For justification to take place, therefore, all three things must cohere. A divine intention to justify the ungodly cannot pass into force without a substitute who provides the righteousness the law requires and bears the pending curse. Justification is not a general amnesty issued automatically by God on the first Good Friday when the Savior died and atonement was accomplished. It differs from that in two important respects. First, it is not universal in the sense that it applies to every individual; rather, it applies only to the elect. Second, and this is really material for our study, the divine verdict is only issued *as and when* people believe the gospel. Just as God did not justify sinners when an atonement was made in accord with his plan, so he did not absolve the elect from guilt along with choosing and predestinating them when the plan was drawn up. In heaven he justifies whoever turns to Christ *on earth*, but only and when he does so *in time and space*. It is an irreversible declaration that, though not made in eternity past, is made with regard to eternity future!

The justification of a sinner by God is therefore on the ground of Christ's active and passive obedience that meets the demands and bears the penalties of his law. God could not justify one sinner, not even the least sinful let alone the worst, without the cross; but, equally, he does not justify any sinner without faith—an accomplished atonement notwithstanding. If words mean anything, faith alone is no less a part of being justified than Christ's work is, although the latter (the ground) is much more important than the former (the instrument). What needs to be asserted, however, is that it is as impossible for a sinner to be justified without his believing as it is for him to be justified without Christ's obeying. Although people were justified before Christ lived and died, it was by means of faith that the Messiah would "bruise the serpent's head."

To conclude, therefore, election and predestination take place in eternity past in Christ; justification takes place in time as people trust in Christ. Election and predestination are not in any way conditional on our believing; justification is. The nature of that connection is vital to understand, so that it may not be incorrectly expressed. Faith is not a condition of justification in the sense in which that word is generally understood by the sinner. It is not something that he must do in order that he might be justified. That would make him his own savior. Even saying that faith is a nonmeritorious condition still leaves things unclear because a condition is something that must be done, and believing is that condition, and it is not something that God will do for the sinner, he must do it for himself. *Sola fide* is, of course, part of God's eternal plan for saving the elect, and it results from his gracious love. Nothing is conditional on human merit or effort. Everything is ordered and sure. Believing is the hinge on which the door into God's favor turns both *really and consciously* for the guilty sinner. It alters his relationship to God and also God's dealings with him. It therefore has two sides. No longer is he the object of God's wrath and displeasure and no longer does he react to God with opposition and impenitence. Being justified is as much "a once-for-all" reality as was the death of the mediator. "There is therefore *now no* condemnation" (Rom 8:1 ESV, emphasis added). Repenting of one's sin and believing in Christ continues throughout the Christian's life, but being justified is not a process. What is more, it is never reversed and never needs to be repeated: "Whom he justified them he also glorified" (8:30 ESV).

Homiletical Directions

Given what has been said, we approach the homiletical part of our task in the realization that the message of *sola fide* forms the nexus between God's truth and man's saving reception of it. Such a connection gives to the preaching of *sola fide* an importance that is second to none from the standpoints of the differing responsibilities of both preacher and hearer. The preacher is "to make the message clear and plain," and the hearer is to receive it with understanding. Luther was right: "This is the truth of the gospel. It is also the principal article of all Christian doctrine, wherein the knowledge of all godliness consisteth. Most necessary it is, therefore, that we should know this article well, teach it unto others, and beat it into their heads continually."[11] This essay is based on the conviction that Luther's directive has not been followed as it should have been—for many a long day.[12]

Many books on preaching either give a noticeable lack of prominence to *sola fide* or omit it altogether. This is due to an *over*attentiveness of a twofold kind. First, there is a concentration with the text in its narrow (immediate) context, noting all the features of its literary character but often neglecting its larger (canonical) context—all in the desire to be expository and say what is actually in the text. This kind of sermon can lack a focus on the centrality of Christ; indeed, he may not be actually mentioned, and so *sola fide* cannot be properly preached. Second, there is a preoccupation with determining the placement of the text in the flow of redemptive history and displaying the interconnecting threads it opens up that lead on and up to Christ. In this kind of sermon, the call to trust Jesus Christ alone can be overlooked, as if to preach Christ will inevitably include *sola fide*. Hermeneutics and homiletics are to be consecrated to the service of

11. Martin Luther, *Commentary on the Epistle to the Galatians* (trans. Philip S. Watson; repr. London: Clarke, 1953), 101.

12. Two books about preaching provide some evidence for this claim: Bryan Chapell, *Christ-Centered Preaching* (Grand Rapids: Baker, 1994); and David Larsen, *The Evangelism Mandate: Recovering the Centrality of Gospel Preaching* (Wheaton, IL: Crossway, 1992). In these valuable works there is *no highlighting* of justification as a subject/theme that is to receive special attention, even though the specifics of evangelistic preaching are dealt with. The same is true of Millard Erickson and James L. Heflin, *New Wine in Old Wineskins* (Grand Rapids: Baker, 1997), which addresses the need for the preaching of Christian doctrine but not the doctrine of *sola fide*.

preaching Christ and the necessity of faith in him. The composition of the congregation is therefore to be as much in the preacher's mind as the text that he is to preach. In our view the best way to do this is by using the categories of law and gospel and certainly not a single, undifferentiated view of covenant.[13]

Given the degree of importance that has rightly been accorded to *sola fide* by Protestants, there is therefore a crying need for its importance to be underlined in courses and writings on homiletics, but nothing can compare with its being preached. That is how it survives in the church and how the church thrives. So how can *sola fide* be preached more effectively in all our churches? Three matters will greatly help in this task.

The Biblical Support for Preaching sola fide

The outline of the essentials of justification, offered earlier, is largely derived from Paul's epistle to the Romans. As is well known, the message of *sola fide* is summarized early in that letter in the immortal words: "The righteous shall live by faith" (1:17 ESV), but it is then unpacked in what immediately follows.

The first part of 1:18–5:21 majors on sin and law, guilt and wrath. Human sin invites divine wrath on account of the law's transgression by ungodliness and unrighteousness: "All have sinned, and come short of the glory of God" (3:23 AV), and "the wages of sin is death" (6:23 AV). No one is without some awareness of God and of his requirements and also of liability to his wrath if they are in any way infringed (1:19–21, 32; 2:14–16). This knowledge is now inscribed on the moral DNA of every human being because of what it means to have been created in the image of God and also to have

13. In Norman Shepherd, *The Call of Grace: Covenant Light on Evangelism* (Phillipsburg, NJ: P&R, 2000), there is no mention of justification by faith as an item in the gospel that is to be preached—in spite of the book's subtitle. There are chapters entitled "Covenant and Election" and "Covenant and Regeneration" but not "Covenant and Justification." Is Shepherd implying that given the reality of the covenant there is no need for the message of justification by faith? Shepherd's definition of *sola fide* is virtually unrecognizable by any confessional measure; see "Justification by Faith Alone," *Reformation and Revival* 11 (2002): 75–90. His definition of faith as it functions in justification flatly contradicts WCF 11.1–2's "resting and receiving" and that of WLC 72.

fallen in Adam. These truths about God and man can be summarized as follows:

1. God demands perfect righteousness from his human creatures and subjects. This includes the majestic holiness and righteousness of God and his kingly authority to legislate, uphold, and execute the sanctions of his law.
2. Man is unable to perform what God requires. This includes man's subservience and accountability to God, his inherited and personal unwillingness and inability to keep God's law, his overweening inclination to sin in all its forms, and his consequent guilt and condemnation before God.

These truths about God, law, and sin are absolutely necessary to the message of *sola fide* and therefore to its proclamation. At one and the same time they are the props on which it rests (theo)logically and the chords that it strikes communicatively. Consequently, the message cannot be preached better if it is disconnected from them, and using them *will* have an effect in the hearer, whatever might be said to the contrary.

These truths are not just to be stated in a generalized form or didactic mode. While they are great and vast truths that must be treated in some depth and at some length, they are to be presented in a pointed way and with some passion. The character of God must be discussed and the character of the sinner must be dissected. The statements in confessions and catechisms on God and sin provide categories for doing this, and the Old and New Testaments contain an abundance of all kinds of material about them by way of proposition and illustration (e.g., Ps 51; Rom 3:9–20). A more thorough use of all this sacred information will contribute greatly to a worthier and more effective preaching of *sola fide*.

The Focus of Preaching sola fide

Every sermon worthy of the name must have a point, one main point to which everything else in it must be connected and to which it moves. That is what is meant by the term *focus*. This main theme or grand point is therefore something other than any of its underpinnings. Applied to *sola fide,* this means that neither human sin nor divine law and justice are the grand theme in the preaching of *sola fide*. Their function in the sermon is to strengthen and sharpen the main point. What then is that point? Is it faith? No! It is "Jesus Christ and him crucified" (1 Cor 2:2 ESV). Changing the analogy, we can say that what is said in Scripture about sin, law, and God can be compared to three roads that run up to Calvary and to what happened there—or they "are the schoolmaster to lead to Christ that [people] may be justified by faith" (Gal 3:24):

Sola fide is therefore all of a piece with *solo Christo,* and so a third point needs to be added to the two sets of truths already mentioned:

3. Jesus Christ provides sinners with righteousness before God. Paul focuses on this in Romans 3:21–5:21. By becoming incarnate, the Son of God became the representative and substitute for sinners, in his life keeping the law of God in all its demands and in his death bearing the full punishment that sin merits in the estimate of God. This provision of righteousness *coram deo* is the supreme expression of the grace of God—not just something undeserved but the opposite of what is deserved.

Jesus, the Christ of God, is to be the focus of every Christian sermon because he is the focal point of the entirety of Scripture. Adumbrated in the Old Testament by what is said, positively or negatively, about servants of God, whether prophets, priests, kings or wise men, whatever Jesus Christ says and does, as reported in the Gospels, is part and parcel of his "fulfill[ing] all righteousness" (Matt 3:15 ESV). As the God-man he is the one and only mediator, both before his birth (that is, by way of promise) and throughout his life on earth and now in heaven, but exclusively and fully in and by his death. That is what Paul highlighted by the term *crucified* in 1 Corinthians 2:2 and the place of importance he gave to it there—not merely referring to "Jesus" or even just to "Jesus [the] Christ," but to "him crucified." The expression indicates that the entirety of his messianic ministry hinges on his accursed and atoning death, and that is pointed up by the amount of space allocated to it in the Gospels.

The message of *sola fide* has therefore to major on the obedient life of Jesus offered up to God in a propitiatory death as the only ground, the only rock of a sinner's righteous acceptance with God. On the basis of that life and death that answers all the law's demands, God remains "just" but can also be "the justifier of the one [i.e., everyone, anyone] who has faith in Jesus" (Rom 3:26 ESV).

The Aim of Preaching sola fide

Although the focal point of a sermon about *sola fide* is the righteousness of the Lord Jesus Christ, this should not diminish the importance of faith but the reverse. Jesus associated both, in John's Gospel, by following his claim to be the "I Am" with "whoever believes in me." The importance of *sola fide* is therefore derived from the significance of *solo Christo*. As a camera lens focuses on an object (other than the photographer) and by adjustment brings it into sharpest relief, so faith uses Scripture to concentrate on Christ. It is extraspective and not introspective.

Imagine that someone were to say "I love" but be unable to answer the question, "Who or what do you love?" Their silence would warrant concluding that such a person knew nothing about love, real love at all—or about the English language. So it is with faith. Faith must have an object outside itself, outside the believer, in order to meet the definition of faith in the languages of the Bible.

The apostle Peter wrote, "Unto you therefore which believe he [Jesus Christ] is precious[ness]" (1 Pet 2:7 AV). If faith were possible without Christ, it would be worthless, but he also described faith as "precious" (2 Pet 1:1), because of course it is by means of it—and it alone—that the merit and worth of the only mediator between God and men is personally and individually received.

The aim of the kind of preaching that we are thinking of is therefore to bring sinners to Christ by faith. This involves a renunciation of any supposed righteousness in self and a reliance on the righteousness of Christ. This touches the sinner's conscience, and so Paul described the ministry that he conducted "in the sight of God" as being addressed to "everyone's conscience" (2 Cor 4:2 ESV), whether to Jew or to Gentile.

What is involved in preaching *sola fide* "to the conscience"? Authentic preaching is never a direct assault on the emotions or the will without a prior address to the understanding. It contains teaching but it cannot be identified with it. Without teaching, preaching becomes a harangue, but preaching cannot be equated with the presentation of true statements taught from the perspectives of biblical exegesis, historical theology, and catechetical reflection, which all too often are couched in general terms. Preaching goes one step beyond all that—a vital step. It goes closer to each individual and also deeper. It digs through the walls of sinners' hearts (Ezek 8:8), carrying the truth beyond the mind to the door of the sinner's conscience, knocking repeatedly there until the whole house (heart) is wakened. It is therefore to the conscience—that critical faculty that alarms the mind (understanding) by means of exposing the disposition and censuring the conduct—that the message of *sola fide* is to be *strongly* addressed. Such preaching is not congenial to any sinner whose innate and idolatrous tendency to self-righteousness has not been illumined or undermined—especially the religious.

The Augsburg Confession of 1530 declares: "This whole doctrine [of justification] must be related to *the conflict of an alarmed conscience, and without that conflict it cannot be grasped*. So persons lacking this experience, and profane men, are bad judges of this matter."[14] And in the following century, the Puritan John Owen wrote about preaching *sola fide*: "It is the practical direction of the consciences of men, in their application unto God by Jesus Christ, for deliverance from the curse due unto the apostate state, and peace with him, with the influence of the way thereof unto universal gospel obedience, that is *alone to be designed in the handling of this doctrine*."[15]

So what is involved in "alarming the conscience"? It is an attempt to bring a sinner into the last judgment ahead of time, issuing a summons to him that he is to appear at the bar of God. The pew becomes the dock, and the pulpit becomes the judge's seat. He is read God's

14. Quoted by Packer in *Here We Stand*, 89 (emphasis added).

15. John Owen, *The Works of John Owen* (repr. Edinburgh: Banner of Truth, 1967), 5.4.2 (emphasis added).

rights—his just demands and threats. The charge of being a transgressor is read; evidence is presented of infringements of the law. He is called to face and answer the charge, but warned that to try and conduct his own defense against the Almighty by way of excuse or mitigation, let alone denial, will but increase the heinousness of his transgression. He is declared to be guilty before God, sentenced to an unbearable and unending punishment in hell, and that most justly.

How can a frail preacher do that? Can it be done? Yes it can, but not by human power or eloquence. It can be done only by the discriminating use of the law and dependence on the power of the Holy Spirit who alone can "reprove the world of sin, and of righteousness, and of judgment" (John 16:8 AV). The law has been given specifically for this purpose. By it, a sinner who thinks he is alive before God (Rom 7:9) is enabled to identify sin for what it is, experience its unmanageable power as he seeks to deal with it by himself, and feel death at work within him. This results from the striking description of the "coming" of the commandment to him. This is not the same as being able to quote the commandment or knowing where to find it in Scripture. It is the result of its reverberating in his conscience and his being unable to silence it. It is the Spirit bringing the given, written Word and using it as a sharp, two-edged sword—and being pleased to do so through frail preaching.

All this is to be pursued as the way to conscience being pacified—before God, through Jesus Christ. When people know what it is to be a "wretched man," they will have had enough of themselves and want to hear only of a "blessed man" who kept the law for sinners and yet bore their curse. They are all to be told that there is nothing left for them to do as a condition of obtaining peace with God and heaven and nothing left for them to fear, though they have sinned (and still will, perish the thought). Jesus has done it all and borne it all. Coming to God as they are by way of trusting in Jesus as he is, God will gladly accept them; he will cancel the sentence, imputing Christ's righteousness to their account in the ledgers of heaven and freely pardoning them all their sins against him.

In the light of all this, better preaching of *sola fide* will not focus on Jesus to the exclusion of God, on his love to the neglect of wrath, on forgiveness to the neglect of righteousness, on assent and decision to the exclusion of trust. It will differentiate between sin and sins and between regret and repentance; it will seek to abase man and exalt God and to present the Lord Jesus Christ in all his mediatorial glory. It will do this by a firm and searching use of the moral law of God as expressed in the Ten Commandments and a winsome description of the life and death of Jesus that fulfilled them. It will focus on the divine transaction completed on Calvary between the Son and the Father and not on a human decision, on a canceled law and not on a filled-in card. Justification by faith cannot be preached at all where texts are used without any doctrinal explanation and where the message is grounded on felt needs rather than on the need that needs to be felt. And it will exult in speaking of faith without works of any kind, whether those done before by way of preparation to receive Christ or done after by way of gratitude, as if they were *part of the basis* on which defiled and condemned sinners are accepted by God unreservedly, not put on probation but installed in his favor.

This kind of preaching needs no defense when it is the unbelieving world that is being addressed. To fail to engage in it there for fear of giving offence and merely to focus on psychological frailty and social alienation (real though these felt needs are) is a dereliction of sacred duty, and it is also the greatest unkindness conceivable.

But what about such preaching *in the church*? Can it be done there—and with good conscience before God and men? Yes, it can—and, what is more, it *should* be done and often. Here perhaps is the real reason why *sola fide* has not been given its due prominence and why this subject is in the crosshairs of this essay. Given the existence of a church as the covenant people of God, an appreciative understanding of *sola fide* can almost be taken for granted. Every preacher should beware of thinking like this because God is said to have "evangelized" Abraham with the message (Gal 3:8)—and, judging from the Genesis record, to have done so more than once.

A basic consideration at this point is that a local Christian congregation is "a mixed company." The largest percentage of those attending is made up of professing believers and their children. Is there any way in which these need to hear the message of *sola fide*? Of course there is. The children certainly do if they have not yet professed faith in Christ. Those who have not yet believed are to be *regarded* as "under the law" and "outside of Christ" though they have a promise that God will be gracious to them if they turn to him. They are covenant children by birth and holy (1 Cor 7:14), and baptism incorporates them into the covenant community (visible church)—but not necessarily into Christ. Regeneration does that, and while that is a secret operation of the Holy Spirit, through the preached gospel (Rom 10:14–15), it becomes conscious and evident via a response to the preached message. Covenant children therefore need to hear the message of *sola fide* desperately, and in any precommunicant class a gentle inquiry is to be made into whether its truth is understood and its worth appreciated.

Adults who have not yet professed faith in Christ, whether brought up in Christian or un-Christian homes, are to be addressed in broadly the same terms. For those who "chance in" on a Sunday morning or evening, not to have a sentence or two addressed to them is serious. (In addition, *sola fide* is the message for those whose membership has lapsed or been withdrawn.)

What of church members? Here, the fact that the composition of a local congregation cannot be identified in all respects with the elect is to borne in mind, for it is not impossible that baptized communicants *may not* actually be "in Christ." This must not lead the preacher to be suspicious of the profession of everyone or to impose extra requirements to satisfy his uncertainty. Such a possibility will be more than sufficiently addressed by a regular preaching of *sola fide* in dependence on the Holy Spirit who knows men's hearts. It will also keep the saints in a humble and grateful spirit, and it is the only salve for a conscience troubled by an awareness of sins committed and duties left undone. *Sola fide* is the only answer to Satan when he sows doubt, accuses of guilt, and even generates a sense of condemnation before God. The message of *sola fide* is by itself almost a panacea for all spiritual ills.

There is, however, but one exception to this connection between Christ's worth and human faith that has been noted and acknowledged in the Reformed tradition (see WCF 10.3–4). Those who are incapable of being outwardly called by the ministry of the Word because they either die in infancy or cannot understand the gospel call because of mental incapacity will be admitted to heaven because they are "regenerated and saved by Christ through the Spirit, who worketh when, and where, and how he pleaseth."

Two things, however, need to be remembered at this point. The first, by way of necessary implication, is that such persons were born in sin and were destitute of spiritual life. Another way of salvation is not therefore being taught, but *sola gratia* is being reinforced in that the one group cannot properly be said to act and the other cannot be said to understand. Here, perhaps, lies the rub of the debate over *sola fide* in every age—no capable and knowledgeable adult likes to have to admit being as helpless in spiritual things as those described.

The second is a matter that is explicitly stated. Westminster Confession of Faith 10.4 forbids that this exception should be extended to cover those who do not profess "the Christian religion . . . be they never so diligent to frame their lives according to the light of nature and the law of that religion they do profess." It also adds that "to assert and maintain that they may [be saved in any other way whatsoever] is very pernicious, and to be detested." Ordinarily, no one can be justified before they themselves actually believe—and that is the standing order for both preacher and church.

The preacher must therefore assert the nature and the necessity of faith alone. Doing this in the church means dissociating it from being faithful. As mentioned earlier, Shepherd omits all reference to justification in dealing with covenant evangelism. He also lacks clarity because he never mentions justifying faith without referring to works or obedience. He comes nearest to doing this when he says that God "forgives us our sins and receives us as righteous because of Jesus Christ and his redeeming activity on our behalf," but he continues immediately:

> At the same time, faith, repentance, obedience, and perseverance are indispensable to the enjoyment of these blessings. They are conditions but they are not meritorious conditions. Faith is required but faith looks away from personal merit to the promise of God. Repentance and obedience flow from faith as the fullness of faith. This is faithfulness and faithfulness is perseverance in faith. A liv-

> ing, active, and abiding faith is the way in which the believer enters eternal life.[16]

We think it is worth reflecting on what the consequences of this emphasis on "active faith" or "faithfulness" might be. Will not Christians think that they ought to keep the law in order that God might accept them? Will not the unconverted be left in worse bondage because having been told to believe and obey, they will try to do so? It is, therefore, distinctly possible that those who have been freed from the law will think they are not, and those who are not will think that they are. Not to close down these gospel-denying options is hardly worthy of the name of evangelism—or of covenant.

The nature of faith is also essentially bound up with "accepting, receiving, and resting upon Christ alone for justification, sanctification, and eternal life, by virtue of the covenant of grace" (WCF 14.2). The term *obey* does not occur. What then shall be said about Paul's use of the expression *the obedience of faith* in Romans 1:5 and 16:26. Should "obey" be added in any sense to the three verbs used by the Westminster Divines? No. The apostle is using the term *obedience* to describe faith as submission to what Christ did (by way of his obedience) and not to refer to anything the sinner is to do by way of contribution to Christ's work or even by way of appreciation of it. To understand it in any other way is to create confusion.

Conclusion

This exploration began with quotations from two respected Reformed theologians of the last century. Since their day the situation has not improved but deteriorated—in spite of all that has been claimed as advances in biblical scholarship and theological study. The need to do better is therefore urgent. In the hope of motivating a ringing clarity in the pulpit on this matter and a joyful, humbling certainty in the pew, we conclude with some words from a theologian and seminary teacher of a slightly earlier date.

16. Shepherd, *Call of Grace*, 50.

B. B. Warfield (1851–1921) gathered Princeton students on Sunday afternoons to explore "the deeper currents of Christian faith and life." On one such occasion he spoke to them from Philippians 3:9, entitling his address "The Alien Righteousness."[17] Toward the end of his talk, he referred to J. A. Froude, professor of history at Oxford University, who used the expression *immorality of evangelicalism* in one of his essays and quoted the following excerpt from a hymn:

> Nothing either great or small,
> Nothing, sinner, no;
> Jesus did it, did it all
> Long, long ago.

Warfield then observed:

> What was particularly offensive to him [Froude] was the assertion that:
> Doing is a deadly thing,
> Doing ends in death.

And he responded by saying:

> It is, nevertheless, the very *cor cordis* of the Gospel that is here brought under fire. The one antithesis of all the ages is that between the rival formulae: Do this and live, and Live and do this; Do and be saved, and Be saved and do. And the one thing that determines whether we trust in God for salvation or would fain save ourselves is, how such formulae appeal to us. . . . *Just in proportion as we are striving to supplement or to supplant His perfect work, just in that proportion is our hope of salvation resting on works, and not on faith*. Ethicism and solafideanism—these are the eternal contraries, mutually exclusive. It must be faith or works; it can never be faith and works. And the fundamental exhortation which we must ever be giving our souls is clearly expressed in the words of the hymn, "Cast your deadly doing down." Only when that is completely done is it really Christ Only, Christ All in All, with us. (emphasis added)

17. See B. B. Warfield, *Faith and Life* (1916; repr. Edinburgh: Banner of Truth, 1974), 323–25.

There is such an intimate connection between *sola fide* and the truly Christian church. In Scripture, the former produced the latter, and this was shown in the sixteenth century when the church that had lost the gospel underwent a reformation when this connection was recovered. New wine and old wineskins do not last long together. Strenuous efforts must therefore be made to regain and retain for the church the good news of *sola fide*, the doctrine by which the church does stand or fall and by which people do pass from death to life.

12
Letter and Spirit

Law and Gospel in Reformed Preaching

R. Scott Clark

Introduction

Preaching begins with Bible reading and interpretation. Before a minister can preach a given text, he must decide what it says. To interpret a passage, the preacher necessarily brings to bear his broader reading of Scripture, a system of doctrine, and the history of interpretation. Theology and hermeneutics, therefore, inevitably find their way to the pulpit. Once there, however, the minister is charged with a particular task, that of proclaiming, that is, announcing and applying to the congregation "the whole plan of God" (Acts 20:27).

Since the sixteenth-century Reformation, the Protestant understanding of that "whole plan," whether understood in redemptive-historical (*historia salutis*) or systematic theological (*ordo salutis*) categories, has been that Scripture contains "two words": law and gospel. This essay will endeavor to explain the meaning and application of these categories more fully, but it is enough here to say that as a hermeneutical and homiletical category law in its pedagogical use speaks of the demand for "perfect, personal and perpetual obedience" (see WCF 7.2; WLC 20, 93).[1]

Traditional Protestant thought distinguishes three uses of the law: pedagogical, civil, and normative. The first use drives sinners to Christ, and the third use structures Christian gratitude. The controversy before us concerns the first use, and thus this essay will focus on that use, which in the language of Heidelberg Catechism 2 teaches us "the greatness of [our] sin and misery" (Schaff 3.308).[2] As a hermeneutical category, gospel speaks of the gracious, sovereign redemption of Christ's people (see HC 19–22, 29, 60–65). Confessional Protestantism is united in its conviction that justification *sola gratia, sola fide,* must produce genuine sanctity. That is, there is a logical and moral necessity for Spirit-wrought sanctity in professing Christians. One has only to read Luther's exhortations to piety and holiness (e.g., in his 1529 Larger Catechism) and those found in *Solid Declaration* 4, where good works are said to be necessary for the one who makes a profession of faith.[3] In the words of Belgic Confession 24, "it is impossible that this holy faith can be unfruitful" (Schaff 3.410–12). According to Heidelberg Catechism 2, the third thing one must know in order to "live and die happily" is "how I am to be thankful to God for such redemption" (Schaff 3.308). Thus, focus on the distinction between law and gospel should not be construed as a slighting of the necessity of sanctity. Rather, it is my conviction that genuine sanctity flows from true faith and is produced "by the preaching of the holy Gospel" (HC 65 [Schaff 3.328]; see also Westminster Shorter Catechism 88). Thus it is imperative that one first understands what the gospel is, how it differs from the law, and

1. References to the Westminster Confession of Faith are taken from S. W. Carruthers, *The Westminster Confession of Faith: Being an Account of the Preparation and Printing of Its Seven Leading Editions, to Which Is Appended a Critical Text of the Confession* (Manchester: Aikman, 1937).

2. The Hebrew Scriptures often use the expression תּוֹרַת יְהוָה (e.g., Ps 19:7 [MT 19:8]) generically for the whole of Scripture. Thus, in this essay "law" stands for a specific grammatical mood—the imperative—not for all of canonical Scripture.

3. See Robert Kolb and Timothy Wengert, *The Book of Concord: The Confessions of the Evangelical Lutheran Church* (trans. Charles Arend et al.; Minneapolis: Fortress, 2000), 386–431, 574–81.

how those two words ought to be preached, before one moves to the doctrine of the Christian life.

In contrast to the historic Protestant hermeneutic, in some contemporary discussion, it has become a datum that the law/gospel distinction is Lutheran and not Reformed.[4] This essay argues, however, that the Protestant law/gospel hermeneutic is not only Reformed, but also a basic part of "interpreting correctly" (ὀρθοτομοῦντα) (2 Tim 2:15) and preaching correctly God's word.

History of Law and Gospel

The Reformed theologians followed Luther's fundamental breakthrough in turning away from the patristic and medieval analysis of Scripture as "old law" and "new law," in favor of seeing the two words of law and gospel throughout the word. And this hermeneutic may be applied in the proclamation of the word toward the recovery of a fully orbed Reformed, covenantal homiletic.

The Prevailing Patristic and Medieval Hermeneutic

The fathers in the postapostolic church spoke frequently about the gospel, but there is disagreement over the degree to which one can find a clear, developed expression of what confessional Protestants would recognize as the gospel. Thomas Oden argues that many

4. Among academic writers, Peter A. Lillback, *The Binding of God: Calvin's Role in the Development of Covenant Theology* (Texts and Studies in Reformation and Post-Reformation Thought; Grand Rapids: Baker, 2001), regards Luther's turn to the law/gospel hermeneutic as introducing an "inescapable tension" (71), which problem Calvin's covenant theology was to resolve. In popular literature, see P. Andrew Sandlin, "Lutheranized Calvinism: Gospel or Law, or Gospel and Law," *Reformation and Revival* 11 (2002): 123–35; and John M. Frame, "Law and Gospel," http://www.chalcedon.edu/articles/0201/020104frame.php (accessed January 13, 2005). On the gratuitous identification of this distinction solely with Lutheran theology, see I. John Hesselink, "Law and Gospel or Gospel and Law: Calvin's Understanding of the Relationship," in *Calviniana: Ideas and Influence of Jean Calvin*, vol. 10: *Sixteenth Century Essays and Studies* (ed. Robert V. Schnucker; Kirksville: Sixteenth Century Studies, 1988), 13–50. On the common Protestant heritage of the third use of the law and the "guilt, grace, gratitude" structure, see Paul Althaus, *The Theology of Martin Luther* (trans. Robert C. Shultz; Philadelphia: Fortress, 1966), 272–73n125. On the contemporary denial of the law/gospel distinction, see Michael Horton, "Law, Gospel, and Covenant: Some Emerging Antitheses," *Westminster Theological Journal* 64 (2002): 279–87.

of the fathers anticipated Luther's doctrine of justification.[5] T. F. Torrance, however, argues convincingly exactly the opposite case, that what one tends to find in the fathers is confusion of law and gospel.[6]

This is not an indictment of the fathers. To criticize the fathers for failing to use Luther's (or Calvin's) language is rather like criticizing Aquinas for not using Einstein's physics. The conceptual framework within which most early postapostolic Christians read the Scriptures made it difficult for them to see the forensic nature of justification. They tended to think in realistic rather than forensic categories.[7] Because Christians were frequently marginalized and criticized as immoral and impious, the fathers placed great stress on piety and morality. They did not, however, always ground their parenesis in the gospel in the same way Paul did.[8]

Beginning with the early apostolic fathers, Scripture was characterized universally not as containing law and gospel throughout, but as comprised of old law and new law. The pseudonymous *Epistle of Barnabas* 2.6 (ca. 70–138) spoke of the abolition of the Mosaic order and the establishment of a "the new law of our Lord Jesus Christ" (ὁ καινὸς νόμος τοῦ κυρίου ἡμῶν Ἰησοῦ Χριστοῦ).[9] Justin Martyr's (ca. 100–ca. 165) *Dialogue with Trypho* (ca. 135) defended the superiority

5. Thomas Oden, *The Justification Reader* (Grand Rapids: Eerdmans, 2002), 40–41.

6. T. F. Torrance, *The Doctrine of Grace in the Apostolic Fathers* (Grand Rapids: Eerdmans, 1959).

7. The fathers were confronted by significant social pressures. From the late first century (e.g., 1 Pet 4:12–19; Rev 2:3, 9, 13, 19; 3:9–10) to the sacking of Rome by the Visigoths in 410, Christians faced a general cultural hostility sometimes erupting into serious persecution (e.g., the Decian persecution). This hostility was the background for the Apocalypse of St. John in the early 90s and Augustine's *City of God* in the early fifth century. See W. H. C. Frend, *Martyrdom and Persecution in the Early Church* (New York: New York University Press, 1967); and Colin J. Hemer, *The Letters to the Seven Churches of Asia in Their Local Setting* (Sheffield: JSOT Press, 1986).

8. Compare 1 Clement to 1–2 Corinthians. Clement spent proportionally much more space on exhortation. See Oscar von Gebhardt et al., *Patrum apostolicorum opera: textum ad fidem codicum et graecorum et latinorum adhibitis praestantissimis editionibus* (3rd ed.; Leipzig: Hinrichs, 1876), 3.1.2–110 (*ANF* 1.5–21). The fathers also faced the doctrinal and moral threat of Gnosticism. Gnostic bifurcation of the Hebrew Scriptures (with its demigod) from the Greek, combined with the Jewish moral and theological criticism of Christians as worshipers of a criminal, created an external stimulus for Christians to emphasize the unity of the church and the covenant of grace and to downplay strong distinctions between law and gospel.

9. Gebhardt, *Patrum apostolicorum opera*, 2.8 (*ANF* 1.138). See also Johannes Quasten, *Patrology* (Utrecht: Spectrum/Westminster, MD: Newman, 1962–64), 1.85–92.

of "the new law" over against Moses.[10] Moses's law was provisional, but Christ's was the "final law" (11.10). For Justin, the new covenant is the new law. In his *First Apology* (ca. 148–61) he contrasted Moses and Christ by speaking of the gospel as a "new law." In his refutation of Marcion's radical dichotomy between Moses and Christ (*Against Heresies*), Irenaeus of Lyon (ca. 130–200) spoke the same way. He affirmed the unity of Scripture by using the old law/new law approach (*ANF* 1.475–78).[11] Even when he spoke (*Against Heresies* 4.12.3) of the "law" and the "gospel," the distinction was not one of kind but purely historical.

Among the Latin fathers, Tertullian and Augustine are representative. In his treatise *Against the Jews*, Tertullian (ca. 155–ca. 225) repeated Justin's argument for the continuity of the faith and used the same old law/new law categories.[12] Augustine (354–430) in *City of God* (413–26) used the now-traditional terminology *lex vetus/lex nova*, though, in his anti-Pelagian writings, *Perfection in Human Righteousness* (ca. 415) and *Proceedings of Pelagius* (417), he was able to describe the entire Mosaic epoch as "law" and Christ's teaching as "gospel."[13] His commitment to soteriological realism virtually required him to see justification as the recognition of inherent righteousness and result of sanctification. Because of the Pelagian and semi-Pelagian controversies, however, Augustine came to ascribe that process to sovereign grace rather than to human cooperation with grace.

Occasioned by the Pelagian controversy, Augustine's *The Spirit and the Letter* (412) was devoted to the question of hermeneutics and especially to the relations between Moses and Christ.[14] His hermeneu-

10. See Quasten, *Patrology*, 1.202–4 (*ANF* 1.200, 211). Quasten (1.202) says that Trypho was probably the Rabbi Tarphon mentioned in the Mishnah.

11. Quasten, *Patrology*, 1.287–313, gives a traditional Roman interpretation of Irenaeus's theology.

12. See especially *Against the Jews* 3, 4, 6 (*ANF* 3.153–56, 157). Quasten, *Patrology*, 2.269, warns that *Against the Jews* 9–14 is spurious, but that does not affect this case. On Tertullian's theology, see Gerald Bray, *Holiness and the Will of God* (Atlanta: John Knox, 1979).

13. *City of God* 10.5; 16.43; 20.21, 26; 21.27 (ed. J. P. Migne; Patrologia latina; Paris: Migne, 1844), 41.13–804 (*NPNF*[1] 2). On *City of God*, see Peter Brown, *Augustine of Hippo* (Berkeley: University of California Press, 1967), 299–329. Augustine uses "law and gospel" in *Perfection in Human Righteousness* 22 (*NPNF*[1] 5.167) and *Proceedings of Pelagius* 13 (*NPNF*[1] 5.196). In this last usage, however, he uses the expression as a synonym for old law/new law.

14. Patrologia latina 44.201–46. On this period in Augustine's ministry, see Brown, *Augustine of Hippo*, 340–75.

tical program was structured by 2 Corinthians 3:6: "The letter kills, but the spirit gives life." For Augustine, the "letter" refers to the law, "which plain forbids whatever is evil" (*Spirit and the Letter* 5 [*NPNF*[1] 5.85]). The "spirit" refers to the Holy Spirit whom God infuses into the elect in order to create inherent righteousness toward justification (3, 5 [5.84–85]). Where the Spirit is not present to infuse righteousness, the letter/law kills (5, 14, 16 [5.86, 94, 95]).[15]

Having argued for the continuity of sovereign, infused, predestinating grace, Augustine turned to a sort of redemptive-historical argument, attempting to address the contrast between Moses and Christ in 2 Corinthians 3:6 (*Spirit and the Letter* 17 [*NPNF*[1] 5.95]). Spirit-wrought sanctity turns the letter into Spirit. The law written on stone was "letter," because it lacked the Holy Spirit (17 [5.96]). For Augustine, when Paul says "Spirit" he means "the law of the New Testament" (18 [5.96]). The great blessing of the new covenant, promised in Jeremiah 31, was the profusion of the Spirit, who would work justifying righteousness within his people (18 [5.97]).

Augustine used a variety of terms. He sometimes recognized a kind of distinction between law and gospel, that the law can be bad news, a killing letter, and distinct from the gospel. More often, however, he wrote of Scripture as one word with differing degrees of grace attached in the old and new covenants. Nevertheless, his recognition that the law per se is unable to justify opened a hermeneutical path that Luther, mutatis mutandis, would take with revolutionary consequences.

For the mainstream of Western medieval theology, represented by Thomas Aquinas (ca. 1224–74), there was little question about how one is justified: by progressive moral transformation through the infusion of a medicinal grace.[16] As in the fathers, there was no law/gospel

15. Hence in *Spirit and the Letter* 6 Augustine described baptism as a "medicine." This conception of the sacraments as conveyors of medicinal grace became a given for Bonaventure and Thomas. Thus, Augustine understood the Pauline phrase "justifies the ungodly" (e.g., *Spirit and the Letter* 7 [*NPNF*[1] 5.86]) to mean "sanctifies the ungodly unto justification."

16. Thomas Aquinas, *Summa theologiae* (ed. Thomas Gilby; London: Blackfriars, 1963), I-II QQ. 109–13. See also Bonaventure's *Breviloquium* 6 in Bonaventure, *Tria opuscala: breviloquium, intinerarium mentis in deum & de reductione artium ad theologiam* (Florence: St. Bonaventure College Press, 1911), 203–51. On medieval hermeneutics, see Beryl Smalley, *The Study of the Bible in the Middle Ages* (Notre Dame: University of Notre Dame Press, 1964); and Henry de Lubac and E. M. Macierowski, *Medieval Exegesis: The Four Senses of Scripture* (Grand Rapids: Eerdmans, 2000).

hermeneutic, but rather an old law/new law hermeneutic. Grace was to help us keep the new law. This much is evident in *Summa theologiae* I-II Q. 107.1, where Thomas considered the relations between the old law to the new. He addressed three objections: (1) that the new and old laws are not distinct, (2) that "there is little difference between the Law and the Gospel" (quoting Augustine) since both Moses and Christ require charity, and (3) that both the old and new laws are laws of faith and works.

In his *Sed contra,* Thomas argued from Hebrews 7:12 that Christ brought a new priesthood and therefore a new law. In his response he elaborated by arguing that both Moses and Christ are law. They have the same purpose, that is, human subjection to God, but they differ in degree of "perfection." The "new is the law of perfection," because it brings with it the grace of charity (with which believers are infused unto final justification) (*Summa theologiae* I-II Q. 112.1).

With the fathers, Thomas rejected a categorical distinction between law and gospel. The *lex vetus* consisted chiefly in "moral and sacramental" deeds. The *lex nova* is so-called only because there is relatively more grace given under Christ the legislator to enable the believer to obey. It is true that, for Thomas, the new law consists chiefly of faith in Christ, but he defined it not as knowledge, assent, and trust in Christ and his finished work, but as an infused grace that exists to the degree that one makes it a reality (*Summa theologiae* II-II Q. 4.3).

The Reformation Breakthrough

Rejecting the old law/new law scheme, Martin Luther capitalized on Augustine's insight that 2 Corinthians 3:6 teaches that the law is a killing letter for sinners.[17] Where Augustine understood the gospel to be Spirit-wrought sanctity *in* the sinner, Luther defined it as Christ's accomplishment of redemption *for* the sinner.[18] In contrast to the

17. On Luther's hermeneutic, see James Samuel Preus, *From Shadow to Promise: Old Testament Interpretation from Augustine to the Young Luther* (Cambridge: Harvard University Press, 1969).

18. Martin Luther, *Luthers Werke Kritische Gesamtausgabe* (ed. J. K. F. Knaake, G. Kawerau, et al. Weimar: Böhlau, 1883–), 2.551–52; Martin Luther, *Luther's Works* (ed. J. Pelikan and H. T. Lehmann; Philadelphia: Fortress/St. Louis: Concordia, 1955–), 27.313. See also Heiko A. Oberman, *Luther: Man between God and the Devil* (London: Fontana, 1993), 78.

patristic and medieval doctrine of justification through sanctification, Luther declared a "joyous exchange" wherein "the rich, noble, pious bridegroom Christ takes this poor, despised, wicked little whore in marriage, redeems her of all evil, and adorns her with all his goods."[19]

The hermeneutical foundation for this doctrine was the law/gospel distinction. It appeared quite early in his Protestant development. In 1518, before Luther himself understood fully the implications of his views, he turned to the law/gospel distinction to explain the Ninety-Five Theses. Regarding thesis sixty-two, he explained that the "gospel is a preaching of the incarnate Son of God, given to us without any merit on our part for salvation and peace. It is a word of salvation, a word of grace, a word of comfort, a word of joy, a voice of the bridegroom and the bride, a good word, a word of peace." In contrast to the gospel, the

> law is a word of destruction, a word of wrath, a word of sadness, a word of grief, a voice of the judge and the defendant, a word of restlessness, a word of curse. . . . Through the law we have nothing except an evil conscience, a restless heart, a troubled breast because of our sins, which the law points out but does not take away. And we ourselves cannot take it away.

The good news of the gospel is understood only in the light of the relentless demand of the law for perfect obedience:

> Therefore for those of us who are held captive, who are overwhelmed by sadness and in dire despair, the light of the gospel comes and says, "Fear not," and "comfort, comfort my people. . . ." Behold that one who alone fulfills the law for you, whom God has made to your righteousness, sanctification, wisdom, and redemption, for all those who believe in him. . . . Therefore those who are still afraid of punishments have not yet heard Christ or the voice of the gospel, but only the voice of Moses.[20]

Whereas only a few years before, with the rest of the medieval church, Luther understood all of Scripture to be law, he was now employing

19. *Luthers Werke* 7.1; *Luther's Works* 31.51.
20. *Luther's Works* 31.231.

different hermeneutical categories to organize various passages from both Old and New Testaments into two distinct words.

In a 1532 sermon on Galatians Luther defined the law as "God's Word and command in which he commands us what we are to do and not to do and demands our obedience." The gospel does not demand our obedience for justification, but "bids us simply receive the offered grace of the forgiveness of sins and eternal salvation." So basic is this doctrine that every Christian "should know and be able to state this difference. If this ability is lacking, one cannot tell a Christian from a heathen or a Jew; of such importance is this differentiation."[21]

In a 1532 sermon entitled "The Sum of the Christian Life," from 1 Timothy 1:5–7, Luther reminded his congregation:

> We must now learn to distinguish between the two parts which are called the law and the gospel. . . . The law brings us before the judgment seat, for it demands that you settle accounts and pay what it requires, there it cancels itself. For even if you have performed what it requires, this still will not stand before God, since before him there will still be much which is lacking and failing. . . . The law keeps harrying you and accusing you through your own conscience, which testifies against you, and absolutely demanding the judgment upon you.[22]

In the gospel, however, Christ says to the terrified sinner, "come to me and have no fear of any wrath. Why? Because, if you believe in me, I am sitting here in order that I may step between you and God, so that no wrath or displeasure can touch you."[23]

In his 1535 lectures on Galatians 3:2 Luther argued that Paul was saying that we receive the Spirit through the gospel, not through the law.[24] Faith comes by hearing the gospel, not by doing the law.[25] The law is a demanding taskmaster, the gospel does not demand but grants freely. It commands us to "hold out our hands and receive what is

21. Ewald M. Plass, ed., *What Luther Says* (St. Louis: Concordia, 1959), 2.732.
22. *Luther's Works* 51.279.
23. Ibid., 51.280.
24. Ibid., 26.202–3.
25. Ibid., 26.203–4.

being offered."[26] In *De servo arbitrio* (1525) Luther lambasted Erasmus for confusing law and gospel, by making God's promise of mercy in Ezekiel 18:23 into law, something we must do.[27] Whenever God offers us salvation (in the Old or New Testaments) that is gospel.[28]

The Reformed Use of the Law/Gospel Hermeneutic

As a matter of history, the assertion that the law/gospel distinction is really Lutheran and not Reformed flies in the face of the overwhelming testimony of the Reformed tradition and confessions.[29] Yet Peter A. Lillback juxtaposes Calvin's "covenantal hermeneutic" with the Lutheran law/gospel hermeneutic.[30] He claims that Calvin replaced Luther's law/gospel hermeneutic with a *spirit/letter* hermeneutic.

The evidence against this conclusion is quite strong however. First, in his 1546 commentary on 2 Corinthians 3:6, Calvin said that Paul was making a "comparison of law and gospel."[31] Calvin did not think that the false apostles were "confusing the Law with the Gospel."[32] Rather, this comparison of law with gospel was intended to demonstrate the superiority of the ministry of the new covenant.[33] Commenting on 3:7 he argued that in this passage "letter" means

26. Ibid., 26.208.

27. Ibid., 33.132–38.

28. Paul Althaus, *The Theology of Martin Luther* (trans. Robert C. Schulz; Philadelphia: Fortress, 1966), 87.

29. Andrew Bandstra, "Law and Gospel in Calvin and Paul," in *Exploring the Heritage of John Calvin* (ed. David Holwerda; Grand Rapids: Baker, 1976), 11–39, is generally correct in his interpretation of Calvin, and his exhortation to read widely in Calvin is well taken, but he overstates the tension between Lutheran and Reformed theology on the law/gospel distinction. The Lutheran orthodox view is represented in Heinrich Schmid, *The Doctrinal Theology of the Evangelical Lutheran Church* (trans. Charles A. Hay and Henry E. Jacobs; 4th ed.; Philadelphia: Lutheran Publication Society, 1889), 508–20.

30. Lillback, *Binding of God*, 125. John H. Leith, "Creation and Redemption: Law and Gospel in the Theology of John Calvin," in *Marburg Revisited: A Reexamination of Lutheran and Reformed Traditions* (ed. Paul C. Empie and James I. McCord; Minneapolis: Augsburg, 1966), 141–51, is a good example of a muddled interpretation of Calvin's use of Luther's law/gospel distinction. For a superior account see Michael S. Horton, "Calvin and the Law-Gospel Hermeneutic," *Pro ecclesia* 6 (1997): 27–42.

31. "Nunc comparationem persequitur Legis et Euangelii"; John Calvin, *Commentarii in secundam pauli epistolam ad corinthios* (ed. Helmut Feld; Ioannis Calvini opera omnia, series 2: opera exegetica; Geneva: Droz, 1994), 53.

32. Ibid., 53–54.

33. Ibid., 54.

"law" and Spirit means "gospel."[34] The law is brittle, but the gospel is a "holy and inviolable covenant because it was struck by the Spirit of God as sponsor."[35] Therefore "from the law they bring back nothing but guilt, because there God demands what is owed to himself, but confers no means of fulfilling it. The Gospel, however, is a ministry of righteousness and hence of life, by which men are regenerated and through the gracious forgiveness of sins are reconciled to God."[36] Despite their similarities, the "distinction is great" between them.[37] The law can do nothing but condemn, that is its "office."[38] The gospel, however, is the *instrumentum* of regeneration and "offers gracious reconciliation with God."[39]

Calvin's account of the law/gospel distinction in 2 Corinthians 3 was actually clearer and more pointed than Luther's. It is evident from this passage and others that Calvin adopted the hermeneutical program of distinguishing between law and gospel. This is evident also in *Institutes* 3.11.14 where he attacked the Roman theologians of the Sorbonne (the *sophistae*) because they "have fun and perverse delights" with Scripture, chiefly by failing to observe the law/gospel "antithesis."[40] "Legal righteousness" (*iustitiam legis*) is obtained by law keeping, whereas gospel righteousness, that is, "the righteousness of faith" (*iustitiam fidei*), is obtained "if we believe that Christ was dead and was raised."[41] This was his argument also in 3.11.17: The "distinction" (*discrimen*) between the law and the gospel is that the

34. Ibid., 57.

35. "Euangelium ergo foedus est sanctum et inviolabile, quia percussum Spiritu Dei sponsore"; ibid., 57.

36. "Lege nihil quam reatum eiusmodi reportant, quia illic Deus exigit, quod sibi debetur, facultatem vero praestandi non confert. Euangelium autem, quo regenerantur homines et per gratuitam peccatorum remissionem Deo reconciliantur, ministerium est iustitiae, et proinde etiam vitae"; ibid., 57.

37. "Longum sit discrimen"; ibid., 57.

38. Ibid., 58.

39. "Offert gratuitam cum Deo reconciliationem"; ibid., 57.

40. John Calvin, *Opera selecta* (ed. P. Barth and G. Niesel; Munich: Kaiser, 1962), 4.198.12–13, 23. On Calvin's relations to medieval Scholasticism and the identity of the "Scholastics" and "Sophists," see David C. Steinmetz, "The Scholastic Calvin," in *Protestant Scholasticism: Essays in Reassessment* (ed. Carl R. Trueman and R. S. Clark; Carlisle, UK: Paternoster, 1999), 16–30. See also Richard A. Muller, *The Unaccommodated Calvin* (Oxford Studies in Historical Theology; New York: Oxford University Press, 2000), 46–61.

41. Calvin, *Opera selecta*, 4.198.25–27.

law "attributes justification to works," whereas the gospel "grants it gratuitously, without [our] works."[42]

Theodore Beza (1519–1605), Calvin's successor in Geneva, announced the Reformed hermeneutical and homiletical program in a popular handbook of the faith, *Confession de foi du chrétien* (1559):

> We divide this Word into two principal parts or kinds: the one is called the "Law," the other the "Gospel." For all the rest can be gathered under the one or other of these two headings. . . . We must pay great attention to these things. For, with good reason, we can say that ignorance of this distinction between Law and Gospel is one of the principal sources of the abuses which corrupted and still corrupt Christianity.[43]

It is of particular interest to us here that Beza made these comments in the course of explaining what ministers ought to preach. He defined the law in distinction from the gospel as a "doctrine whose seed is written by nature on our hearts." In these commandments, God "sets out for us the obedience and perfect righteousness which we owe to his majesty and to our neighbours. This on contrasting terms: either perpetual life, if we perfectly keep the Law without omitting a single point, or eternal death, if we do not completely fulfil the contents of each commandment (Deut 30:15–20; James 2:10)."[44] The gospel, in distinction from the law, "is a doctrine which is not at all in us by nature, but which is revealed from Heaven (Matt 16:17; John 1:13). . . . By it God testifies to us that it is His purpose to save us freely by His only Son (Rom 3:20–22), provided that, by faith, we embrace him as our only wisdom, righteousness, sanctification and redemption (1 Cor 1:30)."[45]

Zacharias Ursinus (1534–83) was primary author and the authorized expositor of the Heidelberg Catechism. In his *Loci theologici*, he argued that the best way to make sense of Scripture is to remember

42. Ibid., 4.201.2–4. He repeated this same point in *Institutes* 3.11.18.
43. Beza, *Christian Faith*, 40–41.
44. Ibid., 40.
45. Ibid., 40–41.

that the "whole of Scripture consists in two parts, Law and Gospel."[46] The first line of his lectures on the catechism declared that "the whole and uncorrupted doctrine of the church is the doctrine of the law and gospel." These are the "two parts of the church's doctrine" in which "the whole of Sacred Scripture is contained."[47] The distinction between law and gospel was no mere *theologoumenon* or abstraction, however, because he explained it in redemptive-historical or covenantal terms. In his *Summa theologiae* (1561), written as a teaching tool and as part of the development of the document that would become the foundation for the Heidelberg Catechism, Ursinus asked, "What distinguishes law and gospel?" The answer:

> The law contains a covenant of nature begun by God with men in creation, that is, it is a natural sign to men, and it requires of us perfect obedience toward God. It promises eternal life to those keeping it, and threatens eternal punishment to those not keeping it. In fact, the gospel contains a covenant of grace, that is, one known not at all under nature. This covenant declares to us fulfillment of its righteousness in Christ, which the law requires, and our restoration through Christ's Spirit. To those who believe in him, it freely promises eternal life for Christ's sake.[48]

It is most significant that Ursinus chose to explain the distinction between law and gospel in terms of the covenants of works and grace. For Ursinus, the covenant of works functions on a different principle than the covenant of grace.[49] It was constituted in

46. Zacharias Ursinus, *Opera theologica* (ed. Quirinus Reuter; Heidelberg, 1612), 1.426: "Quid Sacra Scriptura doceat? . . . totam scripturam duabus constare, Lege et Evangelio."

47. Ibid.: "Doctrina ecclesiae est integra et incorrupta doctrina legis et evangelii"; "partes doctrinae ecclesiae sunt duae, *Lex et Evangelium*, quibus summa totius scripturae sacrae continentur."

48. Ibid., 1.14: "Quod est discrimen legis et evangelli? Lex continet foedus naturale, in creatione a Deo cum hominibus initium, hoc est, natura hominibus nota est; & requirit a nobis perfectam obedientiam erga Deum, praestantibus eam promittit vitam aeternam, non prestantibus minatur aeternas poenas. Evangelium vero continet foedus gratiae, hoc est, minime natura notum existens: ostendit nobis eius iustitiae, quam Lex requirit, impletionem in Christo, & restitutionem in nobis per Christi Spiritum; & promittit vitam aeternam gratis propter Christum, his qui in eum credunt."

49. R. Scott Clark and Joel Beeke, "Ursinus, Oxford, and the Westminster Divines," in *The Westminster Confession into the 21st Century: Essays in Remembrance of the 350th Anniversary of*

nature (hence he described it as a *foedus naturale*). Therefore it is universally known and revealed naturally (Rom 1:18–2:14). It contains promises, but the conditions are legal. In contrast, the gospel (*evangelium*) contains a *foedus gratiae*. It is revealed only in special revelation (not nature). Its promises are not conditioned on *our* doing, but grounded in Christ's law keeping and promised freely to those "who believe in him." Ursinus's construal of the law/gospel distinction would seem to make impossible any disjunction between covenant theology and the law/gospel hermeneutic. In other words, if we follow Ursinus, to preach covenantally is to preach the law (relative to justification) and the gospel as two distinct principles.[50]

Girolamo Zanchi (1516–90), a contemporary of Ursinus and Olevianus, placed relatively strong emphasis in his theology on union with Christ and the logical necessity of sanctity flowing from our union with Christ.[51] Nevertheless, he was unambiguous in his affirmation of the necessity of distinguishing law and gospel. The substance of the law is "only commandments, to which are added irrevocable curses if they are violated in the least."[52] The condition of eternal blessedness under the law is "most perfect obedience" (*perfectissimae obedientiae*). The gospel, however, is "properly a blessed announcement" that "Christ

---

the Publication of the Westminster Confession of Faith (ed. Ligon Duncan; Ross-Shire, Scotland: Mentor, 2004), 2.1–32.

50. Caspar Olevianus (1536–87), Ursinus's colleague and one of the more significant Reformed theologians of the period and a principal author of the Heidelberg Catechism, taught the same hermeneutic: "For this reason the distinction between law and gospel is retained. The law does not promise freely, but under the condition that you keep it completely. And if someone should transgress it once, the law or legal covenant does not have the promise of the remission of sins. On the other hand, the gospel promises freely the remission of sins and life, not if we keep the law, but for the sake of the Son of God, through faith"; Caspar Olevianus, *In epistolam ad romanos notae* (ed. Theodore Beza; Geneva, 1579), 148: "Causa. Ut retineatur legis & Evangelii. Lex non promittit gratis, sed sub conditione, si omnia feceris. Et si quis eam semel sit transgressus, non habet lex seu foedus legale promissionem remissionis peccatorum: evangelium vero gratis promittit remissione peccatorum, & vitam si non praestiterimus legem, propter Filium Dei, per fidem." See also R. Scott Clark, *Caspar Olevian and the Substance of the Covenant: The Double Benefit of Christ* (Rutherford Studies in Historical Theology; Edinburgh: Rutherford House, 2005), 79, 83, 106, 120, 139, 149–53, 159–62, 166, 179.

51. See John L. Farthing, "*De coniugio spirituali*: Jerome Zanchi on Ephesians 5:22–33," *Sixteenth Century Journal* 24 (1993): 621–52.

52. H. Zanchi, *De religione christiana* (London, 1605), 143: "Quia legis materia, tantum sunt mandata, additis irrevocabilibus maledictionibus, si vel minima in parte ea volentur."

our Redeemer, freely forgiving sins and saving us," required nothing of us but "true faith in Christ."[53]

Johannes Wollebius (1586–1629) of Basel is witness to Reformed theology in the period surrounding the Synod of Dort (1618–19). He correlated the antelapsarian *foedus operum* (covenant of works) to the "law" and the postlapsarian *foedus gratiae* (covenant of grace) to the gospel.[54] Law and gospel have much in common—"the Redeemer is known through the law and through the gospel"—but they have different functions. Wollebius even said that they are "opposed" (*opposita*) in justification.[55] From "the law we learn the need for a redeemer, and from the gospel we learn the truth of redemption."[56] Though they have much in common, they differ in that the law is known naturally, but the gospel is known only by God's gracious revelation. The law "primarily teaches what is to be done," but the gospel teaches "what is to be believed." The law drives us to seek Christ, but the gospel reveals him. The law demands "perfect righteousness," the gospel shows it in Christ."[57]

Francis Turretin (1623–87) also articulated this hermeneutic in the high orthodox period. Inasmuch as the law stands for the covenant of works and the gospel stands for the covenant of grace, there is an "opposition" between them (*Institutes* 2.236–37 §12.8.15). The law demands "entire and perfect obedience to the law (Rom 10:5)." The law commands, but does not give righteousness. The law says, "Do this and live." The gospel, however, grants righteousness to those who believe (2.186 §12.3.6). Turretin also correlated law to the covenant of works and gospel to the covenant of grace (2.236–37 §12.8.15).

53. Ibid., 143–44: "At vero Evangelium proprie felix est nuntium, Christum nostrum Redemptorem, peccata gratis remittentem, et servantem, gratis etiam proponens: nihilque a nobis exigens ad salutem consequendam, nisi veram in Christo fidem."

54. Johannes Wollebius, *Compendium christianae theologiae* (ed. E. Bizer; Munich: Moers, 1935), 1.7; idem, *Compendium of Christian Theology* in *Reformed Dogmatics* (ed. and trans. John W. Beardslee III; New York: Oxford University Press, 1965), 64.

55. Wollebius, *Compendium christianae theologiae*, 1.15.7. Johannes Polyander, Andreas Rivet, Antonius Walaeus, and Antonius Thysius, *Synopsis purioris theologiae* (ed. H. Bavinck; 1625; repr. Leiden: Didericum Donner, 1881), shows the same distinctions in disputation 18: "De lege dei (Polyander)," and disputation 22: "De evangelio."

56. Wollebius, *Compendium of Christian Theology*, 75; idem, *Compendium christianae theologiae*, 1.13.

57. Wollebius, *Compendium of Christian Theology*, 85; idem, *Compendium christianae theologiae*, 1.15.

The use of the law/gospel distinction was not a Continental Reformed peculiarity. It is found, for example, in William Perkins (1558–1602), one of the two most outstanding figures of English Puritanism.[58] One of his most well-known works is *The Art of Prophesying* (1592), which remains a valuable resource for ministers who would "preach the word . . . in season and out of season" (2 Tim 4:2 ESV):

> The basic principle in application is to know whether the passage is a statement of the law or of the gospel. For when the Word is preached, the law and the gospel operate differently. The law exposes the disease of sin, and as a side-effect, stimulates and stirs it up. But it provides no remedy for it. However the gospel not only teaches us what is to be done, it also has the power of the Holy Spirit joined to it. . . . A statement of the law indicates the need for a perfect inherent righteousness, of eternal life given through the works of the law, of the sins which are contrary to the law and of the curse that is due them. . . . By contrast, a statement of the gospel speaks of Christ and his benefits, and of faith being fruitful in good works.[59]

The lesson Perkins was trying to teach preachers in the late sixteenth century remains salient. He recognized a clear distinction between the imperative and indicative moods. He took it as a given that there are two distinct but closely related words within the one word of God. He recognized that these two words perform different functions. The law reveals sin and, following Paul (Rom 7:7), stimulates sin. Perkins recognized a distinction in the relative powers of law and gospel to effect salvation. The law "provides no remedy" for sin. The law says "do" and demands perfect, inherent righteousness. By contrast, the gospel "speaks of Christ and his benefits." According to Perkins, the sanctity so evidently desired by those set

58. Perkins's student, William Ames, who exercised massive influence on Continental Reformed theology through his students Gijsbertus Voetius and others, followed his teacher on this point. See William Ames, *The Marrow of Theology* (trans. John D. Eusden; Durham, NC: Labyrinth, 1983), 1.10.6, 1.16.11.

59. William Perkins, *The Art of Prophesying* (repr. Edinburgh: Banner of Truth, 1996), 54–55. See also idem, *The Works of That Famous and Worthy Minister of Christ* (London, 1616), 3.273, 495, which employed the same distinction and definitions in Perkins's exposition of Rev 2:5 and Jude. I am grateful to Brannan Ellis for pointing me to these two places in Perkins's *Works*.

to revise Reformed hermeneutics and homiletics comes through only the gospel. A Christian preacher must know the difference between the two.

William Twisse (1578–1646), the first prolocutor of the Westminster Assembly, opened his 1632 catechism by arguing that the word of God teaches us to come to the kingdom of God in two ways: "Law and Gospel."[60] As for all confessional Protestants, Twisse understood the pedagogical word of the law to be "do this and live." The gospel says, "Believe in the Lord Jesus Christ and you shall be saved."[61] It is not possible for sinners to come to the kingdom "by way of God's law" because the law requires perfect obedience, which no sinner can perform.[62] Therefore, the good news must be preached to sinners. For Twisse, the distinction between law and gospel was basic to Christian faith and piety: "This is the first lesson, to know the right way to the Kingdom of Heaven: and this consists in knowing the difference between the Law and the Gospel."[63]

Britain's greatest seventeenth-century theologian, John Owen (1616–83), used the same hermeneutic. In his Greater Catechism (1645), he argued that, relative to justification, the law is the word of God that teaches us our need of a Savior and the gospel that offers us our salvation.[64] This distinction was even more evident in his *Doctrine of Justification by Faith* (1677). In his preliminary remarks, he reminded the reader that the doctrine of justification was the central concern of the Reformation. He quoted J. H. Alsted (1588–1638), who called the Protestant doctrine of justification "the article by which the church stands or falls." He also quoted and agreed with Luther, who said, "If I lose the doctrine of justification, the whole Christian doctrine has been lost."[65] He recognized that there was a movement during his life to downplay the significance of the doctrine of justification among some Reformed writers.

60. William Twisse, *A Brief Catechetical Exposition of Christian Doctrine* (London, 1632), 3.
61. Ibid.
62. Ibid., 4.
63. Ibid., 5.
64. John Owen, *The Works of John Owen* (ed. W. H. Goold; New York: Carter, 1851–53), 1.476, 485–87.
65. Ibid., 5.67: "Amisso articulo justificationis, simula amissa est tota doctrina Christiana."

Among the issues that Owen addressed was the "order, relation, and use of the law and the gospel." The law is "presented unto the soul with its *terms* of righteousness and life, and with its *curse* in case of failure. Without this the gospel cannot be rightly understood nor the grace of it duly valued." The gospel, in contrast, is the "revelation of God's way of relieving souls of men from the sentence and curse of the law, Rom i.17."[66] In justification, the function of the law is to convict sinners. The gospel, not the law, is the "principal" of faith.[67] Owen was zealous to maintain "the order and use of the law and the gospel, with their mutual relation unto one another."[68]

In view of these examples, on this question (as on most others of its kind) any distinction between British and Continental Reformed theology must be drawn very carefully indeed. The Reformed consensus in the classical period was quite firm on this basic hermeneutical issue.[69]

In nineteenth-century Reformed theology, the distinction was largely assumed by Old School confessionalists and received renewed attention in the early twentieth century among orthodox Reformed such as J. Gresham Machen, Louis Berkhof, and John Murray.[70]

Because the first question before us is whether it is Reformed to distinguish law and gospel and how those two moods ought to be recognized and preached, this essay focuses on their differences. The Reformed have always recognized that, however antithetical law and gospel are to sinners, they are not antithetical to God.[71] It is the basic biblical confession that God is "one" (Deut 6:4). The distinctions we make between God's attributes (e.g., mercy and justice) are for our sakes. We understand that they do not exist in God. There are not

66. Ibid., 5.75.

67. Ibid., 5.76.

68. Ibid., 5.82.

69. It is remarkable that Ernest F. Kevan's widely read *The Grace of Law: A Study of Puritan Theology* (1965; repr. Grand Rapids: Baker, 1976), makes no mention of the distinction between law and gospel. His less well-known volume, *Moral Law* (1963; repr. Phillipsburg, NJ: P&R, 1991), 66–70, does admit the traditional Protestant distinctions affirmed in this essay but manifests some confusion over the history of Reformed covenant theology.

70. Louis Berkhof, *Systematic Theology* (Grand Rapids: Eerdmans, 1941), 612–15; John Murray, *Principles of Conduct* (1957; repr. Grand Rapids: Eerdmans, 1984), 181.

71. Wollebius, *Compendium christianae theologiae*, 1.15.1, 8.

two competing principles in God. So too, the Reformed have recognized that law and gospel have several things in common:[72]

1. Law and gospel do not denote absolutely separate parts of Scripture. Moses and Jesus both preached law and gospel.[73] This is why Reformed theologians consistently quoted Jesus's response to the lawyer in Luke 10:28—"do this and live"—as the prototypical example of law. One could just as easily cite the prologue to the Decalogue (Exod 20:2) as the prototypical example of the gospel word: "I am Yahweh your God, who brought you out of the land of Egypt, out of the house of slavery." The question is not so much *where* these words occur in the canon, but the *mood* (imperative or indicative) with which they speak and the *conditions* attached to their promises.
2. As Wollebius noted, both the law and the gospel urge obedience using promises and curses. They differ in their "proper material" (*propria material*). That is, the stuff of gospel is not the stuff of law. The law is about our "doing" (*facienda*), and the gospel is about our "believing" (*credenda*).[74]
3. It is not that the law is strict and the gospel is lax. Rather, both law and gospel require "perfect obedience."[75] The law demands it of us, and the gospel announces that Christ has accomplished it.
4. Both words are directed at sinners, but, again, with different consequences and conditions or instruments.[76]
5. Both moods glorify God, and both seek to foster Christian virtue in believers. The law, however, is powerless to justify or sanctify; only the gospel achieves those ends.[77] For the unregenerate, law and gospel are antithetical. To believers, however, for whom Christ has satisfied the righteous require-

72. See, e.g., Beza, *Christian Faith*, 41–43; Wollebius, *Compendium christianae theologiae*, 1.15.7; Turretin, *Institutes* 2.233–40 §12.8.

73. Wollebius, *Compendium christianae theologiae*, 1.21.16.

74. Ibid., 1.15.2.

75. Ibid., 1.15.3.

76. Ibid., 1.15.5.

77. Ibid., 1.15.4, 6.

ments of the law, the law is "subordinate" to the gospel.[78] In other words, the gospel is the power of life and sanctity, and the law serves to structure Christian sanctity.

The Twentieth-Century Rejection of Law and Gospel

If the law/gospel *discrimen* was so foundational to Reformed hermeneutics and homiletics in the formative period of our tradition, how has it come into disuse?[79] I venture to offer some general hypotheses. One of the linchpins of the orthodox view was human depravity. According to Reformed orthodoxy, antelapsarian man was able to "do and live." It is postlapsarian man who is unable and unwilling and who needs the gospel. The reigning anthropology of modernity, however, has not featured human depravity. Instead, the Enlightenment taught human progress and perfectibility.

In that same period some of the systematic-theological, confessional, and theological sandbags that provided some protection from the rising modernist tide were called into question even by the orthodox. For example, Reformed orthodoxy correlated the covenant of works with law and the covenant of grace with gospel. With the dismissal of the covenant of works as a category, its corollary—the distinction between law and gospel—was therefore eclipsed.

From the period beginning with end of the nineteenth century until the middle 1980s, the chief issue before us had to do with the knowledge of God and the reliability of Scripture. Due to the distraction created by higher criticism, some traditional categories fell into neglect. Another part of the explanation for the eclipse of law and gospel as hermeneutical and homiletical categories has to do with the shape of Reformed theology in the mainline European and American

78. Ibid., 1.15.8.

79. The loss of this hermeneutical category has impaired some accounts of Reformed hermeneutics. D. L. Puckett, "John Calvin," in *Historical Handbook of Major Biblical Interpreters* (ed. Donald K. McKim; Downers Grove: InterVarsity, 1998), 171–79, asks how Calvin related the Old and New Testaments but ignores this question. A similar approach is also evident in Wayne G. Strickland, ed., *The Law, the Gospel, and the Modern Christian: Five Views* (Grand Rapids: Zondervan, 1993), in which the two of the writers professing to represent the Reformed understanding of law and gospel address them only as *redemptive-historical* categories rather than *hermeneutical* categories. They address the relations between the old and new covenants, not between law and gospel per se, but neither writer seems aware of the distinction.

churches and academies in the twentieth century. In reaction to the nationalism of German liberals, Karl Barth rejected the Reformation and confessional distinction between law and gospel.[80] They are not, he said, two distinct words. As one Lutheran critic wrote, Barth "inverted" the traditional order.[81] There are not, considered hermeneutically, two words in Scripture—"do" and "done for you"—but only one word: grace, which takes different historical forms (Moses and Christ). Of course, for Barth, "grace" means the universal electing favor of God.

This inversion of law and gospel to grace and obligation has found formal acceptance as one of the positions of the mainline Presbyterian Church (USA) and also among conservative evangelicals such as Daniel Fuller and among Reformed theologians such as Klaas Schilder and Norman Shepherd.[82] They neither collapse history into the decree like Barth nor share Barth's doctrine of Scripture. Nevertheless, they do follow his move to obliterate the distinction between the covenants of works and grace and the distinction between law and gospel. Consequently, they establish a grace-and-obligation scheme in which to construct their doctrines of justification. This is the structural impetus for revising the doctrine of justification by rejecting the imputation of Christ's active obedience and to revise the definition of faith as it functions in justification. Having received initial grace, now the emphasis falls on the obligation to cooperate with grace. This move is fundamental to covenantal nomism and is common to the Reformed

80. Originally published in 1935 as *Evangelium und Gesetz*; for English translation see Karl Barth, *Community, State, and Church: Three Essays* (Gloucester, MA: Peter Smith, 1968). Hesselink ("Law and Gospel," 32) concludes that Calvin's use of law and gospel is much closer to Luther's than to Barth's.

81. Thomas Coates, "The Barthian Inversion: Gospel and Law," *Concordia Theological Monthly* 26 (1955): 481–91.

82. This is the basic structure of the Confession of 1967; See *The Book of Confessions* (Louisville: Presbyterian Church USA, 1999), 253–62. See also "Confessional Nature of the Church Report," in *Book of Confessions*, xvii–xviii; W. Robert Godfrey, "Westminster, Justification, and the Reformed Confessions," in *The Pattern of Sound Words: Systematic Theology at the Westminster Seminaries: Essays in Honor of Robert B. Strimple* (ed. David VanDrunen; Phillipsburg, NJ: P&R, 2004), 132–33; idem, "Back to Basics: A Response to the Robertson-Fuller Dialogue," *Presbyterion* 9 (1983): 80–84; O. Palmer Robertson, "Gospel and Law: Contrast or Continuum? A Review Article," *Presbyterion* 9 (1983): 84–91. On Schilder's covenant theology, see A. C. DeJong, *The Well-Meant Offer: The Views of H. Hoeksema and K. Schilder* (Franeker: Weaver, 1954); and A. Strauss, "Schilder on the Covenant," in *Always Obedient: Essays on the Teachings of Klaas Schilder* (ed. J. Geertsma; Phillipsburg, NJ: P&R, 1995), 19–34.

revisers of the doctrine of justification. Any such grace-and-obligation scheme is flatly contrary to the Reformed confessions.

Preaching Law and Gospel

The purpose of this essay is to encourage ministers not only to *read* Scripture correctly, but also to *preach* it correctly. It is not faithful to either the Scriptures or the Reformed faith to adopt a naïve, biblicist approach to the proclamation of the word. Yes, the minister must preach the word, but, according to Scripture as understood by our confessions and theologians, the word has two moods—law and gospel. At any moment, the minister is preaching either law or gospel. Its is not possible to "preach the word" indiscriminately. The faithful minister will be conscious of that fact and adjust his preaching accordingly.[83]

In the Reformed Symbols

It should not seem odd to turn to the Reformed symbols under the heading of "preaching." They are public, ecclesiastically sanctioned expositions of the faith that themselves have preaching very much in view. Heidelberg Catechism 65 says that "the Holy Ghost works [faith] in our hearts by the *preaching* of the holy Gospel" (Schaff 3.328, emphasis added). As will become apparent, when the Heidelberg Catechism says "gospel" it does not mean Scripture generically, but a distinct word and mood. In approaching the work of preaching this way, I hope that other ministers will take the symbols as a guide for their hermeneutics and their homiletics. One of the primary functions of the Reformed confessions and catechisms was to help us preach God's word more faithfully. It is the way the confessions and catechism read the Scriptures and teach us to read and preach the word. The Heidelberg Catechism was quite explicit about the different functions of law and gospel both in the *historia salutis* and in the *ordo salutis*.

83. I am indebted on this point to a 1999 lecture by my colleague Michael Horton, "Preaching Law and Gospel," given under the auspices of the Westminster Institute for Christian Leadership conference entitled "The Glory of Preaching."

Ursinus, the primary author of the Heidelberg Catechism said that the catechism was structured according to the law/gospel distinction.[84] In his lecture on Heidelberg Catechism 92, he turned to covenant theology to explain the distinction made by the catechism. Law and gospel *seem* to agree in that both promise eternal life "freely," since no "obedience can be meritorious in the sight of God." Nevertheless, there is a "great difference between the law and the gospel." They differ as to mode of revelation: the law is natural revelation, and the gospel "was divinely revealed after the fall of man." They differ in doctrine: the law teaches what we "ought to be in order that we may be saved," but the gospel teaches how "we may become such as this law requires, viz: by faith in Christ." The differ in their "conditions or promises": the promises of the law are conditioned on "our own and perfect righteousness, and of obedience in us," whereas gospel promises are conditioned upon "faith in Christ, by which we embrace the obedience which another, even Christ, has performed in our behalf."[85]

According to Ursinus, then, when the Heidelberg Catechism says "law," it means, in the first instance, that word from God that says "love God and love neighbor" (4) and pronounces the curse of death on any who disobeys (10 [Schaff 3.308, 310]). God made Adam (and us in him) able to fulfill the law (6, 9) but sin resulted in depravity and inability so that now, in its first use, the law teaches me only "the greatness of my sin and misery" (2–3 [Schaff 3.308]). Divine justice requires that our good works be completely "conformable to the divine law" (62), a standard that no sinner ever meets (Schaff 3.327).

The Heidelberg Catechism also uses the word *law* in a second, redemptive-historical sense to describe "Moses and the prophets" (19). Here law is contrasted with gospel to describe the types and shadows of the "sacrifices and other ceremonies of the law" that were fulfilled in "his well-beloved Son" (Schaff 3.313).[86]

The Heidelberg Catechism uses the word *law* in a third sense (*tertius usus legis*) to describe God's moral standard for those who have been redeemed (91 [Schaff 3.339–40]). In this instance, obedience

84. Zacharias Ursinus, *Commentary on the Heidelberg Catechism* (trans. George W. Williard; Phillipsburg, NJ: Presbyterian & Reformed, 1985), 13, 14, 20.

85. Ibid., 492.

86. Belgic Confession 25 uses the law/gospel distinction in this sense explicitly.

to the law is not *for* justification, but follows logically and necessarily *from* justification. The fact of human depravity does not ease God's moral requirements. We are "with earnest purpose" to "begin to live not only according to some, but according to all the commandments of God" (114 [Schaff 3.349]).

The law does not change, but one's status relative to the law changes. For those not "under law" but "under grace" (Rom 6:14–15), God continues to "enjoin" the law upon us for two reasons:

> First, that all our life long we may learn more and more to know our sinful nature, and so the more earnestly seek forgiveness of sins and righteousness in Christ; secondly, that we may continually strive and beg from God the grace of the Holy Ghost, so as to become more and more changed into the image of God, till we attain finally the full perfection after this life. (HC 115 [Schaff 3.349])

Therefore, the Heidelberg Catechism has come full circle relative to the law. Having begun with the *usus elencticus* in Heidelberg Catechism 2–3, the catechism returns to it in the third part of the catechism. The law is not good advice for successful living. Human sinfulness is such that even believers, having been justified *sola gratia, sola fide*, need to hear the thunder of the law, need to be driven again to Christ. Only in the law do we see our need for Christ's imputed righteousness and the consequent need for thankful sanctity.

When the Heidelberg Catechism uses the word *gospel* (*evangelium*), it means "how I am redeemed from all my sins and misery" (2) accomplished by a "true and sinless man" (16) who is also "true God" (17) and the mediator of salvation to all who believe (18 [Schaff 3.309, 312]). This gospel was first revealed "in Paradise" (19), after the fall, and proclaimed by the "holy Patriarchs and Prophets" and foreshadowed in the ceremonial types (Schaff 3.313). In the catechism, gospel does not mean, as it meant before the Reformation, "the law before the new law," but rather that word from God announcing our redemption in Christ either prospective or retrospectively.

Heidelberg Catechism 21 gives its definition of the gospel: "That not only to others, but to me also, forgiveness of sins, everlasting righteousness and salvation, are freely given by God, merely of grace, only for the sake of Christ's merits" (Schaff 3.313). Heidelberg Catechism 60 elaborates by adding that God "of mere grace, grants and imputes to me the perfect satisfaction, righteousness, and holiness of Christ, as if I had never committed nor had any sin, and had myself accomplished all the obedience which Christ has fulfilled for me, if only I accept such benefit with a believing heart" (Schaff 3.326–27). The gospel is that message through which the Holy Spirit works "true faith" (21, 65 [Schaff 3.313, 328]).

The gospel is, as Luther reminded Melanchthon, *extra nos* (outside of us), the message concerning Christ's "alien righteousness," that is, what he accomplished *pro nobis* (for us), not, as the medieval church had it, about what is being accomplished "in us." Heidelberg Catechism 66 repeats a similar summary. The gospel is that which, "of free grace," God "grants us . . . the forgiveness of sins and everlasting life, for the sake of the one sacrifice of Christ accomplished on the cross" (Schaff 3.328). The gospel is to be proclaimed by the church on the Sabbath (103) as the key that opens the kingdom to believers (83–84 [Schaff 3.345, 337]). The catechism says it consists of promises (22, 66) that are summarized in the Apostles' Creed and is confirmed by the use of the sacraments (65 [Schaff 3.314, 328]).

It is essential to this discussion to understand that the Heidelberg Catechism defines the gospel *solely* in terms of God's gracious provision of Christ's active and passive obedience, which satisfies the justice for God for all who believe. There is not the slightest shadow over any part of the catechism suggesting that that Christian obedience is either the ground or instrument of justification. Indeed, the catechism (67) says, "The Holy Ghost teaches in the Gospel, and by the holy Sacraments assures us, that our whole salvation stands in the one sacrifice of Christ made for us on the cross" (Schaff 3.328–29). The message of the gospel to believers is that "all their sins are really forgiven them of God for the sake of Christ's merits" (84 [Schaff 3.337]).

The law/gospel hermeneutic of the Heidelberg Catechism could hardly be clearer. One learns the greatness of sin and misery not from the gospel, but from the law. One learns of grace, not in law, but in the gospel (21, 56, 60–61 [Schaff 3.313, 325–27]). Even though the moral law structures Christian obedience, it is the gospel, not the law, that is the stimulus to sanctity.

One finds the very same categories used in the Westminster Standards (1647). What was implicit in the covenant theology of the Heidelberg Catechism eighty-four years earlier was made explicit in Westminster Confession of Faith 4.2, where the law is described as that word of God written on the heart of Adam, who had the "power to fulfill it." To Adam's natural knowledge was added "the covenant of works" (7.2). If our first parents had kept that law, "they were happy in their communion with God" (4.2). Sin is defined as "transgression" of God's law (6.6). Under the covenant of works, the condition of eschatological blessedness was "perfect and personal obedience" (7.2).

Like the Heidelberg Catechism, the Westminster Confession of Faith also reckoned the law redemptive-historically. "Law" stands for those epochs of the *historia salutis* before the incarnation (WCF 7.5). And our Lord Jesus, like Adam, was "made under the law," but unlike Adam, he "did perfectly fulfill it" (8.4).

The first use of the law is to create in a sinner a "sense, not only of the danger, but also of the filthiness and odiousness of his sins, as contrary to the holy nature and righteous law of God" (WCF 15.2). As part of this project, the same moral law (19.3) promulgated to Adam in the covenant of works was "delivered by God upon mount Sinai in ten commandments" (19.1–2). The Reformed orthodox of the period thought of this restatement of the covenant of works at Sinai not as a third redemptive-historical covenant (contra Amyraut), but, in the words of Wollebius, as a "pedagogue to Christ" and as expression of the temporary, typical national status of the Israelites.[87] Following the

87. Wollebius, *Compendium christianae theologiae*, 1.21.17. It was widely held among the Reformed orthodox that the Decalogue was a republication of the covenant of works. To give but a few examples, the following taught it: Herman Witsius, *The Economy of the Covenants between God and Man* (trans. William Crookshank; 1803; repr. Phillipsburg, NJ: Presbyterian & Reformed, 1990), 1.336–37; Leonard Van Rijssen, *Compendium theologiae didactico-elencticae* (Amsterdam, 1695), 89; John Owen, "An Exposition of the Epistle to the Hebrews," in *The Works of John Owen* (ed. W. H. Goold; repr. Edinburgh: Banner of Truth, 1991), 6.85; Johannes Marckius, *Compendium theologiae christianae didactico-elencticum* (Amsterdam, 1749), 345–46; Peter Van Mastricht, *Theoretico-practica theologia* (Utrecht, 1699), 3.12.23. Pace D. Patrick Ramsey, "In Defense of Moses: A Confessional Critique of Kline and Karlberg," *Westminster Theological Journal* 66 (2005): 395, Thomas Boston appealed to the logic implied by the grammar of WCF 19.1–2, which reasserts the doctrine of 7.2 that God "gave to Adam a law, as a covenant of works, by which he bound him and all his posterity to personal, entire, exact, and perpetual obedience; promised life upon the fulfilling, and threatened death upon the breach

mainline of Reformed orthodoxy, Peter Van Mastricht (1630–1706) appealed to the republication of the covenant of works at Sinai as proof of the *foedus operum*.[88] According to the confession, the moral law (which WCF 19.3–5 explicitly distinguished from the civil and ceremonial) reflects the divine nature, it "doth forever bind all" and is not relaxed by the gospel, contrary to the medieval and Tridentine view, but strengthened by it. According to the Westminster Confession of Faith, the gospel is that Christ has met the terms of the law for his elect.

"Receiving and resting" in Christ's active and passive righteousness (WCF 11.1), believers continue to owe obedience to the law, not "to be thereby justified" but "as a rule of life" that informs, directs, and binds the believer to God's revealed moral will and that gives the believer "clearer sight of the need they have of Christ, and the perfection of his obedience" (19.6). For those outside Christ, law and gospel are two radically distinct words. For those in Christ, the law is not opposed to the gospel. As a consequence of justification, "the Spirit of Christ subduing and enabling" the believer is able to "freely and cheerfully" obey Christ out of thanks (19.7).

Like the law, the gospel is something that humans must "obey" (WCF 3.8), but that obedience is not our doing, but "receiving and resting on him and his righteousness" (11.1) in Christ's perfect obedience. In redemptive-historical terms, the word *gospel* denotes promise and fulfillment of the Son's incarnation, obedience, and resurrection (7.5–6). Just as the law was expressed in a covenant of works (or life, so WLC 20), the gospel was expressed in a "covenant of grace" after the fall, "wherein he freely offers to sinners life and salvation by Jesus Christ, requiring of them faith in him that they

---

of it; and endued him with power and ability to keep it. This law, after his fall, . . . was delivered by God upon mount Sinai in ten commandments." The phrase *covenant of works* in WCF 19.1 is appositive to the noun *law*. Thus the law is reckoned here as a covenant of works. Thus when, 19.2 establishes "this law" as the subject of the verb "was delivered," the antecedent can be none other than the law defined as a covenant of works in 19.1. This reading of the confession caused Boston, in his notes in *The Marrow of Modern Divinity* (repr. Scarsdale, NY: Westminster Discount Books, n.d.), 58, to exclaim: "How, then, one can refuse the covenant of works to have been given to the Israelites, I cannot see." These same theologians also held that Moses was an administration of the covenant of grace. The doctrine of unity of the covenant of grace and the doctrine of republication were regarded as complementary, not antithetical.

88. Van Mastricht, *Theoretico-practica theologia*, 3.12.23.

may be saved, and promising to give unto all those that are ordained unto life his Holy Spirit, to make them willing and able to believe" (WCF 7.3).

Preaching the Law

Reformed theologians distinguished law and gospel in order to preach the word. Beza argued that the Holy Spirit has ordained the preaching of both law and gospel. Because of sin, we are "so blind" that we are "ignorant even of our ignorance." We tend to be pleased with those things that ought "to displease us most." Therefore, it is necessary for God to make us know "most clearly the cursed pit in which we are." He informs us of our plight "by the declaration of the law." For this reason "God begins with the preaching of the Law. In it alone we can see what we ought to be; and yet we cannot fulfill a single point of it. In it alone, we can see how near we are to our damnation, unless there comes to us some very strong and sure remedy."[89]

This is the proper function of the law. It was not given to justify, but to condemn, to show us the "hell which is opened wide to swallow us." It is evidence of our blindness that we tend to seek our salvation in the very thing that condemns us. The only remedy for the law's just condemnation is "running to Jesus Christ by faith." Instead, we tend to add to our condemnation by adding "law upon law" to our consciences. "This then is the first use of the preaching of the Law; to make known our innumerable faults so that in ourselves we begin to be miserable and greatly humble ourselves."[90] According to Beza, only those who know their sin turn to Jesus with saving faith and only sinners learn their great need from the law.

One gets a sense from these passages how Beza himself preached the law and to what purpose. Any of the orthodox British Reformed theologians would have given their "amen" to Beza's homiletics.

In the twentieth century, J. Gresham Machen (1881–1937) applied these same principles to the crisis created by modernism and its desire to tame the law in the service of mainline, middle-class American liberalism:

89. Beza, *Christian Faith*, 43.
90. Ibid., 44.

> A new and more powerful proclamation of law is perhaps the most pressing need of the hour; men would have little difficulty with the gospel if they had only learned the lesson of the law. As it is, they are turning aside from the Christian pathway; they are turning to the village of Morality, and to the house of Mr. Legality, who is reported to be very skillful in relieving men of their burdens. . . . "Making Christ Master" in life, putting into practice "the principles of Christ" by one's own efforts—these are merely new ways of earning salvation by one's obedience to God's commands.[91]

To preach, as Machen's liberal contemporaries Harry Emerson Fosdick or Henry Sloan Coffin did or as many conservatives do today, a message of corporate or individual self-improvement is to turn the gospel into law and to remove the sting from the very instrument ordained by God to drive sinners to their Savior.[92]

When a minister comes to a text that proclaims the law, his duty is to "go, and do thou likewise" (Luke 10:37 AV). He must, of course, first recognize the law for what it is—God's unbending moral will requiring "personal, entire, exact, and perpetual obedience" (WCF 19.1) before and after the fall. This is how Paul read Deuteronomy 27:26 in Galatians 3:10: "Cursed is everyone who does not continue to do everything written in the Book of the Law" (NIV).

Jesus was the preacher of the law par excellence, as seen in his encounter with the νομικός (lawyer) in Luke 10:25–37. The encounter follows the commissioning and return of the seventy-two to go into the surrounding cities to preach and demonstrate the kingdom of God (10:1–20). Just then the lawyer rises "testing" Jesus: "Having done what [τί ποιήσας], shall I inherit eternal life?"[93] The question was a test because it contained within it a false premise, namely, that

91. J. Gresham Machen, *What Is Faith?* (Grand Rapids: Eerdmans, 1946), 141.

92. On Machen's liberal contemporaries, see Bradley J. Longfield, *The Presbyterian Controversy: Fundamentalists, Modernists, and Moderates* (New York: Oxford University Press, 1991). On Machen, see D. G. Hart, *Defending the Faith: J. Gresham Machen and the Crisis of Conservative Protestantism in Modern America* (Grand Rapids: Baker, 1995). On the similarities between conservative evangelicalism and modernity, see idem, *The Lost Soul of American Protestantism* (Lanham: Rowman & Littlefield, 2002).

93. This rough translation of the aorist participle is intended to reveal the logic of the lawyer's question, which is perhaps more evident in the Greek text than in the more polished English translations where the question sounds more innocent than it was.

inheritance of eternal life was logical consequence of his "doing." For the sake of discussion and the opportunity presented by this arrogant question, Jesus accepts the unstated premise of the question. He queries Mr. Legality on how he "interprets" (ἀναγινώσκεις) the law (10:26). The lawyer says, in effect, "Love God and love your neighbor" (10:27). Jesus replies, "You have answered correctly" (10:28). Jesus, however, preaches the law when he turns the law on the lawyer: "Do this, and you shall live." The response of the lawyer is worth noting. Rather than accepting the full brunt of the law and acknowledging his own fundamental inability, as a son of sinful Adam, to meet that standard, he attempts to change the standard. Luke says that the lawyer was "wishing to justify himself" by seeking to qualify the class of those humans to whom love is due. He asks, "Who is my neighbor?" (10:29). Jesus again refuses to soften the relentless demands of the law. He tells the parable of the Samaritan (10:30–35) and tests the lawyer by asking who in this story was the true neighbor (10:36). Echoing ποιεῖν κρίμα καὶ ἀγαπᾶν ἔλεον in the Septuagint version of Micah 6:8, the lawyer gets it right: "The one having done mercy" (ὁ ποιήσας τὸ ἔλεος) (Luke 10:37). Again, Jesus preaches the law to the lawyer: "Go and do likewise."

From the vocabulary and movement of the narrative, it seems clear that Jesus defied the lawyer's expectations. The lawyer expected and attempted to tone down the demands of the law. Instead, Jesus intensified the demands of justice. If the lawyer would inherit eternal life through law keeping, Jesus gives him the terms of the law: perfect, perpetual, and personal obedience.

The implications for preachers of Jesus's proclamation of the law are several. First, the law must be proclaimed. It has have been said that "Reformed ministers do not proclaim the law, they proclaim the gospel." It is difficult to know from where such a notion arose, but it did not arise from the Reformed theologians or confessions, and it did not arise from Scripture. The ministers of the old covenant (2 Cor 3:6), Isaiah, Jeremiah, Amos, and others, did nothing if not proclaim the law in precisely the sense and to the ends described in this essay. Amos 1:2 says that Yahweh "roars" (יִשְׁאָג) in his proclamation of the demands of the law.

Second, the law, in both its first (pedagogical) and third (normative) uses must be proclaimed with appropriate vigor and application. Again, one could turn to any of the prophets, especially perhaps to the Minor Prophets, to find dozens of examples of such preaching. Peter's sermon in Acts 2, however, is a good example of the vigorous and pointed preaching of the law.[94] Having explained the meaning of the outpouring of the Spirit, he addresses the crowd directly (for the second time) and directly confronts them about their moral guilt before God's law: "Israelite men, listen to these words . . . this Jesus . . . you condemned, having crucified him" (2:22–23). Peter spoke directly to that congregation, as it were, and spoke about their murder of Jesus. Then he turns to announce the good news that, despite our worst efforts, the Messiah lives and reigns. At the end of the sermon, he preached the law (and the gospel) again, in one sentence: "Let every house of Israel know certainly, this Jesus whom you crucified, God made him Lord and Christ" (2:36). The moods of law and gospel could not be clearer than they are in this sentence. The law comes in the imperative (γινωσκέτω) and with the rhetorical finger pointed in the second-person plural "you crucified" (ἐσταυρώσατε). The gospel comes in the indicative, declarative clause "God has made" (ἐποίησεν ὁ θεός). Sin and law-breaking are *intra nos*, but salvation and righteousness are *extra nos*.[95]

Third, the law must be allowed to be the law. The temptation of our therapeutic, medicated age is to take the edge off the law by making it user friendly. The law is God's demand for justice and obedience, not helpful advice. It was because Peter roared the law to those Israelite men gathered at Pentecost that they were "stabbed in the heart" (Acts 2:37). Peter did not say, "I know you meant well." Rather, he declared in effect, "You shall have no other gods. . . . You shall not murder." Only when directly confronted with the naked righteousness of God did the elect see their need and turn to Christ.[96]

94. Of course, Luke's record of the sermon is telescoped and stylized, but this means that we should pay even closer attention to what is included in the synopsis.

95. The pattern of the sermon also suggests that there need be no artificial separation of law and gospel. Peter moves freely between them in this sermon.

96. Because this essay concerns the existence and nature of the distinction between law and gospel, it focuses on the first use of the law. The reader should not infer from the focus of the essay, however, that the third use of the law is being slighted. To the contrary, by clearly

Preaching the Gospel

Beza said, "We call *Gospel* the Good News, which, from the beginning, and by his grace and mercy alone, God has announced to his Church: those who, by faith, embrace Jesus Christ shall partake of eternal life in him (Rom 3:21, 22; John 6:40)."[97] The gospel refers to the second mood or word to be preached, the announcement that the Second Adam by his one act of obedience (Rom 5:18) has kept the law, fulfilled the covenant of works, and made a new covenant in his blood for us sinners (Luke 22:20) and was crucified, buried, and raised on the third day for our justification (1 Cor 15:1–3).[98] Where the law says to sinners, "Do and live," the gospel announces, "Christ has done." The good news is about justification earned *for us* by Christ, who kept the covenants of works and redemption, and offered freely *to us* (Rom 10:4) in the covenant of grace.

Just after a stern denunciation of "the cities where his acts of power had occurred" (Matt 11:20), Jesus prays, giving thanks for the mystery of God's grace (11:25–26). He announces that he is the sole saving revelation of the Father and that only the elect, those to whom the Son chooses to reveal the Father, know him (11:27). Then he declares, "Come to me all who are laboring and who have been loaded with burdens, and I will give you rest. Take my yoke upon yourselves and follow me, because I am gentle and meek in heart, and you will find rest [ἀνάπαυσιν] for your souls" (11:28–29).

This is a gospel sermon. It has imperatives, but the imperative here is not to fulfill the law, but to come in faith to Jesus the law keeper. This is the indicative voice of God's word, the announcement of "rest," that is, salvation. The gospel comes with urgency—"come," "follow"—but those imperatives are grounded in promises: "I will give

---

establishing the distinction between the law and the gospel the way is prepared for a proper understanding and proclamation of the law as the norm for the Christian life.

97. Beza, *Christian Faith*, 46.

98. In several places (e.g., 2 Sam 4:10; 18:20, 22, 25, 27; 2 Kgs 7:9) the noun for "good news" refers to something that has occurred outside of us that benefits his people. In other places, e.g., Ps 96:2, we are daily to "proclaim the good news" of Yahweh's salvation. Most famous of all such Old Testament passages is Isa 52:7: "How beautiful upon the mountains / are the feet of him who brings good news, / who publishes peace, who brings good news of happiness, / who publishes salvation, / who says to Zion, 'Your God reigns'" (ESV).

you rest," "I am gentle and meek," "You shall find rest." The ground of the gospel is Christ's performance.

Conclusion

Luther's great hermeneutical breakthrough was not that the Bible should be read and preached literally, or that it should be preached redemptive-historically, or even that there is within it an eschatological thread. The church had long taught these things under the *quadriga* (the fourfold system of interpretation). What Luther, Calvin, the Reformed confessions, and Protestant orthodox realized—and what preachers must again understand—is that Scripture contains "two words," or one word with two moods, and that the failure to recognize this distinction has the greatest implications for preaching.

Besides the historical reasons for the eclipse and contemporary criticisms of the law/gospel hermeneutic and homiletics surveyed above, preachers should be aware of another obstacle. According to Scripture, humans *want* their minister to turn the gospel into law because it makes the foolishness of the gospel a little more reasonable. Such an approach, however, minimizes the "scandal of the cross" (Gal 5:11). If Paul had preached to the Galatians how to behave themselves so that God would approve of them, he could have silenced his critics.

The act of preaching is inherently "foolish" (1 Cor 1:21). It is an analogue of the Christian faith: "It pleased God to save those who believe, through the foolishness of the preached message." To those who demanded "signs" and "wisdom" (1:22), Paul deliberately preached "Christ crucified" (1:23), which he knew to be offensive to virtually everyone.

If Reformed churches are going to remain faithful to the Scriptures and their confessions, their ministers must recover the biblical and historic Reformed distinction between letter (law) and Spirit (gospel), for the study and—more importantly—for the pulpit. They must preach the killing letter and the life-giving gospel (2 Cor 3:6–7) because it is this act of faith that God has ordained to bring salvation to his people (Rom 10:1–5).

13

The Rise of Moralism in Seventeenth-Century Anglican Preaching

A Case Study

JULIUS J. KIM

Introduction

The twenty-first century is not the first to witness English-speaking theologians in the Reformed tradition expressing dissatisfaction with the Reformation's doctrine of justification through faith alone on the ground of Christ's righteousness and sacrifice alone. The seventeenth century, in the aftermath of the Puritan Commonwealth that gave us the Westminster Standards, not only found monarchs returning to the British throne but also—even more significantly, in the long run—the rise of a new direction in homiletics, driven by changing theological convictions and a desire for a civil, moral society. This seventeenth-century shift has sobering implications for today's preachers in the midst of the current justification controversy.[1]

In 1678 John Bunyan's *Pilgrim's Progress* introduced to the English-speaking world an unforgettable allegory that would chronicle the great themes of the Christian religion.[2] An early character that emerges in the tale is Mr. Worldly Wiseman, a restful looking gentleman who, upon meeting the protagonist, Christian, offered to him the best solution for removing the burden that was overwhelming his soul. Although his guide, Evangelist, had told Christian to go on a different course on his way to the Celestial City, Christian is invited by this apparent sage to turn aside to a village named Morality. Here he would meet a gentleman by the name of Legality, and his son, Civility, who could help Christian remove his heavy burden through a rational understanding of what brought happiness in this life. Worldly Wiseman thus encourages Christian to forsake the unnecessary suffering that Evangelist had recommended and to pursue happiness through morality and civility. As Evangelist would later explain to Christian, however, Worldly Wiseman represented a religion that would not free him, but ultimately keep him in bondage.[3]

Thinking lightly of sin, and consequently of the cross, Worldly Wiseman thus represented to the Puritan Bunyan the religion of seventeenth-century Anglican Latitudinarianism, which taught that salvation was found in obedience to the chief commands of the law of God and in living a decent moral life, that is, trusting Legality and Civility to remove any remnant of discomfort in this life and in the life to come. How could so sharp a contrast to the soteriology of the

1. I would like to thank Dennis E. Johnson for reading and editing an earlier draft of this essay.

2. Refusing to submit to the new church laws established at the restoration of the Anglican Church in 1660, John Bunyan was arrested and eventually imprisoned for twelve years. Upon his release, Bunyan began to document the problems, as he saw it, of the theology and practice of the new regime that encompassed both church and state. The result was this allegory in which a dreamer describes a man, Christian, on a pilgrimage searching for an escape from the impending destruction that awaits him and his family. In ten short years, *The Pilgrim's Progress* would undergo twelve editions and eventually become so admired that it would be translated into over one hundred languages. See James B. Wharey's introduction to *The Pilgrim's Progress* (ed. James Wharey; 2nd ed. by Roger Sharrock; London: Oxford University Press, 1960), esp. xxv. On the legal penalties against Nonconformist ministers, see Gerald R. Cragg, *Puritanism in the Period of the Great Persecution* (Cambridge: Cambridge University Press, 1957), 50–56.

3. This portion of the tale is found in Bunyan, *Pilgrim's Progress*, 17–25.

Westminster Assembly achieve ascendancy in the pulpits of England within a generation of the assembly's work? To understand the driving motivation and appeal of Latitudinarianism, we need to examine its background and its influential proponents.

In the years following the religious and political tumult of the 1640s and 1650s, a group of young pastors and preachers within the Church of England emerged to take leadership during the period known as the Restoration (1660–89)—the years in which Charles II was restored to the monarchy after some twenty years of Puritan rule under the Lord Protector Oliver Cromwell.[4] Known originally for compromising their ecclesiastical status before and after the Restoration, the Latitudinarians—as they came to be known—numbered among them future leaders of the Restoration Church of England such as Edward Stillingfleet and John Tillotson. In a seminal work on the Latitudinarian movement of the Restoration period, Martin Griffin analyzes this group of seventeenth-century English church divines as sharing similar characteristics:

1. orthodoxy in the historical sense of acceptance of the contents of the traditional Christian creeds
2. conformity to the Church of England as by law established, with its Episcopal government, its Thirty-Nine Articles, and the Book of Common Prayer
3. an advocacy of reason in religion
4. theological minimalism
5. an Arminian scheme of justification
6. an emphasis on practical morality above creedal speculation and precision
7. a distinctive sermon style
8. certain connections with seventeenth-century science and the Royal Society[5]

4. For more on the Restoration see I. M. Green, *The Re-establishment of the Church of England, 1660–1663* (Oxford Historical Monographs; Oxford: Oxford University Press, 1978); and J. Spurr, *The Restoration Church of England, 1646–1689* (New Haven: Yale University Press, 1991).

5. Martin Griffin, *Latitudinarianism in the Seventeenth-Century Church of England* (ed. Lila Freedman; Leiden: Brill, 1992), vii. See also William Spellman, *The Latitudinarians and the Church of England, 1660–1700* (Athens: University of Georgia Press, 1993); John Marshall, "The

Tillotson became one of the foremost leaders representing this new group of Anglican divines, who became known not only for their political concessions but also for their theological moderation and congenial temperament.

For Latitudinarians like Tillotson, there emerged a growing conviction that the true essence of Christianity consisted of preaching and practicing God's moral demands and duties. The hallmarks of the Latitudinarian message were the moral prescriptions of religion, the excellence and necessity of moral virtue, and the reasonableness of Christianity. Though much of their influence came through the press, most Latitudinarians utilized their pulpits to endorse and exemplify the theological ideals that motivated this moralistic message—a message that at the end of the day consisted of a series of "dos" and "don'ts." In doing so, men like Tillotson helped shape the intellectual and ecclesiastical trends of the day. It was primarily through his preaching that Tillotson articulated a clear vision of a religion that possessed the assurance and order that the Restoration mind and soul desired.

Why this analysis of Anglican preaching during the late seventeenth century? The nature and practice of moralistic preaching that occurred during the Restoration seem to have striking similarities to the kind of preaching we often hear today in our pulpits. Though often unintentional, preachers preach messages that implicitly or explicitly state that by practicing virtue, on the one hand, or by avoiding vice, on the other, one can procure divine blessing.[6] One author writes: "It is easy to become moralistic when preaching. While there is nothing wrong with preaching morality, in contrast, moral*ism* is legalistic, ignores the grace of God, and replaces the work of Christ with self-help."[7] Bryan Chapell rightly calls this type of preaching "sub-Christian":

Ecclesiology of the Latitude-men, 1660–1689: Stillingfleet, Tillotson, and Hobbism," *Journal of Ecclesiastical History* 36 (1985): 407–27; John Spurr, "'Latitudinarianism' and the Restoration Church," *Historical Journal* 31 (1988): 61–82; and Barbara Shapiro, *Probability and Certainty in Seventeenth-Century England: A Study of the Relationships between Natural Science, Religion, History, Law, and Literature* (Princeton: Princeton University Press, 1983), 74–118.

6. See the following for more on the problem of moralizing in preaching: Sidney Greidanus, *The Modern Preacher and the Ancient Text* (Grand Rapids: Eerdmans, 1988), 163–66; and Bryan Chapell, *Christ-Centered Preaching* (Grand Rapids: Baker, 1994), 280–86.

7. Jay Adams, *Preaching with Purpose* (Grand Rapids: Baker, 1982), 146 (emphasis original).

> A message that merely advocates morality and compassion remains sub-Christian even if the preacher can prove that the Bible demands such behaviors. By ignoring the sinfulness of man that makes even our best works tainted before God and by neglecting the grace of God that makes obedience possible and acceptable, such messages necessarily subvert the Christian message.[8]

This was exactly the type of preaching Latitudinarians like Tillotson epitomized. This moralistic preaching, however, was not produced in a vacuum. It emerged from particular theological convictions—convictions that included a dismissal of key Reformation doctrines such as the sinful depravity of man, justification by faith alone apart from works, and the imputation of Christ's righteousness to the believer based on Jesus's active obedience to the law of God. The moralistic preaching developed primarily by Anglican Latitudinarians during the Restoration period emerged from a deliberate theological shift away from essential Reformation doctrines.

This historical case study should provide a corrective to the inadequate and insufficient preaching that occurs in pulpits today. My analysis will begin by looking at the two major types of preaching in seventeenth-century England, metaphysical preaching and Puritan preaching, which gave rise to the moralistic preaching found during the Restoration. This will be followed by examination of the nature and practice of moralistic preaching best exemplified by the leaders of Restoration Latitudinarian preaching, Benjamin Whichcote and John Tillotson. And I will conclude with the importance of a Christ-centered hermeneutic and homiletic as a corrective to moralistic preaching.

Seventeenth-Century Preaching in England

Though John Tillotson was a tireless defender of the Anglican religion against irreligion, enthusiasm, and superstition, he saw himself first as a preacher and pastor. As one of the foremost preachers during the Restoration, Tillotson emerged a key figure in the new style of

8. Chapell, *Christ-Centered Preaching*, 268.

preaching that developed during the mid- to late seventeenth century. Gilbert Burnet describes Tillotson's extensive influence:

> His notions of Morality were fine and sublime; His thread of Reasoning, was easy, clear, and solid; He was not only the best Preacher of the age, but seemed to have brought Preaching to perfection; His sermons were so well heard and liked, and so much read, that all the Nation proposed him as a Pattern, and studied to copy after him.[9]

This new "plain style" of preaching, as it came to be known, was part of a larger methodological and stylistic program that included the emergence of the Royal Society and the linguistic contributions of John Wilkins. It was an exposition and rhetoric that eventually dominated late-seventeenth-century Anglican pulpit discourse, though it was also denounced by some High Church Anglicans and exploited by deists.

This new rhetoric of preaching that Tillotson endorsed and exemplified was especially influenced by two elements: the emergence of a new scientific discourse and a reaction to prevailing approaches to preaching.[10] Tillotson, along with other Latitudinarian preachers, reacted to the two major styles of preaching that were popular in the first half of the sixteenth century: the metaphysical preaching of Anglican clergy like John Donne and—what he considered to be—the speculative preaching of the Puritans. As such, the Latitudinarian preaching of Tillotson involved a degree of change not only in content but also in style and emphasis—he hoped to replace the ornate and flowery rhetoric of the metaphysical divines as well as the obscure and intangible doctrinal preaching of the Puritans. Central to this

9. Gilbert Burnet, *History of His Own Time* (2nd ed.; Oxford: Oxford University Press, 1833), 4.242. See also idem, *A Sermon Preached at the Funeral of the Most Reverend Father in God John by the Divine Providence Lord Archbishop of Canterbury, Primate, and Metropolitan of All England* (London, 1694), 13–14.

10. The scientists affiliated with the Royal Society emphatically denounced the prevailing style of ornate language and endorsed the need for a simpler, more direct manner of expression. This plain style was a characteristic feature of the new science at the Royal Society from its very inception in 1662. Richard Jones demonstrates persuasively that this deliberate shift in rhetoric and prose was initiated and carried out by members of the Royal Society, who in most cases were clerics deeply interested in science; see *The Seventeenth Century: Studies in the History of English Thought and Literature from Bacon to Pope* (Stanford: Stanford University Press, 1951), 75–110.

shift in religious language and sensibility during the Restoration was an adjustment from the prominence on biblical mystery and metaphysical doctrines to "tangible" moral exhortations and adages in the preaching of the Latitudinarians.[11] Tillotson stood at the forefront of this change in rhetoric and reality.

To understand this revision of homiletic theory and practice and the consequential shift in religious sensibility, two questions need to be asked: What was this new plain style and how did it differ from previous styles of preaching? Why did Latitudinarian preachers like Tillotson break from these previous styles?

From the early 1660s, a remarkable change emerged in preaching style and method through the influence of prominent preachers such as Tillotson. Isabel Rivers argues persuasively that this change in preaching method and style was a "planned programme" after the Restoration.[12] In the mind of certain Latitudinarian preachers, the elaborate and "witty" preaching of earlier Anglicans like Donne and Lancelot Andrewes, as well as the speculative and enthusiastic preaching of the Puritans, needed be replaced by a simpler style of sermons.[13]

From the book *Ecclesiastes* by John Wilkins (1614–72) to the essays by Edward Fowler (1632–1714), Latitudinarians described not only the differences between Puritan and Latitudinarian modes of preaching but also the anticipated success of this type of preaching for audiences.[14] To understand this "planned programme" of the

11. It is important to bear in mind that for many Latitudinarians this shift was not a complete abandonment of biblical mysteries; rather, it was a change in the emphasis and degree those topics received. For more, see Julius J. Kim, "The Religion of Reason and the Reason for Religion: John Tillotson and the Latitudinarian Defense of Christianity, 1630–1694" (PhD diss., Trinity Evangelical Divinity School, 2003), esp. chap. 5.

12. See Isabel Rivers, *Reason, Grace, and Sentiment* (Cambridge: Cambridge University Press, 1990), esp. 37–59.

13. Some useful studies on this change in preaching include Jackson I. Cope, *Joseph Glanvill: Anglican Apologist* (St. Louis: Committee on Publications, Washington University, 1956), chap. 7; Jones, *Seventeenth Century*, 111–42; Rolf P. Lessenich, *Elements of Pulpit Oratory in Eighteenth-Century England, 1660–1800* (Cologne: Bohlau, 1972); W. Fraser Mitchell, *English Pulpit Oratory from Andrewes to Tillotson* (London: SPCK, 1932), chaps. 8–9; Irène Simon, *Three Restoration Divines: Barrow, South, Tillotson*, vol. 1 (Paris: Les Belles Lettres, 1967), chap. 1; and George Williamson, *Seventeenth Century Contexts* (London: Faber & Faber, 1960), 202–39.

14. John Wilkins, *Ecclesiastes; or, A Discourse concerning the Gift of Preaching* (rev. ed.; London, 1669); Simon Patrick, *A Friendly Debate between a Conformist and a Non-Conformist* (London, 1669); Edward Fowler, *Principles and Practices* (London, 1699); idem, *Design of Christianity* (London, 1668); John Eachard, *The Grounds and Occasions of the Contempt of the Clergy*

men of "latitude," two major preaching styles prior to the onset of the Restoration must be explored: the so-called metaphysical preaching exemplified by Anglicans like Donne and the Puritan preaching of men like William Perkins.[15]

Metaphysical Preaching

For the enigmatic term *metaphysical preachers*, Horton Davies provides the best definition of a particular group of men who dominated English pulpits during the late sixteenth and early seventeenth centuries: "The unfamiliar term describes a large and lively group of at least forty-one Anglican preachers who flourished in the last decade of the sixteenth and the first four decades of the seventeenth century, and who were renowned for their wit, learning, eloquence, and loyalty to the Church and Nation."[16] He continues by noting that the term *metaphysical* does

and Religion Inquired Into (London, 1670); James Arderne, *Directions concerning the Matter and Stile of Sermons* (ed. John Mackay; 1671; repr. Oxford: Blackwell, 1952); Joseph Glanvill, *Essays on Several Important Subjects in Philosophy and Religion* (London, 1676), 41–46 no. 7; and idem, *An Essay concerning Preaching and a Sensible Defence of Preaching* (London, 1678).

15. J. W. Blench writes that three main styles can be differentiated in English preaching in the fifteenth and sixteenth centuries: (1) the plain but not colloquial style, using few illustrative material and artificial word patterns; (2) the colloquial style, using "racy and pungent speech idiom" and illustrations, but avoiding word patterns; and (3) the ornate style with highly embellished word patterns and illustrations "aiming directly at oratorical display"; *Preaching in England in the late Fifteenth and Sixteenth Centuries: A Study of English Sermons, 1450–c. 1600* (Oxford: Blackwell, 1964), 113. The enormous amount of sermons and the length of time covered in the study could weaken Blench's attempt to categorize. Nonetheless, he persuasively argues for these three general kinds of styles. Since, however, the difference between the first and second type of styles is a matter of degree and not kind, I combine the two styles into one category. Thus, generally speaking, the Puritans can be grouped under the first two styles, while the metaphysical preachers can be classified as the third style. Lisa Gordis's new work, *Opening Scripture: Bible Reading and Interpretive Authority in Puritan New England* (Chicago: University of Chicago Press, 2003), though focusing on the New England context, provides helpful background to the sources and development of Puritan preaching. For further study, see some of the works listed in note 6 above and the following works on Dissent: James E. Bradley, *Religion, Revolution, and English Radicalism: Nonconformity in Eighteenth-Century Politics and Society* (Cambridge: Cambridge University Press, 1990); Richard L. Greaves, *"Enemies under His Feet": Radicals and Nonconformists in Britain, 1664–1667* (Stanford: Stanford University Press, 1990); idem, *Secrets of the Kingdom: British Radicals from the Popish Plot to the Revolution of 1688–1689* (Stanford: Stanford University Press, 1992); and Michael Watts, *The Dissenters: From the Reformation to the French Revolution* (Oxford: Clarendon, 1985).

16. Horton Davies, *Like Angels from a Cloud: The English Metaphysical Preachers, 1588–1645* (San Marino, CA: Huntington Library, 1986), 7.

not entail the idea that they were merely philosophical preachers who emphasized the role of the rational mind in the acquisition of truth. Rather, it is a reference to "metaphysical poets" like Donne who used their wit, learning, and striking imagery in their sermons as they did in their poetry.[17] Davies notes eleven characteristics that distinguished this style of preaching from its major alternative—what Davies calls the "Puritan plain" style:

1. wit
2. patristic citations and references
3. the use of classical literature and history
4. illustrations from "unnatural" natural history
5. quotations in Greek and Latin, and etymology
6. principles of biblical exegesis
7. sermon structure and divisions
8. the Senecan style
9. paradoxes, riddles, and emblems
10. speculative doctrines and arcane knowledge
11. relating doctrinal and devotional preaching to the liturgy and the calendar of the Christian year[18]

From one of the earliest and most influential metaphysical divines, Lancelot Andrewes (1555–1626), we have some of these characteristics epitomized in a Christmas-day sermon:

> The Word, by whom all things were made, to come to be made it selfe . . . what flesh? The flesh of an infant. What, Verbum Infans, the Word an Infant? The Word and not be able to speake a word? How borne, how entertained? In a stately Palace, Cradle of Ivorie, Robes of estate? No: but a stable for his Palace; a manger for his Cradle; poore clouts for his array. This was His beginning. . . . Is His end any better, (that Maketh up all:) what flesh then? Cujus livore sanati, blacke and blew, bloudie and swolne; rent and torne;

17. Ibid., 7. The term *metaphysical* was first used by Samuel Johnson (1709–84) in the critical way denouncing the pretentious display of learning, use of artificial images, and cleverness that only obscured the meaning of Scripture's clear and obvious truths. But many others affirmed the style for the challenge it presented to the prevailing methods of preaching, which were facile and unlearned.

18. Ibid., 49.

> the thornes, and nayles sticking to his flesh: And such flesh He was made. . . . Love respects it not, cares not, what flesh he be made, so the flesh be made by it.[19]

In sum, the metaphysical preaching of late-sixteenth- and early-seventeenth-century Anglican England represented the pinnacle of an ornate style of preaching that featured such qualities as clever wit and verbal imagery, complicated sermon structure and divisions, excessive amounts of ancient citations and classical literature, and the use of paradoxes and riddles.

Puritan Preaching

According to J. I. Packer, the label *Puritan* was coined in the early 1560s as a term of derision implying "peevishness, censoriousness, conceit, and a measure of hypocrisy, over and above its basic implication of religiously motivated discontent with what was seen as Elizabeth's Laodicean and compromising Church of England."[20] Many caricatures and misinterpretations have emerged concerning the religious culture of sixteenth- and seventeenth-century Puritanism, but historical scholarship has reassessed what exactly Puritanism was and is.[21] One

19. Lancelot Andrewes, *XCVI Sermons* (London, 1629), 47–48. Another accomplished representative of this style was preacher/poet John Donne (1571–1631), who preached the following sermon the Sunday before Good Friday: "That *God*, this *Lord*, the *Lord of life could dye*, is a strange contemplation; That the *red Sea* could bee *drie*, That the *Sun* could *stand still*, That an *Oven* could *be seaven times heat* and *not burne*, That *Lions* could be *hungry* and *not bite*, is strange, *miraculously strange*, but *supermiraculous* that God *could dye*; but *that God would dye* is an *exaltation* of that. But even of that it is a *superexaltation*, that *God shold dye, must dye*, and *non exitus* (said S. Augustin) *God* the *Lord had no issue but by death*, *oportuit pati* (says *Christ* himself) all this *Christ ought to suffer*. . . . There we leave you in the *blessed dependancy*, to *hang* upon *him* that *hangs* upon the *Crosse*, there bath in his *teares*, there *suck* at his *woundes*, and *lye down in peace* in his *grave*, till he vouchsafe you a *resurrection*, and an *ascension* into that Kingdome, which hee *hath purchas'd for you*, with the *inestimable price* of his *incorruptible blood*. AMEN"; *The Sermons of John Donne* (ed. G. R. Potter and E. M. Simpson; Berkeley: University of California Press, 1953–62), 10.243, 248 (emphasis original).

20. J. I. Packer, *A Quest for Godliness: The Puritan Vision of the Christian Life* (Wheaton, IL: Crossway, 1990), 1.

21. On the resurrection of Puritan studies in this century, see the following significant works: William Haller, *The Rise of Puritanism* (New York: Columbia University Press, 1938); A. S. P. Woodhouse, *Puritanism and Liberty* (London: Macmillan, 1938); M. M. Knappen, *Tudor Puritanism* (Chicago: Chicago University Press, 1939); Perry Miller, *The New England Mind*, vol. 1: *The Seventeenth Century* (Cambridge: Harvard University Press, 1939); Patrick Collinson, *The Elizabethan Puritan Movement* (Berkeley: University of California Press, 1967); Peter Lake,

of these studies, Packer's *Quest for Godliness*, describes a group of generally like-minded English Protestants in the sixteenth and seventeenth centuries leading a spiritual movement that desired to restore to the nation a deeper passion and conviction for God and godliness.[22] Central to this passion was the place of preaching. In fact, one scholar notes that "it was through the pulpit that Puritanism made its mark on the English nation in the early seventeenth century."[23]

Packer concisely distinguishes Puritan sermons from other forms: they were "textual and expository, practical and applicatory, analytical and thorough. They are uniformly doctrinal—that is to say, their real subject is always God and his ways, even when the formal object of consideration is man. And together they show clearly what the Puritans took to be involved in preaching the gospel."[24] As such, these sermons emphasized the primacy of the intellect. Over against the increasing development of uninformed laity from the mere recitation of prepared homilies by ignorant clergy, the Puritans endorsed intellectual depth and precision in their preaching.[25] The primacy of the intellect and the desire for doctrinal comprehensiveness became a hallmark of Puritan preaching.

Despite the emphasis on the intellect and doctrine, Puritan sermons were closely tied to application. Thus, William Ames would say, "First the things contained in the text must be stated. . . . In setting forth the truth in the text the minister should first explain it and then indicate the good which follows from it."[26] Additionally, according to the Directory of Publick Worship of God adopted by the Puritan Westminster Assembly,

---

Moderate Puritans and the Elizabethan Church (Cambridge: Cambridge University Press, 1982); and Harry Stout, *The New England Soul* (New York: Oxford University Press, 1986).

22. Packer, *Quest for Godliness*, 28.

23. Leland Ryken, *Worldly Saints: The Puritans As They Really Were* (Grand Rapids: Zondervan, 1986), 91.

24. Packer, *Quest for Godliness*, 167.

25. Thus Puritans argued in Parliament for "the necessity of preaching and of a learned ministry," and thus proposed "that some good course be taken to have a learned ministry"; Collinson, *Elizabethan Puritan Movement*, 312, 315.

26. William Ames, *The Marrow of Theology* (trans. and ed. John E. Eusden; Boston: Pilgrim, 1968), 191.

> In raising these doctrines from the text, his care ought to be, First, That the matter be the truth about God. Secondly, That it be a truth contained in, or grounded on, that text that the hearers may discern how God teacheth it from thence. Third, That he chiefly insist upon those doctrines which are principally intended, and make the most for the edification of the hearers.[27]

The organization of the Puritan sermon was generally uniform. The outline that appears at the end of Perkins's *Art of Prophesying* serves as a model:

1. To reade the Text distinctly out of the Canonicall Scriptures.
2. To give the sense and understanding of it being read, by the scripture it selfe.
3. To collect a few and profitable points of doctrine out of the naturall sense.
4. To apply (if he have the gift) the doctrines rightly collected, to the life and manners of men, in a simple and plaine speech.[28]

If we take the first point—the reading of Scripture—as preliminary to the sermon proper, the structure took the form of three parts, "the exposition of a passage of Scripture . . . by collecting lessons (or 'doctrines') from each verse and adding the moral applications (or, 'uses') of them."[29] Perkins would expand on this in an excursus in his commentary on Galatians:

> Know therefore, that the effectuall and powerfull preaching of the word, stands in three things. The first is, true and proper interpretation of the Scripture. . . . The second is, savory and wholesome doctrine. . . . The third is, the Application of the said doctrine, either

27. *The Confession of Faith* (Inverness, UK: Free Presbyterian Publications, 1983), 379.

28. William Perkins, *The Workes of That Famous and Worthy Minister of Christ in the University of Cambridge M. William Perkins* (London, 1612–13), 2.673.

29. Horton Davies, *Worship and Theology in England, 1534–1690* (Grand Rapids: Eerdmans, 1996), 304.

> to the information of the judgement, or to the reformation of the life. This is the preaching that is of power.[30]

The Puritan sermon was also characterized by a simple prose style that attempted to appeal to a cross section of society. Its principal spokesman, Perkins, best expresses this plain style:

> Here first wee are to observe the properties of the Ministry of the Word. The first, that it must bee plaine, perspicuous, and evident. . . . Againe, that kinde of preaching is to be blamed in which there is used a mixed kinde of variety of languages, before the unlearned. . . . And in this kinde of preaching wee doe not paint Christ, but . . . our owne selves. It is a by-word among us: It was a very plain Sermon: And I say again, the plainer, the better.[31]

Puritan preachers wanted the deep and rich truths of Scripture to be understood by all. The Puritan plain style was thus a means to the end of clarity.

In sum, a deep conviction and passion for the knowledge of God and the practice of godliness generally distinguished the character of Puritan preaching. Specifically, this preaching utilized a textual and expository model that also emphasized the practical application of truth to life. In style, it attempted to be plain and clear to all members of English society. Thoroughly doctrinal, Puritan preaching also sought to be meticulous and comprehensive, covering all the major doctrines concerning God and his relation to his creatures.[32] One historian sums up the character of Puritan preaching as follows: "It was the genius of the Puritan preaching that in style it was plain without being dull; in emphasis, an admirable balance of doctrine and practice; in character, faithfully devoted to the exposition of the word of Scripture, both letter and spirit, which they loved."[33] By con-

30. Perkins, *Workes of That Famous and Worthy Minister*, 2.222.

31. Ibid.

32. For more on the development of Puritan preaching, see Joseph A. Pipa Jr., "William Perkins and the Development of Puritan Preaching" (PhD diss., Westminster Theological Seminary, 1985).

33. Peter Lewis, *The Genius of Puritanism* (Haywards Heath, UK: Carey, 1977), 47.

trast, Latitudinarian preaching was shaped by Tillotson in reaction to Puritan preaching.[34]

Restoration Latitudinarian Preaching

Leading the development of the plain style of preaching exemplified most clearly during the Restoration was the work and preaching of Benjamin Whichcote (1609–83) and John Tillotson (1630–94).[35] If Whichcote was the theoretician, Tillotson was the exemplar par excellence.

Whichcote and "Ingenuity"

Benjamin Whichcote enjoyed a long and influential career in both the university and the church. First as a student and later as a fellow at Emmanuel College, Cambridge, Whichcote had a hand in mentoring future leaders such as John Smith, John Wallis, and John Worthington during the 1630s and 1640s. Emmanuel at this time had grown not only in size and influence but also in reputation as an ardent patron of Puritanism.[36]

In spite of his Puritan experience and environment, Whichcote began to develop a sermonic discourse that challenged the prevailing emphases on Calvinistic doctrine that not only seemed to bog down the sermons of his Puritan colleagues but also seemed to produce nothing but division among fellow Christian leaders. By 1650

34. For more on the Latitudinarian reaction to metaphysical preaching, see my "Religion of Reason," chap. 5.

35. The influence of John Wilkins must also be noted when discussing the development of Restoration Latitudinarian preaching. As Tillotson's mentor and father-in-law, Wilkins articulated a new mode of language and communication that would revolutionize not only the way scientific papers were read and published by the Royal Society but the use of language in England.

36. In 1644, when Whichcote was appointed provost at King's College, no less than eleven Emmanuel graduates occupied the leadership of colleges in Cambridge. During his time at Cambridge, Whichcote also preached extensively as the lecturer at Trinity Church from 1636 to 1656, succeeding the ministries of Puritans Thomas Goodwin and John Preston. Even after his ejection from the post at King's College in 1660, Whichcote continued his ministry in two London churches: St. Anne's Blackfriars and St. Lawrence Jewry. See James B. Mullinger, "Benjamin Whichcote," in *Dictionary of National Biography* (Oxford: Oxford University Press, 1921), 21.1–3.

Whichcote began to elaborate on the implications of a concept he called "ingenuity," which revealed his desire to showcase the virtue of a reasonable Christianity and the benefits of using "right reason" in religious matters. These views were related to his view that man had essentially a "good nature" and could thus reasonably live a virtuous life based upon both the light of nature and the light of Scripture. Not to be confused with the word *ingenious*, meaning clever, resourceful, or imaginative, *ingenuity* as used by Whichcote referred to man's natural ability of critical reasoning that provided the foundation for religion.[37] He argued that in contrast to the implicit faith endorsed by Rome, the Christian possesses—by virtue of his being created in the image of God—divine rationality. This is evidenced by man being able to comprehend not only natural religion in an intelligible way but also the truths of revealed religion as found in Scripture.[38] Thus, man's religion, from beginning to end, is rational.[39]

Unfortunately for Whichcote, this concept of ingenuity unleashed a series of critical letters from Puritan Anthony Tuckney (1599–1670), his former tutor at Emmanuel College. Tuckney was concerned that the term *ingenuity* carried with it a challenge to the Puritan conviction that grace was necessary for the justification of the helpless sinner. By opposing nature and grace, reason and faith, Whichcote was undermining the Calvinist doctrines of total depravity and imputed righteousness. Tuckney believed that substituting ingenuity and a

37. Robert Greene argues persuasively about the prominence and importance of this word to Whichcote's thinking; "Whichcote, Wilkins, 'Ingenuity,' and the Reasonableness of Christianity," *Journal of the History of Ideas* 42 (1981): 227–52. He notes that the word *ingenuity*, in one form or another, appears 107 times in the course of 97 sermons. Furthermore, Whichcote's contemporaries also noted the importance of this word to his thinking. In fact, the well-known series of letters between Whichcote and Tuckney begins with a sarcastic remark by Tuckney concerning ingenuity: "I doe not fancy as some others, this affected word *Ingenuous*: and I wish, the thing itself was not idolized; to the prejudice of *Saving Grace*"; Whichcote, *Letters*, quoted in *Moral and Religious Aphorisms* (ed. Samuel Salter; London: Payne, 1753), 1–2.

38. Whichcote, *Letters*, 239.

39. It is important to note that Whichcote's optimistic view of man's rational faculties as an alternative to the Reformation's emphasis on sovereign grace and trust in Christ's extrinsic righteousness is different that the alternative to views proposed by Norman Shepherd and those who advocate the federal vision. There is a point of contact, however, in the redirection of the believer back to one's own resources and efforts (aided, of course, by divine grace) and an optimism that these efforts and resources are sufficient to enable the believer to make a significant contribution to the salvation process. I am indebted to Dennis E. Johnson for this insight.

virtuous morality for the saving grace of Christ was misleading and dangerous.

The Whichcote/Tuckney Correspondence

The eight letters that passed between Tuckney and Whichcote in 1651 highlight the distinctions between Puritan and Latitudinarian convictions, methods, and conclusions in preaching.[40] The occasion for Tuckney's first letter to Whichcote was the concern that Tuckney felt about Whichcote's endorsement and example of a religious rationalism that seemed to harm an orthodox view of sin, salvation, and sanctification. Tuckney was referring to two commencement sermons that Whichcote gave in 1651 in which his former student seemed to attack his own commencement sermons delivered in 1650.

After preaching in Boston during the 1630s and 1640s, Tuckney returned to England to serve as a member of the Westminster Assembly from 1643 to 1648. In 1645 he was appointed master of Emmanuel College, which at that time enjoyed the reputation of being the bastion of Puritan faith and learning at Cambridge University. Already by 1648, Tuckney began to criticize those in Cambridge who preached the benefits of ingenuity in religious understanding. He felt that there were dangers in substituting the seemingly salvific use of right reason and virtuous morality for the saving grace of Christ.[41]

40. The letters between Tuckney and Whichcote are found in Whichcote's *Moral and Religious Aphorisms*. The letters have also been summarized and interpreted by the following works: John Tulloch, *Rational Theology and Christian Philosophy in England in the Seventeenth Century* (Edinburgh: Blackwood, 1872), 2.45–98; J. B. Mullinger, *The University of Cambridge* (Cambridge: Cambridge University Press, 1911), 3.588–96; H. C. Porter, *Reformation and Reaction in Tudor Cambridge* (Cambridge: Cambridge University Press, 1958), 414–29; and J. D. Roberts, *From Puritanism to Platonism in Seventeenth Century England* (The Hague: Nijhoff, 1969), 42–65.

41. That this new ethos was a serious problem in and around Cambridge is evident by Tuckney's reference to the spirit that his former student seemed to be supporting and stimulating: "Or if any be more *ingenuous*, and (as you call it) a little *better-natured*, that with him in the Gospel, they be *not far from the Kingdom of Heaven*. Mark 12:34 yet even that, rested in, keeps them from ever coming up to *Jesus Christ*. Pity that *Rachel* should die, when it was now but a *little way to come* to *Ephrath*, that an *Almost* should altogether keep so many a towardly Man from Heaven: But a thousand pities that my *drawing* so *near* the Goal should set me down as having done far enough, and so keep me from ever attaining the *Prize*, that *Ingenuity*, because it's so near akin to Grace, should prove so *Disingenuous*, as to keep a Man from ever being truly *Gracious*"; *Forty Sermons* (London, 1676), 529 (emphasis original).

Later, in his commencement sermon of 1650, Tuckney continued his condemnation of "our ingenuous loving-hearted Arminian's charity."[42] As a prominent figure in Cambridge during these years, Tuckney felt the responsibility to defend what he understood to be the middle way of Calvinism between the twin dangers of the Antinomians, whose rejection of the continuing obligation to the moral law under the gospel involved a rejection of the rational tradition of the natural law, and those who exalted right reason and ingenuity at the expense of free grace and faith.

For his part, Whichcote preached a sermon in 1651 that praised ingenuity.[43] The day after this sermon, Tuckney wrote to Whichcote and initiated the correspondence that lasted only a few short months. The letters show Tuckney's concern that Whichcote's use of the word *ingenuity* was damaging to the Puritan convictions about man's depravity and helplessness and the consequent need for salvation solely by the free grace of God through the imputed righteousness of Christ, received by faith alone. Furthermore, for Tuckney, both the general claims for ingenuity, as well as the apparent opposition of orthodoxy to ingenuity, were nothing but veiled attempts to secure further freedom for a "liberty of speech" that only undercut the solidity of confessional beliefs and of the language of theology, which were essential for maintaining the purity of Christian doctrine.

Whichcote responded by denying that he was attempting to change and harm the doctrines related to salvation by grace: "If I have done prejudice to saving grace, by idolizing natural ingenuity; the Lord reprove it in me."[44] He also reassured Tuckney that he was not elevating nature at the expense of grace: "I abhorre and detest from my

42. Tuckney warned his audience that these are days when "everyone may speake and write the vain Phancies of his own heart, and impune and spread foulest heresies and blasphemies" and when systems, confessions of faith, and forms of belief are rejected in favor of "that Helena of theirs, their *libertas prophetandi*"; *A Good Day Well Improved* (London, 1656), 253, 258, 251; quoted in Greene, "Whichcote, Wilkins," 232–33.

43. Whichcote stated: "The proposal for progress and growth in knowledge—That an ingenuous-spirited Christian, after application to God, and diligent use of meanes to find-out truth; might fairely propose, without offense taken, what upon search he finds cause to beleeve; and whereon he will venture his own soule. This (I said) might be converse to mutual edification; and without disturbance to the world; and so I have long thought; and do continue to think so still" (*Letters*, 13).

44. Ibid., 8.

soul all creature-magnifying self-sufficiencie."[45] Though Whichcote's intent may have been genuine, Tuckney was not convinced. After all, Whichcote would acknowledge Christ "in parts of nature, reason and understanding; as well as in gifts of grace."[46]

One can see the trouble that Tuckney had with Whichcote's convictions, methods, and conclusions. In fact, though the correspondence ended, Tuckney would continue his debate in public. His 1652 commencement sermon includes references to the "Platonick faith (as some call it)," "the sublimated Deists of our Age," and the "compleat Moralist . . . who looks at faith, but as a notion, and at an imputed righteousnesse, as a putatitous ridiculous absurdity. His rational and virtuous morality is his Religion."[47] Tuckney's Puritan convictions of man's sinful state and of his need for alien righteousness are far removed from the language and sentiments of Whichcote's definition of religion: "Religion produceth a sweet and gracious Temper of Mind; calm in its self, and loving to Men. It causeth a Universal Benevolence and Kindness to Mankind. For, these are the things of which it doth consist; Love, Candour, Ingenuity, Clemency, Patience, Mildness, Gentleness, and all other Instances of GOOD-NATURE."[48] In Tillotson's sermons, the repercussions of this shift in religious language and, consequently, Christian doctrine would echo in the years following the Restoration.

Tillotson the Preacher

Though Tillotson's ministry as a preacher began in humble parishes in the countryside, most of his sermons were usually addressed to learned, wealthy, and politically important audiences in the city of London. In the early 1660s, however, after the ejection of more than two thousand Puritan ministers from their pulpits, Tillotson attempted to introduce this new preaching emphasis to his new congregation in the country, who, according to Thomas Birch, did not receive it favorably. After all, they were used to the Puritan way of doing things.

45. Ibid., 100.
46. Ibid., 126.
47. Anthony Tuckney, *None But Christ* (London, 1654), 12, 45, 45.
48. Benjamin Whichcote, *Select Sermons* (London, 1698), 431.

They "universally complain'd, that Jesus Christ had not been preach'd amongst them, since Mr. Tillotson had been settled in the parish."[49] These early hearers of Tillotson sermons would not be alone in their assessment of Tillotson's moralistic preaching devoid of the Puritan emphases on redemption and salvation. Later, however, his preaching in the city gained popularity, especially among the clergy.[50]

Upon hearing his sermons, many Puritans challenged that they were nothing but moral essays. Arguably, many of his extant 254 sermons emphasize not only the rational coherence of the Christian religion but also the practical morality that results from logical scriptural truths. In this, Tillotson continued the thought of one of his mentors, John Wilkins, who wrote in his primer on preaching, *Ecclesiastes*, that the sermon should be divided into three parts: explication, confirmation, and application.[51] Reason plays an important role in confirmation or "proofs." Wilkins recommends that "the Arguments from Reason, should be rendered so plain and so cogent, as may be sufficient to satisfie any teachable man, concerning the truth, or fitness, or necessity of what we would persuade to."[52] In this, Wilkins continued the tradition of Whichcote, who, while sharing the desire to preach logically and plainly with Puritan preaching, emphasized both the rational truths of the Christian religion and the ability of natural man to receive and assent to these truths.[53] Tillotson continued

49. Thomas Birch, "The Life of the Author, Compiled Chiefly from His Original Papers and Letters," in *The Works of John Tillotson* (London, 1752), 1.28.

50. John Beardmore wrote "many, that heard him on *Sunday* at *Lincoln's Inn*, went joyfully to St *Laurence*, on Tuesday, hoping they might hear the same sermon again"; Birch, "Life of the Author," 1.408.

51. Wilkins wrote: "The great End of Preaching, being either to *inform* or *perswade*; This may be most effectually done by such rational wayes of *Explication* and *Confirmation*, as are most fit and proper to satisfie mens judgments and consciences. And this will in all times be accounted good sense, as being suitable to the Reason of Mankind; whereas all other ways are, at the best, but particular fashions, which though at one time they may obtain, yet will presently vanish, and grow into disesteem"; *Ecclesiastes*, preface, A5 (emphasis original).

52. Ibid., 27.

53. There can be no doubt that an important influence upon Tillotson's preaching was the traditional Puritan sermon style. Not only was he raised in a Puritan home and church, Tillotson was also tutored at Cambridge by David Clarkson, the eventual successor of John Owen's influential Puritan pulpit in London. Tillotson was also a member of the Presbyterian delegation that attended the Savoy Conference just prior to the restoration of Charles II to the monarchy and Tillotson's own transfer to the Anglican Church. His first published sermon in 1660, "A Sermon Preached at the Morning Exercises at Cripplegate," was part of a collection of

this agenda of preaching individual moralism for the sake of national civility.

In a sermon entitled "Of Justifying Faith," false speculation, cant terms and phrases, and obscuring the meaning of the gospel are all associated. Tillotson argues that in their attempt to articulate justifying faith, the "enthusiasts" misuse the "resting" metaphor, thereby leading to antinomian tendencies. Restoration historian Rivers states: "For Tillotson (as for all Latitudinarians and almost all Anglicans) active repentance and obedience are conditions of justification: the use of popular non-scriptural metaphors such as 'resting, and relying, and leaning upon CHRIST, apprehending, and laying hold, and applying CHRIST' encourages moral passivity."[54] The language of "resting, relying, and leaning," all come from standard Puritan doctrines found in the Puritan Westminster Confession of Faith (11.1–2). Tillotson's biographer, Thomas Birch, confirms this by stating that Tillotson disliked the potentially confusing language, "as when they taught men to roll upon Christ, and act faith, and the like; the plain sense of which is, to trust in him and believe in him."[55] This was the main problem Tillotson had with Puritan theology: it was too pessimistic about the capacities of fallen humanity and thus necessitated a view of justification that eliminated man's response to divine grace.[56] Following Whichcote, Tillotson elevated the role of mankind's rational and moral abilities so that the apparent antinomianism endorsed by the Puritans could be rooted out of English pulpits.

Tillotson's critique of Puritan preaching continued in his sermon entitled "The Necessity of Repentance and Faith." In responding to a potential objection that the preaching of faith in Christ is unnecessary to those who are already Christians, Tillotson responded by arguing that the faith he preached was one that included the practice of

---

sermons preached by Presbyterian ministers. These factors, along with Wilkins's own affinities with the Puritan plain style, demonstrate how Tillotson was exposed to and influenced by the Puritan sermon style.

54. Rivers, *Reason, Grace, and Sentiment*, 56. See Tillotson, *Works of John Tillotson*, 9.324–27.

55. Birch, "Life of the Author," 1.cclxxxi.

56. Tillotson's view—that *sola fide* disables the motivation to pursue morality—has striking similarities to the views endorsed by critics of the Reformation view of justification.

holiness that faith requires.[57] In this way, Tillotson agreed with other Latitudinarian preachers who emphasized the relationship between faith and works and the importance of conditions for salvation. For disillusioned clergymen like Tillotson who had experienced what he believed to be the antinomian consequences of Puritan theology, religious life was essentially moral and was achieved by active human effort in cooperation with divine grace.[58] In a sermon entitled "The Precepts of Christianity not Grievous," he affirmed that God "hath commanded us nothing in the gospel that is either unsuitable to our reason, or prejudicial to our interest; nay, nothing that is severe and against the grain of our nature, but when either the apparent necessity of our interest does require it, or an extraordinary reward is promised to our obedience."[59] Every law of God was perspicuous, advantageous to our own interest, and able to be kept by the involved believer who utilized the natural and revealed knowledge that was available to every reasonable person. In this way, Tillotson was convinced he was counteracting the precarious notions put forth by Puritan preachers, especially those that were derived from Calvinistic theology.

Tillotson opposed Calvinist doctrines such as irresistible grace and imputed righteousness because they were too God-centered and God-dependent without attributing anything to man. Tillotson, for example, in delineating the four contemporary views on grace, revealed the religious context that influenced his views. The first two opinions he labeled "extreme": (1) irresistible grace was given only to the elect, and (2) sufficient grace was offered to all. The last two views, which he labeled "middle views," stated that (3) irresistible grace was given to the elect and sufficient grace to the rest who reject it, and (4) irresistible grace was given to the elect, sufficient grace to the rest, some of whom may accept it while some may reject it.[60] After rejecting the first three alternatives, he argued that the last viewpoint was the "most agreeable both to the tenor of Scripture and to the

57. Tillotson stated: "This is the faith we would persuade men to, and there is nothing more necessary to be pressed upon the greatest part of Christians than this; for how few are there among those who profess to believe the gospel who believe it in this effectual manner, so as to conform themselves to it?"; *Works of John Tillotson*, 7.251.

58. Rivers, *Reason, Grace, and Sentiment*, 73.

59. Tillotson, *Works of John Tillotson*, 1.468.

60. Ibid., 5.393–96.

best notions which men have concerning the attributes and perfections of God, and gives the greatest encouragement to the endeavors of men."[61] Tillotson articulated here the collective argument of the Latitudinarians: natural and revealed religion demonstrated persuasively what was innately rational, morally acceptable, and ultimately beneficial for man.

Tillotson also repudiated the Puritan idea that faith alone without the "fruits of holiness and obedience" justifies the sinner.[62] The idea of God imputing righteousness to the sinner through the instrument of faith alone only yielded a spirit of lawlessness.[63] Whichcote summarized their objection to Calvinistic doctrine: "Some men put all upon God, and say when He please to come, with Irresistible Grace, the Work will be done; and the Man shall be Converted; for who hath resisted his Will (Rom 9:19)? And till then, the Work will not be done, for they can do nothing." Rather, he stated: "Conversion is a mutual act, and so is Faith."[64] After all, to men like Whichcote and Tillotson, history had already demonstrated the perilous antinomian results that these arcane doctrines yielded.

Tillotson expounded these Latitudinarian ideals in a collection of five sermons that he preached under the title "The Nature of Regeneration, and Its Necessity, in Order to Justification and Salvation."[65] In these sermons Tillotson repudiated the notions that described salvation as an immediate act and the believer as a passive recipient of God's grace unto salvation. Though the importance of grace was never denied,[66] grace contained the idea of virtue, just as faith contained the idea of works. Consequently, the proposal of "conditions" for salva-

61. Ibid., 5.395.

62. The whole quotation reads as follows: "For a bare assent to the truth of the gospel, without the fruits of holiness and obedience, is not a living, but a dead faith, and so far from being acceptable to God, that it is an affront to him; and a confident reliance upon Christ for salvation, while we continue in our sins, is not a justifying faith, but a bold and impudent presumption on the mercy of God"; ibid., 5.422.

63. "To forgive men upon other terms, were to give countenance and encouragement to perpetual rebellion and disobedience"; ibid., 5.423.

64. Benjamin Whichcote, *Several Discourses* (London, 1701–7), 1.314–15 no. 12; 2.137 no. 7.

65. These sermons are found in Tillotson's *Works of John Tillotson*, 5.354–426.

66. Preaching at Whichcote's funeral, Tillotson reported that Whichcote on his deathbed "disclaimed all Merit in himself; and declared that whatever he was, he was through the Grace and Goodness of God in Jesus Christ"; Tillotson, *Works of John Tillotson*, 1.222.

tion was not problematic even for these anti-Roman theologians.[67] To him, the expression *new creature* signified the same idea as the expressions *faith perfected by charity* and *keeping the commandments of God*.[68] Thus he categorically stated at the end of these five sermons: "And our continuance in this state of grace and favour with God, depends upon our perseverance in holiness."[69] Tillotson fused together the source of moral activity and the activity itself into one concept. As a result, grace and virtue were essentially synonymous: "Grace and virtue are but two names that signify the same thing. Virtue signifies the absolute nature and goodness of these things; grace denotes the cause and principle by which these virtues are wrought and produced . . . namely, by the free gift of GOD'S HOLY SPIRIT to us."[70] Which word was used depended upon the perspective, whether human or divine, being considered.[71]

Similarly, faith was usually defined to include works-cooperation with grace. Yet Tillotson refused to be labeled a Pelagian because he did not think that man could act alone without grace. He insisted that man's cooperation with grace was a necessary condition of salvation.[72] In his sermon entitled "Of Justifying Faith," Tillotson noted that the conditions the gospel requires for the pardon and remission of sins consisted of the following: "(1) An assent to the truth of the gospel.

67. "This condition here mentioned in the text [1 John 3:3], of our being new creatures, is the same in sense and substance with those expressions which we find in the two parallel texts to this, where faith, which is perfected by charity, and keeping the commandments of God, are made the conditions of our justification and acceptance with God"; ibid., 5.419.

68. Ibid., 5.419.

69. Ibid., 5.418. Again, Tillotson's view here that one remains in favor with God through holy living has striking parallels with those who advocate the views of the federal vision. Tillotson continues: "As to our acceptance with God, and the rewards of another world, it matters not Jew or gentile, circumcised or uncircumcised; that which maketh the difference, is obeying the truth, or obeying unrighteousness; working good, or doing evil; these are the things which avail to our justification, or condemnation, at the great day. . . . To satisfy us that this is the tenor of the Holy Scriptures, and the constant doctrine of it from the beginning to the end (Gen. iv.7). It is God's speech to Cain, 'If thou dost well, shalt thou not be accepted?' And (Rev. xxii.14): 'Blessed are they that do his commandments, that they may have right to the tree of life, and may enter it through the gates of the city'"; ibid., 5.421.

70. Ibid., 8.476.

71. See Rivers, *Reason, Grace, and Sentiment*, 75–76, for this and the following section.

72. Tillotson, *Works of John Tillotson*, 5.382. Here we find parallels between Tillotson's theology and the Council of Trent on the one hand and Norman Shepherd's *The Call of Grace: How the Covenant Illumines Salvation and Evangelism* (Phillipsburg, NJ: P&R, 2000) on the other.

(2) A trust and confidence in Christ as our only Saviour. (3) Repentance from dead works. (4) Sincere obedience and holiness of life."[73] Elsewhere, he would expound that in the matter of faith and works the apostles Paul and James were not contradictory. In fact, unless faith included works, the truths that both of these biblical authors represented could not be reconciled. Tillotson's biographer noted that the archbishop was planning a new book of homilies that would serve to correct some wrongheaded ideas from sixteenth-century theology: "Some expressions in the first book of Homilies, that seemed to carry justification by faith only, to a height that wanted some mitigation, were to be well examined. Furthermore, the apostle Paul's statements on the subject were to be reconciled with those of James."[74] Tillotson sincerely desired Christianity to be simple, and practical-doctrinal disputes only confused and clouded the important issues.

Tillotson's arguments concerning a simpler, plainer style of preaching were thus a rejoinder to what they saw as Puritan excesses in doctrine, language, and structure.[75] Tillotson, following Whichcote and Wilkins, forged a new paradigm and pattern of preaching that challenged—and eventually displaced in the Church of England—the prevailing approaches of his day: metaphysical and Puritan preaching. In opposition to these styles, Tillotson's preaching emphasized such elements as the clear and rational exposition of biblical truths, cogent argumentation of these truths to the benefit of mankind, and the concrete moral application of these truths for a civil English society. His desire was to make Christianity rationally understandable and ethically practical, regardless of the charge that his preaching was nothing but pure moralism in the guise of Christianity. Indeed, some thirty years after the initial indictment that "Jesus Christ had not been preached amongst them since Mr. Tillotson had been settled in the parish,"[76] Tillotson responded in a sermon on Titus 3:2 by stating

73. Tillotson, *Works of John Tillotson*, 9.312–13.

74. Birch, "Life of the Author," 1.367–68.

75. To some extent Puritan endorsement of a new language was a response to the needs and assumptions of their politically and socially important audiences in the court and city. As such, Burnet could state that Charles II's tastes aided the popularity of this plain style of preaching: "This help'd to raise the value of these men, when the King approved of the style their discourses generally ran in; which was clear, plain, and short"; *History of His Own Time*, 1.91.

76. Birch, "Life of the Author," 1.xviii.

that "I foresee what will be said, because I have heard it so often said in the like case, that there is not one word of Jesus Christ in this. No more is there in the text, and yet I hope, that Jesus Christ is truly preached, whenever his will, and laws, and the duties enjoined by the Christian religion, are inculcated among us."[77]

There is no doubt, then, that Tillotson's view of the Christian religion was fundamentally moralistic. His preaching, along with that of other Latitudinarians, represented a deliberate shift not only in preaching style, but also, more importantly, in theological commitment. Central Reformation truths, such as the sinful state of man, justification by faith alone apart from works, and the imputation of Christ's righteousness based upon his active obedience to the law of God, were rejected and redefined. This intentional program was developed and executed through Tillotson's preaching. George Whitefield would later castigate Tillotson's five sermons entitled "The Nature of Regeneration" in a series of letters he would write to a friend in London:

> [Tillotson] intended to prove, that we must first be regenerated and sanctified, and then on Account of that Regeneration and Sanctification, that God will justify, that is, acquit, accept, and reward us. [But] the Archbishop knew of no other than a bare historical Faith: And as to the Method of our Acceptance with God through Jesus Christ, and our Justification by Faith alone (which is the Doctrine of the Scripture and the Church of England) he certainly was as ignorant thereof as Mahomet himself.[78]

Whitefield is not alone in his assessment that Tillotson's moralism emerged from particular theological convictions. Others describe Tillotson's moralism as one that emphasized a salvation of works over a salvation wrought only by faith—ultimately undermining orthodox English Reformation theology. Tillotson's moralistic preaching, then, developed from particular theological commitments—a commitment that "had no place for a doctrine of original sin and avoided any emphasis upon an evil inheritance transmitted from Adam" and no

77. Tillotson, *Works of John Tillotson*, 3.275.

78. George Whitefield, *Three Letters from the Reverend Mr. G. Whitefield* (Philadelphia: Franklin, 1740), 3.

place for the justification of the believer by faith alone, through the work of Christ alone.[79] As a result of the influence of Tillotson and his fellow Latitudinarians, one scholar writes that "within fifty years Calvinism in England fell from a position of immense authority to obscurity and insignificance."[80] To many historians, the Restoration period was marked by the replacing of Calvinism by Arminianism and perhaps even by outright Pelagianism.[81]

It should not surprise us that the preaching of the Latitudinarians was moralistic. After all, in Matthew 7:17 Jesus taught this commonsense truth: "A good tree bears good fruit; a bad tree bears bad fruit." Latitudinarian sermonic fruit developed from the roots of their theological commitments: a semi-Pelagian scheme of justification by faith plus works naturally led to moralistic preaching.[82] To Latitudinarians, the Reformation had erred in emphasizing the sovereign work of God alone through the extrinsic merit of Christ alone due to its pessimistic views about fallen humanity. Thus, *sola fide* justification naturally leads to antinomian moral passivity. This, to Latitudinarians like Tillotson, was the inherent danger of a Puritan church and nation that was influenced by Reformation theology. The Latitudinarians wanted to reestablish the English church and nation upon principles that were rational, ethical, and civil. In this way, the nation would be spared the bloodshed and turmoil that engrossed the English people for over one hundred years.

So, while the rise of moralistic preaching within the seventeenth-century Church of England is understandable given the theological convictions and political goals of groups like the Latitudinarians, what is surprising is when we hear today—from preachers who profess allegiance to key Reformation truths—messages that call on believers to work out their salvation through good works without grounding

79. R. Buick Knox, "Bishops in the Pulpit in the Seventeenth Century: Continuity and Change," in *Reformation, Conformity, and Dissent: Essays in Honour of Geoffrey Nuttall* (ed. R. B. Knox; London: Epworth, 1977), 101.

80. Gerald R. Cragg, *From Puritanism to the Age of Reason* (Cambridge: Cambridge University Press, 1950), 30.

81. J. H. Plumb asserts that "evil and guilt, sin and redemption—the whole personal drama and appeal of religion—was forgotten or rationalized away"; *England in the Eighteenth Century* (London: Penguin, 1950), 44–45.

82. For a good description of historic semi-Pelagian thought, see J. N. D. Kelly's *Early Christian Doctrines* (New York: HarperCollins, 1978), 370–72.

these efforts in the finished work of Christ in their stead. One author writes, "By making our efforts the measure and the cause of godliness evangelicals fall victim to the twin assaults of legalism and liberalism, which make our relationship with God dependent on human goodness."[83] Yet this is precisely what happens when preachers today have doubts about the power of *sola fide* to produce assurance and holiness. Saved by grace alone, by faith alone, in the work of Christ alone—these were truths that Reformers such as Martin Luther and John Calvin took pains to comprehend and confess. These truths were not developed in a vacuum, however, but were borne out of a faithful reading of Scripture. If sermon titles like "Seven Laws of a Healthy Marriage" or "You Better Be Humble or You Will Stumble" are any indication of the current trends in evangelical preaching today, it seems that a new reformation is needed to recapture the methods and goals of the Reformers in their interpretation of Scripture.

Christ-Centered Hermeneutics and Homiletics

One of the remedies for the lack of Reformation truths heard in preaching today is to be reminded of how to interpret or rightly divide the word of God. It is helpful to recall how the Reformers interpreted the word of God. The Reformers sought to recover the central message of the Bible that Rome had misread and misunderstood. With the apostle Paul, Luther and Calvin believed that the central message of the entire Bible was "that Christ died for our sins according to the Scriptures, that he was buried, that he was raised on the third day according to the Scriptures" (1 Cor 15:3–4 NIV). They believed that the person and work of Jesus Christ must be central to our hermeneutics and our homiletics.

What is Christ-centered hermeneutics and homiletics? Christ-centered interpretation of Scripture resulting in Christ-centered preaching is just that, centered on Christ—his perfect life, sacrificial death, and vindicating resurrection. Only an understanding that the whole Bible is God's story of redeeming humanity from the wages of

83. Chapell, *Christ-Centered Preaching,* 281.

their sin through the person and work of his covenant-keeping Son, Jesus Christ, gives us the right start and finish to all of our sermons. Scripture itself teaches us how to interpret Scripture. From the very beginning of our exegesis to the application of Scripture's truths to the hearts and lives of our hearers, Christ then becomes the alpha and the omega of our sermon preparation and delivery. One author writes:

> To preach the passages . . . as they were intended to be preached, Christ must be exalted as the One who not only has effected our justification (the declaration by God that in Him we are counted perfect), but also has made sanctification possible by sending His Spirit to enable us to understand God's revealed will and to empower us to do it.[84]

As he correctly states, by focusing our interpretation and proclamation on the telos of Scripture, Jesus Christ, we can guard ourselves from the kind of moralistic preaching that plagued the Latitudinarians and threatens to plague the church today. Some key concepts—the role of biblical theology and the function of the law and gospel distinction in our preaching—aid us in the proper interpretation and proclamation of Scripture as it centers on Christ.[85]

In the introduction to his *Biblical Theology*, Geerhardus Vos argues that rather than being a loose collection of unrelated moral stories and religious poems, the Bible itself contains a consistent message.[86] He and others correctly argue that the Bible is God's revelation of his own words and deeds in history to accomplish his redemptive plans for mankind.[87] From the beginning of Genesis to the close of the Revelation, God speaks and acts within time, space, and history

84. Adams, *Preaching with Purpose*, 150.

85. Obviously more than these two themes are important for the proper interpretation of Scripture. Because the law/gospel discussed in chapter 12 below, I will focus on the first of these two.

86. Geerhardus Vos, *Biblical Theology* (Grand Rapids: Eerdmans, 1948).

87. See also the following: Herman Ridderbos, *Redemptive History and the New Testament Scriptures* (rev. ed.; Phillipsburg, NJ: P&R, 1988); Edmund Clowney, *Preaching and Biblical Theology* (Grand Rapids: Eerdmans, 1961); Derke Bergsma, *Redemption: The Triumph of God's Great Plan* (Lansing, IL: Redeemer Books, 1989); and Meredith G. Kline, *Kingdom Prologue* (Overland Park, KS: Two Age Press, 2000).

to reveal his saving purposes for the world through his divine agent of salvation, his own Son, Jesus Christ. Thus, God's word is the Creator's divine, historical, redemptive revelation to his creatures so that they might know him and glorify him for what he has done through Christ.

This revelation of God's redemptive plan, however, is also progressive. That is, God's salvific plan in the Bible is not disclosed all at once, but rather in stages. The Bible unveils God's redemptive revelation from the Old Testament to the New Testament. It moves from promise to fulfillment, from anticipation to realization. From Old Testament to New, God's redemptive-historical story moves from the implicit to the explicit message that God ultimately saves his people from the bondage of sin and slavery in the life, death, and resurrection of the sinless God-man Jesus Christ. The study of Scripture through this redemptive-historical perspective is called biblical theology. It studies Scripture by showing the essential unity among all the seemingly disparate stories and poems, reaching a climax in the person and work of Jesus Christ.

The Lord Jesus himself gives us the warrant to understand the Scriptures through these lenses. Two texts in the gospel of Luke—one in the beginning and one at the end—demonstrate this redemptive-historical pattern of interpretation. Early in Jesus's earthly ministry, Jesus made his way on the Sabbath day to the synagogue in Nazareth (Luke 4:16–21). The Scriptures were read and expounded. On this particular day, the chosen text to be read was from Isaiah 61: "The Spirit of the Lord is on me, / because he has anointed me / to preach good news to the poor. / He has sent me to proclaim freedom for the prisoners / and recovery of sight for the blind, / to release the oppressed, / to proclaim the year of the Lord's favor" (NIV). After having read this portion of Scripture, he began his sermon of that text with these pregnant words: "Today this scripture is fulfilled in your hearing" (NIV). Jesus reveals that he himself is the fulfillment of the promises made to the prophet Isaiah. Starting with this narrative, Luke then begins to unfold the mystery of Christ's purposes as he weaves together the greatest story ever told.[88]

88. As the reader can probably guess, I am indebted to my mentor, Edmund P. Clowney, for this understanding; see especially his *Unfolding Mystery: Preaching Christ in the Old Testa-*

Near the end of Luke's gospel we read a story about Jesus's encounter with two dejected disciples making their way to the town of Emmaus (Luke 24:13–35). Having just explained to this stranger (Jesus) concerning the recent suffering, death, and disappearance of their leader from the tomb, the two disciples hear this: "How foolish you are, and how slow of heart to believe all that the prophets have spoken! Did not the Christ have to suffer these things and then enter his glory?" Jesus then begins the greatest sermon never recorded as he revealed "beginning with Moses and all the Prophets" that he had to undergo all the suffering and shame in order to fulfill "what was said in all the Scriptures concerning himself" (24:25–27 NIV). Jesus continues the same pattern of interpretation as he appears to the eleven disciples: "This is what I told you while I was still with you: Everything must be fulfilled that is written about me in the Law of Moses, the Prophets and the Psalms. . . . This is what is written: The Christ will suffer and rise from the dead on the third day, and repentance and forgiveness of sins will be preached in his name to all nations, beginning at Jerusalem. You are witnesses of these things" (24:44–48 NIV). Jesus thus provides the warrant to understand the Scriptures within this redemptive-historical framework.

Thus, all Scripture must be seen as a testimony to the person and work of Christ. "Biblical theology," as Edmund Clowney states, "serves to unlock the objective significance of the history of salvation. It focuses on the core of redemptive history in Christ."[89] This is the vital role of biblical theology in our interpretative work. Properly interpreting the many and various characters and epochs contained in Scripture requires this understanding of redemptive history culminating in Christ. Clowney states another benefit of biblical theology: "It also opens up for us the subjective aspect, the religious riches of the *experience* of God's people, and its relation to our own."[90] Here Clowney begins to argue against the assumption many have concerning biblical-theological interpretation. That is, some may think that biblical-theological interpretation—and by extension redemptive-

ment (Phillipsburg, NJ: P&R, 1988) and *Preaching Christ in All of Scripture* (Wheaton, IL: Crossway, 2003).

89. Clowney, *Preaching and Biblical Theology*, 78.

90. Ibid., 78 (emphasis original).

historical preaching—precludes ethical demands by the preacher upon the hearer. After all, if, for example, stories about the Old Testament patriarchs focus and culminate in Christ, what does it have to do with me and my life? Again, Clowney is helpful:

> The redemptive-historical approach necessarily yields ethical application, which is an essential aspect of the preaching of the word. Whenever we are confronted with the saving work of God culminating in Christ, we are faced with ethical demands. A religious response of faith and obedience are required. But that response must be evoked by the truth of the particular revelation that is before us.[91]

Several points can be gleaned from this passage. First, ethical applications can never be separated from the exposition of the text. This ethical application, however, must always be based upon the saving work of God in Christ for our sins. Second, the response of faith and obedience are required responses to any text of Scripture. This response, however, must be warranted by a faithful interpretation of that text.

In this way, our preaching will not fall prey to the appeal, for example, of calling God's people to pattern their lives based on the good or bad deeds of biblical characters. Rather, based upon a biblical-theological interpretation of our passage, we call God's people to rest and rely upon the work of Christ in their stead and then, and only then, call them to respond, in gratitude for God's grace in Christ, in faith and obedience. Thus, a clear understanding of the redemptive-historical nature of Scripture will aid us in our desire to preach Christ-centered, nonmoralistic sermons.

Conclusion

In their quest for rational certainty and political stability, Anglican preachers Benjamin Whichcote and John Tillotson modified their former Puritan convictions and adopted a moralistic preaching paradigm that revealed their semi-Pelagian scheme of justification. This rise in

91. Ibid., 80.

moralistic preaching, however, was a direct result of deliberate and intentional adjustments in their theology. The Puritan emphasis on the gospel of free grace, for example, did not have the power to motivate the rational Englishman toward the pursuit of holiness. Thus, the sinful depravity of man, justification by faith alone apart from works, and the imputation of Christ's righteousness to the believer based on Jesus's active obedience to the law of God were deemphasized, ultimately yielding messages that taught that divine blessing could be procured through human efforts that were assisted by God's grace. As a result, these Latitudinarian preachers placed their emphasis on practical morality above creedal speculation and precision. It is through these preachers that a rise in the moralistic preaching would emerge in the Anglican Church that both John Wesley and George Whitefield would denounce a century later during the eighteenth-century evangelical awakening. Through this program of preaching plainly the moral and ethical demands of true religion, the Latitudinarians changed the course of English religious communication and confession.

This seventeenth-century distrust and disposal of the doctrine of *sola fide* parallels those in the twenty-first century caught in the midst of the current justification controversy. Like Tillotson, current critics of the Reformation doctrine of justification by faith alone have produced a theology that not only hopes to provide assurance of salvation but also to motivate ongoing spiritual devotion in the face of apparent antinomianism. What they fail to see, however, is that the assurance of our salvation can be found only in a substitute not only dying in our place but also in this substitute being morally perfect. True assurance of salvation can be found only in placing our faith in Christ alone, who has been raised for our justification (Rom 4:25; 1 Cor 15:20–23). Furthermore, true God-honoring holiness flows out of a gospel of free grace that does not measure our standing before God based upon any degree of moral performance. In fact, the gospel declares that Christ alone fulfilled all the obligations of the covenant on our behalf. Out of gratitude and not fear, then, the Christian, forgiven of sin and declared righteous by faith alone in Christ alone, pursues the kind of holiness that honors and delights God.

These Reformation truths emerged from a reading of Scripture that emphasized the centrality of Christ for the gospel. It behooves preachers today who desire to proclaim Christ in all his fullness without falling into any form of moralism to remember two key hermeneutic methods. The study of Scripture through the discipline of biblical theology will assist the preacher in finding the Christ-centered meaning to each passage of Scripture. In this way, they will be able to herald the gospel in clarity, cogency, and compassion, bringing to bear upon every hearer the glorious message that the believer's status before God has been secured in the life, death, and resurrection of our Lord and Savior Jesus Christ. Upon this foundation of the grace of God in Christ can the preacher then call the once guilty to a life of holiness out of gratitude for the love of God.

14

Simul iustus et peccator

The Role of Justification in Pastoral Counseling

Dennis E. Johnson

Introduction

As shepherds of Jesus's flock, pastors wrestle with the wounds and waywardness of the human heart. They counsel the guilty, who are consumed by self-condemnation. They counsel the defensive, who try to deflect God's heart-piercing word through self-justification and blame-shifting. They counsel those ensnared by deeply ingrained patterns of shameful lust or unbridled rage, trapped souls who derive no pleasure from their sin but despair of finding freedom from it. They counsel the complacent, whose self-absorbed habits of heart sow seeds of dissension into every relationship in home, church, and workplace. Pastoral counseling is, as the older shepherds called it, "the cure of souls," healing the heart of its deep and complex maladies through the wise application of God's infection-exposing law and his conscience-cleansing gospel.

Husband and wife sit glowering at each other, their fires of resentment stoked by years of misunderstanding, offense, and neglect. A middle-aged man reluctantly, despondently unveils the secret shame of his enslavement to impure fantasies. An adolescent hunches over in self-loathing and insecurity, hating her appearance, wounded by the scorn of peers, and terrorized by the prospect of a lifetime without love. Such hurting souls need relief from their inner torment; but the shepherd knows they need more than this. They need to see themselves, their situation, and their God in a fresh way,[1] to glimpse a glimmer of hope that change is possible, and to be gripped with a motive sweet, strong, and enduring enough to overpower the inertia of the status quo and to quicken their pace to "strive for peace with everyone, and for the holiness without which no one will see the Lord" (Heb 12:14 ESV). They need to understand not only the *what* of godly change but also its *why*: to recognize the attitudes, values, and behavior that please God, but also to be moved by the overpowering beauty of this goal of delighting their redeemer and king. How can the pastor not only persuade counselees' minds but also set their wills ablaze with a passion for peace and purity, grounded in the conviction that conformity to Christ is worth the pain and price to be paid, whatever the cost and consequences in the short term?

At first glance, it would appear that the Reformation doctrine that sinful persons are justified, decisively and irreversibly, merely through *relying* on Jesus's covenant keeping (active obedience) and covenant curse bearing (passive obedience) alone, would hamstring Christians' motivation to race toward holiness, thereby depriving the pastoral counselor of much needed leverage to overcome counselees' internal inertia. After all, if we are *assured* that we are not only forgiven but vindicated as upright in God's sight, welcomed as well pleasing to the Father, once for all and irrevocably, why must Christians keep struggling in the uphill battle against our deeply ingrained sin and selfishness? If throughout this life we will be *simul iustus et peccator*,

1. Note the apt title of David Powlison's recent *Seeing with New Eyes: Counseling and the Human Condition through the Lens of Scripture* (Phillipsburg, NJ: P&R, 2003). See also Powlison's persuasive case for a return to biblical categories in the taxonomy through which personal problems are perceived in "Idols of the Heart and 'Vanity Fair,'" *Journal of Biblical Counseling* 13 (1995): 35–50.

"simultaneously righteous [in Jesus's imputed righteousness] and sinner [in our own subjective imperfection]," does not our forensic status, grounded in extrinsic righteousness, obviate the *need* for growth in godliness, while our intrinsic unrighteousness nullifies the *hope* of growth in godliness? By reading Paul as removing Christians' best efforts at loving God and others from the "justification equation," have the Reformers removed from the pastor's arsenal several potent instruments—guilt, fear of divine rejection, a sense of achievement, anticipation of reward and commendation—with which to stimulate and reinforce counselees' commitment to change?

Of course, pastoral counselors could still appeal to other motives for change. The pastor might encourage people to their duty, to safeguard their self-esteem, or to preserve their reputation. Such appeals to common sense and enlightened self-interest might strike a nerve and convince counselees to give change a chance, or they might not. In any case, there is nothing distinctively Christian about such motives, nor can such motives sustain counselees' resolution to persevere in new paths of obedience to God.

Scripture and the church's tested pastoral wisdom point pastors and their counselees to the gospel itself—the good news that this book defends and celebrates, about a mediator who has both obeyed and endured condemnation in our place and who bestows both forgiveness and his own righteousness on those who rest wholly in his achievement—as the foundation and fountain of a God-given, grace-instilled motive that overpowers the appeals of both sin and self-righteousness, producing a freedom to obey for sheer love of the Savior, for God's glory alone. My working assumption is that effective pastoral counseling is the confluence of four necessary factors:

1. an accurate (biblically normed and situationally informed) diagnosis of the problem and its causes
2. a wise (biblically normed) prescription regarding changes needed in the counselee
3. a strong motivation to follow the difficult and distasteful aspects of the prescription
4. a strong hope that changes actually can be made and will yield growth toward holiness and joy in Christ, whatever

adverse consequences, circumstances, or reactions of other people persist

The diagnosis and prescription have at their core the doctrinal seeds of biblical anthropology, soteriology, and ethics, which mature into pastoral wisdom through months and years of caring for Christ's sheep, with all their idiosyncrasies. These diagnostic and prescriptive steps are by no means easy, but the challenge of sustaining counselees' motivation and hope is even more daunting. Here is where the doctrine of justification proves its pastoral worth. Although the assurance that biblical justification imparts may *seem*, both to legalists and to antinomians, to work at cross-purposes to Scripture's summons to strenuously pursue holiness, in fact *only* this assurance can produce a holiness that springs from love for God rather than an exploitation of God for our own ends. In other words, only when our obedience flows from a *justification-secured assurance* of the Father's approval of us for his Son's sake is our obedience an expression of love for God above all, rather than an attempt to obligate through our efforts.

The Scriptural Relation between Justification and the Cure

The power of the gospel of once-for-all justification to motivate passionate pursuit of holiness will be illustrated first in two New Testament case studies in counseling. Then the conclusions drawn from these texts may be compared with the wisdom of representative Reformed pastor-theologians of the six centuries. Finally, a gospel-driven, justification-grounded approach to pastoral care will be applied to the three contemporary case studies described above.

Case Study 1: The Upright versus the Down-and-Out (Luke 7:36–50)

In the home of Simon the Pharisee Jesus ministered to two counselees who appeared to have radically different needs. Simon, Jesus's host, was respectable, affiliated with the sect within Judaism that was recognized for observing God's commands and evidently conscientious in his avoidance of ethically compromising situations. Perhaps he was somewhat judgmental toward others' flaws; but then, who does not disapprove of people who deserve disapproval? He might possibly be charged with breaches of ancient etiquette for failing to attend to the welcome and comfort of his guests, although New Testament scholars debate whether foot washing, a ceremonial kiss, and the anointing of guests' hair were absolute obligations of ancient Near Eastern hosts.[2] Apart from these minor defects, Simon's need for personal change seemed minimal, at least to himself.

The woman who slipped into this semipublic banquet, on the other hand, was notorious for a pattern of behavior that violated God's holy law. She was obviously emotionally overwrought (sobbing, it seems, uncontrollably), oblivious to societal expectations and decorum (releasing her hair in the presence of men), and probably economically imprudent (if her alabaster flask of ointment even approached the value of Mary's in John 12:3). She was, however, en route to a new life. What made the difference in the life of this "woman . . . who was a sinner"?

Jesus's story within a story, disarming in its simplicity and self-evident logic, unveiled the secret that propels radical life change. He introduces one creditor and two borrowers, one owing ten times as much as the other. In a burst of incredible largesse, the creditor erases both debts. The sheer economic imprudence of this action signals that story is really about a different (nonfinancial) category of debt relief

2. Among those interpreting Simon's omissions as serious breaches of expected hospitality etiquette are Kenneth Bailey, *Through Peasant Eyes: More Lucan Parables, Their Culture, and Style* (Grand Rapids: Eerdmans, 1980), 5; and Alfred Plummer, *A Critical and Exegetical Commentary on the Gospel according to St. Luke* (International Critical Commentary; Edinburgh: Clark, 1901), 213, who likewise writes of the Pharisee's "lack of courtesy." Most recent commentators, however, are hesitant to conclude that foot washing, the kiss of greeting, or the anointing of a guest's head were so customary in first-century Judaism that their omission would be construed as insulting. See, e.g., I. Howard Marshall, *The Gospel of Luke: A Commentary on the Greek Text* (New International Greek Testament Commentary; Grand Rapids: Eerdmans, 1978), 311–12, citing H. Schürmann, *Das Lukasevangelium* (Freiberg: Herder, 1969); Joseph A. Fitzmyer, *The Gospel according to Luke (i–ix)* (Anchor Bible 28; Garden City, NY: Doubleday, 1981), 691; John Nolland, *Luke 1–9:20* (Word Biblical Commentary 35A; Dallas: Word, 1989), 357; Robert H. Stein, *Luke* (New American Commentary; Nashville: Broadman, 1992), 237; and Darrell L. Bock, *Luke 1:1–9:50* (Baker Exegetical Commentary on the New Testament 3A; Grand Rapids: Baker, 1994), 701–2.

altogether.[3] Jesus invites his upright host to draw the inference: "Which of them, then, will love him more?" Simon cautiously grasps the logic: "I suppose," he ventures, "the man forgiven the greater debt."

Even if we missed the hint in the creditor's inexplicable generosity that the topic is not a debt of denarii, but rather guilty humanity before God the judge, Jesus's mention of love reveals his real frame of reference. He asks not "Who will be more relieved?" nor even "Who will be more grateful?"[4] The question is: "Who will *love* his creditor-turned-benefactor more?" In the spiritual reality to which Jesus's simple story points, reckless grace binds beneficiary to benefactor with a bond stronger than debt or duty. What now moves the once-indebted recipient of grace is not a lingering sense of obligation, compelling efforts to repay, at least in part, so great a gift—as though the debt still stood on the books. The debt is canceled. No deficit remains to be repaid because the one to whom the debt was owed has fully absorbed the loss. The motive that such grace evokes is spontaneous, uncoerced love—a love that serves the beloved forgiver with a free abandon that neither guilt nor duty could engender.[5]

3. Joachim Jeremias, *The Parables of Jesus* (trans. S. H. Hooke; 2nd ed.; New York: Scribner, 1972), 145: "Surely a *rara avis* among creditors! Where may such a one be found? Clearly Jesus was speaking about God, of his inconceivable goodness."

4. Jeremias, ibid., 126–27, contends that Jesus's choice of the verb *love* was dictated by the absence of a word meaning (strictly) "thank, be grateful" in the Semitic languages spoken in first-century Palestine. Jeremias acknowledges, however, that in some contexts other Semitic verbs—"bless," for example—implied the emotion of gratitude. The selection of the deeply emotive "love" in the parable is primarily explained by the woman's un-self-conscious display of affection and adoration, which Jesus will characterize as great "love" in Luke 7:47.

5. John Piper, *Future Grace* (Sisters, OR: Multnomah, 1995), 31–39, critiques preachers' common appeal to gratitude for past grace as a motive for the pursuit of holiness. He contends that such a backward-looking focus too often produces a "debtor's ethic," in which believers are laden anew with a sense of obligation to "repay" God for his mercy. He makes the provocative (and in my judgment unpersuasive) claim: "The Bible rarely, if ever, explicitly makes gratitude the impulse of moral behavior, or ingratitude the explanation of immorality" (34). Texts such as Matt 18:21–35; 1 John 4:19; Rom 1:21; and Luke 7:36–50 spring to mind as counterevidence against this claim. Nevertheless, Piper rightly critiques those appeals to gratitude that turn reminders of past grace into implements of guilt and duty in order to compel believers' obedience. The genuine gratitude that flows from grace is not a duty or debt that we owe God (like writing thank-you notes for Christmas gifts to unknown great-aunts under our mother's watchful eye). Rather, when we discover Christ's startling mercy lavished on us, our hearts (like the sinful woman's) cannot help but brim over with love for the merciful one (and for others,

Of course Jesus, who knows humanity through and through, had no illusions about our capacity to respond wrongly to grace. Elsewhere he challenged the desire to curtail one's obligation to forgive others, telling a parable that exposes our schizophrenic capacity to cling to grievances against others' offenses even when we have received divine mercy beyond our comprehension (Matt 18:21–35). First-century listeners would have realized immediately the absurdity of the unforgiving servant's request for more time to repay his debt of tens of thousands of talents (18:26). Such an enormous debt would have taken many lifetimes to repay on a servant's (or even a satrap's) wages.[6] Even before the story describes his harsh severity toward his fellow servant, the source of his ruthless justice is revealed: the servant represents those who devalue their "debt" toward God until it seems manageable. As a consequence, they are unfazed by divine grace on the one hand, and on the other hand they are disinclined to extend mercy to fellow servants who are in their debt.

When, however, we see grace to be as gracious as it actually is, our hearts' reflex will be (not merely *ought* to be but *will* be) self-abandoning love. This is what dazzles us in the woman's treatment of Jesus. Jesus reasons back from visible effects to invisible cause.[7]

---

for his sake). Piper endorses true gratitude, in which "there is such a delight in the worth of God's past grace, that we are driven on to experience more and more of it in the future" (39). In his later work, *Counted Righteous in Christ* (Wheaton, IL: Crossway, 2002), Piper argues exegetically and pastorally that the assurance of God's approval, grounded in Christ's imputed righteousness, is the only and indispensable starting point that can stimulate and sustain holy living, motivated by love and hope.

6. Craig S. Keener, *A Commentary on the Gospel of Matthew* (Grand Rapids: Eerdmans, 1999), 458, estimates that ten thousand talents would have represented "30–100 million days' wages for an average peasant—no small amount of labor" and comments on "the impossibly unrealistic character of the debt and the characters' absurd folly." Robert H. Gundry, *Matthew: A Commentary on His Literary and Theological Art* (Grand Rapids: Eerdmans, 1982), 373, notes that even if the servant is portrayed as a king's satrap and the debt as taxes due his sovereign, the parable employs "the indefinite plural of the highest number used in reckoning" and therefore "cannot be calculated," like the American expression *zillions*.

7. Calvin says: "By these words [in Luke 7:47] . . . he does not make her love the cause, but the proof, of forgiveness of sins. For they are taken from the comparison of that debtor who was forgiven five hundred denarii; to him he did not say that they were forgiven because he loved much, but that he loved much because they were forgiven. . . . Her love, by which she gives thanks for his benefit, ought to have convinced you of the forgiveness of her sins" (*Institutes* 3.4.37). Contemporary Roman Catholic commentator Fitzmyer, *Luke*, 686–87,

Where one sees great love for Jesus, one can be sure that behind it—the root from which it springs, the fountain from which it flows—is great forgiveness, great grace. Jesus's parable suggests that the crucial act in the drama being played out at Simon's banquet has already occurred off stage.[8] The woman's tears are not tears of grief, guilt, shame, or despair. They are tears of sheer joy, tears of love for grace already received, forgiveness already granted, justification bestowed by Messiah, assuring her of God's welcome, her shameful past notwithstanding. Her exorbitant gift of ointment likewise expresses an uncoerced, unconstrained love evoked by God's sheer grace in Jesus.

By contrast, Simon's behavior toward Jesus and his attitude toward the woman exhibit no sense of having needed or received forgiveness of a debt of any serious magnitude. Of course Pharisees, like other Jews, were well aware that Scripture and experience indict all of sin, at least those inadvertent missteps for which the law provided sacrificial and cleansing rituals. Whether Simon's omissions at the start of the banquet—no water, no kiss, no oil—were rude or merely indifferent, they showed that, to Simon, Jesus was not worth the effort. And why, after all, should he consider Jesus worth the effort? Simon saw in himself no great need, no insurmountable debt that only Jesus could erase.

Yet the wonderful counselor promised through Isaiah 9:6–7 (MT 9:5–6) would not write off the Pharisee, any more than a welcoming father would refuse to go out to persuade a self-righteous older son who resented undeserved mercy and rejected the joy over the finding of the lost (Luke 15:28–32). The remedy for Simon's subtle idolatry is identical to the cure of the woman's flagrant lawlessness: only the discovery of profound guilt forgiven by utter grace can evoke

---

though acknowledging the antiquity of the interpretation that understands the woman's love as the condition of her pardon, concurs with Calvin's reasoning: "Consequently, it should rather be understood that the sinful woman comes to Jesus as one already forgiven by God and seeking to pour out signs of love and gratitude (tears, kisses, perfume); in this understanding, the love of v. 47b is the consequence of forgiveness, and v. 47c integrates the parable with the narrative."

8. Jeremias, *Parables of Jesus*, 126–27, infers, perhaps rightly, that Jesus would have preached at the banquet given in his honor by the Pharisee (a meritorious act performed for a distinguished teacher-prophet) and that the woman's faith in the forgiveness of her many sins had been evoked by Jesus's preaching.

extravagant, self-forgetful love for Jesus and love for others for Jesus's sake, as our second case study shows.

Case Study 2: Congregations in Conflict (Galatians)

The apostle Paul wrote his earthshaking epistle to the Galatians to address deeply conflicted congregations in central Asia Minor. He observed in the Galatian Christians a host of symptoms indicative of competitive rivalry and interpersonal hostility: they were "biting and devouring each other" (Gal 5:15 NIV), becoming "conceited, provoking and envying each other" (5:26 NIV).[9] Between these two statements the apostle contrasts the deeds and desires of the flesh (5:19–21) to the Spirit's desires and fruit (5:22–23). Competition bred by pride is the dominant motif in Paul's list of the "deeds of the flesh."[10] The list opens and closes with blatantly sensual and pagan vices, overt violations of the law's commandments: "impurity, debauchery, idolatry and witchcraft . . . drunkenness, orgies, and the like." These are the usual suspects, the sins that Paul's Judaizing opponents would expect to see in an inventory of Gentile depravity. At the core of the list, however, perhaps to the Judaizers' discomfort and to the Galatian believers' surprise, is an even longer series of attitudes expressive of competitive rivalry and hostility—"enmities, strife, jealousy, fits of rage, contention, dissensions, factions, envy"—those less visible but more corrosive habits of the heart that were disintegrating interpersonal relationships throughout the Galatian congregations. All such fleshly deeds, whether of body, speech, or thought processes, disqualify those characterized by them from inheritance in God's kingdom, from the blessing promised to Abraham's children (5:21; cf. 3:9, 14, 29; 4:30).

9. In sharp contrast to the aggressive behaviors indicted in Gal 5:15–26 is the apostle's instruction, immediately thereafter, that a person caught in sin should be restored "in a spirit of gentleness," with a humble awareness of one's own vulnerability to temptation (6:1 ESV). He goes on to insist that assessment of one's progress in holiness must be vis-à-vis oneself, rather than by comparison with others (6:4–5).

10. In the church at Corinth, where the spirit of rivalry manifested itself in allegiance to particular human leaders, Paul identified jealousy and discord as symptoms of "fleshliness" (1 Cor 3:1–3).

As master diagnostician, Paul recognized the spiritual disease by its symptoms: under the influence of teachers who claimed that law observance could complete the Gentiles' incorporation as Abraham's heirs (an incorporation begun through belief in the gospel), these believers were inadvertently shifting the weight of their reliance and basis of their boasting from Jesus back to themselves. Through the life-giving work of God's Spirit they had entered into covenant with the living God "by hearing with faith," when Jesus Christ was displayed as crucified in Paul's preaching (3:2 ESV). Having begun in the Spirit by relying on Christ, however, they subsequently succumbed to the plausible lie that their completion as Abraham's heirs could be achieved only by the flesh—by their own performance in adhering to God's commands (3:3). Paul could express only bewilderment at their "bewitchment" (3:1).

Paul's exegetical-theological argument in Galatians sharply contrasts alternative paths to justification and resurrection life: the path characterized by faith in God's promise and the dynamic of the Spirit over against the path characterized by doing "all things written in the Book of the Law" in reliance on the flesh (3:10 ESV). The former secures not only vindication and life, but also the status of sons and heirs as Abraham's promised seed; and it does so for believers of all nationalities, without distinction (3:6–9, 13–14, 26–29). The latter produces curse and death (3:10–12) because the law, though revealing God's holy character and the corresponding obligation of his servants, lacks the power to reverse our spiritual death and enable our compliance with its requirements: "For if a law had been given that could give life, then righteousness would indeed be by the law" (3:21 ESV).

Paul makes two shocking hermeneutical moves to dramatize how alien to the gospel of Christ is a soteriology that shifts the ground of assurance as believers move from the initiation of life in Christ by faith in God's promise to maturation by means of compliance to commandments. First, he identifies the law's commands with the enslaving obligations that the Gentiles have experienced in pagan idolatry, referring to both within a few sentences of each other as "elementary principles" (στοιχεῖα) that enslave (4:3, 9). This term is rare in the Pauline corpus (also in Col 2:8, 20) and the New Testament (Heb 5:12; 2 Pet 3:10, 12). In Galatians 4 Paul applies it first to the law and soon thereafter to the nongods that the Galatians had served prior to faith in order to draw these two religious systems, apparently so different from each other, together under a single categorization. It is common in recent New Testament studies to interpret Paul's use of στοιχεῖα as referring to malevolent spiritual beings and to support this identification by noting Paul's declaration in Colossians 2:15 (between the two occurrences of στοιχεῖα in that epistle) that Christ's death both erased the legal charges against us and disarmed the "rulers and authorities."[11] Even in the context of Colossians, however, the immediate contexts of στοιχεῖα suggest that it refers to human traditions (παράδοσιν τῶν ἀνθρώπων) (2:8) and regulations (δογματίζεσθε) (2:20) rather than to superhuman spirits. In Galatians the law's custodial role in the history of redemption until the arrival of Christ, the object of faith (Gal 3:23), is explained by analogy to the tutors and managers who control an heir as long as he is a minor, making his daily experience like slavery (4:1–2). In this connection Paul describes the law's commands as "elemental principles," that is, controls appropriate to the heir's minority rather than the epoch of maturity and investiture.[12] Now that Messiah has arrived—and with him the era of the heir's liberation—to seek spiritual security in commandment keeping is tantamount to returning to the idols whom the Galatians once sought to placate by their own performance.

Certainly as to their ethical content Paul would never equate the law given by God at Sinai ("holy and righteous and good"; Rom 7:12 ESV) with the Galatians' pre-Christian pagan practices, when they were "enslaved to those that by nature are not gods" (Gal 4:8 ESV). Yet he daringly implies that the Galatians' submission to circumcision (and consequent obligation to keep the whole law; 5:3) as the condition of continuing in covenantal status would entail a "return" to the "weak and worthless" elements that they had left when they turned from idols to Christ Jesus. Since the law was never designed by its

11. See, e.g., the brief discussion in Timothy George, *Galatians* (New American Commentary; Nashville: Broadman & Holman, 1994), 298–99.

12. F. F. Bruce, *The Epistle to the Galatians: A Commentary on the Greek Text* (New International Greek Testament Commentary; Grand Rapids: Eerdmans, 1982), 193: "Whatever else may be said of these στοιχεῖα, they plainly include the law, in the sense of 3:23 (which refers to the same situation): 'Before faith came, we were guarded ὑπὸ νόμον.'"

giver to impart life to fallen human beings, to try to use it as a means of justification is to distort it into an implement of idolatry—to deify one's own obedience as a rival redeemer and justifier in competition to God's provision in the Messiah.

Paul's second move is equally daring: he identifies law reliance with Ishmael, the rejected son born of Abraham's flesh-bound union with the concubine Hagar (Gal 4:21–31). Paul's symbolic interpretation of Genesis 16 and Genesis 21 links Ishmael, the slave woman's son, with Sinai and "the present Jerusalem," capital of the Jewish establishment that had spurned the Messiah Jesus in favor of Torah, temple, and tradition (Gal 4:25). Ishmael was the son born of "flesh" not because sexual intercourse produced his conception (Sarah would conceive in the same way), but because he represents the way of attaining God's promise through *efforts within human capacity and control* rather than through utter reliance upon God's power to confer his promised blessing, which lies utterly beyond human resources, strategies, and efforts. By contrast, Isaac is aptly described as the product of divine promise and the Spirit (who, Paul notes in Rom 4:17, 19, imparts resurrection life to the reproductively dead Abraham and Sarah). Like Isaac, Christian believers are born by Spirit-wrought faith in God's promise and are the free sons[13] who inherit the fullness of covenant blessing promised to Abraham (Gal 4:28–31). The Ishmael/Isaac, flesh/Spirit contrast lays the foundation upon which Paul distinguishes the flesh's divisive deeds from the Spirit's graceful fruit in Galatians 5:16–24.

By making believers' status and tenure in God's favor contingent on their own fidelity in covenant keeping (with divine assistance), the Judaizers' so-called gospel sowed seeds of insecurity or pride or both in Gentile Christians' hearts; and these seeds inevitably germinated into expressions of competition and rivalry, the very antitheses of "faith working through love" (5:6 ESV). Such manifestations of the flesh, no less than libertine sensuality, disqualify people from God's kingdom (5:21). A little reflection clarifies why this is so. When one's assurance of divine approval becomes contingent on one's own track

13. In Christ male and female share equally in the sonship privilege as heirs of the Abrahamic blessing (Gal 3:26–28).

record of obedience (even grace-assisted, leniently assessed obedience),[14] it is natural to seek reassurance of one's spiritual standing through comparison and contrast with the perceived maturity and performance of others.

14. Some federal-vision advocates draw a distinction between God's "strict" justice, which only Christ's perfection can satisfy, and God's "fatherly" assessment, which accepts our less-than-perfect obedience, calling it "pleasing" and "good." Rich Lusk, for example, asserts: "The final declaration God passes over us at the last day will be in accordance with the pattern of life we have lived. There will be a congruence between the life we have lived and the final verdict we receive. Those who have lived lives of faith—meaning lives characterized at their core by loyalty to God—will be justified. . . . The good works believers have done will not merit final justification, but . . . there will be a *basic match* between the verdict rendered and the life lived"; "Faith, Baptism, and Justification," http://www.hornes.org/theologia/content/rich_lusk/faith_baptism_and_justification.htm (accessed August 12, 2004) (emphasis original). In another essay Lusk attempts to soften the daunting prospect of final judgment based on our works: "The Bible nowhere says God will apply absolute justice at the last day. . . . The only places where God enforces strict justice are the cross and hell. For the covenant people, at least, it seems God will use 'fatherly justice' in the final judgment, not 'absolute justice.' He will judge us the way parents evaluate their child's art work, or the way a new husband assesses the dinner his beloved wife has made. The standard will be soft and generous because God is merciful"; "Future Justification to the Doers of the Law," http://www.hornes.org/theologia/content/rich_lusk/future_justification_to_the_doers_of_the_law.htm (accessed August 12, 2004). The problem, however, is that this "soft" paternal "justice," which cuts us some slack in consideration of our weakness, tames and compromises both justice and grace. This kinder, gentler justice approves us as "righteous" as long as we stay loyal—that is, as long as we do not apostatize by abandoning the visible church, but it also introduces our works (all to God's glory and even with the Spirit's assistance, of course!) into the equation that yields our ultimate vindication. Repudiating the word and concept of "merit" as utterly alien to biblical, covenantal thought, federal vision nevertheless insists that believers' behavior must be "congruent with" a justifying declaration of God. It is, however, precisely the point of Jesus's parable of the two debtors in Luke 7 that *only* a lively awareness that our enormous debt, infinitely beyond our capacity to repay, has been forgiven and altogether eliminated can motivate us to serve God out of sheer love, with no ulterior motive (e.g., quelling insecure fears of divine rejection, placing God under obligation by our perseverance in covenant keeping). When the question "why obey?" is approached from the perspective that biblical covenants have two parts, promise *and* command—one for each party (which is true enough)—or from the angle that covenant blessing is *contingent on our fulfilling* the "conditions" of the covenant (either making faith the first condition that we must fulfill, to be accompanied by repentance, new obedience, and church membership, or else expanding the definition of faith in such a way that believers are led to rely, in some sense, both on Jesus's sacrifice and on their own response in repentant obedience and membership), what is obscured is the logic of Jesus's parable and of the woman's service: she did not bring her lavish gift or weep over Jesus's feet out of a sense that these were conditions of the covenant that she needed to keep on fulfilling in order to receive, or even to continue in, the blessing of forgiveness. To speak of conditions to be satisfied misrepresents the whole psychological dynamic that Jesus's parable exposed: it is precisely when our creditor shows himself *so utterly gracious as to absorb our debt* himself, fulfilling the conditions of our liberation from indebtedness, that love (and hence obedience and service) is evoked *inevitably and spontaneously* in the heart of those who discover that they have received such utterly undeserved grace.

By contrast, Paul asserts an alternative that is counterintuitive to the unbelieving heart (whether legalist or libertine). Legalist and libertine agree with each other that, unless one believes that God's approval or rejection is contingent on one's behavior, no plausible motive exists for obeying God's commands. The legalist hears God's summons to pursue holiness (law) and reasons that one *must* obey because God's acceptance is contingent on one's own obedience. The libertine hears God's assurance of forgiveness (gospel) and reasons that, inasmuch as God's acceptance is not contingent on one's own obedience, no one *needs* to obey. Christ's apostle, however, is privy to a stronger, deeper motive that is hidden from legalist and libertine hearts: spontaneous love, the fruit of the Spirit (Gal 5:22).

The Spirit conveys this response of love to our hearts through the gospel of Christ's death and resurrection, the message that the Galatians first heard with faith (3:2). As the reality and implications of our union with Christ in his crucifixion and resurrection increasingly control believers' self-perception, the magnitude of our guilt undercuts the plausibility of our pride: in Paul's terms, all "boasts" are silenced except boasting in the Lord (Gal 6:14; cf. Rom 3:27; 1 Cor 1:31).

Those who have been "crucified with Christ" (Gal 2:20) know that their most shameful secrets are displayed to public view on his cross. Yet our union with Christ in his cross also overwhelms us with the magnitude of divine grace. The law rightly cursed everyone who failed to keep its every command (Gal 3:10, citing Deut 27:26). Grace shocks us when God's anointed, the only law keeper, became the cursed one hanged on a tree (Gal 3:13, citing Deut 21:23), particularly when we are told that as he did he redeemed us from the law's curse and secured for us the blessing of Abraham, the promised Spirit (Gal 3:14). Christ's cross simultaneously broadcasts that we *cannot* rely on our "doing" (flawed as it is) and that we *need* not, for God has provided the surrogate covenant keeper and covenant curse bearer.

It is also believers' union with Christ in his *resurrection* that grounds an assurance that silences both our insecurities and our boasts. Although the cross occupies center stage in Galatians, elsewhere in the Pauline corpus the "centrality of the resurrection" emerges.[15] With respect to Jesus, the resurrection constituted his own "justification" (ἐδικαιώθη) (1 Tim 3:16)—that is, the just judge's declaration that Jesus, having kept the covenant's stipulations flawlessly, is qualified to claim the reward of the righteous, the life of the age to come. Whereas Jesus's violent death under curse was the consequence of his vicarious identification with sinners, his resurrection constituted the Father's certification of and reward for Jesus's personal innocence and perfect fidelity to the law of the covenant.

Jesus's resurrection constituted justification-vindication not only for himself but also for those who are united to him by faith: "Who was handed over [to death] because of our transgressions and was raised because of our justification" (Rom 4:25). In Romans 5 Paul immediately elaborates this compact articulation of the union of Christ with his own, demonstrating why his death has removed our transgressions, and his resurrection—the perpetual witness to his perfect obedience (so Richard Gaffin)[16]—has secured our justification. The reconciliation with God that Christians already experience through Christ's death confirms a fortiori our confident expectation of future, eschatological salvation through his life—that is, through the resurrection life into which he has entered and which he imparts preliminarily to believers by the Spirit (5:9–11). Paul then exposes the covenantal basis of his logic in the comparison and contrast that he draws between Adam and Christ (5:12–21). In both cases a specific response to the divine sovereign's revealed will entails both a legal verdict (guilty or righteous) and a sanction commensurate with the verdict (death or life): just as transgression leads to condemnation (5:16, 18–19) and so to death (5:15, 17), so obedience leads to righteousness (5:16, 18–19) and so to life (5:17–18). Adam's transgression, his breach of the original covenant, justly warranted the verdict of condemnation and the penalty of death for all for whom he acted.

15. Richard B. Gaffin Jr., *The Centrality of the Resurrection: A Study in Paul's Soteriology* (Grand Rapids: Baker, 1978).

16. Ibid., 122: "Consequently, the eradication of death in his resurrection is nothing less than the removal of the verdict of condemnation and the effective affirmation of his (adamic) righteousness. His resurrected state is the reward and seal which testifies perpetually to his perfect obedience."

Because a parallel covenantal-representative relationship binds Christ with those for whom he acts, Christ's obedience warranted the verdict of justification and the commensurate blessing ("reward," as Gaffin aptly calls it) of life—the resurrection life of the age to come. The juxtaposition of death to life throughout this paragraph demonstrates that by the word *life* Paul refers to nothing less than resurrection life. The alternative outcomes announced by Moses—"I have set before you life and death, blessings and curses" (Deut 30:19 NIV)—have been raised to eschatological dimensions. Paul's compact description of the outcome of Christ's righteous action at the end of Romans 5:18, "[leading] to justification of life" (εἰς δικαίωσιν ζωῆς), should therefore be understood as commentary on "he was raised because of our justification [διὰ τῆν δικαίωσιν ἡμῶν]" (4:25). For Paul, Christ's resurrection constitutes the Father's declaration that he had perfectly fulfilled the covenant servant's obligation to express comprehensive loyalty to the sovereign in immaculate obedience to the stipulations of the covenant. Moreover, Christ's resurrection constitutes the Father's declaration that in Christ's obedience on our behalf we too have fulfilled the stipulations of the covenant and are thereby entitled (for Jesus's sake) to vindication in resurrection.[17]

17. The conjunctions drawn by Paul between disobedience, condemnation, and death on the one hand and obedience, justification, and resurrection life on the other should be noted particularly because some who now challenge the classic Reformation understanding of justification as including the imputation of Christ's righteousness to believers contend that for Paul Christ's death and *resurrection*, rather than Christ's death and *active obedience* to the obligations enjoined by the law, constitute the ground of Christians' justification. Norman Shepherd, for example, pointedly contrasts the Reformed emphasis on Christ's active obedience in justification to Paul's statement in Rom 4:25, contending that for Paul justification consists only in the forgiveness of sins; "Justification by Faith in Pauline Theology," in *Backbone of the Bible: Covenant in Contemporary Perspective* (ed. P. Andrew Sandlin; Nacogdoches, TX: Covenant Media, 2004), 86. Shepherd consequently reduces the role of Christ's resurrection in our justification (Rom 4:25) to God's certification "that the penalty for sin has been paid in full and that therefore the justice of God has been satisfied" (88). "His resurrection on the third day testifies to the efficacy of this atoning sacrifice" (89). Consistent with this exclusive focus of justification on forgiveness, Shepherd contends that in Rom 5:18–19 Christ's obedience, set in contrast to Adam's disobedience, consists only of his atoning sacrifice (88). Paul, however, sees Christ as doing far more for his own than removing from them the condemnation and curse earned by Adam, restoring us to the legal status of Adam in innocence. Despite the parallelism in the structure of covenantal representation, Paul insists that God's gift far surpasses the effects of Adam's trespass. The Adam/Christ contrast in Rom 5 shows that, just as Adam's transgression constituted the ground of the negative verdict (condemnation) and the penalty (death) that has fallen on those he represented, so Christ's obedience (not only as

How, then, does such assurance grounded wholly in Christ's work (in Galatians, preeminently in the cross) work its way out in application to the conflicts that threaten to tear apart the Galatian churches? Paul's gospel does not breed passivity or quietism. Rather, he appeals to believers' new, grace-given identity in order to spur them on toward attitudes and actions consistent with who they are in Christ, by grace and through faith. Because believers have been crucified with Christ (Gal 2:20), they have crucified the flesh with its passions and desires—preeminently, in this context, its passion and desire for superiority over others (5:24; cf. 6:14). Because they are children born, like Isaac, of Spirit rather than flesh (4:21–31), they must march along with (στοιχῶμεν) the Spirit rather than return to reliance on the flesh to commend themselves to the Father (5:25). In fact, only the Spirit's sovereign power to enliven and transform keeps the assurance that flows from justification from degenerating into complacency and license, for apart from the Spirit's work we would remain ungrateful even in the face of overwhelming grace. As our hearts, however, are saturated with the gospel of grace, the Spirit bears his sweet fruit (5:22–23) in our lives, not by inducing us to a nervous (or overconfident) attempt to fulfill the conditions of the covenant but by deepening our faith, which operates in love (5:6).

Paul's counsel regarding the attitude and approach to be adopted when a fellow believer is caught in sin illustrates the difference that gospel-grounded assurance makes in our relationships with others (6:1–5). Paul addresses "you the spiritual ones" (ὑμεῖς οἱ πνευματικοί) not to distinguish a mature subgroup from others in the Galatian churches but rather to call *all* believers to recognize their identity as those born of the Spirit (4:28–29), living by the Spirit and walking with the Spirit (5:25). Secure in the Father's favor, they need not and must not see another's sin as an occasion for comparison or boasting over the fallen (6:4). Humbled by the cross's exposure of their sin, they will recognize their own vulnerability to be tempted, either by the sin that ensnared their brother or by the pride that sees itself as impregnable against temptation (6:1, 3). Instead of keeping their dis-

curse bearer but also as obedient covenant keeper) constitutes the ground of both the justifying verdict and the resurrection life that rewards righteousness, both for Jesus and—by amazingly gracious imputation—also for his people.

tance in individualistic isolation, "the spiritual ones" will be so moved by the Savior who gave himself to redeem them that they shoulder the burden that crushes the sinner (6:2), fulfilling Christ's law: "You shall love your neighbor as yourself" (5:14). Instead of standing apart in indifference or standing over in judgmentalism, they will reach down to restore in the Spirit of gentleness (ἐν πνεύματι πραΰτητος),[18] as their master was gentle (Matt 11:29), not breaking bruised reeds or snuffing out flickering wicks (12:20).[19]

Historic Wisdom on the Cure of Souls Grounded in Justification

The investigations of Luke 7 and the epistle to the Galatians offered above seek to trace a connection between justification and the Christian's motivation to pursue change toward holiness. That relation, however, is counterintuitive: Can we really be stirred to strive against sin and for purity by being assured that our acceptance before God is *not* contingent on such striving or succeeding? Such a paradoxical claim may seem unrealistic to those who confront sin's intransigence. Some may think that the classic doctrine breeds antinomianism and thereby obstructs rather than supporting the pastor's task to shepherd people toward Christ-like holiness. The Reformed tradition provides answers to this reservation.

John Calvin (1509–64)

By the middle of the sixteen century the Council of Trent (1546–63) had pronounced its anathema on anyone who says "that by faith alone the impious is justified; in such wise as to mean that nothing else is required to cooperate in order to the obtaining of the grace of justi-

18. English versions generally imply that Paul enjoins simply an attitude ("spirit") of gentleness, but Paul's original readers would understand this expression in light of the immediately preceding verses: "The fruit of the Spirit is . . . gentleness [πραΰτης]" (Gal 5:22–23) and the implicit reference to the Spirit in "the spiritual ones" (οἱ πνευματικοί) in the same sentence (6:1).

19. Paul's "burden bearing" metaphor parallels—and may intentionally echo—Jesus's metaphor of burdens and the yoke in Matt 11:28–29.

fication, and that it is not in any way necessary that he be prepared and disposed by the movement of his own will" (session 6, canon 9) and on anyone who says "that men are justified, either by the sole imputation of the justice of Christ or by the sole remission of sins, to the exclusion of the grace and the charity that is poured forth in their hearts by the Holy Ghost and is inherent in them, or even that the grace, whereby we are justified, is only the favour of God" (session 6, canon 11).[20] Rome thus insisted that justification should be considered contingent not only on Christ's sacrifice and obedience *on behalf of* the believer but also on the Spirit's work of subjective transformation *within* the believer. Only by including the Christian's grace-wrought works in the justification transaction could antinomianism be avoided and could ongoing effort in sanctification be motivated.

Calvin's response to the Roman critics was not to declare the subjective transformation of believers unnecessary. In fact, Calvin began his discussion of "the way in which we receive the grace of Christ" by insisting that "as long as Christ remains outside of us, and we are separated from him, all that he has suffered and done for the salvation of the human race remains useless and of no value to us" (*Institutes* 3.1.1). He went on to affirm that the faith by which God justifies us

> embraces Christ, as offered to us by the Father—that is, since he is offered not only for righteousness, forgiveness of sins, and peace, but also for sanctification and the fountain of the water of life—without a doubt, no one can duly know him without at the same time apprehending the sanctification of the Spirit. . . . Christ cannot be known apart from the sanctification of his Spirit. It follows that faith can in no wise be separated from a devout disposition. (*Institutes* 3.2.8)

He also wrote:

> Now, both repentance and forgiveness of sins—that is, newness of life and free reconciliation—are conferred on us by Christ, and both

20. *Dogmatic Canons and Decrees: Authorized Translations of the Council of Trent, the Decree on the Immaculate Conception, the Syllabus of Pope Pius IX, and the Decrees of the Vatican Council* (1912; repr. Rockford, IL: Tan, 1977), 51–52 (session 6 in 1547).

> are attained by us through faith. . . . Man is justified by faith alone, and simple pardon; nevertheless actual holiness of life, so to speak, is not separated from free imputation of righteousness. (*Institutes* 3.3.1)[21]

For Calvin, Rome's error lay not in insisting that justification and holiness of life are inseparable, but rather in Rome's reversing of the biblical order and logic of the application of Christ's benefits: "For the teaching of the Schoolmen, that love is prior to faith and hope, is mere madness; for it is faith alone that first engenders love in us" (*Institutes* 3.2.41).[22] It is the "taste" of God's goodness that kindles love for God in return: "For truly, that abundant sweetness which God has stored up for those who fear him cannot be known without at the same time powerfully moving us. And once anyone has been moved by it, it utterly ravishes him and draws him to itself" (3.2.41).[23] God's justifying declaration coincides *temporally* with the initiation of our sanctification as the Spirit unites us to Christ by faith, but justification's *logical* priority is essential for believers' assurance and thus for our hope and motivation in the lifelong process of mortification (to sin) and vivification (to God): "The Lord freely justifies his own *in order that* he may at the same time restore them to true righteousness by sanctification of his Spirit" (3.3.19, emphasis added).

Calvin applied the faith-to-love, justification-to-sanctification order of the gospel to the challenge of sustaining motivation as we pursue holiness in the Christian life (*Institutes* 3.6.3). Specifically in response to the objection that justification by faith alone stifles zeal

21. Cf. *Institutes* 3.11.2: "Therefore, we explain justification simply as the acceptance with which God receives us into his own favor as righteous men. And we say that it consists in the remission of sins and the imputation of Christ's righteousness." Regarding the role of faith (versus our love, which in other contexts Paul ranks over faith; 1 Cor 13:13; Col 3:14) in justification, Calvin observes (*Institutes* 3.18.8): "The power of justifying, which faith possesses, does not lie in any worth of works. Our justification rests upon God's mercy alone and Christ's merit, and faith, when it lays hold of justification, is said to justify. . . . We say that faith justifies, not because it merits righteousness for us by its own worth, but because it is an instrument whereby we obtain free the righteousness of Christ."

22. Cf. Trent's decree on justification (session 6, canons 5–6); *Dogmatic Canons and Decrees*, 26–29.

23. Note also Calvin's interpretation (*Institutes* 3.4.37) of the causal order—forgiveness to love—in the woman of Luke 7, cited above.

for good works, Calvin alleged that no "sharper spurs" can be found to arouse Christians to holy living "than those derived from the end of our redemption and calling," alluding to various biblical passages in which believers are summoned to lives of love and purity by such inducements as the love of him "who first loved us," the cleansing of our consciences by Christ's blood, our deliverance from our enemies, our union with Christ in his death and resurrection, and so on (3.16.2). Calvin summarized: "All the apostles are full of exhortations, urgings, and reproofs with which to instruct the man of God in every good work, and that without mention of merit. Rather, they derive their most powerful exhortations from the thought that our salvation stands upon no merit of ours but solely upon God's mercy" (3.16.3). Pastoral counseling in the mold of the apostles builds its rationale for repentance and renewed obedience on the foundation of faith's assurance in God's freely granted and irreversible gift of righteousness, for Jesus's sake.

Guido de Brès (1522–67) and the Belgic Confession (1561)

Two years after the publication of the final Latin edition of Calvin's *Institutes of the Christian Religion*, Guido de Brès published the Belgic Confession on behalf of persecuted Protestants in the Low Countries of Western Europe (now Belgium and the Netherlands). Among its purposes was to affirm to the Roman Catholic monarch Philip II these churches' political submission and also their strong commitment to biblical orthodoxy as defined in their confession. Six years later de Brès himself would be among those who laid down their lives for the sake of the Reformed articulation of the gospel.

Belgic Confession 24, "The Sanctification of Sinners," immediately follows its articles on the righteousness of faith (22) and on justification (23). Article 22 states that saving faith "embraces Jesus Christ, with all his merits, and no longer looks for anything apart from him," emphasizing that reliance on anything within ourselves to commend us to God implies the insufficiency of Christ and his redeeming work. Article 24 therefore pointedly addresses the objection that the Reformed understanding of faith and justification, by excluding the believer's inherent love and good deeds from the transaction, vitiates the motivation to resist sin and pursue conformity to Christ. Like Calvin, the Belgic Confession insists that saving faith is life transforming:

> We believe that this true faith, produced in man by the hearing of God's Word and by the work of the Holy Spirit, regenerates him and makes him a "new man," causing him to live the "new life," and freeing him from the slavery of sin. Therefore, far from making people cold toward living in a pious and holy way, this justifying faith, quite to the contrary, so works within them that apart from it they will never do a thing out of love for God but only out of love for themselves and fear of being condemned. So then, it is impossible for this holy faith to be unfruitful in a human being, seeing that we do not speak of an empty faith but of what Scripture calls "faith working through love," which leads a man to do by himself the works that God has commanded in his Word.

The Belgic Confession implies that Rome's soteriology, by making the individual's justification partially contingent on his own (admittedly grace-assisted) efforts, excludes the only motivation that could ever make a human deed good: love for God. As long as the prospect of divine approval for obedience and divine condemnation for disobedience remain in the picture, self-love and fear remain the driving forces that compel a form of compliance to God's will. Only the purely gracious justification (both atonement of sins and imputation of righteousness) that *removes* one's personal performance as a condition for divine approval produces a genuinely *theocentric* motive for keeping God's commands (grateful love) through the life-producing Spirit of God, God's gift to those who are justified once for all in his Son:

> So then, we do good works but not for merit—for what would we merit? Rather, we are indebted to God for the good works we do, and not he to us, since it is he who "works in us both to will and do according to his good pleasure"—thus keeping in mind what is written: "When you have done all that is commanded you, then you shall say, "We are unworthy servants; we have done what it was our duty to do." . . .

> Moreover, although we do good works we do not base our salvation on them; for we cannot do any work that is not defiled by our flesh and also worthy of punishment. And even if we could point to one, memory of a single sin is enough for God to reject that work. So we would always be in doubt, tossed back and forth without any certainty, and our poor consciences would be tormented constantly if they did not rest on the merit of the suffering and death of our Savior.[24]

Both the awareness that genuinely good works (which spring from trust in Christ and express gratitude to him) are themselves gifts of God's Spirit and the awareness that our best works still bear the stain of our fallenness preclude any reliance on our performance before God's tribunal. Nevertheless, both the insecure apprehension of rejection and the self-confident expectation of reward have been replaced by a new, stronger, and infinitely better motive: love that obeys God for God's sake, not for ours.

The Marrow of Modern Divinity (1627–55)

Emphasis on the freeness of divine grace was misunderstood by some in the seventeenth century as license for antinomian indulgence, which in turn provoked a strongly legalistic reaction from others—although it was a legalism expressed in language heavily laced with grace (as Trent had articulated Rome's position a century before).

The pseudonymous *Marrow of Modern Divinity*, published the same year as the Westminster Confession of Faith, is structured as a four-way conversation among Neophytus (a new Christian), Nomista (a legalist), Antinomista (an antinomian), and Evangelista (a minister of the true gospel).[25] This cast of characters reveals the *Marrow's* purpose to distinguish the biblical gospel from antinomianism on the one hand and from legalism on the other, as well as its pastoral concern

24. *Ecumenical Creeds and Reformed Confessions* (Grand Rapids: CRC, 1987), 101–2.

25. *The Marrow of Modern Divinity*, with notes by Thomas Boston (1726; repr. Swengel, PA: Reiner, 1978).

to guard young believers from the spiritual dangers associated with either extreme.[26]

The *Marrow* was intended to clarify the relationship between saving faith, justification, and obedience to God's commands as the Christian's responsibility in sanctification. Most relevant to the topic at hand is the recurring theme that the only source capable of evoking a genuinely loving obedience to God is confidence in God's promise of forgiveness and right standing, secured by Christ's work and freely given by faith in Christ alone. In answer to Nomista's insistence that repentance (understood as reformation of life) must precede faith, the *Marrow* argued that "the repentant sinner first believes" that God will keep his promise, then after that "cometh alteration of life."[27] Repentance is not an "antecedent of faith," but rather a "consequent." Only believers love God, and it is God's love that "constrains him in Christ."[28]

When Antinomista attempts to excuse himself from obedience to God's commands by observing that the good deeds of many people are self-deceiving, Evangelista concurs that the danger of self-deception is real but insists that Christians will not deceive themselves if they always evaluate their obedience in relation to Christ. A Christian reckons that his sanctity flows "from the habits of grace within him," which in turn flow from his justification, and that from faith "given and embracing Jesus Christ."[29]

Despite the attempt of the *Marrow* to show how the biblical gospel is to be distinguished both from legalism and from antinomian-

26. One example of the pastoral wisdom of the *Marrow* is Nomista's monologue narrating his progressively deepening understanding of the law's demands, from focusing on consistency in devotional practices and visible behavioral reform; to focusing on fervent inward devotion, rigorous self-examination, and confession of sin; to discovering deeper flaws in his obedience as well as the self-centeredness of his motivation. Yet at every stage Nomista reports that ministers reassured him that his accomplishment was sufficient and should satisfy his conscience. The last minister he consulted responded, "Do not fear; for the best of Christians have their failings and no man keepeth the law of God perfectly; and therefore go on, and do as you have done, in striving to keep the law perfectly; and in what you cannot do, God will accept the will for the deed; and wherein you come short, Christ will help you out." Yet such counselors could not quiet the legalist's uneasy conscience (*Marrow of Modern Divinity*, 87–91).

27. Ibid., 145–46.

28. Ibid., 150.

29. Ibid., 187–88.

ism,[30] unease and tension persisted in the English-speaking churches descended from the Reformation.[31]

Thomas Chalmers (1780–1847)

Early in the nineteenth century the preaching of Church of Scotland pastor Thomas Chalmers (later professor of theology at Edinburgh University) stimulated the congregation of St. George's Tron in Glasgow to apply their Christian faith to the growing urban problems being created by the Industrial Revolution and the rampant commercialization of society. His summons to culture-permeating reform, unlike that of the American social gospel in the same century, was grounded in the grace of the gospel—specifically, in the assurance

30. A recent articulation of how the gospel stands over against both legalism and antinomianism is found in one of the foundational statements of Redeemer Presbyterian Church in New York City. Timothy J. Keller explores the implications of the Pauline expression live "in line with the truth of the gospel" (Gal 2:14 NIV), arguing and illustrating that "the Christian life is a process of renewing every dimension of our life—spiritual, psychological, corporate, social—by thinking, hoping, and living out the 'lines' or ramifications of the gospel. The gospel is to be applied to every area of thinking, feeling, relating, working and behaving. . . . All of us, to some degree, live around the truth of the gospel but do not 'get' it. So the key to continual and deeper spiritual renewal and revival is the continual re-discovery of the gospel." Keller proceeds to contrast the gospel with two rivals: religion (moralism, legalism) and irreligion (hedonism, relativism). Both of the rivals are "ways to avoid Jesus as Savior and keep control of their lives," either through strenuous effort to establish one's own moral superiority (religion/moralism) or through a dismissal of the normativity of God's standards and the consequent elimination of one's need for the gospel's radical solution to human guilt (irreligion/relativism). See Timothy J. Keller, "The Centrality of the Gospel," http://www.redeemer2.com/resources/papers/centrality.pdf (accessed January 17, 2005).

31. From the late seventeenth century, in the context of the moralism of Latitudinarian preaching after the restoration of the English monarchy, comes Walter Marshall's *The Gospel Mystery of Sanctification* (1692; repr. Lafayette, IN: Sovereign Grace, 2001), a little-known but powerful restatement of the power of justification-based assurance to motivate growth in sanctification. Marshall's classic has been paraphrased into modern English by Bruce H. McRae under the title *The Gospel Mystery of Sanctification: Growing in Holiness by Living in Union with Christ* (Eugene, OR: Wipf & Stock, 2005). Taking account of the apprehension of some that salvation "by free grace without works" would dampen zeal and promote carelessness in religion (40), Marshall contended that to make any progress toward holiness one must be "well persuaded of our reconciliation with God. . . . And in this I include the great benefit of justification, as the means by which we are reconciled to God, which is described in Scripture, either by forgiving our sins, or by the imputation of righteousness to us (Rom 4:5–7); because both are contained in one and the same justifying act" (14). On the tension between evangelical and legalistic emphases in sanctification as it continued into the eighteenth century in the Church of Scotland, see David C. Lachman, *The Marrow Controversy, 1718–1723: An Historical and Theological Analysis* (Edinburgh: Rutherford, 1988).

of God's gracious acceptance and approval—and based wholly on Christ's redemptive work and received only by faith.

Among Chalmers's most well-known sermons is "The Expulsive Power of a New Affection," which he opens by positing two contrasting strategies for turning people away from sinful desires. The first strategy, that of demonstrating that "the world's" attractions are deceitful and destructive of those who set their hearts on them, can never effect lasting change for the simple reason that it does nothing more than create an affection vacuum in the human heart. To be told, even persuaded, that clinging to a particular pattern of sin or self-righteousness is futile and self-destructive will not, in itself, free the heart from that pattern's allure and control, as both pastors and their counselees can sadly attest.

Only the second strategy, which replaces affection for sin with a new and stronger affection for an infinitely more delightful object, can supply the motivation that sustains ongoing pursuit of holiness. The overwhelming beauty of a "new affection," the discovery of a manifestly more attractive object of desire and occasion of delight, easily displaces the inferior appeal of sin. The transformation of desire that leads to a new course of life, which the law's warnings and prohibitions could not effect, is produced by God's Spirit through the sweetness of the gospel's promise and the assurance of the Father's welcome for Jesus's sake:

> The best way of casting out an impure affection is to admit a pure one; and by the love of what is good to expel the love of what is evil. Thus it is, that the freer gospel, the more sanctifying is the gospel; and the more it is received as a doctrine of grace, the more will it be felt as a doctrine according to godliness. . . . It is only when, as in the gospel, acceptance is bestowed as a present, without money and without price, that the security which man feels in God is placed beyond the reach of disturbance, or that he can repose in Him as one friend reposes in another, . . . the one party rejoicing over the other to do him good, the other finding that the truest gladness of his heart lies in the impulse of a gratitude by which it is awakened to the charms of a new moral existence. Salvation by grace—salvation by free grace—salvation not of works, but according to the mercy of God, salvation on such a footing is not more indispensable to

> the deliverance of our persons from the hand of justice than it is to the deliverance of our hearts from the chill and the weight of ungodliness.[32]

The same utterly gracious grace that erases our guilt, silencing our accusing consciences as it satisfies divine justice, sets our hearts free to pursue joyful holiness in fearless love for the God who has lavished love on us.[33]

Conclusion

Daunting challenges confront pastors in their care for God's people. What does the pastor say to defuse the pent-up resentment that separates a husband and a wife who once vowed to be one throughout

32. Thomas Chalmers, "The Expulsive Power of a New Affection," in *The Selected Works of Thomas Chalmers* (New York: Carter, 1848), 4.271–78.

33. The same insistence on gospel-driven, grace-drawn sanctification was articulated by one of Chalmers's Edinburgh theology students, Horatius Bonar (1809–99), who served as a pastor in the Church of Scotland and a founder of the Free Church in the Great Disruption of 1843. Bonar not only authored well-known hymns extolling divine grace ("Not What These Hands Have Done," "Thy Works, Not Mine, O Christ") but also produced a pair of slender pastoral defenses of the Reformation teaching on justification and sanctification. In the second, *God's Way of Holiness* (1864; repr, Ross-Shire: Christian Focus, 1999), 56, Bonar wrote: "Forgiveness of sins, in believing God's testimony to the finished propitiation of the cross, is not simply indispensable to a holy life, in the way of removing terror and liberating the soul from the pressure of guilt, but of imparting an impulse, and a motive, and a power which nothing else could do. Forgiveness *at the end or in the middle*; a partial forgiveness, or an uncertain forgiveness, or a grudging forgiveness, would be of no avail; it would only tantalize and mock; but a complete forgiveness, presented in such a way as to carry its own certainty along with it to every one who will take it at the hands of God; this is a power in the earth, a power against self, a power against sin, a power over the flesh, a power for holiness, such as no amount of suspense or terror could create" (emphasis original). Bonar went on to argue against those who object that offering assurance of God's forgiveness too freely will lull hearers into complacency in their sin: "A forgiven man is the true worker, the true law keeper. He *can*, he *will*, he *must* work for God. He has come into contact with that part of God's character which warms his cold heart. Forgiving love constrains him. He cannot but work for him who has removed his sins from him as far as the east is from the west. . . . Forgiveness received freely from the God and Father of our Lord Jesus Christ acts as a spring, an impulse, a stimulus of divine potency. It is more irresistible than law, or terror, or threat. A half forgiveness, an uncertain justification, a changeable peace, may lead to careless living and more careless working; may slacken the energy and freeze up the springs of action (for it shuts out that aspect of God's character which gladdens and quickens); but *a complete and assured pardon* can have no such effect. . . . Its tendencies towards holiness and consistency of life are marvellous in their power and certainty" (58, emphasis original; see also 148–54n6).

life? How can the captive of shameful lust be captured by an even stronger hunger for holiness and catch a taste of hope that freedom is possible? And what cure can address the tangle of self-contempt, resentment, and fear that tyrannizes the insecure teenager?

Obviously each counselee and situation have distinctive features that call for great pastoral wisdom, sensitivity, flexibility, and boldness, in humble dependence on the Spirit of Christ to apply the word of Christ to the deep recesses of the heart. No single formula or script can guarantee the desired outcome in the healing of relationships and the cure of souls. (If we pastors thought that our skills or insights could secure the results we seek, we would be succumbing to yet one more expression of works-righteousness and self-justification.) Nevertheless the practical usefulness of the biblical doctrine of justification can be illustrated by suggesting how justification would motivate each of these hurting and hurtful people to pursue the aspects of sanctification that are most needed in view of their distinctive life-dominating problems (both as sinners and as those sinned against).

The battling couple may well need to be shown and held accountable for establishing new patterns of communication: listening before speaking, refusing to resurrect past slights, asking questions before jumping to conclusions, avoiding inflammatory absolutes ("you never . . . ," "you always . . ."). None of these valuable skills will be maintained, however, unless and until the grace of God in the gospel breaks through the hardness of their hearts at new and deeper levels. Their bitterness toward each other may result from unrealistic expectations and hopes shattered by the spouse's failure, from the effort to justify oneself by magnifying the spouse's culpability, from the fear that forgiveness will be misconstrued as a license to perpetuate harmful behavior, or from some combination of these and other factors. Each needs to see the true magnitude of his or her own debt of offense toward God, the abundance of God's mercy in erasing that debt through the cross of Christ, and the invincible assurance of God's approval, grounded on the imputed righteousness of Jesus. As these truths grip their hearts (which often results not from an instantaneous change but from a prolonged struggle), defenses can fall, sins can be confessed (genuinely, not merely as a step in a required formula), forgiveness can flow, and hope can rekindle. John Piper writes:

> What makes marriage almost impossible at times is that both partners feel so self-justified in their expectations that are not being fulfilled. . . . The cycle of self-justified self-pity and anger seems unbreakable. But what if one or both of the partners becomes overwhelmed with the truth of justification by faith alone, and with the particular truth that in Christ Jesus God credits me, for Christ's sake, as fulfilling all his expectations? What would happen if this doctrine so mastered our souls that we began to bend it from the vertical to the horizontal? What if we applied it to our marriages? In our own imperfect efforts in this regard, there have been breakthroughs that seemed at times impossible.[34]

The man unwillingly (yet, in another sense, willingly) enslaved by impure fantasies desperately needs "the expulsive power of a new affection," which only the gospel of God's free grace—"the freer the better," as Chalmers said—can impart. He is painfully familiar with the adverse psychological consequences of his addiction, but has experienced the accuracy of Chalmers's analysis: the merely negative persuasion that sinful pleasure is ephemeral and ultimately self-destructive lacks the strength in itself to break sin's grip on the heart. The pastor will need to probe sensitively but frankly from what stresses or trials of life this man is seeking refuge in thoughts and actions cloaked in shame and then to show him from the gospel that Christ's grace and holiness alone can satisfy his deepest longings. Only as he is ravished by the sacrificial love of Christ and assured of the Father's delighted approval for Jesus's sake will the attractiveness of old lusts lose their luster. This man needs not only a deep redirection of his desires. He also needs strong hope and much reassurance that his seemingly unbreakable cycle of shame and failure cannot withstand the forgiving, justifying, transforming grace of God in Christ Jesus. Piper observes:

> Sin creates a real guilt that makes a person feel despairing and hopeless. That despair and hopelessness is one of the most powerful bondages to sinning there is. You ask such people if they know that the sin's lure is a lie, and they will, amazingly, agree with you

34. Piper, *Counted Righteous in Christ*, 27.

> that it is a lie. But they feel hopeless and therefore say, "It doesn't matter, there's no hope anyway; I am beyond forgiveness." This is a very deep bondage to actual sinning rooted in the despair of guilt. I would argue that this kind of bondage is precisely what [Rom 6] verse 7 can overcome—and is probably designed to overcome. Justification—legal acquittal from and declaration of our righteousness before God—grounds the possibility of liberation from slavery to sin. In wakening hope for acceptance with God by faith alone, it creates the very possibility and foundation for fighting against the bondage of sin that enslaves us.[35]

With the beauty of Christ portrayed before him, the assurance of the Father's welcome for Jesus's sake ringing in his ears and heart, and hope in the Spirit's relentless work to conform God's justified children eventually to the holiness of the Son, this once-defeated sinner can be guided to practical strategies (avoiding occasions of temptation, establishing accountability, etc.) for resisting sin and embracing purity with joy.

Wisdom dictates that the pastor enlist a mature woman who has learned to live "in line with the truth of the gospel" (Gal 2:14 NIV) to participate in counseling to apply the gospel tenderly to the adolescent's deep emotional anguish. This young woman needs to have her heart redirected from false sources and criteria of justification by means within human resources (beauty, cleverness, style, intelligence, personality, popularity). All such systems of justification by works, whether conceived theologically in relation to God or socially in relation to others (whose opinions are valued more highly than God's), ultimately fail not only those whom they condemn but also those whom they seem, for a time, to vindicate. She must be shown the Savior who knows her inmost thoughts and apprehensions yet laid down his life to make her his own beloved. She must be led to rest both her hope for approval and her longing for love in the heavenly bridegroom who loved her and gave himself for her and who by sheer grace clothes her, a member of his church-bride, with his own robes of righteousness (Eph 5:25; Rev 19:8; Isa 61:10).

35. Ibid., 78–79.

Glimpsing, as pastors do, the complexity of the human heart—our resourceful capacity for self-defense and self-contempt, for self-inflated pride and self-absorbed despair—who of us would dare attempt to shepherd others without "the power of God for salvation to everyone who believes" (Rom 1:16–17 ESV), the good news that God sets us right with himself, forgiven and approved forever, by faith alone in Christ alone?

Appendix
Our Testimony on Justification

The Faculty of
Westminster Seminary California

Introduction

The Reformation doctrine of justification has undergone severe criticism in recent decades. Challenges have come from three different sources. First, in the interests of church unity, many ecumenical discussions offer expressions of justification that are more ambiguous than was the Reformation doctrine and implicitly reject the Reformation teaching as too divisive. The statements *Evangelicals and Catholics Together* and *The Gift of Salvation* are examples of such ecumenical compromise. Second, some biblical scholars argue that Luther and Calvin misunderstood what Paul was actually teaching and so construct a false doctrine of justification. The so-called new perspective on Paul offers such an argument. Third, some who claim to be Reformed suggest that too many Reformed people have a Lutheran view of justification and need to develop a distinctively Reformed view of justification. These critics usually claim that they accept the

Reformed confessions, yet at the same time claim that Reformed theology needs to be changed and clarified to be distinctive. Such critics, called neonomians in the seventeenth century, today are perhaps better labeled covenant moralists.

Our testimony is directed primarily to this third group, who claim to be genuinely Reformed. These covenant moralists teach, contrary to the Reformed confessions and/or historic Reformed conviction, some or all of the following:

- that the Reformation doctrine of justification is not fully biblical
- that Lutherans and Calvinists have different doctrines of justification
- that the Reformation misunderstood Paul on justification
- that justification is not by faith alone, but by faithfulness, that is, trust in Christ *and* obedience
- that the idea of merit as a way of explaining the work of Christ for us is unbiblical
- that Christ died for our sins but he did not keep the law perfectly in our place (his active obedience)
- that Christ does not impute his active obedience to us
- that obedience or good works is not only the fruit or evidence of faith, but is also part of the ground or instrument of justification
- that our justification is in some way dependent on the final judgment of our works

As the faculty of Westminster Seminary California we believe that we must issue this testimony especially in relation to those who claim to be Reformed in their attack on the Reformation doctrine of justification and who claim to uphold the teaching of the Reformed confessions.

The confusion found in our confessional Reformed churches among some ministers, elders, and members has reached an alarming level. We recognize that the confessions are standards subordinate to the Holy Scripture. Nevertheless it is our conviction that in the confessions the Reformed churches have summarized the correct understanding of Scripture.

The contemporary confusion in the churches may be due, in part, to a lack of familiarity with our confessions. Therefore, we hope that by highlighting certain statements we will encourage the Reformed churches to uphold the biblical truth presented in them. Our purpose is not to supplement the confessions, which are clear and comprehensive in themselves. Rather we want to underscore the obvious elements of the confessions that the critics seem to ignore or deny.

Human Condition in Sin

The seriousness of our lost condition shows that we need a righteousness that only God can provide.

Heidelberg Catechism 5

I am prone by nature to hate God and my neighbor.

Heidelberg Catechism 8

We are wholly incapable of doing any good, and inclined to all evil.

Belgic Confession 14

Man is but a slave to sin.

Canons of Dort 3/4.3

All men are conceived in sin, and are by nature children of wrath, incapable of saving good, prone to evil, dead in sin, and in bondage thereto.

Westminster Confession of Faith 6.6

Every sin, both original and actual, being a transgression of the righteous law of God, . . . doth . . . bring guilt upon the sinner, whereby he is bound over to the wrath of God, and curse of the law, and so made subject to death.

Work of Christ

The righteousness that sinners need must be the perfect righteousness of Jesus Christ, the righteousness of both his sacrificial suffering (passive obedience) and his perfect life (active obedience).

Passive Obedience

Heidelberg Catechism 56

That God, for the sake of Christ's satisfaction, will no more remember my sins, neither the sinful nature with which I have to struggle all my life long.

Belgic Confession 21

We believe that Jesus Christ . . . hath presented himself in our behalf before his Father, to appease his wrath by his full satisfaction, by offering himself on the tree of the cross, and pouring out his precious blood to purge away our sins.

Active Obedience

Heidelberg Catechism 60

God . . . imputes to me the perfect satisfaction, righteousness, and holiness of Christ, as if I had never had nor committed any sin, and myself had accomplished all the obedience which Christ has rendered for me.

Belgic Confession 22

Therefore, for any to assert that Christ is not sufficient, but that something more is required besides him, would be too gross a blasphemy; for hence it would follow that Christ was but half a Savior. . . . Jesus Christ, imputing to us all his merits, and so many holy works which he has done for us and in our stead, is our righteousness.

Westminster Confession of Faith 8.5

The Lord Jesus, by his perfect obedience and sacrifice of himself . . . hath fully satisfied the justice of his Father, and purchased not only reconciliation, but an everlasting inheritance in the kingdom of heaven.

Westminster Confession of Faith 11.1

Imputing the obedience and satisfaction of Christ unto them.

Westminster Confession of Faith 11.3

Christ, by his obedience and death, did fully discharge the debt of all those that are thus justified . . . and his obedience and satisfaction accepted in their stead.

Westminster Larger Catechism 55

Christ maketh intercession . . . in the merit of his obedience and satisfaction on earth, declaring his will to have it applied to all believers.

Westminster Larger Catechism 70

He pardoneth all their sins, accepteth and accounteth their persons righteous in his sight . . . only for the perfect obedience and full satisfaction of Christ.

Merit of Christ

The work of Christ is meritorious in the sight of God. The idea that sinners can merit anything from God is rejected explicitly (Heidelberg Catechism 60, 63, 86; Belgic Confession 23; Canons of Dort 2.7; 5.8; Westminster Confession of Faith 16.5; Westminster Larger Catechism 193).

Heidelberg Catechism 21

Everlasting righteousness and salvation are freely given by God, merely of grace, only for the sake of Christ's merit.

Heidelberg Catechism 84

All their sins are really forgiven them of God for the sake of Christ's merits.

Belgic Confession 22

Faith, which embraces Jesus Christ with all his merits.

Belgic Confession 24

We do good works, but not to merit by them (for what can we merit?). . . . Our poor consciences would be continually vexed if they relied not on the merits of the suffering and death or our Savior.

Belgic Confession 35

Christ communicates himself with all his benefits to us, and gives us there [at the Lord's Supper] to enjoy both himself and the merits of his sufferings and death.

Canons of Dort, Rejection of Errors 1.3

The pleasure of God and the merits of Christ.

Canons of Dort, Rejection of Errors 2.1

Of the wisdom of the Father and of the merits of Jesus Christ.

Canons of Dort, Rejection of Errors 2.3

[We reject the error of those] who teach: That Christ by his satisfaction merited neither salvation itself for anyone, nor faith.

Canons of Dort, Rejection of Errors 2.4

We by faith, inasmuch as it accepts the merits of Christ, are justified before God and saved.

Westminster Confession of Faith 17.2

The efficacy of the merit and intercession of Jesus Christ.

Westminster Larger Catechism 55

Christ maketh intercession . . . in the merit of his obedience and sacrifice on earth.

Westminster Larger Catechism 174

Feeding on him by faith . . . , trusting in his merits.

Imputation

The righteousness of Christ is reckoned or imputed to sinners, not infused or worked in them, for their justification.

Heidelberg Catechism 60

Though my conscience accuse me that I have grievously sinned against all the commandments of God and kept none of them, and am still inclined to all evil, yet God, without any merit of mine, of mere grace, grants and imputes to me the perfect satisfaction, righteousness, and holiness of Christ, as if I had never had nor committed any sin, and myself had accomplished all the obedience which Christ has rendered for me; if only I accept such benefit with a believing heart.

Belgic Confession 22

Jesus Christ, imputing to us all his merits, and so many holy works which he has done for us and in our stead, is our righteousness.

Westminster Confession of Faith 11.1

Those whom God effectually calleth he also freely justifieth; not by infusing righteousness into them, but by pardoning their sins, and by accounting and accepting their persons as righteous: not for any thing wrought in them, or done by them, but for Christ's sake alone . . . by imputing the obedience and satisfaction of Christ unto them.

Westminster Larger Catechism 71

Inasmuch as God accepteth the satisfaction from a surety, which he might have demanded of them, and did provide this surety, his own only Son, imputing his righteousness to them, and requiring nothing of them for their justification but faith.

Westminster Shorter Catechism 33

Justification is an act of God's free grace, wherein he pardoneth all our sins, and accepteth us as righteous in his sight, only for the righteousness of Christ imputed to us, and received by faith alone.

Role of Faith

Faith and faith alone is the instrument that looks away from self to Jesus and receives the imputation of his perfect righteousness.

Heidelberg Catechism 61

Why do you say that you are righteous only by faith? Not that I am acceptable to God on account of the worthiness of my faith, but because only the satisfaction, righteousness, and holiness of Christ is my righteousness before God, and I can receive the same and make it my own in no other way than by faith only.

Belgic Confession 22

If all things are in him, . . . then those who possess Jesus Christ through faith have complete salvation in him. . . . We do not mean that faith itself justifies us, for it is only an instrument with which we embrace Christ our righteousness. . . . And faith is an instrument that keeps us in communion with him in all his benefits, which, when they become ours, are more than sufficient to acquit us of our sins.

Westminster Confession of Faith 7.3

He freely offered unto sinners life and salvation by Jesus Christ, requiring of them faith in him that they may be saved.

Westminster Confession of Faith 11.2

Faith, thus receiving and resting on Christ and his righteousness, is the alone instrument of justification.

Westminster Confession of Faith 14.2

The principal acts of saving faith are accepting, receiving, and resting upon Christ alone for justification, sanctification, and eternal life.

Westminster Shorter Catechism 30

The Spirit applieth to us the redemption purchased by Christ, by working faith in us, and thereby uniting us to Christ in our effectual calling.

Justification and Sanctification

Justification and sanctification are present together in the redeemed, but are clearly distinct from one another.

Heidelberg Catechism 86

Since, then, we are delivered from our misery by grace alone, through Christ, without any merit of ours, why must we yet do good works? Because Christ, having redeemed us by his blood, also renews us by his Holy Spirit after his own image, that with our whole life we may show ourselves thankful to God for his benefits.

Belgic Confession 24

These works, as they proceed from the good root of faith, are good and acceptable in the sight of God, forasmuch as they are all sanctified by his grace. Nevertheless they are of no account toward our justification, for it is by faith in Christ that we are justified, even before we do good works.

Westminster Confession of Faith 11.2

Faith, thus receiving and resting on Christ and his righteousness, is the alone instrument of justification; yet is it not alone in the person justified, but is ever accompanied with all other saving graces, and is no dead faith, but worketh by love.

Westminster Larger Catechism 77

Wherein do justification and sanctification differ? Although sanctification be inseparably joined with justification, yet they differ, in that God in justification imputeth the righteousness of Christ; in sanctification his Spirit infuseth grace. . . . [In justification] sin is pardoned; [in sanctification] it is subdued. [Justification] doth equally free all believers from the revenging wrath of God, and that perfectly in this life, that they never fall into condemnation; [sanctification] is neither equal in all, nor in this life perfect in any, but growing up to perfection.

The Christian's Sanctification

Sanctification is a work of God's renewing grace by which Christians become more holy over the course of their lives while still confronting real sin in their lives—making it impossible for even our best works to stand in the face of perfect judgment.

Real Progress in Sanctification

Heidelberg Catechism 86

Christ, having redeemed us by his blood, renews us also by his Holy Spirit after his own image, that with our whole life we may show ourselves thankful to God.

Heidelberg Catechism 114

With earnest purpose they [the converted] begin to live, not only according to some, but according to all the commandments of God.

Westminster Confession of Faith 13.1

They, who are effectually called and regenerated, having a new heart and a new spirit created in them, are further sanctified, really and personally, through the virtue of Christ's death and resurrection, by his Word and Spirit dwelling in them; the dominion of the whole body of sin is destroyed, and the several lusts thereof are more and more weakened and mortified, and they more and more quickened and strengthened, in all saving graces, to the practice of true holiness, without which no man shall see the Lord.

Westminster Shorter Catechism 35

Sanctification is the work of God's free grace, whereby we are renewed in the whole man after the image of God, and are enabled more and more to die unto sin, and live unto righteousness.

Continuing Problem with Sin

Heidelberg Catechism 62

The righteousness which can stand before the tribunal of God must be absolutely perfect and wholly conformable to the divine law, while even our best works in this life are all imperfect and defiled with sin.

Heidelberg Catechism 114

Even the holiest men, while in this life, have only a small beginning of this obedience.

Belgic Confession 24

We can do no work but what is polluted by our flesh, and also punishable; and although we could perform such works, still the remembrance of one sin is sufficient to make God reject them.

Westminster Confession of Faith 13.2

This sanctification is throughout, in the whole man, yet imperfect in this life; there abideth still some remnants of corruption in every part.

Westminster Confession of Faith 16.2

These good works, done in obedience to God's commandments, are the fruits and evidences of a true and lively faith.

Westminster Confession of Faith 16.5

And as they [good works] are wrought by us, they are defiled and mixed with so much weakness and imperfection that they can not endure the severity of God's judgment.

Westminster Larger Catechism 78

Their [believers'] best works are imperfect and defiled in the sight of God.

Justification and Final Judgment

Justification occurs when one comes to true faith, giving peace of conscience and assurance of eternal life in the present. God's final judgment is not the justification of his own, but their vindication and perfection.

Heidelberg Catechism 59

But what does it profit you now that you believe all this? That I am righteous in Christ before God, and an heir to eternal life.

Belgic Confession 37

This judgment is . . . most desirable and comfortable to the righteous and elect; because then their full deliverance shall be perfected, and there they shall receive the fruits of their labor and trouble which they have borne. . . . The faithful and elect shall be crowned with glory and honor; and the Son of God will confess their names before God his Father . . . ; all tears shall be wiped from their eyes; and their cause which is now condemned by many judges and magistrates as heretical and impious will then be known to be the cause of the Son of God. And for a gracious reward, the Lord will cause them to possess such a glory as never entered into the heart of man to conceive.

Westminster Confession of Faith 33.2

The end of God's appointing this day is for the manifestation of the glory of his mercy in the eternal salvation of the elect; and of his justice in the damnation of the reprobate, who are wicked and disobedient.

Westminster Larger Catechism 77

[Justification] doth equally free all believers from the revenging wrath of God, and that perfectly in this life, that they never fall into condemnation.

Westminster Larger Catechism 90

At the day of judgment, the righteous, being caught up to Christ in the clouds, shall be set on his right hand, and there openly acknowledged and acquitted.

The doctrine of justification taught in the Reformed confessions is a faithful summary of the biblical teaching, is necessary for the faithful preaching of the gospel in the churches, and is foundational to all Christian assurance and holy living.

Westminster Seminary California
1725 Bear Valley Parkway
Escondido, CA 92027
760.480.8474
www.wscal.edu

Index of Scripture

1 Corinthians

Index of Subjects